Genealogical Fictions

Genealogical Fictions

Limpieza de Sangre,
Religion, and Gender in Colonial Mexico

María Elena Martínez

STANFORD UNIVERSITY PRESS

STANFORD, CALIFORNIA

This book has been published with the assistance
of the University of Southern California

Stanford University Press
Stanford, California

Printed in the United States of America on acid-free, archival-quality paper

Library of Congress Cataloging-in-Publication Data

Martínez, María Elena
Genealogical fictions: limpieza de sangre, religion, and gender in colonial
Mexico / María Elena Martínez.
p. cm.
Includes bibliographical references and index.
ISBN 978-0-8047-5648-8 (cloth : alk. paper)
ISBN 978-0-8047-7661-5 (pbk. : alk. paper)
1. Mexico—Race relations. 2. Racism—Mexico—History.
3. Social classes—Mexico—History 4. Social classes—
Religious aspects—Catholic Church. I. Title.

F1392.A1M37 2008
305.5'12208900972—dc22
2007038751

Typeset by Thompson Type in 10/12 Sabon

To my parents,
Aurelia López Corral and Nicolás Martínez Corral

To my grandparents (mis cuatro costados),
Florentina Corral Esparza, Severo López Avitia,
María de Jesús Corral Corral, and Enrique Martínez Corral

And to the precious land, our patria chica, *that gave us life*

Acknowledgments

As this book comes to fruition I am overwhelmed by the sense of gratitude that I feel toward the people and institutions that in one way or another helped me complete it. I am grateful to my dissertation committee, Friedrich Katz, Tamar Herzog, Claudio Lomnitz, Thomas C. Holt, and Tom Cummins, for the support and guidance they gave me at the University of Chicago, where the book first began to take shape.

I also thank the foundations, institutions, and centers that provided me with the grants that made my research and writing possible. These include the Woodrow Wilson National Fellowship Foundation, the American Council of Learned Societies, the Huntington Library, the American Bar Foundation, the Fulbright-Hays Fellowship Foundation, the John Carter Brown Library, the USC-Huntington Early Modern Studies Institute, the University of Chicago, the Escuela de Estudios Hispano-Americanos (Seville), the James H. Zumberge fund at the University of Southern California, and USC's Center for Law, History, and Culture. I am grateful as well to Dean Wayne Raskind at USC for providing a subvention for the book's publication.

Without the help of librarians and archivists, writing this book would have been difficult, indeed impossible. I want, therefore, to acknowledge the staffs at the Archivo General de la Nación (Mexico City), the Biblioteca Nacional de Antropología e Historia (Mexico City), the Archivo del Ayuntamiento de Puebla (Puebla, Mexico), the Archivo General de Indias (Seville, Spain), the Archivo Histórico Nacional (Madrid), the John Carter Brown Library (Providence, Rhode Island), the Biblioteca Nacional (Madrid), the Huntington Library (San Marino, CA), and the Acervo Histórico del Palacio de Minería (Mexico City). In particular, I would like to thank Roberto Beristáin and Cesar Montoya of Mexico's Archivo General de la Nación (AGN), and Oscar Escamilla of the Acervo Histórico del Palacio de Minería, in Mexico City. Researcher Cecilia Riquelme helped me find and gather important documents at the

AGN. I am also grateful to Socorro Prous Zaragoza, whose knowledge of Mexican documents at the Archivo General de Indias and research leads proved to be extremely valuable to my investigation and who became a good friend in the process. I thank José Hernández Palomo of Seville's Escuela de Estudios Hispano-Americanos for his advice on archives and especially for his hospitality and sense of humor. While conducting research in Spain I also had the good fortune of getting to know Patricia Meehan, whose company in Seville and Madrid I will always treasure. I am thankful to Elisa de Cabo and Teresa Martín for their magical friendship and for always making me feel as though their home, Madrid, is my home as well.

At the History Department of the University of Southern California I have been fortunate to have many dear colleagues and friends, including Paul Lerner, Marjorie Becker, Lois Banner, Ramzi Rouighi, Peter Mancall, Jason Glenn, Lon Kurashige, Lisa Bitel, Kyung Moon Hwang, Charlotte Furth, Judith Bennett, Cynthia Herrup, Terry Seip, Philippa Levine, Deb Harkness, and Karen Halttunen. I feel deeply indebted to Carole Shammas, who was chair of the department when I was hired and who throughout the years has provided me with support to develop as a scholar and teacher. I also thank Steve Ross and Elinor Accampo, for their encouragement as colleagues and chairs of the department. I am extremely grateful as well to George Sánchez for his guidance and friendship. I am blessed to have him in my life. My years at USC have been very much enriched by colleagues in other departments, among them Carol Wise, Judith Halberstam, Karen Tongson, David Román, Judith Jackson Fossett, and Macarena Gómez-Barris. I thank Lori Rogers and Joe Styles for keeping the history department afloat as well as La Verne Hughes and Brenda Johnson for their administrative assistance.

I owe Tamar Herzog and Ilona Katzew for their feedback and suggestions on parts of the manuscript and to the two anonymous reviewers secured by Stanford University Press. I would also like to thank Hane C. Lee for proofreading the manuscript, and Norris Pope, Emily-Jane Cohen, John Feneron, and Margaret Pinette for their help with various aspects of the editing and production process. Of course, the book's shortcomings should be attributed only to its author. I extend a special *gracias* to the participants of the Tepoztlán Institute for Transnational History of the Americas, for providing a congenial intellectual atmosphere, and to Pamela Voekel and Elliot Young for inviting me to be part of such a stimulating project.

Writing this book would have been much more difficult without the companionship, advice, and humor provided by close friends. In particular, I thank Ilona Katzew, Augie Robles, Virginia Chang, David Sartorius,

Carmen Aguilar, Barbara Shaw, Theresa Mah, Clementine Oliver, and Chase Rummonds. Their friendship, generosity, and sybaritic inclinations have sustained me in more ways than I can articulate.

I am profoundly grateful to Sarah Gualtieri for reading and commenting on this book at various stages and most of all for all the years of support, discovery, and joy. I thank the forces of the universe for our strong bonds, which in trying times have nourished us with much courage. I am also fortunate to have shared part of my life with Princesa and Reina, who passed away not long before the book was finished. The affection and playfulness of my two angels kept me sane during difficult periods, and they therefore deserve partial credit for its completion.

Finally, I want to thank my brothers, Jesús, Arturo, Nico, and Enrique, for a childhood full of humor, sports, and history quizzes; and my parents, Aurelia and Nicolás, for instilling in me a love of Mexico that inspires me and my work in more ways than I probably realize. My father's strength, sharp mind, and passion for life and music marked me forever; my mother's gentle soul, optimism, and uncanny ability to see grace in acts big and small gave me a hope in humanity that not even the bleakest of times in this beautiful but suffering planet can ever entirely suppress. I am eternally grateful for the great sacrifices they made for their children to have opportunities in life that they did not.

Contents

Contents

Maps and Illustrations

Genealogical Fictions

Introduction

⋐

PROBLEM AND OBJECTIVES

This book charts the rise of categories of *limpieza de sangre* ("purity of blood") in Spain and their journey from the Iberian Peninsula to the Americas, where they eventually took on a life of their own. Having originated in late medieval Castile, the concept of purity of blood and its underlying assumptions about inheritable characteristics had by the late seventeenth century produced a hierarchical system of classification in Spanish America that was ostensibly based on proportions of Spanish, indigenous, and African ancestry, the *sistema de castas* or "race/caste system."[1] This use of the concept would probably have surprised the Spaniards who first deployed it against Jewish converts to Christianity, the *conversos,* or "New Christians." They defined blood purity as the absence of Jewish and heretical antecedents and, as of the middle of the fifteenth century, they increasingly wielded the notion to deprive the conversos of access to certain institutions and public and ecclesiastical offices. The concept acquired greater force during the next one hundred years, as limpieza de sangre statutes—requirements of unsullied "Old Christian" ancestry—were adopted by numerous religious and secular establishments in Castile and Aragon, the Spanish Inquisition was founded to identify "secret Jews" and root out heresy, and the category of impurity was extended to the descendants of Muslims. By the middle of the sixteenth century, the ideology of purity of blood had produced a Spanish society obsessed with genealogy and in particular with the idea that having only Christian ancestors, and thus a "pure lineage," was the critical sign of a person's loyalty to the faith. Descent and religion— "blood" and faith—were the two foundations of that ideology, and the same would be true in Spanish America.

The transfer of the Castilian discourse of limpieza de sangre to Spanish America did not mean, however, that it remained the same in the new context. As much as Spaniards tried to recreate their society in "New Spain" (colonial Mexico), they had to face circumstances, peoples, and historical developments that inevitably altered their transplanted institutions, practices, and cultural-religious principles. The survival of native communities and part of the pre-Hispanic nobility, the importance of the conversion project to Spanish colonialism and to Castile's titles to the Americas, the introduction of significant numbers of African slaves into the region, the rapid rise of a population of mixed ancestry, the influx of poor Spaniards seeking to better their lot if not ennoble themselves, and the establishment of a transatlantic economy based largely on racialized labor forces—these and other factors ensured that the Iberian concept of limpieza de sangre would be reformulated and have different implications than in Spain. In Castile, for example, it did not produce an elaborate system of classification based on blood proportions as it did in the colonies, though signs that such categories might develop appeared in the sixteenth century, particularly in the Inquisition's genealogical investigations. Furthermore, in Spanish America, the notion of purity gradually came to be equated with Spanish ancestry, with "Spanishness," an idea that had little significance in the metropolitan context. The language of blood and lineage also underwent modifications. Nonetheless, at the end of the colonial period, the concept of limpieza de sangre was still partly defined in religious terms. What were the implications of this religious dimension for colonial categories of identity, racial discourses, and communal ideologies? Answering this question is one of the central aims of this book.

More to the point, the book seeks to expose the connection between the concept of limpieza de sangre and the sistema de castas. Although a number of scholars of colonial Mexico have referred to this connection, they have not fully explained it.[2] They have not clarified how a concept that had strong religious connotations came to construct or promote classifications that presumably were based on modern notions of race. Exactly when, how, and why was the notion of purity of blood extended and adapted to the colonial context? This critical question has received little attention in the literature because, until recently, most historical studies of the sistema de castas have focused on the eighteenth century (when notions of race were starting to become secularized) and in particular on the problem of the saliency of "race" versus "class" as mercantile capitalism expanded.[3] The privileging of the late colonial period in the historiography has meant that both the origins of the system and its relation to the concept of limpieza remain unclear. Works that do refer to the system in the early colonial period generally link the concept of *purity of blood* to *race* without elaborating on what exactly either of these terms meant at that time. Furthermore, they normally describe its rise as a function of the displacement of main peninsular status categories (noble, commoner, and slave) onto the three primary colonial groups (respectively, Spaniards, Indians, and blacks) and explain the disruption of this tripartite order by the growth of populations of mixed ancestry.[4] This rendition of the emergence of the sistema de castas is seductive because of its simplicity; but it is also deceptive because it deprives the process of its contingency, does not explain why more than one category of mixture was created, and obscures the religious dimension of limpieza de sangre and therefore also its implications.[5]

This book provides an analysis, first, of the linkages between the concept of limpieza de sangre and the sistema de castas with special consideration to the role of religion in the production of notions of purity and impurity, the historical specificity of Castilian categories such as *raza* (race) and *casta* (caste), the intertwined nature of peninsular and colonial discourses of purity, and the fluidity and ambiguities that characterized the system of classification throughout the colonial period. It is informed by critical race theory and in particular by scholarship that posits that race is not merely a consequence of material interests (an "effect" of class) but rather is linked in complex ways to economic, political, and ideological structures; social conditions; and systems of signification.[6] Philosopher Cornel West has termed this approach "genealogical materialist." He has stressed the importance of investigating the origins and trajectory of racial ideas within specific cultural and historical traditions and their dynamic interaction with both micro- and macrolevel processes, including those related to political economy (local and global), the reproduction and disruption of power (say, through particular languages, idioms, or representations), and the construction of notions of self. West chose Nietzsche's concept of genealogy because he wanted to underscore the importance of undertaking deep and careful excavations of the meanings of race within the particular cultural-historical context in which it develops and of explaining its connections to different levels of existence.

In this study, the concept of genealogy is central both because it alludes to the process of historicizing race and because in the early modern Hispanic world it was ubiquitous and consequential, the foundation of a multitude of practices and identities that helped mold historical memory at both the individual and collective levels. It does not presuppose the automatic deployment of the concept of limpieza de sangre against colonial populations and simple displacement of peninsular status categories

onto them. Nor does it assume that the meanings of early modern notions of purity and race are self-evident, a mistake that can lead to the
tautological argument that the system of classifying "blood mixture"
arose because "race mixture" occurred, an argument that reproduces
the idea of races as biological givens rather than challenging it by interrogating why categories arise, become reified, and get contested. Instead,
this book prioritizes analyzing the discursive tradition that the concepts
of limpieza and raza were part of and which, together with certain practices, those two notions helped to constitute.[7] It begins by addressing
the following questions. What exactly did the concepts of limpieza de
sangre and raza mean in Spain, when and why did they first start to be
deployed in Mexico, and how were they adapted to the colonial context?
Was their growing usage related to events in the metropole, Spanish
America, or both? Which institutions adopted purity-of-blood requirements and when did they begin to target people of mixed ancestry? Did
definitions of limpieza de sangre change over time, and if so, how? And
what practices and identities did the ideology of purity of blood promote? These are the questions that constitute the first of three main lines
of inquiry in the book.

A second line of investigation pertains to the connections of the concept of limpieza de sangre to gender and sexuality.[8] The book argues
that these connections were strong not just because of the centrality of
biological reproduction (and by extension, female sexuality) to the perpetuation of community boundaries and the hierarchical social order
in general. They were also powerful because Spanish notions regarding sexual and reproductive relations between the three main populations reflected and interacted with other discourses of colonial power.[9]
Recurring ideas regarding blood purity and mixture, for example, construed native people—the transmission of their traits—as weak, thereby
echoing paternalistic religious and government policies that depicted
relations among Spaniards, indigenous people, and blacks in gendered
forms. Political, religious, and genealogical discourses in fact mirrored,
complemented, and reinforced each other through the use of notions of
strength and weakness that by coding different colonial groups as male
or female naturalized socially created hierarchies.

Only in the eighteenth century, however, would invocations of nature
as the basis of difference between men and women as well as between
human groups begin to emerge as a prominent discourse. A growing interest, particularly among natural philosophers, in questions about the
origins of different populations and function of men and women in the
generation of life influenced how the sistema de castas was represented.
As scientific explanations to sexual and racial difference gained ground

over religious ones, colonial Mexico's population became subject, like the animals and plants in natural histories, to increasingly elaborate and visual taxonomic exercises that made the gendering of race and racing of gender as well as social hierarchies seem to be ordained by nature. This penchant for classification and naturalization was manifested in "casta paintings," a genre that illustrated and labeled the unions of different "castes" as well as their offspring and that betrayed both how some of Mexico's artists conceived of the appropriate relationship of gender, race, and class and the lingering importance of the discourse of limpieza de sangre.

A third main line of inquiry tracks the importance of the state-sponsored organization of colonial society into two separate commonwealths or "republics"—one Spanish, the other indigenous—to discourses of blood and lineage. Although strict segregation between the two populations was never achieved and some Spanish jurists and legislation allowed for the day when the native people would be fully incorporated into Hispanic colonial society, the dual model of social organization nevertheless had profound repercussions. At least in central Mexico, the *república de indios* ("Indian Republic") was not just an ideological device, and it continued to have practical significance well into the eighteenth century. It promoted the survival of *pueblos de indios* (native communities) with their own political hierarchies and citizenship regime, the creation of special legal and religious institutions for the indigenous people, and the official recognition of Indian purity. This recognition, which mainly pivoted on the argument that the original inhabitants of the Americas were unsullied by Judaism and Islam and had willingly accepted Christianity, made it possible for some of the descendants of pre-Hispanic dynasties to successfully claim the status of limpieza de sangre, in the long run altering some of their conceptions of blood and history. Their genealogical claims became more frequent in the last third of the seventeenth century, amid increasing efforts to preserve communal lands and histories.

But native nobles and rulers were not the only group to be influenced by the Spanish state's promotion of two polities and corresponding dual citizenship and purity regimes. All colonial identities, after all, were the results of complex colonial processes.[10] Maintaining a system of "proving" purity in the "Spanish republic" necessitated the creation of birth records, classifications, and genealogies and obliged those who wanted access to the institutions or offices with limpieza requirements to submit lineages, produce witnesses, and keep records of their ancestors. Among creoles (Spaniards born and/or raised in the Americas), these administrative and archival practices helped foster a historical consciousness that encouraged their identification with a broader Spanish community of blood even as they developed a strong attachment to the land. By the eighteenth century, they established their purity not so much by stressing their lack of Jewish and Muslim ancestors as by providing evidence of their Spanish descent. Yet this formulation of limpieza de sangre as Spanishness did not entirely undermine the idea that the indigenous people were pure and redeemable because of their acceptance of Christianity. Instead, it produced paradoxical attitudes toward reproduction or *mestizaje* ("mixture") with Amerindians among creole elites,[11] particularly as their patriotism intensified and they began to imagine the merger of the two republics in reproductive and biological terms.

The book, then, centers on three main issues: the relationship between the Spanish notion of limpieza de sangre and Mexico's sistema de castas; the intersection of notions of purity, gender, and sexuality; and the linkages of religion, race, and patriotic discourses. Framing the exploration of these subjects is an emphasis on the role of the state, church, and archives in promoting a preoccupation with lineage in central Mexico, particularly among creole and native elites. In other words, one of the book's thematic threads is how the routinization of genealogical requirements in the secular and religious hierarchies helped shape social practices, notions of self, and concepts of communal belonging. Which is not to say that the Spanish colonial state was powerful and that its laws were always or even frequently obeyed, only that it set guidelines for government and religious institutions and through them shaped the nature of social relations. The term *archival practices* thus generally refers to the record-keeping activities of the state, church, and Inquisition that produced and reproduced categories of identity based on ancestry linked to particular legal statuses (to certain responsibilities, rights, or privileges). These archival practices promoted genealogical ones, including official and unofficial investigations into a person's ancestors—involving examinations of birth records, interrogations of town elders, inspections of tributary lists, and so forth—and the construction of family histories through, among other things, the maintenance, purchase, or falsification of written genealogies, certifications of purity of blood, and copies of baptismal and marriage records.

Another recurring theme in the book is the interaction of metropolitan and colonial notions of purity and, more broadly, discourses about the New Christians—which drew on anti-Semitic tropes—and the converted populations of the Americas. Special attention is drawn to the similarities and differences in Spanish attitudes toward the conversion potential of Jews and native people and especially to how stereotypes that were used to describe one group tended to be mapped onto the

other. Finally, the book underscores the instability of the sistema de castas. It stresses that, like all hegemonic projects, it was a process, powerful and pervasive because it was promoted by the state and the church
but fluctuated and was subject to contestation.[12] The relative fluidity of
the sistema de castas was partly due to inconsistencies in the discourse
of limpieza de sangre, which, for example, characterized native people
as pure and impure, as both perfect material for Christianization and
incorrigible idolaters. Hegemonic discourses tend to derive power from
their construction of subjects in a doubled way.

The sistema's fluidity was also a by-product of the Spanish imperial
structure, which incorporated Spanish America into the Crown of Castile but failed to clearly outline what that meant in terms of the rights
and privileges of different populations. For example, despite the various
compilations of laws for the "Indies" (*derecho indiano*) that Spain produced in the seventeenth century, it did not issue a legal code specifically
for the castas and did not entirely clarify the status of creoles as "natives" of a particular jurisdiction. The political vagueness of imperial
space and piecemeal nature of colonial legislation prompted individuals
and groups to attempt to challenge or redefine statuses, policies, and
classifications. These features also resulted in unexpected political imaginaries, ones that a rigid distinction between a metropolitan core and
colonial periphery cannot begin to capture.

LIMPIEZA DE SANGRE, RACE, AND COLONIALISM
IN THE EARLY MODERN PERIOD

Scholars of early modern Spain have not paid much attention to the
relationship between the concept of limpieza de sangre and Spanish
American racial ideology.[13] Their disinterest in the problem can be
blamed on the lamentably persistent tendency within the profession to
treat the histories of the Iberian Peninsula and colonial Latin America
as separate analytical fields. But it is also indicative of a broader Spanish
denial about certain aspects of Spain's colonial past. I first encountered
this denial when I arrived at the Archivo General de Indias (AGI) in
Seville to conduct research for this book. After I explained the purpose
of my visit, the director of the archive informed me that I would not find
any sources on limpieza de sangre there. The response took me aback
because I had a list of references for documents related to my topic that
other historians had found at that archive. But after being in Spain for
a few months, I realized that it was part of a general reluctance among
contemporary Spaniards to recognize the importance that the concept of

purity of blood had in the Americas, namely because of what it implies for their national history, which has tended to minimize (if not deny) the role of processes of racialization in Castile's overseas territories. This reluctance cannot simply be attributed to ignorance, for even some Spanish historians of colonial Latin America tried to convince me, when at the onset of my research I presented at a reputable research institution in Seville, that the problem of purity of blood was one that never spilled out of the borders of the Iberian Peninsula and that the concept was used exclusively against converted Jews and Muslims. It soon became clear that the organization of archives—the way that many limpieza de sangre documents were classified or not classified, subsumed under other records, or mislabeled—was intimately connected to this national historical narrative.

That the same historians who tried to convince me of the irrelevance of the concept of limpieza de sangre outside of Spain were well acquainted with purity documents produced in Spanish America only added a surreal quality to the discussion that followed my presentation in Seville. But the strangeness of the experience did not end there. To bolster his case, a specialist in Andean history offered the observation that many Spanish colonists had reproduced with native women and, in cases where acquiring land was at stake, even married them! A people concerned with blood purity would not be willing to "mix" with the Amerindians was his point, one that clearly echoed the arguments made by some scholars in the first half of the twentieth century regarding Iberians' relatively benign attitudes toward native people and Africans.[14] This current of thought, which had among its many flaws the propensity to see early colonial sexual relations not as acts of power but as signs of a more gentle or open approach to colonization (sometimes attributed to the history of Spanish and Portuguese "commingling" with Jews and Muslims) is part of the White Legend of Spanish history, an apologetic view of Spain's actions in the Americas. The view to some extent surfaced in reaction to the body of propagandistic literature that began to be produced by Spain's European rivals (especially the British and Dutch) in the late sixteenth century and which gave rise to the Black Legend. Seeking to discredit Castile's claims to the Americas, this legend focused attention on the conquerors' cruelty toward indigenous peoples, their unbridled greed, and their hypocritical use of religion as justification for their deeds.[15]

The Black Legend survived into the twentieth century and colored Anglophone scholarship on both Spain and Spanish America. Its influence is evident, for example, in the modernization studies of the 1950s that compared Latin America's apparent continuity in political, social, and economic forms—its history of authoritarianism, sharp inequalities, and financial dependency—with the more democratic and capital-ist trajectory of the United States.[16] These studies tended to blame the "feudal" and "absolutist" foundations of Spanish colonial societies for the region's troubled path to modernity. Many framed the problems associated with the latifundia (the absence of a yeomanry), the Inquisition (the suppression of freedom of political and religious thought), and the church's collusion with the state (the clergy's ongoing support of absolutism) as medieval holdovers that Castilians took to the Americas, where they obstructed economic entrepreneurship, individualism, and democratic ideals, among other things. The causes of Spain's inability to modernize à la other parts of Western Europe and the United States also explained Latin America's "backwardness."

In the past few decades, the Black Legend has taken on a new twist. Some of the scholarship on the history of race and racism has been casting early modern Iberia as the site of a precocious elaboration of racial concepts and practices. A recent historical overview of the problem, for example, begins by discussing developments in Spain, "the first great colonizing nation and a seedbed for Western attitudes toward race."[17] Iberia's pioneering role in the development of racial ideologies is sometimes linked to its participation in the early stages of the transatlantic African slave trade and in the colonization of the Americas.[18] But it is more often associated with the Spanish statutes of limpieza de sangre. Indeed, particularly in the literature that seeks to excavate the "origins" of race, it has become almost commonplace to postulate that the Castilian concept of blood purity was the first racial discourse produced by the West or at least an important precursor to modern notions of difference.[19] Anti-Semitism was endemic in late medieval Europe, and in the two centuries preceding Spain's 1492 expulsion of its Jews France and England had on repeated occasions tried to do the same with their Jewish populations, but it apparently makes for a much more satisfying narrative when race and racism can be given a single starting point and a linear trajectory. Thanks to its contribution to racism via the purity statutes and Inquisition, early modern Spain can finally make a claim to modernity. It was ahead of its time in something.

Whether the intention of its proponents or not, the argument that credits Spain with establishing the first modern system of discrimination fits neatly into the package of the Black Legend, which might help to explain why Spanish historians would be less than enthusiastic about studying the extension of the concept of limpieza de sangre to the other side of the Atlantic. To acknowledge that a discourse of purity of blood surfaced in the Americas would be to risk adding yet another dark chapter to a history that includes the expulsion of the Jews, the establishment of the Inquisition, the forced exile of Muslims *and* moriscos (Muslim converts to Christianity), and the conquest and colonization of native peoples. Given that the concept of purity of blood was relevant in all of these developments, how does one approach the subject in ways that avoid presenting historical actors in terms of simplistic dichotomies and, more generally, the politicization of history? Perhaps, as the historian Steve Stern has stressed, the conquest and colonization of the Americas can never be disentangled from politics—from the politics of the past and the present, the history and historiography[20]—but the point here is not to vilify Spaniards or suggest that they were worse, as the Black Legend would have it, than other colonial powers, or for that matter better, as the White Legend camp claimed. No expansionist European country could claim the moral high ground with respect to their attitudes toward and treatment of the peoples they colonized and/or enslaved, only some differences in timing, methods, and guiding principles. This book does not intend, therefore, to provide material for the perpetuation of the Black Legend (whether it is used as such is another matter) or to reinforce the tendency in recent studies on the origins of race and racism to single out early modern Iberia, as if those phenomena were unknown in other parts of Europe or somehow spread from the peninsula to the rest of the continent. Its main concern is not with the history of Spain but with that of New Spain, although the two are clearly interrelated, and that in itself is a point that the study tries to reiterate as it charts the transatlantic paths of the problem of limpieza de sangre.

If Spanish historians can be criticized for their failure to recognize the importance of limpieza de sangre in the colonial context, U.S. scholars of Spanish America can be accused of not having paid adequate attention to the complexity of the uses and meanings of the concept in Iberia, which has tended to result in oversimplified and at times anachronistic renditions of the ways in which it shaped racial discourses in the American context. For their part, Mexican and other Latin American academics can be taken to task for their general aversion to treating race as a legitimate subject of inquiry for understanding their region's history. It is fair to say that they tend to regard it as an issue that mainly has had relevance in the United States and other former slave societies (as opposed to "societies with slaves"), whereas they see class as much more salient for understanding the Iberian American past (even when it comes to regions in which slavery was extremely important, such as Brazil and Cuba). Thus, although some Mexican specialists of the colonial period might agree that the notion of limpieza de sangre was of some significance (it is hard to miss references to it in the archives), they commonly dismiss the problem of race by stressing that social organization was based on an estate model.[21] If different groups had distinct rights, privileges, and obligations, it was because of the hierarchical nature of Spanish society, which at the time of the conquest continued to consist of three main estates and numerous corporations with specific functions within the social body, not because of modern notions of biological difference.

The argument that using the notion of race to study the period prior to the nineteenth century is anachronistic has of course not been made exclusively by Latin Americans. Indeed, the standard chronology (and teleology) of the concept is that it had not yet crystallized—assumed its full essentializing potential—in the early modern period because attitudes regarding phenotype usually combined or competed with ideas of cultural or religious difference. According to this account, race did not appear until the nineteenth century, when pseudoscience anchored it in biology, or rather, when biology anchored it in the body much more effectively than natural philosophy and natural history ever did. It is true that the concept of race generally became more biologistic in that period, and it is of course important not to project its modern connotations to previous eras. But arguing that racial discourses took a particular form in the nineteenth century is one thing; contending that they did not operate in the early modern period, quite another. In the past three decades, a number of scholars have demonstrated that the meanings and uses of the concept of race have varied across time, space, and cultures and that even in modern times, it has not relied exclusively on biological notions of difference but rather has often been intertwined with culture and/or class. To elevate "race as biology" to an ideal type is to set up a false dichotomy—to ignore that racial discourses have proven to be remarkably flexible, invoking nature or biology more at one point, culture more at another.[22] The shifting meanings and uses of race simultaneously underscore its social constructedness and suggest that there is no single, transhistorical racism but rather different types of *racisms,* each produced by specific social and historical conditions.[23] The historian's task is precisely to excavate its valences within particular cultural and temporal contexts, study the processes that enable its reproduction, and analyze how it rearticulates or is "*re*constructed as social regimes change and histories unfold."[24]

Several historians of colonial Latin America have argued that it is necessary to keep limpieza de sangre and race analytically distinct for the sake of historical specificity and in particular to attempt to be faithful to the ways in which people of that time and place understood their social identities. Some scholars fear that equating notions of lineage, blood, and descent with race would mean characterizing all premodern societies, and those studied by anthropologists, as racially structured.[25] The argument is compelling, and it is certainly difficult to dispute the point that there is a significant difference between the racial discourses that European colonialism unleashed and indigenous kinship systems. But attempting to draw a rigid analytical line between purity of blood and race is tricky, first, because the two concepts gained currency at about the same time and appear side by side in virtually all *probanzas* (certificates) of lim-pieza de sangre, and second, because the former influenced the latter in no small ways. Indeed, there was no neat transition from early modern notions of lineage to race. In the Hispanic Atlantic world, Iberian notions of genealogy and purity of blood—both of which involved a complex of ideas regarding descent and inheritance (biological and otherwise)—gave way to particular understandings of racial difference.[26]

There is nothing original about asserting that there was a link between European genealogical notions and racial discourses. As the anthropologist Ann Laura Stoler has observed, both Michel Foucault and Benedict Anderson alluded to this link, albeit in different ways. Foucault, who viewed the problem of race mainly as part of Europe's "internal and permanent war with itself" and therefore did not consider colonialism's relevance to it, implied that a discourse of class had emerged from the "racism" of the European aristocracy. For his part, Anderson suggested that race had its origins in ideologies of "class" sprung from the landed nobility.[27] Thus, for one scholar, the aristocracy's racism informed class; for the other, its elitism shaped race. To some extent, these two different formulations stem from confusion over how to characterize the nobility's obsession with "blood," which more often than not was accompanied by concerns with biological inheritance, anxieties about reproduction outside the group, and a series of insidious assumptions about the inferiority and impurity of members of the commoner estate. Medieval representations of peasants, for example, rendered them as a lower order of humanity and associated them with animals, dirt, and excrement.[28] The beastialization of the peasantry could reach such extremes that a historian of slavery has suggested that it was an important precursor to the early modern racialization of Jews and blacks.[29]

Whether medieval and early modern concerns with blood and lineage —in Europe and elsewhere—can be classified as racism will most likely continue to be debated, especially by those who favor using a loose definition of race that makes it applicable to most naturalizing or essentializing discourses and those who opt for a narrow one that basically limits its use to the nineteenth century and beyond. The debate is important but frankly less pressing than analyzing the historical significance of those concerns—the social tensions that produced them, the terms people used to express them, and the ways in which they were reproduced or rearticulated over time and across geocultural contexts. This book therefore uses the word *race* in relation to the discourse of limpieza de sangre but does so with caution, stressing that both concepts were strongly connected to lineage and intersected with religion. Through much of the early modern period, they remained part of a grid of knowledge constituted not by scientific (biologistic) discourses but by religious ones and operated through an "episteme of resemblance" in which similitude dominated the organization of symbols and interpretations and representations of the universe.[30] The book also emphasizes that concepts of blood purity and race were neither contained in Europe nor simply a consequence of the continent's "internal war with itself." They operated in a transatlantic context, and their continued salience and fluctuating meanings over the centuries were partly, if not greatly, determined by colonialism.

In sum, by underscoring the interrelated nature of discourses of purity of blood in Iberia and the Americas, this study undermines the view (especially prominent among Spanish historians) that the problem of limpieza de sangre was primarily an Iberian phenomenon as well as the contention (made by some scholars of Spanish America) that it can be separated from that of race. Furthermore, it problematizes the conceptual division that the literature on race sometimes makes between colonial racism and anti-Semitism. Some studies have argued that the two types of discriminatory regimes are manifestly different: that whereas the former has been characterized by the construction and maintenance of (colonial) hierarchies, the latter has typically promoted exclusion or outright extermination (as in the case of Nazi Germany). But as Étienne Balibar has stressed, a stark distinction between an "inclusive" colonial racism and an "exclusive" (usually anti-Semitic) one is untenable because historically, the two forms have not only exhibited similar characteristics but have depended on each other; rather than having separate genealogies, they have a "joint descent."[31] Few historical phenomena demonstrate this close relationship between anti-Semitic and colonial discourses of difference better than the ideology of purity of blood, which spread while Spain was forging its overseas empire. Like the ships, people, and merchandise moving to and from Europe, Africa, and the Americas, the ideas and practices associated with the notion of limpieza de sangre circulated within, and helped forge, the Hispanic Atlantic world.

If the area to which this book most directly contributes is the study of race in Spanish America, it also has implications for a number of other topics, including ones related to periodization, nationalism, and comparative colonialisms. For one, the centrality of the seventeenth century to the development of the sistema de castas places the focus on a period that historians of colonial Latin America have tended to understudy. Perhaps unduly influenced by anthropologist George Foster's characterization of

colonial Latin American culture as having "crystallized" or acquired
its basic social institutions by 1580, the historiography has generally regarded the years between that decade and 1750 as largely uneventful.[32]
Neglect of this "long seventeenth century" or middle phase of Spanish
colonialism might also be explained by its shortage of events as dramatic
as those of the conquest and its aftermath. How can the period compete, for example, with the years that witnessed the early evangelizing
campaigns and their inspiration in biblical, messianic, and eschatologi-
cal interpretations of history; the Spanish "debates" about the humanity of the Amerindians; and the civil war that erupted among some of
Peru's conquerors? It may also be that the seventeenth-century's difficult
paleography and less extensive secondary literature have made studying
other eras more appealing.

   Whatever the case, the period was anything but static. Seventeenth-
century Spanish America not only had strong connections with Spain
but underwent crucial social and cultural transformations. Included
among these changes was the rise of creole patriotism, a topic that has
been explored by David Brading, Bernard Lavallé, and others and which
is analyzed in the present study in relation to the ideology of limpieza de
sangre. By interrogating the complex relationship of patriotic, religious,
and blood discourses, the book makes an intervention in discussions of
nationalism in Latin America. Nationalism, however, is not an explicit
subject of inquiry, in part because it did not appear until the end of
the colonial period, if then. The region's independence movements were
primarily triggered by Napoleon's invasion of Spain in 1808 and impo-
sition of his brother Joseph as the new king, which on both sides of the
Atlantic led to political assemblies and discussions that quickly became
much more than about the restitution of Ferdinand VII to the throne.
Thus, Latin American nationalism seems to have been the result, not
the cause, of the independence movements, and to speak of eighteenth-
century "creole nationalism" is to walk on shaky argumentative ground.[33]
Furthermore, as a number of historians who responded to Benedict
Anderson's thesis about its rise in Spanish America have pointed out,
not only was creole patriotism compatible with continued loyalty to the
Spanish Crown, but the early modern notion of "nation" (*nación*) was
exceedingly ambiguous with regard to territory and bloodlines.[34]

   That a strong identification with the local community existed prior to
independence does not mean that there was a causal connection between
the two or between *criollismo* (creolism) and nationalism. Assuming
such a connection amounts to "doing history backwards," that is, pro-
jecting modern categories onto a world in which those forms of thinking

had not yet come about.[35] It also forecloses the possibility of studying creole patriotism on its own terms—its meanings, motivations, and political effects at different points in time. But if patriotism and nationalism should not be conflated, examinations of colonial political ideology, social developments, and cultural movements are necessary to understand the form that Mexican nationalism took after independence. By exploring the relationship between the religiously inflected concept of limpieza de sangre and notions of citizenship (*vecindad*) in New Spain, this study seeks to provide a basis for further discussions about how the particularities of colonialism in Mexico shaped its postindependence political projects, gendered and racialized imaginings of the nation, and legal formulations of the citizen.[36]

It also aims to highlight some of the specificities of Spanish colonialism. Although there are continuities and similarities between different colonial projects, colonialism cannot be reduced to a single model; it has multiple historicities.[37] The Spanish colonial project, the earliest in the Americas, was driven by historically and culturally specific forces, and its course was determined by early modern dynamics on both sides of the Atlantic. It differed most from modern imperial projects. For example, unlike Britain and France when they launched the second major phase of European colonialism starting in the second half of the eighteenth century, when Spain invaded the Americas, it was not an industrial power seeking raw materials and markets for its manufactured goods. Its expansion west was initially propelled by the search for gold (increasingly important as a medium of exchange in international commerce), and its economic project came to be based primarily on the exploitation of mineral wealth and on state-controlled systems of extracting labor and tribute from native populations that had few parallels.

Furthermore, Spanish colonialism began long before the emergence of the politics of nationhood, liberalism, and Enlightenment-inspired universalist concepts of freedom, equality, rights, progress, and citizenship. Together with the expansion of capitalist relations, these modern developments generated new ideological frameworks for justifying colonial rule as well as a deep tension between the particularism of colonialism (predicated on the creation and perpetuation of colonial hierarchies) and the universalism of western European political theory.[38] Spanish colonialism in the Americas, based more on the concept of status than on the notion of rights, did not have to contend with this tension, at least not at first. During its first two centuries, its main ideological contradiction stemmed from, on one hand, universalist Christian doctrines that touted the redemptive powers of baptism and the equality of all members of

the church and, on the other, the construction of different categories
of Christians. The extent to which religion played a role in justifying
expansion and colonial rule was another aspect of the early modern
Spanish colonial project that distinguished it from modern ones.

Readily distinguishable in certain respects from nineteenth- and
twentieth-century imperialism, Spanish colonialism becomes less distinctive when it is compared to other formative or early colonial projects
in the Americas. Contrary to what the Black Legend would have us believe, during the initial phase of European expansion, Spaniards did not
have a monopoly on the unbridled use of violence against native peoples. The British and Dutch amply demonstrated their capacity for bar-
barity. Furthermore, Spanish, Portuguese, English, and French colonial
projects shared a number of features, including expansion through settlement; efforts to recreate European ways of life; and religious utopias,
Catholic and Protestant alike.[39] But similarities among these "settler-
type" colonialisms can be overstated, among other reasons because each
power had its own economic, political, and religious agendas, even if
at certain historical moments some of these overlapped. The Spanish
state's control over some systems of labor, its transformation of large
indigenous populations into tributaries, and its collective incorporation
of native people as Christian vassals of the Crown of Castile were exceptional, especially when compared to British policies in Anglo North
America. And although efforts to convert native people to Christianity
were by no means exclusive to Spaniards, no other European colonial
power, not even the other Catholic ones of Portugal and France, relied
on the church to spread the faith, support the government, and structure
colonial society as much as Castile. The historical moment and cultural
context were both crucial. That religion was integral to Spanish colonialism was due in large measure to its importance in sixteenth-century
Spain itself, where Catholicism was the only religion allowed, where the
church and state had developed an extraordinarily strong relationship,
and where the twin notions of "Old Christian blood" and genealogical purity had emerged as powerful cultural principles and exclusionary
weapons. Religion, lineage, and blood would in turn be used to organize
the Spanish colonial world.

In conclusion, Spanish colonialism was shaped by particular economic, political, and religious goals; by historical circumstances in early
modern Spain and Spanish America; and by distinctive principles of social organization. As a result, its categories of discourse, mechanisms of
inclusion and exclusion, and forms of establishing the boundaries of the
Spanish community were unique or, at the very least, substantially different from modern colonial projects in Africa and Asia. Some of the main

differences and reasons for them will be apparent in the chapters that follow, which discuss religious and social developments in early modern Castile, Spanish political ideology in the Americas, and the organization of colonial Mexican society. Before describing the book's content in more detail, a word on sources and methodology is in order.

ARCHIVES, SOURCES, AND CHAPTER DESCRIPTION

Research for this book entailed trips to various Mexican, Spanish, and United States archives in search of documents pertaining to the issue of purity of blood, the most obvious types being the *información de limpieza de sangre* ("information of purity of blood") and the *probanza de limpieza de sangre* ("certification [or proof] of purity of blood"). The former normally consisted of genealogical information that a person (hereafter referred to as either "petitioner" or "candidate") seeking to access an institution or post with purity requirements would provide. The latter generally contained documents from the actual investigation process through which limpieza de sangre was "proven" and certified. Although the informaciones were usually placed in the probanza dossier, it is not rare to find copies of the first without the second, perhaps because at some point they became misplaced or because, for some reason or another, the investigation did not take place. It is also not rare to find documents in which probanzas are called informaciones, which suggests that the two words became somewhat interchangeable. In general, however, an información functioned as a kind of affidavit and did not in and of itself constitute the "proof" of limpieza de sangre, which in theory required a formal investigation into the petitioner's ancestral and religious history. If the results of the investigation were positive, the person received certified copies of the probanza.

Rather abundant in archives with colonial Latin American holdings, probanzas de limpieza de sangre tend to be quite uniform in language and in procedure. Some variations do occur, especially when the officials conducting the investigation suspected "impure" ancestry, but for the most part, the task of reading documents from this genre is repetitive and tedious, which might account for the lack of systematic studies of the problem of limpieza de sangre beyond a particular case or institution. Such studies are made even more difficult by the scattered nature of the sources and the way some have been classified. At times labeled simply "genealogies" or subsumed under other types of documents (such as *probanzas de méritos y servicios,* or "proofs of merits and services"), limpieza-related documents are currently dispersed in archives across

Latin America, Spain, and the United States, and on occasion, tracking a single case can involve research not only in various archives but in several countries. For example, I found several references to and parts of a probanza in Mexico's Archivo General de la Nación and Spain's Archivo Histórico Nacional, but I did not find the actual genealogical investigation until I examined the Mexican Inquisition Collection of the Huntington Library, in San Marino, California. Given that thousands of probanzas were generated in the course of the colonial period (and beyond) and their scattered nature, scholars studying the problem might be tempted to look at the records of one institution, for example, those of the Mexican or Peruvian Inquisition or those of a single guild or convent.

Like studies of specific groups of people (bureaucrats, merchants, women, slaves, and so forth) and of particular places for short periods of time, works on limpieza in one institution might result in important findings but in general do not promise to generate conclusions regarding the workings and evolution of colonial society. The observation that the historian William Taylor made of social historians—that their challenge is to explain how the small picture fits into the bigger one and thus to put "more history into social history"—applies to institutional ones as well.[40] To be sure, documents produced by institutions such as the Inquisition are important, and more than a thousand were analyzed for the present study in order to provide a careful reading of the concept of purity of blood, the language that accompanied it, and changes in its definitions over time.[41] But the issue of limpieza de sangre transcended the establishments that had purity requirements and, whether in New Spain or elsewhere, is therefore not found exclusively in probanzas. Furthermore, the definitions contained in such documents do not tell the whole story. As historians know fully well, the rules, meanings, and prescriptions offered in laws, decrees, institutional constitutions, and other normative instruments cannot be taken at face value, certainly not in a society like that of colonial Spanish America, where the breach between theory and practice was widened by the legally and socially sanctioned distinction between private and public life.[42]

Research for this book therefore involved studying sources produced by the Inquisition and other institutions, but it also entailed mining a wider array of sources that refer to the problem of limpieza de sangre, directly or indirectly. These include inquisitorial correspondence, memorials by theologians and jurists, juridical texts, licenses granted to Iberians to go to the Americas, spatial regulations, land petitions and grants, nobility documents, inheritance records, criminal and civil cases, minutes from town council meetings, indigenous histories, marriage legislation, and in the late colonial period, paintings. Purity information is likely to be provided in applications by Spaniards or creoles wanting an inquisitorial or religious post, but it can also be found in a high-ranking military officer's petition to marry a woman from the colonies, or in legal cases like that of a widow of an eighteenth-century miner from Guanajuato who wished to prove her limpieza status in order to strengthen her claims over certain lands. It might also be found in documents in which a native ruler tried to prove his noble and pure ancestry to defend his right to public office in his town or, indirectly, in portraits of creole or native elites that included genealogies. And so forth. As the eclectic quality of the sources indicates, the problem of limpieza de sangre cut across socioeconomic, religious, and cultural domains and constituted a discourse, a knowledge-producing instrument that promoted certain practices, social relationships, and identities and that was inextricably linked to operations of power.[43]

 To provide a history of this key concept, its relationship to colonial Mexican racial ideology, and its imbrication with religion, the book begins not in America but in the Iberian Peninsula. Chapter 1 provides an overview of the social and political circumstances that in fifteenth- and sixteenth-century Spain helped to produce the statutes of limpieza de sangre and a concept of race intimately tied to lineage, culture, and religion. Chapter 2 underscores the importance of the Inquisition in exacerbating genealogical concerns in early modern Hispanic society and the related emergence of a model of classifying purity that was based on paternal and maternal bloodlines. This dual-descent model heightened Old Christian anxieties over reproduction and marriage with the descendants of Jews and Muslims and also over controlling the sexuality of "pure" women. Chapter 3 focuses on the procedures that, as of about the mid-sixteenth century, many Spanish institutions with purity statutes devised to examine the genealogies of potential members and their creation of a new genre of documents: the probanza de limpieza de sangre. An exclusionary device that was transferred to the Americas by the state, church, and Inquisition, the genre merits close attention because it mobilized a series of archival and social practices that not only made the status of limpieza de sangre highly unstable but helped foster genealogical mentalities in the broader Hispanic Atlantic world.

Shifting the discussion to developments in central New Spain, Chapter 4 focuses on the rise of an Indian republic—separate from but subordinate to the Spanish one—the creation of a special juridico-theological status for the native people, and the production of a discourse of indigenous purity. It argues that lineage became a key reproductive strategy in the "Indian republic," where it was first used by the descendants of pre-Hispanic dynasties to prove their noble status and where the concept of purity, which acquired force in the eighteenth century, was used not just by individuals but also by groups or communities to make certain political and economic claims. Chapter 5 discusses the initial importance of genealogy in Spanish cities. Specifically, it focuses on the rise of a creole aristocracy in central Mexico, its development of local interests, and its increasing preoccupation with ancestry and purity at the end of the sixteenth century. This preoccupation with lineage was encouraged by royal policies pertaining to immigration, by the dispensation of grants for the descendants of conquerors and first colonists, and by the requirements for some religious and public offices. It was also nourished by creoles' belief in their right, as patrimonial sons of the land, to monopolize positions of power and influence and by their willingness to use the concept of purity to curb the political and economic claims of the growing population of mixed ancestry.

Chapter 6 examines New Spain's sistema de castas; its origins, language, and sociocultural logic. It explains its emergence as a function of processes of sociopolitical exclusion as well as of Spanish anxieties about the results of the Christianization project. These anxieties, which increased from the 1560s onward because of the continuation of "idolatry," facilitated the extension of Iberian notions of impurity to colonial populations. The notion of limpieza de sangre, closely tied to the concept of heresy in Spain, essentially entered into the colonial space through the back door of idolatry, generating acute contradictions in the status of the native peoples and their descendants. The chapter also underscores the crucial role that slavery played in shaping the classification of Africans and their descendants and more generally in determining the form that the sistema de castas took. Unlike native people, blacks were not recognized as a community or republic, were not collectively incorporated into the Crown of Castile as free Christian vassals, and were not officially declared pure of blood, all of which affected their ability to make genealogical claims.

Chapter 7 elaborates on the procedures that colonial institutions used for proving purity of blood, their transatlantic dimensions, and their implications for part of the creole population. Initially the products of the Christianization project and anticonverso policies, these procedures served to create the fiction of New Spain's lack of Jewish and Muslim antecedents and, as in Spain, turned the probanza de limpieza de sangre into a part of the public domain and culture of honor. The purity requirements also reproduced archival practices that fostered a genealogical and historical consciousness among elite creoles that throughout the colonial period reinforced their identification with a Spanish Old

Christian community of blood, even as their attachment to the land of their birth intensified and even as they began to forge a nativeness (*naturaleza*) separate from Castile. Chapter 8 closely examines the extension of the discourse of limpieza de sangre to colonial populations and contradictions between how the concept was officially defined and how it operated. It argues that these contradictions emerged not only because prescription and practice were frequently not in harmony, but also because of the ambiguous religious standing of native people and blacks, the elusiveness of the category of Old Christian, and the appropriation of the concept by people of native and African ancestry.

- Chapter 9 outlines some of the changes that limpieza de sangre underwent in the second half of the colonial period, including its identification of more sources of contamination (of more "stains") and the gradual association of purity with Spanishness. It also discusses how this secularization of the concept—made visual in casta paintings—gradually came to link limpieza to white skin color and thus mapped it onto the body. The last section deals with creole patriotic discourses during the period of the Bourbon reforms, a time of greater state intervention in the institutions of marriage and family and in colonial society in general. It argues that the form that these discourses took reflected the weight of the concept of limpieza de sangre in Mexican society and the complex attitudes toward indigenous and black blood it had helped to generate among Spanish elites. Late colonial patriotic vindications and imaginaries were informed by traditional Castilian definitions of political rights, but they were also deeply influenced by religion and race.

PART ONE

Iberian Precedents

CHAPTER ONE

The Emergence of the Spanish Statutes
of *Limpieza de Sangre*

The emergence and spread of the Spanish statutes of purity of blood was a complicated, contested, and drawn-out process. They appeared on a gradual, piecemeal basis and, for one hundred years after the first municipal statute was issued, received only sporadic support from the crown. Some statutes were vigorously challenged, others rescinded only to be reinstated, and yet others were not rigorously implemented. Nonetheless, during the sixteenth century, numerous religious and secular institutions established limpieza de sangre requirements, and these continued to be an integral feature of Spanish society for centuries to come. What implications did the proliferation of the statutes precisely at the time of Iberian expansion to the Americas have on Spanish colonial society? How did they influence religious thought and social dynamics after the conquest? What genealogical beliefs and practices did the requirements of limpieza de sangre bequeath to the Americas? Answering these questions first requires an examination of the meanings of the concept of purity of blood in Spain and the context in which it gained importance. This chapter and the following two (which make up Part 1) provide such an examination.

Specifically, the chapters trace the development of the ideology of limpieza de sangre from its initial appearance in the middle of the fifteenth century to its crystallization one hundred years later and subsequent merger with notions of nobility. The main objective is to discuss general social, religious, and political developments in Castile that help to explain when and why the idea of purity of blood acquired importance and the ways in which it was related to notions of genealogy and race. Although they deal strictly with the discourse of purity of blood in

Iberia, Chapters 1 through 3 focus on those dimensions that would also characterize it in Spanish America. These dimensions include the idea that blood was a vehicle through which all sorts of characteristics and religious proclivities were transmitted, the deployment and reification of the categories of Old Christian and New Christian, the reliance on female sexuality and reproduction to the maintenance of the social order, the link between bloodlines and the honor system, and the establishment of limpieza status through juridical procedures.

This chapter begins with a brief discussion of the social and religious circumstances that prompted the first major waves of Jewish conversions to Christianity in late medieval Spain, the older Christian community's increasingly negative attitudes toward the converts from the 1430s onward, and the passage of the first purity requirements in the middle of the fourteenth century. It then delves into factors that helped give the statutes momentum in the second half of the fifteenth century, including the growth of a discourse about secret or "crypto-Judaism," the revival of a crusading spirit during the reign of Isabella and Ferdinand (monarchs of Castile from 1474 to 1504), and the establishment of the Inquisition. In addition to drawing attention to the political, economic, and institutional dynamics that contributed to the growing significance of the principle of limpieza de sangre, this section stresses that growing social anxieties over conversion, shifting community boundaries, and religious loyalties also played a crucial role in turning lineage into a mechanism for promoting order, fixity, and hierarchy.

MASS CONVERSIONS, ANTI-SEMITISM, AND THE RISE OF THE STATUTES IN LATE MEDIEVAL SPAIN

One current of scholarship on medieval Spain paints the region as a kind of Garden of Eden that for centuries allowed the "coexistence" (*convivencia*) of Christians, Jews, and Muslims and that fostered the rise of a Jewish "Golden Age."[1] According to this current, the convivencia, which was at its peak from the eighth century to the middle of the twelfth, came to a definitive end in the 1400s, when the first statutes of purity of blood were passed and the Spanish Inquisition was established to deal with the supposed problem of crypto-Judaism. Certain scholars also claim that with the systematic use of ancestry against Jewish converts to Christianity, racial, as opposed to religious, anti-Semitism emerged for the first time in history.[2] Although the notion of convivencia with its lingering connotations of tolerance has been challenged by a number of historians, among them David Nirenberg, scholars generally agree that

during the thirteenth and fourteenth centuries, violence against Jews increased in Iberia, as it did in broader Europe, and that it was accompanied by their increasing demonization in Christian popular mythology,
folklore, and iconography.[3] These developments occurred in the context
of heightened social tensions resulting from the transition to a monetary economy and the devastation wrought by the Black Death. The latter struck western Europe between 1347 and 1351 and had several subsequent phases, including one in the years 1388–90. The Spanish purity statutes did not appear until later, but their history is usually traced
to that turbulent period and in particular to the mass conversions that
anti-Jewish movements catalyzed at the end of the fourteenth century.

In 1391, a wave of anti-Semitic attacks that started in Seville spread to
other cities (including Toledo, Valencia, and Barcelona), resulting in the
deaths of thousands of Jews.[4] Violent incidents of the sort had occurred
before, but the late-fourteenth-century pogroms, which occurred amid
a severe economic depression, were particularly significant because they
produced the first major wave of Jewish conversions to Christianity, the
first community of conversos.[5] Faced with the possibility of becoming
the targets of angry Christian mobs once again and subject to a growing number of professional, economic, residential, and sumptuary restrictions, tens of thousands of Jews felt compelled to accept baptism.
Conversion implied assimilating into the dominant society, for it made
them eligible for public and ecclesiastical offices and allowed them to live
outside of Jewish quarters (*juderías*) and to stop wearing distinctive clothing. It also granted the converts the freedom to marry other Christians.
Although the sudden conversions en masse created the impression among
contemporaries that they had been insincere, the church for the most
part accepted them and regarded the conversos as Christians. During the
early fifteenth century, it concentrated mainly on proselytizing in Jewish
communities and maintaining the boundary between Christians (including those who converted from Judaism) and Jews, historically the main
basis of Christian identity.[6]

Aggressive missionary activities by the Dominicans and Franciscans
led to more Jewish conversions to Christianity, especially during the
years 1412–15, but efforts to make the conversos sever their residential,
social, and cultural ties with their former community were generally unsuccessful. Various towns, particularly Valladolid, issued laws aimed at
limiting all kinds of interaction between the two groups, but they apparently did not have the intended results because anxieties over policing
religious boundaries continued to escalate. By the mid-1430s, these anxieties were being manifested in ever-more-disturbing ways. The more
traditional Christians—"Old Christians" (*cristiano viejos*), as they later

called themselves—were not only beginning to express serious doubts about the conversos' commitment to Christianity but were increasingly relying on genealogy to think about and determine identities. The growing concern with lineage was not exclusive to Christians. The conversions of the late fourteenth and early fifteenth centuries were followed by disputations, apostasies, and migrations (sometimes involving various shifts in faith) that posed new classificatory challenges for Spain's three main religious communities. Christians, Jews, and Muslims all responded by turning to new and mutually informed forms of communal identity that privileged ancestry.[7]

Among Old Christians, the newly invigorated concern with lineage was rooted in the idea that "Jewishness" was transmitted in the blood, that it was a natural, inheritable condition. Some therefore came to believe that having even partial Jewish ancestry compromised Christian identity, values, and understandings. This naturalization of a religious-cultural identity coincided with the emergence of a lexicon consisting of terms such as *raza* (race), *casta* (caste), and *linaje* (lineage) that was informed by popular notions regarding biological reproduction in the natural world and, in particular, horse breeding.[8] It was also accompanied by an emergent Old Christian preoccupation with avoiding sexual, reproductive, and marital relations with the converts and their descendants—with protecting "pure" Christian lineages from converso (understood as "Jewish") blood.[9] As the middle of the fifteenth century approached, Spanish genealogical concepts were acquiring particular contours, and social and religious anxieties were beginning to constitute New Christians as a particular *type* of convert.

The reasons for the dramatic shift in Spanish attitudes toward the conversos remain a mystery. Historians who believe that the majority of conversions occurring after the 1391 massacres were not sincere and that at least a portion of the converts' descendants continued to "judaize" (to practice Judaism) tend to argue that religious factors played a role or that worries about the need to safeguard the Christian faith were real.[10] On the other hand, scholars who contend that most conversos became devoted Christians, especially if they had converted before 1492, generally view religion as a pretext. They attribute the hardening of Old Christian views toward that community either to social factors—particularly, resentment of the converts' rapid socioeconomic advancement, ability to secure public and ecclesiastical appointments, and integration into patrician oligarchies—or to sheer racism.[11] Whether the incipient anticonverso movement (whose impetus is identified sometimes more with the noble estate and at others with the Old Christian "masses") was propelled by religious, social, or anti-Semitic factors or all three, by the mid-fifteenth century, the image of the "secret Jew," so central to early modern Spanish thought, was starting to appear alongside a strident Old Christian identity rooted in the traditional military nobility and in the idea of Christian superiority over Jews and Muslims.[12] At the same time, charges of crypto-Judaism were beginning to play a role in political struggles between the crown and nobility, in conflicts over taxation and local autonomy, and in factional competition over control of municipal government. As events in central Castile demonstrated, the confluence of these trends provided the momentum for exclusionary policies that singled out the conversos.

Toledo, seat of the Primate of Spain and host to the most numerically and socially prominent population of conversos, was the site of the first major struggle to establish purity-of-blood policies. In early 1449, as the city's religious and secular leaders encouraged resistance against the repressive tax policies of King Juan II (1406–54) and converso tax collectors were made into the scapegoats of new fiscal impositions, a series of riots erupted that mainly targeted the judería and New Christians. When royal forces arrived to reestablish order, the city found itself in a virtual civil war. Pero Sarmiento, the city's ambitious *alcalde mayor* (chief magistrate) and leader of a group of rebels who accused Alvaro de Luna (the king's minister) of being partial to the conversos, took advantage of his control of the government and, along with other local officials, drew up a decree that made converted Jews and their descendants permanently ineligible for public offices and all municipal appointments.[13] Some political and religious figures raised their voices against the proposal, but they could not prevent the town council from approving it. Historians of early modern Spain consider this decree, the Sentencia-Estatuto, one of the earliest statutes of limpieza de sangre, if not the first.[14] Its supporters, who clearly resented the conversos' prosperity and role in municipal government, claimed that the New Christians could not be trusted because of the insincerity of their conversions; deep hatred of *christianos viejos lindos* ("clean/beautiful Old Christians"); and crimes against God, king, and the public good.[15] The city, they argued, had to protect itself and the Catholic faith by ensuring that only people with unsullied Christian lineages were in positions of power and authority. Pope Nicholas V and a number of Spanish writers, some of whom were Old Christians, strongly condemned the Sentencia-Estatuto for violating the principle of the unity of the church and undermining the redemptive powers of baptism, but to no avail.[16] Juan II, apparently in an effort to gain support at a time of great social instability in Castile, approved it in

August 1451, about five months after he had granted a general pardon to the residents of Toledo for their insubordination.[17]

Toledo's Sentencia-Estatuto had powerful forces behind it, and its language was indicative of the extreme levels that anti-Jewish *and* anticonverso rhetoric was reaching in Spain in the middle of the fifteenth century. Jewish people were increasingly depicted as a hybrid and corrupted lineage, sometimes even as the outcome of monstrous mixtures—of crosses with monsters, demons, and animals—and their supposed traits were being projected onto the conversos.[18] As anticonverso hostility spread from Toledo to other cities (including Ciudad Real, Córdoba, Jaén, and Seville) during the 1460s and 1470s, claims about the treachery and heretical tendencies of the descendants of Jewish converts to Christianity were repeated again and again, and different institutions began to adopt exclusionary measures based on the same genealogical and naturalizing logic as the Sentencia-Estatuto. During these decades, the discovery of cases of (alleged) crypto-Judaism in some religious orders and other establishments, including the Jeronymites, helped to undermine the arguments of the opponents of the Sentencia-Estatuto and to cast suspicions on all conversos. It also convinced a number of church officials that the converts' religious beliefs were still being corrupted by their ongoing contact with Jews, and they therefore called for more intense efforts to separate them. Frustrations over the failure of similar efforts had of course been expressed before, but in the politically and religiously charged climate of the last third of the fifteenth century, they would have extremely grave consequences for both groups.

POLITICAL CENTRALIZATION, CHRISTIAN MILITANCY, AND THE FOUNDING OF THE INQUISITION

The worsening plight of Spain's conversos and Jews occurred during a period of great social and political turmoil and heightened religious zeal. In Castile, the decades between the Sentencia-Estatuto and the establishment of the Inquisition were marked, among other things, by the weak leadership of kings Juan II and his successor Enrique IV (1454–74), royal efforts to curb the political power of the upper nobility, and a crisis of succession that led to a civil war. The nobility included descendants of soldiers who during the period of the Reconquista (the Christian "reconquest" of Iberia from Islamic rule) had received land and status for providing military service to the monarchy. This estate consisted of three main categories: *hidalgos,* who mainly enjoyed local prestige and

exemption from certain taxes; *señores,* owners of small territorial possessions, or *señoríos;* and *grandes,* the titled nobility. In the mid-century,
wealth, land, titles, and political posts were concentrated in the last
category and, more concretely, in the hands of about two dozen noble
families. In a Spain that was still predominantly rural, their economic
and political power rested primarily on their control over large tracts of
territory.[19]

Enrique IV, whose first decade in power was relatively stable but who
nonetheless inherited the problems of factionalism and civil conflicts
that plagued his father's rule, tried to weaken the political muscle of the
grandes through a series of administrative and centralizing reforms.[20]
His attempts were for the most part unsuccessful. Accustomed to governing towns with considerable autonomy, the nobility resisted the push
toward political centralization. The consolidation of royal authority in
Castile had to wait until the reign of Enrique IV's successor and half-
sister, Isabella (1474–1504), whose claim to the throne was solidified
only after a civil war between her supporters and those of her niece,
Juana la Beltraneja. The civil war ended in 1479, the same year in which
the queen's husband, Ferdinand, inherited the Crown of Aragón. The
marriage of the "Catholic Kings," as the couple was later called by Pope
Alexander VI, united the crowns of Castile and Aragon and made a
"double monarchy" possible in Iberia.[21]

The two monarchs, who are perhaps best known for their support
of the voyages of Columbus that eventually resulted in Spain's acquisition of a vast overseas empire in "the Indies," essentially expanded on
Enrique IV's reforms but more effectively dealt with the nobility by simultaneously affirming its socioeconomic preeminence and curbing its
political strength. The weakening of the aristocracy had implications
for the emerging bourgeoisie (composed of merchants, scribes, doctors,
and other urban professionals), for the crown no longer had to rely on
it as much as it had in the past to offset the power of the nobles. The
Catholic Kings also improved and enlarged the administration of justice
(thenceforth centered more on their own regional courts, the *audiencias*
and *chancillerías*), promulgated civil law (most notably, by passing the
Leyes de Toro in 1505), and created a system of councils that included
the reorganized Council of Castile, the Council of the State, the Council
of Finance, the Council of Orders, and the Council of Aragón. Finally,
they increased royal authority by strongly associating the Crown of Castile with the Christian cause, which they did not only by establishing
the Holy Office of the Inquisition but by declaring war on Granada, the
only remaining Muslim-controlled region in the Iberian Peninsula.

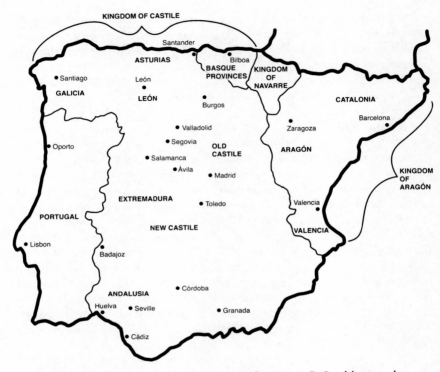

MAP 1. Sixteenth-century Iberia. SOURCE: After James B. Lockhart and
Stuart B. Schwartz, *Early Latin America* (New York: Cambridge University
Press, 1983) p. 21. Drawn by María Elena Martínez.

The Holy Office was not an entirely new institution. Ecclesiastical inquisitions had existed in late medieval Spain and other parts of Christian
Europe. During the twelfth and thirteenth centuries, a rise in spiritual
movements that were considered heretical led the papacy to order bishops and archbishops to conduct regular visits to the parishes within
their jurisdictions where incidences of heresy had occurred, report on
the spiritual life of their communities, and turn in any suspected heretics to secular authorities. When this method of relying on "episcopal
inquisitors" proved ineffective, the Vatican began to appoint judges to
undertake special investigations in designated regions, thus giving rise
to the "papal Inquisition."[22] This institution, which because of a shortage in judges became increasingly dependent on the Dominicans and
Franciscans (Mendicant orders founded in the thirteenth century) for
the investigation of heresy, mainly functioned in France, Germany, and
Italy. Due to the spread of heretical movements in southern France, it

also operated in the Crown of Aragón starting in the year 1232, but by the fifteenth century, it was for the most part inactive. In Castile, a region that apparently did not produce any formal heresies during the late medieval period, inquisitorial tribunals were virtually unknown.[23] But this changed in the last third of the fifteenth century, when concerns over the religious loyalty of the conversos escalated to unprecedented levels and were manipulated by certain groups to further their political and socioeconomic designs.

In the 1460s, support for establishing an inquisition in Castile grew among members of the religious orders who wanted to create an official organism to identify and try conversos suspected of heresy. The Franciscans in particular favored the creation of such a tribunal, and they pressured the Jeronymites into raising the issue with the crown. The general of the Order of Saint Jerome, Fray Alonso de Oropesa, opposed the mushrooming anticonverso movement and the abuses it was perpetrating in the name of the faith but nonetheless considered the problem of religious heterodoxy among *some* of the converts important enough to warrant a solution. After initial hesitation, he supported the proposal of establishing an inquisition in Castile, one that would serve more as a tool of reform and instruction than as a means to punish.[24] Fray Alonso found a sympathetic ear in King Enrique IV, to whom he was a key adviser, and in the early 1460s, the monarch sent a proposal to Rome. But it was not until numerous reports of alleged "judaizers" (crypto-Jews) in Seville and elsewhere reached Ferdinand and Isabella that they pursued, and received, permission from the Vatican to establish the Spanish Inquisition.[25]

The Inquisition was a tribunal set up to investigate charges of heresy among Christians and in particular among conversos. It had little jurisdiction over Jews and dealt not with Judaism per se but with the problem of crypto-Judaism.[26] Signed by Pope Sixtus IV in 1478, the papal bull that granted Castile the right to found its own inquisition referred to the problem of apostasy among the conversos but did not indicate just how serious it was. By 1480, a tribunal consisting of three inquisitors was functioning in Seville. The subsequent discovery of a supposed converso plot against the Inquisition seemed to confirm allegations that the threat of heresy or "judaizing" was real, particularly in Andalusía, and led to the establishment (sometimes temporary) of tribunals in other cities, including Córdoba (1482), Ciudad Real (1483), and Jaen (1483).[27] By 1483, the Inquisition had been extended to Aragón, or rather, the old tribunal and its appointments and salaries were placed more under the authority of the crown than under that of the pope.[28] Two years later, the tribunal that had been operating in Ciudad Real was transferred to

Toledo, where the first permanent court and seat of the Inquisition were established. It was also in that city that the Supreme Council of the Holy and General Inquisition (the "Suprema"), founded between 1483 and 1488, was based. Initially consisting of three ecclesiastical members and a presiding inquisitor general, the first being Tomás de Torquemada, the Suprema was in charge of coordinating activities among tribunals in Castile, León, and Aragón. Later it was also responsible for overseeing all matters handled by the Holy Office in the Americas. The crown selected the members of the Suprema and all other inquisitorial officials. In theory, the pope exerted some influence on the choice of inquisitor general, but he too was presented by the monarchs. Because the crown ultimately determined the inquisitors, a number of historians have regarded the Holy Office as more of a royal than ecclesiastical tribunal, as an instrument of civil power, and even as an expression of Spanish absolutism.[29] And because it consisted of various regional tribunals that were all accountable to one central body—the Suprema was the only governmental agency that had jurisdiction over the entire Spanish empire—it has also at times been viewed as Spain's, if not Europe's, first protonational institution.

Historian Jaime Contreras, for example, views the rise of the Inquisition as a result mainly of the "pseudonationalist" concerns of the Catholic Kings. He concedes that the problem of heresy might have been real but argues that it also provided the crown with the perfect excuse to establish an institution that, while deriving a great deal of authority from its links to the church, was ultimately under royal control. In Contreras's view, the Holy Office was used by Ferdinand and Isabella to strengthen the legitimacy of their rule, which they did on the basis of their defense of the faith.[30] Other scholars grant the Inquisition more of a dual character. They argue that it was mainly created because of the fear that crypto-Jews were trying to subvert the faith from within and that it continued to be concerned with religious issues, but they also stress that as a close ally of the crown, the institution also offered clear political advantages, such as helping to turn the Christian faith into an element of cohesion in a Spain where no real political unity existed.[31] Finally, because the Holy Office confiscated the estates of the persons it prosecuted and disinherited the descendants of those it burned, some historians stress that economic factors also played a role in its founding and perpetuation.[32] Of course, these diverse explanations of the founding of the Inquisition are not incompatible with each other. The institution could have served multiple purposes, depending on the time and place. But its emergence and rapid transformation from a temporary to a permanent institution cannot be fully understood without taking into account the combined effect of anxieties over crypto-Judaism and the militancy that Spanish Catholicism acquired in the 1480s, to which the campaign against Granada strongly contributed.

In 1482, Ferdinand and Isabella responded to a Muslim attack on a Christian town by waging a war against Granada, by then a tributary of Castile. Although the Reconquista had actually ended two centuries earlier, they framed the enterprise as the culmination of the reconquest. The war, which lasted ten years and resulted in victory for the Christians, resuscitated a crusading spirit, bolstered the popularity of the Catholic Kings, and increased the prestige of the monarchy, now solidly identified with Christianity.[33] Roughly coinciding with the Inquisition's first decade of persecutions, it also made Spain's rulers less tolerant of religious minorities, particularly the Jews.[34] Blamed by the Holy Office and some church officials (particularly members of the Dominican order) for the allegedly persistent problem of crypto-Judaism among conversos, they were partially expelled from Andalusía in the early 1480s and in the middle of the decade from certain Aragonese dioceses. These partial expulsions augured the decree of March 31, 1492, which ordered Spanish Jews to leave the region that had been their home since about the first century.

Issued by the Catholic Kings shortly after Granada's surrender and as a fierce religious zeal was sweeping across the peninsula, the expulsion decree of 1492 compelled all Jews who did not convert to Catholicism within four months to leave Castile and Aragón. (Portugal issued a similar decree in 1496 and Navarre in 1498.) As had been the case with the previous decade's partial expulsions, the decision was strongly influenced by the Inquisition and the cases of crypto-Judaism it claimed to have found.[35] At least officially, Jews could not remain in Spain not because they were Jews but because they were thought to be contributing, whether directly or indirectly, to the problem of heresy among the conversos. The decree of expulsion prompted conversions to Catholicism on a greater scale than ever before. At first, church officials, including Cardinal Mendoza and Bishop Hernán de Talavera, undertook peaceful campaigns to indoctrinate the new converts. But the nature of their efforts remains a mystery, as do the reasons for their apparent failure. It is still not known, for example, if the clergy assigned to the evangelization campaign used sermons and catechisms among their new flock.

As for Spanish Muslims, they too were faced with the choice of adopting Christianity or being deported, but this did this not happen until 1502 in Castile and 1526 in Aragón. The treaty signed after the defeat of Granada allowed those who lived there to remain in the town, continue to practice their religion, and enjoy juridical autonomy. During the next

ten years, however, they became increasingly alienated as the relatively
gentle policies of conversion of Bishop Hernán de Talavera were replaced
by the more aggressive methods of Francisco Jiménez de Cisneros, who
served as archbishop of Toledo, the queen's confessor, and inquisitor
general. At the end of the decade, Cisneros's campaigns and burning of
more than one million Islamic texts triggered an uprising in the Muslim
quarter of Granada and the first rebellion of the Alpujarras, which helped
prompt the 1502 expulsion decree. In Aragón, where many Muslims
lived under harsh semifeudal conditions, the Islamic community was
not expelled for another two decades primarily because it was protected
by the nobility, which relied on it for a large part of its income. The
absence of a community of Muslim converts to Christianity might also
have mattered, for it meant that the fear that Muslims would try to win
back former co-religionists did not yet exist.[36] Because most Muslims in
Castile and Aragón chose conversion over exile, by the third decade of
the sixteenth century, Spain not only had an important community of
Jewish converts to Christianity but a significant population of *moriscos,*
Christians of Islamic origin.[37] While the latter community was new, the
conversos had already been in existence for over a hundred years; it was
they who were at the center of fifteenth-century Spanish concerns over
the problem of heresy and who initially provided the Inquisition with
most of its victims.

THE PROBLEM OF CONVERSION DURING
AND AFTER THE REIGN OF THE CATHOLIC KINGS

The Inquisition's treatment of condemned heretics usually involved forc-
ing them to participate in *autos de fe,* public, sometimes private, acts
of religious penitence. Public autos, which over time became elaborate
spectacles involving inquisitors, royalty, and large audiences, featured
a procession to the square and stage where they were held, a mass and
sermon, and a reading of the crimes of the accused. The culminating
moment of the act was the "reconciliation" of sinners with the church.
Punishments were divided into three categories: relaxation, reconciliation, and penance. The first, reserved mainly for unrepentant heretics
or relapsed ones, resulted in the person being handed over to the civil
authorities to be executed (the church could not directly stain its hands
with human blood). When the condemned person escaped or was not
alive, he or she was burned in effigy. The second category, reconciliation,
meant that the person was accepted back into the fold of the church after
confessing, repenting, and undergoing some kind of spiritual penance

or atonement. It involved penalties such as confiscation of belongings, long-term imprisonment, work in the galleys, and the wearing of *sanbenitos* (from *saco bendito*), yellow penitential garments typically with a black Saint Andrew's cross drawn on them. The third type of punishment, penance, was applied to people who abjured their offences—*de levi* in the case of lighter crimes, *de vehementi* when the transgression was more serious—and swore never to commit them again. It tended to imply relatively mild sentences, such as having to wear a sanbenito for a limited time, paying fines, working in the galleys, or being banished from the community for a specified period.

Depictions of early modern Spain as fanatical, especially those produced in Protestant literature, have often focused on the autos de fe—on their supposed popularity, violent spectacles, and high execution rates. But these depictions frequently rest on faulty logic or require qualification. For example, although normally witnessed by large audiences, the actual popularity of the autos de fe is almost impossible to gauge, because attendance was required and not participating aroused suspicions of nonconformity. Furthermore, the main event at autos de fe was not the burning of heretics, which generally took place outside cities and not in the ceremonial itself. The focus, rather, was on the public shaming of religious deviants, beginning with their having to wear sanbenitos while walking in the procession, and on their reconciliation with the church.[38] Finally, the Inquisition did not have as high an execution rate as previously believed, especially when compared with secular tribunals in Spain and broader Europe. In fact, most of the people that the Holy Office "relaxed" were burned in effigy. But if the Inquisition was generally not as bloodthirsty as a tradition of literature had claimed, it did tend to reserve its most extreme punishments for conversos and moriscos. The first fifty years of inquisitorial activities (1480–1530), and in particular the first twenty, were the bloodiest, producing thousands of deaths at the stake and a good number of the relaxations that took place during the Holy Office's entire existence.[39] This was the period in which the Inquisition concerned itself principally with the problem of judaizing conversos.[40]

Was the problem of crypto-Judaism at the turn of the fifteenth century a real one, or was it simply a creation of the Holy Office and fanatical Old Christians? This has been one of the most contentious questions in the literature on early modern Spain. Although few historians dispute that crypto-Judaism existed, there is no agreement about how widespread it was or about whether it was even a problem. Some have argued that many of the descendants of the Jews who had converted in the late fourteenth and early fifteenth centuries continued to practice Judaism during the reign of the Catholic Kings, while others vehemently assert that by then the majority of conversos were true Christians.[41] Neither of these positions does justice to the complexity of the New Christians' religious commitments, and both reify their identities across space and time. As recent studies have convincingly argued, during the fifteenth and early sixteenth centuries, some conversos were crypto-Jews and others were fully committed to Christianity, but most, including those who left the Iberian Peninsula, fell in between these two categories and partook in a variety of Christian and Jewish practices.[42] Between outright acceptance and rejection of the Catholic faith, there were many possible responses, shaped by individual faith and circumstances, the sociopolitical context, life experiences, and certain structural conditions (such as access to knowledge of Judaism, exposure to Christian doctrine, ties to Jewish communities, and so forth). The conversos, furthermore, were not the only ones without clearly defined religious identities. New *and* Old Christians exhibited a wide range of beliefs and practices, and these overlapped with each other.[43] Indeed, the insufficiency of religious instruction among cristianos viejos, particularly in rural areas, led the church to target them, as well as moriscos, in its Christianization campaigns.[44] Despite the religious militancy of the times, the question of who or what was a true Christian did not have a clear answer.

Complicating the problem of religious identity before and after the establishment of the Inquisition was the lack of clarity about how to distinguish a false from a true conversion. Was the sincerity of conversos to be measured by their beliefs, practices, or both, and which ones? Resolving this question proved difficult not only because what constituted the true Christian faith was still open to debate before the Council of Trent but also because of the virtual impossibility of untangling "religious" from "cultural" practices. Whether for Christians, Jews, or Muslims, spirituality was not confined to a few spheres of life during the late medieval and early modern periods.[45] And precisely because culture and religion were not compartmentalized into different domains, conversion to Christianity meant much more than the disavowal of old beliefs and commitment to new ones; it also implied dramatic changes in ancestral traditions, habits, and rituals. Jews who converted to Christianity, for example, were expected to radically alter practices related, among other things, to diet, clothing, and hygiene. Most of these practices did not directly challenge church doctrine and were therefore not technically heretical, but inquisitors and many contemporaries saw them as external signs of an internal affront to Christianity. They assumed that the use of clean linen or clothes on certain days of the week, the refusal to eat pork or to work on Saturday, the lighting of candles on the Sabbath, men does not live b/ bread alone.

the preparation of special food, and the koshering of meat, among other things, were all indications of a commitment to Judaism, Jewish law, and a Jewish way of life.[46] Verbal attacks on Christian dogma were thus not necessary to arouse suspicions of heresy; early modern religion was understood and lived as a system of beliefs as well as practices.

For Muslims, who arguably had less cultural overlap with Christians than Jews (in Spain, the last group tended to speak Castilian or other Romance languages in higher numbers, for example), conversion to Christianity implied an even greater transformation in ancestral practices. Just how sweeping this transformation was expected to be is illustrated in the campaigns to convert Granada's moriscos that took place in the early sixteenth century. The campaigns entailed not just religious instruction but a whole series of efforts to weaken traditional family structures, which were seen as central to the reproduction of the Islamic faith. These efforts included the promotion of "mixed" marriages with Old Christians—the favored arrangement being a "pure" male with a morisca —the creation of special colleges to separate morisco children from their parents, and the banning of polygamy and "double marriages."[47] Legislation in Granada also tried to prevent the use of Muslim names and surnames, circumcision, the survival of Arabic, and certain forms of inheritance and fictive kinship.[48] In short, campaigns to ensure the conversion of former Muslims to Christianity encompassed just about every sphere of life and therefore implied complete assimilation. Some scholars contend that for the moriscos and conversos themselves, cultural practices were inseparable from their religious identities and that their attachment to certain traditions was in fact an indication of a continued commitment to their ancestral faiths.[49] The latter claim is a particularly contentious issue, but the point is that the lack of a clear distinction between cultural and religious identities greatly complicated the process (then and now) of discerning between genuine and false conversions.[50] This problem became especially serious when, as occurred in 1492 with the conversos and in 1502 with Granada's moriscos, conversions occurred en masse and the traditional structures of those two communities could not be immediately dismantled.

Acknowledging the complexity of religious identities in fifteenth- and sixteenth-century Spain does not undermine the thesis that political and economic factors played a role in the establishment of the Inquisition and its subsequent activities, but it does challenge the notion that religion was merely a pretext for the persecution of the converts and their descendants. The instability and vagueness of Christian identity, the presence of conversos (and cristianos viejos) who straddled the categories of Jew and Christian, and the lack of clarity about what religious

Cultural War.

conversion entailed—these and other factors generated real social tensions. To be sure, these tensions had existed before, as had anxieties over crypto-Judaism and ongoing interactions between conversos and Jews. However, they acquired a new importance in the last third of the fifteenth century, as the Catholic Kings used religion to increase their popularity, as different social groups and members of the Mendicant orders mobilized against the conversos, and as the war against Granada intensified Christian zeal. In this context, religion mattered not so much in the sense that crypto-Judaism was a serious problem—perhaps its main importance was that it was perceived to be—but in the sense that it powerfully shaped Old Christian attitudes, motivations, and actions (prompting them, for instance, to interpret almost anything conversos did as "Jewish") and intensified other social conflicts—such as those between segments of the traditional nobility and the wealthy urban classes, the commoner masses and the converso "bourgeoisie," and factions that competed for control of local government.

CONCLUSION

Although their exact origins are still a mystery, Spain's infamous statutes of purity of blood surfaced in the second half of the fifteenth century amid a climate of political and social unrest. Economic and political factors played a role in their emergence, but they cannot fully explain why social strife took the form that it did—why, for example, stigmatization was based mainly on allegations of heresy, why the Inquisition initially targeted not just conversos but heretics in general, and why conflicts between different groups (in religious orders, cathedral chapters, town councils, and so forth) often involved anxieties about conversion. Articulated with various other levels of existence, religion in fifteenth-century Spain cannot be subsumed under other social relations and cannot be underestimated in terms of its ability to influence the actions of various groups as well as individual subjectivities and collective identities. Its central role in Spanish life was due in part to the power of the church in Castile, which had shaped not only politics but juridical culture and civil legislation, and ideas about the body, blood, reproduction, and the self. To paraphrase Stuart Hall, religion was the domain into which all other social relations and ideological structures had to enter.[51]

That some Old Christians manipulated it to ostracize conversos does not minimize its role in establishing the terms of discourse, the acceptable criteria for exclusion and inclusion. The mass conversions of the late fourteenth and fifteenth centuries and subsequent events in fact strengthened Christian, Jewish, and Muslim understandings about the intertwined nature of ancestry and religious identities, about the function of "blood" in the transmission of certain beliefs and practices. The importance of religion, furthermore, only increased after the establishment of the Inquisition. As a "national" tribunal in charge of investigating and punishing heresy and that at any moment could be unleashed against neighbors or rivals, the Holy Office exacerbated frictions between New and Old Christians. And as a knowledge-producing institution that in identifying "crypto-Jewish" and "crypto-Muslim" practices further blurred the line between religious and cultural practices, it also contributed to the preoccupation with purity of blood and displacement of anxieties over contamination onto women.

CHAPTER TWO

Race, Purity, and Gender
in Sixteenth-Century Spain

A la mujer casta Dios le basta
—Popular Spanish expression

¿Y si tu belleza no fuese tu pureza?
—Graffiti scribbled on a street wall in Seville, 1999

The statutes of purity of blood began to spread in earnest in the last decades of the fifteenth century and in the first half of the sixteenth garnered increasing royal and papal support, which in turn made them acquire more momentum. During those years, the idea of limpieza de sangre was not static. Old Christians not only extended it from conversos to other groups, but made it progressively more essentialist by modifying its genealogical formulas and altering its relationship to both race and gender. This chapter discusses those changes in the discourse of limpieza de sangre. After describing the multiplication of statutes during and after the late fifteenth century, it focuses on the meaning and transformation of the concept of purity of blood, its relationship to heresy laws (and attendant notions of cultural and biological inheritance), and its increasing reification of the categories of Old and New Christians. This reification, the chapter argues, was accompanied by the increasing deployment of the Spanish notion of raza and had gendered implications, for it involved not only parting with traditional (patrilineal) genealogical formulas but making women—and the female body in particular—into main sources of "contamination."

THE SPREAD OF THE LIMPIEZA
DE SANGRE STATUTES

Writings on the statutes of limpieza de sangre are usually part of broader studies of the Spanish Inquisition, which has fostered the impression that it was that tribunal that initially promoted them. The Holy Office certainly contributed to the preoccupation with purity of blood once it came into being, but it clearly was not solely responsible for it. When the Inquisition was founded in 1480, hostility toward the conversos had already produced various limpieza requirements and not just in the city of Toledo.[1] Furthermore, the Holy Office did not officially require that its officials submit proof of their purity of blood until about the 1560s. By then, the statutes had reached a number of institutions and corporations in both Castile and Aragón, including the Jeronymite monastery of Guadalupe (1486); Catalonia's Benedictine house of Monserrat (1502); Seville's cathedral chapter (1515); the Spanish province of the Observant Franciscan Order (1525); the church of Córdoba (1530); and the Capilla de los Reyes Nuevos (1530), a chapel in Toledo's Cathedral.[2] The phenomenon was not exclusive to religious bodies, and at least one geographic area, the Basque country's lordship of Vizcaya, passed a law in 1482 that denied entrance to all the descendants of Jews into the region. In 1522, the Suprema ordered Salamanca, Valladolid, and Toledo not to issue university degrees to people with converso or heretic ancestors. The prohibition restricted access to the learned professions and thus also to most public and religious posts.[3] By the middle of the sixteenth century, acceptance to the three great military orders (Santiago, Alcántara, and Calatrava) and a number of greater colleges (*colegios mayores*), brotherhoods, guilds, and cathedral chapters in both Castile and Aragón was conditioned on purity of blood.[4] Limpieza de sangre credentials were sometimes also made necessary for private legal procedures, such as the transmission of noble estates through the institution of *mayorazgo*.

Despite the strong ecclesiastical and bureaucratic nature of the bodies that first had purity-of-blood requirements, neither the papacy nor crown played a direct role in the establishment of the statutes, at least not initially. Under the *ancien régime* (old order), Iberian institutions tended to be of a quasi-private nature, with the juridical capacity to establish their own membership rules. The crown did not have enough authority to order the multitude of "communities" and corporate bodies—each cathedral chapter, military order, guild, and so forth—to implement purity-of-blood policies, which helps to explain why the statutes spread in a piecemeal fashion and why not every Spanish organization adopted them.[5] But even if the sovereign had had the power to make the "statutes" into "laws," that is, to require all establishments to adopt them, it is not certain that it would have done so or when. Up until the mid-sixteenth century, the policies of both Spanish kings and the Holy See on the issue of limpieza de sangre were far from consistent. Pope Nicholas V, for example, condemned the city of Toledo's 1449 statute, as did some top-ranking Castilian secular and religious officials. Conversely, Clement VII and several other popes confirmed the Franciscan order's addition of a purity requirement into its constitution. Starting in 1525 and continuing into the eighteenth century, each time that a candidate for the order was examined for his qualifications, be it in Spain or the Americas, the papal bulls and the guidelines for membership that they sanctioned were invoked as sources of authority. As for Spanish monarchs, after equivocating, Juan II approved Toledo's Sentencia-Estatuto, and Enrique IV supported a similar statute that Ciudad Real issued in 1468. Charles V backed the establishment of purity requirements in greater colleges and Toledo's *cabildo* (town council), among other places.[6]

The Spanish crown and the papacy continued to vacillate during the early decades of the sixteenth century, sometimes opposing, sometimes confirming, the passage of statutes of limpieza de sangre by different institutions. In the late 1540s, however, official support for the doctrine of purity of blood became more explicit. Once again, and almost a hundred years after the Sentencia-Estatuto, the city of Toledo took center stage. After much maneuvering by the city's infamous archbishop, Juan Martínez Silíceo, the top two religious and secular authorities approved the decision of the cathedral chapter to demand proof of purity of blood from its members—the pope in 1555 and King Philip II in 1556.[7] The significance of these developments cannot be emphasized enough. As the primate of Spain, the Church of Toledo was an extremely important religious center in Iberia and Europe in general, in terms of wealth and power second only to St. Peter's Cathedral in Rome. By publicly condoning the cathedral's exclusionary policy, the crown and the Holy See essentially encouraged other institutions, religious and secular, to pass their own requirements of limpieza de sangre.

If Rome continued to be ambivalent about the issue of purity of blood, Philip II for the most part promoted it. In 1566, for example, he ordered Toledo's town council, which had two benches, one for "citizens" and one for nobles, to make limpieza a requirement for the former. It was also at around this time that the king ordered the Inquisition to ensure the purity credentials of its members. His policies, it is true, were not entirely consistent, for he apparently granted some conversos *reha-bilitaciones,* licenses that allowed them to participate in activities and honors from which they were otherwise excluded or dispensations that pardoned their punishments.[8] In addition, toward the end of his life, Phillip II was considering placing a limit on limpieza investigations. Despite these signs of flexibility toward the purity requirements, the king generally supported them and never suggested that they be banned altogether. It should therefore come as no surprise that the number of establishments, particularly churches, that adopted purity requirements during his reign increased. At the turn of the sixteenth century, for example, at least twenty-one cathedral chapters of the thirty-five that existed in Castile had purity statutes.[9]

One of the polemics in the historiography on the statutes revolves around the question of whether they had an official or legislative basis. Henry Kamen, for example, has argued that they were never a part of Spanish public law; had no judicial or legal sanction; and were restricted to a few, mainly private, institutions.[10] Although it may be true that neither the Castilian *cortes* (parliament) nor the crown ever issued a *national* blood law, the statutes cannot be reduced, as he implies, to mere admission requirements by a few organizations in certain parts of Castile. They were in fact publicly legitimated by the royal, ecclesiastical, and legislative support that they eventually received. As the inquisitor Juan Roco Campofrío stated in the early seventeenth century, the requirements acquired a great deal of authority precisely because they were repeatedly confirmed by popes and kings, because those of the university colleges were approved by the general laws of Spain, and because they were sanctioned by Spanish common law and the laws of the kingdom of Castile. It was also no small matter, he added, that limpieza status was necessary for many public honors, dignities, and offices.[11] In short, the absence of a general or national blood law should not obscure the royal support that the statutes received, especially as of the mid-sixteenth century, and the public nature of some limpieza requirements. In Spanish America, where the crown was freer to issue laws for the entire region, official endorsement of the principle of purity of blood was to be even more explicit.

The continuing spread of the limpieza statutes in the second half of the sixteenth century and more overt support that they received from the crown were related to several developments, including the rise of Lutheranism in parts of Castile. Especially from 1559 to 1561, Spain focused on eradicating all manifestations of Protestantism, and this new attack on heresy did not favor the suppression of the purity requirements.[12] Furthermore, during this period, two other groups surfaced that, at least in the eyes of the Inquisition, were threatening to the unity of the faith: the moriscos and the Portuguese conversos (*cristãos novos*).[13] The latter, which tended to have a strong group consciousness and included descendants of Jews who had left Spain in 1492, started to arrive in significant numbers after 1580, when the crowns of Castile and Portugal were united. According to some of the proposals to reform the statutes, Castile was compelled to retain purity requirements after its conversos were no longer engaging in crypto-Judaism because of the emergence of the two new communities of "unstable converts."[14] Finally, the proliferation of the limpieza statutes was also related to Spanish colonialism, which in addition to producing rapid demographic and socio-economic shifts in Iberia, transformed the issue of purity of blood into a transatlantic preoccupation.[15] As discussed in Chapter 7 of this book, not only was Old Christian ancestry made a precondition for going to Spanish America, but many an administrator who was assigned there had to provide genealogical information and proof of his status. The organization of Spain's American colonies thus served as one of the motors that kept the statutes and issue of limpieza de sangre alive in the Iberian Peninsula.

The multiplication of the statutes of purity of blood, dramatic as it was, has detracted attention from other changes that the requirements underwent in the first one hundred years of their existence, particularly in terms of the categories and definitions of impurity. To grasp the nature and significance of these changes, it is first necessary to excavate the concept of purity's initial ideological underpinnings, its early connection with notions of heresy, blood, and culture. The text that follows will consider three main questions. How was heresy defined in late medieval Spain? What factors were thought to influence the transmission of heretical behavior from parents to children? How did treatment of heresy in canon law inform the Spanish statutes of purity of blood?

HERESY, BLOOD, AND
THE ESSENTIALIZATION OF "RACE"

By the time papal inquisitors first became active in the late Middle Ages, the church defined heresy as a doctrinal error, based on an incorrect reading of Scripture and publicly professed, and the heretic as someone who had been baptized and taught the main principles of the faith but rejected some or all of them.[16] Those who were found guilty of the crime were punished in a variety of ways and disqualified from the priesthood and ecclesiastical posts. This disqualification, furthermore, was applied to their children and grandchildren. The "stain" of heresy, which implied the legal status of infamy, was thus passed down to direct descendants for two generations. Certain institutions also denied membership to heretics and their progeny, but there was some variation in how they applied the prohibition. Some religious orders, for example, applied it to two generations by the masculine line and one by the feminine.[17] This meant that a candidate, say, for the Franciscan order, was subject to an investigation of the religious history of his parents and paternal grandparents, but not of his maternal grandparents. Furthermore, some institutions even excluded the great-grandchildren of heretics, thus denying entrance to all those who were within four generations of the source of infamy.[18]

Despite variations in how heresy was punished, policies regarding heretics and their descendants were all based on the belief that people who deviated from church dogma were likely to "infect" the family members with whom they came into contact. As one seventeenth-century Spanish commentator explained, the three-generation prohibition (three after the heretic) was a legacy of Saint Thomas Aquinas and Saint Augustine, both of whom had written that a sinner bequeathed his sins to his great-grandchildren but no more, "because a man can only get to see his descendants as far as the fourth generation, and after this time there is no longer the fear that the successor will imitate the predecessor."[19] Central to the treatment of heresy within canon law was thus the notion that it was within the intimate sphere of the family that religious beliefs and behavior were reproduced. Just what role "blood" was believed to play in this process—and what it stood for—was by no means clear, however. The seventeenth-century commentator implied that heretical tendencies were learned from parents, acquired through early exposure to deviant ideas. In this sense, "blood" was a metaphor for indoctrination within the family rather than for biological reproductive processes. Yet contemporaries seldom articulated a clear distinction between "nature" and "nurture." Rather, they tended to attribute the transmission of beliefs and behavior to both cultural and biological inheritance and to conflate the two.

The conflation of culture and biology in assumptions about heretical behavior partly stemmed from shared understandings about human reproduction, derived from religious texts (including the Bible and works by the church fathers and medieval scholastics) and scientific theories regarding conception and generation.[20] The main physiological theories of the Middle Ages, heavily influenced by ancient Greek science and medicine, tended to accord semen, breast milk, blood, and food a part in the creation and function of life. Food had a role in the generative process because, at least according to the Aristotelian tradition, it was supposed to transmute to blood after consumption. Blood, in turn, changed into sperm in men and into milk in women, the first helping to create life, the second to sustain it. Because body, mind, and soul were seen as connected, the physical constitution of the parents, their bodily fluids, were thought to contribute to the child's physiology and to his or her moral and psychological traits. In short, biology was believed to be crucial in determining the religious and behavioral dispositions of a new life, but cultural factors such as food (and sometimes environmental ones as well) were also deemed important, for they could, for instance, help determine the potency of the male "seed."[21]

Various medieval theories granted both parents a role in the creation of the embryo and in the biological transmission of physiological and behavioral traits to the child. Theories inspired by Galen, for example, held that two seeds, one from the father and one from the mother, contributed to conception and that maternal blood nourished the new life both inside and outside the womb because breast milk was transformed menstrual fluid or "blood twice cooked." Some medieval natural philosophers feared that Galen's ideas about conception actually gave too much credit to the mother, but in general they acknowledged that she contributed to the generation of life and the baby's "physiological stuff."[22] Despite recognition of the role of women in generation, most theories made semen the key agent in the reproductive process and hence posited that children resembled their fathers (exactly how much depending on the "potency" and "movements" of sperm during conception). Some Aristotelian formulations went so far as to claim that female bodies were capable of only making milk because they lost blood through menstruation and were never hot enough to produce the intense "concoction" necessary for the creation of the "thick fluid" or male seed.[23] According to these formulations, the female body was too weak to decisively influence the physiology and personality of the child, and in any event, the mother's breast milk, which at one point had been blood, was the substance through which she herself had received the "physiological stuff" of her male ancestors.[24] For all their emphasis on biological heredity, however, none of the prevailing physiological theories construed the religious, moral, and physiological traits in a given lineage as permanent. Whether or not they privileged paternal descent, they all allowed for the possibility that these characteristics could change over the course of several generations. "Natural" traits were by no means rendered immutable.

The extent to which physiological theories developed by medieval theologians and scientists influenced Spanish popular understandings of how biology and human behavior were related is impossible to determine, but they clearly informed the legal construction of heresy and discourses of blood. For example, beliefs about the role of both biology and culture in the transmission of all sorts of characteristics from parents to child, the more prominent role of the father in this process, and the possibility of mutability over time were partly responsible for the tendency of laws on heretics to transfer "sins" through more generations in the paternal line of descent than in the maternal one. In other words, the punishments that were extended to a heretic's descendants were supposed to be in place for a longer period of time if the culprit was a man because fathers were thought to leave more enduring physiological, behavioral, and psychological marks on their children, especially if they were boys (because they were considered less malleable). This line of thinking is explained in *Diálogos familiares de la agricultura cristiana,* a work by the Franciscan Juan de Pineda completed between 1578 and 1580. Written as a series of "dialogues" between four main interlocutors and modeled on works from classical antiquity, it includes a discussion of the inheritability of customs that renders women as weaker than men and therefore more able to leave behind their parents' values and traditions and adopt new ones. The discussion ultimately suggests that although unions between members of "good" and "lesser" castes should generally be discouraged, if they were to happen, the pairing should involve a male of the superior group and a female of the inferior one. Fathers were supposedly stronger than mothers and therefore their traits were passed down for more generations.

These gendered and temporal assumptions helped shape heresy laws as well as Spanish notions of nobility. Indeed, *hidalguía* (*nobility*) was almost always determined and acquired on the basis of paternal ancestry.[25] Kings could bestow *nobleza de privilegio* (nobility of privilege) on a worthy commoner, for instance, and allow the status to be passed down from father to son. On the third generation, *nobleza de privilegio* became *nobleza de sangre* (nobility of blood), the most valued noble status in Spanish society because it implied being part of a privileged lineage since "time immemorial." The strong Spanish belief in nobility as a natural condition, as an "essence" transmitted by blood, thus did not preclude the possibility that it could be acquired through the paternal line of descent and, after a few generations, transformed into a permanent status. A similar patrilineal and generational logic at first also operated in the discourse of purity of blood and informed the usage of the categories of New and Old Christians.

Initially modeled on the treatment of the children and grandchildren of heretics within canon law, the statutes of limpieza de sangre were

based on the notion that unstable Christians and their descendants had
to be deprived of access to a host of honors, privileges, and posts until
they had proven their loyalty to the faith, a process that was supposed
to require two or three generations. The first statutes thus limited how
far back *manchas* (stains) could be traced to the grandparents or what
contemporaries called the *cuatro costados* (four quarters). That Toledo's
Sentencia-Estatuto did not was certainly a bad omen, but by and large,
the early purity requirements applied a three-generation limit and placed
greater emphasis on the transmission of "impurity" through paternal descent. The influential 1488 Instructions written by Inquisitor General
Torquemada, for example, barred from public office and the holy orders
the children and grandchildren of conversos who had been found guilty
of judaizing. The Catholic Kings approved this policy and in 1501 issued two decrees prohibiting the descendants of convicted crypto-Jews
within two degrees on the paternal line and one on the maternal from
holding any offices of honor and from exercising certain professions, including those of notary public, scrivener, physician, surgeon, and apoth-
ecary.[26] The Church of Seville and other institutions that adopted purity
statutes in the late fifteenth and early sixteenth centuries placed similar
limitations on how far back stains could be traced. At least in theory,
such limitations meant that the great-grandchildren of all converts to
Christianity were eligible for Old Christian status and that the chances
that a person of "mixed" descent would be declared pure were better if
his or her Jewish ancestry ran on the maternal bloodline.

But if the statutes of purity of blood generally followed some of the
gendered and temporal principles operating in canon law's treatment of
the descendants of heretics, they also differed in significant ways. Most
obviously, they identified two separate categories of impurity: descent
from condemned heretics and descent from Jews. Whereas the first category had its antecedents in canon law, the second, based on the argument that many conversos had not yet fully embraced Catholicism and
were therefore *potential* heretics, did not and posed a profound problem
for the Spanish church. As critics of the Sentencia-Estatuto and later
advocates of reforming the statutes pointed out, the distinction between
cristianos viejos and cristianos nuevos undermined the principle of the
equality of all Christians. Apparently invoking Paul's Epistle to the Gala-
tians (Gal. 3:28), they stressed that those who accepted baptism, whether
they descended from Greeks, Jews, or any other "nations," were supposed to be fully incorporated into the Christian community.[27] During
the Middle Ages, it was not uncommon for converts and their immediate descendants to be barred from the priesthood, but that practice
was informal and did not systematically target one particular group.
The statutes did, thereby undermining the notion that conversion was

a means for achieving redemption and a relatively expedient vehicle for transforming ancestral beliefs and practices.

Supporters of the statutes retorted that the blood requirements were temporary measures, mechanisms to ensure that the faith was not endangered by the first generations of converts, and that eventually the conversos would be full members of Christian society.[28] The extent to which these concerns with safeguarding the faith were genuine is difficult to ascertain, but certain institutions and limpieza decrees initially did not classify all conversos as sources of impurity, only those who had actually been convicted of crypto-Judaism or heresy.[29] This restricted definition of the category of impurity was short-lived, however. During the first half of the sixteenth century, the statutes increasingly classified as impure the children and grandchildren of all converted Jews, independent of whether they had been associated with heresy or not. Furthermore, whereas at first they tended to treat only the descendants of persons who had been relaxed or reconciled by the Holy Office as stained, any genealogical connection to individuals (converso or not) who had been in any way penanced, sometimes even just tried, by an inquisitorial tribunal came to constitute a blemish on a lineage.[30] These changes created a significant chasm between the notion of limpieza de sangre and that of heresy, one that became even wider when the statutes were altered in three additional respects.

The most obvious change was the extension of the concept of impurity to people of Muslim ancestry. For decades after the conquest of Granada, some moriscos were able to make the case that they were Old Christians, a category that their descendants continued to cling to when they were expelled a century later.[31] Their ability to claim purity of blood tended to depend on whether they had converted before 1492, because it implied that they had turned to the faith more or less voluntarily, as well as on whether they had Old Christian fathers. Again, the logic operating was one that emphasized paternal descent and the role of the father in shaping the religious and cultural inclinations of children. But by about the middle of the sixteenth century, when religious and secular authorities started to consider the conversion campaigns in Granada a complete failure, descent from a Muslim was systematically included as one of the impure categories. The Second Rebellion of the Alpujarras (1568–70), sparked by Philip II's reissuing of orders to prohibit all sorts of practices that were supposed to be associated with Islam, including the use of Arabic, contributed to this process. The rebellion reinforced the idea that this community was a serious religious and political problem and led the government to try to disperse it throughout the kingdom.[32] These attempts, however, did not dissipate the belief that the moriscos were too wedded to Islam to become sincere Christians.

The statutes also changed in that they began to hinge as much on maternal as on paternal ancestry.[33] Whereas having an Old Christian father had earlier allowed some moriscos to claim purity status, this was no longer the case in the second half of the sixteenth century. Even though the paternal bloodline generally continued to be more important in social and legal terms and in certain types of inheritance, especially as of the 1560s, the purity status of the father no longer prevailed over that of the mother; a stricter dual-descent model of limpieza de sangre classification operated. Finally, the limitations on how many generations back stains could be traced began to disappear. This process started in the 1530s. By the end of the century, the most important religious and secular bodies in Spain, including the Church of Córdoba, Toledo's cathedral, the great military orders, the Inquisition, and the major colleges and universities, did not restrict purity investigations to the cuatro costados.[34] The possibility that the descendants of Jews and Muslims could, after a few generations, claim the status of Old Christian had all but disappeared. The category of cristiano viejo, which had appeared before but entered into regular use only in the sixteenth century, came to be defined as someone whose ancestry was proven to be pure since "time immemorial."[35]

To summarize, the statutes of limpieza, which rested on gendered genealogical and reproductive principles, were modeled on certain heresy laws and their assumptions about the links between kinship, blood, and religious identification, but during the sixteenth century, they came to differ in significant ways. They generally classified as impure not just the descendants of actual heretics but of all Jews and Muslims and of anyone punished by the Inquisition, they placed equal importance on maternal and paternal descent, and they did not establish any temporal limits on the investigation of genealogical stains. Certainly, variations in how different institutions determined the status of limpieza continued to exist. But the general trend was one of rupture with the patrilineal and generational formulas that had informed legal constructions of heresy and nobility and, consequently, a dramatic restriction of the category of purity. The shift to a more rigid dual-descent model of classification, coupled with the elimination of limits on how far back stains could be traced, transformed purity of blood from a naturalist to an essentialist principle,[36] one that no longer allowed for the possibility of the mutability of "natural" traits over the generations—except, that is, through biological "mixture." The overall significance of this transformation was the construction of conversos and moriscos as a particular type of convert, never fully able to rid themselves of their ancestral beliefs and therefore never capable of becoming fully realized Christians.

beginning of "race" ✗

The essentialist nature of the concept of limpieza de sangre was reflected in the deployment of the Castilian word *raza* against the converts and their descendants. Although the exact origins of this term are uncertain, perhaps dating as far back as the thirteenth century, its use started to become prominent only in the 1500s.[37] Like its equivalents in other European languages, *raza* at this time generally referred to lineage.[38] As such, its connotations varied and were not all negative. Sometimes the word simply alluded to the succession of generations, for example, while at others it appeared in phrases such as *good race*. It was also frequently used to distinguish between nobles and commoners.[39] During the sixteenth century, however, the term was strongly attached to religion and came to refer not so much to ancestry from *pecheros* (taxpayers) and *villanos* (commoners) but to descent from Jews, Muslims, and eventually other religious categories. In the process, it shed virtually all of its positive and neutral connotations. Thus, by the early seventeenth century, the Castilian linguist Sebastián de Covarrubias Orozco wrote that when it was used to refer to lineages, the word had a pejorative meaning, "like having some Moorish or Jewish race."[40] For this reason, Old Christians seldom applied it to themselves. Jews, Muslims, and even Protestants were marked through the concept of race, but not the people with putatively long and unsullied ties to the Catholic faith.

To be sure, the early modern concept of race, whether in Spain or other western European countries, operated within a Judeo-Christian system of beliefs still firmly rooted in the idea of monogenesis, of a common creation. Used mainly to "designate a set of persons, animals or plants connected by common descent or origin," the word *race* "was part of a conceptual scheme in which the distinctive characteristics of specimens were explained genealogically, by showing where they belonged in God's creation."[41] The notion that all people descended from Adam and Eve, however, did not prevent the use of putative lineage or imagined biblical origins to create, or account for, human groupings and hierarchies. Certain communities were believed to derive from different biblical ancestors, and thus some were thought to have more privileged lineages than others. As Fray Juan de Pineda wrote in his "dialogue" about the importance of marrying women of good caste (*casta*), the idea that Old Christian males should not marry females of the "Jewish race" (*raza judía*) or Jewish converts to Christianity (*marranas*) was not incompatible with the theory of a common creation. Just as all horses were of the same "race" but some were of a better "caste" than others, human lineages had particular origins and hence specific characteristics. And just as one tried to produce better horses by not breeding those of good caste with lesser ones, so with humans.[42]

If genealogy helped to construct race in the early modern period, it was not deployed in the same way across Europe. For example, in sixteenth-century France, the idea of *noblesse de sang* (nobility of blood) and the word *race* were used primarily to distinguish between nobles and commoners.[43] Espousing quasi-biological notions regarding "natural" inequalities between the two estates, the French aristocracy used the concept of race to justify its domination of nonnobles (*roturiers*) and to discourage marriage and reproduction with commoners, whose "tainted blood" was said to have a corruptive effect on noble lineages.[44] To the extent that ideas about genealogy, noble blood, and race operated jointly, the French concept of race mainly constituted a "class" mode of discourse. Notions of nobility of blood were of course also important in Spain, but as argued above, during the sixteenth century, Castilian conceptions of lineage and race came to be deployed more to religious groups and their descendants than to estates. Linked to sin and heresy, the word *raza* tended to be applied to communities—namely, Jews, Muslims, and sometimes Protestants—deemed to be stained or defective because of their religious histories.[45] It therefore constituted more of a religious mode of discourse. The term *limpieza de sangre* itself is said to have come from Judeo-Christian religious concepts associated with protecting the faith from defilement and the purity of the community.[46] What made the early modern Spanish notion of race distinctive, then, was its direct and powerful link to Judaism, Islam, and heresy, a linkage that the spread of the statutes reinforced and that had solidified by the second half of the sixteenth century.

THE INQUISITION'S PRODUCTION OF HERESY
AND THE FEMINIZATION OF IMPURITY

The transformation that the concept of purity of blood underwent in the sixteenth century—its increasing essentialism and connection to the notion of raza—can partly be attributed to Old Christian attempts to make access to key institutions more difficult in order to reserve positions of power and influence for themselves. But it was also a product of the Inquisition's campaigns to stamp out clandestine Judaic and Muslim practices, which strengthened preexisting assumptions about the transmission, through the blood, of beliefs and behavior from parents to children and also altered them by feminizing religion. Key in this process were the lists of external signs of heresy that were read to the public by inquisitors during the regular announcement of "edicts of grace" and "edicts of faith," periods in which people were encouraged to confess their sins (and/or denounce others) with the promise of receiving relatively mild sentences and of reconciling with the church.[47] These lists included a host of practices that took place in the home, and therefore mainly located religion in a female domain. The disappearance of all Jewish and Muslim institutional life, in which men had played a central role, made the Holy Office turn its gaze to the more private sphere of the household. Not a few inquisitors believed that conversas and moriscas raised their children as Christians until a certain age, and then told them of their Judaic or Muslim origin as well as instructed them how to behave, both secretly and in public.[48] Whether this allegation was true or not, a disproportionate number of the conversos and moriscos that the Holy Office executed or otherwise punished during the sixteenth century were women. Oftentimes denounced by kitchen servants, slaves, or neighbors, these women were tried for reproducing Jewish or Muslim traditions in the home, for turning the domestic domain into a space of cultural-religious resistance through, among other things, cleaning, cooking, dancing, and death rituals.[49]

The Holy Office's persecution of conversas and moriscas as key agents in the reproduction, respectively, of Jewish and Muslim identities roughly coincided with the shift to a dual-descent model of classification, that is, with the modification of previous genealogical formulas and full extension of notions of impurity to women. Was this shift influenced by knowledge of the importance that maternal descent had in Jewish culture? Possibly, but equally or more significant were the Inquisition's particular constructions of crypto-Judaism and crypto-Islam, which shifted the focus of the "heresy problem" to the family and helped to construe women as main sources of impurity. Indeed, the imagery of contamination was ubiquitous in sixteenth-century Spain, and the female body was undoubtedly at the center of it. Concerns that the milk of "impure" wet nurses (*nodrizas*) would contaminate Old Christian children, for example, were at an all-time high during this period. These concerns were most acute with regard to the king, whose nodrizas were supposed to be carefully screened, but they were not exclusive to the royal family. Various authors of Spain's Golden Age of literature wrote that Old Christian infants raised on the milk of conversas would judaize, and popular belief similarly held that even if pure by the four corners, children who were raised and suckled by morisca wet nurses would be "Islamized" (*amoriscados*).[50] Once infected, these children were permanently marked. As a colloquial saying from the period put it, *en lo que en la leche se mama en la mortaja se pierde* (loosely translated as "that which is imbibed in breast milk is retained until death"). Because of its association with blood (the vehicle through which natural traits were supposedly transmitted to children), breast milk in fact became one of the main metaphors of cultural and biological contagion—a clear sign that women's bodies became the symbolic territories in which communal boundaries were drawn.[51]

The frequent allusions to breast milk as a contaminating agent were symptoms of how the ideology of limpieza de sangre had increased concerns with endogamy and created a particular sexual economy, one that assigned separate value to women depending on their purity status. Stated differently, the construction of conversa and morisca bodies as impure was inextricably linked to anxieties about sexual, marital, and reproductive relations between Old and New Christians. These concerns had appeared a century earlier—with the first statutes—but became much more pronounced as the limpieza requirements proliferated, as the inquisitorial eye focused on heretical practices within the sphere of the family, and as the social and material costs associated with marrying impure women increased. Some institutions began to require that members establish their limpieza as well as that of their wives. As of the 1560s, for example, access to almost all inquisitorial offices and titles was in theory denied to applicants who were married to "stained" women. Some confraternities, including that of the Sangre de Jesucristo, also did not accept members who had any "race of confesos [conversos] or Moors" or who were married to women who were not pure.[52] Furthermore, once the status of purity of blood depended equally on paternal and maternal descent, an Old Christian male who wed a New Christian woman could not "redeem" his progeny. Not only were his descendants ineligible for a series of honors, professions, and public and religious offices, and sometimes even for inheriting *mayorazgos* (entailed estates) but his lineage was permanently "tainted." This process was vividly illustrated in the Holy Office's classification of the children of mixed unions. It designated the offspring of a New and an Old Christian as "half New Christians." The children of a "half New Christian" and a "full Old Christian," were considered "quarter New Christians," "quarter Moors," or "quarter Jews." The categories continued until the person was only "one sixteenth of a New Christian"; beyond that, he or she was simply listed as "a part of New Christian."[53] The Inquisition's system of "hybrid" classifications—a key precursor to Latin America's sistema de castas—did not leave much of a terminological legacy in the Iberian Peninsula but was indicative of how the statutes of limpieza de sangre constructed "mixture" between Old and New Christians as an irreversible corruption of pure lineages, as a process of degeneration that not even the "holy seed" of cristianos viejos could prevent. Even if suppressed for a few generations, the "natural" traits and "inclinations" of Jews and Muslims would return: *natura revertura.*[54]

If the statutes produced a sexual economy that generally lessened the desirability of conversas and moriscas as wives,[55] they had different consequences for Old Christian women. Because the status of limpieza was determined by both bloodlines and required legitimate birth in order to establish paternity, marriage to a cristiana vieja became indispensable for the maintenance of genealogical and family preeminence. At the same time, the Old Christian fear that pure women would secretly introduce tainted blood into a lineage made their sexuality more subject to control. The statutes thus reinforced Spanish notions of familial honor that stressed chastity for unmarried women and fidelity for married ones.[56] A number of authors, including Fray Luis de Leon, Juan de Espinosa, Juan Luis Vives, and Juan de la Cerda, wrote texts or "manuals" detailing proper conduct for women, particularly married ones.[57] Their prescriptions, which invariably stressed virtuous sexual behavior, enclosure, and obedience, appeared as the Virgin Mary was being transformed from a symbol of fertility to one of passive motherhood and as the cult of her immaculate conception began to grow, particularly among the Franciscans. In the late sixteenth and seventeenth centuries, she became a powerful symbol of female purity, a transformation that was probably not unrelated to the Spanish society's concerns with safeguarding Old Christian lineages through control of women's sexuality.[58] For a married woman, wrote Vives in 1523, two factors are of utmost importance: chastity and love for her husband. These two virtues, he added, were also those of the church, "which is most chaste and tenaciously preserves unshaken faith in its spouse, Christ. Though harassed internally by suitors, which is to say, baptized heretics, and attacked externally by pagans, Moors, and Jews, it has never been contaminated by the least stain, and it believes and senses that all its good is found in the spouse, Christ."[59]

Given the context in Spain when the author wrote his manual, in which conversos were being tried for heresy by the Inquisition, Vives's reference to the church's being harassed and "courted" by baptized heretics seems to function as a message to Old Christian women to remain loyal to their men as well as to the church. The analogy as well as the language of purity and pollution links religious, sexual, and genealogical contamination. To be sure, the rise in concerns with policing female chastity was not due exclusively to the spread of the ideology of limpieza de sangre. The tridentine reforms' emphasis on regulating marriage and morality strengthened efforts to repress women's sexuality in the whole of Catholic Europe. But in Spain, these efforts (by no means a complete success) were made all the more urgent by the doctrine of purity of blood, its privileging of endogamic marriage and legitimate birth, and its profoundly different implications for men and women as well as for different categories of women. Religion, lineage, gender, sexuality, and reproduction were all integral components of a social and symbolic order premised on the natural superiority of Old Christians over all others.

CONCLUSION

During the first century that the ideology of limpieza de sangre spread across Spain, it was not only extended from conversos to moriscos and other religious categories, but it encouraged a shift in thinking about genealogy and the different roles that men and women played in (biological and cultural) reproduction. Paradigms of sex and gender were altered in relation to changing historical circumstances and dominant notions of social organization. As Christianity became more militant and the Inquisition's investigations of heresy seemed to confirm assumptions about the "intractability" of Jewish and Muslim identities, relatively fluid definitions of purity of blood gave way to more essentialist ones that promoted endogamy and mapped anxieties over contamination onto female bodies. Fears of women as contaminating agents were reinforced by the social and material consequences that, thanks to the spread of the statutes and support they received from the church and state, awaited individuals of "pure" Christian ancestry who mixed with people of "tainted" lineages. By the last third of the sixteenth century, any drop of Jewish or Muslim blood could result in disqualification from important religious and secular institutions and from various public honors and posts. The notion of limpieza de sangre, at first deployed as a temporary tool to ensure the purity of the faith, had been transformed into a mechanism of exclusion that no longer allowed for "purification" through temporal or gendered genealogical formulas.

The features that the limpieza statutes had acquired by the midsixteenth century led a number of historians who saw them as mainly a function of a religious problem—who believed that crypto-Judaism was common—to admit that they had become more about race.[60] But notwithstanding the recent wave of works that locate the origins of racial discourse in early modern Iberia, the claim that race was operating in the sixteenth century continues to be polemical, vulnerable to charges of anachronism by scholars who argue that because the term *race* acquired its modern biological connotations only in the late eighteenth and nineteenth centuries, it should not be applied to earlier periods, when more cultural understandings of difference prevailed.[61] It is true that the concept began to undergo significant changes during the Enlightenment and expansion of mercantile capitalism, as natural philosophers, anatomists, and skull collectors, among others, began to more systematically study, classify, and rank human groups according to supposed biological distinctions and degrees of rationality.[62] But the rise of a particular definition of race during the passage from the ancien régime to modernity does not mean that the term can be used only to describe modern phenomena or that it had salience only from the late eighteenth century onward. Race is not stable, and history has produced not one but many racisms, some of which predate modern capitalism and the Enlightenment.[63] Moreover, no racism is entirely novel; "fragments of its past incarnations are embedded in the new."[64] Rather than preclude the study of race in the early modern period, then, the rise of "scientific racism" makes imperative deeply historical (genealogical) investigations of its past incarnations.

The claim that race can be used only to describe modern phenomena is problematic because it rests on the belief that there is a single, transhistorical racism, and because it is frequently based on the assumption that the notion is operating only when it deploys biological notions of difference. This assumption has in fact framed the debate about whether the statutes of purity of blood were about race (i.e., biology) or religion. To present the problem of limpieza in those terms, however, is to fall into a conceptual trap, to rely on a rigid definition of race that renders biological and cultural/religious constructions of difference as mutually exclusive. The concept does not always need biology to "do its work." Nativist-based nationalisms that have posited cultural differences as timeless and insurmountable have amply demonstrated that even in modern times, culture itself can be essentialized and come to function as race.[65] Indeed, a key feature of racial discourse is that it does not just naturalize or biologize but "allows for a strategic equivocation between nature and culture."[66] Even if appeals to biology were a necessary component of race, the concept would still not have to be reserved for the study of modern phenomena, for no matter how vaguely articulated and protean late medieval and early modern theories of reproduction and generation were, quasi-biological—or rather, genealogical—arguments clearly played a role in shaping notions of purity and nobility of blood.

The point is that there are no compelling theoretical or historical reasons for not using the concept of race to describe conflicts between Old and New Christians and the problematic of limpieza de sangre; after all, early modern Spaniards did. The categories of Old and New Christian, furthermore, were built on binaries, including purity/impurity, beauty/ugliness (*cristianos lindos*), and rationality/sensuality, that are all-too-familiar tropes of racial discourse. That said, it is important to reiterate, first, that Spain was not the only early modern European country where ideas about race were being produced and hence cannot take credit for

giving birth to Western racism. Although the level of institutionalization
that ideas of purity of blood achieved in Iberia might make it tempt-
ing to set it apart from the rest of Europe, anti-Semitism was rampant
throughout the continent, and other countries also relied on genealogy to construct "race." Arising more or less simultaneously in various
countries, the concept's sudden conspicuousness was linked to internal
European dynamics as well as to expansion to the Americas, the establishment of the transatlantic slave trade, and other "global" processes.[67]
Granting Spain a special place in the history of racism while ignoring
or underplaying the phenomenon outside its borders is not only historically problematic but reinforces the Black Legend. Second, it is crucial
to emphasize that the early modern concept of race must be understood
in all of its historical and cultural embeddedness. In Spain, it acquired
its significance in the context of the spread of the statutes of purity of
blood, which constituted a complicated discourse—a system of meaning
production—about lineage, culture, and religion and about conversion,
generation, and degeneration. Applied mainly to Jews and Muslims and
occasionally also Protestants, the notion of raza was incubated in religious cosmologies; informed by late medieval understandings of genealogy and reproduction; and intimately tied to discreet practices within
the familial, domestic domain.

Recognizing the imbrication of race and religion in early modern
Spain is important for the historicization of racial ideologies and for understanding the form that Spanish colonial ideology would take in the
Americas, where casta categories were strongly shaped by metropolitan
ideas about conversion, genealogy, and "blood mixture" and where a
community's purity status was largely determined by its presumed relationship to the Catholic faith. Before venturing into the American context, however, it is necessary to explore one more aspect of the concept
of purity of blood: how it was "proven." The ways in which limpieza de
sangre was certified in different institutions and functioned as a juridical category of personhood had profound implications for early modern Spanish culture. As discussed in Chapter 3, the legal formulas and
procedures used in determining limpieza status made genealogy and
filiation central to the constitution of Spanish identities and made the
juridical process a constant site of contestation and manipulation. These
formulas and procedures also promoted an obsession with origins that
laid the groundwork for the development of particularly strong links, in
both Spain and Spanish America, among religion, race, and "nation."

CHAPTER THREE

Juridical Fictions

The Certification of Purity and the Construction of Communal Memory

⁓

Spanish notions of purity and impurity of blood were fictions, ideological constructs based on religious and genealogical understandings of difference that despite their invented nature were no less effective at shaping social practices, categories of identity, and self-perceptions.[1] If writings by the educated elite, popular literature, and colloquial expressions are any indication, the concept of limpieza was not exclusive to one segment of the Old Christian population but was embraced by significant portions of the nobility and commoner masses. Although there is no consensus on whether the statutes' main impetus came from the lower or upper estate, various scholars stress that the idea of purity of blood had appeal not only for aristocrats who felt threatened by upwardly mobile conversos, but for peasants and other commoners who used it to bolster their sense of honor vis à vis the converso or "mixed" nobility.[2] Resentment toward the converts and their descendants because of religious or social reasons, the leveling effect of the concept of purity among the Old Christian population, and the resonance of the idea of an intractable "Jewish nature" with medieval anti-Semitic discourses all contributed to the spread of the statutes. These factors, however, do not entirely explain the longevity of the ideology of limpieza de sangre in Spanish society. Outliving the Inquisition, some purity requirements were not abolished until the 1860s. How did the concept of limpieza de sangre and its underlying assumptions about religious identities get injected into the everyday life of early modern Spaniards? Through what institutions and practices were they reproduced? And how did purity of blood operate as a juridical category? In short, what social forces, institutions, and legal and archival mechanisms helped reproduce the discourse of purity of blood?

This chapter analyzes these questions and in particular some of the institutional and legal mechanisms that contributed to making the categories of New and Old Christian into salient, ongoing, and taken-for-granted distinctions in early modern Spain. It focuses on the procedures for establishing purity of blood developed by the Inquisition because, thanks to the Holy Office's various regional tribunals and authority on matters of the faith, its genealogical and juridical formulas for proving limpieza de sangre not only became models for other institutions but were disseminated among populations in both Spain and America, in both contexts having a long-lasting effect on racial thought. These juridical procedures were implicated not just in the homogenization of definitions of purity but in making the use of the categories of New and Old Christian enter into the realm of the *habitus,* a form of mediation that by making certain social practices seem natural, part of a commonsense world, turns history "into nature, i.e., denied as such."[3]

The chapter stresses that legal mechanisms for certifying purity arose for a number of reasons, including concerns among some Old Christians that with the passage of time, memory of "stained" lineages would fade; that false genealogies were proliferating; and that persons of Jewish or Muslim descent could not be easily identified through external, physical signs. It also explains the significance that the probanzas placed on nativeness and citizenship for determining the status of limpieza de sangre, a topic that is later elaborated upon in discussions of legal and social hierarchies in Spanish America. Finally, the last section focuses on some of the contradictions and consequences (intended and otherwise) that the process of certifying purity engendered in early modern Iberia. Meant to serve as mechanisms of exclusion and tools through which to detect impurity, the genealogical and juridical formulas involved in the process were not only constantly manipulated but also paradoxically fostered communal memories that helped to produce the myth of a pure Spain.

THE HOLY OFFICE'S PROCEDURES AND THE PROBANZA
DE LIMPIEZA DE SANGRE

The statutes of purity of blood produced the Spanish legal genre called the probanza de limpieza de sangre ("probanza" for short). The origins of this genre were bound up with the problem of memory. Though some institutions had adopted limpieza requirements in the fifteenth century, they did not establish explicit guidelines for the verification of "clean" lineages, apparently because Spaniards still remembered the conversions that took place after Toledo's Sentencia-Estatuto and after the Inquisition began to try cases of heresy.[4] As the memory of these two waves of conversions declined and along with it the ability to identify and winnow out "the impure," certain institutions started outlining and regularizing the procedures that were to be followed in genealogical investigations. The identification of conversos and moriscos was made even harder by their lack of distinguishable characteristics. As the sixteenth-century Spanish writer Juan Gutiérrez remarked, "These descendants of the Mohammedan and Judaic races, cannot be distinguished by any visible extrinsic act, by any ocular external note or sign, from authentic Spaniards."[5] External signs such as skin color and hair would play a more prominent role in Spanish America's discourse of limpieza de sangre, but there, too, legal procedures for certifying pure genealogies would surface.

Spain's Church of Córdoba might have been the first to develop a purity certification process, in 1530, but in terms of setting the tone for other establishments, the 1547 decision by the Capilla de los Reyes Nuevos to require that genealogical certificates be produced and submitted not by the candidates themselves but by designated officials was of greater transcendence.[6] By that time, the shift toward more rigorous procedures was being propelled not just by the need to establish more efficacious ways of tapping into and preserving communal memory of stained genealogies. It was also motivated by the perception among certain religious officials that a growing number of people were using fraudulent documents to access institutions with statutes of purity of blood, by the urgency that the struggle against heresy had acquired as Protestantism spread in Europe, and by Silíceo's relentless efforts to exclude conversos from Toledo's cathedral. In short, the probanza developed in the context of increasing concerns with memory, institutional exclusivity, and religious orthodoxy, all of which, as reflected in the shift to a strict dual-descent model of determining limpieza status, favored the restriction of the category of Old Christian.

Given its mission to protect the faith, its long jurisdictional tentacles, and its burgeoning archival infrastructure, the Inquisition was ideally suited to take a leading role in the development of the probanza system, but as pointed out in the previous chapter, it did not do so immediately. Although orders that Inquisition officials had to be Old Christians had been in the institution's books since at least 1513, they started to be implemented only after Philip II issued several decrees (in 1553, 1562, and 1572) that made purity of blood a requirement for all Holy Office personnel, including inquisitors, *consultores* (advisors on legal matters), *familiares* ("familiars" or lay informants), commissioners, and secretaries.[7] The only official who did not have to abide by this requirement was the inquisitor general, presumably because he was supposed to be more of a papal than royal appointment (he seldom was). The 1572 decree called for the Holy Office to verify, always through trustworthy and respectable witnesses, that its members were Old Christians without any genealogical ties to Jews or Muslims or to persons who had been relaxed, reconciled, or penanced. This verification could not be waived, even if the candidate enjoyed a canonry or other dignities within the church and had submitted proofs of limpieza to other communities or corporations, including the prestigious military orders. The decree also stipulated that all married candidates and those who wed after receiving their titles had to submit proof of purity for their wives. This provision sought mainly to safeguard institutional honor and credibility. A male's marriage to an "impure" woman linked him to an unclean family and "contaminated" his descendants, and the Inquisition, in charge of safeguarding the faith, could not afford to be linked to lineages assumed to have a proclivity to engage in religious subversion. Crucially, the decree did not specify how far back genealogical stains could be traced.

Although the 1572 decree contained a few instructions regarding the purity certification procedure, the Inquisition actually developed many of them during the last third of the sixteenth century. The principal change during this period was the greater emphasis on determining the social status of the candidate and ensuring that neither he nor any other member of his family had been involved in "vile or mechanical trades" ("*oficios viles o mecánicos*").[8] The requirements for familiars in particular became more rigid and exclusive, as the Inquisition sought to eliminate from its ranks individuals of commoner origins. But if by the early seventeenth century a certain degree of wealth was necessary for becoming a familiar, being affluent did not necessarily work in the candidate's favor. Worried that people with means but of humble origins were using bribes to obtain offices and titles, the Suprema in 1602 urged inquisitorial tribunals not only to ascertain that their members were pure of blood and of good social standing, but to protect themselves from infiltration by "new money."[9] Like other early modern Spanish institutions, the Holy Office tried, albeit sometimes without much rigor, to reinforce aristocratic privilege at the expense of merchants, artisans, and other members of the incipient bourgeoisie.

The Inquisition's role in the regularization of the process for certifying purity of blood increased its power. As the only institution with a statute that had extensive and reliable archives, it acquired authority on limpieza issues, especially as memory of stained lineages faded. Though its genealogical investigations were often the source of anxieties, its probanzas were coveted, even by some nobles who did not seek its titles or offices and who had already proven their purity to the military orders.[10] The influence that the Holy Office gained as a result of its development of formal procedures for certifying limpieza extended to the colonial context. As of the 1570s, it began sending detailed instructions and questionnaires to all of its tribunals, including those that were just being established in the Americas. Before long, a transatlantic probanza system was in place that helped spread concerns with purity outside of the Iberian Peninsula. This system operated without interruption until the early nineteenth century and contributed to the longevity and relative uniformity of the discourse of limpieza de sangre in the broader Hispanic Atlantic world.

How, then, did the Inquisition certify limpieza de sangre? The process normally began when the person wishing to be considered for a title, office, or ministerial post petitioned the nearest tribunal. He did this by submitting his genealogical information, called *información de limpieza de sangre, información de genealogía y limpieza de sangre,* or simply "información," and sometimes by also presenting a number of people who could attest to its contents.[11] If the petitioner was married, he also at that time provided an información for his wife. Each genealogical form had to include the names as well as the places of origin or "nativeness" (*naturaleza*), citizenship (*vecindad*), and domicile (long-term or permanent residence) of the parents and four grandparents.[12] This data was supposed to direct officials to appropriate registers and to people who might have information about the petitioner's birth and lineage. Identifying the *lugares de naturaleza* (native towns) of the candidate and all of his ancestors was of special importance to the Inquisition because it believed that it was only there that it could confirm the purity and religious orthodoxy of genealogies. Once the genealogical information was recorded, the inquisitors selected a commissioner (*comisario* or *comisario informador*) to conduct an investigation, and he in turn chose the scrivener or secretary that was to accompany him. If the candidate was applying for a ministerial post rather than to be a familiar or lesser official, the Suprema might assign the secretary itself. The comisario, who performed a variety of duties for the Inquisition (such as filling out paperwork and informing regional tribunals of denunciations of heresy in his jurisdiction), was usually a parish priest from the district in which the probanza was to be done.

The first, and secret, part of the investigation commenced when the commissioner traveled to the petitioner's native town, if different from where the official was stationed, and examined all available public, private, and ecclesiastical records—including parish registers when they existed, Inquisition archives, censuses, and notarial documents (e.g., wills and dowries)—for information regarding the person's birth status, lineage, and general family history. Illegitimacy tended to disqualify the candidate not only because it was considered "infamous" by law (a public dishonor) but also because it called into question his biological parenthood, thus making it impossible to ascertain his purity of blood.[13] If no stain of illegitimacy or any other irregularities were found, the comisario proceeded to the second, oral part of the investigation. His first task was to find the local or district familiars and with their help identify eight to twelve people who could serve as witnesses in the case. Inquisition guidelines instructed commissioners to draw a list of all potential informants and cross out individuals who might be biased toward or against the petitioner (such as close relatives or enemies). In keeping with the gendered Spanish tradition of privileging the *viejos* (elders) of each town as sources of information and authority, the witnesses were to be selected from among the oldest Old Christian males of the community. When women did testify, it was either because no other witnesses could be found or because their husbands were absent and they were asked to represent them. The entire process was supposed to be repeated in different towns if the parents or grandparents had been residents, citizens, or natives in more than one place.

Once the witnesses were selected came the most important and solemn part of the entire process: the depositions. Each testimony was given separately and recorded verbatim by the secretary. In addition to the scrivener, one or more public notaries were present to attest to the legality of procedures. Before the questioning began, witnesses had to swear that they would not divulge any information about the case or their participation in it, in part because the Holy Office liked to shroud most of its operations in mystery but also because secrecy minimized the possibility that those who deposed were bribed, harassed, or punished for their testimonies. They were also asked to take an oath of truth while making the sign of the cross and warned about the penalties for lying, which by the early seventeenth century included the possibility of excommunication. The oath was followed by a tightly controlled interrogation process, one in which the questions were almost entirely scripted (as was generally true in Spanish legal proceedings). As of the late sixteenth century, the comisarios tended to be equipped with an instruction sheet and a questionnaire, complete with the questions that were to be posed to the witnesses and sometimes blank spaces in which the answers were to be recorded. The lists of questions seldom varied, and official instructions dissuaded commissioners from inquiring more than was necessary. One of the questionnaires used by the Inquisition during the first half of the seventeenth century can serve as an example.[14]

How to interrogate witnesses in purity investigations

1. First, [ask] if they know the said person for whom the investigation is being done. [Ask also] how they know him, for how long, and what his age is.

2. [ask] if they know the father and mother of the said person. And if they do, [ask] where they are native to ["*de donde son naturales*"], and where they have lived, and where they have been *vecinos* and for how long, and how they know.

3. [ask] if they know [the paternal grandparents] of the said person. And if they have any information whatsoever about any other ancestors on the paternal line, they should declare how it is that they know them and for how long, and where they are originally from, and where they have been *vecinos* and had residence.

4. [ask] if they know [the maternal grandparents] of the said person, and where they are originally from, and where they have been *vecinos*, and resided, and how they know them and for how long.

5. [ask] the witnesses whether any of the general questions apply. [These basically consisted of whether they were declared enemies or close relatives of the person whose genealogy was being investigated.]

6. [ask] if they know whether the person for which this investigation is being made is the son of the said [parents] and is thought, considered, and commonly reputed to be ["*avidos, tenidos, y comunmente reputados*"] their legitimate son. Ask them to declare the affiliation and how they know.

7. [ask] if they know whether the said person's father and paternal grandparents, and all other ancestors by the paternal line, all and each and every one of them were and are Old Christians, of clean blood, without the race, stain, or descent from Jews, Moors, or conversos, or from any other recently converted sect, and as such have been thought of, and considered and commonly reputed to be. And that there is no fame or rumor to the contrary and if there was, the witnesses would know, or would have heard, because of the knowledge and information that they had and have about each and every one of the said persons.

8. [ask] whether they know that the said person or his father or paternal grandparents which are named in the previous question, or any other ancestor, have not been punished or condemned by the Holy Office

of the Inquisition, and that they have not incurred any other infamies that would prevent them from having a public office and honor. They should say what they know about this, and what they have heard, and what they know about the good habits and prudence and judgment of the said person.

9. [ask] if they know that the said mother of the said person and the named maternal grandparents and all other ancestors by his mother's side each and every one of them have been and are Old Christians, clean and of clean blood, without the race, stain, or descent from Jews, Moors, or conversos, or from any other recently converted sect, and as such have been thought of, and considered and commonly reputed to be. And that as such they are held by public voice and fame ["*pública voz y fama*"] and by common opinion, and that there is no fame or rumor to the contrary and if there was, the witnesses would know, or would have heard, and that there is no possibility that they wouldn't, given the information that they had and have of each and every of the said persons.

10. [ask] if they know whether the mother of the said person and all of the other ancestors which were specified in the previous question have not been condemned or punished by the Holy Office of the Inquisition, and that they have not been associated with any other infamies that would prevent them from having a public office and honor.

11. [ask] if they know that everything that they have declared is public voice and fame.

The person that conducts the interrogation should make sure that the witnesses respond promptly to each point in each question, without accepting general responses to the question. And as for any other questions not in the interrogatory, he should only make those that from the depositions are deemed necessary to investigate the truth, without making impertinent or excessive questions.

As the questionnaire reveals, the first part of the interrogation (questions 1 to 6) sought to verify the candidate's biographical information, namely, his legitimacy, the names of his parents and grandparents, and his ancestors' native towns. The next, and key, part of the process centered on whether his maternal and paternal bloodlines were pure according to the two definitions of limpieza. Specifically, questions 7 and 9 ask whether the candidate had any Jewish, Muslim, or converso ancestors; and questions 8 and 10 ask whether he descended from anyone who had been tried by the Inquisition for heresy or other serious offenses. Although the interrogation process as a whole focused on the candidate's parents and grandparents, *all* maternal and paternal ancestors were included in these purity questions. Finally, in the last part of question 8, witnesses were asked to comment on the petitioner's conduct, values, and character, which afforded them an opportunity to refer to such matters as his religious behavior, marital status, and standing in the community. In the second half of the seventeenth century, some interrogation forms added specific questions about some of these issues as well as about the candidate's occupation, services to the republic, and loyalty to the crown.[15] For the most part, however, the examination of witnesses continued to follow the format and content of the questions listed above, perhaps because tribunals kept old copies of questionnaires.

Since numerous witnesses were questioned, the certification process could take several weeks, sometimes months, and even years. The length largely depended on whether the genealogical investigations had to be conducted in one or several places and especially on whether doubts about the purity of blood of the petitioner or any of his ancestors were raised. In the second scenario, the commissioner had to try to determine on which genealogical branch the stain ran and if there was any "hard evidence" to substantiate the claim, such as the existence of sanbenitos. These were the penitential garments that persons convicted of heresy had to wear and which after they died were left hanging, indefinitely, in local churches with an inscription bearing the name of the heretic and usually describing the nature of his or her crime. Intended to preserve a community's memory of its "stained" lineages—among other things so that "pure" families would avoid being contaminated by them—the sanbenitos served as a visual proof of impurity. Once the comisario finished with the entire investigation, he wrote down his impressions of the proceedings and any other pertinent information and sent the dossier to the tribunal that had commissioned the case. The main job of the inquisitors who received it was to verify that all aspects of the investigation had been conducted according to proper legal form and to evaluate the evidence. If they concluded that enough information had been gathered, they issued a decision, wrote it down in the file, and finalized it with all the required signatures and seals. The case in its original form was stored in the Holy Office's archives (much to the benefit of future historians and genealogists).[16]

When the Inquisition concluded that an applicant was impure, it tended not to inform him of the decision, but its prolonged silence was usually notification enough. The Holy Office refrained from calling attention to these rejection cases in order to avoid hurting the reputation of institutions or corporations with which the said person was already associated. The idea was to protect them from being perceived as havens of conversos, a problem that some religious orders had faced in the late fifteenth century. But despite the Inquisition's efforts to keep its genealogical inquiries secret, communities generally knew when the purity of one of their own was being investigated. The arrival of commissioners, their archival investigations, their conversations with familiars, and their interrogation of witnesses were unlikely to go unnoticed, especially in small towns. And once the case turned into general knowledge, public opinion could play a role in different stages of the probanza process, not just in the witnesses' testimonies. A lengthy investigation process, for instance, could arouse suspicions that the application had been rejected and damage the reputation of the candidate, which could in turn affect the outcome of the case.

As to those who were fortunate enough to have their purity-of-blood status approved, they were generally given three or four official copies (*traslados*) of the probanza, which they could simply keep or try to submit to other institutions with limpieza requirements. But even though their symbolic capital was substantial, inquisitorial certificates were not necessarily accepted by other establishments, and they did not guarantee the holder protection from future accusations of impurity. Individuals and families were sometimes forced to produce several proofs of limpieza, a practice that Philip IV tried to curb with his Real Pragmática of 1623. The pragmatic included a "three positive acts" decree mandating that a candidate for a post or honor who was able to show that his direct ancestors had on three separate occasions had their purity of blood certified by specific institutions (among them the Inquisition, the Council of Orders, certain university colleges, and the Church of Toledo) was exempt from having to prove it himself. However, this decree, which was mainly the result of the Duke of Olivares's efforts to gain supporters by making it easier for individuals to enter the military orders, did not have significant consequences.[17] If anything, it underscored how difficult "proving" limpieza and having it count had become in early modern Spain. Unlike the status of nobility, which after being transmitted for three generations could become a permanent and therefore "natural" condition, that of purity of blood could at any point be lost.

THE PROBATORY AND UNSTABLE NATURE
OF PURITY OF BLOOD

The Inquisition's procedures for certifying purity of blood were of course its own and not necessarily those adopted by the other institutions. Because of the corporate nature of early modern Spanish society, each "community," secular or religious, had the right to determine not only whether to have a statute but the terms by which limpieza was confirmed. For this reason, certification procedures differed somewhat by institution. The Inquisition's probanzas were considered rigorous, but not as much as those of Spanish university colleges, which in some cases required not only extensive genealogical information but details about the family's estate and a minimum income level. These colleges were extremely important institutions because they basically produced the lettered (*letrado*) bureaucracy, professional civil servants who usually had degrees in law or theology. Procedures for obtaining military habits were also quite elaborate because the Council of Orders (a mainly royal body that assessed, administered, and advised the military orders) required that the candidates prove their purity and nobility of blood. In these investigations, a minimum of twenty-four witnesses were needed for establishing limpieza and at least another twenty for verifying nobility and other qualities; some involved as many as five hundred interrogations.[18] In the case of candidates for ecclesiastical posts or benefices, who in general did not need to have noble ancestry but who sometimes did have to prove that they were not associated with any "vile or mechanical trades," the certification process resembled that of the Inquisition. Cathedral chapters acted as the tribunals in charge of the limpieza investigation and assigned a commissioner (sometimes the same one who served the Holy Office) to examine public registers, interrogate witnesses, and submit a report. The chapter made sure that proper procedures had been followed and made a decision on the case.[19] Other certification processes were less demanding and mysterious. For example, in some confraternities the candidate played more of a role in the investigations, and the decision was made not by a committee or tribunal but by all the members of the sodality.[20]

Despite the corporate nature of the statutes, they were not limited to "private bodies" or to a nonpublic sphere. Some town councils, including that of Toledo (1566), established limpieza requirements and were of course not private institutions. Candidates for local public office presented their genealogical information to the *corregidor* (a royal municipal official), and the latter submitted a report to the Royal Chamber (Real Cámara). The Inquisition made use of public notaries in its purity certification procedures, sometimes also alcaldes mayores and other figures of local government. It also habitually presented town councils and local judges with the names of familiars, and this list became a part of the community's records. To be sure, not all institutions implicated the municipal government and the justice system in their certification processes, but a number of them (such as military and religious orders) relied on services of both secular and religious officials, thus making the "private" probanza system intersect with the public domain. Furthermore, despite variations in their purity investigations, these different institutions followed similar procedures and developed a general pattern or model for "proving" Old Christian ancestry. As the inquisitor Diego Serrano de Silva explained in the early seventeenth century, because the limpieza statutes had no precedent in canon or any other type of law, the certification process had to be created, but new practices gradually were regularized and a particular form of proceeding emerged.[21]

At least three aspects of this procedural pattern made purity-of-blood status fundamentally unstable. First, as mentioned by Serrano de Silva, the probanza represented an atypical type of legal procedure, one that hardly ever settled the matter of limpieza once and for all. Within Spanish common law (*ius commune*, an amalgam of canon, Roman, and feudal law), the traditional type, used in criminal cases, was the *proceso en forma*, in which a judge studied and announced the charges against the accused, the different parties had the right to present evidence, defendants could argue their own cases or hire lawyers to represent them, a sentence was pronounced, and it was possible to appeal. Limpieza de sangre cases, however, fell under the category of *expediente*, which was meant to be a more expedient legal process.[22] Although a committee acting as a tribunal could be involved, the case was not in the hands of a judge, no lawyers were allowed to participate, the questions posed to the witnesses were almost entirely predetermined, and no sentence was issued, only approval or rejection. Furthermore, all that the person whose lineage was "on trial" was normally allowed to do was present his genealogical information and, when applicable, that of his wife, and pay the required fees. He did not have the right to know who the witnesses in his probanza were, let alone the substance of their allegations.[23] In addition, most bureaucratic establishments with the statute did not allow the candidate to appeal decisions nor for investigations to be reopened, although in the case of the Inquisition, it did make some exceptions.[24]

One such exception occurred in the early years of the seventeenth century. Diego Gonzales Monjarrés applied to be a familiar and submitted his genealogy and that of his wife to the inquisitorial tribunal in Valladolid. After a series of lengthy investigations in various towns, he was granted the title. Subsequently, several people went to the inquisitors to urge them not to allow Gonzales Monjarrés to be a familiar because he descended, on his maternal bloodline, from Diego de Castro, who was reputed to be a New Christian—mainly because he was a clothes merchant and moneylender, professions that in the popular imagination were strongly linked with Jews and conversos. The Suprema reviewed the testimonies and ordered that his title be removed and his name be withdrawn from Valladolid's list of familiars. Contending that his accusers were unjustly trying to strip him of his honor, Gonzales Monjarrés took matters into his own hands and met with elders from the city of Valladolid who had information about his ancestors, in the process uncovering copies of a power of attorney, dowry, and other legal documents that demonstrated that even though a brother of his great-grandfather had married the daughter of Diego de Castro, he himself was not a direct descendant of the alleged New Christian. He was related to him, but by "transversal," not "direct," bloodlines. Armed with this new information, Gonzales Monjarrés appealed to the Suprema, which ordered a new investigation, the result of which supported his contentions. The councilors concluded that the people who had denounced the familiar had been mistaken about his genealogy and ordered that his title be reinstated. They also ordered all local justices and other municipal authorities (*regidores* and *corregidores*) of Valladolid to reinsert his name in the local list of familiars, record the outcome of the case in the town council's registers, and grant him a copy of the decision.[25]

Gonzales Monjarrés's appeal to the Suprema demonstrates that it was possible to contest the Inquisition's decision on a limpieza case and that in some instances written records carried more weight than oral testimonies. The late sixteenth century and early decades of the seventeenth, when memorials in favor of reforming the statutes proliferated, when Spanish monarchs were somewhat receptive to trying to curb some of the worst abuses of the probanza system, and when at least one converso lineage was made eligible for Old Christian status, was a particularly propitious time to challenge unfavorable decisions in purity investigations. Still, Gonzales Monjarrés's successful appeal was exceptional, and he must have known that himself, just as he was aware that his title of familiar did not guarantee that the purity of his lineage would not again be challenged in the future. Wanting to spare his descendants the trouble he had gone through to clear his name, Gonzales Monjarrés left them a written statement describing the reinstatement and listing the archives and documents that they should consult if anyone tried to link them genealogically to Diego de Castro, the alleged New Christian. He also advised them to make sure to select spouses that were pure Old Christians, "because only on that foundation can one aspire to make more money and not lose one's entire estate."[26] Finally, Gonzales Monjarrés deposited a copy of his title at the Congregación del Señor San Pedro Martir, a confraternity associated with the convent of San Pablo that tended to accept only familiars, in case any of his descendants wanted to enter into it. It is as if he anticipated that in the future the purity of his lineage would once again be questioned, probably with good reason.

Because the probanzas and other legal processes that fell under the category of expediente did not result in a sentence, approval of a genealogy by one institution, though considered juridical because it followed a certain form, did not have to be accepted by other establishments, hence

the need to keep proving it. The Pragmática of 1623 and its "three positive acts" decree, which constituted the first attempt by Spanish kings to
regulate an aspect of the purity certification process as a whole, tried to
apply principles of common law, in particular, of the *proceso en forma*,
to the probanzas de limpieza by declaring that purity of blood could
under certain circumstances be considered a judged, and therefore permanent, status. But the legislative effort failed precisely because of the
reluctance by different institutions to relinquish their autonomy to decide on such matters.[27] Corporatism, at least in this instance, prevailed
over royal authority. The status of limpieza de sangre thus continued
to be unstable, accessible but easily lost, depending on one's reputation
within the community (which was not necessarily fixed), personal relationships, and the outcome of the next probanza.

A second feature of the certification process that made limpieza a
fragile status was its reliance on the "public voice and fame."[28] As the
Inquisition's probanzas suggest, purity-of-blood cases primarily admitted two main types of evidence (three if one counts visual forms such as
the sanbenitos). The first came from written records, namely, registers
and archives, and attested mainly to the legitimate birth of the candidate and his immediate ancestors, sometimes also to other genealogical
information. The second was oral and relied on the memory of a select
group of men who were supposed to be authorities on their community's
past generations and on the public reputation of its members. Because of
the importance that early modern Spanish society placed on a person's
social standing according to the "public voice and fame," it was the oral
type of proof that usually established the purity or impurity status of
the individual. As historian Antonio Domínguez Ortiz observed, this aspect of the process was the most radical as well as the most problematic,
because it essentially meant that the whole case relied on the presumed
impartiality of witnesses.[29] The Inquisition and other institutions tried
to ensure objectivity and truth by not allowing "intimate friends," "declared enemies," or relatives of the person for whom the probanza was
being made to testify and by warning witnesses that lying could result in
their excommunication, but these measures were not foolproof devices.
Furthermore, beyond the problem of objectivity was the critical issue of
how deponents acquired, constructed, and communicated their knowledge. Some Spanish kings tried to discourage the indiscriminate use of
hearsay as evidence in the probanzas de limpieza. The 1623 Pragmática,
for example, stressed that rumors and other information provided by
witnesses had to be verified. But for both commissioners and witnesses,
discerning between what was "public voice and fame" and what was
merely rumor or gossip was probably easier said than done.

The probanza system's privileging of public opinion made it open to abuse by all parties involved in the investigations. Witnesses sometimes accepted bribes; at others they demanded them in return for positive testimonies. By the end of the sixteenth century, the statutes had produced a new social category: the *linajudo,* or expert in local lineages (*linajes*). Prominent in Seville and other major Spanish cities, linajudos volunteered their services to various institutions that had purity and/or nobility requirements, among them the military orders, the Inquisition, and the religious orders, and tried to extort money from candidates in return for providing favorable genealogical records and testimonies in their investigations.[30] Inquisition officials and familiars were themselves not immune to corruption. As key informants in the web of investigations in which so much privilege and symbolic capital was at stake, the latter were in fact among the most susceptible to accepting bribes.[31] Notwithstanding the precautions that the Inquisition and other bodies took to prevent corruption and perjury, then, the probanza system was fraught with problems. For the petitioner, the best scenario was that the familiar and witnesses selected held him in high regard and would not try to profit from the case; the worst was that anyone involved in the investigation had a vendetta against him or his family. Either way, the process could turn out to be quite expensive, especially because for some institutions it generated income.[32] All of this meant that those individuals who had their purity of blood certified were not necessarily those who were pure but those who could afford to pay for a probanza and were well connected.

Given the high cost of obtaining a certificate of purity, the possibility that the process could result in the discovery of stained ancestors, and the limited transferability of the probanzas, why would anyone apply for one? In addition to the obvious reason that they provided access to certain institutions and posts—which for some might mean securing a place in the privileged estate—and represented symbolic capital, applicants were also motivated by the desire to preserve, or rather construct, a certain memory of their past. Gonzales Monjarrés, for example, claimed to have applied for the title of familiar because he did not want his descendants to become the victims of attempts by others to defame them, to paint them with the brush of impurity. Concretely, he wanted to create a paper trail and public record that his children could resort to in order to preserve and defend their honor as well as their estates. Although the probanzas were intended to preserve memory of stained lineages, they also could serve to create different histories, in some cases even to manufacture clean lineages out of "impure" ones. The manipulation of memory could work both ways.[33] The promise of establishing an archival record favorable to a family and its progeny could compensate for the expense and anxiety that subjection to the probanza implied. As to the incentives that institutions had for requiring the proofs, there were many. Not only did the probanzas allow them to have a tightly controlled admission process that theoretically allowed them to select good Christians of a certain social and religious background, but they sometimes generated revenue. Moreover, having purity requirements protected secular and religious establishments from accusations that they were harboring conversos, whereas not having them tended to be interpreted as being lax about admitting stained people. The need to safeguard institutional honor partly explains why the statutes remained in place long after the original motive for establishing them—the threat that conversos supposedly represented to the Christian faith—had disappeared.

A third aspect of the certification process that rendered the status of purity of blood unstable, even farcical, was that ultimately, the category of Old Christian was established on the basis of negative proof. Detecting impure ancestry—through records of people tried by the Holy Office, sanbenitos, hearsay, and so forth—was much easier than finding positive or conclusive proof of limpieza de sangre. The latter was in fact not feasible because it involved verifying that a person did not have any Jewish or Muslim ancestors and no links to people who had been associated with heresy. But genealogies, particularly those of ordinary people, could be traced only to a certain point, and there were obvious limits to the memory of a local community. Thus, the best that the Inquisition and other establishments could do to establish someone's purity of blood was to show that there appeared to be no evidence to the contrary. For this reason, the system was somewhat favorable to individuals with obscure origins, those who were less likely to have genealogical documents and other historical records. That limpieza could be established only through negative proof also meant that the system placed as much of a burden on the "pure" as on the "impure."[34] While the latter were in theory the targets of the investigations, the former were also obliged to show that they were untainted, but again, this was virtually impossible and even the most loyal Christian lineages could be falsely accused and defamed. The system essentially turned the search for security in matters of purity of blood into a quixotic quest, which was one of the reasons why Miguel de Cervantes and other writers of the Golden Age could not resist but to satirize it.[35] Their fascination with reality and illusion, a central theme not only in literature but in painting, dioramas, and other optical devices of the period,[36] was rooted in the disconcerting realization that their relationship was dialectical.

The impossibility of proving limpieza beyond a shadow of a doubt was not acknowledged by the formulaic language that witnesses in probanzas were compelled to use. As many of the *tratadistas* (authors of treatises or memorials) who wrote about the statutes observed, usually in reference to the Inquisition's 1572 requirements, in order for purity status to be approved, people who deposed could not simply state that they did not know that the candidate was not an Old Christian; rather, they had to assert that they knew that he was and "that there [was] no fame or rumor to the contrary and if there was, the witnesses would know, or would have heard, because of the knowledge and information that they had and have about each and every one of the [the candidate's ancestors]." In legal terminology, Old Christian ancestry could be not presumptive but affirmative and positive ("*no es presumptiva sino afirmativa y positiva*").[37] Why this stress on the unambiguous affirmation of limpieza de sangre? In part it can be attributed to linguistic legal formulas meant to secure testimonies that, by being framed in categorical terms, enabled commissioners and inquisitors to arrive at conclusions about the case. But the carefully controlled language and procedures used in the interrogations, which created a kind of staged environment evocative of Cervantes's "theatre of marvels" (*teatro de las maravillas*)—a short play about a "magic play" mounted and viewed exclusively by those who were "pure" in which no one acknowledges that nothing happens for fear of being declared tainted—was also implicated in the creation of a particular historical memory. For by exalting Old Christian ancestry and favoring those with obscure origins (the masses), over the long run, the probanzas also paradoxically contributed to the production of a teleological historical fiction: the Christian foundation of Spanish communities.[38] The statutes might have sought to limit the activities of conversos in some secular and religions institutions and in politics, but what mattered most was the abstract ideal,[39] that is, the appearance of a pure Christian realm, achieved through the legal fiction of having pure blood.

TELEOLOGICAL FICTIONS

The Spanish crown, which during most of the sixteenth and seventeenth centuries claimed to have a providential mission to protect the church and faith, relied on this fiction, structuring society not only around the principle of nobility, as other European monarchies did, but around that of purity of blood. The second principle extended the concept of honor to the masses and was initially directed mainly against those segments of the noble estate that had been tarnished by intermarriage with upwardly mobile converso families. The purity movement's antiaristocratic (and antibourgeois) dimension was evident in Silíceo's struggle to establish a statute in Toledo's cathedral chapter, which a number of scholars consider paradigmatic of the popular sector's resentment of the conversos' rapid social mobility. Silíceo was an Old Christian of commoner (peasant) origins who studied his way to the upper levels of the church and who, once in power, turned against the New Christians. According to Jaime Contreras, he represented the victory of the *villano* and the *castizo*, and his struggle stood for that of peasant masses against the urban bourgeoisie.[40]

The antiaristocratic thread within the purity movement was also manifested in the linajudos' policing of noble lineages and in the production and circulation of numerous books and compilations identifying "infected" families of the privileged estate, including the notorious *Libro Verde de Aragón* (1507) and *Tizón de la Nobleza de España* (1560). The former, "The Green Book of Aragón," was written by an assessor of the Zaragoza Inquisition and targeted the Aragonese aristocracy; the latter, "Blot on the Nobility of Spain," was a memorandum written by Cardinal Francisco Mendoza y Bobadilla to Philip II that claimed that virtually all of the Spanish nobility were stained.[41] Popular resentment toward the aristocracy grew in tandem with the commercialization of nobility, which was at its height in the last quarter of the fifteenth century. In this period the Catholic Kings sold patents of nobility, *cartas de privilegio* (or *privilegios de hidalguía*), mainly to persons who had provided military and personal services. Involvement in transatlantic commerce also opened up new avenues to the privileged estate. Some wealthy merchants, for example, obtained offices (*regimientos*) in the town council and then either acquired noble titles or married into the Old Christian aristocracy. In Seville of the late fifteenth and the whole sixteenth centuries, a good number of conversos who had been enriched by the transatlantic trade ennobled and "purified" themselves by these means.[42] The *Carrera de Indias* (navigation and commerce between Spain and its colonies) became a promising track to wealth, public office, and ennoblement.

Despite this "bourgeoisification" of Spain's nobility (or "feudalization" of the bourgeoisie?) the inflation of honors did not sit well with Castilian rulers, especially those who followed Isabella I and Ferdinand V, because it decreased the value of noble status. However, financial need and pressure from the Council of Finance compelled them to continue the practice. After 1557, sales slowed down. The patents became more expensive, and therefore less accessible, and Philip II, like his father before him, made it illegal for the patents to be sold to the descendants of heretics, Jews, and *comuneros* (citizens of Castilian communities who rebelled against the rule of Charles V and his administration between April 16, 1520 and February 3, 1522), among others.[43] It was at about this time that the crown began to reconstitute its ties to the aristocracy. According to the historian Juan Antonio Maravall, after pacifying and defeating the nobles during the late fifteenth and early sixteenth centuries, the monarchy forged a kind of deal with them that allowed it to consolidate its power.[44] This pact essentially consisted of reserving most public offices and certain professions for the Old Christian nobility, particularly hidalgos, at the expense of the wealthy urban classes, among which the conversos were well represented. The limpieza statutes, argues Maravall, were part of the process by which the medieval Spanish nobility, with the help of Spanish kings, became a relatively closed ruling elite.

Early modern Spain thus produced two discourses of limpieza: one based on the "feudal" notion of pure aristocratic lineage (nobleza de sangre), the other on that of pure Christian ancestry. If initially the second generally favored commoners of obscure origin, their victory was ephemeral. In the middle of the sixteenth century, the two discourses began to merge.[45] The traditional nobility reacted to the attack on its honor and to the infiltration of conversos and members of the commoner estate into its ranks by making purity of blood a prerequisite for noble status, thereby not only safeguarding its prestige but spearheading a "refeudalisation" of Castilian society.[46] Especially after 1600, seignorialization in Castile expanded, reinforcing the traditional social structure as well as the bond between the crown and the landed aristocracy. This process revived the notion that noble qualities were inherited through the blood, which had been weakened by the Spanish monarchy's sale of patents of nobility as well as by the Renaissance's stress on personal and achieved nobility. Thus, by the seventeenth century, Spanish genealogical texts usually made a strong distinction between nobility of blood (nobleza de sangre) and nobility of privilege (nobleza de privilegio), and in general, popular opinion did not look favorably upon noble status that did not date from "time immemorial" or that the holder had been compelled to prove through *ejecutoria*, a legal process resulting in a public document that consecrated decisions or sentences made by tribunals of justice. In short, the sale of privilegios de hidalguía led to a certain "bastardization" of the noble estate, but the inflation of honors was strongly resisted by the traditional aristocracy and in the end did not weaken either traditional social hierarchies or notions of nobility and purity of blood but just the opposite.[47]

Although the revival of "feudal" notions of blood occurred in varying degrees throughout western Europe, in Spain it took a particular

form because of the prominence of the discourse of purity that had been
brewing there since the mid-fifteenth century. The merger of the two
limpiezas—one referring to the absence (or remoteness) of commoner
ancestry, the other to the lack of Jewish, Muslim, or heretic ancestors—
produced the uniquely Iberian paradigm of the "hidalgo-cristiano viejo"
and with it a whole culture of social differentiation based on blood
and religion.[48] Because this paradigm crystallized in the context of the
Counter-Reformation and was nourished by the strong links that the
church and Castilian crown had forged in the fight against heresy, it
exalted not only traditional noble notions relating to genealogy, pre-
cedence, and civic virtue but also religious orthodoxy, loyalty to God
and king, and the complex of sexual and family values promoted by
the Council of Trent.[49] Human perfection was thus embodied in an Old
Christian male of legitimate birth, honorable lineage, and impeccable
Catholic credentials who expressed loyalty to God and king, policed
and defended the sexual virtue of the women in his family, and obeyed
(or at least appeared to obey) the church's main views on morality. The
construction of this ideal, which reinforced concepts of familial honor
and male authority over the sexuality of women, is discernible in the
system of probanzas. Not only the Inquisition but other institutions began to demand proof of various limpiezas and to inquire about the morality, behavior, and political inclinations of candidates.

By the late seventeenth century, a number of key bodies required proof
of legitimate birth and of purity of blood, purity of noble ancestry, and
"purity of profession" (limpieza de oficios). The multiplicity of manchas—
a blatant rejection of personal and meritocratic nobility—exacerbated
the Castilian obsession with blood and genealogy. This obsession was
manifested in the pervasiveness of a language of blood constituted by
terms such as sangre (blood), casta (breeding), generación (lineage), raíz
(root), tronco (trunk), and rama (branch),[50] as well as in the privileging
of "Gothic" ancestry. To "descend from the Goths" (descender de los
godos), a common expression during this period, meant to derive from
the ancient lineages of the north of Spain, regions never conquered by
the Muslims and which initiated the Reconquista. Because those lineages
were considered the most pure, Christian, and noble in the whole of the
peninsula, seventeenth- and eighteenth-century genealogists, magicians
in their own right, often undertook extraordinary feats of historical reconstruction to locate the origins of aristocratic families in Asturias, the
mountains of Burgos, Navarra, and especially the Basque provinces of
Vizcaya and Guizpúzcoa.[51] Reality shaped illusions and illusion shaped
realities. The manipulation of history and genealogy created a climate
of distrust of external appearance, masterfully captured in some of the
literature of the Golden Age.[52]

To the extent that the statutes of purity ensured that only people of a certain status and ideological and religious disposition could have access to the power, wealth, and honor that being associated with certain institutions implied, they not only made Castilian society more exclusive but promoted the cultural-political projects of the church and state (as well as of the traditional aristocracy).[53] However, the system was also riddled with contradictions and engendered a host of unanticipated consequences. Some inconsistencies have already been mentioned: The probanzas were considered juridical instruments, yet they did not result in the legal judgment of limpieza; the statutes were membership requirements voluntarily adopted by "private" bodies, but they helped make limpieza into a public matter; and the proof of purity was required of certain religious and public officials (such as inquisitors, royal scribes, and canons in many cathedral chapters) but not for others (the inquisitor general, parish priests, bishops, archbishops, aldermen, corregidores, and so forth).[54] But these contradictions in the way that the statutes operated were minor when compared to those that they as a whole produced, which threatened to undermine the Catholic image of Spain, the power of the king, and the very underpinnings of the concept of purity of blood.

Although in theory the probanzas were supposed to promote the purity of the Spanish population (by excluding the impure from positions of power and privilege and discouraging marriages between Old and New Christians), the chronic abuses in the certification system by people with personal or political motives, the rise of the linajudos, and the absence of limitations on genealogical investigations resulted in the discovery (or invention) of so many ancestral "blots" that by the early seventeenth century, not only the honor of the nobility was in jeopardy, but that of the Iberian Peninsula as a whole. As the Dominican fray Agustín Salucio and other advocates of reforming the statutes pointed out, the manner in which they were being implemented was producing a vision in Europe of Spain as a predominantly "Jewish" nation. He proposed that his country learn from the example set by France two hundred years earlier, when it allowed the Jews who chose to convert rather than leave the country to forget their ancestry and become full members of the body social. By not placing limits on how far back stains could be traced, Fray Salucio observed, the statutes helped keep the memory of stained lineages alive and promoted divisions with the realm. He proposed that allowing converts to become Old Christians, "Christians since time immemorial," was the best way to erase the memory of their Jewish past and hence resolve the problem of crypto-Judaism.[55] Some Spanish monarchs expressed a willingness to ameliorate the problems that Salucio and others identified, but because their plans were never actualized (Philip II died before the junta that he convened to analyze the limitation of the statutes finished), were too timid, or were too unacceptable to the most important institutions with purity requirements, the system was not altered in any significant way. The obsession with purity and genealogy therefore continued unabated throughout most of the seventeenth century.

Furthermore, even though the purity statutes legitimated the Spanish monarchy's role as protector of the faith and increased its social base because of the popularity they ostensibly enjoyed among the masses as well as sectors of the aristocracy, they might also have inadvertently lessened the power of kings. Although the statutes did not deny rulers their traditional ability to help their subjects transcend their birth status,[56] to redeem their "blood," Spain's monarchs apparently did not make much use of this power with regard to conversos and moriscos. The descendants of some conversos, most notably, those of the Bishop Pablo de Santa María (former rabbi of Burgos Solomon ha-Levi),[57] were granted royal dispensations that entitled them to purity and Old Christian status, but studies have yet to demonstrate that these cases were numerically significant. In any event, some seventeenth-century advocates of reforming the statutes frequently stressed that the probanza system had undermined the crown's ability to confer grace and called on the king to exercise his power to remove genealogical stains, which they argued would help deify him. One of Cuenca's inquisitors, for example, argued that just as Roman emperors had granted slaves the opportunity to transcend their condition and eradicate blots in their past, and just as rulers had the authority to ennoble their vassals, so should His Majesty grant "karats of purity and pure blood" to erase the "race of Moors and conversos." This power should not only beautify his vassals and benefit the republic as a whole, he added, but make His Majesty act in the likeness of God.[58] Part of an extensive number of discussions and debates about the role of "blood" in Spanish politics and society, the inquisitor's arguments did not have much effect, probably because Spain's seventeenth-century Habsburg kings did not enjoy absolute power or assumed that exercising it in that way would make them unpopular.

Finally, the statutes also exposed and exacerbated contradictions inherent in the notion of purity of blood, a naturalizing concept that both presupposed and promoted the idea that descent (and thus the "natural" process of biological reproduction) determined a person's behavior, beliefs, and identity. The belief that Judaism and "Jewishness" were "communicated" through the blood, transmitted by nature, not nurture, had of course been one of the initial justifications for the statutes—some of which distinguished between the conversos and "Old Christians by nature" (*cristianos viejos de natura*)—and it was still thriving centuries later. Even if he converts to Christianity, wrote one late-seventeenth-century supporter of the statutes, the Jew continues to be a threat to Catholicism because he "begets" (*engendra*) children with heretical inclinations.[59] However, the concept of limpieza was not as essentializing as this construction of an intractable Jewish nature would suggest. Even after the changes that the notion underwent in the sixteenth century, when various institutions turned to a more rigid dual-descent model and removed limits on genealogical investigations, it continued to accommodate a temporal and cultural-religious definition, that is, to allow for the possibility that the descendants of conversos would eventually be fully committed to the faith and be eligible for equality with Old Christians. For example, the Inquisition, which like other institutions with the limpieza statute conflated "purity of faith" and "purity of blood," had to recognize that even if they were inherited, Jewish and Muslim beliefs and "inclinations" could be transcended; otherwise how could it explain the reconciliation of converso and morisco heretics with the church? From the point of view of some members of the Holy Office and of the ecclesiastical hierarchy, Judaism, Islam, and heresy were transmitted in the blood, but they were ultimately spiritual "maladies" that baptized Christians could overcome. Through extraordinary efforts and dedication to Catholicism, faith could prevail over nature.[60]

Tensions between the notions of purity of faith and purity of blood were an integral part of the limpieza certification process. As the questionnaires that were used in probanzas reveal, the status of purity had to be determined not just by the absence of Jewish, Muslim, and heretic blood but also by religious orthodoxy, usually measured by the lack of encounters with the Inquisition but by behavior more generally. The two definitions of purity of blood—as descent and practices—created a deep ambiguity in the concept of limpieza as a "natural" condition, all the more heightened by the probanza system's privileging of the "public voice and fame." According to some of the authors of treatises on the statutes, purity of blood was not a natural condition but could be gained or lost, depending on one's actions and reputation, thus the need to keep proving it. Whether a person actually had Jewish ancestry or other genealogical "imperfections" simply did not matter as much as whether it was the common opinion in his or her place of origin.[61] Some Spanish thinkers did prefer to define limpieza as a "natural" essence transmitted from parents to child through the blood and to rely on genealogical information contained in written records more than on hearsay, but the legal procedures established for the probanzas tended to favor the public voice, thus further thinning the line between purity of blood as a status

determined by biology and one that was determined by behavior and
social perceptions. This slippage between biology and culture, rather
than destabilizing the concept of limpieza, made it more powerful, for it
could be deployed in multiple ways, here against people because of their
descent, there because of their actions and reputation. The "strategic
equivocation between nature and culture"—to borrow the words of the
anthropologist Peter Wade—in the process of certifying and defining
purity produced a discursive flexibility that facilitated the preservation
of social hierarchies and structures of inequalities in periods of change.

In the end, the multiple contradictions of the discourse of purity of
blood did little to undermine the statutes during the Golden Age. The
century of baroque literature that captured the deep skepticism about
external appearances in early modern Spanish society as well as its ob-
sessive genealogical concerns was also the period in which the ideology
of limpieza de sangre was at its apogee. Not until the late seventeenth
century did the controversies over the probanza system start to die down
and the purity requirements begin to be relaxed. Scholars tend to stress
that although statutes were still being implemented, some even adopted
for the first time, the probanzas and issue of limpieza lost much of their
importance because Castile's converso community was by then numerically insignificant or had almost fully assimilated into Old Christian
society, because the problem of crypto-Judaism was no longer deemed
a serious one (the last major wave of Inquisitorial prosecution was during 1720–33 and it mostly targeted Portuguese New Christians), and
because the monarchy was not focused on fighting heresy anymore.[62]
Despite these developments, however, purity requirements remained in
force for a variety of titles, posts, and professions and in numerous institutions throughout the eighteenth century and into the nineteenth.[63]
That the Bourbon kings did not abolish the statutes and that the Cortes
of Cádiz did not even raise the issue could be interpreted as indications
that the probanzas had become unimportant. But an equally plausible
explanation is that even if they were a dead letter, the requirements were
still serving to reproduce a symbolic order premised on the irreducible
otherness of Jews and Muslims and the Christian foundation of Spanish
communities. The abstract ideal is what mattered most.

CONCLUSION

The rise and spread of the statutes of purity of blood was a complex
phenomenon that took place from the mid-fifteenth century to the mid-
seventeenth century, a period in which a semifeudal Spain tried to grap-
ple, among other things, with the expansion of an incipient urban bour-

geoisie, the integration of relatively large numbers of conversos and moriscos into the rest of Christian society, the administration of a large overseas empire, the spread of heresy in broader Europe, and the struggles between the crown and parts of the nobility. Determining the significance of limpieza during this turbulent period and its connections with different social forces is a daunting challenge, all the more so because there are still many unanswered questions regarding the system of probanzas. For example, how did the certification process operate in the fifteenth century and early sixteenth century, before it became systematized? When were the procedures first developed, by which institutions, and what legal sources inspired them? In what ways did their implementation differ by both institution and period? And most important, what purposes did purity requirements serve? Naturally, the answer to this last question will differ somewhat by corporate body and temporal context, but a growing number of studies are suggesting that as mechanisms to exclude conversos (moriscos are seldom the focus of the scholarship), the statutes were not always effective and that frequently a wide gap existed between how they were supposed to be operating and how they actually were.

In sixteenth-century Toledo, for example, some members of prominent converso families, despite having been tried by the Inquisition, were able to sidestep purity requirements and access both public offices and military habits.[64] In Seville, not even the high number of linajudos could prevent New Christians from obtaining military habits, becoming Inquisition familiars or officials, and entering religious orders.[65] In some institutions, conversos were able to prevent the adoption of the purity statute altogether. This occurred, for example, in Burgos's cathedral chapter, which in the second half of the sixteenth century tried to establish a statute modeled after that of Toledo's cathedral.[66] In Lorca and Murcia, efforts to remove conversos from municipal government and the local oligarchy between 1550 and 1570 also failed.[67] The growing body of evidence suggesting that the statutes did not represent an insurmountable barrier for those of Jewish ancestry has led some historians to conclude that limpieza de sangre was an instrument through which to control upward mobility that had little to do with either religion or race.[68] Marxists historians in particular tend to characterize the statutes as weapons that the traditional aristocracy (or in some cases, Old Christian commoners) deployed against a converso bourgeoisie. To a certain extent they are right. The contention that the statutes were "social weapons" has some validity, and various scholars agree that especially after 1560, they helped make Castilian society more exclusive. The merger of nobility and purity requirements in some institutions and growing exclusion of those associated with "vile or mechanical" work are signs that increasingly the statutes were attempting to reserve domains of power, honor, and privilege for Old Christians of aristocratic stock.

But the statutes did not merely serve as weapons of social exclusion. They operated within a contested field, one in which limpieza was used in different ways by various groups and was not the exclusive tool of any one "class" or estate. Probanzas were sometimes used, for instance, to produce clean genealogies out of impure ones, and the extent to which they benefited the traditional aristocracy is by no means clear, especially prior to the mid-sixteenth century. Furthermore, having Jewish or Muslim ancestry *was* sometimes an obstacle for accessing offices, professions, and institutions that had purity statutes, and having "stained" ancestors probably dissuaded many from even attempting to enter those establishments. Those cases of people being discouraged would not be part of the historical record, making the significance of the statutes even more difficult to gauge. Finally, the religious and anti-Semitic arguments and sentiments that inspired the statutes continued to serve as their rationale long after the original reason for establishing them, the so-called threat that "backsliding conversos" posed to the Christian faith, existed in any serious form. Social strife can take many forms; that in early modern Spain it was often cast in theological and genealogical terms suggests that the issue of purity of blood was much more than an instrument of exclusion, more than a tool of this or that class—in short, more than an epiphenomenon. The ideology of limpieza became pervasive precisely because of its articulation with different social relations and its ability to rearticulate levels of religious, social, and political life in times of change.

The reproduction of the statutes and ideology of limpieza de sangre cannot be attributed to any one source or single domain. The mass conversions and rise in anxieties over threats that the recent converts posed to the unity of the faith (whether real or not but which the Inquisition's "discoveries" and autos de fe seemed to confirm), the resonance of Old Christian representations of the New Christian as a backsliding Jew with long-standing constructions of the Jews as obstinate adherents of their faith and enemies of Christianity (passed down through such things as religious sermons, Passion plays, and tropes), the commoner estate's appropriation of concepts of purity to bolster its sense of honor, the nobility's own reclaiming of the concept of limpieza in order to restore its prestige and exclusivity in the face of a mercantile class (expanded thanks largely to transatlantic trade networks) with aristocratic pretensions— these were among the religious and socioeconomic factors that provided initial and ongoing momentum for the discourse of limpieza de sangre. Political dynamics also played a role, particularly the crown's more explicit support of the statutes in the mid-sixteenth century, but also local struggles in which the issue of limpieza was often used and abused to discredit enemies and to try to compel the Inquisition to act against them.

Finally, the discourse of purity also derived its lifeblood from the archival and genealogical practices that the system of probanzas established and routinized. The presence of familiars in many towns across Spain, the visits and investigations by commissioners, and the countless testimonies that community elders provided from the sixteenth century to the end of the eighteenth helped not only to create local memories but also to reproduce notions of limpieza and make the disavowal of Jewish and Muslim ancestry into a taken-for-granted aspect of everyday life. Early modern Spanish society came to accept as normal that a candidate for a religious order would present the hierarchy with genealogical information about his Old Christian antecedents, that a Holy Office commissioner would inspect local archives and conduct interrogations about a certain lineage, and that a nobleman or wealthy commoner would pay a genealogist to invent him a pure pedigree. These and other behaviors and personal interactions were embedded in the discourse of purity of blood and the way it shaped individual and collective practices. This discourse was energized by Spain's establishment of a transatlantic empire that was also structured around the concepts of recent convert and Old Christian but that in addition produced a whole range of intermediate categories of purity.

PART TWO

Religion, Genealogy, and Caste
in Early Colonial Mexico

Nobility and Purity
in the *República de Indios*

⤳

At the time of expansion to the Americas, the Castilian crown was characterized by its close relationship with the church, partly a function of the Reconquista, and by its sizeable bureaucracy, mainly the result of the centralizing reforms begun by Enrique IV and brought to fruition by the Catholic Kings.[1] These two aspects of the monarchy strongly influenced the nature of Spanish colonialism, which was never exclusively concerned with extracting mineral wealth for the metropole or with promoting mercantile interests. From virtually the beginning, the crown set out to establish a much more encompassing relationship between its Spanish subjects and the native population, one that implicated a host of agents, institutions, and ideological weapons. In central Mexico, the defeat of the Mexica ("Aztecs")[2] by Hernán Cortés and his minions in 1521 was quickly followed by the arrival of church officials, government bureaucrats (the top being the viceroy), and colonists, who along with the conquerors waged a multifaceted assault on the peoples and landscape of Mesoamerica.[3] Early experiments with different forms of labor extraction were accompanied by the religious orders' conversion campaigns; the establishment of Castilian-styled town councils (*cabildos*), municipalities (*ayuntamientos*), and high courts of justice (*audiencias*); the building (or rebuilding) of cities according to the Spanish urban grid plan; the surveying and parceling out of lands; the intensive study of native languages; and the collection, organization, and production of knowledge about indigenous societies and histories.[4]

By the middle of the sixteenth century, the Spanish state—the crown and its public institutions for administration, justice, and finance—was creating a political, economic, and institutional framework that simultaneously obstructed the rise of a feudal colonial aristocracy (the subject of Chapter 5) and extended its own jurisdiction over the native population. This framework, which consisted of two separate but interrelated polities or "republics," the Indian and the Spanish, was one of the most distinctive aspects of Spanish colonial rule. It essentially allowed for the political and socioeconomic subordination of the indigenous people at the same time that it granted them a special status as Christian vassals of the Crown of Castile. According to Spanish colonial ideology, the native people's acceptance of the Catholic faith made them into a spiritually favored and unsullied population while their voluntary subjection to the Castilian monarch earned them rights similar to those enjoyed by natives of Spanish kingdoms. The colonial relationship of vassalage was peculiar, however, in that it was between the king and indigenous communities (not individuals).[5] Construed as contractual and voluntary, this relationship required that native towns pay tribute and remain loyal to the Catholic faith and the Spanish crown in return for the right to maintain internal hierarchies, retain their lands, and enjoy relative political autonomy.

Although efforts to maintain a strict segregation between the two republics failed,[6] the dual model of social organization had long-term social consequences. It not only led to the establishment of special legal and religious institutions but extended notions of citizenship to the native population and produced a discourse of Indian purity that throughout the colonial period promoted a concern with blood among indigenous elites. This chapter focuses on these three processes. It begins with an overview of the significance of genealogy among the Mexica before the conquest, explains the ideological and institutional foundations of the república de indios, and describes some of the ways in which Spanish colonialism made blood figure into the reproductive strategies of indigenous rulers and nobles. The last sections analyze the consequences of these strategies on central Mexican notions of genealogy, history, and race.

THE RISE OF THE MEXICA IN THE LATE POSTCLASSIC
AND THE COLONIAL "REPUBLIC OF INDIANS"

When the Spaniards arrived in the Valley of Mexico (actually a basin), the region was dominated by the Mexica, who had risen to power during Mesoamerica's Late Postclassic period (1200–1521). The fall of Tula (ca. 1168), seat of the Toltec culture which thrived from the tenth to the twelfth centuries, was followed by the arrival of refugees from the northern Mesoamerican frontier into the area and by the emergence of various "city-states"—independent political units consisting of a city and surrounding countryside—many composed of militaristic bands of diverse cultural origins. During that period of political fragmentation, which lasted about one hundred and fifty years, the different polities came to idealize the Toltecs and adopted elements of their culture, government, and religious ideology, including the cult of kingship. The obsession with Tula, generated mainly by the relative newcomers' need to establish their authority in the region, extended into the realm of kinship and genealogy. Wanting to claim direct ties with the polity that central Mexican legends associated with the arrival of civilization, local leaders eagerly married members of its royal and noble dynasties, some of whom had survived in Culhuacan, the last remnant of the Toltec state.[7] Those unions occurred mainly between rulers and Toltec royal women and therefore increased the importance of matrilineal descent for the transmission of posts, titles, and estates. They also produced nobles (*pipiltin*) who were favored for high offices in the individual city-states and who began to marry among themselves. Kinship ties among the ruling groups of different polities in turn facilitated the creation of military coalitions. By the early fourteenth century, two main confederations had been formed in the central valley: the Tepanecs, centered in the town of Atzcapotzalco, and the Acolhua, consisting of various capitals including Texcoco. In this increasingly militaristic context, a few small polities—Xochimilco, Chalco, and Culhuacan—struggled to remain independent and maintain peace with threatening neighbors—the last one by marrying off sons and daughters of Toltec noble blood to rulers of other city-states.

The Mexica, a migratory people from the northern frontier who arrived in the Valley of Mexico around the early twelfth century, were initially not troubled by their lack of Toltec pedigree and continued to rely on their traditional leaders until the last third of the fourteenth century, when members of the upper classes started to marry into Tula's prestigious lineages. In 1376 they selected the son of a Mexica warrior and Culhua princess as ruler, Acamapichtli, their first true monarch (*tlatoani*).[8] Conflicts between the new lineage groups and the traditional leadership ensued and endured until the reign of Itzcóatl, which began in 1426 (or 1427) and lasted until 1440. Itzcóatl's ascension marked the triumph of dynasties boasting Toltec ancestry and led to a remarkable effort on the part of the new leadership to rewrite the past, to construct a historical narrative that made the Mexica the direct heirs of Tula's civilization and rulers. One of the most dramatic moments of this effort came when the tlatoani and one of his main advisors, Tlacaélel, ordered the burning of all pictograms and ancient codices (pictographic histories) because these assigned a minor and unflattering historical role to the Mexica. In subsequent years, new codices, as well as songs, stories, and monuments, gave birth to migration narratives that began with the departure of the group from its homeland (Aztlán) and ended with the foundation of Tenochtitlan (in 1325 or 1345) on an island in the southwestern part of Lake Texcoco, the "promised land."[9] These narratives contained new historical myths and new conceptions of space and time, all suited to the Mexica project to cast themselves (and their religion) as protagonists in the Valley of Mexico and as the political, cultural, and genealogical heirs of the Toltecs.[10]

The myths promoted by Itzcóatl and his advisors not only created a cosmological vision that turned the Mexicas into the chosen people of the Sun, but also signaled the beginning of a powerful warrior ideology, one that developed in tandem with the group's violent rise to power. Although they initially served as mercenaries and allies in conquests, during the reign of Itzcóatl they helped form the Triple Alliance (consisting of Tenochtitlan, Texcoco, and Tlacopan), which between 1428 and 1433 defeated the Tepanec confederation. The Mexica eventually asserted their supremacy over the other two members of the Triple Alliance by conquering a number of surrounding polities, including Tlatelolco (1473), Tenochtitlan's sister city. Thanks to the frenetic pace of their military campaigns, by the last third of the century they had subjugated much of the central region, parts of the arid north and lowlands of Tehuantepec (southern Oaxaca), and large stretches on both coasts. The Mexica made conquered peoples into tributaries, but allowed some local rulers, especially those based in more remote lands, to retain political control, never quite absorbing their polities into the "empire."[11] Although the conquest of a few groups, such as the Tarascans and Tlaxcalans, remained elusive and towns frequently rebelled because of onerous tribute demands, they became the undisputed power in Mesoamerica. Imperial expansion made possible a dramatic increase in tribute and the establishment of extralocal commercial networks at the same time that the reforms instituted by Itzcóatl and his nephews Tlacaélel and Moctezuma I accelerated the concentration of power, wealth, and lands in the hands of the state and upper social classes (rulers, warrior elites, and the nobility).[12] The Mexica thus developed into a highly stratified society whose economy was based on state-oriented tribute (most in the form of commodities rather than labor), the local market, and long-distance trade.[13]

Therefore, when Cortés and his men arrived in central Mexico, they encountered not only a highly militaristic and religious society, but a complex political economy and hierarchical social order that included a number of social and occupational groups. At the summit of this order were rulers and nobles who lived mainly from tribute rendered by con-

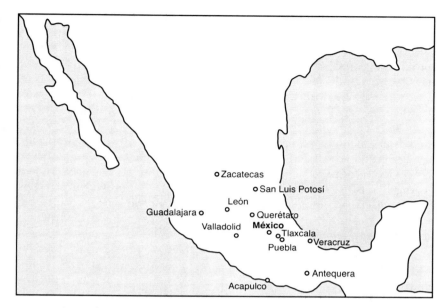

MAP 2. Central New Spain and surrounding cities. SOURCE: After Peter Bakewell, *A History of Latin America: Empires and Sequels, 1450–1930* (Malden, MA: Blackwell, 1997), p. xxi. Drawn by María Elena Martínez.

quered regions and their own communities, associated "blood" with descent and political authority, and considered genealogy and marriage affiliation extremely serious matters. All of these characteristics of the upper crust of Mexica (and more broadly Nahua) society survived the Spanish conquest, and in particular, the last two. Aristocratic concerns with blood were actually reinforced by the colonial administrative system's dependence on preexisting social and political structures and by the crown's recognition of pre-Hispanic dynasties. This recognition made genealogy central to the reproduction of indigenous political and economic elites as well as to the symbolic and cultural codes of the república de indios.

New Spain's "two-republic model" came about gradually and imperfectly and was the result of a Spanish political ideology that initially justified the colonial enterprise on the basis of the need to convert the indigenous people, of the crown's desire to deter the emergence of colonial lordships, and of the royal interest in reproducing a population of tributaries. The Christianizing mission of colonization was spelled out in the 1493 papal bull *Inter Caetera,* which granted Castile jurisdiction over most of the lands that came to be known as the Americas. Inspired by a providential conception of history that was strongly fortified by the 1492 defeat of Granada and the Columbian voyages, Spain initially linked its right to rule "the Indies" to its responsibility to spread the Catholic faith,[14] a task that, after the military conquest of the Mexicas, it took to accomplishing with a small but tenacious army of friars. These friars were mainly selected from the Franciscan and Dominican orders, which like the Spanish church as a whole had undergone important reforms in the late fifteenth and early sixteenth centuries. Reformist currents were especially strong among the Franciscans, a branch of which, the Observants, was completely devoted to a life of austerity, simplicity, and poverty. It was from this branch that the twelve friars who arrived in Mexico in 1524 to preach the Gospel were chosen. As is well known among historians of colonial Mexico, when the friars were greeted by Cortés, he—the conqueror and representative of the king—kneeled before them, a dramatic gesture symbolizing the subordination of the political order to religion.

Known for their religious zeal, commitment to saving souls (the Observants had been active in the evangelization of moriscos in rural Spain), and messianic millenarianism, Mexico's early Franciscans suffused the colonial religious project with an intense utopianism.[15] They were convinced that the dramatic events of 1492, including the expulsion of the Jews, prefigured the unification of humanity under Christianity, the second coming of Christ, and the apocalypse. The friars also believed that Spaniards had been selected by God to convert as many non-Christians as possible in order to save their souls. Delighted with the initial results of their efforts, some regarded Mexico's indigenous inhabitants as prime material—"soft wax" in the words of the Franciscan Gerónimo de Mendieta—for Christianization because they had "willingly" accepted conversion and because they were "uncontaminated" by Islam and Judaism.[16] Both of these claims would strongly influence the juridico-theological status of the native population and set it apart from other colonial groups, particularly blacks, and from Iberia's New Christians. Although those who successfully resisted being "reduced" (*reducidos*) to the Spanish Christian order were labeled "barbarians," "infidels," or simply "gentiles," during the second half of the sixteenth century, indigenous people in general came to be officially regarded as recently converted Christians who did not have tainted blood in their veins.[17]

As *gentiles no infectados* (uninfected gentiles) who, at least according to the official view, had accepted Spanish rule and embraced the Christian faith, the Indians became free vassals of the Castilian king. Their freedom, however, was not a foregone conclusion. Spanish monarchs at first wavered between allowing and prohibiting native enslavement, a situation that conquerors and colonists fully exploited. Part of the problem was that the legal and ideological justifications for Spanish rule, on which the issue of slavery hinged, were not fully developed until about the middle of the sixteenth century and in fact continued to be revisited throughout the next one hundred years. The papal bulls that had granted Castile sovereignty over most of the Western hemisphere and declared its missionary enterprise proved to be an insufficient foundation for Spain's titles because they were not based on natural law, which unlike Christian law was supposed to apply to all nations. Furthermore, Protestant countries did not recognize the papacy's authority. Spanish monarchs therefore convened various juntas to discuss the nature of their jurisdiction over the territories and peoples on the other side of the Atlantic. Jurists and theologians who participated in these meetings or "debates" were in charge of coming up with moral and legal justifications for Spain's right to property (lands and bodies) in the Americas.[18] Their arguments, particularly those of the Dominican Bartolomé de las Casas, strongly influenced Spanish legislation regarding the native people's rights and status, particularly the New Laws of 1542.

These laws, the most important body of legislation during the early colonial period, consecrated the native people's right to freedom. Specifically, they stipulated that Indians who accepted Christianity and Spanish rule were entitled to their liberty. Although some Spaniards continued to enslave natives, especially in areas such as Sonora and Pánuco, indigenous people were supposed to be freed, and not a few religious officials fervently defended that right on both religious and legal grounds. As a group of Franciscan friars asserted in 1594, the Indians "are in their own lands, where they were taught the Holy Gospel, which they received with great enthusiasm, and for having accepted it, they should not be treated like slaves but remain free as before, and [in] their republic with its permanent set of privileges."[19] As this passage suggests, the native people's right to freedom and to communal existence was defended on the grounds that they were in their territories and had collectively welcomed Christianity. Of course, not all Spaniards embraced the notion that indigenous persons were entitled to freedom and their own republic. Indeed, the various debates that took place in Spain about the nature of its overseas rule gave way to a variety of formulations about the Castilian crown's right to sovereignty (*imperium*) and property (*dominium*) in the Americas, a number of which continued to garner support even after the passage of the New Laws.

These formulations, which were developed as the lands and economic privileges of native lords in central Mexico started to be transferred to Spanish hands, fell into three main lines of thought. One current, espoused by the Dominicans Francisco de Vitoria and Bartolomé de Las

Casas, argued that although native people had come under a new sovereign, they were entitled to retain their own institutions, lands, and laws as well their governors. The role of the Castilian crown was therefore of a foreign prince, and its main responsibility was to promote the evangelization enterprise.[20] A second line of thought, represented by Gerónimo de Mendieta and other early Franciscan missionaries, was in some respects similar to the first, but tended to advocate the creation of two separate commonwealths, each with its own institutions and law. Many of the first Franciscans in Mexico believed that the presence of lay Spaniards was counterproductive to the conversion project and general well-being of the native population. They were the first, therefore, to articulate the idea of dual republics.[21]

At the opposite extreme of the Franciscans' utopian and millenarian vision was the position held by some jurists, viceregal officials, and colonists who wanted the native people to be placed under Castilian institutions and law and in the same republic as the Spaniards. Advocates of Spain's "civilizing" mission ("civility" here associated mainly with Christianity and urbanity), they claimed that the Amerindians had lost property rights because some of their institutions and alleged practices, particularly, cannibalism and human sacrifice, were against nature.[22] Juan Ginés de Sepúlveda, Las Casas's main ideological foe, articulated his argument against native property rights in Spain, but his ideas reached New Spain and were enthusiastically received by members of Mexico City's town council and many of the colonists. These parties opposed the Franciscan project to segregate the indigenous population because it made their access to laborers more difficult; they were also receptive to arguments that could be used to undermine efforts by native rulers to claim rights to the land.

Although the general tone of the New Laws and other mid-sixteenth-century legislation reflected the strong influence of Las Casas and the Salamanca scholars, the crown never clearly defined its position on the issue of creating one or two republics, and its policies on the matter lacked consistency. Whether the native people should be exposed to Spanish culture and to what degree, whether it was possible or even desirable to Christianize without Hispanicizing them, and whether proximity to the colonists would provide them with examples of virtuous life or simply result in unbridled exploitation—all of these questions, which had first been raised in the Caribbean, continued to be controversial through the end of the sixteenth century.[23] Spain's objectives in the Americas were also not clearly explained. Were religious goals going to dictate government policies, or did political and economic concerns have priority? At once medieval and Thomistic (because it was based on the ideal of a hierarchical society in which religion was at the apex and which was governed by the principles of Christian justice) and Renaissance and Machiavellian (because it contained a humanist and utopian strand and favored the creation of a strong state), the political model that surfaced never entirely resolved tensions between the different objectives.[24]

The absence of uniform royal policies was in large part due to the different colonial groups and interests that the crown had to take into account and try not to alienate.[25] Spanish colonialism was not a monolithic enterprise; the conquest and its aftermath consisted of related but competing Spanish ideological frameworks of "multiple paradigms, fantasies, and utopias."[26] Furthermore, official positions on a given issue could shift in accordance with changing social, political, or economic circumstances. The process of creating a stable order was thus one that involved a degree of political and social experimentation, the careful balancing of different Spanish interests (ecclesiastical, royal, and civilian), and the ability to respond to unforeseen events, including the actions and reactions of indigenous peoples, whose initiatives at times altered the terms of colonial power relations. Nonetheless, the crown generally favored the existence and reproduction of a república de indios, separate from Spanish colonial society. It encouraged the perpetuation of this republic through spatial segregation policies and through numerous laws and institutions that separated the indigenous people from the rest of colonial society and subjected them directly to royal authority. By recognizing citizenship rights within native communities, namely, access to lands and office holding, the crown also promoted the creation of parallel citizenship regimes.[27]

The project to forge a dual spatial order had its origins in the 1530s and was linked to the government's efforts to phase out the *encomienda* system, by which individual Spaniards (*encomenderos*) received grants of native laborers in return for promising to oversee their Christianization. In those years, Mexico City's second audiencia (1530–35) started to experiment with the creation of separate towns for native people and Spaniards, a project that initially resulted in the almost simultaneous foundations of Puebla de los Ángeles and Santa Fe.[28] The first was built exclusively for Spaniards; the second, conceived by the Franciscan Vasco de Quiroga with Thomas More's utopian ideas in mind, for native people in the province of Michoacán.[29] In subsequent decades, a more systematic project to create separate towns for Amerindians and Spaniards took place, even as the question of what the proper relationship between the two republics should be continued to be debated. The project was greatly propelled by the *congregaciones* program, an aggressive effort to nucleate native communities and transform them into Spanish-style municipalities that as of the 1540s was facilitated by the decline of central Mexico's native population. Nucleation, the government discovered, made it easier not only to offer religious instruction to the newly converted but to control native laborers and rationalize the collection of tribute.

Maintaining the two republics separately, however, proved to be a formidable challenge. Colonial officials simply could not prevent the flow of native people to Spanish towns, where they provided all sorts of labor services, and of Spaniards to *pueblos de indios* (Indian towns). Municipal authorities thus resigned themselves to the presence of Indians in *pueblos de españoles* (Spanish towns), but they insisted on reserving the *traza*, the "checkerboard" grid area that designated the urban space, exclusively for Spaniards and ordered indigenous people to live in outer wards, or *barrios*. The ideal of order was thus to have separate urban centers for the two populations, but when economic and other factors made it impossible, colonial officials tried to apply the principle of segregation within the cities themselves. Thus, in the 1550s, Viceroy Luis de Velasco (1550–64) issued several decrees that were supposed to keep all non-Indians, excepting priests and a few royal officials, from residing in the pueblos and wards that had been designated for the native people. The viceregal government also allowed the populations of the barrios to have their own town councils and to function as relatively autonomous political districts. Therefore, a number of Spanish colonial towns had two cabildos, one for each republic.

The Spanish crown also encouraged the establishment of the república de indios through the creation of a different juridical status for the native people. They not only had distinct rights and obligations (such as paying tribute), but were placed under the jurisdiction of separate legal and religious institutions, including the Juzgado de Indios.[30] This secular court was not formally established until the 1590s, but its origins date back to the years of Viceroy Antonio de Mendoza (1535–50), who used to set aside days of the week to deal with native petitions. With permission from Philip II, Viceroy Luis de Velasco II transformed those previously informal procedures into a more coherent and structured judicial system.[31] The supreme judge of the Juzgado de Indios continued to be the viceroy. Because the tribunal was intended to simplify legal processes for the native people and reduce their legal costs, it eliminated fees (costs were covered by a special tribute levy) and some of the formalities of Spanish law. All native people had the option of taking their cases to the Juzgado de Indios, but those who had the means to resort to the audiencia could still do so, and those who sued Spaniards were obliged to go through the normal channels of justice.

New Spain's government also created separate institutions and inquisitorial procedures for treating native religious issues. Despite initial enthusiasm with the conversion project's results, the friars had to recognize that acceptance of baptism did not necessarily translate into full, or even partial, acceptance of the Christian faith. Especially troubling to them was the realization that some native rulers and nobles—generally the most Hispanicized segments of the indigenious population—had not relinquished their old religious beliefs and gods. Trying them for heresy through familiar methods seemed to be the natural solution. Because a formal inquisitorial tribunal did not yet exist, during the period from 1530 to the mid-sixteenth century, investigations of religious heterodoxy were undertaken by bishops and members of the monastic orders, just as they had been in late medieval Europe. The most well-known prosecution during these years was that of the *cacique* (native lord) don Carlos de Texcoco, grandson of Nezahualcóyotl (the poet-king of Texcoco) and one of the many sons of Nezahualpilli. In the late 1530s, don Carlos was accused of prompting his people to reject Catholicism and retain their ancient beliefs. He was tried by the bishop and inquisitor Fray Juan de Zumárraga, convicted of being an idolater and "heretical dogmatizer," and executed.[32] After he was declared guilty, don Carlos was forced to participate in a procession and ceremony that resembled an auto de fe. He was paraded around the city wearing a sanbenito before being taken to the central square, where his alleged transgressions and punishments were read publicly (and translated to him in Náhuatl) in front of a large audience that included viceregal and ecclesiastical officials. After the cacique's execution, his sanbenito was taken to Mexico City's church, where it was displayed until 1570.

Don Carlos's case was followed by similar trials of native religious heterodoxy, most involving indigenous rulers and nobles. Almost every aspect of these early cases indicated that indigenous people were going to be policed and punished for religions transgression like Spain's conversos and moriscos. However, shortly after the Tribunal of the Holy Office was formally established in New Spain (1571), royal instructions, backed by apostolic briefs, decreed that the native people were to be removed from its jurisdiction. The king and some top church officials apparently had not approved of the execution of don Carlos and subsequently decided that it was not appropriate to subject a people who were just learning the principles of the faith to inquisitorial prosecution.[33] Although the reasons for the removal of the indigenous population from the jurisdiction of the Inquisition have never been entirely clear, religious leaders and the crown were concerned about the violent excesses of zealous friars in the colonies, a worry that seemed all the more justified after news of the Franciscan Diego de Landa's "idolatry trials" and autos de fe in Yucatán arrived in Spain. The trials, which took place in the 1560s, resulted in the torture of more than forty-five hundred Mayas, of whom at least one hundred fifty died.[34] (A strong commitment to the missionary project was not incompatible with excessive cruelty toward "strayed" flock.) The decision to remove the Indians from the Inquisition's jurisdiction was also influenced by fears that the Holy Office's public execution of native leaders would produce martyrs and fuel anti-Spanish rebellions. Another factor might have been the rapid demographic decline of the indigenous population and consequent shortage for labor, problems that would not have been ameliorated by completely unleashing the Inquisition on them.

For all of the questions surrounding the exemption of the native people from inquisitorial prosecution, the decision was actually quite consistent with other royal efforts to constitute them as a separate estate and place them under the tutelage of the state and the church.[35] Although the Holy Office functioned as a royal and ecclesiastical tribunal, it nonetheless retained some autonomy. As it was, the indigenous people were placed under the jurisdiction of vicar generals and an institution that operated just like the Holy Office: the *provisorato de indios* or Office of the Provisor of Indians. This institution—which has also been called, among other things, the Ecclesiastical Inquisition, the Natives' Court, the Secular Inquisition, the Tribunal of the Faith of the Indians, and the Ordinary—was in charge of handling religious and moral matters in indigenous communities throughout the colonial period and beyond.[36] Specifically, the responsibility for dealing with native heterodoxy fell on the bishops and archbishops, who delegated it to their vicar generals or *provisores* (provisors). The provisors in turn appointed commissioners and other officials in provincial areas. It was not at all unusual for these officials to call themselves "inquisitors ordinary," to establish tribunals to try native people, and even to stage autos de fe. Thus, in terms of their activities, ceremonies, titles, and at times even personnel, there was little difference between the Holy Office and the provisorato de indios. Furthermore, the Inquisition continued to study native affairs, particularly, idolatry and paganism, well into the seventeenth century, which is why there is extensive documentation in Mexican inquisitorial archives on indigenous religious and moral practices and why there were many cases of jurisdictional conflict between the two institutions.[37]

The Spanish government's creation of special secular and religions institutions for the indigenous population was accompanied by the deployment of the categories of *nuevamente convertidos* (recent converts) and *miserables* (wretched). Between the mid-sixteenth century and Mexico's Third Provincial Council (1585), the church in New Spain adopted a policy of not ordaining Indians on the basis that they were "tender plants in the faith." This claim enabled the exclusion of native people from the priesthood and from certain religious offices and institutions without necessarily contradicting the official discourse regarding their "purity of blood." In other words, it allowed for their construction as not quite "impure," but also as not quite "Old Christians." To be sure, some native people who were considered exceptionally qualified on theological and moral matters were ordained, especially in the later colonial period. But the idea that as a whole they were recent converts, indeed even "neophytes," left ambiguous the issue of when they could be considered full Christians. How many years before they were no longer considered new to the faith? How many generations before they could claim Old Christian status? These questions did not have clear answers.

If their status as recent converts placed the indigenous population in a special religious category, their classification as miserables implied a particular juridical and social position. The classification, which began to be used around the time that the Office of the Protector of Indians was created, promoted an image of the native people as lacking the rational capacity to either fully comprehend the Catholic faith or to govern themselves. According to the seventeenth-century jurist Juan de Solórzano Pereira, the term *miserable* was applied to those persons who Spaniards "naturally [felt] sorry for because of their condition, quality or hardships." The Indians' wretched condition, he explained, placed them in a kind of state of grace that implied special privileges and protections, thus the special legal tribunals and religious supervision.[38] And because they were supposedly easily induced into alienating their properties and losing all of their estates, viceregal officials had the power to annul—without their permission—the contracts that Amerindians signed. Spanish legislation also included indigenous lords in the category of persons who could be fooled and exploited by others, which meant that they too lost part of their ability to act as free subjects and to dispose of their properties as they pleased and were not considered legal adults. In theory, the classification of miserables was meant to lessen the possibility that the native people would be the victims of fraud, violence, and other types of abuses. But it also implied that they were placed in a particularly strong paternalistic relationship with the Spanish state and the church, akin to children and women within the patriarchal family unit because of their supposed need for legal supervision. Even as native communities were granted a degree of political autonomy and their internal hierarchies were recognized, Spanish laws construed indigenous people as dependent and weak,[39] concepts that were coded female and that would be echoed in discourses of blood.

The creation of separate legal and religious bodies and of a special juridico-theological status for the native people might not have presented much of a problem for the Spanish colonial government had it not been for the rise of a significant population of mixed ancestry that blurred the boundary between the categories of Spaniard and Indian. The emergence of this population made it increasingly difficult to establish institutional jurisdictions, tributary obligations, and the citizenship rights and privileges that were accorded to the members of each republic, a problem that led to the growing use of mechanisms to determine "Indian purity." The Holy Office, for example, frequently had to conduct lengthy investigations to establish its jurisdiction over persons whose identities were for some reason unclear or disputed. Problems arose for a number of reasons. Individuals of mixed ancestry who ran afoul of the Inquisition sometimes claimed that they were pure Indians in order to escape the grip of the Holy Office.[40] Native people who committed moral offenses were at times accused by their enemies of having Spanish-Indian parentage in order to have them tried by inquisitors.[41] And so forth. Whenever jurisdictional confusion arose, Inquisition officials attempted to establish the ancestry of the individuals in question, often by adapting procedures and legal formulas that were used for determining purity and nobility of blood in Spain.[42] Usually officials inspected baptismal records, took testimonies of community elders, and checked to see if the person was included in local tributary lists. The same methods and principles were used, furthermore, by other institutions in which Indian purity (as well as nobility) was an issue.[43]

But how exactly was a "pure Indian" defined? An invention of Spanish colonialism, the category of indio did not have much meaning for native people themselves, at least not at first. Particularly during the sixteenth century, they tended to use it mainly when dealing with Spanish authorities. For the latter, a pure Indian was technically someone who descended only (or mostly) from pre-Hispanic peoples. For this reason, formal procedures for determining native purity prioritized the examination of baptismal and marriage records. But when these records did not exist or did not provide the necessary information, officials were compelled to rely more on the declarations of local community members, who on most occasions referred not just to the person's public reputation but to factors such as physical appearance, language abilities, clothing, and tributary status.[44] Because most native people had to pay tribute, the last factor in fact became one of the most important social signs of being a pure Indian. Even though its definition privileged bloodlines, then, the category of "indio puro" was frequently determined through a combination of genealogical, sociocultural, economic, and physical characteristics. It was thus as much a historical and social construct as "Spaniard," "black," and "mestizo."

The social meanings of the category of indio did not prevent the elaboration of a discourse of native purity, premised on lineage and on the idea that being a pure Indian meant having certain rights (as well as duties) within indigenous communities. The project to create two republics essentially produced dual citizenship and dual purity regimes. It also heightened the already strong concerns with blood among segments of the native population. These concerns did not remain the same, however, as they had been in pre-Hispanic times. By introducing new ways of determining nobility, succession, and blood purity, Spanish colonialism also led to significant changes in understandings and uses of lineage among central Mexican indigenous elites.

SPANISH COLONIALISM AND THE RECONSTITUTION OF PRE-HISPANIC DYNASTIES

The Spanish government initially relied on pre-Hispanic settlement patterns and hereditary rulers for the administration and control of indigenous populations. Although central Mexico's larger units of organization, the *altepetl,* or "ethnic states," were divided into their constituent parts, the early colonial arrangement of indigenous communities into *cabeceras* ("head" towns), *sujetos* ("subject" or dependent towns), and *estancias* (outlying hamlets of principal towns, consisting mainly of tenants of the nobility) at first conformed to traditional political and spatial configurations.[45] And although the pre-Hispanic political leadership suffered losses at the highest levels, a good number of hereditary rulers were allowed to keep their statuses because Spanish colonial authorities, at this point relatively small in number, were strongly dependent on them not just for control of the native population but for the collection of tribute. Generically called caciques (a term of Caribbean origins) by the Spaniards, these hereditary leaders were in some cases even able to expand the areas and number of people under their jurisdictions.

The reconstitution of local power began during the years of Mexico City's second audiencia (1530–35).[46] This institution was vested with the authority to recognize the titles of males with legitimate claims to the rank of tlatoani. In the early 1530s, the heirs to Tenochtitlan's main ruling dynasties, the *tlatoque* (plural form of "tlatoani"), recuperated political power and, together with the descendants of rulers and nobles of lesser rank, gained access to public offices, particularly in the city's native cabildo. In Tlaxcala, all four of the altepetl composing the larger confederation of the same name were granted to their respective royal lineages, which were then able to perpetuate themselves in power for at least another hundred years.[47] In Michoacán, where Charles V confirmed the status of the pre-Hispanic royal dynasty after the Tarascan king submitted to the Spanish crown, the rulership of the province was transmitted through the same noble bloodlines for about a half century.[48] The pattern of continuity was repeated in Teotihuacán and other parts of central Mexico as well as in southern regions. In Oaxaca, local caciques who had helped the Spaniards conquer the region fared exceptionally well. They were allowed the creation of great *señoríos*, regional-political jurisdictions with large populations of dependent tenants. Between 1520 and 1540, Oaxaca's native rulers also seized the opportunity to acquire large landed estates, thereby establishing a solid base for their rulerships, which lasted until the final years of Spanish domination.[49]

Other pre-Hispanic ruling groups fared less well, including those of Cholula and Tacuba.[50] In various parts of central Mexico, traditional rulers and nobles—groups which overlapped and were affected by royal polices in similar ways—began to lose political power in the middle of the sixteenth century, when many of the conditions that had favored the reconstitution of the preconquest ruling dynasties began to change. Several factors contributed to the downward trend, but the central ones were the establishment of Spanish-style municipal government (which allowed for reconfigurations of political power), the decline of the indigenous population (which eroded the caciques' social base of support), and Philip II's reforms to the tribute and labor regimes. Implemented in the 1560s and 1570s, these reforms sought to make tributary payments universal and to have them paid more in cash than in kind; they also aimed to acclerate the transition from encomienda to *repartimiento*, a system of corvée labor organized by royal officials, the corregidores.[51] Changes to the tributary and labor regimes had a leveling effect on native communities, particularly those in the Náhua zone, but this process was gradual and by no means absolute. Despite an overarching pattern of decreasing internal differentiation within indigenous towns, important social divisions, namely, among nobles, commoners, and tenants, managed to persist in numerous places during and beyond the sixteenth century.[52] As late as the 1700s, descendants of *la nobleza mexicana*, whose blood was admittedly diluted through generations of intermarriage with Spaniards or natives of lesser status, continued to request recognition of their status and privileges on the basis of both their nobility and "purity" of blood.[53] The lingering importance of genealogy among them was due to the deep roots that this notion and tool had in Mesoamerican culture and to the adaptation of rulers and nobles to colonial conditions. But it was also a function of royal policies, which paradoxically provided legal mechanisms for perpetuating pre-Hispanic dynasties at the very same time that governmental reforms were undermining their economic and political power.

In the course of the sixteenth century, Spanish colonial legislation consecrated three principles that would continue to be upheld throughout the next two hundred years: the hierarchical nature of political organization within indigenous communities, the equality of native rulers and nobles with hidalgos, and the "pure" blood of the indigenous population as a whole. These principles, which crystallized after the Valladolid debate between Las Casas and Sepúlveda (1550–51), were linked to the ways in which the subjection of the native population to Spanish rule and Christianity was construed as a voluntary and contractual relationship of vassalage with the crown. In 1557, for example, a royal decree affirmed the property rights and privileges of indigenous elites on the ground that they had accepted the Castilian king and the Catholic faith.[54] Colonial officials were ordered to recognize two noble ranks: caciques and principales. In central Mexico, the former category was applied to the legitimate successors of pre-Hispanic rulers (the tlatoque) and the latter to descendants of the nobility (the *pipiltin* and *teteuctin*). Spanish authorities at first equated caciques with the Castilian titles of duke, marquise, and count, and principales with hidalgos and caballeros, that is, with the gentry or nontitled nobility. Both categories were therefore of noble rank, but the first was of higher status and initially referred to those with hereditary rights to rulerships.[55] As to their economic privileges, caciques and principales were entitled to receive tribute, and most were exempt from paying it themselves. Both categories were also permitted to have tenants and *indios de servicio* (retainers), at least until the 1570s, and were in theory not to provide any personal services themselves. Those in public office enjoyed the additional benefit of being able to complement their tribute earnings with salaries from the community treasury. Finally, in the 1590s, the right to request royal lands (*mercedes de tierra*) was extended to native elites and communities, which among the former promoted private property ownership.[56]

Attached to the titles of cacique and principal were a set of honor privileges, or *privilegios de honra*. These included the right to carry arms, to wear Spanish clothes, to ride horses, and to use the formal designation of don.[57] Noble status and honor privileges were not exclusive to men. The Spanish government not only created special houses for the female descendants of pre-Hispanic dynasties in order to indoctrinate

them in Catholic and Spanish cultural values, but recognized their nobility and allowed them to use the honorific *doña*. Social status for
indigenous men and women was also marked by naming practices.
Whereas commoners generally gave their children two first names (such
as "Domingo Francisco") when they were baptized, elites generally combined a Spanish ("Christian") name with pre-Hispanic surnames. Some
caciques and principales adopted native and Hispanic surnames or did
away with the former altogether, but the more common practice was to
retain the name of a key ancestor in order to preserve the memory of
precolonial noble lineages. For example, in 1533, a royal decree allowed
Quetzalmamalitzin Huetzin, son of the ruler of Teotihuacan at the time
of the conquest, to assume the title of cacique. By then he had become
don Francisco Verdugo Quetzalmamalitzin Huetzin.

Dynastic surnames survived in part because of the *cacicazgo,* the key
political-economic institution established for the descendants of pre-
Hispanic rulers. This institution referred to "the ensemble of rights
and holdings surrounding the [cacique's] rulership," including having
access to the tribute extracted from his jurisdiction and to communal
and patrimonial lands.[58] The cacicazgo, which established the legal
framework for the entailment of indigenous estates and thus also for the
perpetuation of native wealth, property, and status, fused pre-Hispanic
and Castilian traditions. In preconquest central Mexico, the institution
that most resembled it was the *tlatocáyotl,* a seigniorial estate or rulership that provided the political and economic structure for administering production, land tenure, and tribute collection within a territorial
jurisdiction and whose main function was to reproduce the dominant
classes, particularly, the tlatoque.[59] Kinship and marriage ties were central to this institution and system of governance because they helped
forge internal cohesion as well as relations between different tlatocáyotl.
Rulerships were frequently transmitted from father to the firstborn son
of the ruler's most important wife. If inheritance through primogeniture
was not possible, the tlatocáyotl was usually passed down to the oldest
daughter, contingent on her marrying a person of equal social status
(usually a paternal uncle), and then to her oldest son. Rulerships were
also sometimes bequeathed to a daughter or a niece when the tlatoani's
sons did not live in his community.[60] According to Guillermo Fernández
de Recas, the tlatocáyotl resembled Castilian traditions of noble succession and inheritance as embodied in the *señorío* (seigniorial estate) and
the mayorazgo.[61] In its most basic form, the latter institution referred
to a civil entailment that enabled the generational transmission of an
estate—which could include titles, properties, rents, pensions, jewelry,

works of art, and even certain public offices—through established rules of succession and ownership. The most conventional type of mayorazgo privileged the oldest son (*hijo mayor*), who would typically be required to continue using the last name of the founders (*mayores*) of the entail.[62]

Parallels between the mayorazgo and the tlatocáyotl led Spaniards to immediately equate the two. Ignoring that forms of succession and inheritance had actually varied considerably in preconquest times and that maternal descent was important on various social and political levels,[63] Spanish laws gradually made indigenous rulerships subject to the same regulations as Castilian ones, most notably by consecrating the principle of primogeniture. The adoption of this principle included the patronymic practice of conserving the last name of the male founder of a lineage. The tlatocáyotl was thus transformed into the mayorazgo, or rather, cacicazgo (a neologism). The *principalazgo* was an analogous institution for native nobles, but was less subject to rules that made cacicazgo properties indivisible and inalienable. Older Mesoamerican practices did not entirely disappear, however. Native traditions were too rooted and resilient. Furthermore, Spanish colonial policies were initially flexible and under certain circumstances permitted indigenous noble women to inherit cacicazgos. Thus, during the sixteenth century, women in different regions were recognized as legitimate *cacicas* and granted a series of rights with the title, mainly economic.[64] Their numerical and social significance subsequently tended to decline, among other reasons because Spanish law (which did not recognize native kinship systems) favored the transmission of titles and estates through primogeniture and legitimate birth.

The mid-sixteenth century formalization of procedures for accessing and transmitting cacicazgos and principalazgos led to a flurry of petitions for titles. Some petitions were fraudulent, made by individuals of commoner origins, and in some instances their recognition led to the replacement of traditional local aristocracies.[65] Colonial authorities were aware of the problem and implemented measures to ensure that individuals of genuine noble ancestry were distinguished from those whose high social status had been acquired through means other than birthright. Pursuant to a 1554 law that specified that the title of cacique could be issued only to those who merited it because of their lineage, colonial officials attempted to more carefully investigate and record whether indigenous authorities were *principales de linaje y sangre* or *principales de gobierno*—noble by virtue of blood or by virtue of office holding. To make the distinction, they turned to their own procedures and traditions for determining noble ancestry, and more concretely to the Castilian

prueba de hidalguía (proof of nobility).[66] The juridical process for validating native titles thus came to involve presenting, among other things,
extensive genealogical information, testimonies by important members of the community, and increasingly as of the seventeenth century,
baptismal and marriage records. Acceptable proof also included copies
of prior royal decrees recognizing the person's noble status, tribute exemptions, and/or right to carry arms.

The process of acquiring the title of cacique began with the candidate's
submitting the body of evidence (the genealogical información and related proof) to the district magistrate or corregidor, and then to the audiencia, which in 1558 was granted sole power to determine the validity of
petitions for cacicazgos.[67] Once the judges examined the petition, they
summoned and questioned the interested parties, as well as the *gobernador* (the governor or appointed head—normally a native person—of an
indigenous municipality), cabildo members, and principales of the petitioner's community. When considering cacicazgo cases, the audiencia
was foremost concerned with verifying that the petitioner did indeed descend from the ancient lords of the land. For this purpose, the testimonies of other caciques and principales were central (as well as baptismal
records, when they began to exist). A second priority was to determine
whether the lands being requested as part of the cacicazgo had in fact
belonged to the petitioner's ancestors since "time immemorial."[68] If exact jurisdiction of a rulership could not be established through available
documentation, colonial officials leaned heavily on "tradition," that is,
on the information provided by witnesses deemed knowledgeable and
reliable—usually the community's male elders. Pictographic documents
with information about towns and their lands were sometimes accepted,
but Spanish officials discouraged the practice because they suspected
that many were being forged.

Once the audiencia felt that the evidence and depositions sufficiently
established the petitioner's royal ancestry and holdings of the cacicazgo,
the case was given to the viceroy for final approval. Similar procedures
were followed for people seeking noble privileges, such as tribute exemptions, and here as well a main concern was establishing lineage. Because
the privileges and statuses of new generations had to be confirmed (and
were sometimes contested), documentation submitted by members of a
lineage tended to expand over time. By the eighteenth century, it was
not unusual for petitioners to present copies of prior recognitions given
to several of her or his ancestors, sometimes as far back as the 1500s.
Petitions for cacicazgos and noble status hence contained genealogical
information as well as records of royal grants and of the lineage's services to the crown. As such, they were testaments to the periodic affir-

mation of the contractual relationship between native communities and the king, and reminders of the monarch's ability to dispense privileges, honor, and grace to his loyal vassals.

Among the main beneficiaries of the crown's policies toward native nobles were the descendants of the Mexica's last supreme ruler (*hueytla-toani*), Motecuhzoma II Xocoyotzin ("Moctezuma"), many of whom married Spaniards and moved to the Iberian Peninsula. Throughout the colonial period and as late as the twentieth century, members of this royal lineage in Spain received the titles of count, viscount, duke, and marquis, along with rights to wear royal insignia, bear arms, hold ceremonial acts proper to their rank, collect annual pensions, enjoy tax exemptions, and so forth.[69] Two of the Mexica ruler's male heirs, don Pedro Desifor de Moctezuma, Viscount of Tula (who became a member of the Spanish court), and don Diego Cano de Moctezuma, were admitted into the Order of Santiago, which along with the two other main Castilian military orders had both purity and nobility statutes. Another descendant, don Diego Luis de Moctezuma (son of Pedro Tlacahuepantzi and grandson of the hueytlatoani), was sent to Spain, where he married doña Francisca de la Cueva. The couple's son, don Pedro, was the first Count of Moctezuma, a descendant of whom returned to New Spain as viceroy at the beginning of the eighteenth century. As various Spanish colonial writers were to point out in response to Enlightenment thinkers' dismissal of the cultural and historical achievements of native people, Mexica (and Inca) royal blood had merged with, and even ennobled, some of the most prominent lineages in Spain and other parts of Europe. Such claims would have carried less weight had Spanish law not recognized the nobility of pre-Hispanic dynasties and nourished certain codes regarding native blood.

The Moctezumas who remained in New Spain were also honored. For example, Hernán Cortés granted doña Isabel de Moctezuma, daughter of the ruler he had just defeated, the cacicazgo of Tacuba.[70] It included the right to receive tribute from several towns. Another Moctezuma who was generously rewarded was don Gonzalo, one of the tlatoani's many grandsons. After helping Cortés conquer provinces near Oaxaca and other parts of the Mixteca, he received a cacicazgo in Tepeji de la Seda, a town belonging to the jurisdiction of Puebla. Two hundred years later, doña Ursula García Cortés y Moctezuma, a *vecina* (citizen) of the city of Puebla de los Ángeles, would petition the Castilian crown for confirmation of the privileges, honors, and annual rent that she and her children were entitled to receive by virtue of their ancestral ties to the distinguished don Gonzalo de Moctezuma. Naturally, not all descendants of the pre-Hispanic ruling elite were as fortunate as the Moctezumas, but other Mesoamerican dynasties received economic and symbolic recognitions.

For example, in the 1590s, don Constantino Huitziméngari, grandson of the Tarascan ruler at the time of the conquest, asked the crown for a grant of 4,000 annual pesos and the right to bequeath it to his descendants in perpetuity, but he was issued a considerably more modest sum of money. Nonetheless, he was not in a precarious economic position. An illegitimate descendant of the Tarascan king, he inherited the main cacicazgo of the province of Michoacán in 1577 when the only legitimate successor was a woman of mixed ancestry. That the woman did not inherit the title was apparently due less to her gender than to her dual (Spanish-Indian) descent, for by the last third of the sixteenth century only "pure Indians" were allowed to inherit cacicazgos.[71] When don Constantino requested an increase in his annual pension, he was also building a case to have his royal lineage officially certified, along with the corresponding grants, privileges, and honors.

The crown's recognition of pre-Hispanic dynasties and legal mechanisms it implemented to reproduce them effectively co-opted the upper echelons of central Mexico's indigenous society. It is true that not all caciques and principales were seduced by the trappings of Spanish culture and legitimation, and many struggled to protect their communities' lands and traditions. But in general, native rulers and nobles came to have a stake in a colonial system that allowed them to retain a degree of political and economic power. Another, less perceptible consequence of the crown's policies toward the descendants of royal and aristocratic lineages was the transformation, through the legal formulas accompanying the transmission of the cacicazgo and proof of nobility, of native notions of genealogy and the past. On one hand, the colonial government's system for recognizing titles and promotion of pre-Hispanic dynastic histories shaped formulations of communal origins and rights; on the other, its policies of making office and landholding in the república de indios exclusive to "pure Indians" influenced elite constructions of "blood mixture" and "race."

HISTORY, GENEALOGY, AND THE NEW
SYMBOLICS OF BLOOD

The Spanish legal system not only homogenized native forms of succession but ushered in profound changes in the everyday life of the Mexica, and specifically in their notions of property, inheritance, gender, family, and kin. By the seventeenth century, those changes included a simplification of native genealogies, the replacement of varied forms of transmitting inheritance and property with more of a patrilineal model, and a stress on the nuclear family and married couple as social and moral units at the expense of the multihousehold complex typical of the pre-Hispanic period.[72] Furthermore, Mexica women generally lost authority and independence because under the colonial legal system they were no longer considered "jural adults," capable of taking social and legal responsibility for themselves.[73] The law considered them legal minors to a greater degree than indigenous men, who as explained earlier had to obtain permission from viceregal officials to sell their properties and who juridically were also considered "miserables." Accompanying these dramatic changes in the areas of dynastic succession, inheritance, and kinship were transformations in historical narratives, the elaboration of which was encouraged by the system of cacicazgos and principalazgos.

The Spanish government began encouraging the construction of pre-Hispanic dynastic histories almost immediately after the conquest. New Spain's first viceroys even demanded proof of noble status in the form of historical texts. Viceroy Mendoza, for example, requested a history of the governing families of the province of Chalco-Amaquemecan. The result was an account written by the rulers and elders of the community that later became the basis of Chimalpahin's magisterial text, written in classical Náhuatl, on his hometown of Chalco.[74] In 1557 and subsequent years, Philip II ordered all towns in the viceroyalties of New Spain and Peru (as well as in Castile) to provide information about their populations, geography, lands, traditions, and histories. New Spain produced more than four hundred of these accounts, or *relaciones geográficas*.[75] These not only provided the government with a great deal of knowledge about the pre-Hispanic past—at least as it was understood by a small group of relatively privileged and Christianized native males in the post-conquest period—but many would also later serve (indeed some still do) in the reconstruction of communal histories and defense of village lands.

Dynastic histories produced by colonial native historians, including Chimalpahin and Tezozómoc, for the most part did not reflect the rules of succession that operated during pre-Hispanic times—which could involve the transmission of titles from the tlatoani to a son from one of his wives, to one of his brothers, and even to a daughter or niece—but instead tended to adopt Castilian ones and their emphasis on monogamous marriage, legitimate birth, and primogeniture.[76] The introduction of Spanish values of nobility and traditions of inheritance thus resulted in a recasting of the native past, in indigenous histories and genealogies increasingly framed in European and Christian terms. Indeed, in their historical accounts and in correspondence with the crown, Nahua chroniclers often compared the *teccalli* (noble houses) of their *altepelt* (kingdoms) with the mayorazgos of Castile. For example, Chimalpahin—who was born Domingo Francisco but later in life changed his name to don Domingo Francisco San Antón Muñon Chimalpahin Quauhtlehuanitzin—equated the distinguished lineages of the Kingdom of Chalco with the noble houses of Europe.[77] The dynastic histories that he and other native elites produced were in large part products of colonialism and the way it introduced and routinized certain principles of political legitimation and certain understandings of the past.

If the influence of Christianity and Spanish culture is discernable in the historical works of Chimalpahin and Tezozómoc, it is much more apparent in those of Diego Muñoz Camargo, Juan Bautista Pomar, and Fernando de Alva Ixtlilxóchitl.[78] Their texts are permeated with European terms, values, and temporal concepts.[79] A late-sixteenth-century description of Tlaxcala, probably written by Muñoz Camargo, even referred to the conquest as ordained by divine providence and as having freed the native people from the "enemy of humankind," presumably the devil.[80] Ixtlilxóchitl (1578–1648), a descendant of rulers from Texcoco, emphasized his ancestors' supposed collaboration with the conquerors in his *Historia de la nación chichimeca,* a historical account of that altepetl and its dynasties.[81] The works of these three historians reveal not only just how rapidly the discourse of vassalage—of subjection to the Crown of Castile and the Catholic faith—had insinuated itself into local histories, but also the importance that pre-Hispanic ancestry had for accessing colonial offices, posts, and privileges. All three had Spanish fathers but had received a number of social and economic benefits thanks to their maternal noble native bloodlines and their cooperation with colonial authorities.

The works of Muñoz Camargo, Bautista Pomar, and Ixtlilxóchitl functioned as appeals to a higher authority in which claims were based not just on services to crown and faith but on the worthiness of bloodlines originating in the pre-Hispanic past and conquest period. These legitimating claims were characteristic of the broader body of colonial historiography. Perhaps nowhere are they as prominent as in the writings of Peru's El Inca Garcilaso de la Vega, whose mother was a noble Incan and father a Spanish conqueror. He authored *Comentarios reales de los Incas,* about the Inca and their achievements, and complemented it with *Historia General del Perú,* about the conquest and early colonial period. Both works amounted to petitions to gain legitimation: the first on the basis of the author's mother's noble indigenous past, the second on the basis of his father's military services, which had helped pave the way for Christianity in Peru.[82] Colonial Spanish American literature thus shared rhetorical formulas with probanzas, petitions (e.g., for cacicazgo titles), and accounts (*relaciones*) submitted to the Spanish king. Law, history, and literature converged and helped to produce certain (genealogical) narratives of the past. The descendants of pre-Hispanic dynasties and Spanish conquerors were particularly invested in the construction of those narratives because it gave them a double claim to political and economic privileges.

New Spain's Ixtlilxóchitl, for example, did not inherit his mother's cacicazgo because it was passed down to his older brother, but he was appointed governor and judge of various regions, including Texcoco, Tlalmanalco, and the province of Chalco. He also served as interpreter in the Juzgado de Indios. At the time that Ixtlilxóchitl was writing his dynastic history, he was also helping his mother put together a dossier to prove the family's direct descent from the pre-Hispanic rulers of Teotihuacan and Texcoco. The family had in fact already received a number of royal recognitions, including the title to a cacicazgo, but wanted another, presumably more definitive, probanza because its lands and tribute were constantly being threatened by relatives and other people.[83] These recognitions began in 1533, when a royal decree granted don Francisco Verdugo Quetzalmamalitzin Huetzin the cacicazgo of San Juan Teotihuacan, an altepetl that had belonged to Texcoco's jurisdiction during the time of the Triple Alliance. Don Quetzalmamalitzin Huetzin married the daughter of the king of Texcoco, doña Ana Cortés Ixtlilxóchitl, a union that greatly enhanced his lands and tribute. Not having a male successor when he died, he left his cacicazgo to his wife and daughter. The latter, Francisca Verdugo Ixtlilxóchitl, wed the Spaniard Juan Grande (an interpreter in Mexico's audiencia) in 1561 but kept the title of cacica because by this time Spaniards were not allowed to appropriate the title of cacique (though they sometimes did anyway). This couple also did not produce a male successor. Thus, when doña Francisca Verdugo Ixtlilxóchitl died, her daughter, doña Ana Cortés, succeeded her. Doña Ana Cortés also married a Spaniard, don Juan Pérez de Peraleda, another interpreter in the royal audiencia. The pair gave birth first to don Francisco de Nava Huetzin and then to don Fernando Alva Ixtlilxóchitl, the author of *Historia de la nación chichimeca*.

Having three Spanish grandparents did not prevent Ixtlilxóchitl from reclaiming his pre-Hispanic royal blood and from attempting to preserve the history of his native ancestors' altepetl. He as well as Muñoz Camargo and Bautista Pomar were all engaged in the creation of indigenous regional histories and vindication of their maternal bloodlines, through which they had status, honor, and privileges. Despite the Spanish government's stress on paternal descent, then, their histories and genealogies preserved an important matrilineal dimension. Not by coincidence, the construction of these histories and appropriation of the native past by the three writers occurred at a time when the crown was attempting to disenfranchise mestizos, the descendants of Spanish and Indian unions. During the early decades of colonial rule in which the government did not have or did not enforce purity requirements, some rulerships and offices in native cabildos were transferred to Spaniards and people of mixed ancestry,[84] but in the second half of the sixteenth century, royal legislation tried to slow down this process. In 1576, for example, the crown decreed that individuals could not become caciques by marrying cacicas and that only pure Indians could inherit cacicazgos.[85] Those mestizos who had acquired the title were to be removed from the post, even if they were of legitimate birth.

Eligibility for cacicazgos thus became contingent not only on pre-Hispanic noble ancestry but also on native purity. Not just rulerships but all municipal offices in the Indian republic as well as governorships were in theory limited to individuals of pure ancestry. Various laws to that effect were passed in the late sixteenth and early seventeenth centuries. That they continually had to be reissued reflects their ineffectiveness as well as the inconsistent nature of royal policies with regard to the descendants of Spanish-Indian unions.[86] Religious officials in central Mexico often complained that laws designed to protect the native population were not being implemented, and in 1647, Juan de Palafox y Mendoza, the bishop of Puebla and interim viceroy, passed an ordinance stressing the need to uphold the principle of purity because mestizos, mulattos, and others of mixed ancestry ("*de nación mezclada*") were taking over indigenous government. He argued that only "true Indians" by both father and mother ("*meramente indios de padre y madre*") should be allowed to hold offices in native cabildos, or great harm would come to that population. A short time later, the crown made Palafox's ordinance a general law for New Spain, thereby reiterating and expanding the requirement of "purity" for positions in native government.[87]

Palafox's defense of the rights of the Indian republic, which he too based on their eager reception of the Christian faith and remarkable loyalty to His Majesty,[88] was made urgent by the threatened condition of many native communities. Sociodemographic shifts, including the rapid growth of the population of mixed ancestry and the beginning of a steady rise in indigenous numbers, coupled with the expansion of the latifundium, placed enormous pressure on patrimonial and communal properties and led to numerous conflicts between Spaniards and caciques. These conflicts compelled the crown to establish a legal process called *composición de tierras*, through which caciques applied to the audiencia for titles to their lands or those of their communities, that is, when they did not already have them or when the ones they had were not considered legitimate. Often local leaders based their claims on sixteenth-century titles granted to their ancestors and on the historical accounts provided by their communities to Philip II. The composiciones, the first phase of which lasted from 1643 to 1647, thus provided a stimulus for the production of more histories and specifically for a genre of documents that came to be known (probably as of the nineteenth century) as *títulos primordiales* (primordial titles).

The títulos primordiales, some of which historians are still discovering in local communities and archives, appeared throughout central Mexico, the Mixtec and Zapotec regions, and the southern Maya zone. Written primarily in indigenous languages, they were somewhat like land titles but were mainly produced by and for communities and thus not all were presented to Spanish authorities. The títulos served three central functions: They preserved the town's memory of its foundation, territorial boundaries, and traditional land and water rights; they strengthened the sense of corporate identity and entitlements; and, especially as of the late seventeenth century, they helped defend communal lands and those of the native aristocracy from encroachment by external forces.[89] Because they also sought to establish the noble and pre-Hispanic origins of the local ruling group, they often included genealogical information. Thus, by the eighteenth century, the genre had sprouted indigenous genealogists, experts in the production not just of lineages but also of coats of arms (potent symbols of communal autonomy) and land titles. Some of these "experts" were tried for falsification of documents.[90] Reminiscent of Spain's linajudos, they mined earlier royal decrees, relaciones geográficas, and other historical records and mastered Spanish genealogical and juridical formulas for the recognition of landholdings and other indigenous corporate rights. These formulas generally privileged native bloodlines that were pure, which helps to explain the rising concerns with lineage in the late colonial period as well as attempts by some caciques and principales to reclaim Náhuatl surnames that their families had not used for generations and to disavow those that exposed their mixed bloodlines.[91]

As a whole, the títulos primordiales vividly illustrate the importance that genealogy had for the late colonial native nobility's imagination and the extent to which the written word was complementing, and in some cases supplanting, oral and pictographic traditions of maintaining communal memory. They also reflect the degree to which the pre-Hispanic past had either receded into the background of that memory or become fully intertwined with events of the postconquest period. If those that were produced in central Mexico are any indication, by the late seventeenth century, the conquest had become the main reference point for indigenous reconstructions of their past and their acceptance of the Catholic faith, the principal source of colonial legitimation.[92] Clearly, indigenous corporate rights and history were shaped by colonial legal discourses and in particular the Spanish patrimonial state's contractual relationship with the "Indian republic." This relationship was confirmed by late-seventeenth-century royal legislation and especially by a 1697 *real cédula* (royal decree). Issued by Charles II, the decree upheld the privileged status of the descendants of pre-Hispanic nobles and rulers and the principle that the native population as a whole had "clean" blood because they descended from "uninfected gentiles" who had accepted the Catholic faith.[93] Significantly, it stipulated that all the privileges and rights that were reserved for indigenous people also applied to mestizos ("*indios mestizos*"). The real cédula thus expressed one of the apparent paradoxes of Spanish colonial ideology: its ability to reconcile concepts of purity and mixture, especially if the "mix" involved Spanish and noble native blood. If indigenous purity was in theory necessary for accessing public offices in native government, its definition turned out to be relatively flexible. Two examples, one from the region of Oaxaca, the other from central Mexico, will serve to demonstrate how notions of purity and mixture operated in parts of New Spain during the eighteenth century.

In 1722, the caciques don Diego González de Chavez and doña Josefa María de Zarate, a husband and wife from a town in the Valley of Etla (in Oaxaca) founded a chaplaincy naming one of their sons, don Joseph Antonio González de Zarate, as chaplain.[94] Wanting the chaplaincy to be transmitted as a mayorazgo (or cacicazgo), they requested a probanza from the district's alcalde mayor and presented him with proof of the value of their estate, of their legitimate birth as well as that of their son Joseph Antonio, and of the family's pure Indian blood, unblemished by any bad "race" (raza) or any other stains. The proof included the testimonies of six Spanish-speaking caciques and nobles from the region, all of whom attested, among other things, to the couple's nobility, legitimacy, purity, and solvency as well to the absence of any stains of idolatry in their bloodlines. Once the testimonies were recorded and approved, the husband and wife also left instructions that after their son don Joseph Antonio died, the chaplaincy was to continue to be passed to their direct descendants or, in their absence, to other relatives who met the requirements of purity, legitimacy, and nobility, with preference given to those who were virtuous, studious, and poor. When no descendants were left, the chaplaincy was to be granted to other caciques from the region who met those qualities.

The chaplaincy was transmitted to the direct descendants of don Diego González de Chavez and doña Josefa María de Zarate for a couple of generations, but in 1772, there were apparently no eligible ones left, and it was contested by three different parties. One of the parties, don Lazaro López Pacheco, argued that the chaplaincy should be granted to his son because the other candidate, Joseph C. Carrasco, had a grandmother who was reputed to be a *mulata*, a woman of partial African blood, which automatically made him ineligible because "such a quality is inherited (*comunicable*), and is passed down to all of the descendants of the trunk."[95] Don López Pacheco also claimed that the third contender was neither pure nor a descendant of caciques. The other parties fought back with accusations of their own and, even though at least one (Carrasco) acknowledged having some Spanish ancestry, submitted documents to defend their purity and nobility. These documents included various probanzas that had been granted to their ancestors (one a sixteenth-century cacique who had converted to Christianity and allied with Cortés) as well as copies of the 1697 decree upholding the rights of Indians and "indios mestizos." Like numerous late-seventeenth- and eighteenth-century native conflicts over titles, office holding, or estates, this case illustrates that in "indigenous" (rural) communities, concepts of lineage and purity could be quite strong among elite sectors; that although undiluted Indian ancestry was clearly privileged, mestizos could also be construed as pure; and that notions of "impurity" and "race" were frequently linked to African ancestry. As the next example reveals, these aspects of the colonial Mexican discourses of blood were also marked in the more hispanicized urban contexts.

In 1751, doña Ursula García Cortés y Moctezuma asked her husband, Capitán don Manuel del Toro y Santa Cruz, to petition Mexico City's audiencia for confirmation of her noble privileges. The request was accompanied by a two-hundred-folio probanza containing, among other things, numerous declarations regarding her lineage and social status, copies of royal decrees that two centuries earlier had granted her family the right to bear arms ("*el privilegio de Armas*"), and information from her baptismal records verifying her genealogical ties (and those of her children) to don Gonzalo de Moctezuma, the sixteenth-century cacique of Tepeji de la Seda. The judge who examined the documentation noted that all of the testimonies submitted by her fellow *vecinos* (citizens) in Puebla de los Ángeles had alluded to the petitioner's "*calidad de mestiza*," her mixed Spanish and indigenous ancestry. But he added that they had also stressed that all of doña Ursula's ancestors had remained "pure": "*sin mescla de sangre infecta*" ("without the mixture of contaminated blood").

The judge's own assessment was that the body of evidence effectively demonstrated that doña Ursula's progenitors consisted of, on one hand, caciques and principales, and on the other, conquerors, noble "Old Christians."[96] He therefore recommended that the petitioner and her children be granted all of the privileges, exemptions, honors, and liberties to which their distinguished lineage entitled them. The judge sent the case, along with his recommendation, to Viceroy Revilla Gijedo, who in turn approved the petition on May 12, 1751. Doña Ursula's probanza, as well as the judge's assessment of the case, stressed her family's descent from conquerors and from don Gonzalo de Moctezuma, a direct blood descendant of the emperor Moctezuma (*"como descendientes de tales conquistadores, y de don Gonzalo de Moctezuma inmediato en sangre al emperador Moctezuma"*). They both also alluded to the moment in which don Gonzalo and his family converted to Catholicism. This, in fact, turned out to be the key moment of legitimation. Notwithstanding eighteenth-century discourses about the degenerating effects of "blood mixture" (a topic to be elaborated in subsequent chapters), acceptance of the faith, loyalty to the crown, noble blood, and the passing of generations had earned the descendants of the caciques and principales of Tepeji de la Seda the status of "pure" and noble "Old Christians."

CONCLUSION

Scholarship on colonial Spanish America often describes the "two-republic" model of social organization as a failure, mainly because segregation policies were constantly violated.[97] This characterization has some validity. Creating an apartheidlike order never entirely worked, especially not in areas of significant Spanish populations, because Spaniards depended on native labor and because for a number of other reasons individuals frequently defied residential laws. The project to create dual republics was not simply a spatial one, however. It also encompassed the establishment of separate civil and ecclesiastical institutions and a distinct theological-legal status for the native population, as well as the recognition of their right to live in semiautonomous communities with their own rulers and lands. Initially part of a utopian missionary project, the idea of an Indian republic was supported by the crown for political, economic, and religious reasons. The existence and reproduction of native towns not only facilitated the siphoning of tribute to royal coffers but enabled placing their population under the tutelage of the crown and the church, thereby strengthening the relationship between the Spanish state and indigenous communities. This relationship, which was cast as voluntary and contractual and was constantly invoked in legal procedures for validating indigenous political and economic claims, strongly shaped central Mexican communal histories and notions of blood among native elites.

Although central Mexico's native rulers and nobles experienced a general decline during the second half of the sixteenth century, and royal legislation construed them along with the entire indigenous population as "miserables," the Spanish crown recognized pre-Hispanic lineages and tried to ensure that their blood would continue to have a privileged place within the colonial order of symbols. Fashioned after the Spanish proof of nobility, the process for recognizing titles enhanced the concern with genealogy among caciques and principales and made primogeniture increasingly important in their succession and inheritance practices. It also altered their constructions of the native past. By the late seventeenth century, central Mexican historical narratives had by and large come to center on sixteenth-century rulers and the moment in which they and their communities accepted Christianity and Spanish rule. Pre-Hispanic forms of thinking about the past survived, at times providing inspiration for alternative historical imaginings and anticolonial rebellions (although less in central Mexico than in Peru). But Christianity and the discourse of vassalage that accompanied recognition of the native republic and its traditional leaders led to profound transformations in native historical narratives, succession and inheritance practices, and understandings of corporate rights. These transformations may not have been as conspicuous as the more material changes that colonialism wrought—namely, the systems of labor and tribute, the demographic decline, and the nucleation programs—but they were just as important both in terms of their role in legitimating Spanish political authority and in reconfiguring indigenous memory, social relations, and identities.

At least at the elite level, Spanish legal procedures influenced native historical and genealogical narratives as well as notions of purity, mixture, and race. As will be discussed in later chapters, these notions were initially all linked, as in the Iberian Peninsula, to religious discourses but came to be deployed mainly against people of African ancestry. Spanish colonial ideology deemed blacks capable of becoming good Christians but never accorded them the same spiritual status as the indigenous people. The official recognition of Indian purity, its transformation into a precondition for certain privileges and corporate rights, had deep implications for colonial Mexico's constructions of "race" and "caste." Together with the recognition of native nobility, it made blood matter, especially among caciques and principales; and it discouraged mixture, particularly with "black blood." Although the creation of dual citizenship and purity regimes implied that the descendants of Spanish-Indian unions were disenfranchised and sometimes considered "impure," some were nonetheless able to access honors, titles, and other privileges reserved for the native population. This occurred because succession and inheritance laws were sometimes simply ignored, because royal policies were especially ambiguous about the status of mestizos (and frequently upheld the rights of those with aristocratic bloodlines), and because the belief in the right of blood was strong in both indigenous and Spanish cultures. Furthermore, as the 1697 cédula confirmed, within Spanish colonial ideology, notions of purity and mixture were not necessarily opposed.

Like native rulers and nobles, the descendants of Spanish-Indian unions produced histories and petitions that stressed their linkages to pre-Hispanic dynasties and that centered on their ancestors' unbroken loyalty, starting in the sixteenth century, to the Catholic faith and Spanish king. The Castilian crown's recognition of an Indian republic, its establishment of legal processes and formulas for validating the titles of caciques and principales, and its extension of the concept of purity to the native population thus left a deep imprint on indigenous and mestizo notions of political legitimation, history, and blood. Those processes, however, also had consequences for the Spanish population. Spaniards too were transformed by the organizing principles, laws, institutions, and material conditions of colonial rule, indeed "creolized." Aspiring to become a colonial aristocracy, they too produced genealogical histories, colonial fictions that in due time would merge with those of the descendants of central Mexico's native rulers and nobles, in the process-shaping discourses of political legitimation as well as of race.

CHAPTER FIVE

Nobility and Purity
in the *República de Españoles*

The Spaniards were not unique in their transplantation of metropolitan concerns with lineage and blood purity to the Americas, but they were distinguished by the extent to which they relied on categories of blood to organize colonial society. Chapter 4 examined how the crown's recognition of pre-Hispanic dynasties and native purity promoted a preoccupation with genealogy and purity within central Mexico's indigenous communities. Chapter 5 analyzes how royal policies contributed to similar concerns among the Spanish population. It argues that there were strong connections between the reproductive strategies used by Spanish elites, particularly in the clergy and administration, and those used in the república de indios and more generally between the perpetuation of hierarchies in both republics and the rise of a social order based on "blood." This chapter first describes the importance of the institution of encomienda to creole class formation and the establishment of a system of *probanzas de méritos y servicios* through which the descendants of conquerors and first colonists claimed economic rewards and status on the basis of the worthiness of their bloodlines. It then discusses the early significance of the concept of purity of blood in New Spain and its appearance as a requirement for travel from Spain to the Americas and for certain public and religious offices. Together, the probanzas de méritos y servicios and probanzas de limpieza de sangre promoted archival practices that helped generate a creole historical consciousness with a strong genealogical component. Finally, the chapter discusses some of the tensions that arose toward the end of the sixteenth century between Spaniards born in the colonies and those born in Spain, especially as the former started to defend their right to have preferential access to the secular and religious administrations on the basis of both their bloodlines and ties to the land.

DESCENT AND TERRITORIALITY:
THE PROBANZA DE MÉRITOS Y SERVICIOS

One of the most well-documented dramas of sixteenth-century Spanish America was the struggle between the crown and the conquerors over the encomienda. Having recently managed to suppress the rebellion of the comuneros in Spain and to limit the power of the Castilian nobility,[1] the monarchy immediately perceived the permanent distribution of native workers to individual Spaniards in the colonies to be a threat to its interests. The encomienda was not technically a feudal institution, first, because it did not involve land grants and, second, because it did not imply civil and criminal jurisdiction over the tributary population. Recipients were given the right to extract tribute and labor from their assigned native subjects and in return were expected to care for their spiritual and temporal well-being, but all indigenous converts were first and foremost vassals of the Crown of Castile.[2] Nonetheless, the virtually unlimited control over labor and tribute that encomenderos first enjoyed promised to transform them into a powerful regional aristocracy, and that was something that the Spanish monarchy, an ocean away, could not afford. Therefore, as early as 1532, the Council of the Indies ordered Mexico City's audiencia to attempt to stop distributing encomiendas.

Depriving the conquerors of grants of native workers proved to be a difficult task because, having risked their own properties, not to mention their lives, they expected rewards worthy of their sacrifices and achievements. As the principal source of wealth in Mexico during the first three decades of colonial rule,[3] the encomienda was at the heart of a feeling of entitlement that sprang from the conquerors' implicitly contractual relationship with the crown. This relationship was reflected in the tenor of petitions for encomiendas, which uniformly cast the grants being sought not as gifts, but as payments for services rendered, indeed, as the "wages of conquest."[4] Abolishing the institution would clearly have meant alienating the conqueror-encomenderos, which the crown could not do without jeopardizing colonial rule. Because Spain did not have a standing army in the Americas until relatively late, it initially had to rely on them to maintain control over conquered regions. The encomenderos kept horses, men, and arms ready at all times to defend the territory, and they generally settled around their town's central square or *plaza de armas,* where they would periodically perform military drills and rituals. But the encomenderos did not limit themselves to military roles. They gradually took over some of the offices in the town councils of main colonial cities, among them Mexico City and Puebla. Together with *primeros pobladores* (first colonists), they would not only consti-tute central Mexico's own group of *beneméritos de la tierra* (meritori-ous sons of the land) but would become the core of its aristocratic elite.

The growing economic and political power of the conqueror-encomenderos only strengthened the crown's resolve to limit their power. In 1542, it issued the New Laws, which mandated the extinction of the encomienda after all the holders had died and which sought to substi-tute the institution with the *repartimiento,* the system of rotating labor that shifted control over the distribution of workers to royal officials. Like elsewhere in Spanish America, Mexico's encomenderos vehemently protested and forced the crown to compromise.[5] The Spanish monarch allowed the institution to continue for "two lives"—to be passed down through a direct line of descent and with preference given to the oldest legitimate son—as it had previously been doing and promised to con-duct a *repartimiento general,* a general distribution of native tributar-ies to all the Spaniards who through their services had earned, but not yet received, encomiendas. The crown also established mechanisms to reward the descendants of conquerors and first colonists with pensions, public and religious offices, and lands.[6]

The infrastructure for receiving petitions for royal grants began to be established relatively soon after the conquest. Viceroy Antonio de Men-doza asked all the conquerors and first colonists to formally record their accomplishments, thus setting the stage for the vast number of *informes* (reports) and *probanzas de méritos y servicios* (proofs of merits and services) that were produced during the rest of the colonial period.[7] In the middle of the sixteenth century, as it became increasingly difficult to identify the meritorious sons of the land (also called *hijos patrimoniales de la tierra,* or "patrimonial sons of the land"), the government stepped up efforts to create an archival infrastructure for preserving their histori-cal and genealogical information and to regularize the process by which they petitioned grants.[8] This increasing systematization of the reports oc-curred precisely around the time that the government formalized chan-nels for recognizing the descendants of pre-Hispanic rulers and nobles. The criteria and mechanisms for reproducing the elite sectors of both "republics" thus surfaced in the same period, each system contributing to the construction of a colonial social and symbolic order strongly based on descent and territoriality. In the reports of merits and services, contri-butions to maintaining Spanish rule in a given region and the worthiness of bloodlines became virtual mantras, the typical reasons provided when requesting honors, rewards, and public or religious offices.

The reports of merits and services consisted of sworn statements pre-sented before the audiencia by the interested party and various witnesses.

Individuals who submitted them underscored military and/or colonization services, such as participation in exploration or conquest expeditions, in the founding of towns or in local government. Maintaining a
"populated house" with many servants and slaves as well as keeping
arms ready at all times in case of a rebellion were also considered contributions and therefore usually mentioned. In addition, the reports tended
to include details about the petitioner's regional origins, lineage, social
status, and properties. Over time, the *informes* tended to become more
extensive because new generations had to submit not only their own
reports but also those of their ancestors. Thus, the documents became
family histories of a sort: chronological and genealogical reconstructions that reinforced the aristocratic mindset of New Spain's creole elites
and that shared as their main reference point participation in the conquest and colonization of the land. The archive produced by the descendants of Juan de Cervantes Casaús and his descendants is a case in
point. Cervantes Casaús, a conqueror who became *capitán general* of
the province of Pánuco in 1529, produced numerous reports of merits
and services with remarkable historical depth. Indeed, some of these reports linked the conquest of Mexico with the Reconquista; they stressed
the military services provided by members of the lineage not only in New
Spain but in Spain, in struggles against Muslims going as far back as the
eighth century.[9] Cervantes Casaús's documentation became part of the
informes de méritos y servicios submitted by his descendants, thus con-
stituting the basis of a particular historical and genealogical consciousness that would continue to be strong into the eighteenth century and
beyond.

The reports of merits and services were not colonial innovations but,
rather, were part of the Spanish system of nobility. They derived from
the legal tradition of granting noble status, normally "nobility of privilege" or "nobility of office," to men who had performed heroic military deeds on behalf of the crown or who had rendered other services
that were considered beneficial to the republic. If the status was granted
in perpetuity, it became "nobility of blood" (hidalguía) on the fourth
generation, that is, after it was established juridically on three separate
instances.[10] In Spanish America, however, the crown did not intend to
use the reports of merits and services to dispense noble titles. Breaking
with the Reconquista tradition of granting the status of caballero or
hidalgo to those who made significant contributions to the colonizing
and christianizing mission, it issued only a handful of noble titles during
the sixteenth century (thirteen to members of Pizarro's first expedition
in Perú). Most explorers, conquerors, and first colonists had to settle
for *hidalguía americana,* a mostly de facto noble status marked by tax

exemptions, coats of arms, and preferential treatment with regard to accessing land, cabildo offices, and the post of corregidor.[11] But of all prizes that the crown initially handed out to its soldiers and colonizing agents in New Spain, it was the encomienda that became most strongly associated with noble status, and for this reason encomenderos insisted on extending them beyond the stipulated "two lives." Indeed, by the late sixteenth century, some encomienda holders began to attempt to turn their grants into mayorazgos, to entail them and make them transmittable generation after generation through a "straight male line" (*línea recta the varón*).[12] The Council of the Indies, however, generally did not indulge them.

One of the most notable petitions the Council of the Indies received was a 1564 letter from New Spain's conquerors and first colonists stating that they were all anxiously waiting for the prize of perpetuity.[13] Three years later, Mexico City's cabildo asked that the encomenderos be given the right to entail their encomiendas and consolidate their estates, which would enable them to petition for titles of nobility. This and similar requests must have had an effect, because in 1575, Philip II ordered Viceroy Martín Enríquez to discreetly extend the encomiendas to a third life. But the question of perpetuity was not settled. At the end of the sixteenth century, the Council of the Indies was still studying the issue, and only about three encomiendas had been given the title of mayorazgo.[14] The rest were mainly in their second or third generation and therefore targeted for repossession by the crown. The failure of royal policies to definitively resolve the fate of the encomiendas only fed the resentment of families of the conquerors and first colonists, whose laments for what seemed to be an inexplicably tragic fate were accompanied by a defiant vindication of the privileges, honors, and sources of wealth that they considered theirs by virtue of their ancestors' contributions to winning the land.[15]

For example, at the end of the sixteenth century, Gonzalo Gómez de Cervantes, son of the conqueror Juan de Cervantes Casaús, completed a *memorial* (historical account) describing New Spain's social and economic conditions. His account had two main goals: to persuade the crown to finally fulfill its promise of making a distribution of tributaries to all the beneméritos who had not yet received any and to make all new and existing encomiendas perpetually transmittable. Gómez de Cervantes considered the distribution and perpetuation of grants of native tribute necessary to protect the families of conquerors and first colonists, whose status was being threatened by the rapid upward mobility of a group of more recent immigrants from the Iberian Peninsula, individuals who had contributed little to the conquest but were amassing fortunes, whether thanks to royal favors or their mining and commercial enterprises.[16] His memorial, the arguments of which were echoed by other American-born Spaniards, signaled the rise of "creolism" (*criollismo*) or what Bernard Lavallé has called the creole "spirit of possession," a sense of entitlement that grew as the crown began to favor European-born Spaniards for high public and religious offices and certain royal grants.[17] Representing a rupture with the Castilian practice of granting the natives of a jurisdiction a monopoly on access to office holding and ecclesiastical benefices, the policy was one of the factors that prompted the rise of a creole discourse of "nativeness." This discourse developed alongside, and in constant tension with, that of purity of blood, which privileged (Spanish) bloodlines as the basis for making political and economic claims and which set in motion its own set of social, archival, and genealogical practices.

BLOODLINES AND RELIGION:
THE PROBANZA DE LIMPIEZA DE SANGRE

Given the importance that the issue of limpieza de sangre enjoyed in early modern Spain, it is not surprising that it acquired significance in the Americas and that purity requirements would be implemented there too. But the use of the concept in the conquered lands was immediately linked to the cultural politics of Spanish colonialism. The tight relationship between the Spanish state and the church and the prevalence of Castilian providential notions of history at the time of the conquest produced a vision of the "Indies" as a privileged space of purity, a region where Old Christians would make their faith flourish and the seeds of heresy would never sprout. This religious utopia led the crown to bar untrustworthy converts from going to its new territories, thereby making the concept of limpieza de sangre important there before statutes of purity of blood and the Inquisition were formally established. In New Spain, a first edict forbidding the arrival of people who were "stained" was issued in 1523.[18] Various other decrees targeting Jews, Muslims, conversos, moriscos, Gypsies, heretics, and the descendants of those categories were to follow.[19] Together these laws amounted to a de facto purity-of-blood statute for going to the Americas.[20]

If corporate society and local *fueros* (laws) prevented the passage of a general blood decree in the metropolitan context, the incorporation of Spanish America into the Crown of Castile and the importance of the project to convert the native population prompted Spain's monarchs to pursue a more aggressive limpieza policy in the colonies, one that in theory did not even tolerate the presence of New Christians. It is true that the Catholic Kings at one point considered the possibility of allowing converted Jews to migrate to the Americas, for a price, but fears that they would become a source of "contamination" led them to change their minds. As the Mexican inquisitor Alonso de Peralta was later to explain, His Majesty did not allow New Christians in the Indies because of concerns that the indigenous people would unite with them or follow their ways.[21] The colonial discourse of purity of blood was therefore initially propelled by the Christianization project and by Spanish distrust of the religious loyalties of Jewish converts—by religious utopias and anticonverso sentiment.

Excepting a few categories, emigrants to the Americas were required to present certificates of purity of blood, along with royal licenses to travel, at Seville's Casa de Contratación (Royal House of Trade). These certificates were normally obtained from local judges. Some of the emigrants' purity documents date back to the early 1530s, which suggests that people departing for the Americas submitted some of the first informaciones de limpieza de sangre produced in Spain. Not all travelers obtained the required limpieza certification from local judges in their hometowns, however, and the bureaucratic mechanisms set up in Seville, especially during the early decades, were not efficient enough to prevent some New Christians from traversing the Atlantic.[22] News of their growing presence in New Spain led to legislation such as the 1535 royal decree ordering Viceroy Antonio de Mendoza to make sure that people barred from practicing medicine and obtaining university degrees in Spain were also not allowed to do so in Mexico.[23] Occasionally the king excused the limpieza certification requirement for travelers to the Americas. Philip II did so, for example, in 1574 with Santiago del Riego, who he named *oidor* (judge) of the Audiencia of Nueva Galicia. Del Riego was the illegitimate son of a nun whose ancestry could for obvious reasons not be investigated without damaging her honor and that of her convent.[24] In general, however, purity requirements for passengers became stricter during the reign of Philip II and in particular after the approval of the Cathedral of Toledo's statute, which sent an unmistakable message about the importance that limpieza de sangre was acquiring in the secular and religious administrative hierarchies. In New Spain, it was precisely in these two spheres that the issue of purity of blood first gained prominence.

But exactly which government and ecclesiastical offices required proof of purity? In Spain, the lack of a blanket limpieza policy had created some striking inconsistencies. Proof of purity was required in a large number of institutions and for certain royal posts, but not for regidores and corregidores nor for judges, priests, counts, and dukes.[25] In the colonial context, the situation was slightly different because only Old Christians were allowed to migrate there. However, whether religious and public officials had to submit a probanza depended on the office and institution with which they were associated. Proof of purity was necessary for a number of imperial posts, including councilors in the Council of the Indies, audiencia judges, and royal secretaries (*escribanos reales*). At the municipal level, practices varied more because government institutions like the cabildo largely functioned as independent bodies and their membership requirements could change. The most important town councils, those of the capital and Puebla, had mechanisms to monitor the purity of their members, but it is unclear whether they had a formal statute. Proof of Old Christian lineage was thus required of some corregidores, regidores, and alcaldes—officials that apparently were not obliged to prove their limpieza in Spain. Because the religious orders and cathedral chapters also enjoyed some autonomy, probanza requirements for the clergy varied as well.

During the early colonial period, the limpieza certification process for public and religious officials normally involved audiencias and cabildos, bodies that were authorized by the crown to handle those cases.[26] These institutions received petitions and genealogical information and determined whether or not to submit the case to the Council of the Indies for examination and possible further investigations. For example, not long after Puebla's town council was founded, it was accepting petitions such as that of Francisco Gutiérrez de León, a priest whose parents were among the city's earliest settlers. In the late 1530s, he submitted his genealogical information before the cabildo's alcalde ordinario in order to have it sent to the Council of the Indies.[27] He also presented five witnesses, all of whom attested to his unblemished Catholic lineage, admirable religious practices, and virtuous conduct, as well as to his overall eligibility for a royal grant. Done well before the Inquisition had regularized purity investigations, the probanza included the main questions (regarding legitimacy, limpieza, place of birth, moral conduct, and reputation) later contained in Holy Office questionnaires.

Another probanza initiated in Puebla's town council was that of Alonso Pérez, who in the middle of the sixteenth century presented his genealogical information to Antonio de Almaguer, the city's alcalde ordinario. A priest and canon in Puebla's cathedral who hoped to be named precentor (*chantre*), Pérez also submitted a purity certification from the Villa de la Puebla de Sancho Pérez that his father had secured for him from the alcaldes of that Spanish town in 1548.[28] That probanza included the testimonies of eight witnesses, all of whom confirmed that

Alonso Pérez was legitimate and pure of blood and that the public voice and fame held him as such. The father was given copies of the certification, which he promptly sent to his son in New Spain. In 1552, Alonso Pérez presented one of those copies to Almaguer and requested another probanza to establish his qualifications to be precentor. The entire dossier—including the genealogical information, the probanza done in Spain about his blood purity, and the one completed in New Spain about his qualifications and character—was sent to the Council of the Indies, which approved his petition.

The probanza of Pedro García Martínez, another priest, followed the same bureaucratic trajectory. In 1569, he requested a canonry in Puebla's cathedral and presented the cabildo with an información attesting to his experience as a priest and his "clean lineage and caste."[29] After interrogating seven witnesses, the alcalde approved the probanza and sent it to the Council of the Indies. Not long thereafter, García Martínez was issued three legal copies of his purity certification. In those same years, the priest García Rodríguez Pardo initiated a similar process with the cabildo of Michoacán. Wanting a canonry in the city's cathedral, he presented the local judge with a probanza made in the town of Guayangareo (Michoacán) that attested to his qualifications as a priest. He also submitted a certificate of purity of blood that he had received from an alcalde in Spain in 1548, just before migrating to the Americas.[30] In 1549, Nicolás Garcia, a priest in Mexico City, began to submit paperwork to the cabildo in order to prove that he was an Old Christian.[31]

An example of a probanza that was petitioned not at a town council but at Mexico City's audiencia is that of Juan Cabrera, a priest in the capital and son of one of its "ancient settlers." In 1565, he requested a purity investigation from the tribunal, which he said he needed because he wished to be considered for a post and prebend in the cathedral chapter of Mexico City, Puebla, or Michoacán.[32] To that end, he submitted proof of his purity of blood as well as documentation of the services that he and his father had provided for the crown. Cabrera's certification process thus combined the probanza de limpieza de sangre with the probanza de méritos y servicios. After Cabrera presented his genealogical information and four witnesses to support it, one of the judges conducted an interrogation and a royal secretary recorded the testimonies. The interrogation consisted of five questions, the first of which focused on the candidate's lineage, legitimate birth, purity of blood, and nobility. Cabrera, who had been educated at the recently founded University of Mexico and who described himself as a "patrimonial son" of the capital city, claimed hidalguía for his father and himself on the basis of their services to the crown. Other questions tried to verify that the candidate was a priest, lived a peaceful and prudent life, and set good examples for others, as well as that he could communicate in native languages. The following year, Cabrera presented another información and four witnesses at the audiencia, this time to prove that he had received the Holy Orders. Both probanzas were sent to the Council of the Indies.

In addition to receiving petitions for probanzas de limpieza de sangre from religious officials, Mexico City's audiencia also handled requests from candidates for royal posts. For example, in 1601, Antonio Rueda applied for the post of escribano real and presented his genealogical information to the corregidor, who in turn relayed it to the tribunal.[33] The probanza, which involved interrogations and the typical questions of legitimacy, ancestry, and purity, was approved by an audiencia judge and sent to the Council of the Indies. Also sent was a copy of a limpieza certification that Rueda had obtained in 1548 from the corregidor of Alba de Tormes (near the Spanish city of Salamanca) and which he presented at the Casa de Contratación before embarking for the Americas. Another applicant for the post of royal secretary in 1601 was Pedro de Salmerón, a native of Castile.[34] Six witnesses, most from Salmerón's hometown of Villanueva de la Fuente, declared before Mexican audiencia officials that he was of pure and Old Christian ancestry. The second witness, from a neighboring village, testified that he knew that the applicant was clean because the elders from his town and from Villanueva de la Fuente had known his parents and grandparents and would often refer to the purity of their lineage. When all the testimonies were recorded, the información was sent to Spain, where a second probanza was made in Salmerón's native town. There the alcalde ordinario interrogated four people who had known him and his family and who attested to their purity of blood.

That government officials (including corregidores, oidores, and alcaldes ordinarios) on both sides of the Atlantic intervened in the purity certification of religious officials is partially explained by the Real Patronato, which gave Castilian monarchs the right to regulate the movement of clergy to Spanish America and to nominate candidates for all religious appointments, from archbishops down to priests. Popes could reject appointees but they rarely did, and when it came to the lower clergy, their approval usually was not even requested. Petitions for ecclesiastical benefices were normally sent to the Council of the Indies, at least until the passage of the Ordenanza del Patronazgo in 1574. This important piece of legislation sought to curb the influence and parochial duties of the regular orders in favor of the secular (Episcopal) clergy and to consolidate the king's control over the colonial church.[35] It therefore reiterated that the crown was in charge of all ecclesiastical benefices, including cathedral chapter appointments. The official responsible for implementing the Ordenanza del Patronazgo's reforms was Pedro Moya de Contreras, the viceroyalty's first formal inquisitor and one of its arch-bishops (1573–89). Besides introducing a system of competitive exams, *oposiciones,* for new rural benefices, he convened a tribunal to select parish priests and to examine candidates for the Holy Orders and for the job of ecclesiastical notary. Participants in the competition (which later was supervised mostly by bishops rather than by a tribunal) were to render informaciones de limpieza de sangre and "relaciones [or infor-maciones] de oficio y parte."[36]

Moya de Contreras's reforms sought both to ascertain that priests were pure and to encourage the appointment of the descendants of the conquerors and first settlers to new posts and benefices. Because the king and the Council of the Indies could not consider all petitions alone, they delegated the responsibility to the viceroy. As of 1575, then, most recipi-ents of religious benefices received them from the highest colonial secu-lar official, who was in charge of ensuring that they met all of the profes-sional and genealogical requirements. Although the Spanish church as a whole did not have a purity statute (cathedral chapters were a different matter) and bishops and pastors were not technically required to submit proof of their purity of blood, in New Spain, members of the secular clergy were generally expected to be Old Christians. Thus, in the early seventeenth century, a scandal broke out because the archbishop was ru-mored to have stained ancestors. He was not removed from his post, but the Holy Office reported that his religious order had tried to expel him when it received news of his tainted lineage and that one of his nephews had not been admitted into the Order of Santiago for the same reason.[37] As to the regular clergy, by the start of the seventeenth century, at least two religious orders—the Franciscans and the Jesuits—required that ap-plicants in New Spain submit proof of purity of blood.[38]

During the last third of the sixteenth century, the number of proban-zas de limpieza de sangre requested in Mexico sharply increased. As in the metropolitan context, the rise was related to the religious-political climate of the Counter-Reformation. Catholicism was clearly on the de-fense at this time and nowhere was this truer than in Spain, which en-visioned itself as the divinely chosen guardian of the faith. Its efforts to enforce a post–Tridentine Catholic orthodoxy within Hispanic society at large inspired more aggressive policies to prevent both the spread of heresy and the revival of idolatry in Spanish America. These concerns with ensuring that the Indies remained "uninfected" and that the native people did not relapse into their pagan practices helped justify entrust-ing colonial governance, both civil and spiritual, only to Old Christian

Spaniards. Another factor influencing the numerical rise in probanzas de limpieza de sangre in Mexico was the union of the crowns of Portugal and Castile (1580–1640), which accentuated fears among colonial officials about Portuguese conversos (*cristãos novos*) making their way to the Americas. The migration of a significant number of cristãos novos to Spain (from which their ancestors tended to derive in the first place) led Castilians to equate the term *portugués* with that of *judío* and to look upon their growing presence, and that of Portuguese people in general, in both the metropole and colonies with great suspicion.[39] It soon became clear to some colonial officials that they needed better mechanisms to ensure the purity of passengers to the Americas. Inquisitor Peralta intimated as much in 1604 when he warned that many New Christians had been evading limpieza requirements and arriving in New Spain. He referred specifically to members of the Carvajal family, many of whom were burned for practicing Judaism in one of the first autos de fe "celebrated" in Mexico. With the arrival of more Portuguese conversos to New Spain and ensuing increase in the number of Inquisitorial prosecutions, Mexico City's cathedral ran out of room for sanbenitos and instead of hanging them had to put the names of the sanbenitados on small strips of cloth.[40]

Finally, the probanzas de limpieza de sangre became more commonplace because of the formal establishment of the Tribunal of the Holy Office of the Inquisition, which transferred its concerns with policing religious and genealogical purity to New Spain's landscape. Indeed, almost as soon as it was founded, the Mexican Inquisition began to produce these certifications and to receive and disseminate instructions on how commissioners should proceed.[41] Following royal orders, it sought to ascertain that its officials and familiars provided proof of blood purity for themselves and, if married, for their wives.[42] New Spain's Holy Office even conducted genealogical investigations for deceased spouses, but the Suprema ordered an end to the practice in 1612.[43] The Inquisition's mandate to scrutinize family genealogies at first did not seem to dissuade many individuals from trying to join its ranks. The title of familiar was especially coveted because, though unsalaried, it gave the holder automatic local influence by transforming him into an official informant of one of the most important institutions in central New Spain. Applicants for the title therefore often consisted of recent immigrants who hoped to infiltrate established circles of power. But the Holy Office did not simply conduct genealogical investigations for candidates to its ministerial posts and *familiaturas* (familiar titles). Although town councils, cathedral chapters, and religious orders with purity requirements had their own certification procedures, members of the political and ecclesiastical hierarchies sometimes requested probanzas from the Inquisition because its procedures were considered more rigorous. Aristocrats who simply wanted to obtain proof of their unsullied lineages and persons dissatisfied with the results of investigations done by other bodies also at times resorted to the Holy Office.[44] The establishment of the Inquisition thus led to the spread of probanzas and facilitated the transfer of the obsession with purity of blood to New Spain. By the end of the sixteenth century, this obsession was particularly marked among creoles who aspired to secure their place within the religious or secular administration but whose limpieza de sangre and fitness for office were starting to be questioned by the Spanish born. It was a period that witnessed the rise of new regional identities, sociocultural tensions, and political claims.

CREOLES AND THE STRUGGLE FOR RELIGIOUS AND PUBLIC OFFICES

When people from the Iberian Peninsula migrated to the Americas and established permanent domicile there, they not only were exposed to landscapes, climates, flora and fauna, and foods different from those in the Old World but became integrated into new social relations that tended to lessen differences among themselves. It was, after all, thanks to Spanish policies on immigration and trade with the Americas that the category of "natives of the kingdoms of Spain" emerged at the end of the sixteenth century.[45] This category had little meaning in the homeland itself, where several kingdoms and therefore several communities of natives continued to coexist for at least another hundred years. But if the concept of "Spanish natives" first operated in Spanish America, peninsular regional identities were by no means automatically transcended in the colonial context. Furthermore, new cleavages among Spaniards emerged, one of the earliest being between those who were born or raised there, the *criollos* (creoles), and *peninsulares* (peninsulars), or those who were born in the metropole.

In Mexico, the word *criollo* first appeared in Puebla de los Ángeles, where it initially referred to native-born slaves and livestock but was also quickly displaced onto Spaniards who had been born there.[46] Although the exact origins of the word are disputed, scholars generally agree that it came from the verb *criar*, to raise (as in to be raised in), and that it was first applied to black slaves who were born and raised outside of Africa, so as to distinguish them from those who were born in that continent, who for their part were called *bozales*. The term referred to the place where one was born or raised, and more generally to the process by which transplanted individuals became immersed in new social relations and acquired new habits, beliefs, and local interests. As scholars have remarked about the same phenomenon in the Andes, the displacement of the term onto the colonists was by no means an innocent linguistic exercise.[47] By the latter half of the sixteenth century, Spaniards equated blacks with slavery and thus deemed them to be at the bottom of the social hierarchy. Containing connotations of inferiority, the word *creole* or *criollo* marked the growing tension between Spaniards born or raised in the Americas and more recent migrants from the Iberian Peninsula.

This tension surfaced in the context of the growing competition over public and religious offices and relative socioeconomic decline of the families of the conquerors and first colonists. Notwithstanding earlier promises made to them by the crown, the tenure of Viceroy Luis de Velasco marked a shift in policy in favor of more recent arrivals to New Spain. Royal officials and other nonconquerors with ties to the court and Castilian nobility seemed to fare especially well.[48] These Spaniards received considerable viceregal patronage, and much to the dismay of the first generation of colonists, some were even issued encomiendas. The son of Viceroy Luis de Velasco, who also became viceroy, was one such recipient. The policy of favoring newer arrivals was precipitated by the discovery of a conspiracy against the viceregal government by Martín Cortés (the conqueror's son) and of his plans to declare himself king. After an investigation that resulted in the execution of some of the conspirators and Cortés's forced exile in Spain, the loyalty of the meritorious sons of the land was put into question, and this suspicion, in turn, was used to justify denying them access to the highest political and ecclesiastical offices. But creoles had their advocates, including Diego Romano, the bishop of Tlaxcala. In a 1579 letter to Philip II, he argued against allowing Spaniards who had been born in Spain to make their religious posts perpetual, a policy he feared would damage the native people because those officials were not prepared to teach them in their languages. He admitted that criollos who were not entirely qualified had been ordained, but many of them spoke indigenous tongues and had demonstrated they were virtuous and with the capacity to excel in letters.[49]

The shift in political climate in favor of more recent arrivals was most noticeable in Mexico City, where the membership profiles of the audiencia and the cabildo underwent a gradual but nonetheless important transformation. By the second decade of the seventeenth century, the capital's town council was characterized by an almost complete absence of members of New Spain's "traditional" colonial families.[50] The role of these families and of creoles in general also declined in the religious administration, which among the regular clergy created intense frictions. By 1606, a report submitted to the crown described all of the orders in New Spain as being divided into two camps: criollos and *castellanos* (Castilians).[51] Spanish friars accused creoles of excessive ambition, of wanting to control not just the religious orders but the cathedral chapters and town councils, and of claiming the "kingdom of New Spain" as their own. The latter responded by accusing Castilians in the orders of conducting secret investigations (informaciones) to prove that the locals were not sufficiently qualified for positions of authority and by attempting to produce their own proofs of their abilities, intellectual and otherwise.[52]

Creole struggles within the religious orders continued into at least the 1620s, eventually resulting in various orders establishing the *alternativa*, a system in which access to the novitiate, offices, and benefices was given on a rotating basis to Spaniards, creoles, and in some cases to a third category: those who had been born in Spain but had taken the habit in Mexico.[53] For creoles, the system was not ideal, but they were nonetheless able to play an important role in the religious orders and, indeed, in both the public and religious hierarchies, which in the course of the seventeenth century became increasingly creolized. Even though they were not normally named to the top public and church posts, royal policies continued to support granting the descendants of the conquerors and first colonists preferential access to certain posts (particularly in the administration of justice in native communities),[54] in part to appease them and in part to limit the possibility that they would unite with other populations.[55]

In any case, the first wave of rivalries between creoles and peninsulars over religious and public offices coincided with the beginnings of European theories of colonial degeneration, the terms of which reveal some of the cultural tensions that arose in the Americas and significance that the concept and certification of purity of blood would acquire in central New Spain. These theories were primarily based on the idea that the American climate, environment, and skies made people lazy, unstable, superstitious, and prone to a series of vices, including lasciviousness and lust.[56] The climate of the Indies, proposed the cosmographer Juan López de Velasco at the end of the sixteenth century, made native bodies weak, thin, fragile, and lazy and had similar effects on the children of Spaniards, whose temperament, habits, and corporal qualities would eventually mutate.[57] Decades later, the friar Gregorio García discussed indigenous men's lack of facial hair and wondered if this would happen to Spaniards as well as if their skin color would change.[58] Would geography and climate make them effeminate and dark like the Indians?

Various other writers speculated whether climate explained the external and internal characteristics of the native people and, if so, whether life in the colonies would eventually transform the descendants of Europeans.[59] According to some of their works, the warm and humid climate of the Americas changed the physiological makeup of Spaniards, their bodily humors, and from these changes followed others in their temperament, intellect, complexion, and even rhetorical wit. The environment shaped physiology, and physiology in turn determined everything else. The logical conclusion of this environmental and physical determinism was that, whether they "mixed" with the indigenous people or not, Spaniards would with time become more and more like them, a process that could only be slowed down by the constant infusion of more Europeans into the colonies.

Theories that posited that the children of Europeans in the colonies underwent a physiological and moral decline sometimes attributed the process not just to the effects of the American physical environment and skies but also to the use of native or black wet nurses by creole families.[60] Spaniards degenerated in the Indies, argued the theologian José de Acosta, because of the constellations and because they had been nourished by the breasts of Indian women. Just as in early modern Spain breast milk figured prominently in notions of social contamination—as a metaphor for exposure to certain cultural and religious practices and for the biological transmission of all sorts of qualities to the child—so too in Spanish America. And just as in the metropolitan context women's bodies came to mark cultural and biological boundaries, so too in the colonies, as anxieties over converso and morisco wet nurses were displaced onto the African and indigenous women in charge of raising Spanish children. As in other imperial contexts, degeneration was a mobile concept—applied first to certain metropolitan groups and then colonial populations or vice versa—and served to establish citizenship status (or at least its prerogatives) as well as to assign gender to race, among other things.[61]

Another and related dimension of the emerging discourse of creole degeneration revolved around charges of biological "mixture," which at first were made primarily against the children of conquerors and first colonists (a good number of whom were the products of unions, mostly informal, between Spaniards and indigenous women). Already by the 1570s, religious and secular authorities started to express concerns that some people who claimed to be Spaniards had traces of native, or in some cases black, ancestry and were therefore inferior in quality to persons who were born in the Peninsula and ineligible for public and religious offices. For example, in 1571, the bishop of Antequera wrote to the crown suggesting that Cristóbal Gil should not have the post of treasurer in the cathedral because he was a mestizo and not "pure Spaniard" and because for that same reason the chapter's constitution made him ineligible for benefices.[62] About a decade later, Madrid ordered New Spain's viceroy to make sure that certain audiencia offices (particularly that of receptor) be sold only to the sons of conquerors and first colonists, but to ascertain that they were not mestizos or mulatos.[63]

Whether they stressed the effects of climate, wet nurses, or biological reproduction with colonial populations, Spanish charges that life in the colonies had a degenerating effect did not go unchallenged. For example, when at the end of the sixteenth century Juan de Cárdenas wrote his *Problemas y secretos maravillosos de las Indias* in order to familiarize a European audience with some of the many "marvels" of the New World, he mounted a defense of the colonial Spanish population. A medical doctor who was born in Spain, Cárdenas was educated and for the most part raised in Mexico and thus qualified as a creole. Influenced by classical and medieval sources (including Aristotle, the Greek physician Galen, and the Arab scholar Ibn Rushd), he argued that the Indies' environment, namely, the heat, sun, and humidity, altered aspects of Spaniards' physiologies and generally made human bodies hotter, softer, and more prone to disease. But Cárdenas refuted the notion that colonists would eventually become like the native population. On the contrary, he insisted that their fundamental "nature" (*naturaleza*) remained the same.[64] That Cárdenas argued for the basic unity of creoles and peninsulars as the question of who should have access to political and ecclesiastical offices started to be raised was not a coincidence. Myths of nature have historically been deployed to legitimate the social order and help to naturalize power.[65] In Spanish America, these myths arose at a time when colonial hierarchies were emerging and their ideological basis was being elaborated in the minds, policies, and writings of colonial and peninsular Spaniards.

For creoles, particularly those who descended from the first colonists, the main religious and public institutions of the viceroyalty belonged to them because of the efforts of their forefathers and, increasingly, their rights and qualifications as natives of the jurisdiction. At the end of the sixteenth century, they began to conceive of the territory of New Spain as a kingdom—a kingdom under the Spanish crown but independent of Castile—and to stress both their ties to the land and knowledge of indigenous languages; they also began to construe Spaniards as "foreigners," that is, as people who were not integrated into the local community and who were therefore not entitled to the rights of either vecindad or naturaleza.[66] Thus, the creole spirit of possession was gradually extended from the encomienda to public and religious offices, to the prerogatives of "nativeness." The stage was apparently set for the rise of a distinct creole identity and protonational consciousness. But this growing sense of "nativeness" and separateness from Castile did not ultimately erode their sense of being part of a broader community of Spaniards.

Indeed, objections to the use of the word *criollo* (made as writings associating American-born Europeans with the native people proliferated) usually stressed the idea that it created a damaging separation, one that made no sense given that creoles were Spaniards.[67] The crown and Spanish jurists for the most part agreed. Juan de Solórzano Pereira, for example, rejected theories that the sky and climate of the Indies and the breast milk they drank from native women made Spaniards who lived there lose the good qualities that they received from their Spanish blood. Pointing out that those theories had been elaborated mainly by theologians who wanted to exclude creoles from the rights enjoyed by Spaniards, and in particular to deny them access to the prelacy (body of prelates) and honorific posts, he affirmed the former's essential "Spanishness."[68]

The probanzas de limpieza de sangre played a critical role in this construction of a broader sense of Spanishness as well as in the creoles' struggle to secure their place in the religious and political hierarchies. Along with the informes de méritos y servicios and relaciones de oficio y parte, they were used to prove educational preparation, services to crown and faith, and purity of bloodlines. Especially as questions about the "nature" of Europeans who lived in the Americas and their suitability for certain offices began to surface, the probanza de limpieza de sangre acquired new meanings. As elaborated on in the last three chapters of this book, it allowed creoles to vindicate their religiosity, Old Christian ancestry, and Spanish bloodlines and thus to claim to be part of a broader community of "pure Spaniards."

CONCLUSION

By the second half of the sixteenth century, New Spain had a regional elite composed of conquerors, first colonists, and their descendants. Members of this group felt entitled not just to the perpetuity of their encomiendas but to the viceroyalty's public offices and ecclesiastical benefices and more generally to aristocratic privileges. Not only did they have to face the specter of losing their grants of native laborers and tributaries, however, but they also encountered growing competition from more recent arrivals for jobs in the government and church, as well as accusations that life in the colonies had somehow made them inferior to

Spaniards born on the Iberian Peninsula. Nonetheless, the crown continued to recognize, albeit less than in the past, the contributions of the meritorious sons of the land and established bureaucratic mechanisms that ensured that they had access to certain religious and public offices. These mechanisms mainly consisted of the probanza de méritos y servicios, which granted a de facto nobility status, and which was frequently submitted with the probanza de limpieza de sangre.

Transplanted from Spain, the concept of purity of blood did not operate in the same way as it did in Iberia and came to occupy a particularly important role in creole power struggles and discourses. It first gained importance as part of efforts by the Castilian crown and the church to ensure that the project to establish the Catholic faith in the Americas would not be undermined by "suspect" Christians. The colonial discourse of limpieza de sangre thus differed from the metropolitan one in that it was inextricably linked to the Christianizing mission, which led Spanish kings to make the status of purity of blood a precondition for going to its newly acquired territories and a requirement for certain colonial officials. By the end of the sixteenth century, the state, the Inquisition, and some religious orders were routinizing genealogical investigations that helped to transfer the metropolitan obsession with lineage to Spanish America and in particular to enhance the colonial elite's concern with bloodlines. Fueled by the role that lineage played in gaining access to various religious and public offices, this concern allowed creoles to identify as part of a broader community of Spaniards and, in general, to forge the myth of Spanish unity.

The creole use of the concept of purity of blood and its unifying function developed in constant tensions with the emerging colonial discourse of nativeness, which began to construct Spaniards born in the Iberian Peninsula as foreigners and which was tied to a deep sense of entitlement and attachment to the land. Originating with the conqueror-encomenderos, this sense of territoriality and local patriotism would in the seventeenth century start to produce a literature that exalted the climate, topography, and wealth of the viceroyalty. But creoles would continue to maintain a strong sense of their purity of blood—a concept that they deployed not just to reclaim their Old Christian Spanish identity but to draw boundaries between themselves and the growing population of mixed ancestry.

CHAPTER SIX

The Initial Stages and Socioreligious
Roots of the *Sistema de Castas*

Testimonies to the Spanish colonial project to create a dichotomous model of social organization, the first Mexican parish books containing baptismal, marriage, and death registers were divided into *libros de españoles* (books of Spaniards) and *libros de indios* (books of Indians). During the first half of the seventeenth century, however, parishes in different parts of New Spain started to keep separate records for people of mixed ancestry, the "castas," who previously had tended to be included in the books of Spaniards. Scholarship on colonial Mexico has generally interpreted this change as a sign that the sistema de castas had crystallized.[1] The system began to unfold in the second half of the sixteenth century, a period that witnessed the growth of a "mixed" population as well as a nomenclature referring primarily to descent. By the end of the century, main colonial categories of difference, including *mestizo* and *mulato,* started to appear in administrative records on a regular basis.

Spanish colonial categories of "mixture" partly drew on metropolitan traditions. Beginning with the Council of Elvira (circa 314 C.E.), sexual intercourse between people of different religions was the subject of continual ecclesiastical prohibitions, and eventually marriages between Christians, Jews, and Muslims were not permitted. The persistence of interreligious sexual unions during the medieval period gave way to new terms for their "hybrid offspring" (*híbridos*), including that of *mozárabe* (mixed Arab), which initially referred to the children of a Christian and a Muslim.[2] This classificatory impulse intensified when the Spanish Inquisition began its genealogical investigations and efforts to determine people's degrees of Jewish, Christian, and Muslim blood. Given early modern Spain's acute concerns with lineage, purity, and categorization, the emergence of the colonial sistema de castas was perhaps to be expected. But the rise and form of that system can be explained only by social, political, and religious developments in Spanish America and the dynamic interaction of local and transatlantic processes, among them those set in motion by the African slave trade.

This chapter charts the origins of the sistema de castas in central New Spain. It first discusses main classificatory trends in sixteenth-century parish records, particularly the shift from a somewhat fluid system of categorization in which paternal ancestry was privileged, but not always, to a more rigid model based on both bloodlines. Focusing mainly on mestizos, this section attributes the shift at the end of the sixteenth century to processes of economic and political exclusion as well as to the establishment of the Inquisition and accentuation of Spanish anxieties over the religious proclivities and genealogical origins of the native populations. The chapter then examines the role of slavery in determining the juridical-theological status of blacks vis-à-vis that of the native people and more generally the place that African descent occupied within colonial society and its gendered order of blood symbols. The final section analyzes the Spanish colonial language of "race," particularly the concepts of raza and casta, and the influence that religious notions of blood purity had on the system of classification's principal categories.

CATEGORIES AND ARCHIVES: BOOKS OF SPANIARDS, INDIANS, AND CASTAS

Although insufficient in and of themselves as a source of information about the origins and functioning of the sistema de castas, sixteenth-century parish records provide important clues about early colonial classificatory trends. One of their limitations, besides their incomplete nature, is that they generally list more information for men than for women and children. Marriage records, for example, often qualify grooms with terms such as *español* or *indio*, but don't provide the background of the bride. Similarly, baptismal records include more information about the father (and godfather) than about the mother and child. This gendered asymmetry in parish registers was the result of the Castilian tradition of determining the sociopolitical status of family members according to that of the head of the household, normally the father. A patrilineal logic reigned, that is, not just in the discourse of nobility (which established noble status through the paternal bloodline) but in processes of establishing vecindad ("citizenship" or membership in the local community) and naturaleza ("nativeness" or membership in the kingdom).[3] In Spanish America, this logic tended to operate in accordance with the dual model of social organization, for at least initially, belonging in one or the other "republic" was largely, though by no means exclusively, determined on the basis of the status of the father.

Patrilineal classificatory patterns are evident in birth records from sixteenth-century central Mexican cities. For example, the baptismal registers of Puebla's Sagrario Metropolitano (Cathedral Parish), which had *libros de bautismos de españoles* as early as 1544, tend only to specify the Spanish status of the father, as such suggesting that the mother and child were Spaniards too. Yet other colonial sources, including a 1534 report sent by the city to the Council of the Indies, confirm that some of the children being registered had indigenous mothers. The report stated that out of eighty-one male heads of households, twenty-seven were married to native women.[4] As far as can be determined, the children produced by these unions were registered in libros de bautismos de españoles, without any indication that they were not Spanish.[5] In the early period, what seems to have mattered most were the status of the father and the legitimacy or illegitimacy of the child. Although the category of mestizo does appear in one register from the 1540s, its use continued to be rare through most of the sixteenth century.[6] That the term was scarcely utilized was not due to a lack of a population of mixed ancestry. A demographic count sent to the Suprema at the end of the sixteenth century estimated the total nonnative population of Puebla to be 20,100, including 14,400 Spaniards; 3,000 "mestizos, mulattoes, and free blacks" working in the *obrajes,* or textile mills (silk, cotton, and wool); 200 religious; and 2,500 black and mulatto slaves.[7] The absence of the category of mestizo in parish records also did not mean that it was not used, for it did quickly appear in a number of municipal ordinances, town council records, and colonial reports. In the 1540s and 1550s, for example, various mestizos were granted lots of land in Puebla's *traza* (colonial urban grid plan) as well as in some native barrios.[8]

As to the use of the categories of *negro* and *mulato* in the Sagrario Metropolitano's baptismal records, they started to appear with some frequency in the 1560s. Few of these entries include last names, but they tend to apply the qualifiers *negro* and *mulato* to both men and women.[9] Thus, on July 9, 1560, Juan, son of "Lucrecia negra y de Diego de Ojeda," was baptized. His godparents were Luis Hidalgo and *"una mulata Mendoça."*[10] That the patrilineal trend determining the classification of the children of Spanish males and native women did not operate in unions involving women of African ancestry was partly a function of the institution of slavery and the Spanish legal principle of the "free womb" (*vientre libre*), which in order to protect the property rights of masters made the status of newborns follow that of their (enslaved) mothers.[11] It was also an early sign of Spanish colonial society's reluctance to fully incorporate blacks and their descendants as vecinos and naturales, to include them in the principal categories of sociopolitical belonging.

By contrast, early policies toward the offspring of Spanish–Indian parents encouraged their integration into Spanish society. In the 1550s, for example, the crown mandated that New Spain's officials take mestizos who were living in native towns and link them with their fathers, who were to raise them as good Christians, cultivate their love for Spain and all things Spanish, and distance them from the "vices" and rituals of the indigenous population.[12] Royal decrees also ordered the establishment of institutions aimed at integrating the children of Spanish–native unions into the república de españoles. Though not always carried out, various projects to found orphanages, boarding schools, monasteries, and dowry foundations for those who were destitute surfaced in Mexico City, Puebla, and other Spanish colonial towns.[13] The crown promoted the incorporation of mestizos into the Spanish community in order to lessen demographic imbalances as well as to cultivate their loyalty to Spain. But its early orders to transfer them to Spanish cities and parents were mainly aimed at those who were orphaned and not at those who were already being raised by families in native towns, whose classification varied.

Indeed, the offspring of colonists and native women could be considered Spaniards, mestizos, or Indians depending on such factors as their birth status (legitimacy), paternal recognition, and level of Hispanicization as well as on the community in which they were raised. Self-perceptions also played a role. Some individuals, especially those who had noble pre-Hispanic blood, identified more with their Indian ancestors. Ixtlilxóchitl, for example, was a mestizo (actually a *castizo*) according to the emerging Spanish system of classification, but he for the most part considered himself part of the indigenous nobility and was recognized as such. He recast native history largely in Spanish terms and to a certain extent distanced himself from the indigenous world of both the past and present, but he nonetheless claimed noble Indian status and the colonial privileges that it implied.

A more telling example of how children of Spanish and native parents could be classified is provided by some of the descendants of the conqueror Diego Muñoz, who was married to a Castilian but fathered at least two children with an indigenous woman. When he settled down to live in Mexico City, he apparently helped raise his illegitimate offspring, one of whom was Diego Muñoz Camargo (ca. 1528–99), the future historian of Tlaxcala.[14] In the 1580s, the historian accompanied a group of Tlaxcalan officials to Madrid and met with Philip II, who recognized him as the son of a conqueror. Muñoz Camargo married Leonor Vázquez, a native noblewoman of Ocotelulco, and had two legitimate children with her, Isabel and Diego. The historian became the *teniente* (deputy) of the Tlaxcalan municipal magistrate in 1583 and, being fluent in Castilian and Nahuatl, often acted as official interpreter for colonial administrators. Though he worked for Spanish authorities, Muñoz Camargo identified with native interests. As the son of a Spaniard, however, he could not hold a post in Tlaxcala's indigenous government. Muñoz Camargo's son, on the other hand, was able to take over the post of "Indian governor" of Tlaxcala after he married the highest-ranking native woman in the province.[15] At least some of the descendants of the union between Diego Muñoz the conquistador and an indigenous woman were thus absorbed into the category of indio. As this and other examples demonstrate, Spanish patrilineal principles, while dominant, did not always prevail. Official recognition of New Spain's native nobility and the establishment of a dual system of rights and privileges based on blood made a return to the "pure Indian" pole not only possible but, under certain circumstances, desirable.

In sixteenth-century central Mexican cities, then, the classification of the descendants of Spaniards and native people was not determined by descent alone (as it seldom was to be), or for that matter by gender, but by a variety of factors. Despite an overarching patrilineal trend, legitimacy, parental recognition, social rank, the initial demographic imbalances, strategies on the parts of both Spaniards and Indians, and level of acculturation could all play a role. At the end of the sixteenth century, however, patterns of classifications began to be based more squarely on ancestry. The term *mestizo*, for example, started to be applied to the children of Spanish and native unions on a more regular basis, regardless of legitimate birth and other factors. The shift from a patrilineal but relatively fluid model of classification to one that was based on both paternal and maternal bloodlines was manifested in the parish archives of various cities, which began to keep separate books for people of mixed ancestry: *libros de castas*. Mexico City's Sagrario Metropolitano started to keep separate baptismal records for the castas in 1603. Puebla's sagrario began to do so in 1607, and by 1661, it had also started to keep different marriage books for that population.[16]

Was the shift to a dual-descent model of classification related to developments in Spain, where maternal descent had become increasingly important due to the merger of requirements of nobility and purity of blood and the Inquisition's activities? Possibly, but more important were a series of sociodemographic, political, and religious trends in central Mexico that lessened the overall status of mestizos. These trends

included the growth of a Spanish population through natural reproduction and migration, which reduced the need to absorb the children of
mixed unions into the Spanish group. Furthermore, marriages between
Spanish males and noble indigenous women, never common in the first
place, became even less common as pre-Hispanic lineages declined,
which meant that the mestizo population was not only increasingly illegitimate but also more distanced from noble blood.[17] Another sociodemographic factor influencing the status of mestizos was the emergence
of a population of poor Spaniards. The problem was already considered
serious in the mid-sixteenth century, and in 1553 led Viceroy Luis de
Velasco to order Puebla's officials to attach all the Spaniards who did
not have professions, properties, or employers ("*oficios, haciendas, o
amos*") to masters.[18]

Nonetheless, the number of poor Spaniards continued to increase.
The growth of this population may not have been perceived as a problem
had it not been for the presence of persons of mixed descent who were
taking advantage of available economic opportunities or creating their
own. The historian Muñoz Camargo had several large properties as well
as cattle ranches and commercial enterprises, and Andrés Rodríguez, described by a contemporary source as an "Africano," was a merchant who
regularly made trips to and from Tlaxcala and Zacatecas.[19] These two
cases might have been exceptional, but it is well documented that persons of mixed descent acquired a strong presence in craft guilds and that
many engaged in petty commerce.[20] In Puebla, free blacks and mulattos quickly discovered that they could buy maize, wheat, chickens, salt,
fish, and various other products from the native population and then sell
them to Spaniards for a decent profit. The cabildo tried to put an end to
the practice in 1555 and subsequently made several attempts to prevent
persons of African ancestry from selling anything in the city.[21] As has
been suggested for Mexico City, the increase in poor Spaniards during
a period in which a small but significant portion of the population of
mixed ancestry was showing signs of economic advancement might have
made ancestry increasingly important for the maintenance of colonial
boundaries.[22] State policies, for one, reflect a desire to make that population into a free wage-labor force.

It would be misleading and reductionist, however, to attribute the
rise of the sistema de castas simply to socioeconomic tensions and processes, for there were other important dynamics at work. Politically,
the government started to consider mestizos a liability, especially after
the attempted rebellion of Martín Cortés, and to limit their rights and
privileges. The crown deemed the descendants of conquerors and noble
Indians an especially dangerous group because they had a double claim

to the land. Seeking to curb their power but not alienate them, it issued policies that sometimes affirmed their special status and at others undermined it. Although the process had started earlier, in the last third of the sixteenth century, a series of legal restrictions diminished the rights of mestizos and started to make them into "second-class citizens."[23] In the 1570s, for example, royal decrees prohibited them from carrying arms; from becoming public notaries, caciques, and municipal magistrates; and from holding the title of Protector of Indians.[24] Furthermore, in 1582, Philip II ordered New Spain's viceroy to sell certain offices in the audiencia (particularly that of receptor) only to the sons of conquerors and to ascertain that they were not *"mestizos o mulatos."*[25] Persons of mixed ancestry were also gradually not permitted to enter the most prestigious trades and guilds and particularly were barred from becoming masters in them.

Fears that mestizos would turn into a political threat combined with suspicions about their religious loyalties. Usually described simply as a system of social control that served to divide and rule colonial populations,[26] the sistema de castas emerged during the formal establishment of the Inquisition and was inseparable from rising concerns (and mendicant pessimism) over the persistence of pre-Hispanic religious practices and beliefs. Although the Holy Office did not receive permission to prosecute native people, the discourse of indigenous idolatry—to which both the formal inquisitorial tribunal and the provisorato de indios contributed—that surfaced after the mid-sixteenth century fed the Spanish interest in determining the origins of the Indians and in studying theories about the pre-Columbian inhabitants descending from one of the lost tribes of Israel.[27] Many of these theories linked the two groups by arguing that both had a predisposition to idol worshipping and that they had similar traditions of ritual sacrifice and cannibalism. Some Spanish writers made much of the fact that the words *judio* and *indio*, as written in sixteenth-century Spanish, were virtually indistinguishable. For the Carmelite friar Antonio Vázquez de Espinosa, for example, the orthographical similarity was not exactly evidence that the Indians derived from Jews, but it was certainly consistent with the theory.[28] The friar, who returned to Spain around 1622 after spending time in Peru and New Spain, also claimed that passages in the Bible indicated that the native population descended from one of the lost tribes of Israel, the one, incidentally, that had been condemned, "like mules," to perpetual servitude.[29]

The Spanish colonial discourse of idolatry, which drew heavily from anti-Semitic thought and tropes, had implications not only for the native people but for mestizos and other casta categories, some of which were revealed in a 1576 letter written by Mexican inquisitors to the Suprema. The letter, which made a case for depriving people of partial indigenous descent from inquisitorial offices and posts, stated that Spaniards in New Spain avoided the company of "indios mestizos or castizos" because they generally considered them "vile and despicable" and incorrigible liars. For that same reason, the authors continued, these categories of people were not admitted into monasteries nor allowed to take the habit, but some were able to do both because of their white skin color, which allowed them to conceal their "true descent." And if their negative characteristics were not enough to deny them access to posts in the Holy Office, there was also the matter of their ancestry, which some writers had speculated had its origins with the Palestinians (the term used in the letter). The issue was not resolved, the inquisitors noted, but there was "persuasive evidence" linking the two populations, such as similarities between Hebrew words and indigenous ones, and their "likeness in habits, rituals, sacrifices, dress, blankets [and] long hair":

and because many things that happened to these [Indians] were announced for the Jews by the Prophets; and also because they [the people that speculate about this issue] see the name Indio, and presume that it has been altered, and that the N should be joined at the bottom so that it says Judio. These rumors and general thinking and assumptions, together with the vileness and baseness and depraved customs of the descendants of these [Indians], seem sufficient reason not admit to them into the offices of the Inquisition nor to any other ministerial post, and if the contrary was done it would come as a great surprise and shock.[30]

The Mexican inquisitors' letter, which oozes anxieties over the possible Semitic origins of the Indians, was written as the notion of purity of blood was starting to be adapted to the colonial context and ancestry was becoming an exclusionary tool. The issue of idolatry played a crucial role in this exclusionary process because, at least in the minds of religious officials, it associated the native people not only with the ancient Hebrews but also with the conversos. Technically, the veneration of idols was considered a different type of religious transgression than heresy, the persistent rejection of the church doctrine by those who were baptized and taught the main principles of the faith.[31] But because the indigenous people had been "cleansed" by holy water and in theory indoctrinated, some colonial authorities argued that their lingering allegiance to their old deities, by breaking with Christianity's monotheistic precept that *latría* (adoration) is owed exclusively to God, constituted not only apostasy but heresy. Frustrated by the removal of the mass of native people from their jurisdiction, inquisitors in particular insisted that the Holy Office should be allowed to try idolaters as heretics.

Indeed, in a 1619 letter to the Suprema, Mexican inquisitors claimed that some "ladino Indians" were returning to their idolatry, superstitions, and sorcery and spreading their ideas not only among native people but also among Spaniards.[32] These and other wrongdoings, the authors lamented, were common in New Spain but could not be dealt with properly because the Holy Office could not try Indians. The officials pointed out that if in Europe the Inquisition had been given authority to deal even with "infidel Jews and Moors, when they carry out their rituals and ceremonies in Christian lands, [thereby] providing bad examples [for Christians]," with more reason should it be able to try a population that had been baptized. Their requests were not heeded, but various Spanish priests and writers continued to link the idolatrous traditions of the Indians to those of the ancient Jews, and their refusal to completely relinquish their old gods and beliefs to the "heresy" of the conversos, thus pulling the native people and their descendants into the discourse of purity of blood.

Initially the connection between pre-Hispanic native religious practices and impurity was not explicit. But by placing the indigenous people and their descendants on a lower spiritual plane than Old Christian Spaniards, the supposedly recurring problem of idolatry prompted religious authorities to question native qualifications not only to work for the Inquisition but also to be ordained as priests and have access to ecclesiastical offices and benefices. By the 1570s, some cathedral chapters had constitutions that made mestizo priests ineligible for ecclesiastical posts and benefices. Thus, when in 1571 the bishop of Antequera wrote to the crown proposing that Cristóbal Gil should not have the post of treasurer in the cathedral because he was not a "pure Spaniard," his letter included a list of other priests who had "raça de mestizos" and were therefore disqualified from accessing benefices.[33] The descendants of Spanish–Indian unions were allowed to enter the priesthood in the 1580s, but only if they were exceptionally qualified. Because there was a shortage of priests who spoke native languages, this acceptance was understood to be a matter of necessity and strongly contingent on candidates' submitting proof of their qualifications in the form of "*informes de calidad y méritos*," which included birth and genealogical information. Not yet addressed directly in relation to colonial populations, the issue of limpieza de sangre nonetheless loomed in the background.

The Mexican historian Francisco Morales believes that the first Spaniard to explicitly link the indigenous people to both the ancient Jews and the issue of purity of blood was the Franciscan Gerónimo de Mendieta.[34] In his *Historia Eclesiástica Indiana*, finished in 1604, the friar stated that just as those who had converted from Judaism were prevented from joining religious orders because they were "new" Christians, so too should the Indians, for they also were new to the faith.[35] He pointed out that even though the primitive church had allowed recently converted gentiles and Jews as priests and bishops, experiences with New Christians (meaning the conversos) had led the papacy to bar the descendants of "infidels" within the fourth degree from professing in the religious orders and the Franciscans to codify this exclusion in their statutes. According to Mendieta, a few Indians had been given the habit in the early phases of evangelization, but during their novitiate year they had proven to be "unsuitable" for the order. Therefore, the Franciscans—the same order that had helped lead the campaign to create the Spanish Inquisition and which by 1525 had installed purity requirements—had established a statute against accepting them altogether. Arguments about insufficient knowledge of the Catholic faith and unproven loyalty to it were also used against mestizos. Although both groups had already been barred from the Franciscan Order in central Mexico, their exclusion became part of the order's purity statute in 1614.

Spanish concerns with the issue of native idolatry, which increased from the 1560s onward, were accompanied not only by the extension of Iberian notions of impurity to colonial populations but also by the construction of indigenous women's bodies as vehicles of contamination. The ability of the discourse of limpieza de sangre to turn women into sources of impurity had already manifested itself in Spain. In Mexico, the prohibition of indigenous religions ("idolatry"), which like Christianity and Judaism were not confined to a series of beliefs but encompassed various levels of social life and were inscribed in everyday rituals and practices,[36] enhanced the importance of spirituality in the household. That is, the colonial church's efforts to annihilate pre-Hispanic cults, priests, and public rituals lessened the role that native men played in perpetuating indigenous forms of understanding and experiencing the sacred. Religious officials were not as effective at policing the indigenous household, in which women tended to be more crucial in the transmission of knowledge about the natural and supernatural.

In the more private domain of the home, traditional practices related to the keeping of sacred household objects, celebrating rites of passage and marriage, dealing with sickness, and so forth tended to survive. Women were prominent in these activities and in particular in rituals to ward off sickness, to prevent the dangers of childbirth, to protect children from malignant supernatural forces, and to heal. Their critical role in the process of "acculturation and counter-acculturation"[37] enabled the projection of Spanish colonial anxieties over the failure of the conversion project, and indeed, over impurity, onto their bodies. Like conversas and moriscas, native women became strongly associated with the transmission of their ancestors' cultural-religious forms. And just as Old Christian concerns with safeguarding purity of blood were expressed in terms of anxieties about the fluids of impure women in the metropole, so too in the colonial context, where the metaphor of contaminating breast milk also became common. This metaphor served to refer to the transmission of all sorts of practices from native (and later black) wet nurses to children, and in particular to mark mestizos and creoles as impure.

At the start of the seventeenth century, the category of mestizo, like that of Indian, was deeply embedded in discourses of religious conversion and being linked, more often than not implicitly, to the concept of limpieza de sangre. This development, along with the socioeconomic and political trends that were sketched out above, explains the declining status of people of Spanish–Indian ancestry and the increasing preoccupation with ancestry at the end of the 1500s. But it does not entirely clarify the emergence of the sistema de castas and more specifically the form that it took. Explaining the nature of the system requires a deeper understanding of the impact of the formal recognition of native purity on patterns of categorization and of the consequences of the institution of slavery on the classification of blacks and their descendants.

CASTE, SLAVERY, AND COLONIAL MEXICO'S GENDERED SYMBOLICS OF BLOOD

The construction of casta categories and processes of political and economic disenfranchisement that accompanied it escalated in the seventeenth century. During the early decades, for example, vecindad was transformed, at least in Spanish towns (native ones had their own citizenship regime), from an administrative to an informal status and made virtually exclusive to Spaniards.[38] Moreover, in the 1630s, in response to a petition from professors at the University of Mexico, the crown prohibited the matriculation of Indians, mulattos, and illegitimate mestizos and made them ineligible to hold university degrees. The decision was extremely important in terms of constructing religious and political hierarchies because university degrees were necessary for most high-ranking posts in the church and state. Restrictive legislation, however, generally did not lump all the castas together. Mestizos, especially if legitimate, tended to occupy a different place within the "republic of Spaniards" than mulattos.

Irrespective of how certain institutions were operating and the linkages that some colonial officials drew between Indians and Jews, and between idolatry and heresy, the crown and key jurists and theologians continued to uphold the notion that native people were pure and thus to allow for their possible access, and that of their descendants, to the category of Old Christians and, indeed, to that of Spaniard. Thus, when the Dominican friar Gregorio García discussed the theory that the native people descended from ancient Hebrews in his early seventeenth-century treatise, titled *Origen de los indios del Nuevo Mundo*, he made sure to stress that even if it turned out to be true, their blood was nonetheless pure. He reasoned that if the Indians did indeed have Jewish ancestors, it was possible that they had arrived in the New World before the death of Christ. The implication was that the indigenous population did not descend from deicides—an aspersion commonly cast on Jews in Christian Europe—and thus that their genealogies were not stained.[39] This affirmation of Indian purity enabled García not only to defend the right that mestizos had to access offices in the government and the church (prerogatives of natives of a jurisdiction) but to include them in the "Spanish nation" (*nación*):

When uniting that part of the Indians that such Spaniards have with the Spanish Nation, said part loses whatever negative association it had, and gains much from the one that now accompanies it, from which, since it is better, and more honorable, the said descendants take the surname and name Spaniard, even if they are mestizos and have the same percentage of Indian and Spanish parts, and as [Spaniards] they are admitted in the Republic's honorable posts and government, and to other places and things of honor and Religion, and are not excluded because of having Indian parts . . . [which they ordinarily derive] from their maternal line.[40]

In the early modern period, the term *nación* (from the verb *nacer*, "to be born") had different connotations, one of its most common referring to a group with the same origin, sharing birthplace and lineage as well as language and culture. Thus, Old Christians sometimes described converted Jews as members of the "Hebrew nation," as in *"los de nación hebrea descendientes de Judios"* ("those of the Hebrew nation descending from Jews").[41] In Spanish America, the concept of nación also usually meant an ethnolinguistic group, and it was in this sense that Gregorio García used it when he asserted that mestizos were eligible for honors and offices in the republic because of their "Spanish parts." Colonial archives provide ample examples of Spaniards who disagreed, and as previously discussed, certain institutions and royal policies did limit their rights. Nonetheless, the friar's construction of mestizos as Spaniards was articulated in different colonial laws and texts and reflected the adaptation of the generational and genealogical formulas of the Castilian concept of limpieza de sangre to the colonial context. Thanks to the belief that blood was a vehicle for the transmission of all sorts of qualities, the descendants of Indians could become Old Christians by demonstrating, for several generations, their devotion to the faith, and by reproducing with "pure" Spaniards.

This construction of the Spanish-Indian "mixture" was gendered because it coded Spanish blood as stronger and masculine. Its logic was that Indian blood could be completely absorbed into Spanish blood not only because it was unsullied but because it was "weak." García thus alluded to the mestizo's purported physiological weakness and "feminine" characteristics (such as the inability to grow a beard), which the friar argued derived from his "Indian parts." Drawing from Galenic theories of humors, he claimed that the climate of the region had made native bodies humid, like those of women, and thus not conducive to the growth of facial hair, as well as intellectually and physically weak, and in general "effeminate and pusillanimous" (*"afeminados, i pusilanimes"*).[42] García's characterization of Spanish–Indian unions was thus built on certain binaries that were coded female and male and that implied an imbalance of strength and power between the two groups. Spanish colonial society's dominant "symbolics of blood" thus echoed the sociopolitical relationship between the two republics as compatible but hierarchical and paternalistic. It simultaneously reflected the gendering effects of power and the powerful effects of gender, instrumental not only for conceptualizing but for constructing and reproducing colonial hierarchies.[43]

The colonial discourse of native weakness was prominent in Spanish colonial society. It originated in the sixteenth century at the time that the indigenous population began to decline. To deal with the resulting shortages of labor for Spanish mining, ranching, and sugar enterprises, the crown allowed the importation of black slaves into its American territories. A single black, some Spaniards claimed, was three or four times stronger than an Indian—a claim that helped them to rationalize both the system of enslavement and the demographic drop among the indigenous population. Thus, Viceroy Martín Enríquez described with awe the strength of mulattos (here referring to children of black men and indigenous women) when compared to mestizos. Thanks to the "nature" of his black father, he claimed, a mulatto was to a mestizo like "a man to a doll."[44] The viceroy's depiction of the two castas—his use of a gendered simile to mark a relationship of power—was not unique, but rather reflected larger discourses that feminized native people and masculinized blacks and that were linked to Spanish political, economic, and religious projects.

Whereas Spanish colonial ideology generally construed sexual reproduction between Spaniards and the indigenous population as a redemptive process—one in which Indian blood could be completely absorbed into Old Christian lineages—it seldom allowed blacks the possibility of full "redemption" and their full incorporation into the "Spanish nation." The lower status of African ancestry within colonial Mexico's blood symbolism owed much to slavery, which in the sixteenth century was still understood, as in the late medieval period, as an economic and religious institution. According to the Siete Partidas, the thirteenth-century legal code that constituted the juridical basis of the Spanish monarchy, freedom was the natural human condition, and only three types of people could be deprived of it: enemies of Christianity who were captured in "just wars," children of slave women, and individuals who sold themselves under certain circumstances. The prevailing notion that co-religionists should not be enslaved, which the late medieval Christian world had borrowed from Muslims, rhetorically framed slavery as a religious institution and connected slaves to infidelity, paganism, and sin.[45]

By the time of Spanish expansion to the Americas, Iberians already had a long history of enslaving Africans and of developing negative attitudes toward people with dark skin. In the second half of the fifteenth century, antiblack imagery intensified on the peninsula due to the establishment of the Portuguese African slave trade, which began in 1441 and was stimulated by the 1453 capture of Constantinople by Ottoman Turks. The fall of the city cut Christian Europe's access to slaves from the Black Sea and Balkan regions and led to a clear shift to sub-Saharan Africa as the main source of forced labor for western Europeans. Although Spanish cities such as Seville and Valencia (main recipients of African slaves) had populations of free blacks, the shift reinforced pre-existing Castilians associations of slavery and "blackness."[46] These associations, however, need not have determined the nature of slavery in Spanish America. During and after the conquest, not all slaves were black and not all blacks were slaves.[47] Persons of African descent participated in Spanish expeditions and conquests, and after the foundation of cities including Havana, Mexico City, and Puebla, some were allowed to obtain titles of vecindad (especially if they had Spanish fathers).[48] But their status generally declined after the mid-sixteenth century, when the New Laws helped make the condition of inheritable slavery exclusive to blacks.

The momentous decision to ban the enslavement of native people was prompted by numerous factors, among them the fear that the practice would lead to their extinction, the role of the church in defending indigenous rights, and the crown's desire to prevent the encomenderos from becoming a feudal nobility. That Spaniards did not prohibit the use of black slaves, on the other hand, was partly due to the growing European perception of Africa as a land of infidels and barbarians, Iberia's experience and familiarity with black slaves, the prior establishment of trading networks in West Africa by the Portuguese, and the cooperation of African slave traders.[49] Also of crucial importance were the political responsibilities that Spain had in the Americas. As the jurist Solórzano y Pereira later declared, because conversion could take place only through gentle means and persuasion, the crown's responsibility for delivering the Indians to Catholicism, on which its titles to lands in the Americas depended, could be achieved only by respecting their natural and ancient liberty.[50] The very application of the concept of *naturales* (natives) to the indigenous population drew from the Scholastic tradition and implied recognition of their right, as a people who were in their lands and had submitted to Christianity, to live in their own polities, with their own political leaders, institutions, and hierarchies.[51] Although in some regions the enslavement of Indians continued even after the passage of the New Laws, the principle of their freedom became a crucial component of Spanish colonial ideology, central to Spain's justification of its continued presence in the Americas.

Perhaps because Spanish sovereignty in the Americas did not rest on the idea of respecting the freedom of Africans, who after all were not in their own lands, relatively little thought was given to the legitimacy of the transatlantic slave trade. Bartolomé de Las Casas, one of the main advocates of the liberation of the native people, was apparently not as troubled by the brutal treatment of Africans and owned some himself. Although he modified his views toward the end of his life, he along with other colonial officials proposed that labor shortages be resolved through the importation of black slaves.[52] To be sure, a few theologians did voice strong opposition to the enslavement of blacks, including Archbishop Alonso de Montúfar. In 1560, he wrote to Philip II asking how a Christian king could allow for the enslavement of blacks when there appeared to be no just cause for it. Noting that His Majesty and his predecessors (Charles V and the Catholic Kings) had acted in a noble and just manner when they freed the baptized Indians, the archbishop wanted to know why the merchandising of slaves from Guinea and other areas "conquered" by the Portuguese was being permitted.

In a remarkable statement for its time, Archbishop Montúfar challenged the principal arguments that Spaniards used to justify slavery. He pointed out that the claim that blacks could be enslaved because they were enemies of Christianity did not have much validity because those who were introduced to it seemed to be accepting it in good faith and were not waging war against Christians. Responding to writers who excused the practice on the basis that it was controlled by Africans themselves, Montúfar added that if enslavement was common in Africa, it was because it had been stimulated by the large profits that resulted from satisfying European demand. "[N]or does it seem to be sufficient cause," he continued, "that said blacks receive spiritual and corporal benefits from their captivity under the Christians, in particular because in such captivity they are often times or routinely subject to harms that are antithetical to their salvation."[53] Montúfar could not reconcile the enslavement of peoples who had accepted baptism with Christian principles—the last potentially liberating because they posed freedom as the natural condition of humanity—and urged the crown to condemn the institution. If saving the souls of blacks was the goal, the archbishop wrote at the end of his letter, instead of "rescuing" them through slavery in order to convert them, the Holy Gospel should be preached to them in their lands, where both their bodies and souls were free and thus more open to receiving the message of God.

During the following decades and early seventeenth century, a few other Spanish voices were raised against the transatlantic slave trade. Particularly strong critiques of slavery were written by Bartolomé Albornoz in the 1570s and by the Jesuit Alonso de Sandoval in 1627.[54] Sandoval, who described in great detail the horrific conditions under which Africans were captured and transported to the Americas, defended the intellectual capacities of blacks. If they did not have mental faculties, he argued, no one would be bothering to try to convert them. But notwithstanding the arresting image of bodies and souls in captivity that critics of the slave trade sometimes painted, the system was allowed to continue, in part because the sale of licenses to the Portuguese for importing blacks into the Americas had by the late sixteenth century become an important source of revenue for the Castilian crown.[55] But despite the obvious economic interests behind the transatlantic slave trade, Spaniards continued to justify their enslavement partly in religious terms and, more concretely, to mark slaves as Muslim infidels. Thus, some bills of sales of Africans contained the inscription "captured in just war, subject to servitude." The linkage with Islam was not entirely fictitious, for most of the slaves that the Portuguese shipped to Spanish America during the fifteenth and sixteenth centuries were from the Upper Guinea region (now Senegambia), which had a significant population of Muslims.[56] Although Spanish laws stipulated that all slaves had to be baptized and taught the basic principles of the faith, the persistent presumption that they retained their "infidel" ways led to various efforts to try limit their contact with native people.[57] Their efforts were on the whole not successful, in part because the principle of the free womb encouraged unions between black men and indigenous women and quickly led to the rise of a free population of mixed African and native ancestries (labeled "mulatto" at first).

The association of blackness with infidelity also facilitated the extension of Castilian concepts of limpieza de sangre to persons of African descent. As the transatlantic slave trade was consolidated, various Spanish writers on both sides of the Atlantic, including Juan de Torquemada, started to identify dark skin color as a marker of divine punishment and, more specifically, to attribute the enslavement of blacks to the curse of Ham.[58] Some also began to refer to blacks in terms of "race" and "impurity." Early records of passengers from Spain to Spanish America reveal that blacks and mulattos were sometimes listed in Seville's Casa de Contratación's registers as Spaniards (as well as *negros* and *mulatos*) and that some were even classified as *cristianos viejos*, particularly when their fathers were Old Christians.[59] Thus, although people of African descent were already being marked by their skin color, they were not yet uniformly considered genealogically impure. This situation began to change in the late sixteenth century. In his chronicle of the life of Charles V, for example, Fray Prudencio de Sandoval compared the supposed inability of the descendants of converted Jews to rid themselves of their "Jewish race" with that of the descendants of blacks to separate themselves (even with "thousands" of white ancestors) from the "accident of their negritude."[60] Who would deny, wrote the friar and bishop of Pamplona, "that in the descendants of Jews remains and lasts the bad inclination of their ancient ingratitude and failed beliefs, like in blacks the inseparable accident of their negritude? For if one thousand times they are with white women their children are born with the dark skin of their parents."[61] Tellingly, Sandoval's comments not only construe Jewish and black ancestries as ineffaceable stains, and hence threatening to Old Christian lineages, but betray a particular anxiety about sexual relations between black males and white women.

In the colonial context, just as in the metropolitan one, anxieties over genealogical contamination were largely displaced onto the field of women's sexuality, the privileged site for the containment of race/caste ambiguities. Within the emerging sistema de castas, in which classification based on both bloodlines and the status of purity implied having access to economic resources and political rights and offices, control of female reproductive capacities was crucial for perpetuating the hierarchical and racialized social order. Unions between black men and Spanish women were the most threatening to that order because they undermined one of its main psychological premises, the inaccessibility of the latter to all but Spanish men. They were also problematic because if they became commonplace, they would compromise the dominant group's limpieza de sangre. Black blood was more threatening to Spanish lineages than that of native people because Spanish men who reproduced with indigenous women could, over the course of a few generations, reproduce their purity status. What they could not do was to completely "redeem" or "purify" their children with black women—the "seeds" of blacks were, like those of Jews and Muslims, apparently too potent to be completely assimilated.

That women of African descent could not produce "pure Spaniards" was a legacy of the institution of slavery and the way it tried to ensure that children of female slaves remained the property of masters, that is, by making their status follow that of their mothers. It was also a product of efforts to deny the descendants of blacks the political and economic privileges that the status of purity implied and in general any genealogical claims. As property, slaves were not able to make many claims based on birth and their masters and government officials normally tried to prevent them from creating a communal identity. Through a process that Orlando Patterson calls "natal alienation," they were to relinquish their heritage as well as the possibility of bequeathing it to their descendants.[62] This denial didn't mean that slaves did not forge ties to the past and among themselves, just that Spanish society seldom recognized them as legitimate or binding. The absence of slave surnames in many parish records in a sense reflected an ideology that sought to obstruct or destroy black communal identities and memory of the African past.[63] African-descended people were strongly discouraged from congregating, creating their own associations, and in general from engaging in activities that would allow them to nurture a collective identity.[64] Several colonial Mexican cities allowed blacks to form *cofradías* (religious brotherhoods) for the sake of fomenting their Christian religiosity, and some of these confraternities thrived, becoming important and ongoing sites of religious and cultural expression for blacks and their descendants.[65] But the Spanish population's persistent fears that such institutions would enable free and enslaved people of African ancestry to unite and plan rebellions periodically led government officials to attempt to outlaw them and on various occasions led to their temporary suspension.

Freedom did not necessarily make it easier for blacks to either exist as communities or make genealogical claims. Because their progenitors were generally assumed to have arrived as slaves, they were not recognized as a community that had willingly accepted Christianity and Spanish rule and that was in a contractual relationship with the Castilian crown. Lacking the status of a "republic" and marked as descendants of natives of distant, infidel lands who had lost their freedom, African Mexicans were denied access to full vecindad rights and to the category of Old Christian. Thus, the issuing of vecino titles to blacks and their descendants, which although on a limited basis had taken place before, became increasingly rare in the late sixteenth century. They were also normally not allowed to serve as witnesses in civil or ecclesiastical tribunals because, civil and religious authorities argued, their Old Christian status could not be confirmed. Spanish laws and institutions tended not to validate claims that the descendants of slaves had been Christians since "time immemorial." As late as the eighteenth century, people of partial African ancestry were described by some colonial officials, and sometimes presented themselves, as deriving from slaves and having infidel origins.[66]

Spanish colonial discourses regarding persons of African ancestry, which rendered their political ties and religious loyalties as suspect, were immersed in contradictions. Parts of Africa (mainly in the Kongo and Angola) had accepted Christianity, for example, and some blacks in Spain and the Americas had proven, and were acknowledged, to be sincere Christians. Spanish secular authorities constantly worried that African-descended people would use confraternities to plan rebellions, but some black sodalities became known for their piety. Furthermore, although colonial reports tended to construe blacks as disloyal and subversive elements,[67] a significant number served in colonial militias, which were avenues to honor and social advancement. In central New Spain, people of African descent provided military services as early as the sixteenth century and in subsequent centuries played a critical role in the Spanish defense of the Circum-Caribbean.[68] Moreover, even though Spaniards associated persons of African descent with slavery and tried to relegate them to the lowest socioeconomic levels, their place in Mexican society was at no point monolithic. At the end of the sixteenth century, they not only participated in a number of crucial rural and urban economic activities[69] but also had a significant presence in Spanish households and were highly prized by their masters not just as a source of labor. According to various viceregal reports, even Spaniards of modest backgrounds made it a priority to purchase posts in local government for no other reason than to acquire black retinues and the symbolic capital that they embodied.[70] Indeed, in Mexico, where no separate planter class emerged, many colonial officials had slaves, thus turning them into a part of the theater of domination, into public symbols of the economic, social, and military might of their masters.

By the early seventeenth century, both Mexico City and Puebla had rising numbers of free and enslaved Africans who were relatively integrated into Spanish colonial society. Many lived in close proximity to Spanish residents and tended to be relatively acculturated, especially those who had been raised in the Americas and worked in Spanish households. Spaniards referred to these blacks and mulattos as either *criollos* (creoles) or *ladinos,* the latter term having been used in Spain to refer to Muslims and Jews who mastered the Castilian language or were

Hispanicized to the point that they could not be distinguished from "authentic Spaniards."[71] No matter how "creolized" or "Latinized" persons of African ancestry in central Mexico were, their strong presence in the dominant culture's intimate, familial sphere made Spanish men anxious and distrustful, constantly on guard that at any moment their male slaves and servants would try to kill them, usurp power, and take their white women. In 1612, Spanish fantasies of racial and sexual violence in Mexico City played a prominent role in the circulation of rumors about a "black conspiracy" that led the audiencia to conduct an investigation, convict thirty-five blacks and mulattos, and order their executions.[72] Because cofradía leaders were implicated in the alleged plot, the tribunal also ordered the temporary dismantling of all black sodalities.

Spanish fantasies, or rather nightmares, of racial violence and dispossession surfaced periodically in Mexico. Tending to take a similar form, they reflected the existence of an arena of competing patriarchies in which power was symbolized by the phallus and enacted upon on the bodies of women, particularly their wombs.[73] These fantasy-nightmares usually conjured up a world in which it was no longer the labor, sexual, and reproductive power of women of African descent that was being appropriated and transferred to the dominant group, but that of Spanish women; in which it was not blackness but whiteness that was marked as inferior and targeted (through reproductive and classificatory patterns) for extinction; and in which black men were not stateless but had their own kingdom and, with it, privileged access to all women. The phantasmagoria of a black republic was clearly a product of a racialized sociopolitical order that denied the patriarchal rights of black men and transformed the bodies, children, and labor of black women into the property of Spanish men. It betrayed the particularly deep connections that slavery had created between racial, gender, and economic subordination as well as Spanish colonial society's chronic anxieties over "black blood." These anxieties were reflected in the very categories of the sistema de castas, which mainly marked as impure people of African descent.

RAZA, CASTA, AND LIMPIEZA DE SANGRE: THE SPANISH COLONIAL LANGUAGE OF RACE

Raza and *casta,* terms central to early modern Spain's lexicon of blood, both referred to breed, species, and lineage, and could thus be used interchangeably to describe groupings of animals, plants, or humans.[74] Their uses and connotations were not identical, however. Whereas the first became strongly identified with descent from Jews and Muslims and acquired negative connotations, the second remained more neutral and was hence more frequently applied to Old Christians.[75] But *casta* also had multiple meanings. If as a noun it was usually linked to lineage, as an adjective it could allude to chastity, nobility ("good breeding"), and legitimacy, and more generally to an uncorrupted sexual and genealogical history. *Casta* was thereby able to give way to the term *castizo*, which referred to notable ancestry.[76] By implication, the mother of a castizo would have been casta, a woman who had remained faithful to her husband. When applied to humans, then, the sixteenth-century Spanish word *casta* and its various connotations were alluding to a system of social order centered around procreation and biological parenthood, one in which reproducing the pure and noble "caste" was mainly predicated on maintaining the chastity of its women. Whether in Spain or Spanish America, notions of genealogical purity and their privileging of endogamic marriage and legitimate birth were never divorced from discourses of gender and female sexuality, from a sexual economy constituted by gendered notions of familial honor.

In the colonial context, Spaniards came up with even more uses for the word *casta*, for by the mid-sixteenth century it was functioning, in the plural, as an umbrella term for the children of "mixed" unions.[77] In Mexico, this application of the term began around the mid-sixteenth century, almost simultaneous with the rise of a nomenclature distinguishing people of different lineages, its first and most enduring terms being *mestizo* and *mulato*. Hence, when later in the sixteenth century Diego de Simancas, a man of Spanish and native parentage, was tried by the Mexican Inquisition for allegedly believing that Jesus was not the true son of God, he was asked to declare not his "race," but his "caste."[78] The dominant colonial usage of the term *casta* simultaneously signaled the importance of reproduction and sexuality to the colonial order and the increasing anxieties about being able to control them. The Augustinian friar Nicolás de Witte expressed these anxieties in 1552, when he wrote about the difficulty of maintaining peace in Mexico. The land, he noted,

is engendering and is being populated by a mixture of evil people. For it is clear that this land is full of mestizos, who are [born] so badly inclined. It is full of black men and women who derive from slaves. It is full of black men who marry Indian women, from which derive mulattos. And it is full of mestizos who marry Indian women, from which derive a diverse caste [casta] of infinite number, and from all of these mixtures derive other diverse and not very good mixtures.[79]

The emerging system of classification relied on the idea that each of the three main colonial categories—Spaniards, Indians, and blacks—

was characterized by a unity of substance that was maintained through endogamy but could be broken through sexual intercourse outside the group. As other naturalizing discourses, the sistema de castas held sex as a productive act that could pollute or dilute blood, which in turn could generate sick and degenerate beings, or at the very least pose classificatory problems within the hierarchy of allegedly natural categories.[80] Indeed, the system allowed for a virtually infinite number of castes to be produced. Did the premises of the sistema de castas and in particular the belief in discreet human groups challenge the theory of monogenesis? Not according to Gregorio García. Realizing the dangerous theological implications of applying the concepts of purity and mixture to people, he pointed out that mestizo animals could come from distinct creatures but be part of the same species. Likewise, individuals could belong to different "nations" or "lineages" but be part of the same Adam-derived human species.[81] García seemed to be echoing Fray Juan de Pineda's discussion, in his *Diálogos familiares de la agricultura cristiana* (1578–1580), of marriages between Old Christians and New Christians and in particular his comparison of horse breeding with human reproduction to argue that even though all people derived from the founding biblical couple, some lineages were better than others and therefore should avoid mixing with lesser ones. The influence of understandings of reproduction in the natural world on Spanish thinking about human reproduction proved to be even stronger in the colonial context, as evidenced, for example, by the numerous casta categories created from zoological terms.

Once the term *casta* was applied to people of mixed ancestry, it began to acquire negative connotations, but it remained distinct from the concept of raza and its religious undertones. Hence, mestizos, mulattos, and in a general sense also Spaniards and Indians were considered castes, lineages, but not necessarily races. Or rather, not all of these categories were thought to have "race." Anthropologist Laura Lewis is thus partly correct when she asserts that early modern Spain elaborated an exclusionary discourse on race within its peninsular borders at the same time that it created a more inclusive system of caste in the Americas, one that allowed the different castas to claim to be connected through genealogical or symbolic kinship ties.[82] Such a rigid distinction between the two systems of differentiation cannot be drawn, however. Not only did caste in the colonies become racialized over time, an increasingly naturalizing discourse, but as stressed earlier, by the late sixteenth century, Iberian notions of race and impurity had started to be used against persons of African ancestry. This use was captured in the probanzas de limpieza de sangre. In 1599, for example, Cristóbal Ruiz de Quiroz submitted his genealogical information to the Franciscan Order in Puebla

in order to prove that he descended from "a clean caste and generation, without the race or mixture of Moors, mulattoes, blacks, Jews or
the newly converted to the Holy Catholic Faith."[83] The following year,
Pedro Serrano, a native of Seville who applied to be a royal secretary in
the Philippines, submitted his genealogical information in order to establish that his ancestors had not been tried by the Holy Office and that
they were pure Old Christians, "clean from the races of moriscos, Jews,
blacks and mulattoes."[84]

The extension of Castilian notions of race and impurity to persons
of African ancestry was also reflected in casta nomenclature. For example, the term *mestizo*, which surfaced in the 1530s and by the next
decade had become almost synonymous with illegitimacy, simply meant
"mixed" and had been used in Spain mainly to refer to the mixture of
different animal species.[85] The category of *mulato*, which in the Spanish
colonies appeared on a regular basis only as of 1549, referred to the
children of Spaniards and blacks and in general to anyone with partial
African ancestry. In both Mexico and Peru, it was initially applied to
persons of either black–Spanish or black–native parentage, but in the
seventeenth century, a separate, though sporadically used, category for
the latter was created, that of *zambahigo* (*zambo* in Peru).[86] According
to Solórzano Pereira, the term *mulato* was used to describe the offspring
of Spaniards and blacks because they were considered an uglier and more
unique mixture than mestizos and because the word conveyed the idea
that their nature was akin to that of mules.[87] Although both *mestizo*
and *mulato* derived from a zoological vocabulary and implied cross-
breeding, their use marked an important difference in Spanish attitudes
toward reproduction with blacks and indigenous people.

Covarrubias, who also linked the word *mulato* to that of *mule*,
pointed out that mules were bastard animals, a "third species" that was
produced by the crossing of horses with donkeys and that could reproduce only under extraordinary circumstances.[88] As such, the term was
reminiscent of *alboraico* (or *alboraique*), a pejorative name for conversos. Originally the word referred to the Prophet Muhammad's fabled
animal, which was neither horse nor mule, but in fifteenth-century
Spain, it was used to convey that the New Christians were neither Jews
nor Christians but a kind of unnatural or third species, one that presumably had difficulties reproducing. In the case of the term *mulato*,
its trope of infertility perhaps served the same function in the Spanish
colonial world that it had in the French colonies: simultaneously easing
white anxieties about the uncontrolled growth of populations descending from slaves and sanctioning the continued sexual exploitation of enslaved women by their masters.[89] What is clear is that the word *mulato*,

which for some Spaniards connoted ugliness, was inextricably linked to social and reproductive relations promoted by the institution of slavery and incipient Western notions of beauty and race.

Spanish views about reproduction with blacks versus native people become even more evident in the next two casta categories that surfaced in central Mexico: castizo and morisco. These for the most part did not appear in early parish registers but were used in some colonial administrative and Inquisition documents. *Castizo*, which emerged in the last third of the sixteenth century, referred to the child of a Spaniard and a mestizo, that is, to someone who was three-quarters Spanish and one-quarter Indian.[90] *Morisco* was at first more ambiguous, for it was associated with Islam, blacks, or both.[91] In New Spain, it continued to be applied to Muslim converts to Christianity. Thus, in the early 1600s, María Ruiz, a morisca residing in Mexico City and native of Granada, Spain, was tried for being a follower of the "sect of Muhammad."[92] In subsequent decades, the word *morisco* increasingly referred to the children of Spaniards and mulattos. For example, in 1631, the Mexican Inquisition tried Agustín, a "morisco or mulatto," for idolatry; in 1658, it reviewed the case of Beatriz de Padilla, "an unmarried morisca, daughter of a Spaniard and a free mulata"; and in 1693, it tried Francisca de Chiquacen, a "mulatto of the morisco race" ("*mulata de raza morisca*") for sorcery.[93]

Needless to say, the terms *castizo* and *morisco* carried significantly different cultural baggage. In Spain, the first had been used to describe a person of good lineage and caste and the second to designate ex-Muslims, thus carrying connotations of religious infidelity. It is true that when Mexican Inquisition officials first explained the meaning of *castizo* in their 1576 letter to the Suprema, they did not associate the category with any redeeming qualities. Nevertheless, the displacement of a word that in Castile mainly had positive connotations onto the children of mestizos and Spaniards was no linguistic accident. It not only acknowledged the aristocratic bloodlines of some castizos, descendants of Spanish conquerors and noble native women, but also signaled the construction of a specific type of discourse of "mixture," one that recognized the purity, or potential purity, of native lineages (especially if they were noble).

Indeed, in the last decades of the sixteenth century, royal policies began to privilege castizos over other castas, namely, by making them eligible for the priesthood and (like mestizos) exempt from paying tribute.[94] Furthermore, the Holy Office started to consider them eligible for the status of purity of blood. Thus, in 1590, the canon Santiago was commissioned by the Mexican Inquisition to investigate the purity of blood of Juan de Reina and his wife in order to determine if he was eligible to work for the Holy Office. After some inquiries, Santiago wrote to the Suprema requesting instructions because he had discovered that Reina's wife was not a *"castiza hija de mestiza,"* but a *"mestiza hija de India."* She was not the product of a union between a Spaniard and a mestiza, as he had assumed, but rather of a union between a Spaniard and an Indian woman.[95] Santiago's letter clearly implied that the category of castizo was compatible with the status of purity of blood. In the early seventeenth century, the Suprema received a number of similar letters, which led it to instruct colonial Inquisition officials to grant purity certification to those candidates for offices or familiaturas who had no more than one-fourth Indian blood (*cuarto de indio*). Other colonial establishments, including the Franciscan Order, instituted the same policy.[96]

Although the sistema de castas lent itself to the production of a great number of classifications, only a handful appeared in a consistent fashion in Mexican colonial records such as parish registers, tax lists, and censuses. Besides Spaniard, Indian, and black, these categories mainly consisted of mestizo, mulato, castizo, morisco, and zambahigo (or zambaigo), and in the eighteenth century, also *lobo, coyote, pardo, moreno,* and occasionally *chino.*[97] That a relatively small number of terms figure in legal records does not mean, however, that others were not in everyday use. As numerous documents containing legal petitions or witness testimonies indicate, categories such as "mestiza coyota," "mulato lobo," and "coyote mestizo" circulated among the population, and composite zoological names became increasingly common in the second half of the colonial period.[98] But the appearance and relevance of certain terms varied by region and period. The system of classification was even less rigid in the northern Mexican frontier, for example, than it was in central New Spain.[99] Even within the same region, their use was often inconsistent and influenced by a number of subjective and situational factors.[100] The process of recording caste classifications in parish archives was itself fraught with complications. Ancestral information provided at the time of a birth or marriage was not always trustworthy, for example, and parish priests were sometimes less than rigorous in their use of categories.

If in practice the use of classifications tended to be anything but systematic, the sistema de castas was nonetheless a system, an ideological complex constituted by a set of underlying principles about generation, regeneration, and degeneration. These principles linked main casta categories with specific proportions of Spanish, Indian, and black blood; made certain mixtures compatible with purity; and distinguished between people who descended from Spaniards and Indians and those who had African ancestry. Although they did not go unchallenged, the organizing assumptions behind the sistema continued to operate throughout the colonial period, influencing colonial power relations, individual and group identities, and Mexican definitions of purity, race, and nation.

CONCLUSION

Although genealogical investigations and concerns with "blood mixture" surfaced in both Spain and its colonies, a system of classification based on caste differences did not blossom in the metropole, at least not an enduring one. Perhaps the difference was due to the relatively small population of conversos and moriscos, especially vis-à-vis the numerical significance of people of African and native descent in the Americas. Perhaps the absence of discernible physical differences between New and Old Christians made it difficult for such a system to operate other than on paper. And perhaps the bureaucratic and archival revolution that Spain began to experience near the middle of the sixteenth century also played a role in the reproduction of the sistema de castas in the Americas. For all their flaws, parish archives, which separated Indians and Spaniards and eventually castas, became increasingly systematized in the following two hundred years. Although similar efforts to create and organize parish records took place on the Iberian Peninsula, colonial archives became a main source of creating and reproducing knowledge about caste, so much so that by the late seventeenth century most probanzas de limpieza produced in New Spain offered a certified copy of the candidate's baptismal record or an affidavit from a priest attesting to birth information.

The rise of the sistema de castas in Mexico and other parts of Spanish America was ultimately related to colonial developments and the interplay of local and transatlantic processes. The increasing salience of the casta categories, in parish records and elsewhere, was part of the larger process of disenfranchising people of mixed ancestry, of limiting their political and economic claims and making the prerogatives associated with vecindad and naturaleza exclusive to Spaniards and, to a lesser extent, native people. The emergence of the sistema de castas and growing use of the categories were also related to the extension of Iberian religious notions of impurity to colonial populations, particularly those that had African roots. At the end of the sixteenth century, European theories about the origins of the Indians proliferated, and Spanish thinkers considered the possibility that not just blacks but native people descended from stained biblical genealogies. Some attributed the darker skin color and servile condition of colonial populations to their descent from Ham's cursed son Canaan, while others blamed it on their being one of the lost tribes of Israel. Insofar as they linked black and Indian blood to ancestral sin and condemned lineages, these theories contributed to the recasting of early modern Castilian concepts of purity and race.

The colonial notion of limpieza de sangre was not clearly defined, however, and remained vague throughout most of the seventeenth century, especially with regard to the native people and their children with Spaniards. Some institutions included Indians and their mixed descendants in the categories of impurity, and Spaniards occasionally deployed the word *raza* against them (as in *raça de mestizos*). But the extension of the concepts of limpieza de sangre and race to the indigenous population did not prevail or at least had to contend with its official status as pure. That native people and blacks occupied different places within New Spain's "symbolics of blood"[101]—evidenced in probanzas de limpieza de sangre and in numerous colonial texts, reports, and legislation—was partly due to the ideological importance of conversion for the Spanish colonial project and in particular to the Amerindians' status as free Christian vassals of the Crown of Castile. It was also determined by the transatlantic slave system, and its role and legacy in perpetuating ideas about the so-called religious infidelity and supposed debased origins of African-descended people. Colonial racial ideology was influenced, furthermore, by the survival of a small but important number of pre-Hispanic lineages and by the strong kinship and social ties established between native elites and Spaniards in the early colonial period. Finally, the importance of the two-republic model of social organization also cannot be underestimated. It provided the legal and political framework for constructing a "contractual" relationship between the crown and indigenous communities and for extending notions of purity and citizenship, albeit on a limited basis, to the native population and their mestizo descendants, thereby strongly influencing the form and categories of the sistema de castas.

The early history of these categories reveals several important aspects of Mexico's sistema de castas. First, Spaniards had begun to use some of the classifications and to place them in hierarchies by the late sixteenth century. By that time, they had also started to articulate some of the sistema's main ordering principles—including that reproduction between different castas produced new castas; that black blood was more damaging to Spanish lineages than native blood; and that the descendants of Spanish–Indian unions could, if they continued to reproduce with Spaniards, claim limpieza de sangre. From its inception, the dual-descent system of classification promoted a sexual economy in which control of the sexuality of Spanish women (and to a certain extent also of native noblewomen) was necessary for the reproduction of the hierarchical social order. It also produced a gendered symbolics of blood. These symbolics construed native blood as unsullied but weak and tended to masculinize black blood. The colonial discourse of limpieza de sangre was thus connected to gender not only through sexuality and reproduction, but through its coding of different colonial groups as masculine or feminine, which served to construe certain unions and castes as compatible and redeemable and not others.

Second, when the metropolitan discourse of limpieza de sangre started to be extended to colonial categories, it was during a period of increasing inquisitorial activities and growing Spanish pessimism (especially among the friars) regarding the conversion of the native population. The problem of purity was therefore initially framed, as in Spain, in religious and generational terms. Thus, when Gerónimo de Mendieta argued that the Indians could be excluded from institutions that had limpieza requirements because, like the conversos, they were not yet secure in the faith, he implied that at some point they would be eligible for Old Christian status. Thanks to the early modern belief that blood was a vehicle for the transmission not just of physical but of moral and spiritual qualities, "mixture" with Spaniards could accelerate that process. These temporal and biological formulations could have been applied to blacks as well because they too were relatively recent converts (especially if they arrived directly from Africa), but their associations with slavery and infidelity generally prevented their descendants from making legally binding genealogical claims, a crucial part of the process of certifying purity of blood. At the end of the seventeenth century, persons of African ancestry would nonetheless begin to try, using the religious and generational formulas of the concept of limpieza de sangre, to appropriate the category of cristiano viejo.

Finally, the early history of casta classifications in central Mexico indicates how rapidly the discourse of limpieza de sangre and its genealogical practices and procedures were adapted to the colonial situation. The Inquisition, which since the 1560s had established guidelines in Spain to verify the purity of blood of its officials and familiars, exemplified and led this discursive adaptation. Not long after the Mexican Holy Office tribunal was formally established and began to conduct investigations to certify Old Christian ancestry, its commissioners resorted to genealogical formulas for granting or denying the status of limpieza to people of mixed ancestry. These formulas were necessary because, as the Holy Office's early disparaging remarks about castizos indicated, ongoing reproduction between Spaniards and castas had quickly turned skin color (and phenotype in general) into an unreliable index of descent. As discussed in Chapter 7, the purity requirements of the Inquisition together with those of other institutions served to routinize exclusionary practices based on notions of religious and genealogical purity, to transform lineage into a central component of colonial identities, and ultimately to turn limpieza de sangre into a transatlantic discourse.

PART THREE

Purity, Race, and Creolism in Seventeenth- and Eighteenth-Century New Spain

CHAPTER SEVEN

The *Probanza de Limpieza de Sangre* in Colonial and Transatlantic Space

In 1594, Pedro Hernández de Asperilla, a native of a town near the Spanish city of Toledo and resident of Puebla de los Ángeles, appeared before New Spain's inquisitors to request a familiatura, a title of familiar. As was by then standard practice, he submitted his genealogical information and that of his wife, daughter of doña María Gómez de Vasconcelos and Diego de Carmona, the latter an alderman who was also in the process of applying for a familiatura. To bolster his case, Asperilla submitted the royal license that he had obtained in 1579 to travel to the Americas and which certified that he had established his purity of blood before a judge from the jurisdiction in which his family lived, along with a note from the master of the ship in which he crossed the Atlantic asserting that he had provided all the information required to make the trip. He also presented informaciones from Puebla and Mexico City containing testimonies from other natives of his town regarding his ancestry and purity of blood. The entire case was forwarded to the Toledo Inquisition, which sent officials to various towns to comb through archives and question community elders for information about the petitioner's bloodlines and those of his wife.

In many ways typical of early colonial petitions for purity certification in New Spain, Asperilla's case exposes several important dimensions of the colonial procedures for proving limpieza de sangre. First, it illustrates the transatlantic nature of the process, the back-and-forth circulation of knowledge about lineages between the Iberian Peninsula and Spanish America and the practices, archival and otherwise, that the system of investigations promoted on both sides of the Atlantic. Second, the case reveals how colonial administrative and institutional requirements made it necessary for those who wanted to have access to certain spheres of power and honor to keep proving their limpieza status. Certificates obtained in Spain before migrating were usually not enough. And third, Asperilla's petition and that of his father-in-law hint at the integral part that purity documents were starting to play in the life of leading creole families, most of which were interrelated and would come to have a strong presence in the town councils and religious orders. This chapter explores these and other dimensions of the system of probanzas de limpieza de sangre in central New Spain prior to the eighteenth century.

Concretely, it elaborates on the procedures for certifying purity of blood in the colonial context, patterns in their implementation during the seventeenth century, and their implications for part of the creole population. In the first section, the chapter discusses the Inquisition's transatlantic system of probanzas, obstacles to the certification process in New Spain, and the requirement that genealogical investigations be made in the petitioners' Spanish towns of origin. The next part explains how these investigations functioned and how the Holy Office proceeded when it found evidence of impure blood. It stresses that the system of probanzas not only had implications for the discourse of limpieza de sangre in Spain but made the status of purity fundamentally unstable, subject to change depending on such factors as whether witnesses defined Old Christians through descent or (perceived) behavior and more generally on how communal memory was reconstructed. Finally, the chapter describes some of the difficulties that creoles faced, especially if their families had been in the Americas for several generations, when they tried to fulfill the requirement that their genealogical information be investigated in Spain. It argues that the Castilian crown's creation of a transatlantic empire premised on the fiction of purity and dependent on Old Christian Spaniards for the political and spiritual projects not only ensured that concerns with blood remained strong in both the metropole and the colony but enabled the rise of a particular creole historical consciousness. Rooted in Christian providentialism and a strong sense of belonging to a Spanish community of blood, this consciousness grew at the same time that some criollos claimed kingdom status for the land of their birth and developed a notion of nativeness distinct from that of Castile.

THE MEXICAN INQUISITION AND THE TRANSATLANTIC CERTIFICATION OF PURITY

European notions of blood purity and race operated in imperial contexts, flowing from metropole to colony and back; they "were never contained in Europe alone."[1] This statement is especially true for the Spanish empire, because members of the secular and religious hierarchies had to provide proof of their limpieza de sangre, and the process normally required that investigations be made in their native towns. The administrative procedures crisscrossed the Atlantic and implicated officials and communities in both colony and metropole. The probanzas de limpieza de sangre, which in Mexico began to appear within a decade after the conquest and which often included investigations in Spain (either for people traveling to the Americas or who were already there), thus vividly illustrate some of the bureaucratic mechanisms that made genealogical information circulate between metropole and colony. They also demonstrate the provisional or "probational" nature of limpieza status. Candidates for certain royal posts and public and religious offices normally had to establish their purity of blood more than once, which increased the possibility that stains would be found in their genealogies. Dependent on information derived from archives and on reconstructions of family histories by the "public voice and fame" of local communities, the status of purity was a precious but precarious commodity. Finally, early probanzas reveal the involvement of royal and government officials and institutions in the certification process and thus in promoting colonial purity concerns. Corregidores, oidores, and alcaldes ordinarios on both sides of the Atlantic were implicated as was the Council of the Indies, and their participation points to the public nature of the limpieza de sangre discourse.

More than any other institution, the Inquisition established transatlantic informational networks that helped bridge metropolitan and colonial discourses of limpieza de sangre. Its methods for certifying purity of blood in Mexico essentially followed those that had been established in Spain. In both places, the probanzas were characterized by the irregular nature of legal proceedings, a focus on negative proof, the importance of the public voice and fame, a formulaic interrogation process, and high costs. But colonial societies presented new challenges for the certification process, including the shortage and newness of archives.[2] When the Inquisition was founded, local genealogy books did not yet exist, and most parishes were barely building their birth, marriage, and

death records. The Suprema ordered the three Spanish American tribunals (in Mexico City, Lima, and Cartagena de Indias) to keep registers
of all the people they processed and of all the lineages they investigated,[3]
but until a solid infrastructure for tracing ancestries was created, the
genealogical evidence gathered in the colonies had mainly to consist of
oral testimonies. Yet finding an adequate number of witnesses was also
not easy. As the Peruvian inquisitors pointed out in 1603, in the Indies,
everyone was a newcomer except the Indians, which meant that identifying enough people from the same Spanish town as the petitioner who
could testify about his lineage was sometimes a formidable challenge.[4]

The distance between Mexico and Spain, the size of the Spanish American territories, and the migration process presented a series of other
problems. For one, these factors facilitated the falsification of names and
fabrication of new identities, indeed, the multiplication of genealogical
fictions. According to some inquisitors, upon arriving in the port of San
Juan de Ulua, many commoners added a *don* to their names, and just as
many conversos and other prohibited categories altered their surnames
in order to erase all traces of their past. The Holy Office sent inspectors
to monitor the people and cargo arriving in Spanish ships, but it was
not easy to detect false genealogies and in particular to identify probanzas that had been secured through the purchase of favorable testimonies.[5] Tacitly acknowledging the inefficiency of immigration controls,
Veracruz's alcalde mayor remarked in 1601 that the title of familiar was
not valid proof of limpieza de sangre because it was especially sought by
conversos in order to claim that they descended from Old Christians.[6]
A related problem was that the distance involved in transatlantic genealogical investigations increased not only the costs of probanzas but also
the possibilities of corruption and foul play. Inquisition officials on both
sides of the ocean sometimes did not hesitate to use their power to punish enemies, accept bribes, or fill their pockets with money that petitioners had deposited for their investigations. Even relatives in the Iberian
Peninsula could not be trusted, for as the Spanish inquisitor who was
sent to conduct a mid-seventeenth-century *visita* in Mexico reported,
"There is not a person in Spain who does not consider it a virtue to take
as much as possible from the *indianos* [a pejorative term for Spaniards
who went to the Indies]."[7]

Moreover, the constant movement of people within the Iberian Peninsula (a process that accelerated in the early modern period) and between Spain and the Americas made the verification of genealogies increasingly problematic. Investigations were supposed to be undertaken
in all the places of origin and long-term residence of each petitioner's

parents and grandparents, which meant that a single probanza could entail inquiries in various towns, oftentimes by different tribunals.[8] Thus, when Juan Esteban applied to be a familiar in the late 1630s, his genealogy had to be certified in the Spanish towns of Logroño, Valladolid, and Jerez de la Frontera and in Mexico itself.[9] If the petitioner was married, the investigations could easily multiply, making the process of certification even longer and more expensive than in Spain. Because the process was never the secretive affair the Inquisition touted it to be, a long delay tended to produce suspicions and rumors within communities and deep anxieties in the petitioner. Desperation drove Martín de Birbiesca Roldán to write to members of the Suprema in 1595. Having waited for four years for his limpieza certification, he feared that he would be removed from his Inquisition post or simply be kept in the dark indefinitely. Urging the Suprema to make a decision on his case, Birbiesca Roldán explained that nothing less than his personal and family honor were at stake, for the whole "Kingdom of New Spain" knew that he was awaiting confirmation of his title. His sense of urgency was compounded by the upcoming wedding of one of his daughters, which he knew would be jeopardized if news of a stain in the family surfaced.[10] As in Castile, the probanzas were part of the public domain and deeply enmeshed in a culture of honor that placed a high premium on reputation in the establishment of marriage and kinship ties.

Delays in the certification process were often related to the Inquisition's requirement that genealogical information be verified in *lugares de naturaleza,* a term that is loosely translated as "native towns" but that conflated geographical origins (birthplace), caste (lineage), and "nature" (character). The word *naturaleza* was interchangeable with *natura,* wrote Covarrubias, and could refer to a person's condition or being (as in a person "of strong nature") as well as "to caste and to birthplace or nation" ("*[n]aturaleza se toma por la casta y por la patria o nación*").[11] Thus, to describe someone as "a native of Toledo" (*natural de Toledo*) was to imply that she or he had been born and had kinfolk in that city and that the person's "nature" originated or was somehow located there. Within the probanza system, the strong emphasis on conducting investigations in native towns rested on the assumption that the most reliable source of information about a lineage's limpieza de sangre was the community of origins. It was in that community that commissioners expected to find elders who could speak with authority about the family's religious behavior, kinship ties, and public reputation beyond a few generations and that was also the most likely to have written and visual sources for reconstructing its history, such as baptismal and marriage records, genealogical books, and sanbenitos. In short, the native or "natural" community—its elders and archives—was the privileged repository of genealogical memory.

The testimony of eighty-year-old María de Inestrosa Cobarruvias—unusual not only because witnesses were almost always men but because it was taken at her home while she was bedridden and dying and because there was a higher degree of spontaneous dialogue than in similar interrogations—further clarifies the relationship between nativeness and purity. Declaring in the probanza of Francisco de Cobarruvias, who in 1586 solicited a familiatura and who was from her Spanish place of origin, the town (*villa*) of Cobarruvias, she said she remembered that his father and family had been pure and reputable people. Asked how she knew, she responded that their hometown consisted of no more than eighty vecinos, did not have a single converso or Moor, and had never had anyone tried for heresy. Pressed on how she could be certain that the petitioner was pure given that she did not know his grandparents, María de Inestrosa Cobarruvias stated that she had heard that they were all villanos and Old Christians, that the public voice and fame held them as such, and that there was no rumor or knowledge to the contrary. Furthermore, the town of Cobarruvias was small enough that everyone knew each other and easily identified those who had "raza."[12]

Numerous other probanzas included references regarding the ability of the community, because of its elders and size, to know when someone was not pure, including that of Pedro de Vega. A *procurador* (procurator) in Mexico City's audiencia who in 1585 applied for a familiatura, he was a native of the town of Martimuñoz de las Posadas in Castile. The witnesses for the case, from his hometown, stressed that everyone knew each other there and that the place had only three vecinos who were conversos (*confesos*), all of them held in contempt. Implying that impurity and foreignness went hand in hand, they added that all three New Christians were *advenedizos*—that they had arrived from elsewhere.[13] Suffering a much different fate than the probanza of Pedro de Vega was the información of Fray Alonso de Gironda, a Dominican friar who in 1621 applied to be a *calificador* (censor) in the Mexican Inquisition. Born in Tehuantepec, Mexico, to parents from the Spanish city of Trujillo, his genealogies were sent to Spain and investigated by the Llerena tribunal. Twelve witnesses testified, all of them alluding to the New Christian ancestry of both bloodlines and to the converso association of the paternal and maternal last names, respectively, Camargo and Gironda. They also mentioned that the town's elders often repeated that no one from the Girondos had held a post that had limpieza requirements, which in and of itself was suspicious. One witness alluded to a failed probanza that the petitioners's uncle had attempted to obtain, and another to an old refrain and verse that was often repeated in the streets of Truijillo: *"quien quisiese comprar judíos de los buenos y excelentes, comience por los Camargos y acabe por los Vicentes"* ("whoever wants to purchase a good Jew should begin with the Camargos and end with the Vicentes").[14] The Inquisition denied Fray Alonso de Gironda's probanza and declared him ineligible for inquisitorial posts. The public voice and fame in his parents' *lugar de naturaleza* held him to be impure.

The strong connection between purity and nativeness made it difficult but not entirely impossible for non-Spanish Europeans to be recognized as unsullied Old Christians. If they derived from Catholic families, their purity could be proven by sending commissioners to their places of birth (or those of their parents) and conducting archival and oral investigations there. Such an investigation was really feasible, however, only if the petitioner derived from a Catholic part of Europe and that region allowed Spanish inquisitors to enter and undertake their inquiries. The Spanish Inquisition could operate, for example, in parts of the Crown of Aragón's "Mediterranean empire," which included Sicily, Sardinia, and the kingdom of Naples in southern Italy.[15] Even in those places, however, the process was probably a logistical nightmare. Therefore, when the Inquisition had to verify the purity of blood of a naturalized foreigner or of a Spaniard of foreign parentage, it tended to base its decision on testimonies gathered from members of the Spanish communities in which the petitioner had spent significant periods of time. These cases were not common in Spanish America, among other reasons because foreigners were not allowed to live there, but a few did occur. For example, in 1597, Juan de la Rocca, canon in Lima's cathedral chapter, applied to be a minister in the Holy Office. The Peruvian Inquisition admitted that his limpieza status could not be determined "with certainty" because his father was Genoese but nonetheless sent his genealogy to Spain so that his mother's ancestry could be investigated. As to Rocca's paternal bloodline, the Holy Office accepted testimonies from people who had known the petitioner for some time and who therefore could share information about his behavior, public reputation, and possibly about his father's antecedents.[16]

Cases in which the Inquisition investigated and certified the limpieza de sangre of persons of foreign descent underscore the importance that local reputation had in the probanza system. In the Juan de la Rocca example and similar probanzas, witnesses usually stressed that they believed the petitioner to be an Old Christian because he acted like one and there were no rumors to the contrary. Testimonies gained credibility if they came from persons who had emigrated from the same town as the integrated foreigner, but the latter could be classified as pure simply if the vecinos in his adopted community could attest to his "Old Christian" ways. Indeed, in many of the probanzas that were approved, witnesses tended to highlight not only that they had information about petitioner's ancestors but that he and his relatives had good habits (*buenas costumbres*), were practicing and honorable Christians, and were fearful of God. They also frequently stressed that members of the lineage had earned a positive local status, for example, because they had served in the government or church. Thus, if in theory limpieza de sangre was primarily determined by descent, in practice it could just as equally be determined by behavior and standing within the community.

Inquisitors and authors of treatises on limpieza de sangre occasionally reflected on which was more important: what one "really" was according to birth and ancestry or what one was believed to be according to the community. More often than not, they opined that the public voice and fame was the last word on the matter. That the status of limpieza largely hinged on public reputation meant that it could hardly be considered a permanent condition. It also implied that it had a performative dimension. Whether in probanzas done in Spain or the Americas, the holding of public or religious offices normally worked in the petitioner's favor. In these cases, testimonies referred to the official's participation in political and religious rituals and in such events as public processions. In short, partaking in certain activities could be read as signs of limpieza de sangre. The extent to which certain public practices and "common" opinion (*común opinion*) played a role in the construction of limpieza de sangre thus cannot be overestimated,[17] and neither can their part in making the status of purity of blood highly unstable.

NATIVENESS, COMMUNAL MEMORY, AND THE INSTABILITY OF LIMPIEZA DE SANGRE

Despite its occasional flexibility with regard to integrated foreigners or Spaniards of foreign parentage, the Inquisition clearly preferred that genealogical investigations of persons living in Spanish America be made in their lugares de naturaleza, and in fact many were. The numerous probanzas that were sent to Spain to be completed kept breathing life into the memory and discourse of limpieza de sangre in Iberian towns, while the investigations that they resulted in, sometimes in various places, contributed to the instability of the status of limpieza de sangre. An example of a probanza that was done in Spain was that of Dr. Santiago de

Vera, who in 1582 applied to be an advisor for the Mexican Holy Office. A native of Madrid, he was a judge in Mexico City's audiencia, and when his probanza was being made, he was named president, governor, and general capitan of the audiencia that was just being established in the Philippines. It is not clear whether Vera had already submitted his genealogical information in order to be appointed as alcalde de corte or whether he had to show proof of purity to assume the presidency of the new tribunal.[18] In any event, he did have to establish his limpieza to work for the Holy Office, and that process involved investigations in different Spanish towns, including Seville (for his paternal bloodline) and Madrid (for the maternal one).[19] To strengthen his case, Vera submitted a stack of documents with a number of probanzas that had been made for his parents and grandparents as well for the ancestors of his wife, doña Isabel Rodríguez. Specifically, he presented a purity certification that in 1554 had been made in Seville by an alcalde ordinario for his father, Juan de Santiago, and his paternal grandparents, Diego Hernández and Isabel de Cazalla. He also submitted one for his mother and maternal grandparents that had been made in Madrid in 1555 and approved in the audiencia by the *teniente de corregidor* (corregidor's deputy). Vera also submitted two probanzas for his wife, both of which had been made by Valladolid's audiencia and attested to the purity of her parents and four grandparents.

Notwithstanding the arsenal of genealogical documents that Vera submitted when he applied to be consultor, the Inquisition ordered new investigations for him and his wife in Spain. As it was, the commissioner in charge of the inquiry in Seville quickly declared his paternal bloodline to be unclean. According to some of the witnesses and the Holy Office's local archives, Diego Hernández (a royal secretary) was the son of Juan de Sevilla and Violante Ruiz, who had both been tried for crypto-Judaism and reconciled with the church. The family's history with the Inquisition did not end there. Juan de Sevilla's parents had purportedly also been reconciled, and those of Violante Ruiz had been condemned for heresy. The witnesses made similar claims about the parents of Vera's paternal grandmother, Isabel de Cazalla. Since the Inquisition's archives confirmed their statements, there was no need to wait for the results of the investigation of the maternal bloodline in Madrid. Vera was a "confeso, descendant of people condemned and reconciled for following the law of Moses" and therefore clearly not eligible for purity-of-blood status.[20] The investigation of the alcalde de corte's mother and maternal ancestors in Madrid (made by the Toledo tribunal) had more positive results, but that did not matter because his paternal bloodline had been declared impure. That his "stain" derived from his paternal great-grandparents and great-great-grandparents was apparently irrelevant. But even if Vera's probanza had been approved, he still would not have qualified as a consultor, for the Inquisition determined that his wife, a native of Valladolid, was impure. The witnesses who testified in her probanza (one of whom was an alderman and familiar) declared that doña Isabel Rodríguez, her parents, and her grandparents descended on all lines from conversos and that all of this was public and notorious knowledge. Apparently no one in her lineage had been directly associated with heresy, but in order to be considered impure, all that sufficed was to descend, or be known to descend, from Jews.[21] Descending from impure categories, however, did not necessarily prevent individuals from playing a role in the colonial administration, for Vera and a number of his relatives continued to do so even after his failed attempt to secure a probanza from the Inquisition.

Another case that sheds light on how the link between purity and nativeness and the privileging of communal memory operated within the Inquisition's probanza system is that of Lucas de Madrigal, who in the early seventeenth century was residing in Puebla de los Ángeles.[22] The Inquisition ordered an inquiry in Madrid, where the petitioner claimed to have been born, and instructed the commissioner, don Diego de Guzmán, to make sure to determine the exact "naturalezas" of Madrigal's ancestors. He first interrogated six people. None gave any indication that Lucas or any of his relatives were impure, but their testimonies were insufficient to complete the probanza. The fourth witness, Luis Sánchez García (a notary for the Holy Office), declared that he had known the petitioner's brother because he lived in Madrid, and that he had a good reputation. But he was reluctant to remark about Madrigal's purity of blood because he did not know the origins of his parents ("*como no sabe su naturaleza no puede decir con certeza acerca de su limpieza*"). The next witness, a priest, said he had not seen the petitioner for forty-eight years but knew his brother and parents and that his father had for a time served as a shoemaker to the empress in Vienna and Germany. He added that he thought of all of them as Old Christians because that was their reputation in Germany and in Madrid, but that he did not really know where they originated. Lucas's brother, Juan de Madrigal, was also interrogated, but even he could not help establish the family's real origins. He testified that his parents had been born in Madrid, but they had died when he was still young and did not tell him much about their naturalezas.

Because none of the witnesses could establish Madrid as the native town of Lucas de Madrigal's parents and were therefore reluctant to speak

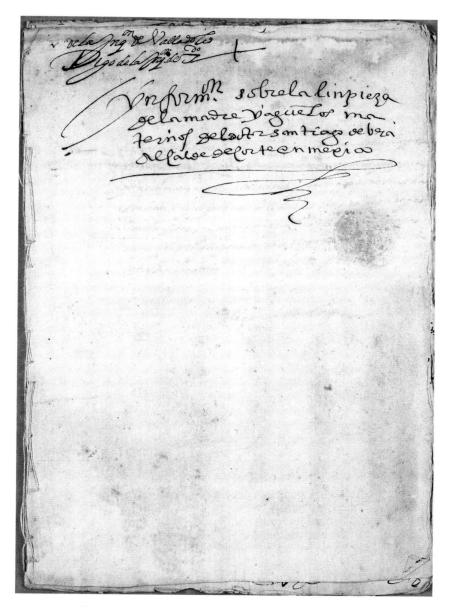

FIG. 1. Page from the purity of blood investigation of Dr. Santiago de Vera, who in 1582 applied to be an advisor for the Mexican Holy Office. SOURCE: Huntington Library, MS 35145. This item is reproduced by permission of the Huntington Library, San Marino, California.

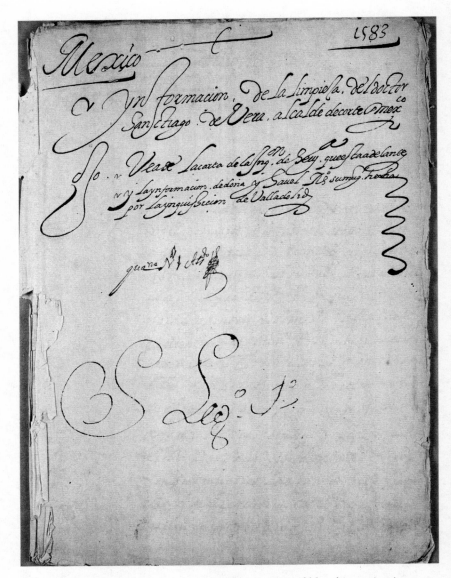

FIG. 2. Cover page of Dr. Santiago de Vera's purity of blood investigation, 1583. SOURCE: Huntington Library, MS 35145. This item is reproduced by permission of the Huntington Library, San Marino, California.

with conviction about their limpieza, commissioner Guzmán continued to investigate. As he pursued leads about the family's residences and burial sites, he discovered that Lucas had acquired a purity certification before he left for New Spain in 1602 and, furthermore, that when his parents had returned to Spain from Germany, the emperor had rewarded them with noble status (nobleza de privilegio). The commissioner also confirmed that some of the family members had lived in Madrid and had been buried in its cemeteries. Lucas's sister, furthermore, was a nun in the convent of San Ildefonso de Talavera and had had to submit a probanza de limpieza de sangre. Still, Guzmán was not satisfied because doubts about the family's geographical origins remained. The investigation therefore continued. Guzmán interrogated at least ten additional people from the area in which the parents of Lucas de Madrigal were said to have lived, but none was able to remember them, let alone establish their origins. The commissioner was also unable to find records for Lucas and his brother in the house where as children they would have had their religious instruction (doctrina). He therefore concluded that the family was foreign to Madrid (forasteros) and that Lucas de Madrigal's purity status had to remain unresolved, at least for the time being.

Meanwhile, the Seville tribunal was studying the bloodlines of Madrigal's wife, María Dávila. Inquiries were conducted in Cádiz for her maternal ancestors and in Medina Sidonia for her paternal ones. In the first town, the commissioner was informed that María Dávila's maternal grandparents, Pedro de Sierra (a priest) and María de Paredes, had arrived from elsewhere and had not been married. Furthermore, of the twelve potential witnesses that the commissioner identified, only two were willing to testify. The other ten said that because María de Paredes had a reputation for being "loose" ("no de las mas recogidas"), they could not be certain that the father of her child was really the priest Pedro de Sierra. At least from her maternal bloodline, María Dávila's limpieza could not be established, but neither had it been directly challenged. In Medina Sidonia, the story was different. Twelve witnesses were interrogated, all of whom declared that María's father, Alonso Jiménez Dávila, and all of her other paternal ancestors were neither pure nor Old Christians. The first witness (who like three others was a familiar) said that he had heard from many community elders that both of Alonso Jiménez Dávila's parents derived from conversos and that for as long as he could remember he had been hearing just that. He thus took the family to be New Christians. The same witness added that he had never known of anyone in the family being penanced or condemned by the Holy Office or of having any other infamy. He did recall, however, that the town's viejos and others used to say that Catalina Rodríguez (Alonso Jiménez Dávila's mother) descended from a "fulano" (So-and-so) Mantillo who had been forced to wear a sanbenito that the Inquisitors later hanged on the walls of the church. Other witnesses gave similar testimonies and mentioned hearing about the ancestor who had been "*sanbenitado*" (forced to wear a sanbenito). When the interrogations in Medina Sidonia were over, the comisario wrote in his report that María Dávila was not pure of blood because her father's community considered him to be a descendant of New Christians. The case was sent to Seville and from there to Mexico, where presumably Lucas de Madrigal was not issued a certificate of limpieza de sangre.[23]

Like that of Dr. Santiago de Vera, Lucas de Madrigal's investigation not only reveals the tight connection between limpieza de sangre and naturaleza, but provides a sense of how it led commissioners to tap local memory in Spain, reviving or reinforcing a community's knowledge of its lineages and reproducing genealogical mentalities. The two cases also point to some of the bureaucratic processes by which information about families traveled from the old world to the new, creating transatlantic flows of knowledge that sometimes jeopardized a person's chances of securing a certification of purity of blood or simply damaged his or her social standing (even if just for a brief time). But information did not flow in just one direction, and the Holy Office's genealogical investigations did not necessarily end in Spain. After all, limpieza de sangre was not a permanent status or condition. Even if a family was recognized as notoriously Old Christian in its native town, its members could move to new places and marry the wrong person, decide to reject the main principles of the church, or for a variety of other reasons acquire a reputation of being impure. It was mainly for that reason that applicants for titles and offices were asked to provide the names of all the towns in which they and their immediate ancestors had been natives, residents, or citizens and that probanzas often entailed investigations in Spanish American and Spanish towns.

For example, to determine the purity of blood of doña Juana de Orellana (wife of a candidate for a Holy Office post at the turn of the sixteenth century), the Inquisition ordered investigations in Spain as well as in Havana and Mexico. The investigation in Cuba, where she had lived, yielded two testimonies in which witnesses said that from her paternal side she was known to descend from moriscos and thus held as an impure "*morisca berberisca*" (Berber morisca). Furthermore, in her maternal bloodline she had Jewish ancestors. As a result, the Mexican Inquisition sent doña Juana de Orellana's genealogical information to Seville with instructions that officials there conduct an in-depth investigation as to who her parents and grandparents were, when and where they had married, where they had been vecinos, when they had moved to Cuba, and so forth.[24] Knowledge about limpieza de sangre traveled across the Atlantic, and the Holy Office did its part to disseminate it not only through its inquiries but through its efforts to spread information about "tainted" lineages to different regions when it convicted a New Christian for heresy or backsliding. Thus, when in 1582 it found Juan González and his wife guilty of "Judaizing" in Spain and burned him in effigy (he had died while in one of the Holy Office's prisons), it sent information about his fate to Mexico where he had descendants.[25] That persons who were deemed pure might suddenly have their reputations tarnished by events thousands of miles away must only have reinforced anxieties about the fragility of the status of Old Christian.

Stains mattered regardless of whether they were discovered in Spain or Spanish America and independent of how remote they were. Few cases illustrate these two points better than that of don Bernardino Vázquez de Tapia and his wife, doña Antonia de Rivadeneira, a novohispanic (colonial Mexican) couple with ties to important conqueror families. In the second decade of the seventeenth century, Vázquez de Tapia requested a familiatura. The Inquisition did not uncover negative information about his background, but his wife was a different story. The Holy Office became aware of a potential problem when it discovered that her maternal uncle, Francisco de Rivadeneira, had had difficulties becoming a familiar. It is not clear from available documentation what the problem was, but the three inquisitors from the Valladolid tribunal who reviewed the case could not agree on whether to issue the certification. The Suprema intervened, an unusual move, and ruled that the decision should be based on the majority opinion, which was to grant Francisco de Rivadeneira title. In New Spain, inquisitors conducted their own investigation of doña Antonia de Rivadeneira's genealogy and reported that she:

lists as her paternal grandmother doña Catalina de Salazar, daughter of Gonzalo de Salazar . . . who is said to have married doña Catalina de la Cadena, daughter of Pedro de Maluenda [Macuenda?], resident of the town of Covarrubias. After inquiring about the lineage of the said Pedro de Maluenda most of the witnesses held to be true and to be a matter of public voice and fame that he is a direct descendant of doña María de Cartagena, sister of the bishop don Pablo de Santa Maria y Cartagena, a Jewish conversa.[26]

Based on the information provided by the Mexican inquisitors and the witnesses, some of the "branches" connecting doña Antonia de Rivadeneira to the converso don Pablo de Santa María y Cartagena would look similar to those shown in the accompanying genealogical chart.

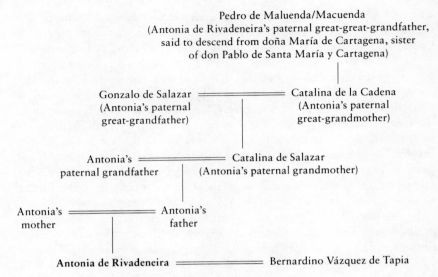

Pedro de Maluenda/Macuenda
(Antonia de Rivadeneira's paternal great-great-grandfather,
said to descend from doña María de Cartagena, sister
of don Pablo de Santa María y Cartagena)

Gonzalo de Salazar ═══════ Catalina de la Cadena
(Antonia's paternal   (Antonia's paternal
great-grandfather)   great-grandmother)

Antonia's ═══════ Catalina de Salazar
paternal grandfather   (Antonia's paternal grandmother)

Antonia's ═══════ Antonia's
mother   father

Antonia de Rivadeneira ═══════ Bernardino Vázquez de Tapia

Don Pablo de Santa María y Cartagena was the famous fifteenth-century rabbi, Solomon ha-Levi, who converted to Christianity, changed his name, and became bishop of Burgos. His son, Alonso de Cartagena, also devoted himself to the church and succeeded him in the post. In 1604, Philip III granted all the direct descendants of don Pablo de Santa María a rehabilitation allowing them to participate in activities and professions reserved for Old Christians and nobles, that is, to enter institutions that had purity and nobility requirements. But the public voice and fame had not forgotten doña Antonia de Rivadeneria's distant Jewish ancestry—not even in the remote region of New Spain. Anticipating problems, don Bernardino Vázquez de Tapia submitted copies of the royal decrees and papal briefs that had rehabilitated don Pablo de Santa María's descendants. Although doña Antonia de Rivadeneira was not a direct descendant of the bishop but of his sister, the decrees might help explain why the Mexican Inquisition requested permission to do another investigation in its district. The tribunal's *fiscal* (prosecutor) was inclined to reject the certification—the testimonies made it clear that she was not known as an Old Christian—but the three inquisitors felt that the extremely high regard in which the Vázquez de Tapia and Rivadeneira families were held in New Spain warranted another investigation, one that presumably would help to confirm their religiosity and good standing in the community. It is not clear from the records whether other investigations were done or not, but the couple's descendants went on to enjoy important religious and public posts and to compose part of the aristocratic circles of Puebla and Mexico City. Perhaps eventually the public voice and fame forgot about their connection to the fifteenth-century converso and allowed them to claim that they were Old Christians.

Needless to say, the genealogical investigations conducted by the Mexican Holy Office normally did not go as far back as the one for doña Antonia de Rivadeneira. Most people who applied for purity-of-blood certification were not linked to lineages as famous as that of don Pablo de Santa María y Cartagena. Furthermore, the newness of town, archives, and populations as well as other colonial realities made it impossible for inquisition tribunals in the Americas to conduct probanzas according to all of the regulations. Indeed, they often adopted pragmatic responses to problems associated with doing genealogical investigations. Sometimes commissioners were flexible on the number of witnesses and, following the Suprema's early instructions, simply gathered as much information as they could about the person's reputation and purity-of-blood status in their new communities.[27] At others, the Inquisition issued titles before informaciones were completed, a decision they regretted more than once. For example, in the early years of the seventeenth century, Gaspar de Rojas Victoria, Diego Jiménez de Ayala, and the brothers Diego and Juan de Monroy became familiars (the first two in Puebla, the third in Mexico City, and the fourth in Zacatecas) after their genealogies were investigated in Mexico. They received their titles, but the Holy Office grew concerned when rumors continued to circulate about their lack of purity. The genealogical information of each of the four familiars was therefore sent to the appropriate Spanish tribunals, which upon conducting investigations declared that all were found to be "*notorios confesos.*"[28] The probanza of the wife of Juan Pérez de Aparicio, a familiar in the city of Veracruz, was also approved in Mexico, but lingering doubts about her ancestry led inquisitors to request an investigation of her genealogy from the Valladolid tribunal in Spain.[29]

The Holy Office sometimes also exercised flexibility with regard to the purity requirement of the wives of its familiars. Technically, it was supposed to ascertain that such women had unblemished ancestries, which sometimes resulted in probes about the kind of lives they had led, and specifically about whether they had "good habits."[30] But this rule was not set in stone. For example, in 1632, Cristóbal Hernández de Colchero applied for a familiatura in the city of Puebla and submitted two genealogies, one for himself and the other for his wife. Both were natives of Spanish towns. Hernández de Colchero's case went to Sevilla and was approved in 1634. That of his wife was sent to the Inquisition's tribunals in Llerena and Toledo. After the commissioner in the second town discovered converted Jews in her maternal bloodline, the Holy Office declared her impure but, as it was prone to do, did not reveal the results to the petitioner. The year 1640 therefore arrived and Hernández de Colchero still had not received word of his case. Having grown extremely anxious that his public reputation and honor were being compromised, he appealed to the Mexican Inquisition, which because his wife had died allowed him to obtain a dispensation from the inquisitor general to receive a familiatura. Hernández de Colchero's petition was approved contingent on his agreeing to pay additional fees and promising not to remarry without first submitting proof of the limpieza of his betrothed.[31]

Another area in which the Holy Office could be flexible was in the requirement that all genealogies be investigated in Spain. Technically incomplete, those that were done only in Mexico were most common in probanzas made for creoles. Because in Spain certifications of limpieza de sangre were not done on a regular basis until after the middle of the sixteenth century, including for emigrants, many of the first colonists and settlers did not have any genealogical documentation. Their descendants therefore often had difficulties accounting for their origins. Obviously, the longer a family had been in Spanish America, the harder tracing its ancestry in Spain tended to be. The Mexican Inquisition was alerted to this creole predicament a year after it was founded. In 1572, the commissioner conducting the genealogical investigation of Damián Sedeño, a consultor in the Holy Office, found it difficult to verify the candidate's ancestry in his parents' native towns because so much time had elapsed since they had lived there.[32] The problem of investigating genealogies in the metropole became more serious in the early seventeenth century, when the number of creoles who solicited offices and titles started to increase. The Holy Office sometimes opted to approve probanzas in which only some of the grandparents had been studied in proper form or which had been done only in Mexico. This flexibility allowed creoles to monopolize familiaturas and certain inquisitorial posts and to start to locate their nativeness, purity, and history in the colonial context.

CREOLE NATIVENESS, PURITY, AND HISTORY
IN THE "KINGDOM OF NEW SPAIN"

By the beginning of the seventeenth century, central Mexico's "traditional" aristocracy was intermarrying with Spanish immigrants who were members of merchant, mining, and manufacturing groups.[33] This pattern of intermarriage between members of the conqueror-encomendero nucleus and the emerging bourgeoisie emerged in Mexico City, Puebla, and Morelia, and the families of these cities together comprised New Spain's ruling class.[34] The novohispanic aristocracy, which itself was but a minute percentage of the overall Spanish population was highly endogamous. As opposed to the early years of colonization, when some of the conquerors married noble indigenous women (to acquire lands and cacicazgos), by the seventeenth century, there was little intermarriage at the top level of colonial society. These aristocratic lineages, for which honor and noble status were of primary importance, effectively reproduced their estates and last names through at least the eighteenth century. Furthermore, throughout the colonial period, they provided daughters for convents and sons for the church and local government, effectively creolizing various colonial institutions. In the Inquisition, this process accelerated in the first decades of the seventeenth century, when tensions about how nativeness was defined started to surface.

Juan de Altamirano was a creole who in 1606 requested a probanza from the Mexican Inquisition in order to be confirmed as its *alguacil mayor* (chief constable). His father, also born in New Spain, had been a corregidor in Texcoco and a familiar; his mother, Juana Altamirano Pizarro, was Hernán Cortés's first cousin. Altamirano's connections to important local figures did not end there. His wife (and blood relative) was doña Mariana de Ircio y de Velasco, daughter of Viceroy Velasco (the son). Neither his kinship ties to the top colonial official nor his military habit from the Order of Santiago exempted Altamirano from having to submit proof of limpieza for himself and his wife. When the two informaciones were sent to Spain, however, Inquisition officials were unable to find people who could testify about doña Mariana de Ircio y de Velasco's ancestry. Anxious because his title did not arrive, Altamirano wrote to the Suprema in 1608 explaining that he had been born in New Spain, as had his parents, and that his grandparents had spent a good number of years there. His wife was in a similar predicament. More than seventy years had passed since her grandparents had arrived in Mexico, which is why no one in Spain could remember them.[35] Altamirano therefore requested that his wife's probanza be completed in the "kingdom," where her parents and most of her relatives had been born. The members of the Suprema agreed, and the inquisitor general even wrote a letter to Viceroy Velasco requesting that he and his wife provide their genealogical antecedents so that their daughter's limpieza could be investigated.[36]

Other creoles petitioned to have their investigations completed in Mexico, but the Suprema did not always indulge them. The question was delicate because it implied bending one of the principal rules regarding probanzas: that they be done in the petitioner's lugares de naturaleza.

But how exactly was a creole's "nativeness" defined? Was it defined by birthplace, lineage, or both? Framed differently, where was creole nativeness located? Was it in the place of birth and integration or in the ancestral community? Spanish expansionism and establishment of colonial communities raised these and other questions about how nativeness was constituted. Some Spanish jurists contended that creoles were natives of Spain because of their lineage and therefore entitled to the prerogatives of naturaleza. Solórzano Pereira, for example, affirmed that the Indies were considered equal to other parts of Spain and that the Spaniards who lived there were equal to those that lived in the peninsula, eligible for the same rights, honors, and privileges. Even though they lived far from Spain, creoles had their beginnings there, and their status was determined not by their domicile but by the "natural origin of their parents." [37]

The crown, however, never clarified either the status of Spanish America or that of criollos. The incorporation of the Indies into the Crown of Castile in 1523 precluded the possibility that Spanish America might enjoy a legal identity analogous to that of Aragón, Navarre, Naples, or Milan,[38] and the uncertainty of the territory's political standing extended to creoles. Castilian tradition dictated that natives of the jurisdiction had a monopoly on public and ecclesiastical offices, but some royal policies had been sending signals that peninsulars were favored for the top ones. And since creoles could not hold civil office in Spain, they did not enjoy the full prerogatives of nativeness on either side of the Atlantic. Underlying their predicament was the problem that if by lineage they were "natives of the kingdoms of Spain," by birthplace (or integration) they were natives of the jurisdiction. But what were the boundaries of that jurisdiction? Was the relevant unit the "Indies," the viceroyalty, or the audiencia? Only in the eighteenth century would creoles themselves start to define those boundaries and even then not with much precision. In the meantime, the dual and fundamentally vague character of Castilian naturaleza—which like the concept of nación could refer to both birthplace and bloodlines—produced constant tensions among American-born Spaniards and heightened their rivalries with peninsulars.[39]

These rivalries, which in the early seventeenth century were especially strong within the religious orders, managed to reach the Inquisition. Indeed, at the very moment when Altamirano received permission to complete his wife's probanza in New Spain, the Holy Office was becoming the site of struggles between peninsulars and creoles to control it. The Inquisition's role as the guardian of the faith and the influence of its officials and familiars in all sorts of local matters dragged high-ranking religious authorities into the controversy. Thus, in 1612, the archbishop of Mexico sent an unsigned letter to the Suprema urging it to conduct genealogical investigations for creoles in both the Iberian Peninsula and New Spain.[40] The archbishop, who disliked American-born Spaniards and wanted to exclude them from establishments that had purity statutes, argued that inquiries had to be made locally because it was there that the "infamies" of their birth were better known. His efforts to prevent creoles from becoming members of the Holy Office failed, however. Their access to familiaturas increased, especially after 1620, and by 1640, they were probably in possession of the majority of the titles.[41] Creoles also gained a foothold in inquisitorial posts. Hence, in 1636, the Suprema received another anonymous letter from New Spain, this time complaining that criollos were becoming officials, not just familiars. The letter alleged that their presence in the Holy Office threatened the honor and prestige of the institution because "by nature" they were lazy and not as rigorous in their endeavors as the Spanish born. Clearly influenced by the theories that were circulating about the long-term degenerating effects of the Spanish American physical environment on the physiological, moral, and psychological characteristics of Europeans, the author suggested that the Inquisition should follow the example of Mexico City's audiencia, which did not have any creoles serving as judges, procurators, or alcaldes.[42]

Despite Spanish diatribes against creoles and theories about their degeneration in the Indies, the crown's policy of reserving some offices and honors for the descendants of the conquerors and first colonists together with the probanza system's initial flexibility facilitated the creolization of the Inquisition. Petitions by criollos were given a special boost when the Suprema gave Spanish American tribunals permission to accept probanzas that were done according to the guidelines for all but one of the "four quarters." This early seventeenth-century decision was based on "the difficulties that those of the Indies have in knowing the origins of all their grandparents."[43] One of the probanzas that was approved even though the required information had been obtained for only three of the grandparents was that of the creole Francisco de Bazán Albornoz. In 1609, he was waiting for certification of his purity in order to become an inquisitorial official. The commissioner assigned to his case in Spain could not certify the purity of his paternal grandmother, Francisca Verdugo, because he could find no one who had known or even heard of her in the town where she supposedly was born. Having to settle for an investigation of the name Verdugo, he did uncover that it was one of five local hidalgo lineages, all of which were reputed to be pure of blood. Since the other three bloodlines had been investigated in proper legal form and found to be clean, the Inquisition tribunal in Valladolid was of the opinion that the case was complete and sent it as such to the Suprema. The probanza must have been approved because Bazán Albornoz became an inquisitor, who on several occasions expressed his opinion regarding the creole–peninsular struggle in the religious orders and his own bias against peninsular Spaniards, whom he called *gachupines*.[44]

The Suprema's willingness to be flexible with regard to some creole probanzas waned in the mid-seventeenth century when due to a change in political climate in Spain it tried to reinstate rigor to the whole system of genealogical investigations. New Spain felt the change in policy soon after the arrival of the inquisitor Pedro Medina Rico, who was sent to conduct a visita. This official had just spent years investigating complaints of abuses by inquisitors in Cartagena de Indias and had concluded that they were guilty of corruption and of accepting bribes from Portuguese merchants. When the scrupulous visitador inspected the Mexican Holy Office's archives in the latter half of the 1650s, he also claimed to have found many abuses. According to his numerous reports to the Suprema, local officials had been pocketing the money that was supposed to be sent to the various places where the investigations had to be conducted. A number of probanzas that were requested were thus never made, dissuading other eligible candidates for familiaturas from applying. Not only did they face losing money, but they risked bringing on to themselves all the public shame that petitioning for limpieza certification and not having it confirmed implied.[45]

Medina Rico also reported that of about one hundred and fifty limpieza files that he had had a chance to review, only seven or eight were technically complete. Consequently, he spearheaded efforts to make the investigations conform to the original guidelines. Medina Rico wanted to enforce early provisions that had stressed that limpieza investigations were to precede, not follow, the granting of any Inquisition title, that they were supposed to be done not just in Mexico but in the peninsula, and that the bloodlines of all four grandparents had to be studied in their native towns. Because many probanzas fell short of some of these requirements, the visitador asked familiars and officers to return their titles and to refrain from using them until their investigations were in fact complete. The orders affected members of New Spain's aristocratic families and hence immediately erupted into a public scandal.[46] Even the reputations of familiars whose probanzas were complete ended up tarnished, and they did not hesitate to express their outrage. Juan de Aguirre, for example, sent an angry letter to the Suprema contending that he had rendered many services on behalf of the crown and the faith, and that his family was of "notorious purity" and Old Christian ancestry.[47]

Like his mother, Aguirre was a creole, but all of his grandparents were peninsular Spaniards. That not all of his family's roots in New Spain were very deep made him somewhat unique among those singled out by Medina Rico. Indeed, what upset the visitador the most was that the genealogies of officials and familiars whose families had been in Mexico for several generations had not been investigated thoroughly. According to Medina Rico, many of their probanzas were incomplete because the birthplace of one or more of the grandparents had remained unknown. Commissioners had simply gathered testimonies where said grandparents had lived, not in their naturalezas.[48]

The archbishop of Mexico did not approve of Medina Rico's actions and accused him of abusing his power and of manipulating the issue of limpieza to enrich himself. The visitador in turn accused the archbishop of wanting to undermine the Holy Office's authority.[49] The three Mexican inquisitors were also outraged by Medina Rico's interventions. Prior to his visit, they had already expressed their disagreement with the Suprema's increasingly rigid guidelines and had warned that the majority of people whose "grandparents and great grandparents had shed their blood conquering the lands" in the service of God, the Catholic faith, and the crown were now unable to account for their Spanish origins. These individuals were not able to prove their purity of blood according to new guidelines, which meant they would not qualify for anything:

All we have to report to Your Highness is that there are families in these Kingdoms of New Spain that are so ancient that they almost arrived with the conquest. . . . The sons of those that first populated these Kingdoms cannot give their grandparents' exact origins [*naturaleza*] in Spain because they came more than one hundred years ago to these parts, where their purity status has been maintained in the highest opinion.[50]

The Mexican inquisitors' letter then discussed the detrimental effects that having to prove the purity of their bloodlines in Spain would have on the descendants of the conquerors and first settlers, many of whom, they claimed, were experiencing an economic decline. In the process, they described a system of inquisitorial posts and familiaturas that had been controlled by the same creole families that tended to monopolize town council and religious posts in central Mexico. Indeed, in the preceding decades, titles had frequently been passed down in patrimonial fashion.[51] The inquisitors also described a colonial gentry whose historical and genealogical memory was no longer principally linked to Spain but to the "Kingdoms of New Spain" and that claimed nativeness in the land.

Bernabé Álvarez de Hita, a public official from Puebla who applied for a familiatura in the 1660s, embodied this emerging creole consciousness. For more than two decades he waited for his purity certification.

Aware that the main obstacle in his probanza had been the commissioner's failure to find any information about his wife's paternal grandmother (Violante López) in her native town of Trujillo, he wrote to the Suprema in 1684 explaining that more than one hundred and fifty years had passed since she and her husband, the Capitan Juan de Vargas, had left Spain to become first colonists of New Spain. Because the memory of men was incapable of remembering that far back, Álvarez de Hita continued, no one in Trujillo could testify regarding López's purity. But evidence of her unsullied and noble ancestry could be found, he claimed, in an información that had been made for her and her husband in 1594, at the request of the couple's son-in-law. Álvarez de Hita asked the Suprema to review that información and to order that new probanzas be made in New Spain, where the couple had lived and died. He closed by listing the services he had rendered as a public official, by stressing his children's descent from the first nobility of the land, and by reminding members of the council that many of the viceroyalty's most important lineages, those founded by conquerors and first colonists, were now in their fifth or sixth generation. How was their purity to be proven? To honor those noble families, Álvarez de Hita suggested, the Inquisition and the religious orders should conduct their genealogical investigations in the kingdom.[52]

Álvarez de Hita's remarks were one manifestation of an emerging creole historical and genealogical consciousness and more generally of the patriotic discourse that had begun to surface at the start of the seventeenth century, in both New Spain and Peru, among the descendants of the first conquerors and settlers.[53] By the middle of the century, Mexico's patrimonial sons of the land began to demand that they be granted a monopoly on office holding and thus to more aggressively attempt to construe a nativeness separate from Castile. The increasing militancy of their claims was reflected in their more frequent deployment of the term *kingdom* (sometimes *kingdoms*) for their territory. Although the term had already surfaced in some creole writings of the late sixteenth century, it appeared more regularly around the 1650s and became increasingly specific with regard to the cultural and territorial boundaries. A century later it would start to appear in the form of "Kingdom of Mexico," along with the phrase "Mexican nation."[54]

Creole attempts to constitute a nativeness separate from Castile and to claim kingship status were accompanied by the construction of historical narratives that centered not on the conquest but on the imperial pre-Cortesian past. This past was the subject of Juan de Torquemada's *Monarquía Indiana* (1615), for example, and would only increase in importance in the writings of other creole authors, among them those of the polymath Carlos de Sigüenza y Góngora (1645–1700). A professor of mathematics at the University of Mexico who came into possession of Ixtlilxóchitl's manuscripts when he was helping his descendants reclaim properties, Sigüenza y Góngora helped to give literary expression to the growing cult of the Virgin of Guadalupe—a major watershed in the criollo sacralization of the soil and indigenous inhabitants of New Spain—and was also a key contributor to the creation of a mythic Aztec past.[55] This mythification of the Mexica had few, if any, real parallels. Creoles from other Spanish American regions also relied on the figure of the Indian to create historical narratives, but not in the same way and not to the same degree as those of New Spain. As the historian Anthony Pagden has observed, "Indians, both ancient and modern, were perhaps the most important single element in the criollo interpretation of the history of 'New Spain' and thus in the creation of their own national [sic] identity."[56] By the late seventeenth century, the Mexica past and in particular the figure of the heroic Aztec warrior had helped creoles forge a classical antiquity for their kingdom.

The transformation of the pre-Hispanic past into New Spain's classical antiquity enabled creoles to create deeper roots in Spanish American lands than those that the conquest afforded them and thereby to begin to rupture their history from that of Spain.[57] Those roots were not just historical but genealogical. As of the late seventeenth century, central New Spain began to produce memorials, some of them anonymous, that highlighted the political and kinship alliances that the conquerors and first colonists had forged with caciques and principales and to revive the early colonial idea that noble indigenous blood had an ennobling effect on Spanish lineages. It also began to generate probanzas de limpieza de sangre in which ancestry from elite Amerindians was not an impediment to certification.[58] Mexican creoles, and in particular, the descendants of the conquerors and first settlers, thus started to develop a historical narrative in which they figured as the "natural" rulers of the polity, as heirs to the imperial Mexica past by virtue not just of their colonization and Christianization services but of their birthplace and bloodlines. In essence, they tried to advance their rights as natives of the kingdom by simultaneously appropriating Indian history and Indian "nativeness"—by grounding their claims to naturaleza in both the soil and "blood" of the land. Religion was central to the creoles' patriotic project not only because they claimed to be the bearers of Christianity but because their cult of the Virgin of Guadalupe served to rid the land of any lingering connotations of idolatry and by extension to "purify" the indigenous people.

But in spite of the gesture to redeem the "blood" of the indigenous people and the related move to appropriate their historical *and* genealogical claims, creoles who acknowledged having native ancestry did so with caution. They usually made sure to emphasize not only that their indigenous relatives were remote and noble but that they had little connection to contemporary Indians, whom they generally perceived as impoverished and imperfect versions of their pre-Hispanic progenitors. This effort to establish links with the imperial indigenous past while simultaneously underscoring the distance between the Indians of the past and those of the present gave rise to "criollo antiquarianism," which began to flourish in the second half of the seventeenth century as part of the creole patriotic project.[59] It also led to an affirmation of the generational formulas of the discourse of purity of blood, which allowed for converts to become Old Christians after three generations, and the principle that indigenous blood could be completely absorbed into Spanish lineages. In the eighteenth century, those formulas and that principle would start to appear in political tracts and probanzas de limpieza de sangre and come to be visually represented in the casta paintings.

CONCLUSION

The notion that only Old Christians could migrate to the Indies and that they alone could become colonial officials was clearly a fiction, and not only in the sense that the category of cristiano viejo was a social and not a "natural" construct. It was also a fiction in that the crown occasionally granted conversos (especially merchants) special licenses to go to the Americas; in that purity requirements were sometimes overlooked or not firmly monitored; and in that many genealogies were fabricated, the products of falsifications, bribes, or plain ingenuity. Nonetheless, enough probanzas were made and investigated through transatlantic information networks to feed the idea of Spanish purity and concomitant fiction of Spanish America's lack of Jewish and Muslim antecedents. The rhetorical, not historical, force of the claim is what mattered.

The Holy Office played a crucial part in both transferring the metropolitan blood concerns to the colonies and reinforcing them in the Iberian Peninsula because of its insistence, throughout the colonial period, that probanzas had to be done in all of the lugares de naturaleza of the petitioner and his ancestors. The hundreds, perhaps thousands, of investigations that it ordered for its officials and familiars involved inquiries in towns all over Spain that examined, ignited, and reproduced communal memories about conversos and moriscos long after the two groups were considered serious threats to the Catholic faith. Historical genealogies of European racial concepts and racism that present the problem as entirely internal—its origins tending to be attributed to the aristocracy's concerns with blood—clearly do not work well for Spain. Thanks to the multiple agents, practices, and institutions that were part of the transatlantic system of probanzas, the metropolitan and colonial discourses of limpieza de sangre strongly shaped and reinforced each other. These discourses allowed the crown to continue to present itself as the unrivaled guardian of the Catholic faith, and it permitted Spaniards in the colonial context to construct themselves as unsullied Old Christians, as such exceptionally qualified to guide the indigenous people in spiritual and secular matters.

And yet, the relationship of creoles to the concept of purity of blood was a tortured one. Their limpieza was sometimes questioned, and because of the nature of the certification system, the status was fundamentally unstable, indeed, probational. Perhaps for this reason the ideology of purity of blood had an especially potent, and in some ways unexpected, effect on part of the creole population. The ubiquity of purity requirements, their centrality to the crown's creation of secular and religious hierarchies, and the archival practices that they set in motion produced a particularly strong preoccupation with bloodlines among the descendants of Spaniards, which in turn made their patriotic and "nativeness" discourses profoundly ambivalent with regard to issues of race. Indeed, the emergence of these discourses accentuated colonial concerns with limpieza de sangre. The concept was woven so tightly into the fabric of colonial relations that criollo elites apparently could not bring themselves to question its primacy. As discussed in the following chapters, their incapacity to imagine their kingdom without recourse to ideas of lineage and purity and reluctance to do away with colonial hierarchies led to an increase in probanzas in the second half of the colonial period, to a gradual secularization of the notion of limpieza de sangre, and to the formal extension of the concept of impurity to the castas.

CHAPTER EIGHT

Religion, Law, and Race

The Question of Purity in Seventeenth-Century Mexico

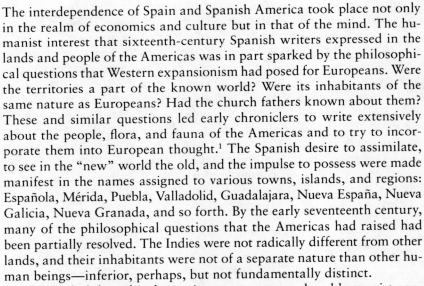

The interdependence of Spain and Spanish America took place not only in the realm of economics and culture but in that of the mind. The humanist interest that sixteenth-century Spanish writers expressed in the lands and people of the Americas was in part sparked by the philosophical questions that Western expansionism had posed for Europeans. Were the territories a part of the known world? Were its inhabitants of the same nature as Europeans? Had the church fathers known about them? These and similar questions led early chroniclers to write extensively about the people, flora, and fauna of the Americas and to try to incorporate them into European thought.[1] The Spanish desire to assimilate, to see in the "new" world the old, and the impulse to possess were made manifest in the names assigned to various towns, islands, and regions: Española, Mérida, Puebla, Valladolid, Guadalajara, Nueva España, Nueva Galicia, Nueva Granada, and so forth. By the early seventeenth century, many of the philosophical questions that the Americas had raised had been partially resolved. The Indies were not radically different from other lands, and their inhabitants were not of a separate nature than other human beings—inferior, perhaps, but not fundamentally distinct.

As initial philosophical questions were answered and humanist concerns receded, the interest in studying contemporary Amerindians was replaced by antiquarianism, particularly popular among creoles. Nonetheless, Spanish thinking about the "nature" and rights of the native people continued, only now in more obscure writings. Not only jurists and theologians but also inquisitors and physicians, many of them based in Spain, provided their opinions about the place of the indigenous people and other colonial populations within the sociopolitical and religious order, which sometimes led them to tackle the question of purity of blood. A little-known fact, a number of memorials and other writings on the statutes directly addressed the problem of whether people of native and African descent could claim limpieza de sangre. Although previous Castilian monarchs had already issued pronouncements with respect to the status of the original inhabitants of American lands, the growing prescience of questions of purity of blood in Spanish America at the end of the seventeenth century compelled the crown and the Suprema to reassess and clarify the matter. Thus, just as the preoccupation with limpieza de sangre was declining in Spain, colonialism helped keep it alive in the Hispanic Atlantic world, long after the original motives for the statutes had dissipated.

This chapter continues the discussion of the transplantation of the discourse of purity of blood to the colonial context of Mexico and the contradictions in which it was immersed. It first focuses on official interpretations of the limpieza status of colonial populations, particularly the views expressed by the Suprema at the end of the seventeenth century and the relationship that the question had to Spanish political imperatives. The chapter then analyzes the gap between official definitions of purity of blood and those that tended to operate in the colonial context, contradictions that were exacerbated by the ambiguous religious standing of Indians and blacks and uses of the category of Old Christian. It stresses that these contradictions did not make the sistema de castas any less potent, that hegemonic discourses are seldom cohesive and tend to be constituted by overlapping and conflicting ideas. Finally, the chapter argues that even though the status of people of African descent within the discourse of limpieza de sangre was ill defined, the Spanish association of "blackness" and "impurity," which had started to surface in the late sixteenth century, had only grown stronger a hundred years later.

THE OFFICIAL LINE: THE INQUISITION AND THE CROWN ON THE ISSUE OF LIMPIEZA DE SANGRE

Sometime toward the end of the seventeenth century, the Supreme Council of the Inquisition convened to assess whether mestizos and mulattos in Spanish America should be allowed into institutions with purity-of-blood statutes.[2] The starting point of the discussion was a typology of the different types of people or "nations" that lived in the colonies. Referring to Solórzano Pereira's classifications in *Política Indiana*,[3] the

Inquisition identified four categories: "criollos," or people who were born in the Indies and "whose father, mother, and entire ancestry were Spanish"; "mestizos," the children of Indians and Spaniards; "mulatos," those who were "engendered by Spanish males and black females, or the other way around"; and "zambahigos," or the descendants of unions between native people and blacks.[4] The problem entailed assessing the status of Indians and blacks vis-à-vis Spaniards, but the primary aim was to determine the nature of intermediate groups, whose numbers had been increasing throughout the century. With regard to creoles, the Suprema stated, there was no doubt that they should be admitted into institutions that had the statute, because by virtue of their bloodlines they met the dual requirement of being pure and Old Christians. Some Spaniards had wanted to exclude them from noble status, the priesthood, and religious orders by arguing that the constellations of the Indies had made them acquire the "natural ailments," "deceitfulness," and "sensuality" of the Indians:

But His Majesty has issued various orders so that they be ordained by bishops and admitted into honorific posts, and the friars have come to agreements whereby [they alternate between admitting creoles and Spaniards], because the Indies are incorporated into the kingdoms of Castile and Leon and the Spaniards born in Spain and in the Indies enjoy the same [rights and privileges].[5]

As to mestizos, mulattos, and zambahigos, the Suprema admitted, the issue was much less clear, for as descendants of blacks and Indians, they had "gentile blood" in their veins. The main task, therefore, was to determine which of these colonial categories were pure under Spanish laws, and of those that were not, which were eligible for royal dispensations. What ensued was a revealing discussion of legal and popular definitions of the concepts of limpieza de sangre and cristiano viejo, the original reasons for the establishment of the purity statutes in Spain, and the official status of communities that had converted to Christianity in both the metropole and its Spanish American territories.

The Suprema's exposition of the problem, which drew from the writings of various theologians and jurists, began with a clarification of official policies regarding the ability of converts to serve in the church. Under Spanish common law, noted the council, neophytes, whether originating from gentiles, Muslims ("Moors"), or Jews, could not be admitted into religious orders or the priesthood, nor granted ecclesiastical benefices, if they were not well instructed and firm in the faith. The eligibility of a candidate was normally determined by individual bishops, but as a general rule, only those that were at least two generations removed from the conversion could be considered, that is, those whose parents and grandparents had been Catholic all their lives. However, as the Suprema observed, the statutes of limpieza generally did not follow common law on this matter but called for purity of blood *in infinitum:* exclusive Christian lineage. To enter institutions that had purity requirements, individuals therefore had to be considered Old Christians, which in Spain amounted to proving that they did not have *any* Jewish or Muslim ancestors. This definition had come about, the document continued, because Jews and Muslims had historically demonstrated a marked readiness to return to the practices and beliefs of their ancestors, a phenomenon that various authorities attributed to their "infected" blood (*la infección de la sangre*). Because "experience" had shown that Judaism and Islam were transmittable stains, Jewish and Muslim converts to Christianity were by definition all potential heretics, a threat to the faith and therefore ineligible for Old Christians status and positions of authority.

Having reviewed the original motive for the statutes, the Supreme Council of the Inquisition noted that some Spanish jurists had argued that the descendants of Indians and blacks—the latter sometimes generically called "Ethiopians"—could also be excluded from institutions that had limpieza requirements because they too were not Old Christians. In Spain, the Suprema added, the term *cristianos viejos* was commonly understood to refer to the descendants of gentiles who in the distant past had converted upon hearing the Gospel, or as one source had put it, to "those for whom there is no mention and no memory of the origins of their conversion."[6] This was the definition employed by Alfonso Pérez de Lara in his early seventeenth-century treatise on purity of blood to argue that individuals descending from Indians and blacks could not be accepted into places that had the statute because of the impossibility of verifying that they were Old Christians.[7] He observed that this way of thinking was already quite common in Spain and for some time had been prompting various institutions to deny admission to people of African and indigenous ancestry.

Pérez de Lara's views regarding native people and blacks were subsequently rejected by a number of important Spanish jurists and theologians, including Solórzano Pereira and Juan Escobar del Corro. The latter, notoriously anti-Semitic, had served as inquisitor at the Holy Office's tribunal in Llerena.[8] In his own treatise on limpieza de sangre, Escobar del Corro stressed that laws intended for certain groups could not simply be extended to others, especially if the original motivation for the legislation was not applicable to them. According to the inquisitor, the statutes had arisen out of a need to deal with converted Jews, Moors, heretics, and "other groups like them," presumably with the propensity to slide back to their old religious beliefs and practices. The Indians did not fit into this category, argued Escobar del Corro, because they had from the beginning embraced the faith and remained firmly loyal to it. They were fundamentally different from Muslims and Jews, he concluded, and should be recognized as such by Spanish laws.[9] Concurring with Escobar del Corro, the Suprema asserted that native people might be recent converts, but were nothing like the New Christians of the Iberian Peninsula. Like Old Christian Spaniards, they descended from gentiles or people who had lived only under natural laws and not under a religion and were therefore able to embrace Christianity.

The Suprema essentially argued that gentiles remained Catholics once they converted because they had no religion to which to return; unlike Jews and Muslims, they were a tabula rasa. To be sure, some Spaniards did not like the idea of comparing the pre-Christian condition of the native people to that of their own ancient ancestors and argued that idolaters were just as difficult to convert to Christianity as Semitic peoples. But the Supreme Council of the Inquisition did not see it that way, at least not at the end of the seventeenth century. At most, noted the councilors, there might be one Indian who relapsed into the beliefs of his ancestors, but the rest had not, and for that they should be rewarded, not punished: "Experience has shown that [the Indians] have retained the Catholic faith that they received and remain firmly committed to her. And there has hardly been one that has returned to heathenism." Following Escobar del Corro's strict interpretation of the limpieza de sangre statutes, the Suprema thus concluded that purity requirements could be used only as originally intended, that is, against converted Jews and Muslims and other "potential heretics."

As to the more technical matter of whether indigenous people and blacks could claim to be Old Christians, the Suprema stressed that the statutes should follow ius commune and ascertain only that a person's parents and grandparents had been Catholic all their lives. The purity "in infinitum" requirement, if it was going to be applied, could only serve to cast the descendants of Jews and Muslims as perpetual New Christians. Although the document containing the Suprema's deliberations on the matter appears to be missing pages (or these were misplaced), it is probable, given the points that it had already made, that its final thoughts on who was allowed to use the concept of cristiano viejo were similar to those of Solórzano Pereira. The jurist, whose opinions the Supreme Council repeatedly cited and clearly respected, had argued that because most Indians descended from people who had converted in the sixteenth century, they were no longer "neophytes" as many people still claimed, but in fact already "ancient" Christians.[10] They were, in other words, both "limpios de sangre" and "cristianos viejos." And if by now native people had both the qualities of purity of blood and Old Christian ancestry, then the mestizos who descended from them and (Old Christian) Spaniards had them even more so.[11] It is unclear whether the councilors applied the same logic to blacks because they gradually drop out of their discussion and toward the end are hardly mentioned at all.

The Supreme Council of the Inquisition's deliberations about the applicability of the limpieza de sangre statutes to colonial populations raises a number of important issues, among them that of timing. Why the need to define who was pure or not in Spanish America at that particular moment? The topic had on occasion already been raised by some jurists and colonial religious officials, but it clearly took on more importance toward the end of the second century of Spanish colonialism. Indeed, at roughly the same time that the Suprema deliberated on the matter, Charles II issued the decree that affirmed the purity status of native people and their descendants and the legal equality of caciques and principales with Spanish hidalgos (1697). Given the timing of this decree, it is entirely feasible that the king had solicited the Suprema's opinion on the problem of limpieza in Spanish America and that the results were the deliberations discussed above. As to why the crown felt a need to address the problem at that particular moment, the reasons are not difficult to surmise.

One reason was that after about a century of allowing Spanish America relative autonomy, Castilian monarchs were starting to take a greater interest in colonial affairs, in large part because they wanted to make their overseas territories more lucrative for Spain. The second half of the seventeenth century had witnessed the aggressive expansion of large landed estates in parts of New Spain, mainly to the detriment of native communities. To ensure the steady flow of tribute, the crown had to try to offer them some protection, which it did in part by confirming their rights and privileges through several pronouncements, including the 1697 decree. Another development compelling clarification of the colonial purity question was the growth, throughout the seventeenth century, of the population of mixed ancestry and restrictions on their participation in certain professions and institutions.[12] The proliferation of exclusions targeting people of native and African ancestry by virtue of their "stained" blood, to which metropolitan authorities were not oblivious, obliged the crown to intervene and clarify the status of its colonial subjects. That it prioritized affirming the limpieza de sangre of the indigenous people and their descendants and made no reference to blacks was consistent with its previous pronouncements and a function of the close linkage of politics and religion in the Spanish colonial enterprise.

Spain's debates about its political obligations in the Americas by no means ended with the discussions of Bartolomé de Las Casas and Juan Ginés de Sepúlveda. Its struggle to establish solid legal and ideological grounds on which to defend its titles continued, and kept reviving the topic of the indigenous people's rights and privileges under the Crown of Castile. This struggle in fact intensified in the seventeenth century, when the construction of the Black Legend by other European countries forced Spain to explain why it continued to occupy Spanish American territories and govern their populations. Protestant powers in particular accused Castile of basically committing genocide, of not curbing the greed of its conquerors, of not protecting its overseas subjects, of using evangelization as a pretext to further its own financial interests, and of illegitimately claiming dominium in the Indies on the basis of papal donations and the Requerimiento.[13] The growing challenge to Spain's New World titles was one of the factors that led Juan de Solórzano y Pereira to start compiling all the laws that Castilian monarchs had passed for their overseas possessions. Both his *De Indiarum Iure* (a two-part work published, respectively, in 1628 and 1639) and his *Política Indiana* (1648) were political works ultimately concerned with legitimizing the conquest and Spain's right to govern Spanish American territories.[14] As a defender of the crown, the jurist aimed to argue that Castile had respected the natural rights of native people, allowing them to live in their own polities, and that the principal goal of conquest and colonization was evangelization. His insistence on the purity status of the indigenous population and their mestizo descendants followed the official line and had clear political motivations.

That is to say, given the ideological centrality of religion to Spanish colonialism—its importance in justifying expansion, conquest, and colonization—the native people *had* to be recognized as pure. Both the crown and the church had to support the idea that they had the quality of limpieza de sangre and were in a different category than Jews and Muslims. After all, if the indigenous people were lumped with conversos and moriscos—communities generally regarded as reluctant and backsliding converts—what was Spain doing in the Americas? Why should the church attempt to convert populations that could not be converted? In 1576, the Jesuit Antonio Possevino (1533–1611) had hinted at these tensions in a memorial in which he insinuated that the society's adoption of a purity statute would jeopardize its missionary agenda.[15] For Spain, the broader implication of the continued division of Christians into two categories was that it would not be able to make a convincing case for its conversion campaigns. Especially if the concept became part of its imperial policies pertaining to indigenous populations, the ideological basis of colonial rule would be completely undermined. The tight linkage of politics and religion in Hispanic expansionism thus could not but make native purity into a part of the official Spanish discourse, recognized by the state, the church, and the Inquisition.

Of course, formal pronouncements about purity of blood were one thing; how they were applied was quite another. Limpieza de sangre was not only a mobile discourse that could be transferred to the Americas but also a flexible one in which new groups could be incorporated and marked as impure, even if it meant contradicting the official line. By the Suprema's own admission, despite the legal definition of limpieza de sangre, various establishments, in both Spain and the colonies, had for a time been using the concept to exclude people who did not have any ties to either Judaism or Islam (and for that matter to any heretical movements). As an example, the councilors pointed out that Seville's Colegio Mayor had been denying entrance to blacks, mulattos, gypsies, and *guanches* (the native people of the Canary Islands) on the basis of their lack of blood purity. The colonial discourse of purity of blood was rife with contradictions, many of which emanated from the ambiguous religious status of colonial groups and the elusive category of Old Christian.

IDOLATRY, HERESY, AND THE AMBIGUITIES OF THE COLONIAL DISCOURSE OF NATIVE PURITY

The Suprema's discussion of the different opinions of jurists on the purity statutes and the category of Old Christian stressed two main issues. The first was the fundamental distinction that Spanish authorities tended to draw between Jewish and Muslim conversions to Christianity and those of gentiles—a distinction that, as already emphasized, Spain needed in order to keep framing its presence in the Americas (and elsewhere) as a fundamentally religious enterprise. The second was the temporal dimension associated with being a cristiano viejo. Old Christians, the councilors had noted, were generally understood to be people who did not descend from Jews and Muslims but instead derived from gentiles who in previous generations had accepted the faith, ideally so far back in time that no one remembered their conversions. Needless to say, this definition left substantial room for ambiguity. Although the Suprema favored allowing people whose parents and grandparents had been Catholic all their lives to claim the category, the more popular definition made it much less accessible, dependent on whether there remained memory of a non-Christian past. As far as the colonial population was concerned, the status of Old Christian thus mainly hinged on one question: was loyalty to Christianity measured by whether a person was part of a lineage that had adhered to Catholicism for at least three generations or by whether he or she belonged to a community—a caste—whose conversion no one remembered? The absence of a clear answer to this question made the category of Old Christian both accessible and slippery and generated deep fissures within the discourse of purity of blood.

Complicating the issue of who could claim Old Christian status was the lack of consensus about the results of the church's Christianizing efforts in Spanish America. By the second half of the seventeenth century, some jurists and theologians argued that the native people were eligible for the status of cristianos viejos because most derived from families that had converted to Catholicism soon after the conquest and because most remained loyal to the faith, but other Spaniards were far more skeptical. The indigenous population's status as converts was in fact still very much contested and provoked strikingly different and passionate responses. For example, in the 1670s, the Mexican Inquisition was still referring to the native people as being "tender in the faith," as "new Christians" in need of the "milk of the Holy Gospel."[16] Furthermore, if some priests were convinced of their devotion to Christianity, others not only maintained that idolatry was still rampant, but continued to link it to heresy. Indeed, at the very moment that members of the Suprema were asserting that one would be hard-pressed to find a native who had relapsed into his ancestors' "gentile" practices—which in their eyes made them fundamentally different to the conversos and moriscos—church officials in Mexico were expressing a heightened concern over the persistence of pre-Hispanic religious rituals and beliefs and resuscitating theories that linked the indigenous people to the Jews.

One such official was don Isidro de Sariñana y Cuenca, a seventeenth-century bishop of Oaxaca who gained notoriety for his harsh policies toward native "dogmatizers" in his jurisdiction, and who contended that idolatry was deeply rooted in the hearts of the indigenous people; that even if they appeared to be good Catholics, they continued to adore their idols; and that they were like "idolatrous" Jews who concealed the true objects of their devotion. His writings and in particular his warnings to priests regarding the untrustworthy nature of indigenous religiosity influenced Diego Jaymes Ricardo de Villavicencio. A priest who served the church and the Inquisition in the archbishopric of Puebla, Villavicencio was also *juez comisario* (commissioner judge) in Santa Cruz Tlatlaccotepetl, where he was in charge of supervising native people on religious and other matters. In 1692, he published a treatise titled *Tratado de avisos y puntos importantes de la abominable seta [secta] de la idolatría*, which was to help priests identify and uproot pre-Columbian religious beliefs through the development of better confession methods, based on experience rather than on information gathered from books.[17] In this revealing text, Villavicencio lamented that after a century and a half of evangelization efforts in indigenous communities, "the abominable sect of idolatry" had still not been eradicated. On the contrary, the priest stated, the problem had only worsened, and not only in his bishopric but in the whole of the viceroyalty. Though the native population partook in the rituals of Catholicism and on the outside manifested the signs of the faith, inside they continued to keep alive the "superstitions" and beliefs of their gentile past.

Permeated with imagery that predictably links light and visibility to Christ and the dark and blindness to the devil, Villavicencio's book provided a list of techniques for how to detect idolatry. In addition to helping priests recognize the signs of heathenism, the new methods were supposed to improve confessional strategies. The goal was to probe the internal, moral world of native people and to instill notions of sin and guilt that would prompt those who had deviated from the faith to confess. But beyond what it reveals about the slippage between religious and cultural practices—in the sense, for example, that the name given to a child was to be interpreted as a sign of religious orientation—and the development of a more efficacious "moral science" at the end of the seventeenth century,[18] the manual is remarkable for an additional reason: the author's relentless efforts to link the indigenous population to the Jews. Basing his discussion on passages from the Bible and writings of the church fathers, Villavicencio dedicated not just one but several chapters of his treatise to discussing the pagan cults and sacrificial practices of the ancient people of Israel, their refusal to relinquish their idols when they were called upon to do so, and the punishments that God cast upon them for their sins.[19]

The depiction of the ancient Hebrews as idolaters who regularly engaged in all sorts of carnal excesses is followed by a similar one of Mexico's pre-Columbian peoples. Villavicencio's text renders the Aztec capital a den of vices, sin, and abominations, a veritable meat market where despotic rulers, the worst being Moctezuma, constantly indulged their insatiable appetites for women and human flesh. Through this description of unbridled depravity, the author sought to convey the message that punishment was not only imminent but also well deserved. Just as the ancient Israelites had to pay for their errors, so too had the Indians. Thus, when Cortés, like a New World Moses, arrived to liberate that blind "Indian Egypt" (*indiano egipto*) that was Tenochtitlan, the Mexica rulers were killed and their people forced to endure plagues, hunger, and finally, defeat. Clearly attempting to interpret the Spanish conquest through the Holy Scriptures, Villavicencio went so far as to contend that biblical prophecies regarding the ancient Jews had prefigured the destruction of the idols in the Templo Mayor and the punishments of the Indians. He was suggesting that the fall of the Mexica, as well as their subjection to the Spaniards, had been divinely ordained. This reading of the conquest of Mexico allowed the priest to interpret the tribute imposed on the native people as both a marker of their sin and as a symbol of their spiritual debts to the Iberians for leading them out of satanic darkness and into the light of salvation.

But according to Villavicencio, indigenous people were still paying for their mistakes not so much because their ancestors had practiced idolatry, but because they continued to do so. Far from being loyal newcomers to the faith, he argued, the Indians were false Christians, people "in whose veins still runs and moves, and lives, the blood of their ancestors, who in their gentility gave themselves so blindly to Idolatry."[20] Villavicencio claimed to have received numerous reports about native people in the bishoprics of Puebla and Mexico who frequently escaped to the mountains in order to sacrifice animals and even humans in secret caves. He also wrote that he had news that a priest in charge of evangelizing Indians in the jurisdiction of the town of Atlixco (near Puebla) had found out that some of his parishioners were regularly going to a spring to commit idolatries. The said priest claimed to have gone to the scene of the crime incognito and to have seen some native people pour water from the spring in a ceramic container and place it in on a cart that they covered with branches and flowers. They then burned copal incense around the container and moved the cart in a festive procession. As the people rejoiced, the priest and his assistants supposedly removed their disguises and took the group of idolaters to jail. They were all publicly punished, and the leaders were sold as temporary slaves in Puebla's textile mills.

For Villavicencio, idolaters were like beasts and they should be treated as such. He even blamed the persistence of gentile practices for the high price of wheat, the epidemics of measles, and the overall instability that had been plaguing the viceroyalty and which in 1692 resulted in a riot in Mexico City.[21] Furthermore, the priest attributed the repression and the militarization of the viceregal capital that followed the riot to the Indians' deviation from Catholicism. But Villavicencio did not blame the entire native population for the recent chain of disasters, especially not its nobility. The problem of idolatry, he stressed, was limited to the poorer, and predominantly rural, sectors, which he claimed were more rustic and ignorant and therefore more susceptible to superstitions and to the devil. This vulnerability was enhanced, Villavicencio observed, by the drinking of *pulque,* an alcoholic beverage from pre-Columbian times that at that moment was being linked to all sorts of social disorders.[22]

Villavicencio saved his strongest indictment for native religious specialists, whom he called "rabbis" (*indios rabies*) and accused of spreading demonic and subversive thoughts. The priest believed that it was necessary to identify and remove these "dogmatizers" from their communities, but he admitted that the task was not going to be easy because they "wore rosaries" and exhibited other exterior signs that made them seem like good Christians. After warning other church officials not to be fooled by the "artifice" of "wolves pretending to be sheep," he advised those working among native populations to learn from past experiences with the Jews, who he claimed had pretended to convert to Christianity but secretly kept alive their old beliefs and practices. Through the notions of "artifice" and "dissimulation," the priest thus made discursive connections between the Indians and the conversos. His discussion of the religious lives of indigenous people relied not only on the trope of the backsliding Jewish convert but on that of the carnal Jew. In Villavicencio's view, Mexico's indigenous population shared with the ancient Hebrews an almost innate inclination to practice idolatry and with Spain's New Christians an ability to conceal, under the veneer of Catholicism, the real objects of their devotion. From his use of the term *rabbi* to refer to native religious specialists, to his equation of Jewish and indigenous "idolatry," to his comparison of the conversos' allegedly recalcitrant nature and the Indians' adherence to their ancestors' beliefs, the priest's understanding of religious problems in New Spain were strongly shaped by Spanish anti-Semitic thought.

Bishop Sariñana y Cuenca and Villavicencio were certainly not the first to try to establish connections between the Jews and the Indians, nor were they the first to use biblical passages about the ancient Israelites as parables of what could happen to "incorrigible sinners." Indeed, during the period in which theories about the pre-Columbian inhabitants descending from one of the lost tribes of Israel began to proliferate, some colonial officials made concerted efforts to transfer their contempt of the Jew to the native people. As Inquisitor Peralta revealed in a 1604 letter in which he discussed the clandestine arrival of conversos to New Spain and their alleged crypto-Judaism, autos de fe served as good examples for the local population, especially for the Indians, who were learning to hate Jews and others who were publicly humiliated and punished by the Inquisition.[23] The clergy in both Mexico and Peru also made the topic of Jewish idolatry a prominent theme in their sermons. Together with the dramatic autos de fe in which people convicted of crypto-Judaism were punished, the colonial priesthood's anti-Semitic invectives ultimately served as examples or "teaching devices" through which native people and other groups were to learn of the penalties that awaited those who committed idolatry (embodied by the ancient Jews) and heresy (embodied by the conversos).[24] Villavicencio's manual even advised priests to begin the first of several talks that they were to have with those who confessed to religious deviations by discussing the prevalence of idolatry among the Hebrews and stressing that those who had not converted with Saint Paul (which had been most) were burning in hell.

The clergy's ongoing obsession with the topic of Jewish idolatry reveals not only its efforts to frighten the native population into relinquishing their old rituals, but its gradual and often subtle adaptation of notions of impurity to the colonial context. As argued in Chapter 6, some religious officials did not make a distinction between heresy and idolatry, thereby helping to produce a de facto discourse of native "impurity." The exclusion of the indigenous people from the jurisdiction of the Inquisition thus did not prevent members of the clergy—especially those not satisfied with the results of the conversion project—from drawing cultural, historical, and even genealogical linkages between the Indians and Jews. Periods during which New Spain's religious officials turned their attention to the problem of idolatry tended to be times in which speculation about the native population's possible Hebrew origins increased and in which Spanish writers and institutions raised questions about its purity status. Although various seventeenth-century Spanish thinkers rejected the theory of the Indians' Jewish descent, it nonetheless remained popular. According to both Solórzano Pereira and the friar Gregorio García, it was particularly appealing to common Spaniards, especially those living in the Americas, as well as to some jurists. In the last third of the seventeenth century, the theory once again became the subject of a number of different texts, which suggests it was experiencing a kind of revival. Even the document containing the Suprema's discussion of the purity of blood of colonial populations hints at a continued fixation with the topic, for it has the words *judío* and *indio* scribbled next to each other on the bottom of a page, probably not by the original authors because it is upside down and more legible.

The continued popularity of the Indian Jewish-descent theory made manifest some of the contradictions inherent in the Spanish colonial discourse of purity of blood. The native people were officially considered

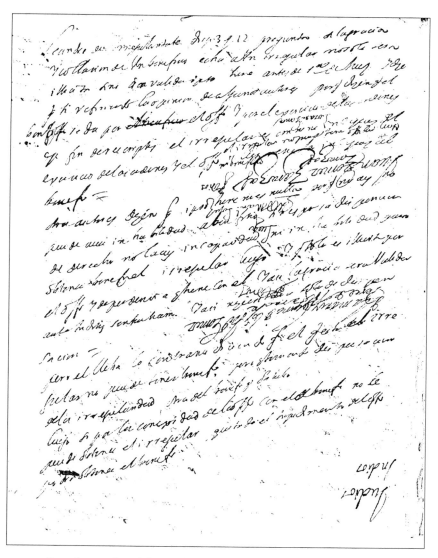

FIG. 3. Page from a Spanish Inquisition document containing deliberations on whether mestizos and mulattos in Spanish America should be allowed into institutions with purity of blood statutes. Undated. SOURCE: Archivo Histórico Nacional, Inquisición, libro 1266.

unblemished and perfect candidates for Christianity, but in the writings of theologians and priests, they often figured as fragile converts who if misguided could easily regress to idolatry. The two images complemented each other and together served a crucial political need, because if in the seventeenth century Spain no longer defended its titles on the basis of the papal donations and evangelization mission, it nonetheless insisted that it had a responsibility to ensure that the indigenous population did not revert to pre-Columbian rituals. According to this line of reasoning, which Solorzáno y Pereira used in *De Indiarum Iure,* abandoning the Americas would be tantamount to a sin because it would enable native religious specialists to take control of the government and spearhead a return to idolatry. The argument that Spain had a moral and political obligation to continue its rule in Spanish America in order to fulfill its religious mission meant that the crown and its supporters had continuously to construct the Indians at once as ideal material for Christianization and as fragile converts, always susceptible to sliding back to their ancestral beliefs and practices. Ambiguities in the purity status of native people thus emanated from the very contradictions of Spanish colonialism, from a political ideology that on one hand announced that they were untainted because they lacked Jewish, Muslim, and heretical antecedents and had willingly accepted the faith, and on the other constantly iterated that they would revert to idolatry if left to their own devices and in the hands of misguided leaders.

Religion thus continued to be central to the discourse of limpieza de sangre at the end of the seventeenth century, but in deeply inconsistent ways. While the native people were depicted by some religious officials and metropolitan thinkers as ideal Christians and declared pure, their real or presumed linkage to idolatry in the colonial world made their access to purity status provisional, problematic, conditional, and at times highly contradictory. Which is not to say that the official discourse of limpieza de sangre did not have important social and political consequences. Quite the contrary. Native political and economic elites used it in their communities, where a discourse of purity parallel to that which was in place in the republic of Spaniards and which also relied on religious ideas survived into the eighteenth century and beyond. Echoing the formal definition of limpieza de sangre, caciques and principales proclaimed their purity in probanzas, genealogies, and títulos primordiales on the basis of their abandonment of idolatry and oftentimes also their lack of black blood. Furthermore, within Spanish colonial cities, people of partial native ancestry were sometimes able to claim both purity of blood and Old Christian ancestry. A few examples from the admission records of the Franciscan Order can illustrate the point.

After it established its limpieza statute in Spain in 1525, the Franciscan Order theoretically did not accept anyone who descended from Jews within four generations on either the father's or the mother's side. The purity requirement continued to be the source of controversy until 1583, when the order held a general chapter in Toledo and incorporated it into its legislation, where it was to remain unchanged for more than two centuries. In central Mexico, the Franciscan chapter, called the Province of the Holy Gospel, initially created two novitiates, one in Mexico City, the other in Puebla. Later a third one was established in the Convent of San Cosme, also in the capital. In Puebla, the Convent of San Francisco was accepting novices by 1569. Most of its admission records, the earliest produced in the Province of the Holy Gospel, have survived and therefore allow for a close analysis of the process and language involved in the certification of purity of blood and to chart changes over time.[25] Shortly after the Franciscan Order's constitution containing the purity statute was published in Mexico in 1585, candidates for the novitiate began to submit *informaciones de limpieza, vida y costumbres* (information of purity, lifestyle, and habits).[26] These informaciones were the first step in the probanza or purity certification process.

The Franciscan Order's purity certification process closely resembled that of the Inquisition, but there were some differences. A purity investigation conducted by the religious order began when the candidate submitted his genealogical information to the friar in charge of receiving novitiates. By then, the candidate had already informed the head of the province of his desire to profess and passed an examination on religious matters. The friar receiving the candidate's information (who oftentimes also served the Holy Office as a calificador) first reviewed the papal bulls that had confirmed the purity statute of the order and all the criteria that were necessary for membership in the order. Among ineligible categories were illegitimates; the children of clergymen, friars, and nuns; people with substantial debts; and murderers. Naturally, married candidates were also disqualified. Technically the purity statute targeted two main types of people: descendants of "Moors, Jews, or the recently converted" within the fourth degree, and persons who had been punished by the Inquisition (or other religious tribunals) and their relatives. Those who professed were warned that they would be expelled if at any point it was discovered that they fell under any of the prohibited categories.

After the genealogical information was presented, a commissioner and a notary were assigned to the case and, as with the Inquisition, two investigations were conducted. The first, or *información secreta*, involved checking public and parish records in order to verify genealogies and to identify those who were automatically disqualified, for example, because they were married or had criminal records. Illegitimate birth was sometimes excused if the candidate was otherwise deemed a strong candidate. The second, or *información jurídica,* focused on the issue of purity of blood and hence involved the interrogation of witnesses, usually three or four, occasionally more. The questioning normally took place at one of the Franciscans' convents. The interrogations differed from those of the Inquisition mainly in two regards. First, they were initially shorter than those of the Holy Office, although by the mid-seventeenth century they too consisted of eleven questions. And second, the Franciscan Order explicitly inquired into more aspects of the candidate's life (e.g., criminal record, marital status, and infectious diseases) in order to determine his suitability for monastic life and missionary work. With regard to the issue of purity of blood itself, the order in theory limited genealogical investigating to the great-grandparents, but as had occurred with the Inquisition's probanzas, when the interrogations took place, witnesses were normally asked to declare whether they had information about the person having any Jewish, Muslim, or heretic ancestors. Once the interrogations were finished, the case was submitted to the prosecutor (*promotor fiscal*) of the order, who examined the documentation and determined whether anything else was needed. The last step was a review of the case and decision by a committee of friars.

After 1614, the year that the Province of the Holy Gospel's purity statute was amended to read that "no Indian or mestizo may be received into this Province or anyone who is not pure Spanish reverting to the fourth generation,"[27] commissioners regularly asked witnesses whether the candidate for the novitiate was a mestizo or *cuarterón* (quadroon) or had any other "Indian part." Often they framed the question indirectly, by inquiring whether the petitioner derived from "newly converted gentiles within the fourth degree." Categories referring to proportions of different bloods used by the Franciscans as well as other colonial institutions evoke those that the Spanish Inquisition had started to use in Spain ("half New Christians," "quarter New Christians," "one sixteenth of a New Christian," and so forth) to refer to the children of Old and New Christians. The similarity reflects the strong influence that Iberian notions of lineage and purity had not only on Mexico's sistema de castas but on colonial genealogical and archival practices. Suspicions that a candidate for the Franciscan Order had "native parts" were likely to lead to lengthy investigations to determine his exact ancestry that mirrored those that were done to detect Jewish and Muslim descent.

For example, in 1672, the purity of blood of Francisco de Lara, a novice in Puebla's Convent of San Francisco who had already had his probanza approved, came into question.[28] The witnesses had all declared that he was pure and that his ancestors were Spanish. The case, furthermore, contained an affidavit from a priest certifying that the candidate was entered in Toluca's baptismal records for españoles. During Lara's first year in the novitiate, however, "trustworthy people" informed the convent's authorities that he was not a pure Spaniard. The friars in charge therefore undertook a second investigation. A commissioner was sent to the city of Toluca, Lara's place of birth, to do the interrogations. He questioned three witnesses, all of whom indicated that Francisco's limpieza had been challenged because his mother's ancestors were unknown and were rumored to have "some mixture from the land," albeit not much. In the end, the seven friars who assessed the case accepted Lara into the order because whatever native ancestry he had appeared to be remote and not "within the fourth degree."

But what exactly did the stipulation that candidates could not have native ancestors to the fourth generation mean? It might have simply implied that that no one with an Indian ancestor to the fourth generation or as a great-grandparent could be accepted into the order, that is, no one with more than "one-eighth native blood." However, the Province of the Holy Gospel was vague on the matter and seems to have followed the Holy Office's example of using the exclusion mainly against those who had more than one-fourth of indigenous ancestry ("*cuarto de mestizo*"). Adding to the confusion was the appearance of the phrase "newly converted gentiles within the fourth degree" in some genealogical investigations, which implied that limpieza de sangre could be defined according either to degrees of mixture ("no more than one-eighth Indian") or to timing of conversion ("no idolaters within four generations"). According to the first definition, the descendants of native and Spanish unions could, after several generations, be eligible for purity status; according to the second, "pure Indians" could, too, providing that they and their parents, grandparents, and great-grandparents had been good Catholics. The lack of clarity created spaces for individuals with indigenous ancestry to enter the Franciscan Order, which they began to do in the last third of the seventeenth century.

One such individual was Miguel Osorio Moctezuma, who submitted his genealogy to the friars in Puebla's Franciscan convent in 1679. He was a descendant of the Mexica ruler defeated by Cortés, and his parents were Nicolas Osorio Moctezuma and doña Ana de Morales, identified by the witnesses as "good and noble people of Tlaxcala." According to the testimonies, the community considered the candidate and his family to be faithful Catholics without Muslim, Jewish, and infidel ancestors and without any "vulgar infamies." One witness said that he had not known the candidate's paternal grandparents, but that he had heard that they were Old Christians and that they were all notable gentlemen who had played a role in the government and administration of justice. The other witnesses also emphasized the candidate's ancestors' adherence to the faith, their Old Christian credentials, and their participation in local politics. Miguel Osorio Moctezuma was thus held to be a loyal Catholic and pure of blood. His baptism was recorded in Tlaxcala's Spanish registers in the list of bautismos de españoles, suggesting that his indigenous ancestors were remote and that he was known as a Spaniard.[29] Once the investigation of his genealogy was complete, he was accepted into the novitiate and eventually became a Franciscan friar.

A few other Moctezumas from Puebla's surrounding regions were admitted into the city's Franciscan convent, including Diego Valdés Moctezuma, who had his genealogical investigation done in the 1690s.[30] The witnesses in his información testified that he descended from "Catholic Christians" and that he had no ancestors who were Jews, Mohammedans, or heretics, and also none who were "modern Gentiles" within degrees that would disqualify him from entering the order. They also stressed that he did not have any "stains of vulgar infamies," such as slavery, and that he had not held any "vile" trades or professions.[31] The commissioner also inspected Valdés Moctezuma's baptismal record in the convent of San Matheo de Hueychiapan. Like that of Miguel Osorio Moctezuma, it too was included in the libros de españoles. Both informaciones suggest that the two Moctezumas were considered Spaniards and that they were accepted into the order because whatever native ancestry they had, it was noble and remote. Equally important, they were known in their respective communities as honorable Old Christians. Ancestry, religious behavior, and participation in government and public rituals could all play a role in the determination of limpieza de sangre.

Another candidate who claimed to have noble native ancestry and was accepted into the Franciscan Order was Manuel de Salazar, who described himself as a descendant of Citlalpopoca, lord of Quiahuixtlán (one of the four divisions, or *cabeceras*, of Tlaxcala).[32] When he submitted his genealogical information in 1675, he stated that his parents, don Bernabé de Salazar y de los Santos and doña Felipa Isabel, were principales in the city of Tlaxcala. The commissioner conducted the secret investigation and, not having found any impediments, such as illegitimate birth, proceeded with the interrogation of the witnesses (which according to the order's rules had to be Spaniards). Three people, all native to Tlaxcala, testified that Salazar's parents and grandparents were among the most noble of the city, had held offices in its government, and did not have any vulgar or infamous stains. The witnesses also stated that the candidate's parents were "faithful Catholics and did not descend from Jews, Mohammedans, or heretics in any degree whatsoever, nor from modern Gentiles within the fourth degree." The third and final declarant added that Salazar's parents had not been tried for idolatry or for any other crime that would have been punished by the Inquisition. Together the testimonies thus established that Salazar's parents, grandparents, and great grandparents had been Catholic; that they were not commoners; and that they did not have any other stains in their bloodlines, such as slave or illegitimate antecedents. In this case, the claim that the candidate did not descend from "modern Gentiles within any degrees that would impede his candidacy" implied that he did not derive from *unconverted* Indians within four generations because, at least from his maternal line, his ancestors were all said to derive directly from one of the "Kings of the Indies."

Like the previous two cases, that of Salazar demonstrates that within the Franciscan Order, indigenous descent—depending on how far removed it was and on the social status and Christian reputation of the members of the lineage—did not necessarily hinder the recognition of purity. Salazar's acceptance into the novitiate suggests that the Franciscans were sometimes even willing to receive individuals who had native relatives "within the fourth degree" if they were otherwise deemed to be worthy candidates. Although there is no reason to believe that persons of partial indigenous ancestry were entering the religious order in significant numbers, the fact that some were did not sit well with creoles who had come to believe that they should have exclusive access to that institution as well as to the viceroyalty's public offices and ecclesiastical benefices. In 1702, for example, the friar Agustín de Vetancour (also spelled Betancur), a writer and theology teacher in Puebla's Franciscan convent, argued that people of Spanish–Indian parentage should not be admitted into the Franciscan Order because they were not Old Christians.[33]

Vetancour, who for a while had been in charge of receiving the genealogical information presented by candidates for the novitiate, had been born in Ayotzingo and was one of New Spain's principal creole patriots.[34] In a letter addressed to another friar, he stressed that mestizos descended from "new converts" on their indigenous line and were therefore neophytes who should not be accepted into the order. It did not matter that their Indian ancestors had been Catholics for generations, he stated, because the ordinario (the Provisorato, or "Native Inquisition") knew of their crimes and of how deeply ingrained in their blood were the rituals and ceremonies of their gentile past. Allowing mestizos into the Franciscan Order would therefore "stain the creole nation" (*a la nación criolla se mancha*). Some people argued that accepting a few would not make a difference, noted Vetancour. But for him, a single mestizo was enough to tarnish the reputation of his order, which he claimed was composed exclusively of religious individuals who descended from Old Christians and nobles. Of those who differed, the friar asked, "If a mulatto that was born in Spain, being a neophyte descendant of new converts, was received, would it not be an affront to the Spanish nation?" For Vetancour, being an Old Christian was not a matter of years or generations; it was fundamentally a matter of religion and lineage.

As Vetancour's views suggest, faith and bloodlines continued to be integral to the discourse of limpieza de sangre, and their growing sense of patriotism did not prevent some creoles from harboring a profound disdain for the native people and mestizos and from using lineage to secure their privileges. In their version of the argument that Spain could not abandon the Americas because it had to ensure that there was no retreat from Christianity, it was they, the "natives" of the kingdom and descendants of the conquerors and first colonists, who were to be in control of the government and church. In the mid-eighteenth century, they would produce a mural in Mexico City depicting Cortés as an American Moses, thereby turning the conquest and Christianization project into a visual image of their patriotic history.[35] Creole patriotism generally did not challenge the ideology of limpieza de sangre but rather sought to reinforce it by redeploying the late medieval argument that blood was a vehicle through which all sorts of "natural" qualities were transmitted and by inserting the descendants of native people and especially blacks into the same category of impurity as conversos and moriscos.

BLACKS, CASTAS, AND THE EXPANSION
OF THE CATEGORY OF IMPURITY

Although colonial Spaniards generally regarded blacks as recently converted Christians or not yet fully instructed in the faith, the Spanish crown did not remove them from the jurisdiction of the Holy Office like it did with native people. Extending its reach to Africans and their descendants, the Inquisition tended to prosecute them for moral and religious transgressions such as bigamy and blasphemy and for practicing pagan rituals. It tried them especially for renouncing God or the Virgin or making other blasphemous remarks that the clergy viewed as an expression of ingratitude toward the divine.[36] Blasphemy cases usually resulted in the accused being paraded through the streets of the viceregal cities, subjected to some kind of public humiliation or torture, and forced to confess their transgressions against the faith. The punishments for those whom colonial officials accused of plotting rebellions were much more severe, sometimes resulting in executions. The periodic violence that the state perpetrated on black bodies—usually in the viceregal plaza and in front of the palace and church—served to reinforce

Spanish suspicions about the disloyalty of blacks to crown and faith, and thus also to justify depriving them of the rights that were supposed to be granted to all Christians, among them that of freedom.[37]

In 1640, Mexico had the largest population of free blacks in the Americas and second-largest of enslaved ones.[38] However, as of the mid-seventeenth century, the number of slaves declined, in large part because the separation of the crowns of Castile and Portugal (1640) led Spain to prohibit the purchase of Africans from the Portuguese. But New Spain's free black population continued to increase and to be one of the groups targeted by the Inquisition. That Africans and their descendants were included in the jurisdiction of the Holy Office did not mean that they were somehow considered long-standing Christians or more trust-worthy converts than the native people. As Spain's conversos and moris-cos knew fully well, being subjected to the Inquisition did not translate into being accepted as faithful or "old" Christians but just the opposite. The crown's decision to allow the Holy Office to try blacks and not indigenous people was in consonance with its project to create a dual model of social organization and the concomitant establishment of spe-cial secular and religious institutions for the latter.

Because they were associated with slavery and not recognized as a re-public of their own, blacks and their descendants had less clearly defined rights than the native population, whose status as free Christian vassals of the Crown of Castile was in practice not always upheld but nonethe-less constantly invoked in colonial policies and legislation. As far as can be determined, Spanish kings did not issue a decree or formal statement regarding the rights of African-descended individuals as vecinos or con-firming their purity-of-blood status, and if they did, the proclamation did not become a prominent part of colonial legislation. It was therefore easier for colonial institutions to include black blood as a source of im-purity, which they began to do as of the late sixteenth century.

For example, in what was perhaps the first genealogical investigation done by Puebla's Convent of San Francisco, dated 1594, the commis-sioner sought to determine whether Bartolomé de Mancillas's progeni-tors were of a lineage that was "stained by Jews, Moors, slaves, heretics"; had been reconciled or burned by the Holy Office; or had any other blemish.[39] By the turn of the sixteenth century, blacks and mulattos were identified as impure with no apparent limit on how far back the "stain" could be traced. Thus, in 1599, the Franciscan Order made a probanza for Cristóbal Ruiz de Quiroz in Tepeaca in which the witnesses were asked whether he was of "a clean caste and generation, without the race or mixture of Moors, mulattoes, blacks, Jews and the newly converted to the Holy Catholic Faith and with no ties to persons punished by the Holy Office."[40] In some probanzas, the phrase "does not descend from mulattoes within the fourth degree" appears, but more often than not, it was used by witnesses and candidates rather than by the commissioners, which would suggest that there was no limitation on the exclusion.

Despite the early construction of slave and black antecedents as impure in colonial genealogical investigations, neither the state nor the Inquisition issued a formal statement regarding the practice, at least not until the second half of the eighteenth century. The results of this conceptual vagueness were discursive spaces and fissures that allowed people of African ancestry on both sides of the Atlantic to attempt to claim the category of Old Christian by defining it according to its original religious and genealogical terms. For example, on 30 March 1606, Catalina Reyes requested a probanza before a judge in Seville in order to establish that she was the daughter of a "free and Old Christian white male" (*hombre blanco libre y cristiano viejo*) and an "Old Christian woman of dark skin" (*morena ateçada y cristiana vieja*) who had been a slave. Reyes wanted to accompany her employer Isabel Cervantes to New Spain, but because she was a "morena" (of partial black ancestry), she first needed to obtain a special travel license, which meant that she had to prove that she was both free and pure of blood. To that effect, she claimed that her mother had been liberated before giving birth to her, which thanks to the principle of the free womb meant she too was free. As to her purity status, Reyes declared, "I and my son and my parents are and were Old Christians of clean caste and generation, without any stains or races from Moors or Jews nor from the newly converted to our holy Catholic faith," and presented two witnesses to support her statement.[41] Relying on the original meanings of the notions of limpieza de sangre and cristiano viejo, Catalina Reyes did not see her mother's slave (and presumably also African) past as an impediment to claiming purity of blood.

Although the possibility that African-descended people would be able to obtain purity of blood and Old Christian status became more remote as the seventeenth century unfolded and the plantation revolution shaped racial ideologies across the Atlantic world, some nonetheless continued to try. At the end of the century, for example, Nicolas Cortés, whom the Inquisition tried for bigamy and described as a "free white mulatto," claimed that he was born in Jalapa to a Spanish father and a woman of the "mulatto nation" and that he was of a "caste and generation of Old Christians," unblemished and (until then) untouched by the Inquisition. When he gave his genealogy to the Holy Office, he added that he had been baptized and was a good Christian who regularly went to mass, confessed, and took communion.[42] Diego Velásquez de Tasada, a mulatto slave working in the mines of Guadalajara who was tried for blasphemy roughly at the same time as Cortés's prosecution, made similar claims. He stated that his father was a Spaniard and his mother a *mulata* from Guadalajara and that all of his ancestors and collaterals had been Old Christians. He too asserted he was a good Christian.[43] These and similar cases make evident that there were competing definitions and understandings of the category of Old Christian, some of which stressed religion and genealogy and challenged the association of black blood with impurity.

Although the above examples seem to suggest otherwise, having a Spanish father was not necessary for people of black ancestry to see themselves as pure Old Christians. For example, the *información* of Diego Joseph Rodríguez Vargas, a candidate for the novitiate in the Convent of San Francisco, contains a copy of a certification of purity of blood that his mother, Petrona Vaquero, requested on his behalf from Puebla's alcalde mayor in the 1690s.[44] When Vaquero submitted her son's genealogy, she stated that she was a Spaniard but that her husband, Diego de Covos, was of "*color pardo*" (a category increasingly used for people of partial African ancestry).[45] As if attempting to compensate for his origins, she added that Covos was an honest man, a good Christian, and a person who was "clean of all bad race." Vaquero also stressed that her husband was free and had been a battalion captain in Puebla's *compañía de pardos*. Some of the witnesses for Rodríguez Vargas's probanza claimed that his mother was a *parda* herself. Others, however, regarded both of his parents as Old Christians, and a priest certified that he was registered in Puebla's cathedral parish in the book of Spanish baptisms.

Clearly, what "bad race" meant and who could claim purity and Old Christian ancestry were highly contested issues in colonial Mexico. In appropriating both categories, African-descended people challenged some of the principles of colonial racial ideology as well as the social hierarchies they were meant to reproduce and rejected the idea that they could not make lineage claims. That they did so by using concepts of limpieza de sangre speaks not only to their participation in the construction of a common discursive field.[46] It also points to how African diasporic identities were "by definition creole, but also simultaneously tortured and creative" and their struggles almost always interstitial, "found in spaces and cracks within ostensibly hegemonic structures."[47] In the end, however, claiming the category of purity of blood and having it recognized were two separate matters. As the eighteenth century began, the assumption that black ancestry was incompatible with the status of limpieza de sangre was firmly in place and operating in a host of institutions across central Mexico.

For example, in 1702, the authorities of a Franciscan convent in Querétaro began to investigate the antecedents of two brothers, Fray Nicolás de Velasco and Fray Miguel de Velasco, who were suspected of having "the bad race of mulattoes." The investigation started with interrogations of community elders, many of whom reported that they knew or suspected that the brothers were not pure because of the skin color and hair texture of their mother and some of their grandparents. After a three-year investigation, which involved examining many juridical instruments (copies of marriage and birth certificates) presented by the father and several waves of interrogations of different witnesses, the Velasco brothers were allowed to remain in the order and declared "pure and legitimate Spaniards of good social status and blood" (*limpios y legítimos españoles de buena calidad y limpieza*). The friars in charge of the investigations determined that the Velascos were being confused with two other brothers, whose last name was Velázquez and who had been expelled from their religious order because of the "defect" of their lineage. They also declared that some of the rumors about their ancestry were motivated by malice.[48]

The Velasco case includes a detailed discussion by theologians regarding the Franciscan Order's prohibition of blacks and the proper course of action when a "mulatto pretending to be a Spaniard" had been accepted. The theologians concluded that when acceptance into the order occurred under false pretenses, the culprit could be deprived of the habit and expelled. They also determined that if the said friar had black blood, he could not be granted dispensation because it would contradict the statute against accepting mulattoes that had been approved by the pope. The convent's authorities could not ignore what higher authorities had mandated. By the time this discussion took place, few institutions, religious or otherwise, questioned the association of black blood with impurity, and black skin color had become a marker of impure ancestry. As the testimonies of witnesses in the Velasco case suggest, colonial Spaniards had come to link limpieza de sangre to physical appearance. In the course of the seventeenth century, the concept had gone from being mainly associated with having Old Christian ancestry to being connected to whiteness. This link would become stronger in the eighteenth century.

CONCLUSION

In seventeenth-century New Spain, purity of blood was still officially defined as a religious and genealogical concept that referred to whether individuals had ties to Judaism, Islam, or heresy. This enduring legal definition led prominent Spanish jurists and theologians to argue that indigenous people and in some cases also blacks were technically "untainted." Nonetheless, as the archival practices, interrogative procedures, and genealogical formulas associated with purity investigations came to be adapted to the colonial context, the concept of limpieza was deployed against people of African and native ancestry on the basis of their "gentile origins." Furthermore, references to candidates not descending from blacks, mulattos, and mestizos became commonplace in seventeenth-century genealogical investigations, as did the claim that they did not derive from anyone associated with the "stain of vulgar infamies, such as slavery or the exercise of any base trade within the republic."[49] As Spaniards in the Americas mapped the notion of impurity onto certain colonial populations, they came to relate it to phenotype and social status.

Nonetheless, the meaning of the concept of limpieza de sangre continued to be vague and inconsistent. Its main inconsistency stemmed from the official status of the native people, which despite claims about their alleged continued association with idolatry allowed some of the descendants of pre-Hispanic lineages to claim both purity of blood and Old Christian ancestry. At the end of the seventeenth century, it was not difficult for them to make the case for having Catholic ancestors beyond the grandparents, and the crown confirmed their limpieza status. The status of blacks was less inconsistent, in large part because the state never declared their blood to be unsullied, but some African-descended people nonetheless attempted to use religious and genealogical formulations to proclaim their purity of blood and Old Christian ancestry. Limpieza de sangre was to a certain extent in the eye of the beholder, and the notion's intrinsic vagueness—its equivocating references to descent and generational formulas and also to religious practices and beliefs—almost encouraged appropriations.

But if the concept was at times employed in unexpected ways, redeployed by persons generally marked as impure, the power to create definitions, archives, and classifications ultimately resided with the Inquisition and a host of other colonial institutions linked to the state and the church. To a considerable degree, these institutions and the practices they routinized established the parameters of the categories that were possible and legitimate. They not only had the power to define, classify, and order but to exclude on the basis of those categorizations. Over time, colonial institutions came to increase the role that baptismal records played in establishing limpieza status. Some purity informaciones done in the sixteenth century contain written copies of the candidate's baptismal information (with affidavits from priests), but in the latter half of the colonial period, which began in the 1670s, they became a standard feature. As the seventeenth century closed, these parish records were increasingly using the formula "people of reason," as in "baptisms of Spaniards and other castes of people of reason" (*bautismos de españoles y demas castas de personas de razón*). The discourse of limpieza de sangre and the colonial sistema de castas that it inspired had entered the Age of Reason.

CHAPTER NINE

Changing Contours

'Limpieza de Sangre' in the Age of Reason and Reform

About two decades ago, a series of paintings that are unique to eighteenth-century Spanish America began to attract the attention of students of the region. The genre, which modern scholars have labeled "casta paintings," originated and was developed in the viceroyalty of New Spain.[1] Stimulated by a growing metropolitan curiosity over the nature and inhabitants of the New World, Mexican artists produced the vast majority of these paintings to represent the different "types" of people that sexual relations among Amerindians, blacks, and Spaniards had engendered in the Americas. The main subject of the paintings, in other words, was the population of mixed descent. The painters, a good number of whom were creoles,[2] shared a concern with depicting how reproduction among the three main colonial combinations (Spanish–Indian, Spanish–black, and black–Indian) unfolded in the course of several generations. To illustrate this process of generational mestizaje, they relied on multiple panels—normally three to five for the first two units and several more for the third—and on the family trope. A typical series consisted of sixteen panels, each featuring a mother, father, and a child (sometimes two); an inscription providing the casta terminology for the particular family members; and a focus on skin color distinctions. The intended audience for at least some of the paintings was European, because several of the series were commissioned by colonial officials who intended them as gifts for relatives or institutions in Spain.[3] Casta sets were also destined for the Real Gabinete de Historia Natural (Royal Cabinet of Natural History), which Charles III founded in Madrid in 1771 in order to display objects from different parts of the world, including Castile's overseas territories. Together with minerals, fossils, rocks, flora, and other products from the Americas, various paintings were shipped across the Atlantic and consumed by a Spanish public. Yet some sets stayed in Mexico, implying that there was a local market for them as well.[4]

With the possible exception of only one series, by Luis de Mena, casta paintings situated the different colonial lineages in secular contexts. They also have a strong ethnographic flavor. The European interest in observing, recording, and classifying, which in the eighteenth century inspired a number of scientific expeditions to the Americas, was not new. In previous centuries, the Western ordering impulse had led to the "natural histories" of all sorts of things, including plants, animals, and humans. What became increasingly common in the eighteenth century was the emphasis on the visual, on recording difference not only through taxonomic systems but also through the catalogue.[5] As a genre that most certainly privileges vision in the production and representation of ethnographic distinctions, casta paintings appear to be a part of the Enlightenment project. But it would be a mistake to see them simply as a product of that project and of European encyclopedic and taxonomic trends more generally. Rather, as art historian Ilona Katzew has argued, casta paintings were largely the result of the growing sense of creole identity and identification with the local.[6]

They must also be understood in connection to the socioeconomic context in eighteenth-century central Mexico, the changing relationship between metropole and colony, and the discourse of limpieza de sangre. This chapter focuses on these issues. It stresses that casta paintings, which emerged during a period of deepening anxieties about the shifting social order, construct a narrative of mestizaje informed by the discourse of purity of blood. They also reflect some of the changes that the concept of limpieza de sangre had undergone in colonial Mexico, most notably its association with whiteness. The chapter emphasizes that the existence of multiple definitions of purity of blood, some religious, others more secular, helped fuel a creole patriotic defense of Spanish–Indian unions at a time of growing concerns about mestizaje and its supposed degenerating potential.

AN ICONOGRAPHY OF MESTIZAJE: CASTA PAINTINGS AND THE INTERSECTION OF RACE, CLASS, AND GENDER

At the end the seventeenth century, various Spanish *arbitristas* (authors of treatises on economic and fiscal reform) were convinced that both the Castilian state and economy were in crisis. They mainly attributed the country's lamentable economic situation to its failure to develop its industries and to its being reduced to exporting agricultural products in return for manufactures. Politically, the monarchy was weak and the death of Charles II in 1700 plunged the country and other parts of Europe into a war of succession (1701–13) between supporters of Archduke Charles of Austria and those of Philip of Anjou, respectively, the Habsburg and Bourbon contenders. By the second decade of the eighteenth century, Spain had not only a new king, Philip V (1701–46), but a new dynasty in power. The Bourbons would devote a great deal of time trying to explain why the country had fallen behind other parts of western Europe and strategizing about how to strengthen the crown and the economy. Their efforts would yield a series of reforms that had sweeping ramifications in both Spain and its colonies.

The "Bourbon reforms," however, did not begin in earnest until after the middle of the eighteenth century. By then, Mexico had already been undergoing important socioeconomic and cultural changes. Demographically, the region went from having a population of about 1.5 million in 1650 to having between 2.5 and 3 million people in the early 1740s. The native population's "recovery" played an important role in this increase, as did the rapid numerical growth of people of mixed ancestry.[7] The demographic upsurge together with shifts in the economy, including a rise in silver production that stimulated economic activities in northern Mexico,[8] resulted in an expanded market for internal goods. These goods included textiles, most of which were produced in *obrajes* (textile manufactories) or domestic artisan establishments; pulque, the alcoholic beverage of pre-Hispanic origins; and tobacco, which until the crown brought the industry under its control in 1765 was sold by small shopkeepers and street vendors. The virtual self-sufficiency and expanding market and productive capacity that Mexico enjoyed in the first decade of the eighteenth century, not to mention the economic influence it still had on other parts of Spanish America, made its political and economic elites confident about its future and not a little arrogant about their capital's place in the hemisphere. The most prominent of these elites lived in Mexico City and Puebla, which had emerged not only as the viceroyalty's main sociopolitical centers but as its principal sites of artistic production.[9] It was in these two cities that many of the artists who produced casta paintings were trained and in the former that the genre was born.

The first paintings to exhibit conventions of the casta genre were done by a member of a family of artists from Mexico City, the Arellanos, at the request of the Viceroy Alencastre Noroña y Silva. Two works in particular, both dated 1711, are considered early manifestations of the art form. The first is titled *Sketch of a Mulatto, Daughter of a Black* [Woman] *and a*

FIG. 4. Manuel Arellano. *Diceño de Mulata yja de negra y español en la Ciudad de Mexico. Cabesa de la America a 22 de Agosto de 1711* (Sketch of a Mulatto, Daughter of a Black Woman and a Spaniard in Mexico City, Capital of America on the 22 of August of 1711). SOURCE: Courtesy of Denver Art Museum: Collection of Frederick and Jan Mayer. © photograph Denver Art Museum.

Spaniard in Mexico City, Capital of America (Fig. 4), and the second, *Sketch of a Mulatto, Son of a Black [Woman] and a Spaniard in Mexico City, Capital of America.*[10] The *mulata* is dressed in sumptuous clothing and wears pearls around her neck and wrist, a figure certainly worthy of representing the "seat" of the Americas. Her male counterpart, the *mulato* (not shown), is likewise adorned with fancy attire, including a Spanish cape and hat that rest on his left shoulder and arm. The figure looks directly into the eyes of the viewer as he holds a substance up to his nose, the scent of which he is clearly appreciating. The substance is tobacco, the first exotic import from the Americas to become a product of mass consumption in western Europe,[11] but one that Mexico produced exclusively for the internal market. Standing beside the male mulatto is a little boy grasping a wooden horse with one hand and a flag or streamer with the other. The two canvases were meant to function as a unit, thus rendering the family triad that was to become characteristic of casta paintings.[12]

While the two Arellano representations of mulattos anticipated casta paintings, it was the work of the Mexico City artist Juan Rodriguez Juárez (1675–1728) that first exhibited the principal traits of the genre. Foremost among these traits was a concern with depicting how reproduction between people of different ancestries unfolds in the course of several generations. This process of ongoing mestizaje was represented through a sequence of separate images or family vignettes. Starting with Juárez, works belonging to the casta genre were produced as series, each normally consisting of separate canvases or copper plates. A few depict the different images on a single surface. Each image normally features a man, a woman, and their child.[13] Some include two children, but the standard family unit of casta paintings was a trinity. Series were sometimes numbered in order to facilitate the ordering of the images. Furthermore, each vignette included an inscription providing the nomenclature for the family members. Most casta sets, for example, begin with the representation of an elite Spanish male, an indigenous woman also of high socioeconomic status, their offspring, and a title that reads something like *From a Spaniard and Indian [Woman] a Mestizo Is Born* (*De Español e India nace Mestizo*) (Fig. 5).

Casta sets are somewhat different depending on the painter and period in which they were produced, but they nonetheless share a number of underlying principles that produce a particular narrative of mestizaje. One of these principles is the idea that blood is a vehicle for transmitting a host of physical, psychological, and moral traits. The most explicit series in this regard was by José Joaquín Magón, an artist from the city of Puebla who worked during the second half of the eighteenth century. One of the two casta sets that he completed includes inscriptions listing the qualities that children supposedly received from one or both parents.

FIG. 5. José de Ibarra, *De español e india, mestizo* (From Spaniard and Indian, Mestizo), ca. 1725. Oil on canvas, 164 × 91 cm. SOURCE: Courtesy of Museo de América, Madrid.

The first painting, for example, starts with the message that in "the Americas people of different colour, customs, temperaments and languages are born" and then describes the mestizo born of a Spaniard and Indian woman as "generally humble, tranquil and straightforward." The third and last vignette in the unit explains that the Spanish boy, born of a Spanish man and a *castiza,* "takes entirely after his father." He apparently inherited nothing from his indigenous great-grandmother or any of her ancestors. The next sequence of images begins by announcing that the "proud nature and sharp wits of the Mulatto woman come from the White [male] and Black woman who produce her" and ends with a vignette that features a child called *torna atrás* (return backwards) and an inscription that describes him as having "bearing, temperament and tradition."[14]

Another idea present in casta paintings is that while mixture is a potentially infinite process, it is not irreversible; returning to one of the poles of purity is possible. In particular, they allow for the possibility that a Spanish–Indian union can on the third generation result in a "Spaniard" if its descendants continue to reproduce with persons of Iberian descent. However, while admitting that reproduction with Spaniards can also Hispanicize or whiten blacks, casta paintings as a whole suggest that black blood inevitably resurfaces, that "blackness" cannot be entirely absorbed into Spanish lineages, or native ones for that matter. The last generational unit of a typical series, which is characterized by the total or near-total absence of Spaniards and by ongoing reproduction between people of African and indigenous descent, normally links mestizaje to incomprehensibility (as conveyed by terms such as "hold yourself in mid-air," "return backwards," "lobo return backwards," "mulatto return backwards," "lobo once again," and "I don't get you") and in some cases to moral degeneration.[15]

The narrative of mestizaje constructed by casta paintings also depends on the strong interdependence of race and gender. The first sequence of a typical set normally begins with the family of a Spanish male and an indigenous female, and the second, with that of a Spaniard and a black woman. Some representations of black men with Spanish women do appear, but these are not common, and rarer still are images of Spanish women with Amerindians.[16] That in the majority of casta sets the Spanish–Indian and Spanish–black unions involve Spanish males not only promotes the notion that elite white men were in command of the sexuality of all women (thereby emasculating other men), but construct a gendered image of New Spain's three main populations. Sexual subordination essentially functions as a metaphor for colonial domination. However, casta paintings gender indigenous and black people differently. Whereas the genre links the former to biological "weakness"

FIG. 6. Andrés de Islas [Mexican], No. 4. *De español y negra, nace mulata* (From Spaniard and Black, Mulatto), 1774. Oil on canvas, 75 × 54 cm. SOURCE: Courtesy of Museo de América, Madrid.

when it implies that their blood can be completely absorbed into Spanish lineages, it associates blacks with strength and thus codes them more as male. The casta iconography imbues them with the power, for example, to transmit their qualities to their descendants.

In some of the paintings that have images of domestic violence (Fig. 6), it is black and mulatto women in particular who are masculinized. These paintings tend to feature Spaniards serving black or mulatto women or as the victims of female aggression; they thus reverse traditional gender roles and figure women of African ancestry primarily as atavistic and violent forces.[17] Not all images of African-descended people in casta paintings are negative, but the genre's inclusion of violent black women and absence of similar representations of indigenous women are consistent with its overall privileging of the Spanish–Indian family, the images of which are generally characterized by patriarchal domestic harmony, noble rank, and a return to purity. The implication that Spanish blood can be restored when it mixes with that of native people but corrupted by that of blacks suggests that the paintings draw on a set of notions about generation, regeneration, and degeneration.

In a sense, the genre offers a secularized recasting of Christian mythology, not only in that the family images are obviously a product of a Trinitarian imagination (Joseph, Mary, and Jesus; Father, Son, and Holy Spirit) but in that the degeneration narrative can be read as a kind of fall from grace, one that always begins with the sexual act. As in Christian thought, "the fall" is not irrevocable; redemption is possible. The Edenic ideal, embodied in the actual body of the Spanish male, can descend into a state of "barbaric heathenism" (if his descendants continue to reproduce with native and black people), but it can also be restored. Spanish (Christian) blood has redemptive power. But again, the possibility of complete redemption is admitted only for Spanish–Indian unions and not for those involving blacks. From this perspective, the focus of casta paintings is not so much the castas but the Spanish male, who is warned that reproducing with black women can lead to the loss of status, purity, and identity, to the corruption of his "seeds."

Few paintings reveal the importance of the Spanish male within the mestizaje narrative as dramatically as the first canvas (Fig. 7) of a 1763 set by Miguel Cabrera (1695–1768).[18] It features a Spanish male to the left, an indigenous woman to the right, and their daughter in the middle.[19] In the background is a wall, and between it and the figures, a stall with neatly arranged, luxurious Mexican textiles, indicating that the scene takes place in a marketplace. The male, who stands perfectly erect, is turned toward the adult female. His right hand rests on his daughter, and with the left he points toward the indigenous woman, displaying her

FIG. 7. Miguel Cabrera [Mexican], 1. *De español y de india, mestiza* (From Spaniard and Indian, Mestiza), 1763, oil on canvas, 132 × 101 cm. SOURCE: Private collection.

to the viewer of the painting. The Spaniard's face is not shown, but his posture and hand gestures leave no doubt as to where his eyes are fixed. The object of his gaze is the native woman, who returns the look with a slightly raised eyebrow and somewhat flirtatious expression on her face. She holds her daughter by the hand and is standing in front of the array of finely detailed textiles, as if she herself were a commodity. The little girl, who is holding a Spanish fan and like her mother is dressed in Hispanic attire, looks at her father with an expression of deference.

Both the positioning of the figures in relation to each other and their body language create an idealized patriarchal order, one based on Aristotelian formulations of family and polity in which children are subordinate to adults and women to men and in which the authority of the father is linked to that of the king. The painting consists of four imaginary lines of vision: that of the Spanish man, which is directed at the indigenous woman; that of the latter back toward the Spaniard; that of the girl, also directed at the male figure; and that of the viewer of the painting, whose eyes are first led to the mother and then to the child and other exoticized products from New Spain (the textiles in the background and the pineapple on the lower right corner of the frame). These four lines paradoxically position not the woman and child, which are being displayed, but the Spanish male as the center of the painting. Indeed, it is he who through the whole visual rhetoric of the painting—the three figures' body language, the deployment of the male gaze, and the spatial arrangement of humans and objects—is rendered as in command not only of the wealth and products of New Spain, but of the sexuality and reproduction of the native female, his most valued possession.

Through its fetishized portrayal of both the textiles and the indigenous woman, Cabrera's painting hints at the process of creole class formation. The one fetish conceals the work that produced New Spain's economic enterprises and therefore most of its wealth; the other hides the labor, domestic and reproductive, that gave rise to a good number of Spanish colonial estates. The implied phallus in the painting, the instrument through which some indigenous women were inseminated and through which Spaniards were able in the course of a few generations to reproduce themselves, stands as a symbol of patriarchal control, economic exploitation, and racial dispossession—a signifier of multiple and overlapping structures of domination. Through the iconography of productive sexuality in the domestic sphere, Cabrera's casta set thus exposes the dynamic relationship of race, class, and gender and the importance of the Spanish appropriation of the labor and reproductive capacity of native women to the colonial order.

Cabrera, born in Antequera (now Oaxaca), was eighteenth-century Mexico's most prominent painter. He produced a large body of officially sponsored works featuring religious themes as well as portrait paintings, including one of the Virgin of Guadalupe and another of the seventeenth-century Mexican writer Sor Juana Ines de la Cruz. Credited by some art historians with taking casta paintings to their highest levels of artistic sophistication, Cabrera also was involved in introducing important changes into the genre. These changes include more attention to emotion and physical contact between the figures, a stronger reliance on clothing to mark socioeconomic differences, and a greater stress on order and hierarchy.[20] Nonetheless, sets from the second half of the century continued to convey the message that parents transmit a series of traits to their children through their blood, that after three generations the descendants of Spanish–Indian unions can return to the Spanish pole, and that black blood eventually stains pure lineages—ideas that were all part of the discourse of limpieza de sangre as it had developed in New Spain. The paintings also still generally offered a vision of Mexican society in which race, gender, and class intersected and in which Spanish men's control over female sexuality, especially over that of their own women, enabled the survival of colonial hierarchies. Paradoxically, the period in which casta paintings were produced was one in which those hierarchies and the very category of Spaniard were becoming highly unstable.

THE SISTEMA DE CASTAS IN FLUX AND THE PROLIFERATION OF STATUTES AND STAINS

This instability of the sistema de castas in central Mexico was partly due to changes in marriage patterns and legitimacy rates. In the capital and Puebla, for example, marriages between Spaniards and women of partial African descent experienced slight but significant increases in the final decades of the seventeenth century. The church might have played a role in these increases, for it intensified its campaign to compel couples in informal unions to marry by threatening them with excommunication.[21] Thus, when in 1695 the Inquisition asked the bishop of Puebla to compile a list of the couples that had wed under those circumstances, it learned that during the preceding five years, twenty Spanish men had married African-descended women, free and enslaved.[22] By the start of the next century, legitimacy rates among the broader casta population were rising, and Spanish women were taking men from other groups as husbands at higher rates than before.[23] Because the church had a history of upholding the principle of free will in choice of marriage partners over parental wishes (a policy that the state had supported for most of the seventeenth century), families had no legal or institutional mechanisms to halt such unions, at least not yet.[24]

The growing instability of the sistema de castas was also due to the greater complexity of colonial society, which witnessed a dramatic surge in the population of mixed ancestry, the beginnings of a working class culture (especially in the northern mining towns and in Mexico City and Puebla), and increasing social mobility due to the expansion of mercantile capitalism. Mobility went in both directions, however, and economic trends were by no means uniform. Improvements in mining and agricultural production and greater integration into the Atlantic economy gave Mexico modest but steady economic growth rates. But not all regions followed the same trajectory, and some experienced more decline than growth. In Puebla, for example, signs of economic problems appeared relatively early. In 1724, a number of Puebla's residents testified regarding the city's downturn and the flight of many of its affluent vecinos, namely, business owners and merchants, to Mexico City and Oaxaca.[25] The out-migration had been so large that a section of the capital, comprised of several neighborhoods, came to be known as "Little Puebla."

According to those who testified, many of the Spaniards that remained in Puebla had become impoverished, and the city itself had lost some of its charm. Previously opulent homes had fallen into disrepair; the population had dropped significantly; and many private citizens, convents, and obrajes had been unable to collect rents on their properties (some of them in the most exclusive streets) because of the shortage of currency in the city. Viceroy Fernando de Alencastre Noroña y Silva (1711–16), the Duke of Linares, called attention to similar problems. Puebla, he wrote in a 1723 report, was blessed with good agricultural production, but many of its industries, including its wool, soap, and glass workshops, were suffering because of competition from other regions and moving elsewhere. Only the city's craft guilds were doing well.[26] Economic conditions in Puebla took a turn for the worse in 1736, when harvest failures and an epidemic that hit the central region created a food crisis.[27]

As the viceroy suggested, during these decades of economic problems and fluctuations, colonial officials looked to the craft guilds as models of order and regimentation. Especially strong in Mexico City and Puebla but also important in other cities, these bodies were in charge of regulating a good portion of the working population and thus played a part in reproducing social hierarchies. In the capital, for example, one-third to one-half of working males participated in artisan crafts, which despite the growing number of non-Spaniards owning their own shops tended to be structured according to racial lines.[28] Even if master artisans were no longer all Spaniards and creoles, and even if workers were by no means exclusively people of indigenous and black ancestry, the most important trades and obrajes were still controlled by people of European descent, which gave the semblance of order and the sense that the sistema de castas was alive and well. For example, the textile workshops in the Puebla-Tlaxcala basin, the Bajío, and the Mexico City area were almost all owned by Spaniards (who in the case of the first two regions were mainly peninsulars married to wealthy creole wives), but their workforce consisted primarily of people of mixed ancestry and black slaves.[29] The surviving hierarchical nature of certain trade occupations might explain why a number of them are represented in casta paintings of the second half of the eighteenth century. The vision of order that the paintings project, however, was more illusion than reality, and this became especially evident as the colonial period drew to a close.

The instability of the sistema de castas was parodied in a 1754 manuscript titled "Ordenanzas del Baratillo de México" ("Decrees of the Baratillo of Mexico"), which turned the system of classification on its head, poked fun at its failure to work as intended, mocked its effort to create institutional exclusivity on the basis of blood-purity laws, and invented castalike categories based on the marking of Spanishness ("one-half Spanish," "one-quarter Spanish," and so forth).[30] Although the manuscript correctly identified cracks in the system, the fluidity that it conveyed did not apply to the entire population. Social mobility did not really affect the upper class, which was constituted by the owners of large estates and mines, wholesale merchants, high-ranking royal officials and clerics, and large-scale retailers; nor did it apply to the bottom social levels, which mainly consisted of unskilled indigenous manual laborers. Fluidity primarily characterized colonial society's growing middle strata, which included creoles and peninsulars in artisan and retail occupations, people of mixed descent, and acculturated Amerindians. Although mobility among these groups could go in both directions, in the second half of the eighteenth century it mainly went downward.

This downward trend was accelerated by the Bourbon reforms, which were first aggressively promoted during the reign of Charles III (1759–88). One of the central goals of the king and his enlightened advisors was to promote "free trade"; another was to make Spain's political and economic domination over its colonies more efficient. The relative autonomy that Spanish America had enjoyed during the previous century had allowed for the different provinces to be under the control of creole elites (namely, lawyers, landlords, and churchmen), peninsulars who had served in the region for a long time, and great merchants. To impose a mercantilist policy that worked, the crown believed it was necessary to curb the power of these regional elites as well as to launch a major program of administrative, fiscal, and social reform.[31] In Mexico, the main architect of the reforms was the visitador José de Gálvez (1765–71), whose accomplishments included creating a new military district in the northern frontier, introducing a system of intendancies, and tripling public rents. Gálvez was also responsible for creating royal monopolies on certain colonial products (including tobacco and pulque),[32] for decreasing the power of Mexico City's *consulado* (merchants' guild), and for reorganizing the system of *alcabalas* (sales or excise taxes).

Together with Spain's new trading policies, Gálvez's changes to the tax system, reconfiguration of certain interests and industries, and establishment of royal monopolies on some colonial products led to a dramatic increase in Mexican commerce. The region's exports included cochineal (a red dyestuff used for textiles), sugar, hemp, cacao, vanilla, indigo, and hides, that is, mainly raw materials that were in high demand because of the Industrial Revolution. But by far the most important product New Spain sent abroad was silver, the production of which the Spanish crown had increased by lowering taxes on it and on mining supplies. It constituted about three-fourths of the value of the region's exports and toward the end of the colonial period represented two-thirds of the crown's income in the Americas. Silver remittances from New Spain and Gálvez's revenue-raising policies led to a significant improvement in Spain's fiscal yields. In the 1730s, the Royal Treasury of Mexico's yearly tax collections amounted to about 6.3 million pesos; by the 1780s, they had jumped to between 10 and 20 million pesos and would continue to rise.[33] Mexico had become the indisputable "jewel in the imperial crown."

Whereas the Bourbon reforms were a fiscal success for Spain, their effects on the Mexican economy were much more mixed. Economic expansion created more wealth for some but did not lead to noticeable structural and institutional changes, the modernization of manufacturing sectors, or a significant increase in wages.[34] Some enterprises, such as the obrajes or textile manufactories, flourished for a time because of internal demand, but were technologically stagnant and suffered as New Spain became increasingly integrated into the Atlantic economy.[35] Furthermore, the dramatic assertion of the state's extractive role did not help spread economic wealth within colonial society. By the late eighteenth century, New Spain's population paid 70 percent more in taxes than that of Spain.[36] Because approximately 40 percent of tax revenues went to Madrid and because colonial governments had to absorb the costs of greater defense obligations and bureaucratic reconfigurations, Mexico's budget deficit grew at an alarming rate.[37] At the same time, the already acutely uneven distribution of wealth worsened.[38] Indeed, the little upward mobility there was tended to favor peninsulars (main beneficiaries of the crown's expansion of the bureaucracy), while surging royal tax and tribute demands elevated pauperization rates among the rest of the population. Among the most affected were rural working people, who underwent a decrease in their real wages and incomes. But creoles also experienced some downward mobility. Toward the end of the century, they were increasingly joining the lower ranks of the *"gente decente"* (respectable people).[39]

Far from providing an accurate picture of the social order, then, casta paintings presented a highly distorted view. Spanish men were never in full command of female sexuality, but whatever control they had decreased in the eighteenth century, when they did not even have a monopoly on their own women in the marriage market. The upper crust of society might have consisted almost exclusively of Spaniards and creoles and the lower one of unskilled indigenous laborers, but the relationship between race and class—never clear-cut to begin with—was becoming messier, especially as more and more whites joined the lower middle ranks. The racialized order that characterized some craft guilds was no longer as representative of the larger society as before, and a number of artisan occupations did not uphold strict racial hierarchies. Given the circumstances in which casta paintings were produced, their ongoing production and the interest they generated might have been tied to nostalgia for a more stable, hierarchical past, and more concretely to elite anxieties about the changes that were threatening to radically alter the social order. Rather than calming these anxieties, however, the paintings made them worse.

By the 1740s, some creoles began to express concern that casta paintings were creating the impression that most of New Spain's population was mixed and, more unacceptable from their point of view, that much of it had black ancestors. One such creole was Andres de Arce y Miranda, a theologian who was born to an established family from Huejotzingo (near Puebla) and enjoyed various high-ranking offices in Puebla's cathedral chapter. In 1746, he sent a manuscript entitled "Noticias de los escritores de la Nueva España" to Juan José de Eguiara y Eguren, professor and rector of Mexico's university, in order to help him compile his *Biblioteca Mexicana*, a bio-bibliography of Mexican writers meant to undermine European claims regarding the lack of intellectual production in the Americas.[40] In a letter that accompanied the manuscript,

Arce y Miranda cautioned Eguiara y Eguren to treat as "incidental" the "mixture of lineages" that had occurred in the viceroyalty in order not to encourage the perception on the other side of the Atlantic that everyone in the colonies was the product of mestizaje. Referring explicitly to some casta sets, the theologian regretted that they reflected only the "functional" (*útiles*) and not "noble" minds of New Spain, and that they did not include the best pairing of all, that between Spaniards and creoles. If casta paintings were initially a manifestation of pride in the local, by the 1750s they had clearly become a source of consternation for colonials who did not want to be perceived as anything but pure.

The perception that creoles were impure had been growing not just in Europe but in New Spain itself, among peninsular Spaniards. For example, in letters from the 1730s, the Mexican Inquisition explained to the Suprema that the shortage of applicants for familiaturas in the region stemmed from the prohibitive costs of the probanzas, the obscure genealogy of those who had been born in Spain, and the uncertainty about the social status (*calidad*) and purity of blood of the wives of candidates owing to the "mixture of castes" (*mezcla de castas*) in the viceroyalty.[41] Referring to the same shortage again in 1753, the inquisitors observed that the most qualified individuals were those who came from overseas but that they were usually not interested in being ministers or familiars because they did not have a fixed residence. Creoles, on the other hand, were generally not eligible because in New Spain many were illegitimate or lacked the quality (calidad) of pure Spaniard due to the high rates of "mixture" in the viceroyalty. Turning to candidates from other parts of the kingdom did not resolve the problem because conducting genealogical investigations in faraway places was difficult and opened the possibility of accepting "illegitimates as legitimate" and "mulattos as Spaniards."[42]

Other colonial officials expressed similar concerns about the rising incidence of mestizaje and in particular about Spanish lineages' being corrupted by black blood. In their reports and correspondence with the crown or Suprema, they convey an almost paranoid fear of "blackness," of its capacity both to be invisible (hidden in the blood) and to influence phenotype and other biological traits. The reasons for this fear are not entirely clear. Although Mexico's population of slaves had been declining since the middle of the seventeenth century, people of African descent (free and enslaved) continued to have a strong presence in Mexico throughout the end of the colonial period, particularly in Mexico City.[43] This presence, however, does not in and of itself explain the elite preoccupation with black blood. Perhaps the preoccupation was linked to increases in marriages between creoles and castas, or perhaps simply to fears that those types of unions might become more common as social mobility for the latter became more feasible.[44] Whatever the case, as the Mexican Holy Office's correspondence suggests, some peninsular Spaniards were linking creoles with illegitimacy and mixture, singling out those who had African blood as impure, and focusing on women as the sources of contamination. Similar to what had occurred in Spain two centuries earlier, the rising obsession with safeguarding limpieza de sangre resulted in the feminization of impurity and masculinization of women deemed to be impure.

The increasing marking of creoles as impure made the use of the word *criollo* become the subject of debate. Arce y Miranda, who was troubled by the failure of casta paintings to convey the message that unions between Spaniards and creoles took place, proposed expelling the word from the dictionary and from the language altogether. Because it had been created for the "sons of slaves born in America," he considered its application to American-born Spaniards to be "ridiculous," "derogatory," and "inflammatory."[45] Casta paintings do not include the term *criollo*, thus giving the category of Spaniard a unity it was clearly lacking. Chronically unstable due to the absence of a clear legal distinction between metropolitan and colonial space and the slippage between blood and culture in Spanish definitions of purity, the category became even more problematic as the eighteenth century unfolded and Mexico's preoccupation with black blood and mestizaje in general continued to rise. This preoccupation not only compelled colonial institutions to attempt to become more exclusive, but led religious and secular officials to become more aggressive about discouraging Spanish and native unions with people of African descent.

CREOLE FICTIONS: PURITY, THE VIRGIN, AND THE RISE OF A CATHOLIC MESTIZO PATRIA

The exclusivist trend in colonial institutions was manifested in the proliferation of categories of impurity. By the end of the eighteenth century, many probanzas de limpieza produced in New Spain identified four stains: descent from Jews, Muslims and heretics; descent from blacks and (some) native people; descent from slaves ("stains of vulgar infamies"); and descent from people who had engaged in "vile or mechanical occupations." Furthermore, a greater assortment of secular and religious bodies introduced or formalized purity policies. These bodies included town councils, guilds, academies, convents, colleges, and seminaries.[46]

It is as if society was going in one direction and these institutions were trying to go in another. The number of statutes and stains grew in part because of efforts by creole and Spanish elites to stem the tide of people of African and mixed ancestry attempting, in some cases successfully, to enter the more prestigious occupations, the medical profession, and the universities as well as to further restrict their access to ecclesiastical and public offices.[47] But the rising obsession with purity and genealogy was also fueled by the crown's social and administrative policies, and in particular its passage of the 1776 Royal Pragmatic on Marriages (or Pragmatic Sanction).

A key moment in the history of the Spanish state's curtailment of the church's independence on matters of marriage, the Pragmatic Sanction made parental consent necessary for matrimony for people under twenty-five, stressed the importance of encouraging marriages between "equals," and shifted the power to mediate disputes between parents and children over spousal choice from ecclesiastical to royal courts.[48] This law was extended to the Americas in 1778 along with other decrees that ordered royal officials (especially those in the armed forces) wishing to marry in the colonies to provide proof of purity of blood for themselves and their betrothed.[49] Marriage, however, was not the only domain that felt the crown's interference in limpieza de sangre matters. State-sponsored educational bodies also adopted purity requirements, including Mexico City's Real Colegio de Abogados (Royal College of Attorneys) and the Colegio de Minería (Mining College). The latter, which opened its doors in 1792, demanded proof of limpieza for students admitted into its mining seminar. By the end of the eighteenth century, purity requirements had become so pervasive that some parents secured purity certifications for their young children in order to improve their future marriage and professional opportunities.[50]

What do the probanzas produced in the century of the Enlightenment reveal about the ways in which the Spanish discourse of purity of blood had transformed in the course of the colonial period? As has already been stressed in previous chapters, one of its first and most significant transformations was its extension to colonial populations and in particular to people of African descent—an innovation that the Inquisition acknowledged and approved in 1774.[51] Although various institutions had a statute of purity that explicitly barred Africans and their descendants, the Inquisition did not formalize its own until that year. The change came about because of a case involving the limpieza de sangre of Josef Thomas Vargas Machuca, an alderman and chief constable (alguacil mayor) in the Mexican town of Salamanca who had applied to be a familiar a couple of years earlier.[52] The commissioner assigned to the case had gone to Vargas Machuca's native town and interrogated nine witnesses, all of whom said that the petitioner's maternal bloodline was pure and among the most noble of the region, but that his paternal one was mixed with "the vile caste of mulattoes," specifically the branch that carried the last name of Zavala. The stain in his genealogy, they added, was a matter of public knowledge, as were the problems that some members of his family, including an uncle who had entered the priesthood, had faced when attempting to certify their purity status.

The commissioner did not uncover evidence of impurity in the birth records that he examined, however, and therefore sent the case back to Mexico City with a recommendation that Vargas Machuca be granted the title of familiar. Finding the case to be incomplete because not enough witnesses had been interrogated and because an investigation had not been done in the hometown of the allegedly "infected branch," the Holy Office's prosecutor ordered that further inquiries be made, particularly on the paternal grandparent who carried the surname of Zavala and the uncle whose purity had been questioned when he entered the priesthood. This second investigation unearthed more damaging details about Vargas Machuca's bloodlines, including various probanzas for the uncle that contained contradictory information about his purity. It also revealed that the petitioner's paternal grandmother, Brígida Zavala, had been granted a dispensation to marry a man who was related to her within the third degree. The dispensation referred to her as the daughter of a mestizo and "coyote," which meant that she had native and black ancestry. The commissioner also turned up evidence that another of the candidate's relatives, also a descendant of Brígida Zavala, was known to have the "race of mulattoes."

When the case was complete, the Mexican inquisitors declared the candidate to be impure because of the "prolonged stain that his direct ancestors and collaterals carried for having mixed with mulattoes." They also used the case to ask the Suprema to amend the purity statute and questionnaire. The inquisitors explained that their tribunal had raised the issue on repeated occasions because the form they used in interrogations continued to adhere to the traditional categories of limpieza. In most cases, what they had opted to do was add a handwritten question about whether the petitioner descended from "mulatos, coyotes, lobos, mestizos," and other castas. The inquisitors justified the addition on the basis of numerous past occasions in which the Suprema had approved their rejection of candidates who had black blood as well as on popular opinion regarding the effects of reproducing with blacks. These opinions, they added, held that "blackened blood [*sangre denegrida*] never disappears, because experience shows that by the third, fourth, or fifth generation it pullulates, so that two whites produce a black, called *tornatrás* or *saltatrás*."[53]

The question of mulattos and other castas had not been included before, the Mexican inquisitors observed, because the issue of limpieza, a matter of faith, had been intended for the descendants of Jews, heretics, and Saracens, groups that were hostile to the Christian faith. Basically repeating what the Suprema had stipulated at the end of the seventeenth century, they pointed out that strictly speaking, the statute did not affect people who descended from gentiles unless their gentility was recent, within the cuatro costados (their parents and grandparents), but even then mainly on the basis of illegitimacy. Because Vargas Machuca's genealogical "stain" originated with his great-great-grandparents (*rebisabuelos*), he was technically eligible for limpieza status. Therefore, if the Suprema wanted to reject his petition and others like it (as it had done with similar requests in the past), it should finally resolve, first, whether the purity requirement could be used against the descendants of gentiles without limitations on how far back the stain ran and, second, whether to add African ancestry to the categories of impurity in the limpieza questionnaire. The Suprema agreed, but it took a definitive stance only on the second issue. On January 8, 1774, it gave the Mexican Inquisition permission to add a question regarding mulattos "and other castes held there in disdain."[54] After more than a century and a half of having a de facto purity policy against people of African ancestry, the Holy Office formally included blacks and mulattos as impure categories.

Another change in the discourse of limpieza de sangre was the growing interaction of the notion of purity with concepts related to "class" or social status. The acceleration of mercantile capitalism and greater possibilities of social mobility that it created and the growing acceptance of individual achievement and other principles of enlightened rationalism gradually peppered the language of purity of blood with terms such as *calidad, condición,* and *clase.* The change, which went hand in hand with the proliferation of stains, is obvious in probanzas de limpieza de sangre. In these documents, phrases such as "calidad de mulato" and "calidad de español" started to appear almost as often as "casta de mulato" and "casta de español," and both Inquisition officials and witnesses began to use *calidad* (which had multiple connotations) and *casta* interchangeably.[55] Furthermore, the ancient regime's lexicon of purity of blood increasingly merged with "bourgeois" concepts of diligence, work, integrity, education, and utility to the public good. In 1752, for example, don José Tembra (or Tenebra), a cleric from the diocese of Tlax-cala, argued that in order to ensure the "public good," the state should discourage unequal marriages, that is, unions between honorable men and women who were not of the right condición because they lacked the three limpiezas of social status, caste, and occupation.[56] His example typically framed the problem of inequality as one that involved Spanish or creole men and women of a lower status. Inquisitors, members of the clergy, and casta painters all appeared to share a concern with preserving the purity of the white male.

The concept of limpieza de sangre also underwent partial secularization. If the declarations of people who testified in eighteenth-century genealogical investigations are a good indication, the meaning of blood purity moved farther and farther away from religious practices and became embedded in a visual discourse about the body, and in particular about skin color. Spanish concerns with phenotype were present during the early stages of Iberian colonialism,[57] but these became much more acute in the Age of Reason, and not just in Spanish America. A growing scientific and philosophical interest in determining the effects of living in the Americas on people, animals, and plants and in a related set of questions about human generation and evolution led to the production and circulation of numerous theories of skin color in the Atlantic world as a whole.[58] In Mexico, these theories reinforced the concept of purity of blood's links to "Spanishness" and "whiteness," which had begun to appear with regularity in the second half of the previous century. Purity certifications indicate that witnesses increasingly used the category of "pure Spaniard" (*español puro*) and expressions such as "Old Christians, whites of pure blood" (*cristianos viejos, blancos de limpia sangre*).[59] They also suggest that the colonial body started to become the main text through which ordinary people read the issue of purity of blood.

For example, several of the witnesses who testified in the 1702 Franciscan investigation in Querétaro to determine if the Velasco brothers were of "the bad race of mulattoes" declared that they were impure not only because of the skin color and hair texture of some of their ancestors, but because of the two siblings' own pigmentation and "physiognomy."[60] In 1748, two of the witnesses in the probanza of Donado Francisco Mariano Gómez, a candidate for the novitiate in Puebla's Franciscan convent, declared that questions about the status of the petitioner's maternal grandfather as a "mestizo," "castizo," or "Spaniard" had been raised because of his skin color, which was *trigueño* (olive).[61] The commissioner, however, turned to generational formulas to argue that even if the grandfather was a "mestizo," the father was a "castizo" and the petitioner therefore a "Spaniard." He added that if the candidate was indeed within four degrees of the "stain," the defect had disappeared because only two witnesses had mentioned it; the others saw him as a Spaniard. For the commissioner, public reputation trumped ancestry.

Purity of blood could be established, as in the past, by descent or reputation but also by skin color or phenotype in general. But as Donado Francisco Mariano Gómez's probanza and numerous other purity cases suggest, witnesses tended to rely more on phenotype than did Spanish religious and secular officials, who generally tried to adhere to more traditional genealogical and reputational formulas. The breach between official definitions of limpieza de sangre and more popular ones points to the extent to which the concept had taken a different course in the colonial context and had become strongly intertwined with Spanishness and skin color. This transformation of the concept is illustrated, literally, in casta paintings, which recast the notion that it took three or four generations for New Christians to become Old Christians and for the descendants of Spanish–Indian unions to claim purity in terms of "whitening." And just as the discourse of limpieza de sangre seldom allowed the descendants of Spanish–black unions the status of purity of blood, the paintings suggest that they could never become Spaniards or fully white. Thus, the union of an *albino*—a person with predominantly Spanish blood but some African ancestry (usually one-eighth)—with a Spaniard, does not produce a "white" child, as one would expect given the overall logic of the genre, but one of dark complexion.

Despite the various transformations that the notion of limpieza de sangre underwent, it retained old layers of meaning. For one, religion continued to be important to its definition. Spaniards and creoles who requested probanzas almost always emphasized their loyalty to the faith and impeccable Old Christian ancestry. Religion also continued to be the basis of the concept of native purity, which despite the association of limpieza and Spanishness was still recognized in royal legislation and some colonial establishments. The purity status of the indigenous population and its religious basis were actually invigorated in the first half of the eighteenth century, when the government tried to uphold the special privileges of pure and noble Indians and along with the church established new institutions for them. These institutions included Mexico City's convent of Corpus Christi, which was founded in 1724 exclusively for indigenous women of cacique or principal rank. It required that candidates submit proof of their purity, nobility, and legitimacy; confirm that they did not have idolatrous antecedents; and ascertain that their parents did not engage in disdainful occupations.[62] In the following two decades, convents with similar requirements were founded elsewhere, including Valladolid and Oaxaca.

FIG. 8. José de Ibarra [Mexican], *De mestizo y española, castizo* (From Mestizo and Spaniard, Castizo), ca. 1725. Oil on canvas, 164 × 91 cm. SOURCE: Courtesy of Museo de América, Madrid.

FIG. 9. José de Ibarra, *De castizo y española, español* (From Castizo and Spaniard, Spaniard), ca. 1725. Oil on canvas, 164 × 91 cm. SOURCE: Courtesy of Museo de América, Madrid.

One of the factors motivating the establishment of these institutions was a strain of Catholic thought that the religious utopias of the sixteenth century had turned indigenous people into a theologically privileged community. This current of thought was strengthened with the spread of the cult of the Virgin of Guadalupe, believed to have appeared to the humble indigenous convert Juan Diego in 1531. Her image, which had been taken from the hill of Tepeyac to Mexico City in 1629, had grown in popularity throughout the seventeenth century, and in particular after the 1648 publication of Miguel Sánchez's *Imagen de la Virgen María Madre de Dios de Guadalupe milagrosamente aparecida en México*.[63] It was officially recognized in 1737, the year that it was placed in the capital's cathedral and formally named by the city council as its new patron. Several other cities subsequently made the same pronouncement. In 1746, Archbishop Antonio de Vizarrón y Eguiarreta (1730–47) and delegates from all dioceses held a meeting that resulted in her being declared their universal patron, a decision that the papacy approved in 1754. During these decades, countless copies of her image were painted, including one by Miguel Cabrera in 1756, the same year that he authored *Maravilla Americana*. In this work, he made a case for the divine nature of the original image and supported it with the opinions of other painters, including some who were also producing casta sets and renditions of the Virgin of Guadalupe.[64]

As the cult of Guadalupe reached its apogee, her image became part of an increasingly complex symbolism. Not only did her apparition to Juan Diego come to represent the promise of a renewed Christendom in Mexico and a kind of collective baptism of its disparate populations,[65] but members of clergy incorporated it into a vision of New Spain as a product of two spiritually unsullied communities: one brought the Catholic faith; the other was redeemed by it. Within this vision, it was the latter community, the indigenous people, that at a symbolic level was the more important. The Virgin's appearance on the hill of Tepeyac had accelerated the eradication of idolatry, thereby sacralizing both the land and its original inhabitants; she had made Mexico into the new Holy Land and the Indians her chosen people. Thus, when Francisco Antonio de Lorenzana (1722–1804), a Spanish prelate who served as archbishop of Mexico from 1766 to 1772, referred to Spaniards and native people as "Mexicans" favored by the Virgin of Guadalupe, he stressed that although her image protected both groups, it especially cared for the latter, "the last to convert but the first to enter [God's] kingdom."[66]

The spread of the cult of the Virgin of Guadalupe and its exaltation of the native people's theological status enabled the rise of a creole vision of a Catholic mestizo kingdom under her protective image. This vision

FIG. 10. Andrés de Islas, No. 5. *De español y mulata, nace morisco* (From Spaniard and Mulatta, a Morisco is Born), 1774, oil on canvas, 75 × 54 cm. SOURCE: Courtesy of Museo de América, Madrid.

FIG. 11. Andrés de Islas, No. 6. *De español y morisca, nace albino* (From Spaniard and Morisca, an Albino is Born), 1774, oil on canvas, 75 × 54 cm. SOURCE: Courtesy of Museo de América, Madrid.

FIG. 12. Andrés de Islas, No. 7. *De español y albina, nace torna-atrás* (From Spaniard and Albino, a Return Backwards is Born), 1774, oil on canvas, 75 × 54 cm. SOURCE: Courtesy of Museo de América, Madrid.

is captured in Luis de Mena's 1750 casta painting, to date the only one of the genre known to have overt religious iconography. Produced four years after Mexico declared the Virgin of Guadalupe its universal patron, the painting is dominated by her image, which spills over into the first sequence of family vignettes. The first vignette atypically features an indigenous man with a Spanish woman. Because he wears almost no clothes and carries a bow and arrow—conventions that were used to represent "heathens" and "barbarians"—the image functions as an allegory for the "civilizing" and Christianizing process. The second vignette, *From Spaniard and Mestizo, Castiza (De Española y Mestizo, nace Castiza)*, shows the mother and daughter staring adoringly at the Virgin; and the next, *From Castiza and Spaniard, Spaniard (De Castiza y Español, nace Española)*, depicts the Spanish girl—the final product of the Spanish–Indian union—also captivated by the image.

Together the first three family images in Mena's painting allude not only to the Christianizing process but to the redemptive powers of Old Christian Spanish blood and the divinely sanctioned "marriage"—literal and metaphorical—of the Spanish and indigenous communities. By contrast, the next sequence, which deals with the Spanish–black union, results in an "Albino tornatrás" ("albino return backwards"). The painting thus includes people of African ancestry within the Virgin's fold but, like the rest of the genre, renders their blood as ineffaceable, as not quite compatible with Old Christian Spanish blood and incapable of entirely transmuting into "whiteness." The work therefore captures the anxieties that Spanish and creole elites were expressing about Spanish–black unions as well as some of the implications that the indigenous people's exalted place in New Spain's spiritual economy had for the region's symbolics of blood and dominant notions of communal belonging. Stated differently, it illustrates how the religious dimension of the concept of limpieza de sangre influenced central Mexico's constructions of race as well as its patriotic imaginaries.

Perhaps at no point in the colonial period was the Mexican vision of a Catholic mestizo patria and its roots in the discourse of purity of blood expressed more clearly than after the passage of the Royal Pragmatic on Marriages. The law, which stipulated that in Spanish America social inequality referred primarily to racial or "caste" disparity, prompted prominent creoles and Spaniards (mostly members of the clergy) to defend unions with the indigenous population. Reviving the early missionary idea of creating "one people out of two" through intermarriage and reproduction,[67] this defense was passionately articulated by the exiled Jesuit priest and historian Francisco de Clavijero. In addition to romanticizing the achievements of the pre-Columbian Aztecs and portraying

FIG. 13. Luis de Mena, casta painting, ca. 1750. Oil on Canvas, 120 × 104 cm.
SOURCE: Courtesy of Museo de América, Madrid.

their empire as New Spain's classical antiquity, he strongly lamented
that the biological ties between creoles and native people had not been
strong enough to create a single (mestizo) people.[68] Other religious and
lay figures expressed similar vindications of Spanish–Indian marriages,
among them Archbishop Lorenzana and the enlightened creole polymath
José Antonio de Alzate y Ramírez (1737–99). Clearly favoring certain

biological mixes over others, both men proposed that native people should be encouraged to marry Spaniards but not blacks, mulattos, or zamboes (zambahigos) because of the negative consequences that unions with the last three categories would have on their lineages.

Mexico City's audiencia must have agreed, for in 1784 it prompted priests to warn their indigenous flock that if they married persons of African ancestry, their descendants would not have access to municipal honorific positions.[69] Although some religious and secular officials worried about shielding the native population in general, they were always more protective of indigenous noblewomen, whom they saw as having a particular claim to religious virtue, honor, and genealogical purity. As Archbishop Lorenzana explained in his sermons, if the Virgin of Guadalupe favored the Indians as a whole, she was most protective of *indias,* for whom various convents, including that of Corpus Christi, had been founded.[70] Native noblewomen occupied a special place in Mexico's order of signs, a consequence of the extension of the concept of limpieza de sangre and attendant ideas about endogamy, legitimate birth, and female chastity to the "Indian republic" as well as of the role of the daughters of caciques and principales in Spanish ennoblement and creole class formation.

Although the urgency with which some creoles and Spanish clerics defended Spanish–Indian marriages in the last decades of the eighteenth century would suggest otherwise, the emerging Mexican vision of a Catholic mestizo patria was not incompatible with the Bourbon government's social policies. Indeed, even though the Pragmatic Sanction's provision of inequality caused some confusion among colonial officials who were not certain or disagreed about which unions they were supposed to discourage, the 1778 order and subsequent decrees emphasized that the prohibition was to be applied primarily to Spaniards or native people who planned to marry people of African descent. In other words, marriages were "unequal" when they involved unions between blacks and nonblacks.[71] The Pragmatic Sanction and related marriage legislation thus did not erode, but rather consecrated, the principle of indigenous purity.

Other Bourbon social policies did so as well, including those pertaining to the legal instruments called *gracias al sacar.* These instruments were part of a Spanish tradition in which monarchical authority superceded laws about legitimacy and various other matters related to birth status and ancestry. They allowed, for example, those who were illegitimate, impure, or (in the colonies) not white to purchase edicts (*cédulas de gracias al sacar*) erasing the "defect" of their birth. The edicts, which reflected the legally sanctioned distinction between the private and public domains, had existed for centuries, but in 1795, the crown for the first time issued a list of prices for purchasing them.[72] That the list focused on dispensing the status of *pardo* (dark skinned) and of *quinterón* (one-fifth black) amounted to a tacit recognition that black ancestry was that which was deemed legally and socially impure and, by extension, that native descent was not.

And indeed, Bourbon institutional policies continued the tradition of equating black ancestry with impurity and recognizing the principle of native limpieza. For example, the Royal College of Attorneys included "mulatto ancestry" and "vile or mechanical trades" as stains, but made no mention of indigenous descent as a cause for disqualification. The Mining College encouraged applications from "noble Indians" and, in consultation with the viceroy, determined that because mestizos were allowed to receive the sacred orders and were exempt from tribute, there was no reason to exclude them either, especially if they were of the "first order" (half Spanish, half indigenous).[73] Accordingly, the informaciones and probanzas submitted by candidates to the seminar include "negros, mulattos, Jews, and Moors" as impure categories but not "indios" or "mestizos." As Archbishop Lorenzana and Alzate y Ramírez had insinuated when they argued that native people should avoid marrying blacks, the continuing stigma of black blood was clearly related to the purity-of-blood requirements and the greater social implications they had for the descendants of Africans than for other colonial populations.

Eighteenth-century Mexico's discourse of purity of blood had been created primarily by the laws, institutions, religious cosmologies, and social and archival practices that accompanied Spanish colonialism. But native people had also participated in its construction. The passage of the 1697 decree confirming their purity of blood and the privileged status of caciques and principales led to a rise in the production of indigenous genealogical documents. Following the traditional definition of limpieza de sangre but with a colonial twist, caciques and principales made purity claims primarily on the basis of the absence of any stains of idolatry in their lineages since their (sixteenth-century) ancestors had converted to Christianity and oftentimes also their lack of black blood.[74] Furthermore, indigenous communities throughout central Mexico created images and histories that made baptism, the vassalage pact with the Crown of Castile, and the conversion of the collectivity into main cornerstones of their founding myths. Energized by local cults to the Virgin and other Catholic symbols that made the native population into a new chosen people, these patriotic narratives strongly interacted with creole ones.[75]

Needless to say, creole attitudes toward the native population were not uniform. Indeed, as Mexican responses to Gálvez's efforts to appoint mainly peninsulars to senior posts in the political and ecclesiastical hierarchy make clear, the emerging vision of a Catholic mestizo patria did not eliminate the strong ambivalence that novohispanic political elites tended to have toward mestizaje.[76] This ambivalence is palpable in the Mexico city council's 1771 Representación, or address to the crown, which complained about the exclusion of American Spaniards (the word *criollo* was not used) from the viceroyalty's top honors. Like previous creole appeals to Spain,[77] the document argued that access to public offices was supposed to be exclusive to natives of the jurisdiction and contrasted the "nativeness" of the American Spaniard with the "foreignness" of the European one. It also emphasized that creoles were just as noble as peninsular Spaniards and, in a transparent attempt to claim a historically deeper local pedigree, even referred to the pre-Columbian imperial blood of some of the members of the ayuntamiento. Yet the author was quick to point out that Spaniards on both sides of the Atlantic constituted one political body and that American ones were as "pure" as those in Old Spain.[78]

The 1771 Representación, the "last grand statement of the traditional themes of creole patriotism in New Spain before the debates of 1808,"[79] vehemently denied accusations that all Spaniards in the Americas were "Indians" or "mixed." These accusations, the document contended, were false because native women were too "ugly," "dirty," and "uncultured," among other things, and because the children of mixed unions would not have access to the honors, rights, and privileges granted to Spaniards and pure Indians. Mixture with blacks was even less likely, it pointed out, because it implied higher social costs. The author then rejected the notion that the mixture of Spaniards with blacks was common in New Spain, as had been "painted" (probably a reference to casta paintings). It was true, he conceded, that in the first years Spaniards had fathered children with Indian women, but because the latter had tended to be noble, their descendants did not suffer any social or legal consequences. The Spanish–Indian combination was "a mixture that by the fourth generation has no importance in nature or politics; for anyone who has one Indian great-grandparent out of sixteen is by nature, and for all civil purposes, a pure Spaniard, without the mixture of any other blood." In fact, the author continued, many noble houses in Spain had that particular "mix."

The town council's 1771 statement to the king was but one of a number of documents from the time that reflect both the growing sense of creole patriotism and the deep apprehensions that some Mexican creole elites had about native blood and mestizaje. Their identification with a Spanish community of blood continued to be reinforced in the eighteenth century by the system of probanzas de limpieza de sangre, which remained in place for the ecclesiastical and secular hierarchies even though conducting transatlantic investigations for both creoles and peninsulars had become more difficult.[80] The proliferation of purity and nobility requirements in the face of growing social instability not only led to an increase in the number of probanzas but enhanced the creole elite's obsession with genealogy and the past. Their genealogical trees and claims became more and more elaborate.[81] Thus, in 1767, Francisco Antonio de Medina y Torres applied to be the Holy Office's alguacil mayor. Just a decade earlier, one of his relatives, a secretary in Mexico's audiencia who tried to have his purity and nobility certified, boasted that he was able to produce genealogical proof for thirty-eight of his ancestors.[82]

Together with the reports of merits and services, the probanzas de limpieza de sangre helped sustain the creole preoccupation with blood. They also served to reproduce the myth of Spanish origins and to generate a historical narrative that linked the Christian "reconquest" of Spain and the conquest of Mexico. For example, in 1730, don Antonio Joaquín de Rivadeneyra y Barrientos, the future author of the Representación of 1771, competed for a prebend in Mexico City's Colegio de Todos Santos, for which he submitted proof of his purity of blood, nobility, and respectable behavior. In his información, he stressed that all of his ancestors from both bloodlines had been "Old Christians, clean of all bad race, and notable gentlemen and hidalgos" and that his parents and grandparents had held honorific posts in Mexico City and Puebla. Don Rivadeneyra y Barrientos also provided extensive information regarding his ancestors from his mother's side. He claimed that they had belonged to some of the most illustrious Spanish families, dating back at least to the eleventh-century king Alfonso VI, and had participated in the wars against the "Moors" as well as in the conquest of New Spain.[83] The history of Mexico and its pre-Hispanic "classical" past thus became part of a broader providential narrative that allowed creoles to simultaneously claim kingdom status for their place of birth, construct a nativeness that was separate from Castile, and vindicate their Spanish bloodlines. As a mural produced in the capital in the middle of the eighteenth century revealed, Hernán Cortés was a central figure in this narrative, a New World Moses who brought about a new religious order and whose legacy criollos claimed.[84]

Don Rivadeneyra y Barrientos's 1730 información became part of a report of professional and academic merits that he compiled in 1752, when he was serving as an oidor in Guadalajara's audiencia, and that he continued to use as he climbed the ranks of government administration. Beyond recording the elite preoccupation with lineage at a time of social change, his *probanzas* and other genealogical histories from the period suggest that the hidalgo–cristiano viejo cultural paradigm—first promoted centuries earlier by the state and church—was alive and well in late colonial Mexico. This paradigm only added to the complexity of New Spain's racial ideology, which even at the height of the construction of a Catholic mestizo patria oscillated between including native people in the category of purity and marking them as impure.

CONCLUSION

Eighteenth-century New Spain gave birth to casta paintings, a genre that reveals a great deal about how colonial artists (most of whom were creoles) conceived of the sistema de castas, the relationship between race and gender, and colonial hierarchies. The paintings' representation of a social order neatly structured by overlapping race and class lines and maintained by white male control over female sexuality was deceptive, for the period was one in which the system of classification became more unstable due to demographic, economic, and marriage trends. As socio-economic shifts made the lower border of Spanish society even more permeable than it had been in the past, not only did the term *creole* acquire connotations of impurity but the concept of calidad began to compete with that of casta within the lexicon of purity of blood—a sign that the categories of the sistema de castas, including that of Spaniard, were increasingly defined by social status and bloodlines.

The growing instability of the sistema de castas prompted a variety of colonial institutions to attempt to increase their exclusivity by issuing or enforcing purity and nobility statutes, which only intensified the Mexican elite's obsession with genealogy and anxieties about mestizaje, particularly about the mixing of Spanish and black blood. These anxieties culminated in 1774, when the Inquisition formally added black ancestry to its categories of impurity. By then, the Spanish marking of blackness as an indelible genealogical stain was widespread. Inquisitors, friars, painters, and government officials (including audiencia judges) deemed black ancestry to be impure, and if the Holy Office is to be believed, so did "popular opinion." In a variety of written and visual sources, impurity was not just Africanized but feminized, mapped, as it were, onto black women. The century that opened with the production of an image of a *mulata* dressed in sumptuous clothing and representing the seat of the Americas thus closed with an affirmation of the impure status of blacks not only by the Inquisition but by the Bourbon government's institutional policies and social legislation, including the Royal Pagramatic on Marriages.

In New Spain, this law not only raised questions about what constituted racial inequality but encouraged the production of more limpieza de sangre certificates. These late colonial documents reveal that even though the concept of purity of blood had undergone important transformations—among them becoming increasingly linked to "Spanishness" and "whiteness"—religion continued to be important to the ways in which some church and government officials defined it. The survival of the religious-spiritual dimension of limpieza de sangre enabled the continued extension of the concept to the Christianized native population, shaped central Mexico's patriotic defense of Spanish–Indian marriages, and allowed criollo clerics, intellectuals, and painters to elaborate a vision of a Catholic mestizo patria. Primarily but not exclusively a function of creole imaginings, this vision was expressed in Luis de Mena's 1750 depiction of New Spain's diverse populations under the image of the Virgin of Guadalupe. Although this was apparently the only casta painting with overt religious iconography, the genre as a whole contributed to the patriotic vision by reproducing the underlying principles of the limpieza de sangre discourse, which granted the indigenous population a favored spiritual and genealogical status, especially vis-à-vis blacks.

The directionality of influences in eighteenth-century Mexican thinking about race and mestizaje was extremely complex, however. On one hand, the generational principles and ideas about which descendants of mixed unions could claim Spanishness that are present in casta paintings came from the practices and legal formulas that institutions had been using to determine limpieza de sangre status; on the other, the paintings were viewed by government and inquisition officials and seem to have influenced the way some of them thought about lineage and biological inheritance. As the creole vision of Catholic mestizo patria was emerging, the political and cultural spheres were clearly shaping each other, as were the material and representational.

Despite its message of redemption through faith, this vision was one that betrayed a strong ambivalence toward native blood; after all, it imagined not only Hispanicizing and Christianizing the indigenous population but whitening it, fusing its blood into Spanish lineages until rendering it invisible. It was therefore a vision very much produced by colonialism as both a system of economic, patriarchal, and racial subordination and a fantasy of sexual domination and biological dispossession. This fantasy became more elaborate as mercantile capitalism expanded, made population a main source of national wealth, and turned colonial bodies into virtual commodities, and as creole patriots tried to reconcile their identification as a community on the basis of territory with their identification as a community on the basis of bloodlines. The form that late colonial Mexican patriotic and racial imaginings took owed much to institutional policies, power struggles, and social relations that by routinizing certain archival practices made a set of assumptions about blood and lineage purity—a series of genealogical fictions—seem natural, taken for granted, and thus the consequence of history denied as such.

Conclusion

⁑

This book has analyzed the concept of limpieza de sangre from its origins amid the complex sociopolitical climate of early modern Spain to its deployment in colonial Mexico, where it served as the ideological foundation of the sistema de castas. It has emphasized that in both places, the concept of limpieza de sangre was mediated by religion and linked to a set of beliefs about lineage, legitimate birth, and honor. In the Iberian Peninsula, the notion was closely connected to the idea that Jewish and Muslim converts to Christianity were not yet secure in the faith and were therefore potential heretics. This idea became the basis of the purity-of-blood statutes, which gave rise to genealogical investigations to ascertain that a person's parents and grandparents had all been Christians. Between the middle of the fifteenth century—when Toledo issued what was perhaps the first municipal purity decree—to the middle of the sixteenth—when the same city's cathedral chapter issued a similar requirement—the generational limitations on such investigations declined, and the relatively flexible definition of limpieza was replaced by a more rigid one requiring equally unsullied paternal and maternal bloodlines. By the end of the sixteenth century, the concept of limpieza de sangre had become a common (albeit not always effective) mechanism of exclusion and had served to construe conversos and moriscos as New Christians, as converts indefinitely suspended between two religions.

The Inquisition played a major role in spreading the ideology of limpieza de sangre, at first by targeting converted communities (thereby helping to associate them with heretical tendencies) and, as of the 1570s, by standardizing and disseminating the legal procedures for establishing a person's Old Christian bloodlines. Through the literature it produced for its different tribunals and the genealogical interrogations it conducted in towns all over Spain, the Holy Office not only accentuated concerns with purity, but promoted a certain understanding of it, one in which religion and lineage were strongly linked. The extent to which the two were collapsed in early modern Spain was manifested in the commonly held assumption that religious beliefs, values, and practices were transmitted from parents to children, in part through indoctrination within the family, in part through physiological processes. Blood thus came to function as a metaphor for both biological and cultural inheritance and along with breast milk figured prominently in early modern Spain's imagery of (Old Christian) purity and (heretical) contamination. The female body was at the center of this imagery because of women's roles in biological and cultural reproduction, which took on more importance as the Inquisition disproportionately prosecuted conversas and moriscas for religious transgressions.

Spain's requirements of limpieza de sangre promoted an obsession with lineage that led to the rise of linajudos, a market in false genealogies, and investigations into family histories that only called attention to Spain's Jewish and Muslim past. Paradoxically, the statutes helped to invent the Christian foundations of Spanish towns. As some of the jurists and theologians who commented on them observed, whether someone had Jewish or Muslim ancestry mattered less than whether anyone remembered they did. Experts on the statutes did not actually agree on whether genealogical investigations should place more weight on oral testimonies or written records, but by placing a high premium on reputation, the requirements became implicated not just in controlling access to certain institutions and corporations but also in constructing local and historical memory. As the seventeenth-century Spaniard Gonzales Monjarrés realized when he left his title of familiar at a confraternity for his descendants to use as well as a list of archives and papers they should consult if they were ever accused of being related to the alleged converso Diego de Castro, probanzas de limpieza de sangre and other purity documents could be used to create unsullied family histories and thereby to shape understandings of the past. Thus, although at first the statutes produced a frenzy of genealogical investigations that led to the discovery of countless "stains," over the course of the early modern period, the pressure to conceal Jewish and Muslim antecedents shaped individual and collective memories and helped to generate the myth of a pure Christian Spain. Not until the writings of Américo Castro in the middle of the twentieth century did this myth start to be dismantled.[1]

The concept of limpieza also shaped historical myths in Mexico, where it too functioned, at least initially, as a religious mode of discourse. Indeed, the first colonial purity requirements, those that demanded that emigrants to the Americas provide proof of their Old Christian status, were ostensibly part of the Christianization project. Although they made exceptions, Spanish monarchs claimed that they wanted to prevent conversos and moriscos from going to their new territories because they might try to undermine the church's overseas conversion efforts. Charles V and especially Philip II leaned on the same justification when they issued decrees making purity of blood a requirement for certain posts in the colonial religious and secular administrations. Their policies facilitated the transfer of peninsular concerns with blood and genealogy to the colonial context, as did the Inquisition's establishment of procedures for certifying the Old Christian status of its officials and familiars in the Americas. The emergence of a colonial system of probanzas de limpieza de sangre, which often required genealogical investigations in Iberian towns and archives, in turn reinforced the metropolitan obsession with blood purity. Spanish policies on emigration to the Americas, colonial bureaucratic requirements, and the Inquisition's investigative mechanisms all contributed to the spread and reproduction of the discourse of limpieza de sangre in the Hispanic Atlantic world as a whole.

Although this discourse enjoyed a certain unity and continuity throughout the early modern period, the meanings of limpieza de sangre were adapted to local and historical circumstances. For the more than three centuries that it was in use in Mexico, for example, the concept retained its stress on bloodlines uncontaminated by Jews, Muslims, or heretics. But in the last decades of the sixteenth century, some probanzas began to list blacks, mulattos, and occasionally mestizos and indios within the category of impurity. This intersection of limpieza de sangre and the sistema de castas—of the discourses of raza and casta—occurred because of a series of transatlantic and local developments that enabled the displacement of Spanish anxieties about religious conversion onto people of African and indigenous descent. Particularly important among these developments was the importation of black slaves to Spanish America, which as evidenced in the growing popularity of the myth of the curse of Ham to explain enslavement practices, strengthened Iberian associations of slavery with black skin color and ancestral sin. More important from a long-term perspective, slavery made it difficult for blacks to make genealogical claims, which in turn affected their descendants' ability to successfully claim that they were Old Christians. The extension of notions of limpieza de sangre to people of indigenous ancestry was precipitated by different socioreligious developments, including the clergy's disillusionment with the conversion project, the decline of the pre-Hispanic nobility, and the arrival of more European women to the Americas. These factors made marriages between Spanish men and native women even rarer than they had been in the decades after the conquest and lessened the status of mestizos, who in addition to being marked by the stain of illegitimacy were increasingly distanced from pre-Hispanic noble blood and, like their indigenous parents, perceived by church officials as fragile Christians.

Because of their (real or alleged) pagan practices and beliefs, because they could not yet claim that they were Old Christians, or simply because Spaniards saw them as unstable converts, blacks and people of mixed ancestry were gradually included in the category of impurity by various colonial institutions. This inclusion, which occurred in spite of the official and more restricted definition of limpieza, accelerated in the seventeenth century and was accompanied by the production of more casta categories and concomitant (if irregular) creation of separate baptismal, marriage, and death records for Spaniards, Indians, and castas in parishes throughout New Spain. The transfer and adaptation of the discourse to the American context also resulted in the association of purity with Spanishness and white skin color. A colonial innovation, this association emerged almost surreptitiously and was recorded in the declarations of witnesses in probanzas de limpieza de sangre. Their testimonies suggest that, at least in the Spanish mind-set, skin color came to function as an index of behavioral, religious, and biological characteristics and that phenotype in general came to play an informal role in how pure bloodlines were measured. Witnesses to the gradual crystallization of a Christian, Spanish, and white identity in Spanish America, the probanzas point to the interrelated nature of the histories of anti-Semitism and colonial racism as well as to the centrality of colonialism to modern definitions of race and nation.

It was the colonial situation that in the seventeenth century forced Spanish jurists, theologians, and inquisitors to reflect on the rationale, meanings, and applicability of the statutes of purity of blood, and it was pressure from Mexico's Holy Office that led the Suprema to formally include African-descended people in the category of impurity. The trajectory of the concept of limpieza de sangre in New Spain thus serves as a reminder that just as histories of colonialism that don't take into consideration how metropolitan markings of peasants, Jews, and other marginalized groups were mapped onto colonized populations are insufficient, histories of race that don't consider how fundamental colonial rule was to the rise of modern racial (and national) ideologies are equally problematic. That the transformation of the concept began in earnest in the 1600s also calls attention to the need to reconsider the importance of the seventeenth century in various areas of social and intellectual life. Some historians of Latin America have begun this reevaluation, but there is much more to do in terms of studying, for example, the fate of the Christianization project after the religious orders lost power to the secular clergy, the reconstitution of indigenous communities within the context of an emerging capitalist global economy, the rise of significant numbers of free African-descended people and their relations with and impact on other colonial populations, the effects of shifts in the political economy on women's socioeconomic roles and gender in general, and the relationship of science and religion. Future studies of these topics will help put to rest the view in the historiography of the seventeenth century as a relatively static period and raise new ways of thinking about how ideas and social practices functioned in a local and transatlantic context and about the reproduction of Spanish colonial rule.

As the probanzas de limpieza de sangre hint at, social change in central Mexico accelerated as of the middle of the seventeenth century. Not only did the concept of purity of blood become associated with Spanishness and whiteness, but it came to work together with socioeconomic categories. Especially in the second half of the colonial period, some probanzas added not just black and slave ancestries into the category of impurity but also descent from people who engaged in "vile or mechanical trades." Appearing in Spain as well, this trend was related to the expansion of mercantile capitalism, which by increasing the possibility of social mobility prompted numerous religious, secular, and educational institutions to attempt to become more exclusive by establishing narrower admission requirements. In central Mexico, the growing exclusivity was also due to changes in demographic and marriage patterns, which along with economic ones made the lower border of Spanish society more permeable and the sistema de castas more fluid. The proliferation of purity requirements and of genealogical stains in the context of socioeconomic reconfigurations both manifested and exacerbated the existing tension between, on one hand, an incipient structure of class stratification and, on the other, a system of determining access to key public and religious offices and institutions based primarily on bloodlines, in other words, a system that could be abstracted to caste.

The instability of the sistema de castas grew in the latter half of the colonial period, but it was actually built into it because of the multiple ambiguities of the concept of limpieza de sangre, which made different forms of classification and incorporation into the category of Spaniard possible. For one, widespread use of the concept never resolved, in Spain or Spanish America, whether purity was a natural condition, that is, carried in the blood and therefore established by genealogical records, or a social one and thus determined more by oral testimonies.[2] In colonial probanzas, this lack of clarity meant that Spanish and casta categories were sometimes defined more by birth (by lineage and legitimacy), at others more by religious behavior, reputation, social status, phenotype, and so forth. Furthermore, neither religious nor secular authorities produced hard rules about how far back to look for stains, nor about whether the category of gentile, which could encompass black and native people, could be treated as impure. Questions about whether to rely more heavily on public reputation than on genealogical records, about how many generations back investigations could probe, and about whether the descendants of gentiles could be excluded from the status of purity and for how long tended to be raised in institutional contexts because it was there that admission requirements were sometimes put to the test. These questions were never definitively resolved, and perhaps could not have been, given that the existence of a juridical model for determining purity status did not prevent each institution or corporation from coming up with its own rules and procedures.

Thus, in the second half of the colonial period, multiple, overlapping, and even competing discourses of blood purity operated in Mexico. Some stressed Christian bloodlines, some Spanish ancestry, and some skin color. The multivalence of the concept of limpieza de sangre stemmed from its definitional ambiguities as well as from the chameleonic and parasitic nature of race, from its capacity to adapt to new circumstances and attach itself to new social phenomena while retaining shades of its past incarnation. No racial discourse is ever entirely new; as social and historical conditions change, race builds on old beliefs, tropes, and stereotypes. In Mexico and the rest of the Iberian Atlantic world, the expansion of mercantile capitalism and advent of new understandings of the body and biological reproduction within the natural sciences began to secularize the concept of limpieza de sangre. Its association with Spanishness and whiteness and its interaction with class enabled the exclusion of people who were not officially considered impure and who could claim Christian ancestry for several generations from institutions with statutes and from some religious and public offices. But as has been stressed repeatedly in this book, the inconsistency between royal definitions of purity of blood and exclusionary practices did not mean that the original and more religious meanings of the concept did not have major ramifications in colonial Mexican society. Not only did these meanings continue to shape understandings of Spanish purity, but throughout the colonial period, they informed the legal-theological status of the native population. The principle of Indian limpieza was periodically expressed in royal legislation, but more important, it operated in native communities, where local caciques and principales were granted a set of privileges and rights on the basis of their pre-Hispanic noble bloodlines and acceptance of the Catholic faith.

Spanish colonialism's production of parallel discourses of purity was in consonance with the two-republic model of sociopolitical organization. This model led to the creation of separate religious and secular tribunals, town councils, fiscal obligations, and parish records for native people, and insofar as it granted them the right to hold office and to claim vecindad in their communities, it resulted in two citizenship regimes. The establishment of two systems of local government and corresponding dual requirements of blood purity also led to the introduction of the legal formulas of Spanish probanzas into the process of confirming caciques and principales and into Indian limpieza cases, the latter frequently arising because of jurisdictional disputes or struggles over the inheritance of land titles, political offices, and cacicazgos. Native nobility and purity cases both came to involve genealogical investigations to the second or third generation, declarations by community elders, and claims regarding unwavering loyalty to the Catholic faith. Lineage—the need to prove descent from certain families, the need to prove purity of bloodlines—thus became a central strategy of social reproduction in main indigenous towns just as it did in Spanish colonial society, where it was used to access the clergy and administration. There were strong connections between the mechanisms used by Spanish and native elites to obtain political and economic privileges and more generally between the reproduction of hierarchies in the two republics and a social order based on blood.

Instead of affirming lack of Jewish and Muslim blood and the absence of any heretical antecedents, however, indigenous rulers and nobles who had to prove their purity would normally declare that they did not have ancestors or relatives who had practiced idolatry, presumably since the sixteenth-century conversions had taken place. They also routinely emphasized their lack of black and mulatto blood. In a society strongly shaped by a political ideology that construed Spaniards as Old Christians and native people as a spiritually unsullied (albeit religiously fragile) community and that established similar mechanisms of social reproduction for their elites, black blood became the main source of impurity almost by default. Not that Spaniards never recognized individuals of African descent as good Christians, only that unlike the indigenous population, blacks did not have a collective legal status as free Christian vassals of the Crown of Castile, which shaped cultural codes about their place in the spiritual and sociopolitical order. Moreover, their alleged slave origins made it virtually impossible for them to claim purity of blood. The condition of slavery's curtailment of genealogical claims meant that it was inherently antithetical to the concepts of cristiano viejo and hidalgo, contrary to the spirit of purity and nobility, because both notions were constituted by a set of ideas regarding legitimate birth, lineage, and temporality. For these reasons, certain religious orders and other institutions included descent from slaves as an impure category, one that made a person ineligible for admission. The status of impurity could have real social consequences.

Colonial documents, and in particular, the probanzas de limpieza de sangre produced by the Inquisition and other Spanish institutions, do not reveal much about how blacks viewed or challenged the ideology of purity of blood. But some sources do suggest that African-descended people had alternative definitions of purity and rejected the idea that they were unable to make genealogical claims and become Old Christians. Though not numerous, these sources provide clues as to how relatively disempowered people tried to carve social and spiritual spaces for themselves in a society that generally marked them as impure. At certain times, persons of African descent demonstrated a strong sense of lineage and tried to appropriate and redeploy the very concepts and definitions of the discourse of purity of blood to capitalize on its ambiguities about the importance of religious faith versus bloodlines and about the ability of the Christianized descendants of gentiles to be accepted as cristianos viejos. But mainly because of their restricted access to institutional and political power, their efforts as a whole did not prevail, and they were systematically included in the category of impurity. This inclusion had profound implications for the place of blacks and their descendants in novohispanic society and in Mexico's historical narratives.

Power is constitutive of history, among other reasons because different groups have unequal access to the means of historical production, and this inequality plays a part at every step of the construction of the past. Specifically, it is involved in the making, assemblage, and retrieval of sources and in the forging of their contents into narratives.[3] In New Spain, the restricted ability that African-descended people had to produce, organize, and reproduce categories; to create sources and structure archives and therefore influence the recovery of facts; and to leave written traces of feelings, thoughts, and practices generated deep silences about their significance in Mexican history. These silences were made all the more powerful by the ideology of limpieza de sangre. Just as the purity statutes both exposed and denied Spain's Jewish and Muslim past, colonial forms of marking blackness through classifications, genealogical investigations, and institutional exclusions had paradoxical consequences. These forms of marking aimed to make black ancestry visible while simultaneously encouraging its erasure from the historical record, thus laying the groundwork for modern Mexico's myth of its pure Spanish and Indian foundations. Although the works of the anthropologist Gonzalo Aguirre-Beltrán in the 1940s and 1950s and more recent studies by scholars in the United States and Mexico have begun to recover the history of New Spain's black populations by examining, for example, slavery, Inquisition, town council, military, church, and confraternity records, the myth continues to shape the country's nationalist thought, its teleological and genealogical fictions.

In part because of their recognition as a republic under the Crown of Castile—subordinate to the Spanish one but entitled to their own government and hierarchies—indigenous communities, or rather their political and economic elites, contributed to the construction of those fictions. The concept of purity was deployed by caciques and principales who had to submit probanzas, but it was also used in communal histories that emphasized the moment of the group's acceptance of Christianity and the authority of the Spanish king. These histories framed indigenous entitlement to land and political autonomy in terms of a contract between the Castilian crown and the Mesoamerican ruling and noble dynasties that had converted to the Catholic faith, thus revealing how the issue of purity—as one of loyalty to the faith across generations—was important not just for individuals but for the group. In time, the incorporation of Spanish notions of political and religious fidelity into native petitions for land and titles and into town histories influenced New Spain's broader historical narratives. Tlaxcala's indigenous political leaders, for example, integrated Christian concepts of baptism, conversion, and vassalage into their textual and visual histories, and the imagery and narratives they produced colored creole representations of the conquest and its political and religious consequences.[4]

The construction of New Spain's discourse of native purity had many agents—members of the religious and secular administrations as well as caciques and principales, indigenous artists, and other members of the "Indian republic"—and was achieved through a variety of legal, visual, and social mechanisms. A more comprehensive history of this construction awaits more detailed studies of local religious and political developments, the role and language of lineage claims in native petitions for land and public office, and the creole appropriation of indigenous religious and genealogical iconography. It is clear, however, that this appropriation intensified in the eighteenth century and laid bare the implications of the religious dimension of the concept of limpieza de sangre for Mexico's racial ideology. As the sistema de castas became unstable, as the elite obsession with safeguarding its purity of blood reached new heights, and as the government passed laws attempting to control intermarriage, religious and secular officials and creole patriots expressed deep concerns about unions between Spaniards and blacks but tended to articulate a strong defense of marriages between the former and native people.

As had occurred two centuries earlier in the Iberian Peninsula, the obsession with limpieza de sangre and the concept's stress on purity from both bloodlines displaced Spanish anxieties over impurity onto women; in New Spain, onto black women in particular. It is difficult to determine whether these anxieties were a result of actual marriage and reproductive patterns between white men and African-descended women or simply of fears of such unions. Whatever the case, the political and cultural establishment left evidence of its urgent concern with preventing Spanish men from corrupting their "seeds" by reproducing with black women in a variety of written and visual sources, including casta paintings. Conveying systematicness to categories that no longer had much, the masculinization of blackness, and in general the intersection of race, class, and gender within the logic of the sistema de castas, the paintings reveal the creole elite's ordering and classificatory impulse at a time of flux. By privileging the Spanish–Indian union and implying that black blood could not be fully assimilated into Spanish lineages, they also attest to the ongoing importance of the ideology of limpieza de sangre and its extension of the status of purity to the native population. This status, which had been reinforced by royal legislation, the founding of convents for indigenous noblewomen (a recognition of their privileged place within the spiritual and genealogical economy), and the spread of the cult of the Virgin of Guadalupe, enabled the emergence of a vision of a Catholic mestizo patria, the main contours of which appear in some probanzas; in the works of clerics, government officials, and writers; and in Luis de Mena's mid-eighteenth-century casta painting.

Despite its potency, the patriotic vision of a Catholic and mestizo New Spain did not undermine the creole sense of being part of a Spanish community of blood. Creole patriots appropriated pre-Hispanic history and some even claimed to have remote noble Indian ancestors to strengthen their arguments for their right to access upper levels of the government and ecclesiastical administrations. But for all their identification with the land and the Mexica empire, novohispanic elites generally continued to strongly identify as Spaniards, an identification that throughout the colonial period was fed by the probanzas de limpieza de sangre and the set of archival practices they promoted. Facilitating access to main political and religious offices, educational institutions, familiaturas, religious orders, craft guilds, military academies, and so forth, these probanzas generated family and group narratives that in their privileging of

Spanish bloodlines were in tension with the discourse of native purity. As the ayuntamiento's 1771 address to the crown suggests, Mexican elites dealt with the contradictions inherent in wanting to make historical and genealogical claims that bolstered their "nativeness" (and thus their argument for having full naturaleza rights) and to reject the view that they were "mixed" by rendering mestizaje a phenomenon of the early colonial period, by stressing that it had mainly involved Spanish unions with indigenous noblewomen, and by suggesting that mixture and purity were compatible.

This compatibility was by no means a product of their imagination. As Spanish colonial legislation and various religious and secular institutions had been recognizing for about two centuries, the descendants of Spanish–Indian unions could return to the Spanish pole. The juridico-theological status of the indigenous people, the survival of pre-Columbian royal and noble lineages, the legacy of the religious utopias of the early missionaries, the social relations that Spaniards established with caciques and principales, the adaptation of Castilian legal and genealogical formulas to the colonial context, and the appropriation of Catholic concepts and imagery by indigenous communities were among the factors that had made that return possible. These colonial developments, a vivid example of how historical processes and ideological constructs—especially if backed by the force of religion and law—influence a society's understandings of biological reproduction and race, enabled the emergence of a Mexican vision of a Catholic mestizo patria, one that simultaneously recognized the favored place of the native people within New Spain's spiritual economy and betrayed the creole elite's privileging of Spanish bloodlines and whiteness. That vision and all of its ambivalences toward native and especially black ancestries would survive independence and continue to haunt Mexican political imaginaries throughout the nineteenth and twentieth centuries and beyond.

Reference Matter

Appendix

Questionnaire Used by the Spanish Inquisition

The following questionnaire was used to interrogate witnesses in purity of
blood investigations in the first half of the seventeenth century. It is in AHN,
Inquisición, libro 1056, fols. 439–439v. Author's transcription.

Como se han de interrogar a los testigos en investigaciones de limpieza
1) Primeramente, si conocen al dicho de cuya información se trata. Declaren
como es el conocimiento, y tiempo y la edad que tiene.

2) Si conocen al padre y madre del dicho. Y si saben de donde son naturales,
y han vivido, y sido vecinos, de cuanto tiempo y como es el conocimiento.

3) Si conocen al padre, y madre del dicho, abuelos por parte del dicho y si
tienen noticia de los demás ascendientes por parte de padre del dicho declaren
como es el conocimiento. Y de que tiempo, y de donde son naturales, y han sido
vecinos y tenido domicilio.

4) Si conocen al padre, y madre de la dicha, abuelos de partes de madre del
dicho y de donde son naturales, y han sido vecinos, y tenido domicilio, declaren
como es el conocimiento, y de que tiempo.

5) Sean preguntados los testigos por las preguntas generales.

6) Si saben que el dicho de cuya información se trata es hijo de los dichos y
por tal su hijo legítimo es habido, y tenido, y comúnmente reputado. Digan y
declaren los testigos como lo saben, y la filiación.

7) Si saben que el dicho su padre y los dichos sus abuelos por partes de
padre, y los demás sus ascendientes por partes de padre, todos, y cada unos
de ellos, han sido, y son Cristianos viejos, de limpia sangre, sin raza, mácula,
ni descendencia de Judíos, Moros, ni Conversos, ni de otra secta nuevamente
convertida, y por tales han sido, habidos y tenidos, y comúnmente reputados,
y de lo contrario no ha habido fama, ni rumor, que si lo hubiera, los testigos
lo supieran, o hubieran oído decir, según el conocimiento y noticia que de los
susodichos, y cada uno de ellos han tenido y tienen.

8) Si saben que el dicho y el dicho su padre y abuelos de partes de padre,
contenidos en la pregunta antes de ésta, ni ninguno de los demás sus ascendientes,
han sido penitenciados, ni condenados por el Santo Oficio de la Inquisición, ni
incurrido en otra infamia, que le prohíba tener oficio público y de honor: digan

los testigos lo que acerca de esto saben, y han oído, y lo que saben de las buenas costumbres, cordura, y opinión del dicho.

9) Si saben que la dicha madre del dicho y los dichos sus abuelos por partes de madre, y los demás ascendientes por partes de la madre del dicho todos y cada uno de ellos, han sido, y son Cristianos viejos, limpios de limpia sangre, sin raza, mácula, ni descendencia de Moros, Judíos, ni Conversos, ni de otra secta nuevamente convertida, y que por tales son habidos y tenidos, y comúnmente reputados, y tal es la pública voz y fama, y común opinión, y de lo contrario, no ha habido fama, ni rumor, que si la hubiera, los testigos lo supieran o hubieran oído decir, y no pudiera ser menos, según la noticia que de los susodichos, y cada uno de ellos han tenido y tienen.

10) Si saben que la dicha madre del dicho y los dichos sus padres y ascendientes contenidos en la pregunta antes de esta, ni ninguno de ellos ha sido condenado, ni penitenciado por el Santo Oficio de la Inquisición, ni incurrido en otra infamia que le prohíba al dicho tener oficio público, y de honor.

11) Si saben que todo lo susodicho es pública voz y fama.

El que hiciere la información ha de hacer que los testigos respondan puntualmente a cada artículo de la pregunta, sin contentarse con responder generalmente a toda la pregunta como en ella se contiene. Y demás de las preguntas del interrogatorio, hará las que de las deposiciones de los testigos resultaren, necesarias para averiguación de la verdad, sin exceder a preguntas impertinentes.

Glossary

alcalde   A first-instance judge who was also a member of the town council. Also called *alcalde ordinario*.

alcalde mayor   Chief magistrate of a given town or area. Appointed by the crown. In Spanish America, the term was frequently used interchangeably with *corregidor*.

alguacil mayor   Chief constable in charge of executing the orders of the district magistrate (alcalde mayor). Also an official within the Inquisition.

audiencia   Royal tribunal; acted as an appeals court and governing body.

auto de fe   A public or private act of religious penitence. Over time, public autos became elaborate spectacles involving inquisitors, royalty, and large audiences and featuring a procession to the square and stage where they were held, a mass and sermon, and a reading of the crimes of the accused.

ayuntamiento   The main Spanish American local governing body; a municipal corporation in charge of administering an urban center and the territory under its jurisdiction. It was composed of a royal official or *corregidor* (also called *alcalde mayor* or *justicia mayor*), two *alcades menores*, and a town council (*cabildo*).

cabildo   Town council. The number of aldermen (*regidores*) in a cabildo tended to be six, but in the case of prominent cities such as Mexico and Puebla, it was twelve.

cacicazgo   A political and economic institution established by the Spanish government for the descendants of pre-Hispanic rulers (*caciques*) that fused pre-Hispanic and Castilian traditions. It referred to a set of rights and holdings attached to the rulership of a cacique, including having access to communal and patrimonial lands and bequeathing his property and titles to his descendants. Like the Spanish *mayorazgo*, the cacicazgo provided a legal framework for the consolidation and perpetuation of estates because they could not be divided and were supposed to be transmitted from patriarch to single heir.

cacique   Native dynastic ruler. Spaniards first applied the term to the legitimate successors of pre-Hispanic rulers.

cartas de privilegio   Patents of nobility, sold by the crown to worthy commoners. Also called *privilegios de hidalguía*.

casta Lineage, caste.

cofradía Religious brotherhood.

comisario Commissioner. Comisarios were normally parish priests who worked for the Inquisition in major cities and ports and were in charge of a variety of duties, such as filling out paperwork, informing Holy Office tribunals of religious transgressions in their jurisdictions, and conducting genealogical investigations in limpieza de sangre cases. Also called *comisario informador*.

comuneros Citizens of Castilian communities who rebelled against the rule of Charles V and his administration from 1520 to 1522.

consultor Advisor. A jurist who advised inquisitors on matters of law.

conversos Converts to Christianity, initially Jewish but eventually Muslim ones as well (the latter also called *moriscos*). Interchangeable with the term *New Christians*.

convivencia The coexistence of Christians, Jews, and Muslims in medieval Spain.

corregidor A district governor and judge (also called *alcalde mayores* and *gobernadores*). In Spanish America there were two types: *corregidores* (in charge of jurisdictions with Spanish and other populations) and *corregidores de indios* (in charge of native jurisdictions and matters).

criollismo Creolism, the strong identification with the local that surfaced among the descendants of Spaniards in Spanish America.

criollo Creole. A Spaniard who had been born or raised in Spanish America. Spaniards at first applied the term to black slaves who were born and raised outside of Africa.

derecho indiano Spanish laws for Spanish America.

encomienda Grant of native laborers awarded by the Spanish crown to individual Spaniards in return for promising to oversee their Christianization.

familiar A lay informant working for the Inquisition who technically had to be pure of blood.

familiatura Title of familiar.

fiscal Prosecutor.

fueros Laws. The term was used to refer to traditional community charters in Spain, where different regions had their own code of laws. It also referred to the distinctive legal status of a particular group, such as the clergy, the military, or the native people.

gobernador Governor; in a native municipality, the highest office held by an indigenous person.

hacendados Owners of haciendas or large landed estates.

hidalgos The Spanish gentry or nontitled nobles.

hidalguía Nobility. Spanish nobles consisted of *hidalgos,* who mainly enjoyed local prestige and exemption from certain taxes; *señores,* owners of small territorial possessions (*señoríos*); and *grandes,* the titled nobility

información de limpieza de sangre Genealogical information provided by a person seeking to prove his or her purity of blood.

ius commune Common law. A European legal science that originated in the twelfth century and combined Roman, canon, and feudal law.

juderías Jewish quarters (in medieval Spain).

ladino In Spain, the term initially referred to Muslims and Jews who mastered the Castilian language. The word was also eventually applied to the language spoken by the Sephardim. In the colonial context, depending on the region, it referred to Hispanicized native people, mestizos, or blacks and others who were fluent in Spanish and had adopted other elements of Castilian culture.

limpieza de oficios Purity of occupation or trade.

limpieza de sangre Purity of blood; the absence of Jewish, Muslim, and (in the Americas) black ancestors.

linajudos Experts on lineages (*linajes*).

marranos A pejorative name for conversos. Of uncertain etymology, the term meant "pigs" and might have been applied to the converted Jews because some refused (or found it difficult) to eat pork.

mayorazgo Entailed estate; allowed for the indivisibly and transmission of different forms of property, normally to the oldest son, or *hijo mayor*.

memorial Historial account.

mestizaje A term coined in the nineteenth century that referred to the "mixing" of different castes or races in colonial and postindependence Latin America.

mestizo Person of Spanish and indigenous descent.

Mexica A migratory people from the northern Mexican frontier who arrived in the central valley around the early twelfth century and through military might became the most powerful group in the region in the course of the fifteenth century. When the Spaniards arrived, they dominated most of central Mexico, parts of the arid north, the lowlands of Tehuantepec, and large stretches on both coasts. Popularly known as "Aztecs."

mulato A person of Spanish and black ancestry. The term was sometimes applied more loosely to anyone of partial African descent.

nación Nation. In early modern times the word had numerous meanings, among them an ethnolingustic community.

Nahuas The Náhuatl-speaking people of Central Mexico.

Náhuatl An Uto-Aztecan language family indigenous to Mesoamerica.

naturaleza Nativeness. In Spain, generally a status that accorded certain exclusive privileges within the kingdom, namely eligibility for office holding and ecclesiastical benefices. The native monopoly on public and religious offices was called the *reserva de oficio*.

nobleza de privilegio Nobility of privilege. Granted by kings to commoners who provided important military or public service or who were able to purchase patents of nobility. If the crown allowed for its transmission from father to son, the status would become *nobleza de sangre* (nobility of blood) on the third generation.

nobleza de sangre Nobility of blood. The most valued noble status in Spanish society because it implied being part of a privileged lineage since "time immemorial."

oidor Judge on an audiencia.

peninsular Peninsular; a Spaniard who was born in Spain.

pipiltin Náhuatl word for nobles.

prebend A stipend or income provided by cathedrals or churches to clergymen in their chapters.

principales Spanish term applied to the legitimate successors of the pre-Hispanic nobility.

probanza de limpieza de sangre Certification or proof of purity of blood. Normally done for persons trying to access institutions or posts with purity of blood requirements or trying to migrate from Spain to Spanish America. Sometimes the term was used interchangeably with *información de limpieza de sangre*.

probanza de méritos y servicios Proof of merits and services. Provided by Spanish conquerors, colonists, and their descendants to the Spanish Crown to be rewarded for their military, political, or religious accomplishments in Spanish America.

procurador Procurator/attorney. A person in charge of representing parties in legal proceedings or the interests of a body such as the Inquisition, an audiencia, or a cabildo.

provisor Chief ecclesiastical judge.

pueblos de indios Indigenous communities

pulque A pre-Hispanic alcoholic beverage made from the maguey plant.

raza Lineage, race.

reconquista The Christian "reconquest" of Spain or effort to reclaim Iberian lands under the control of Muslims after 711, the year that much of the Peninsula fell under Arab rule.

regidor Alderman.

regimiento Town council office; aldermanship.

repartimiento The Spanish colonial system of corvée labor. Called *mita* in the Andes.

república de indios Indian Republic, a term used in Spanish colonial sources that reflected Spain's recognition of the right of indigenous communities to retain their lands, political leaders, and social hierarchies.

sanbenitos Yellow penitential garments worn by people who were convicted by the Inquisition during and sometimes after an auto de fe. They typically had a black Saint Andrew's cross drawn across them. From *saco bendito* (sacred sack).

sistema de castas The colonial system of classification that was theoretically based on proportions of Spanish, indigenous, and African descent but that in practice tended to take social factors into account and therefore to be fluid.

tlatoani Náhuatl for dynastic ruler or "king." Plural: *tlatoque*.

vecindad Local citizenship. A status determined primarily by integration in the local community and implying certain rights and duties.

vecino Head of household. Citizen.

Abbreviations

These abbreviations for the most part follow those used by the archives from which the documents were derived, but for the sake of consistency the AGI's abbreviation of *legago* (L.) was changed to "leg."

AAPAC	Archivo del Ayuntamiento de Puebla (Puebla), Actas de Cabildo
AGI	Archivo General de Indias (Seville)
AGN	Archivo General de la Nación (Mexico City)
AHN	Archivo Histórico Nacional (Madrid)
AHPM	Acervo Histórico del Palacio de Minería (Mexico City)
BNAHMC	Biblioteca Nacional de Antropología e Historia (Mexico City), Microfilm Collection
BNM	Biblioteca Nacional (Madrid)
doc.	Document
exp.	Expediente (file)
fol.	Folio
fols.	Folios
HL	Huntington Library
JCBL	John Carter Brown Library
JCBL/LI	John Carter Brown Library, Rare Book Collection, Libros de Informaciones (novitiate records of the Franciscan Order in colonial Puebla)
LBESP	Libros de Bautismos de Españoles del Sagrario de Puebla (Consulted in the Family Archives of the Genealogical Society of Utah)
leg.	Legajo (file; bundle of papers)
legs.	Legajos
MS.	Manuscript
MSS.	Manuscripts
n. or no.	Number
r.	Ramo (section)
vol.	Volume

Notes

INTRODUCTION

1. The term *sistema de castas,* frequently translated into English as the "race/caste system," refers to the colonial system of classification theoretically based on proportions of Spanish, indigenous, and black ancestry. To draw attention to the social dimensions of race, some historians of colonial Latin America prefer to use the term *sociedad de castas.* The phrase *sistema de castas* is preferred here because, although the system was fluid, it was constituted by underlying principles that gave colonial Mexican racial ideology a measure of coherency and that continued to operate through most of the colonial period.

2. For example, Lyle McAlister, "Social Structure and Social Change in New Spain," *Hispanic American Historical Review* 43, no. 3 (1963): pp. 353–54; Magnus Mörner, *Race Mixture in the History of Latin America* (Boston: Little, Brown, 1967), pp. 54–55; Julio Caro Baroja, "Antecedentes españoles de algunos problemas sociales relativos al mestizaje," *Revista Histórica* (Lima, Peru) 28 (1965): pp. 197–210; and Douglas Cope, *The Limits of Racial Domination: Plebeian Society in Colonial Mexico City, 1660–1720* (Madison: University of Wisconsin Press, 1994), pp. 14–26.

3. See John K. Chance and William B. Taylor's "Estate and Class in a Colonial City: Oaxaca in 1792," *Comparative Studies in Society and History* 19 (1977): pp. 454–87; Robert McCaa, Stuart B. Schwartz, and Arturo Grubessich, "Race and Class in Colonial Latin America: A Critique," *Comparative Studies of Society and History* 21, no. 3 (July 1979): pp. 421–42, esp. p. 433; with reply from John K. Chance and William B. Taylor, "Estate *and* Class: A Reply," *Comparative Studies of Society and History* 21, no. 3 (July 1979): pp. 434–41; Patricia Seed and Philip F. Rust, "Estate and Class in Colonial Oaxaca Revisited," *Comparative Studies of Society and History* 25, no. 4 (October 1983): pp. 703–10; and Robert McCaa and Stuart B. Schwartz, "Measuring Marriage Patterns: Percentages, Cohen's Kappa, and Log-Linear Models," *Comparative Studies of Society and History* 25, no. 4 (October 1983): pp. 711–20. Studies focusing on different aspects of Mexico's sistema de castas in the seventeenth century have started to emerge. They include Cope, *The Limits of Racial Domination;* and

Laura A. Lewis, *Hall of Mirrors: Power, Witchcraft, and Caste in Colonial Mexico* (Durham, NC, and London: Duke University Press, 2003).

4. See McAlister, "Social Structure and Social Change in New Spain," pp. 349–70, which provided a discussion of the system of estates and corporations in Spain and colonial Mexico that influenced a number of subsequent descriptions of the sistema de castas.

5. The work of Claudio Lomnitz, which argues that Mexican racial ideologies and nationalism both have their foundations in Spanish Catholic cosmologies and the idea of purity of blood, is a notable exception to the rule and has been an important reference point for the present study. Claudio Lomnitz-Adler, *Exits from the Labyrinth: Culture and Ideology in the Mexican National Space* (Berkeley and Los Angeles: University of California Press, 1992), pp. 261–81.

6. Scholarship that grants race relative autonomy stresses its complex articulation with the economic, political, ideological, and cultural domains of a particular "social formation." Although it generally challenges economic reductionism, it by no means dismisses the importance of material relations in how race operates. As Stuart Hall remarks, opposing "economism"—a type of theoretical reductionism in that it treats "the economic" as the sole determining structure—does not mean denying the influence of the dominant economic relations of a society on the whole of social life. Stuart Hall, "Gramsci's relevance for the study of race and ethnicity," in *Stuart Hall: Critical Dialogues in Cultural Studies,* ed. David Morley and Kuan-Hsing Chen (London and New York: Routledge, 1996), p. 417. Also see Cornel West, "Race and Social Theory: Toward a Genealogical Materialist Analysis," *The Year Left 2: An American Socialist Yearbook,* ed. Mike Davis et al. (London: Verso, 1987), pp. 74–90; Thomas C. Holt, "Marking: Race, Race-making, and the Writing of History," *American Historical Review* 100, no. 1 (Feb. 1995): pp. 1–20; and Paul Gilroy, *'There Ain't No Black in the Union Jack': The Cultural Politics of Race and Nation* (Chicago: University of Chicago Press, 1991).

7. For a recent discussion of the importance of studying the meanings and connections of certain words, concepts, and practices within the cultural and historical context in which they are embedded, see Saba Mahmood, *The Politics of Piety: The Islamic Revival and the Feminist Subject* (Princeton, NJ, and Oxford: Princeton University Press, 2005), esp. pp. 16–17.

8. On the role of gender in the historical constitution and signification of power, see Joan W. Scott's pioneering discussion, "Gender: A Useful Category of Historical Analysis," *Gender and the Politics of History* (New York: Columbia University Press, 1988), pp. 28–50. Also refer to the vast interdisciplinary literature on the intersection of gender with race and class, in colonial situations and otherwise. The literature is too vast to do it justice here, but it includes Ann L. Stoler, "Rethinking Colonial Categories: European Communities and the Boundaries of Rule," *Comparative Studies in Society and History* 31, no. 1 (January 1989): pp. 134–61; Stoler, "Carnal Knowledge and Imperial Power: Gender, Race and Morality in Colonial Asia," in *Gender at the Crossroads of Knowledge: Feminist Anthropology in the Postmodern Era* (Berkeley: University of California Press, 1991), pp. 51–101; Anne McClintock, *Imperial Leather:*

Race, Gender and Sexuality in the Colonial Contest (New York and London: Routledge, 1995); Philippa Levine, ed., *Gender and Empire* (Oxford and New York: Oxford University Press, 2004); and Verena Martínez-Alier [now Verena Stolcke], *Marriage, Class and Colour in Nineteenth-Century Cuba: A Study of Racial Attitudes and Sexual Values in a Slave Society* (Ann Arbor: University of Michigan Press, 1989 [1974]).

9. On the links between gender and political culture in eighteenth-century New Spain and how gender relations shaped broader forms of understanding authority, see Steve J. Stern, *The Secret History of Gender: Women, Men, and Power in Late Colonial Mexico* (Chapel Hill and London: University of North Carolina Press, 1995).

10. Lewis, *Hall of Mirrors*, pp. 173–76.

11. The term *mestizaje* is sometimes translated into English as "miscegenation," but it does not have the same cultural baggage as the latter, which was coined in the American Civil War period and referred in particular to unions between blacks and whites. Although the Spanish word was not widely deployed in Mexico until the modern period, it is used here in relation to the process that colonial Spaniards described as *mezclas de castas* ("the mixing of castes"). On the concept of miscegenation, see Martha Hodes, *White Women, Black Men* (New Haven: Yale University Press, 1997), pp. 2, 9, and 144–45.

12. William Roseberry, "Hegemony and the Language of Contention," in *Everyday Forms of State Formation: Revolution and the Negotiation of Rule in Modern Mexico*, ed. Gilbert M. Joseph and Daniel Nugent (Durham: Duke University Press, 1994), pp. 355–66.

13. A notable exception is Henry Méchoulan, *El honor de Dios,* trans. from the French by Enrique Sordo (Barcelona: Editorial Argos Vergara, 1981).

14. Scholars and nonscholars alike have for a long time tended to contrast Latin America and the United States on matters of race by stressing that the former has always had more of a class problem than a racial one. The argument, which in the case of Brazil gave way to the myth of racial democracy, was normally accompanied by the claim that the Iberian cultural heritage made Spaniards and Portuguese more open to having sexual and concubinage relations with native and African women. According to scholars such as Frank Tannenbaum, Gilberto Freyre, and Carl Degler, this and other factors led to more "intermingling," tolerance, and manumission. Although almost every element of Brazil's myth of racial democracy has been challenged since the 1950s (by Charles R. Boxer, Florestan Fernandes, Thomas Skidmore, and many others), the argument that class or socioeconomic barriers are more important than race to understanding the history of Brazil and the rest of Latin America continues to shape scholarship in the field. For a brief introduction to the topic, see John Burdick, "The Myth of Racial Democracy," *Report on the Americas* (NACLA) 25, no. 4 (February, 1992): pp. 40–44; and Emilia Viotti da Costa, *The Brazilian Empire: Myths and Histories* (Chicago: Dorsey, 1988), pp. 234–46.

15. Benjamin Keen, "The Black Legend Revisited: Assumptions and Realities," *Hispanic American Historical Review* 49, no. 4 (1969): pp. 703–19; Lewis Hanke, "A Modest Proposal for a Moratorium on Grand Generalizations:

Some Thoughts on the Black Legend," *Hispanic American Historical Review* 51, no. 1 (1971): pp. 112–27; Benjamin Keen, "The White Legend Revisited: A Reply to Professor Hanke's 'Modest Proposal,'" *Hispanic American Historical Review* 51, no. 2 (1971): pp. 336–55; William S. Maltby, *The Black Legend in England: The Development of Anti-Spanish Sentiment, 1558–1660* (Durham: Duke University Press, 1971); Charles Gibson, ed., *The Black Legend: Anti-Spanish Attitudes in the Old World and the New* (New York: Knopf, 1971); Henry Kamen and Joseph Pérez, *La imagen de la España de Felipe II: 'Leyenda negra' o conflicto de intereses* (Valladolid: Universidad de Valladolid, 1980); Sverker Arnorldsson, *La conquista española de América según el juicio de la posteridad: Vestigios de la leyenda negra* (Madrid: Insula, 1960); Miguel Molina Martínez, *La Leyenda negra* (Madrid: Nerea, 1991); and Ricardo García Cárcel, *La leyenda negra: Historia y opinión* (Madrid: Alianza Editorial, 1992).

16. See Jeremy Adelman, "Introduction: The Problem of Persistence in Latin American History," in *Colonial Legacies: The Problem of Persistence in Latin American History,* ed. Jeremy Adelman (New York and London: Routledge, 1999), pp. 6–8.

17. George M. Fredrickson, *Racism: A Short History* (Princeton, NJ, and Oxford: Princeton University Press, 2002), pp. 17–47 (citation from pp. 12–13).

18. See James H. Sweet, "The Iberian Roots of American Racist Thought," *William and Mary Quarterly* 54, no. 1 (January 1997): pp. 143–66; A. J. R. Russell-Wood, "Before Columbus: Portugal's African Prelude to the Middle Passage and Contribution to Discourse on Race and Slavery," *Race, Discourse, and the Origins of the Americas: A New World View,* ed. Vera Lawrence and Rex Nettleford (Washington, DC, and London: Smithsonian Institution Press, 1995), pp. 134–65; and Sylvia Wynter, "1492: A New World View," *Race, Discourse, and the Origin of the Americas,* pp. 5–57.

19. See, for example, Ivan Hannaford, *The Idea of Race: The History of an Idea in the West* (Washington, DC: Woodrow Wilson Center Press and John Hopkins University Press, 1996), esp. pp. 122–26; and Ronald Sanders, *Lost Tribes and Promised Lands: The Origins of American Racism* (Boston: Little, Brown, 1978), pp. 16 and 64–71. For Fredrickson, an antiblack racial ideology was unnecessary in late medieval and early modern Spain because religion and the legal status of blacks sufficed to justify their enslavement. The same was not true, he argues, of the Spanish Jews who converted to Christianity, because their new religious status in theory made them equal to other Christians. Fredrickson, *Racism: A Short History,* pp. 30–31.

20. Steve Stern, "Paradigms of Conquest: History, Historiography, and Politics," *Journal of Latin American Studies* 24 (1992): pp. 1–34, esp. p. 6.

21. The work of Gonzalo Aguirre-Beltrán, pioneering in many respects, was among the first to take the issues of limpieza de sangre and race in colonial Mexico seriously. See *La población negra de México: Estudio etnohistórico* (Mexico City: Fondo de Cultura Económica, 1989 [1946]).

22. Peter Wade, *Race, Nature and Culture: An Anthropological Perspective* (London and Sterling, VA: Pluto, 2002), pp. 14–15.

23. Hall, "Gramsci's relevance for the study of race and ethnicity," p. 435; Stuart Hall, "Race, Articulation and Societies Structured in Dominance," *Unesco Reader, Sociological Theories: Race and Colonialism* (Paris: Unesco, 1980), p. 338; Étienne Balibar, "Racism and Nationalism," in *Race, Nation, Class: Ambiguous Identities,* ed. Étienne Balibar and Immanuel Wallerstein, trans. of Étienne Balibar by Chris Turner (London and New York: Verso, 1991), p. 40; and West, "Race and Social Theory," pp. 74–90.

24. Thomas C. Holt, *The Problem of Race in the 21st Century* (Cambridge and London: Harvard University Press, 2000), p. 19.

25. See, for example, Verena Stolcke, "A New World Engendered: The Making of the Iberian Transatlantic Empires" in *A Companion to Gender History,* ed. Teresa A. Meade and Merry E. Weisner-Hanks (Oxford: Blackwell, 2003); and Stuart B. Schwartz, "Colonial Identities and the *Sociedad de Castas,*" *Colonial Latin America Review* 4, no. 1 (1995): p. 189. Also refer to Stuart B. Schwartz and Frank Salomon, "New Peoples and New Kinds of People: Adaptation, Readjustment, and Ethnogenesis in South American Indigenous Societies (colonial era)," *The Cambridge History of the Native Peoples of the Americas III (2): South America* (Cambridge: Cambridge University Press, 1999), pp. 443–501, esp. p. 444.

26. Peter Wade has pointed out that studies of "generation" (notions about the generation of life in a given culture) don't deal all that much with race and, vice versa, studies of race usually don't examine notions of heredity. As a result, the question of how genealogy helps to construct racial identity has been understudied. *Race, Nature and Culture,* pp. 11–12 and 39–40.

27. Ann L. Stoler, *Race and the Education of Desire: Foucault's "History of Sexuality" and the Colonial Order of Things* (Durham, NC, and London: Duke University Press, 1995), pp. 29–30; Michel Foucault, *The History of Sexuality,* vol. I, trans. from the French by Robert Hurley (New York: Vintage, 1990), pp. 124–25; and Benedict Anderson, *Imagined Communities* (London: Verso, 1991), pp. 149–50. Also see Colette Guillaumin, *Racism, Sexism, Power and Ideology* (London and New York: Routledge, 1995), pp. 29–60.

28. Paul Freedman, *Images of the Medieval Peasant* (Stanford, CA: Stanford University Press, 1999), pp. 133–56.

29. David B. Davis, "Constructing Race: A Reflection," *William and Mary Quarterly* 54, no. 1 (1997): pp. 12–13.

30. On the episteme of resemblance and the gradual decline, starting in the early seventeenth century, of similitude in the constitution of knowledge, see Michel Foucault, *The Order of Things: An Archaeology of the Human Sciences* (New York: Vintage, 1973), pp. 17–25 and 51–58.

31. Balibar, "Racism and Nationalism," pp. 39–45.

32. George Foster, *Culture and Conquest: America's Spanish Heritage* (New York: Wenner-Gren Foundation for Anthropological Research, 1960), pp. 1–20. James Lockhart and Stuart B. Schwartz refer to the years between 1580 and 1750 as the "mature colonial period" to underscore the stabilization of earlier conquest patterns, at least in the main centers and nearby regions. They stress,

however, that the period was one of gradual transformations. Lockhart and Schwartz, *Early Latin America* (New York: Cambridge University Press, 1983), pp. 122–25.

33. For a recent work that makes these points, see Jeremy Adelman, *Sovereignty and Revolution in the Iberian Atlantic* (Princeton, NJ: Princeton University Press, 2006).

34. See Anderson, *Imagined Communities*, pp. 47–65. Critiques of Anderson's treatment of Latin American creole nationalism include Claudio Lomnitz, "Nationalism as a Practical System: Benedict Anderson's Theory of Nationalism from the Vantage Point of Spanish America," in *The Other Mirror: Grand Theory Through the Lens of Latin America*, ed. Miguel Angel Centeno and Fernando López-Alves (Princeton, NJ: Princeton University Press, 2001), pp. 339–43; and Tamar Herzog, *Defining Nations: Immigrants and Citizens in Early Modern Spain and Spanish America* (New Haven, CT, and London: Yale University Press, 2003), pp. 10–11. Also refer to François-Xavier Guerra, "Identidades e independencia: La excepción americana," in *Imaginar la nación*, ed. François-Xavier Guerra and Monica Quijada (Münster and Hamburg: Lit, 1994), pp. 93–134, esp. pp. 107–14; and John Charles Chasteen, "Introduction: Beyond Imagined Communities," in *Beyond Imagined Communities: Reading and Writing the Nation in the Nineteenth-Century Latin America*, ed. Sara Castro-Klarén and John Charles Chasteen (Washington, DC, Baltimore, and London: Woodrow Wilson Press and Johns Hopkins University Press, 2003), pp. ix–xxv.

35. Frederick Cooper, *Colonialism in Question: Theory, Knowledge, History* (Berkeley: University of California Press, 2005), p. 18.

36. As various scholars have argued, all national identities have been construed on gendered and racial terms. It is therefore imperative to study the ways in which different nationalisms presuppose, institutionalize, and reproduce gender and race differences. See, for example, Anne McClintock, " 'No Longer in a Future Heaven': Gender, Race and Nationalism," in *Dangerous Liaisons: Gender, Nation and Postcolonial Perspectives,* ed. Anne McClintock, Aamir Mufti, and Ella Shohat (Minneapolis and London: University of Minnesota Press, 1997), pp. 89–112; and Nancy P. Appelbaum, Anne S. Macpherson, and Karin Alejandra Rosemblatt, eds., *Race and Nation in Modern Latin America* (Chapel Hill and London: University of North Carolina Press, 2003), especially the prologue by Thomas C. Holt (pp. vii–xiv) and the introduction by the editors (pp. 1–31). And although it does not deal with the colonial question, also see Carole Pateman, *The Sexual Contract* (Stanford, CA: Stanford University Press, 1988), which argues that the principle of patriarchal right (central to European civil society) underpinned the social contract among men and defined the individual and citizen as male.

37. Frederick Cooper and Ann L. Stoler, "Tensions of Empire: Colonial Control and Visions of Rule," *American Ethnologist* 16, no. 4 (1989): p. 617.

38. Cooper and Stoler, "Tensions of Empire," pp. 610–11.

39. Bernard Bailyn, *Atlantic History: Concept and Contours* (Cambridge, MA: Harvard University Press, 2005), pp. 62–81. Comparative works include Patricia Seed, *Ceremonies of Possession in Europe's Conquest of the New*

World, 1492–1640 (Cambridge: Cambridge University Press, 1995), which stresses differences among the ceremonies of possession of the British, Spanish, French, and Dutch; and Jorge Cañizares-Esguerra, *Puritan Conquistadors: Iberianizing the Atlantic, 1550–1700* (Stanford, CA: Stanford University Press, 2006), which emphasizes similarities between English and Spanish societies' concerns with demons.

40. William B. Taylor, "Between Global Process and Local Knowledge: An Inquiry into Early Latin American Social History, 1500–1900," in *Reliving the Past: The Worlds of Social History,* ed. Oliver Zunz (Chapel Hill and London: University of North Carolina Press, 1985), p. 120. Taylor's claim that Latin American social histories have not produced either a *longue durée* type of history or works of broad synthesis and theory also continues to have considerable validity. Taylor, pp. 119–21.

41. The sources consulted include more than 964 probanzas and informaciones and dozens of other documents containing purity information, including reports of merits and services, royal decrees, correspondence, and so forth.

42. As Ann Twinam stresses in various works, the distinction is reflected in the king's ability to erase birth "defects" such as illegitimacy. *Public Lives, Private Secrets: Gender, Honor, Sexuality, and Illegitimacy in Colonial Spanish America* (Stanford, CA: Stanford University Press, 1999); Twinam, "Pedro de Ayarzo: The Purchase of Whiteness," in *The Human Tradition in Colonial Latin America,* ed. Kenneth J. Andrien (Wilmington, DE: Scholarly Resources, 2002), pp. 194–210; and Twinam, "Racial Passing: Informal and Official 'Whiteness' in Colonial Spanish America," in *New World Orders: Violence, Sanction, and Authority in the Colonial Americas,* ed. John Smolenski and Thomas J. Humphrey (Philadelphia: University of Pennsylvania Press, 2005), pp. 249–72.

43. The concept of discourse generally refers to knowledge, its production and dissemination, and the way it shapes power relations. Foucault stresses that it cannot be reduced to language and to speech (to the use of signs to designate things) but rather is linked to complicated webs of relations and "practices that systematically form the objects of which they speak." Discourse is thus related both to the operations of power and the production of subjectivities. Michel Foucault, *The Archaeology of Knowledge,* trans. A. M. Sheridan Smith (New York: Pantheon, 1972), pp. 44–49.

CHAPTER I

1. The term *convivencia* (most associated with the Spanish philologist Américo Castro) simply means "living together," but a number of scholars have interpreted it as implying peace and mutual respect among medieval Spain's three main religious communities. The literature is too extensive to cite here, but for examples of works that describe the period prior to the fifteenth century as one in which Spanish Jews flourished, see María Rosa Menocal, *The Ornament of the World: How Muslims, Jews, and Christians Created a Culture of Tolerance in Medieval Spain* (Boston: Little, Brown, 2002); Norman Roth, *Conversos,*

Inquisition, and the Expulsion of the Jews from Spain (Madison: University of Wisconsin Press, 2002), pp. xi–xiii, xix, and 9–10; and Cecil Roth, *The Spanish Inquisition* (New York: Norton, 1964), pp. 18–21. And for studies that posit that Spanish Jews continued to thrive well into the fifteenth century (at least in some parts of Iberia), see E. William Monter, "The Death of Coexistence: Jews and Moslems in Christian Spain, 1480–1502," in *The Expulsion of the Jews: 1492 and After*, ed. Raymond B. Waddington and Arthur H. Williamson (New York and London: Garland, 1994), pp. 5–14; Benjamin R. Gampel, "Does Medieval Navarrese Jewry Salvage Our Notion of *Convivencia?*" in *In Iberia and Beyond: Hispanic Jews Between Cultures*, ed. Bernard Dov Cooperman (Newark: University of Delaware Press, 1998), pp. 97–122; and Mark D. Meyerson, *A Jewish Renaissance in Fifteenth-Century Spain* (Princeton, NJ: Princeton University Press, 2004).

2. Some historians distinguish between medieval "anti-Judaism," based on religious prejudice and in existence since the early days of Christianity, and "anti-Semitism," which they argue only arose when invidious notions of blood purity were used against Christians of Jewish descent. Such a sharp distinction is difficult to sustain, however, when one considers that assumptions about Jewish identity or "Jewishness" being intractable were common in medieval Europe long before the Spanish purity statutes arose, even if individual Jews were encouraged to convert. See Steven F. Kruger, "Conversion and Medieval Sexual, Religious, and Racial Categories," in *Constructing Medieval Sexuality*, ed. Karma Lochrie, Peggy McCracken, and James A. Schultz (Minneapolis and London: University of Minnesota Press, 1997), pp. 164–76; Anna Sapir Abulafia, "The Intellectual and Spiritual Quest for Christ and Central Medieval Persecution of Jews," in *Religious Violence between Christians and Jews: Medieval Roots, Modern Perspectives*, ed. Anna Sapir Abulafia (Houndmills, Basingstoke, Hampshire, UK, and New York: Palgrave, 2002), pp. 61–85; and Joshua Trachtenberg, *The Devil and the Jews: The Medieval Conception of the Jew and its Relation to Modern Antisemitism* (New Haven, CT: Yale University Press; London: H. Milford and Oxford University Press, 1943).

3. David Nirenberg, *Communities of Violence: Persecution of Minorities in the Middle Ages* (Princeton, NJ: Princeton University Press, 1996), esp. pp. 8–9; R. I. Moore, *The Formation of a Persecuting Society: Power and Deviance in Western Europe, 950–1250* (Oxford: Basil Blackwell, 1990), pp. 29–45; Léon Poliakov, *The History of Anti-Semitism*, vol. 1, trans. from the French by Richard Howard (New York: Schocken Books, 1974), pp. 99–154; and Michael Alpert, *Crypto-Judaism and the Spanish Inquisition* (New York: Palgrave, 2001), pp. 10–11. Julio Caro Baroja refers to the existence of an anti-Semitic "cosmogony" in Spain prior to the fifteenth century in *Los judíos en la España moderna y contemporánea*, vol. 1 (Madrid: Ediciones Arión, 1961), pp. 104–10.

4. The vast literature on the 1391 pogroms includes Emilio Mitre Fernández, *Los judíos de Castilla en tiempo de Enrique III: El pogrom de 1391* (Valladolid: Secretariado de Publicaciones, Universidad de Valladolid, 1994); and Philippe Wolff, "The 1391 Pogrom in Spain: Social Crisis or Not?" *Past and Present* 50 (1971): pp. 4–18. Numerous scholars have stressed the role that the anti-

Jewish sermons of the archdean Ferrán Martínez played in inciting the pogrom in Seville. See, for example, Cecil Roth, *The Spanish Inquisition*, pp. 20–22.

5. The term *conversos*, like *New Christians*, eventually encompassed both Jewish and Muslim converts to Christianity. It was initially and most frequently applied to the former, however, while the latter were generally identified as moriscos. For the sake of clarity and consistency, the word *conversos* is used throughout this study to designate only Jewish converts to Christianity and their descendants. This group was also labeled *marranos*, a term whose etymology and meanings remain uncertain but which by the end of the sixteenth century was strongly associated with swine. Covarrubias speculated that it might have been applied to the converted Jews because they had refused (or found it difficult) to eat pork or that it might have been borrowed from the Muslims, who used it to refer to a one-year-old pig. Because of its dehumanizing connotations, the term *marranos* is not used here. See Sebastián de Covarrubias Orozco, *Tesoro de la lengua castellana o española*, 2nd ed., ed. Felipe C. R. Maldonado (Madrid: Editorial Castalia, 1995 [1611]), pp. 738–39.

6. See Antonio Domínguez Ortiz, *La clase social de los conversos en Castilla en la edad moderna* (Madrid: Instituto Balmes de Sociología, Consejo Superior de Investigaciones Científicas, n.d.), p. 10; and Norman Roth, *Conversos, Inquisition, and the Expulsion of the Jews*, pp. 12 and 49.

7. David Nirenberg, "Mass Conversions and Genealogical Mentalities: Jews and Christians in Fifteenth-Century Spain," *Past and Present* 174 (2002): pp. 18–33.

8. David Nirenberg, "El concepto de la raza en la España medieval," *Edad Media: Revista de Historia* 3 (Spring 2000): pp. 50–54.

9. For Benzion Netanyahu, Old Christian concerns about limiting intermarriages between members of their community and conversos were the main cause of the rise of "racism" (in the form of the statutes) in mid-fifteenth-century Spain. Netanyahu, *The Origins of the Inquisition in Fifteenth Century Spain* (New York: Random House, 1995), pp. 987–89. Also see David Nirenberg, "Conversion, Sex, and Segregation: Jews and Christians in Medieval Spain," *American Historical Review* 107, no. 4 (2002): pp. 1478–92.

10. See, for example, Yitzhak Baer, *A History of the Jews in Christian Spain*, trans. from the Hebrew by Louis Schoffman (Philadelphia: Jewish Publication Society of America, 1978), vol. 2, esp. pp. 272–74; Haim Beinart, *Conversos on Trial: The Inquisition in Ciudad Real*, trans. Yael Guiladi (Jerusalem: Magnes Press, 1981), pp. 53–55; and Alpert, *Crypto-Judaism*, pp. 12–20.

11. See, among others, Roth, *Conversos, Inquisition, and the Expulsion*, p. 51; Henry Kamen, *The Spanish Inquisition: A Historical Revision* (New Haven, CT, and London: Yale University Press, 1998), pp. 28–36; Antonio Domínguez Ortiz, *Los judeoconversos en España y América* (Madrid: Ediciones Istmo, 1971), pp. 19–28; Albert A. Sicroff, *Los estatutos de limpieza de sangre: Controversias entre los siglos XV y XVII*, trans. Mauro Armiño (Madrid: Taurus Ediciones, 1985), p. 48; and Netanyahu, *The Origins of the Inquisition*, pp. 964–70 and 975–1004. Also see the pioneering article by Francisco Márquez Villanueva, "Conversos y cargos consejiles en el siglo XV," *Revista de Archivos,*

Bibliotecas y Museos 63 (1957): pp. 503–40, which discusses the strong presence of conversos in town councils and resentment it generated among the Old Christian masses.

12. Edward Peters, *Inquisition* (Berkeley: University of California Press, 1989), pp. 81–85.

13. For details on the rebellion, see Eloy Benito Ruano, *Toledo en el siglo XV: Vida política* (Madrid: Consejo Superior de Investigaciones Científicas, Escuela de Estudios Medievales, 1961), pp. 33–81, and for a copy of the decree, pp. 191–96.

14. Although Albert A. Sicroff regarded the Sentencia-Estatuto as the first statute of purity of blood, some historians contend that the "classic" statutes (those issued by private or semiprivate institutions instead of town councils) appeared later. Others have argued that the requirements first appeared in Castilian colleges during the fourteenth century, or even earlier in the military confraternities of Andalucía (where they were mainly used against Muslims). See Sicroff, *Los estatutos de limpieza de sangre*, pp. 51–56; Antonio Domínguez Ortiz, *La clase social de los conversos en Castilla*, p. 53; and Kamen, *The Spanish Inquisition: A Historical Revision*, p. 233.

15. The term *lindo*, used in the Sentencia-Estatuto, was interchangeable with *limpio* ("pure" or "clean") and also connoted beauty. See Antonio Domínguez Ortiz, *Los Judeoconversos en España y América*, p. 26, n. 14; and Covarrubias Orozco, *Tesoro de la lengua castellana*, p. 717.

16. See Sicroff, *Los estatutos*, pp. 56–85; and Roth, *Conversos, Inquisition, and the Expulsion*, pp. 92–100. One of the most important critiques of the Sentencia-Estatuto was by Alonso de Cartagena, bishop of Burgos and son of the converso and former rabbi Pablo de Santa María, who had also served as bishop in that city. Cartagena's text, titled *Defensorium Unitatis Christianae*, influenced converso arguments against the purity-of-blood concept for generations to come. See Cartagena, *Defensorium unitatis christianae (tratado en favor de los judíos conversos)* (Madrid: C. Bermejo, Impresor, 1943).

17. The Sentencia-Estatuto was probably not implemented on a consistent basis because Toledo continued to try to bar conversos from all public offices. Furthermore, in 1566, the crown issued a decree ordering the town council to adopt purity requirements. See Ruano, *Toledo en el siglo XV*, p. 134; and Linda Martz, "Implementation of Pure-Blood Statutes in Sixteenth-Century Toledo," in *In Iberia and Beyond: Hispanic Jews Between Cultures*, ed. Bernard Dov Cooperman (Newark: University of Delaware Press, 1998), pp. 246–47 and 251.

18. Nirenberg, "Mass Conversions," pp. 25–27. An anti-Jewish polemic written sometime in the second half of the fifteenth century compared the *alboraico*, Muhammad's fabled animal that was neither horse nor mule, to the conversos, who were depicted as neither Jews nor Christians. See Netanyahu, *The Origins of the Inquisition*, pp. 848–54.

19. At the end the fifteenth century, four-fifths of Spain's population of approximately 5,300,000 people worked the soil, albeit from a wide range of social and economic positions. The nobility, which was increasingly entailing estates, used land for agricultural and pastoral pursuits and for the production of basic export commodities. See William D. Phillips Jr. and Carla Rahn Phillips, "Spain

in the Fifteenth Century," in *Transatlantic Encounters: Europeans and Andeans in the Sixteenth Century,* ed. Kenneth J. Andrien and Rolena Adorno (Berkeley: University of California Press, 1991), pp. 15–18.

20. The reforms included the use of *corregidores,* royal officials assigned to main Castilian towns with authority over urban councils; the creation of the Santa Hermandad, an organized police force hired by some municipalities; the appointment of *letrados* (university-educated men) to public posts and royal councils; and the distribution of land grants, offices, and incomes to high nobles in order to win their support. The reign of Enrique IV thus actually witnessed an increase in the number of grandes. See William D. Phillips Jr., *Enrique IV and the Crisis of Fifteenth-Century Castile, 1425–1480* (Cambridge, MA: Harvard University Press, 1978), pp. 47–53 and 58–62. On debates regarding the nobility in late medieval Spain, see María Concepción Quintanilla Raso, "Nobleza y señoríos en Castilla durante la baja edad media: Aportaciones de la historiografía reciente," *Anuario de Estudios Medievales* (Barcelona) 14 (1984): pp. 613–39; and Quintanilla Raso, "La nobleza en la historia política castellana en la segunda mitad del siglo XV: Bases de poder y pautas de comportamiento," in *Congresso Internacional Bartolomeu Dias e a sua época: Actas,* vol. 1 (O Porto: Universidade do Porto, 1989), pp. 181–200.

21. In the mid-fifteenth century, Iberia included five independent kingdoms: Portugal, Aragón, Granada, Navarre, and Castile. The last was the largest and became even more dominant in geographic and demographic terms after it defeated Granada (1492) and annexed Navarre (1512). Like that of Aragón, the Crown of Castile was divided into smaller political entities, including the northern coastal areas of Galicia, Asturias, and Cantabria, and the Basque regions of Vizcaya, Guipúzcoa, and Alava. It also included León and Castile (Old Castile) to the north of the central mountains, La Mancha and Extremadura (New Castile) to the south, and the kingdoms of Andalusía and Murcia in the extreme south and southeast. Although some historians have interpreted the dynastic linkage of the crowns of Castile and Aragón as the first step toward the creation of the Spanish state, the union was more symbolic than real. The political institutions, economies, monetary systems, customs barriers, and cultural traditions of the two crowns remained distinct for at least another two centuries.

22. Peters, *Inquisition,* pp. 44–58. Peters stresses (p. 68) that although medieval inquisitors and "inquisitions" (formal investigations) existed, the Inquisition as an institution—as a centralized office of authority—did not exist until the fifteenth century. Spain established its Inquisition in 1480; Portugal, in 1536; and Rome, after 1542.

23. Kamen, *The Spanish Inquisition: A Historical Revision,* pp. 5–7. For a contrasting view of the problem of heresy in medieval Castile-León, see Norman Roth, *Converso, the Inquisition, and the Expulsion,* p. 223. Teófilo F. Ruiz explains the absence of an Inquisition in Castile before the 1470s as a function of the unsacred nature of kingship and politics in that kingdom. Because the crown's authority came from the sword more than from religion, he argues, it did not need to embark on religious campaigns to uproot heresy or to follow the mandate of Rome as other medieval kingdoms did. Ruiz, "The Holy Office in Medieval France and in Late Medieval Castile: Origins and Contrasts," in *The*

Spanish Inquisition and the Inquisitorial Mind, ed. Angel Alcalá (Highland Lakes, NJ: Atlantic Research and Publications, 1987), pp. 37–38.

24. See Gretchen D. Starr-LeBeau, *In the Shadow of the Virgin: Inquisitors, Friars, and Conversos in Guadalupe, Spain* (Princeton, NJ: Princeton University Press, 2003), pp. 112–16; and Sicroff, *Los estatutos,* pp. 92–96.

25. See Kamen, *The Spanish Inquisition: A Historical Revision,* pp. 43–44; and Juan Gil, *Los conversos y la Inquisición sevillana,* vol. 1 (Seville: Universidad de Sevilla, Fundación El Monte, 2000), pp. 41–92. Although it is probable that the Catholic Kings' aggressive diplomatic efforts in Rome and expressed commitment to defend and expand the Christian faith influenced the papacy's decision to allow the creation of a Spanish inquisition under royal control, the factors that led to the passage of the 1478 bull that founded the Holy Office have yet to be explained. What is known is that after receiving numerous complaints from conversos about the abuses and violence of the first tribunals, Sixtus IV tried to revoke the bull, but the Catholic Kings ignored his petitions. Spain's ecclesiastical hierarchy was also ambivalent about the founding of the Holy Office because the institution usurped some of the bishops' authority on matters of heresy and appropriated the papal principle of theological infallibility. Some church officials regretted supporting it, including Cardinal Mendoza, and others, such as bishop Talavera, never did (for which the latter was almost burned). It was the lower clergy that expressed more of a willingness to participate in the Inquisition's activities, at least in Seville. Francisco Márquez Villanueva, "Noticias de la Inquisición sevillana" (plenary address, conference titled "Los conversos y la historia de España de 1248 a 1700," Saint Louis University (Madrid Campus), May 21–22, 2004.

26. The Inquisition could try some Jews, including those who proselytized among Christians, blasphemed against Christianity, engaged in sorcery or usury, or received apostatizing conversos back into the Jewish fold.

27. Tribunals proliferated through most of Spain mainly from 1478 to 1495. See Jaime Contreras and Jean Pierre Dedieu, "Estructuras geográficas del Santo Oficio en España," *Historia de la Inquisición en España y América: Las estructuras del Santo Oficio,* ed. Joaquín Pérez Villanueva and Bartolomé Escandell Bonet, vol. 2 (Madrid: Biblioteca de Autores Cristianos, Centro de Estudios Inquisitoriales, 1993), pp. 5–7.

28. On the establishment and operation of the Holy Office in Aragón (vigorously resisted by towns zealous of their independence and traditional rights), see E. William Monter, *Frontiers of Heresy: The Spanish Inquisition from the Basque Lands to Sicily* (Cambridge: Cambridge University Press, 1990); Stephen Haliczer, *Inquisition and Society in the Kingdom of Valencia, 1478–1834* (Berkeley: University of California Press, 1990); and Ricardo García Cárcel, *Orígenes de la inquisición española: El Tribunal de Valencia, 1478–1530* (Barcelona: Ediciones Península, 1976). And on the Inquisition in Galicia, see Jaime Contreras, *El Santo Oficio de la Inquisición en Galicia, 1560–1700: Poder, sociedad y cultura* (Madrid: Akal, 1982).

29. See, for example, Roth, *The Spanish Inquisition,* pp. 72–73; and Haliczer, *Inquisition and Society,* pp. 12–17. Some scholars disagree with the character-

ization of the Inquisition as a tool of royal absolutism. López Vela, for example, argues that the Holy Office maintained some autonomy from the crown because the inquisitor general, in theory under papal control, had ultimate authority over the institution, not the Suprema, which was not fully recognized by the Vatican. Roberto López Vela, "Inquisición y monarquía: Estado de la cuestión (1940–1990)," *Hispania* 3, no. 176 (1990): pp. 1133–40.

30. Contreras, Jaime, *Historia de la Inquisición Española (1478–1834)* (Madrid: Arco/Libros, 1997), pp. 17–26.

31. See John H. Elliot, *Imperial Spain 1469–1716* (London: Edward Arnold, 1963), p. 97; and John Lynch, *Spain Under the Habsburgs*, vol. 1 (New York: Oxford University Press, 1964), pp. 23–24. That the Catholic Kings had a clear plan of religious and political unification has been challenged on several grounds, including that the two processes did not exactly coincide. As Kamen and others have pointed out, the monarchs protected the Jews up to the expulsion and allowed Muslims to remain in Castile for another ten years and in Aragón until 1526. Kamen, *The Spanish Inquisition: A Historical Revision*, p. 61.

32. Juan Gil, for example, recently argued that independent of the religious and political motives that the Catholic Kings might have had for founding the Inquisition, the tribunal in Seville quickly became a weapon to deprive the conversos of their wealth and resulted in the (figurative) decapitation of the local economic oligarchy. Gil, *Los conversos y la Inquisición sevillana,* vol. 1, esp. pp. 60–70 (on the early confiscations of converso estates) and pp. 123–37 (on the economic effects of the Inquisition on the church and city). Whether the Inquisition's arrival followed the same pattern in other cities, however, has yet to be proven; some scholars doubt that the wealth the Holy Office acquired through its confiscations, part of which went to the royal treasure, became a significant source of revenue.

33. See Peggy Liss, *Mexico under Spain, 1521–1556: Society and the Origins of Nationality* (Chicago: University of Chicago Press, 1975), p. 4.

34. Monter, "The Death of Coexistence," pp. 8–9. Monter suggests that the war against Granada created fiscal needs that the crown partly resolved by increasing its taxes on Jews and using the Inquisition to confiscate the wealth of conversos.

35. See Haim Beinart, "The Expulsion from Spain: Causes and Results," in *The Sephardi Legacy*, vol. 2, ed. Haim Beinart (Jerusalem: Magnes Press, Hebrew University, 1992), pp. 19–20 (and pp. 28–31 for a copy of the 1492 expulsion decree); Beinart, *The Expulsion of the Jews from Spain,* trans. Jeffrey M. Green (Oxford and Portland, OR: Littman Library of Jewish Civilization, 2002); Kamen, *The Spanish Inquisition: A Historical Revision*, pp. 18–21; and Roth, *Conversos, Inquisition, and the Expulsion*, pp. 271–316. Both Kamen and Roth reject theories that attribute the expulsion of the Jews to the Catholic Kings' religious fanaticism and suggest instead that the Inquisition's findings played a key role in bringing about the decision.

36. Mark D. Meyerson, *The Muslims of Valencia in the Age of Fernando and Isabel: Between Coexistence and Crusade* (Berkeley: University of California Press, 1991), pp. 56–57.

37. The term *moriscos* derived from the pejorative Spanish word for Muslims, *moros* (Moors). Between 1609 and 1614, the moriscos were forced to leave the Iberian Peninsula, a fate that the conversos were able to escape. See Bernard Vincent, *Minorías y marginados en la España del siglo XVI* (Granada: Diputación Provincial de Granada, 1987); Antonio Domínguez Ortiz and Bernard Vincent, *Historia de los moriscos: Vida y tragedia de una minoría* (Madrid: Alianza Editorial, 1997, [1985]); Roger Boase, "The Morisco Expulsion and Diaspora: An Example of Racial and Religious Intolerance," in *Cultures in Contact in Medieval Spain,* ed. David Hook and Barry Taylor (London: King's College London Medieval Studies, 1990), pp. 9–28; and Stephen Haliczer, "The Moriscos: Loyal Subjects of his Catholic Majesty Philip III," in *Christians, Muslims, and Jews in Medieval and Early Modern Spain: Interaction and Cultural Change,* ed. Mark D. Meyerson and Edward D. English (Notre Dame, IN: University of Notre Dame Press, 1999), pp. 265–89.

38. See Kamen, *The Spanish Inquisition: A Historical Revision,* pp. 204–13. Also see Francisco Bethencourt, "The Auto da fe: Ritual and Imagery," *Journal of the Warburg and Courtlaud Institutes* 55 (1992): pp. 155–68. The first auto de fe took place in Seville in February 1481. Although autos continued to be staged throughout the sixteenth and seventeenth centuries (one of the most spectacular was held in 1680), in Castile they reached their apogee from 1559 to the 1570s, the period of intense persecution of Protestants. "Judaizers" of Portuguese origin tended to be a standard feature of autos de fe as of the last decade of the sixteenth century and figured prominently in those of the last quarter of the seventeenth.

39. For estimates, see Kamen, *The Spanish Inquisition: A Historical Revision,* pp. 59–60, 198, 203.

40. As of about the middle of the sixteenth century, the inquisitors shifted their attention to other groups. They continued to be concerned with identifying crypto-Jews, particularly Portuguese ones, but after 1550, they concentrated also on Protestants and moriscos (the latter especially from 1560 to 1614) as well as Old Christians. The Inquisition thus went through several stages in which it targeted different groups. See Jean Pierre Dedieu, *L'administration de la foi. L'inquisition de Tolède XVIᵉ–XVIIIᵉ siècle* (Madrid: Casa de Velázquez, 1989), pp. 240–41; and Bartolomé Bennassar, *L'Inquisition Espagnole XVᵉ–XIXᵉ* (Paris: Hachette, 1979), pp. 15–41.

41. Besides Yitzhak Baer and Haim Beinart, scholars who have argued that a significant number of conversos during and after the founding of the Inquisition were crypto-Jews or Judaizers include Renée Levine Melammed, *Heretics or Daughters of Israel? The Crypto-Jewish Women of Castile* (New York: Oxford University Press, 1999); and Alpert, *Crypto-Judaism.* Historians who deny that crypto-Judaism was a serious problem in fifteenth-century Spain include Netanyahu, *The Origins of the Inquisition;* and Kamen, *The Spanish Inquisition: A Historical Revision,* pp. 36–42 and 61–6.

42. See, for example, Starr-LeBeau, *In the Shadow of the Virgin,* pp. 50–110; and David L. Graizbord, *Souls in Dispute: Converso Identities in Iberia and the*

Jewish Diaspora, 1580–1700 (Philadelphia: University of Pennsylvania Press, 2004), esp. pp. 8–12. Also see Nathan Wachtel, *Foi du Souvenir: Labyrinthes Marranes* (Paris: Éditions du Seuil, 2001), which not only problematizes arguments that present conversos as either stable Christians or secret Jews but also analyzes the complex role of memory in shaping their identities. These points are also made in Wachtel, "Marrano Religiosity in Hispanic America in the Seventeenth Century," in *The Jews and the Expansion of Europe to the West 1450–1800*, ed. Paolo Bernardini and Norman Fiering (New York and Oxford: Berghahn Books, 2001), pp. 149–71.

43. Starr-LeBeau, *In the Shadow of the Virgin*, pp. 89–90.

44. The campaigns to "Christianize" Old Christians began in the 1540s and intensified during and after the Counter-Reformation and Council of Trent. See Jean Pierre Dedieu, "'Christianization' in New Castile: Catechism, Communion, Mass, and Confirmation in the Toledo Archbishopric, 1540–1650," in *Culture and Control in Counter-Reformation Spain*, ed. Anne J. Cruz and Mary Elizabeth Perry (Minneapolis: University of Minnesota Press, 1992), pp. 1–24.

45. Norman Roth points out, for example, that for medieval Jews, the term *Judaism* would not have made much sense because they did not see themselves as adherents of a religion but as a people, an understanding encouraged by Jewish law, which makes no distinction between religious and secular levels of existence and encompasses just about every aspect of life. Roth, *Conversos, Inquisition, and the Expulsion*, p. 29.

46. Haim Beinart, "The Conversos in Spain and Portugal in the 16th to 18th Centuries," in *The Sephardi Legacy*, vol. 2, ed. Haim Beinart (Jerusalem: Magnes Press, Hebrew University, 1992), pp. 62–63.

47. Because men enjoyed more authority in the household, marriages between Old Christian males and moriscas did not pose as significant a threat to the social order as the alternative "mixed" arrangement. See Mary Elizabeth Perry, "Moriscas and the Limits of Assimilation," in *Christians, Muslims, and Jews in Medieval and Early Modern Spain: Interaction and Cultural Change*, ed. Mark D. Meyerson and Edward D. English (Notre Dame, IN: University of Notre Dame Press, 1978), p. 275.

48. Vincent, *Minorías y marginados*, pp. 25–99. Although Old Christian authorities tended to claim otherwise, polygamy was not a widespread practice among the moriscos. Vincent notes that the more common arrangement was the double marriage or acquisition of two wives, one an Old Christian, the other a morisca (pp. 56–57).

49. See, for example, Vincent, *Minorías y marginados*, pp. 25–99.

50. Significantly, historians of the Inquisition and the limpieza statutes, including Benzion Netanyahu, have tended to avoid the critical issue of how to distinguish between a true and false conversion. Even those who have argued that religious tensions were real, such as Henry Charles Lea, Cecil Roth, and Albert A. Sicroff, did not demonstrate that crypto-Judaism was widespread; they simply assumed it was on the basis of Spanish sources that complained about the problem. See Lea, *A History of the Inquisition in Spain*, vol. 2 (New

York: Macmillan, 1906), p. 314; Roth, *The Spanish Inquisition,* pp. 30–32; and Sicroff, *Los estatutos de limpieza de sangre,* p. 49. For a recent Spanish edition of Lea's classic work on the Inquisition, one that includes a prologue and updated bibliography, see Lea, *Historia de la Inquisición española,* vol. 2, trans. Angel Alcalá and Jesús Tobio, ed. Angel Alcalá, prologue by Angel Alcalá (Madrid: Fundación Universitaria Española, 1982–1983).

51. Stuart Hall, "On postmodernism and articulation," in *Stuart Hall: Critical Dialogues in Cultural Studies,* ed. David Morley and Kuan-Hsing Chen (London and New York: Routledge, 1996), pp. 141–43.

CHAPTER 2

1. For example, one of Córdoba's private chapels established a purity statute in 1466, and by about 1473, one of its confraternities, the Brotherhood of Charity, had as well. Its town council also adopted a limpieza statute, but it was suppressed by the Catholic Kings. See John Edwards, "The Beginnings of a Scientific Theory of Race? Spain, 1450–1600," in *From Iberia to Diaspora: Studies in Sephardic History and Culture,* ed. Yedida K. Stillman and Norman A. Stillman (Leiden, Boston, and Cologne: Brill, 1999), p. 182; and Edwards, *Christian Córdoba: The City and its Region in the Late Middle Ages* (New York: Cambridge University Press, 1982), pp. 182–88.

2. The Order of Saint Jerome's 1486 decision to establish purity-of-blood requirements was subsequently suspended, but by 1515 it had a statute firmly in place. See Starr-LeBeau, *In the Shadow of the Virgin,* pp. 235–36, 240, and 249. With regard to other religious orders, the Dominicans' efforts to establish a general limpieza statute in the 1480s did not succeed, but some of the order's priories did adopt the requirement. The Jesuits resisted adopting the purity requirement until the end of the sixteenth century. Even though efforts to revoke the statute did not end, the order thereafter tended to implement it with rigor. Sicroff, *Los estatutos de limpieza de sangre,* pp. 326–29.

3. See Lea, *A History of the Inquisition in Spain* (1906), vol. 2, p. 287.

4. Lea, *A History of the Inquisition in Spain* (1906), vol. 2, pp. 285–90; Juan Hernández Franco, *Cultura y limpieza de sangre en la España moderna: Puritate sanguinis* (Murcia: Universidad de Murcia, 1996), pp. 38–39; Domínguez Ortiz, *La clase social de los conversos en Castilla,* pp. 54–68; and Peré Molas Ribalta, "El exclusivismo de los gremios de la Corona de Aragón: Limpieza de sangre y limpieza de oficios," in *Les sociétés fermées dans le monde Ibérique, XVIe–XVIIIe siècles. Définitions et problématique: Actes de la table ronde des 8 et 9 février 1985* (Paris: Editions du Centre National de la Recherche Scientifique, 1986), pp. 63–80. By the 1560s, the Military Order of San Juan had also adopted a purity statute. See Biblioteca Nacional (Madrid) [hereafter BNM], MSS 11410–14: "questions that are included in the purity of blood investigations of candidates for the military habit of San Juan."

5. See Hernández Franco, *Cultura y limpieza de sangre,* p. 63.

6. Domínguez Ortiz, *La clase social de los conversos en Castilla,* p. 35.

7. See Sicroff, *Los estatutos de limpieza de sangre,* pp. 132–72.

8. Lea, *A History of the Inquisition in Spain* (1906), vol. 2, p. 306. At first, rehabilitaciones were sold mainly by the Inquisition, but as of 1501, the crown began to issue them (usually for steep amounts of money) for the exercise of public posts and certain professions. The Holy Office retained the right to grant them mainly for sumptuary restrictions or personal punishments. The sale of rehabilitations to conversos and moriscos peaked under Ferdinand, the Catholic king, and Charles V. On the pardons sold to conversos in Seville from the late fifteenth century to the reign of Philip II, see Gil, *Los conversos y la inquisición sevillana*, vol. 1, pp. 189–92 and 229–25.

9. Hernández Franco, *Cultura y limpieza de sangre*, p. 68.

10. Kamen, *The Spanish Inquisition: A Historical Revision,* p. 239; and Kamen, "Limpieza and the Ghost of Américo Castro: Racism as a Tool of Literary Analysis," *Hispanic Review* 64, no. 1 (1996): p. 20. Kamen's point about the statutes and public law was part of his revisionist argument about the problem of limpieza de sangre, which he contends historians of early modern Spain have grossly exaggerated. His revisionist arguments are offered in *The Spanish Inquisition: A Historical Revision,* pp. 230–54, and "Limpieza and the Ghost of Américo Castro," pp. 19–29. For Kamen's earlier and different views on the problem, see *Inquisition and Society in Spain in the Sixteenth and Seventeenth Centuries* (Bloomington: Indiana University Press, 1985), pp. 114–33. For the view that the statutes acquired the force of law and constituted "the first example in history of legalized racism," see Léon Poliakov, *The History of Anti-Semitism,* vol. 2, trans. Natalie Gerardi (Philadelphia: University of Pennsylvania Press, 1973), pp. 221 and 228.

11. BNM, MS 10918, fols. 1–129r: discourse (*discurso*) on the statutes of purity of blood by Juan Roco Campofrío, president of the Council of Finance. Campofrío was a bishop of Zamora at the start of the 1620s and later of Soria.

12. Gil, *Los conversos y la inquisición sevillana,* vol. 2, p. 132.

13. A discussion of the literature on the Portuguese New Christians is provided in Bruce A. Lorence, "The Inquisition and the New Christians in the Iberian Peninsula—Main Historiographic Issues and Controversies," in *The Sepharadi and Oriental Jewish Heritage Studies,* International Congress on the Sepharadi and Oriental Jewry, and Issachar Ben-Ami (Jerusalem: Magnes Press, Hebrew University, 1982) pp. 13–72.

14. See, for example, BNM, MS 10431, fols. 131–150v.

15. Spanish expansionism generated significant migration to the Americas (initially mainly from southern Spain) and spurred internal population movements. Because of their paramount role in transatlantic commerce, Seville and Cádiz became magnets for people from other regions in Spain and broader Europe. Through much of the sixteenth century, they experienced sustained demographic growth. See Antonio García-Baquero González, *Andalucía y la Carrera de Indias, 1492–1824* (Seville: Biblioteca de la Cultura Andaluza, 1986), pp. 17–20 and 56–57. And for other good studies of the effects of migration to America on local Spanish society, see Ida Altman, *Emigrants and Society, Extremadura and America in the Sixteenth Century* (Berkeley: University of California Press, 1989); and Juan Javier Pescador, *The New World Inside a*

Basque Village: The Oiartzun Valley and Its Atlantic Emigrants, 1550–1800 (Reno: University of Nevada Press, 2004).

16. On the gradual classification of religious dissent as heresy in secular law, theology, and canon law during the late medieval period, see Peters, *Inquisition*, pp. 40–71.

17. AHN, Inquisición, Libro 1247: Memorial on the statutes of limpieza de sangre, 1655.

18. The extension of divine punishments to third- or fourth-generation descendants appears in the Bible. See, for example, Exodus 34:6–7.

19. AHN, Inquisición, Libro 1247, fols. 156–76: Memorial on the statutes of limpieza, 1655. Translation mine. Note that unless otherwise indicated, all subsequent transcriptions and translations are also mine.

20. See Edwards, "The Beginnings of a Scientific Theory of Race?" pp. 184–96; and Françoise Héritier-Augé, "Semen and Blood: Some Ancient Theories Concerning Their Genesis and Relationship," *Fragments for a History of the Human Body*, vol. 3, ed. Michel Feher with Ramona Naddaff and Nadia Tazi (New York: Urzone, 1989), pp. 159–75.

21. The slippage between nature and culture was especially evident in the theory of pangenesis, which originated in ancient Greece and became one of the most influential theories of heredity in the West. According to this theory, the "male seed," formed by all parts of the body, was the most potent of the generative fluids and therefore determined the characteristics of the child. Although pangenesis clearly stressed the role of nature (biology) in human conception and heredity, it also took culture into account, for it posited that semen could be influenced by food intake and climate. See Wade, *Race, Nature and Culture*, p. 47. Juan de Pineda, a sixteenth-century Spanish Franciscan friar, discussed theories about the role of food in the creation of life (by authorities such as Hippocrates, Galen, and Aristotle) in *Diálogos familiares de la agricultura cristiana*, vol. 3, ed. Juan Meseguer Fernández (Madrid: Ediciones Atlas, 1963–64), Biblioteca de Autores Españoles, vol. 163, pp. 32–33.

22. See Caroline Walker Bynum, "The Female Body and Religious Practice in the Later Middle Ages," in *Fragments for a History of the Human Body*, vol. I, ed. Michel Feher with Ramona Naddaff and Nadia Tazi (New York: Urzone, 1989), p. 182; and Edwards, "The Beginnings of a Scientific Theory of Race?" p. 185. The notion that women's breast milk was "cooked blood" probably sprang from theories regarding reproduction in the animal world. Covarrubias, for example, defined milk as the "juice of the cooked blood that, among animals, nature sends to the udders of the female, so that she can raise her offspring." Covarrubias Orozco, *Tesoro de la lengua castellana*, p. 705.

23. Héritier-Augé, "Semen and Blood," p. 168.

24. According to Thomas Lacqueur, women were seen as imperfect men and their sexual organs as inverted male genitalia until about the eighteenth century, when natural sciences started to produce two categories of male and female as opposite biological sexes. Although theories of sexual and reproductive organs were never as uniform as he suggests, notions of female weakness and imperfectability were prominent in Western medical thinking about sex throughout the medieval and early modern periods. Lacqueur, *Making Sex: Body and Gender*

from the Greeks to Freud (Cambridge, MA, and London: Harvard University Press, 1990), pp. 148–92, *passim*. For an introduction to the historical relationship between theories of biological difference and the construction of gender and sexuality, see Anne Fausto-Sterling, *Sexing the Body: Gender Politics and the Construction of Sexuality* (New York: Basic Books, 2000).

25. The traditional avenue to Spanish ennoblement, military service, experienced its last important phase during the reign of the Catholic Kings. Subsequently, ennoblement entailed either a legal process in which candidates sought to prove that they were already noble or the purchase of patents from the crown. The latter process resulted in the status of *nobleza de privilegio* (or *privilegio de hidalguía*).

26. Lea, *A History of the Inquisition in Spain* (1906), vol. 2, p. 287.

27. See, for example, AHN, Inquisición, Libro 1247, fols. 156–76: Memorial on the statutes of limpieza, 1655.

28. Roberto López Vela, "Estructuras administrativas del Santo Oficio," in *Historia de la Inquisición en España y América*, ed. Joaquín Pérez Villanueva and Bartolomé Escandell Bonet, vol. 2 (Madrid: Biblioteca de Autores Cristianos, Centro de Estudios Inquisitoriales, 1993), p. 231.

29. Kamen, *The Spanish Inquisition,* p. 234.

30. Lea, *A History of the Inquisition in Spain* (1906), vol. 2, p. 299.

31. Julio Caro Baroja, *Razas, pueblos y linajes* (Madrid: Revista de Occidente, 1957), p. 108.

32. See Julio Caro Baroja, *Los moriscos del Reino de Granada* (Madrid: Diana, 1957), p. 65; and Vincent, *Minorías y marginados,* pp. 25–28.

33. The same shift to a more rigid dual-descent model of classification occurred in the process of acquiring military habits. After the 1550s, Castile's main military orders required examinations of both bloodlines, mainly because of the influence of the limpieza requirements. See Elena Postigo Castellanos, *Honor y privilegio en la corona de Castilla: El Consejo de las Órdenes y los Caballeros de Hábito en el s. XVII* (Almazán, Soria: Junta de Castilla y León, 1988), pp. 134 and 138; and Caro Baroja, *Los judíos en la España moderna y contemporánea,* vol. II (Madrid: Ediciones Arión, 1961), pp. 301–02. Nonetheless, patrilineal ideas periodically reappeared in discussions of limpieza. In the 1620s, for example, the inquisitor Campofrío argued that genealogical investigations in purity cases should be limited, because if it was true that all the conversos who descended from Jews on the paternal line were now secure in the Christian faith, "much more are those who have [Jewish ancestry] on their maternal line, since they never had much zeal [for Judaism] to begin with." BNM, MS 10918, fol. 73v. Also see Domínguez Ortiz, *La clase social de los conversos en Castilla,* p. 201.

34. Lea, *A History of the Inquisition in Spain* (1906), vol. 2, p. 298.

35. The concept of *tiempo immemorial* was vague but initially seems to have referred—at least in the legal determination of nobility—to three or four generations. Within the discourse of limpieza de sangre, however, it became elusive.

36. Naturalizing concepts invoke "natural" processes, including biological ones, but do not discount the possibility of change; essentializing ones always presuppose immutability, that is, unchanging essences. Wade, *Race, Nature and Culture,* p. 18.

37. As far as can be determined, the word *raza* was not systematically deployed against conversos in the fifteenth century, at least not until the purity statutes had managed to spread. The Sentencia-Estatuto, for example, does not contain the term. It describes the conversos as a "lineage," not a "race," and specifically as "the descendants of the lineage and caste [*ralea*] of the Jews." See the copy of the statute in Ruano, *Toledo en el siglo XV,* pp. 191–96.

38. See Michael Banton, *Racial Theories* (Cambridge: Cambridge University Press, 1998), pp. 4–5 and 17–43.

39. Some of Spain's military orders, for example, granted habits only to persons whose ancestors had been of noble blood and without the "race or mixture of commoners" (*"hijosdalgo de sangre, sin raza ni mezcla de villano"*). Postigo Castellanos, *Honor y privilegio en la corona de Castilla,* p. 139.

40. Covarrubias Orozco, *Tesoro de la lengua castellana,* p. 851. According to Corominas, when the word *raza* was being linked to Jewish and Muslim descent, it incorporated the meanings of an older Castilian term (*raça*) that connoted defectiveness (as in "defect in the fabric") and guilt. See Joan Corominas, *Diccionario crítico etimológico de la lengua castellana,* vol. III (Berna, Switzerland: Editorial Francke, 1954), pp. 1019–21; and Verena Stolcke, "Conquered Women," *Report on the Americas* (NACLA) 24, no. 5 (1991): pp. 23–28. After the mid-sixteenth century, the term increasingly appeared as part of the phrase *mala raza* ("bad race").

41. Banton, *Racial Theories,* p. 4.

42. de Pineda, *Diálogos familiares de la agricultura cristiana,* vol. 3, pp. 410–11.

43. Verena Stolcke writes that the French word *race* originally referred mainly to "belonging to and descending from a family or house of 'noble stock' or *stirpis nobilitas* which was translated as *noblesse de sang* ('nobility of blood') in 1533." See Stolcke, "Conquered Women," *Report on the Americas* (NACLA) 24, no. 5 (1991): p. 24.

44. See Guillaume Aubert, "'The Blood of France': Race and Purity of Blood in the French Atlantic World," *William and Mary Quarterly,* 3rd series, vol. LXI (July 2004): pp. 439–78. Aubert also notes that because the early modern French believed that "blood-mixing" between nobles and commoners resulted in new lineages or "races," the French word *métis* was first applied to the children of those "unequal" unions, or *mésalliances.*

45. In the case of Jews, their "stained" blood was sometimes attributed to their supposed role in the death of Christ but more often than not to a long history of rejecting Christianity in the Iberian Peninsula. Similar arguments were applied to Muslims, especially as of the middle of the sixteenth century. They too were considered a "blemished race" and "infidels" because they had heard the message of Christ and refused it. Caro Baroja discusses early seventeenth-century depictions of moriscos as incorrigible infidels in *Razas, pueblos y linajes,* pp. 83–98.

46. Elaine C. Wertheimer claims that the Spanish notion of limpieza de sangre was based on the Judaic concept *taharot,* but stresses that the two were used for rather different ends. Wertheimer, *Jewish Sources of Spanish Blood Purity Concerns* (Brooklyn, NY: Adelantre, the Judezmo Society, 1977), esp. pp. 6–8.

Américo Castro was among the first to propose that biblical concepts as well as the Jews' strong sense of purity and caste served as the basis for the Spanish idea of limpieza. See, for example, Castro, *España en su historia: Cristianos, moros y judíos* (Barcelona: Editorial Crítica, 1984 [1948]), pp. 512–15. Several scholars subsequently refuted Castro's attribution of the origins of the concept of limpieza de sangre to Jewish thought. See, for example, Benzion Netanyahu, "The Racial Attack on the Conversos: Américo Castro's View of Its Origins," in *Toward the Inquisition: Essays on Jewish and Converso History in Late Medieval Spain* (Ithaca, NY: Cornell University Press, 1997), pp. 1–39.

47. Effective at spreading fear, the edicts of grace produced a significant number of confessions and accusations, which in turn fortified the Inquisition's belief that there was indeed a serious problem of heresy among the conversos and, later, among the moriscos. For a translated copy of a 1519 edict of grace, see Roth, *The Spanish Inquisition*, pp. 76–83.

48. Domínguez Ortiz, *Los Judeoconversos en España y América*, pp. 156–157.

49. Echoing arguments made by the Inquisition, some scholars have tended to explain the relatively high number of conversas and moriscas prosecuted by the Holy Office as a function of the disappearance of all Jewish and Muslim institutional life, which they argue made the household into the locus of crypto-Jewish and crypto-Muslim practices. See Levine Melammed, *Heretics or Daughters of Israel?* p. 32; Perry, "Moriscas and the Limits of Assimilation," pp. 274–89; Flora García Ivars, *La represión en el tribunal inquisitorial de Granada, 1550–1819* (Madrid: Ediciones Akal, 1991), pp. 196–98 and 236–38; Haliczer, *Inquisition and Society in the Kingdom of Valencia*, pp. 271–72; and Renée Levine Melammed, "Crypto-Jewish Women Facing the Spanish Inquisition: Transmitting Religious Practices, Beliefs, and Attitudes," in *Christians, Muslims, and Jews in Medieval and Early Modern Spain*, pp. 197–219. On problems associated with relying on Inquisition sources for evidence of crypto-Judaism, see, for example, Avita Novinsky, "Some Theoretical Considerations about the New Christian Problem," in *The Sepharadi and Oriental Jewish Heritage Studies,* International Congress on the Sepharadi and Oriental Jewry, and Issachar Ben-Ami (Jerusalem: Magnes Press, Hebrew University, 1982), pp. 4–12.

50. See de Pineda, *Diálogos familiares de la agricultura cristiana*, vol. 3, pp. 102–10; Caro Baroja, *Los moriscos del reino de Granada*, p. 159; Edwards, "The Beginnings of a Scientific Theory of Race?" p. 185; and Méchoulan, *El honor de Dios*, p. 113. The term *Golden Age* is sometimes applied to Spain during the years between 1500 and 1650, when it became a powerful empire thanks to the mineral wealth it extracted from its colonies. It is also sometimes used to refer to the flourishing of Spanish arts and letters during the early modern period and especially between the years 1550–1650.

51. As Mary Douglas pointed out in her classic discussion of boundary rituals, the symbolic meaning assigned to bodily fluids such as breast milk, blood, semen, and saliva—substances that figure into the imagery of purity and contagion because they leave the body and become a potential source of, or vulnerable to, contamination—in different cultural contexts will tend to reflect dominant

ideas regarding the proper social order. Mary Douglas, *Purity and Danger: An Analysis of the Concepts of Pollution and Taboo* (London: Routledge, 1995), esp. pp. 115–16.

52. Refer to AGI, México 281: Petition for an ecclesiastical benefice by Cristóbal San Martín, 1567.

53. See Caro Baroja, "Antecedentes españoles de algunos problemas sociales relativos al mestizaje," pp. 201; Roth, *The Spanish Inquisition*, p. 199; and Wertheimer, *Jewish Sources of Spanish Blood Purity Concerns*, p. 15. The classificatory impulse that the obsession with purity of blood generated was also manifested in Portugal, where the Inquisition also conducted genealogical investigations and deployed categories such as *"meio-cristão," "quarto de cristão novo," "mais de meio cristão novo,"* and so forth for the children of marriages between New and Old Christians. Maria Luiza Tucci Carneiro, *Preconcepto Racial: Portugal e Brasil-Colônia* (São Paolo: Editora Brasiliense, 1988), p. 102.

54. The expression is used by one of Juan de Pineda's interlocutors in a discussion on the effects of wet nurses on Old Christian children, which mentions the likelihood that Jewish or Muslim ancestry would eventually prevail over Old Christian descent (a belief that some conversos and moriscos allegedly shared). de Pineda, *Diálogos familiares de la agricultura cristiana*, vol. 3, p. 103.

55. Dominguez Ortiz, *La clase social de los conversos en Castilla*, pp. 201–04.

56. Verena Stolcke, "Invaded Women: Gender, Race, and Class in the Formation of Colonial Society," in *Women, 'Race' and Writing in the Early Modern Period*, eds. Margo Hendricks and Patricia Parker (London: Routledge, 1994), pp. 277–78; Mary Elizabeth Perry, *Gender and Disorder in Early Modern Seville* (Princeton, NJ: Princeton University Press, 1990), pp. 5–6; and Susan Socolow, *The Women of Colonial Latin America* (Cambridge: Cambridge University Press, 2000), pp. 8–9. On honor, female enclosure, and social order in early modern Spain, also see José Luis Sánchez Lora, *Mujeres, conventos, y formas de religiosidad Barroca* (Madrid: Fundación Universitaria Española, 1988).

57. Juan Luis Vives's manual for women, first published in 1524, has recently been translated into English. See Vives, *The Education of a Christian Woman: A Sixteenth Century Manual* (Chicago: University of Chicago Press, 2000). Also see Perry, *Gender and Disorder*, pp. 53–54.

58. Perry, *Gender and Disorder*, esp. pp. 37–43.

59. Vives, *The Education of a Christian Woman*, p. 180.

60. See, for example, Lea, *A History of the Inquisition in Spain* (1906), vol. 2, pp. 286 and 314; Domínguez Ortiz, *Los judeoconversos en España y América*, p. 96; and Domínguez Ortiz, *Los judeoconversos en la España moderna* (Madrid: Editorial MAPFRE, 1992), p. 137.

61. Debates over whether race was operating in late medieval Spain tend to become more heated when those who argue in favor of that position are scholars trained in the United States, which (in both Europe and Latin America) often arouses suspicions that they are universalizing their country's particular histori-

cal experience with "race" and letting their "obsession" with the topic influence their analyses of cultures where it is presumably weak. For a recent and particularly strong condemnation of such "imperialist" uses of the notion of race, see Pierre Bourdieu and Loïc Wacquant, "On the Cunning of Imperialist Reason," *Theory, Culture and Society* 16, no. 1 (1999): pp. 41–58; and the response by John D. French, "The Misteps of Anti-Imperialist Reason: Bourdieu, Wacquant and Hanchard's *Orpheus and Power*," *Theory, Culture and Society* 17, no. 1 (2000): pp. 107–28.

62. On the rise of a secular, pseudoscientific, biologistic discourse that gradually eroded the idea of monogenesis and that to a great extent continues to shape modern understandings of human difference, see Colette Guillaumin, "The Idea of Race and its Elevation to Autonomous Scientific and Legal Status," in *Sociological Theories: Race and Colonialism* (Paris: UNESCO, 1980), pp. 37–67; Lucius Outlaw, "Toward a Critical Theory of 'Race,'" in *Anatomy of Racism*, ed. Theo Goldberg (Minneapolis: University of Minnesota Press, 1990), pp. 62–68; Elazar Barkan, "Race and the Social Sciences," in *Cambridge History of Science*, vol. 7 (2003), p. 696; and Michael Banton, *Racial Theories*, pp. 44–80.

63. West, "Race and Social Theory," pp. 82–83.

64. Holt, *The Problem of Race*, p. 20.

65. See Gilroy, *'There ain't no Black in the Union Jack'*; Paul Gilroy, "One Nation under a Groove: The Cultural Politics of 'Race' and Racism in Britain," in *Anatomy of Racism*, ed. David Theo Goldberg (Minneapolis and London: University of Minnesota Press, 1990), pp. 263–82; Étienne Balibar, "Is there a 'Neo-Racism'?" in *Race, Nation, Class: Ambiguous Identities*, ed. Étienne Balibar and Immanuel Wallerstein, trans. of Étienne Balibar by Chris Turner (London and New York: Verso, 1991), pp. 17–28; and Faye V. Harrison, "The Persistent Power of 'Race' in the Cultural and Political Economy of Racism," *Annual Review of Anthropology* 24 (1995): pp. 48–50.

66. Wade, *Race, Nature and Culture*, pp. 14–15.

67. Wade, *Race, Nature and Culture*, p. 12; and Banton, *Racial Theories*, p. 17.

CHAPTER 3

1. On how social practices result from the mutually influential relationship between the material and the representational and come to operate through unstated assumptions, see Pierre Bourdieu, *Outline of a Theory of Practice*, trans. Richard Nice (Cambridge and New York: Cambridge University Press, 1977), pp. 78–86. And on how race and racism in particular function through "agreed-upon fictions," that is, conventional or unconscious aspects of social practice, see Holt (who partly draws on Bourdieu), *The Problem of Race in the 21st Century*, pp. 13 and 22–23; and Stuart Hall (who draws on Gramsci's discussion of how ideologies become "organic" and transform popular thought), "Gramsci's Relevance for the Study of Race and Ethnicity," in *Stuart Hall: Critical Dialogues in Cultural Studies*, pp. 430–31.

2. See, for example, Sicroff, *Los estatutos de limpieza de sangre*, p. 48; and Domínguez Ortiz, *Los judeoconversos en España y América*, pp. 22–28.

3. Bourdieu, *Outline of a Theory of Practice*, pp. 78–79.

4. López Vela, "Estructuras administrativas del Santo Oficio," p. 238; Sicroff, *Los estatutos de limpieza de sangre*, p. 268.

5. The passage reads, "*Estas descendencias de las razas mahometana y judaica, por ningún acto extrínseco visible, por ninguna nota o signo ocular externo se distinguen de los auténticos españoles.*" Cited in Domínguez Ortiz, *La clase social de los conversos en Castilla en la edad moderna* (Madrid: Instituto Balmes de Sociología, Departamento de Historia Social, Consejo Superior de Investigaciones Científicas, 1955), p. 142.

6. Sicroff, *Los estatutos de limpieza*, pp. 121, 129–30 and 268–71.

7. López Vela, "Estructuras administrativas del Santo Oficio," pp. 238–39. For copies of the 1553 and 1572 decrees, see Archivo Histórico Nacional (hereafter AHN), Inquisición, libro 1240, and AHN, Inquisición, libro 1243, fols. 400–01; and for a detailed discussion of Toledo's inquisitorial personnel, see Jean Pierre Dedieu, *L'administration de la foi. L'inquisition de Tolède XVIᵉ–XVIIIᵉ siècle* (Madrid: Casa de Velázquez, 1989), pp. 159–211.

8. See, for example, Jean Pierre Dedieu, "*Limpieza,* Pouvoir et Richesse: Conditions d'entrée dans le corps des ministres de l'inquisition. Tribunal de Tolède, XIVᵉ–XVIIᵉ siècles," in *Les sociétés fermées dans le monde Ibérique (XVIᵉ-XVIIIᵉ siècle)* (Paris: Editions du Centre National de la Recherche Scientifique, 1986), pp. 168–87. "Oficios viles" (sometimes "oficios vulgares") basically referred to trade and money lending, while people who were linked to the "mechanical trades" included silversmiths, painters, embroiderers, stonemasons, innkeepers, tavern owners, and scribes (except royal ones). The Holy Office did not always succeed in excluding merchants from its ranks, especially during the eighteenth century, when mercantile activity shed many of its negative associations.

9. López Vela, "Estructuras administrativas del Santo Oficio," p. 243. The Inquisition's increasing exclusivity was extended to its American tribunals. In 1604, for example, the Suprema ordered the Mexican Holy Office and the other colonial tribunals not to accept any butchers, shoemakers, bakers, and in general anyone that had been involved in "vile or mechanical" trades or that descended from such individuals. AHN, libro 1050, fol. 50.

10. López Vela, "Estructuras administrativas del Santo Oficio," p. 247.

11. In institutions in which the process of certification was not as rigorous (and sometimes in the Holy Office itself), the testimonies provided by the first group of witnesses, those presented by the candidate, constituted "the proof." However, as of the second half of the sixteenth century, the production of the probanza tended to be controlled more by designated officials than candidates and to consist of more than one group of depositions.

12. The translations of the nativeness and citizenship offered here admittedly simplify what in early modern Castile were rather multivalent, interrelated, and fluctuating terms. Generally, naturaleza was a status that accorded certain exclusive privileges within the kingdom, namely eligibility for office holding and

ecclesiastical benefices. (The native monopoly on public and religious offices was called the *"reserva de oficio."*) Nativeness was commonly established by place of birth, but it was also socially and legally negotiated and it could be acquired from the king. Vecindad was a status determined primarily by integration in the local community. Implying certain rights and duties, it amounted to a more local type of citizenship. For more on the two concepts and their relationship, see Herzog, *Defining Nations,* pp. 6–9, 17–42, and 64–93.

13. See AHN, Inquisición, libro 1266.

14. AHN, Inquisición, libro 1056, fols. 439–439v. This questionnaire was sent to inquisitorial tribunals in Spain and Spanish America. It is included in its original language (Spanish) as an appendix to this book. Other copies of the questionnaire can be found in various Spanish and Spanish American Inquisition archives. After 1623, the year that Philip IV issued a decree that sought to curb the number of times that an individual and members of the same family were subjected to genealogical investigations, some interrogation forms included a question about whether any of the petitioner's ancestors had proven their purity of blood. Questionnaires differed somewhat in terms of the language or questions, but the sections on limpieza de sangre remained essentially the same throughout the seventeenth century and well into the eighteenth century. For copies of questionnaires that were sent to the Zaragoza, Valencia, and Barcelona tribunals in the seventeenth century, see AHN, Inquisición, libro 1243; and for a questionnaire that was sent to Mexico in the early part of the seventeenth century, see AHN, Inquisición, libro 1053, fol. 39.

15. Sometimes questions were added on the recommendation of inquisitors visiting and reporting on tribunals. In 1661, for example, Visitador Medina Rico, who had been sent to inspect the activities and records of the Mexican Holy Office, proposed changing the interrogation to explicitly inquire into the candidate's marital status, occupation, religious behavior, and peaceful or restless nature (the last alluding to political activities). AHN, Inquisición, libro 1058, fols. 581–582v. The inclusion of more questions in purity-of-blood certifications in the second half of the seventeenth century also characterized questionnaires used by cathedral chapters. The questionnaires used by Murcia's cathedral chapter in 1672, for example, asked whether the candidate or any of his ancestors had engaged in "vile or vulgar work" (*oficios viles o bajos*), whether they had been *comuneros* or traitors to the king, and whether they had practiced witchcraft or sorcery. The questionnaire is reproduced in Hernández Franco, *Cultura y limpieza de sangre,* p. 135.

16. For a good introduction to the Spanish Inquisition's archives, see Gustav Henningsen, "The Archives and the Historiography of the Spanish Inquisition," trans. Lawrence Scott Rainey, in *The Inquisition in Early Modern Europe: Studies on Sources and Methods,* ed. Gustav Henningsen, John Tedeschi, and Charles Amiel (Dekalb: Northern Illinois University Press, 1986), pp. 54–78.

17. López Vela, "Estructuras administrativas del Santo Oficio," pp. 257–74.

18. See Postigo Castellanos, *Honor y privilegio en la corona de Castilla,* pp. 141 and 144–55. For an example of the Council of the Orders' certification procedures, see BNM, MS 9881, fols. 261r–264v, which describes the

investigations conducted in the early seventeenth century in five different Spanish and Mexican cities to certify the purity and nobility of blood of don Francisco Pacheco de Cordoba y Bocanegra. And for a description of the procedures followed by the military order of San Juan, see BNM, MSS 11410–14, fols. 187–90. Like other main military orders, the Order of San Juan required proof of nobility and excluded people who were or had engaged in mercantile activities, money lending, and "vulgar or mechanical" trades.

19. References to the certification procedures of cathedral chapters can be found in a memorial written by don Francisco de Cueva y Silva regarding the statutes. See AHN, Inquisición, libro 1266.

20. López Vela, "Estructuras administrativas del Santo Oficio," p. 251.

21. BNM, MS 10431, fols. 131–150v.

22. See López Vela, "Estructuras administrativas del Santo Oficio," pp. 248–52.

23. Needless to say, the certification system was supposed to work one way, but in practice it sometimes functioned differently. For example, although the Suprema had already tried to bar petitioners from selecting the witnesses who were to be examined in their probanzas, in 1604 it acknowledged that this continued to be a problem.

24. During the 1620s and 1630s, the Suprema did grant candidates for offices and titles the right to appeal decisions on their limpieza cases, but according to López Vela, the policy did not have much effect. "Estructuras administrativas del Santo Oficio," p. 270.

25. BNM, MS 12053, fols. 304–311v: Memorial of Diego Gonzales Monjarrés, regarding his ancestry and purity of blood, 1605. For another example of an appeal to the Suprema on a purity of blood probanza, this time from New Spain, see the case of Gregorio Romano, a familiar and alderman in the city of Puebla who had his title removed after the Holy Office discovered that he was married to a woman whose grandmother was known to be a "*confesa*" (conversa). The Suprema revoked the sentence of the Mexican tribunal, which according to New Spain's inquisitors sent shock waves among Puebla's vecinos, not only because Romano was going to be allowed to continue being a familiar but because they were aware that his brother Diego Romano had been removed from the Inquisition due to his impurity and (as consolation?) granted the bishopric of Puebla. AGI, AHN, Inquisición 1729, Exp. 8: Case of Gregorio Romano, familiar of the Holy Office in Puebla de los Ángeles, against the Mexican Inquisition, October 5, 1602. For more on the case, see AGI, AHN, Inquisición 1728, Exp. 10; and AHN, libro 1049, fol. 473v: Letter from the Mexican Inquisition to the Suprema, March 23, 1603.

26. BNM, MS 12053.

27. The Council of Orders, the Cathedral of Toledo, and the Colegios Mayores rejected the three positive acts decree shortly after it was passed and refused to accept the probanzas of the Inquisition because its partial acceptance of the law (it vacillated) was perceived as a sign of lax procedures. The decree was also met with reluctance by some sectors of the traditional aristocracy as well as of the Holy Office, who feared that the measure would wrest rigor and legitimacy from the probanzas. As of the naming of a new inquisitor general in 1643, the Inquisition began to reassert its institutional autonomy, gradually

rejecting a number of royal orders regarding the purity procedures. By 1654, it too had rejected the positive acts component of the 1623 Pragmática. See López Vela, "Estructuras administrativas del Santo Oficio," esp. pp. 258–59, 267–68, and 271–74.

28. In both Spain and Spanish America, the "public voice and fame" was a social and legal category that stemmed from the system of honor and that generally referred to how a community judged a person according to its system of values. A mechanism of social control and part of local oral histories that were subject to change and manipulation, it mainly entered the legal sphere through the witnesses who were asked to testify about a given person's public reputation. On the distinction between rumor and reputation and the way the latter (which had more validity as evidence) functioned in the Spanish colonial administration of justice, see Tamar Herzog, *Upholding Justice: Society, State, and the Penal System in Quito* (1650–1750) (Ann Arbor: University of Michigan Press, 2004), pp. 208–20.

29. Domínguez Ortiz, *La clase de los conversos*, p. 75.

30. According to Ruth Pike, linajudos (who tended to be doctors, lawyers, and even former inquisitors) were most numerous in Seville because of the scores of wealthy converso merchants who in the fifteenth century had married into its aristocracy. The "mixed" nature of the city's nobility, in other words, provided plenty of work for genealogists who either dedicated themselves to policing lineages for Jewish ancestry or who simply wanted to profit in any way they could from their "expertise." Pike, *Linajudos and Conversos in Seville: Greed and Prejudice in Sixteenth- and Seventeenth-Century Spain* (New York and Washington, DC: Peter Lang, 2000), pp. 15–16. Also see Postigo Castellanos, *Honor y privilegio*, p. 149.

31. Though unsalaried, the title of familiar was eagerly sought. It automatically bestowed honor and local political leverage and after 1518 removed the holder from civil jurisdiction.

32. In the Inquisition, when the petitioner initiated the process, he had to make a deposit, the sum of which was based on the estimated costs of sending commissioners to one or various places and of compensating all other local officials involved in the process. To this payment might be added others, depending on how long and labyrinthine the investigation turned out to be. According to Lea, the probanzas sometimes provided important revenues for royal officials. *A History of the Inquisition*, vol. 2, pp. 302–06.

33. Jaime Contreras, "Limpieza de sangre, cambio social y manipulación de la memoria," in *Inquisición y conversos* (Toledo: Caja de Castilla-La Mancha, 1994), pp. 81–101.

34. I thank Tamar Herzog for this insightful observation.

35. Cervantes satirizes the Inquisition and Spanish cult of purity of blood in *Don Quijote de la Mancha*, but also in "Le elección de los alcades de Daganzo," a short comedy that ridicules the transformation of poverty, ignorance, and laziness into Old Christian "values"; and in his "El retablo de las maravillas," a more explicit critique of his society's obsession with clean and legitimate birth. Miguel de Cervantes, *Entremeses* (Mexico City: Editorial Porrúa, 1968), pp. 27–40 and 73–86.

36. Antonio Dominguez Ortiz, *The Golden Age of Spain, 1516–1659*, trans. James Casey (New York: Basic Books, 1971), p. 254.

37. AHN, Inquisición, libro 1266.

38. On the statutes' manipulation of time and privileging of obscure genealogical origins, see Jaime Contreras's excellent prologue in Hernández Franco, *Cultura y limpieza de sangre*, esp. pp. iii–iv.

39. Peggy Liss, *Mexico Under Spain*, pp. 13–14.

40. Jaime Contreras, *Sotos contra Riquelmes: Regidores, inquisidores y criptojudíos* (Madrid: Anaya & M. Muchnik, 1992), pp. 23.

41. The crown tried to suppress these and other genealogical compilations (generically called *Libros verdes* or *Libros del becerro*), but even after they were banned by Philip IV's 1623 Pragmatic, they continued to circulate and were constantly being amended as they passed from hand to hand. See Sicroff, *Los estatutos de limpieza de sangre*, p. 255; and Kamen, *The Spanish Inquisition: A Historical Revision*, p. 32.

42. Pike, *Linajudos and Conversos in Seville*, pp. 6, 16, 78, and 154. One quarter of all noble titles issued by the crown (19 out of 77) between 1552 and 1602 were purchased by men who had been in the Americas or whose fathers had spent time there. Most of these men claimed nobility on the basis of military contribution, but a good number also acquired it through their involvement in transatlantic trade. I.A.A. Thompson, "The Purchase of Nobility in Castile, 1552–1700," *Journal of European Economic History* 11 (1982): p. 347.

43. Thompson, "The Purchase of Nobility in Castile," pp. 323–26.

44. See José Antonio Maravall, *Poder, honor, y élites en el siglo XVII* (Madrid: Siglo Veintiuno Editores, 1984), pp. 173–250.

45. See, among others, Contreras, *Sotos contra Riquelmes*, pp. 26–27; Maravall, *Poder, honor, y élites en el siglo XVII*, pp. 173–250; Hernández Franco, *Cultura y limpieza de sangre*, pp. 12–17, 25–26, and 62–65; Kamen, *The Spanish Inquisition: A Historical Revision*, pp. 28–36; and Postigo Castellanos, *Honor y privilegio en la corona de Castilla*, pp. 133–37.

46. See Ignacio Atienza Hernández, " 'Refeudalisation' in Castile during the seventeenth century: A cliché?" in *The Castilian Crisis of the Seventeenth Century: New Perspectives on the Economic and Social History of Seventeenth-Century Spain*, ed. I.A.A. Thompson and Bartolomé Yun Casalilla (Cambridge and New York: Cambridge University Press, 1994), pp. 249–76, esp. 254–56; and, in the same volume, Bartolomé Yun Casalilla, "The Castilian Aristocracy in the Seventeenth Century: Crisis, Refeudalisation, or Political Offensive?" pp. 277–300. Spain was not technically a "feudal" society since serfdom, which in medieval Castile had been limited thanks in part to the nature of colonization and land distribution that accompanied the Reconquista, had expired by the late fifteenth century. William D. Phillips Jr. and Carla Rahn Phillips, "Spain in the Fifteenth Century," p. 17. Also see Helen Nader, *Liberty in Absolutist Spain: The Habsburg Sale of Towns, 1516–1700* (Baltimore: Johns Hopkins University Press, 1990), pp. 8–9.

47. See Atienza Hernández, " 'Refeudalisation' in Castile," esp. p. 254. Also see Thompson, "The Purchase of Nobility in Castile," which argues that the

extent and impact of the Habsburg sale of *privilegios de hidalguía* has been exaggerated in the historiography; and the response by James Amelang, "The Purchase of Nobility in Castile, 1552–1700: A Comment," *Journal of European Economic History* 11, no. 1 (1982): pp. 219–26.

48. Hernández Franco, *Cultura y limpieza de sangre,* pp. i–v and 61–62.

49. On the Counter-Reformation's influence on Spanish sexual attitudes and practices, see Stephen H. Haliczer, "Sexuality and Repression in Counter-Reformation Spain," in *Sex and Love in Golden Age Spain,* ed. Alain Saint-Saëns (New Orleans: University Press of the South, 1999), pp. 81–94.

50. I.A.A. Thompson, "*Hidalgo* and *pechero:* The language of 'estates' and 'classes' in early-modern Castile," in *Language, History and Class,* ed. Penelope J. Corfield (Cambridge: Basil Blackwell, 1991), pp. 70–71.

51. Caro Baroja, *Razas, pueblos y linajes,* pp. 147–51.

52. See, for example, Francisco de Quevedo, "El mundo por de dentro" ("The World from the Inside"), in *Dreams and Discourses,* introduction and trans. by R. K. Britton (Warminster, UK: Aris & Phillips, 1989), pp. 187–89. Like other works of the Spanish literary Baroque, Quevedo's *sueños* are characterized by self-doubt, skepticism, and pessimism and in particular by a deep suspicion of external appearances; their main themes are illusion and disillusionment, *engaño* and *desengaño.* See the introduction to *Dreams and Discourses,* esp. pp. 13–14.

53. Hernández Franco, *Cultura y limpieza de sangre,* p. 15.

54. According to Poole, bishops and pastors were not required to have limpieza de sangre because Rome opposed it. Stafford Poole, "The Politics of Limpieza de Sangre: Juan de Ovando and his Circle in the Reign of Philip II," *The Americas* 55, no. 3 (January 1999): p. 367. However, as Domínguez Ortiz points out, the Cámara de Castilla was aware of this situation and took measures to ensure that the family background and genealogical purity of candidates for the priesthood were investigated while they were in seminaries. Domínguez Ortiz, *Los judeoconversos en la España moderna,* p. 149.

55. Fray Agustín Salucio, *Discurso sobre los estatutos de limpieza de sangre,* ed. Antonio Pérez y Gómez (Valencia: Artes Gráficas Soler, 1975 [1599]), esp. fols. 1v–4v, 26v–28r, and 36v. For two seventeenth-century memorials that also complained that all Iberians (Spaniards and Portuguese) were called Jews and marranos in the rest of Europe, especially France and Italy, see AHN, Inquisición, libro 1247, fols. 156–76 and fols. 177–80.

56. For a discussion of the mechanisms that Spanish kings had to erase "defects of birth," see Twinam, "Pedro de Ayarzo: The Purchase of Whiteness"; and "Racial Passing: Informal and Official 'Whiteness' in Colonial Spanish America."

57. The dispensation was granted by Philip III in 1604 and applied only to his direct descendants. See Norman Roth, *Conversos, Inquisition, and the Expulsion,* pp. 136–44 and 148.

58. The inquisitor supported limiting the statutes and removing the historically unprecedented third division that had arisen in Spain, that of conversos. The distinction between Old and New Christians, he claimed, created a

"monstrous" situation, in which plebeians, simply for being Old Christians, could claim superiority over patricians. See BNM, MS 10431: Memorial of don Diego Serrano de Silva. Similar arguments are made by Juan Roco Campofrío in his discourse on the statutes. BNM, 10918.

59. AHN, Inquisición, libro 1266: Opinion of the licenciado don Francisco de Cueva y Silva about why his Majesty should continue to support the statutes of limpieza de sangre, ca. 1690s.

60. Graizbord, *Souls in Dispute,* pp. 116–20.

61. See, for example, Opinion of the licenciado Francisco de Cueva y Silva, op. cit.

62. See, for example, Domínguez Ortiz, *Los Judeoconversos en España y América,* pp. 109–14; Domínguez Ortiz, *La clase de los conversos en Castilla en la edad moderna,* pp. 126–30; and López Vela, "Estructuras administrativas del Santo Oficio," pp. 273–74. Both authors also stress that by the eighteenth century, the concept of purity came to operate mainly as a nobility requirement and as tool to check for *limpieza de oficio.* If their contention is correct, then Spain's dominant notions of blood were once again operating in similar ways to those of the rest of Europe.

63. Although the 1812 liberal Constitution of Cádiz established the equality of all Spaniards under the law, proof of purity continued to be required in some public and private corporations for at least two more decades. (The Inquisition was suspended during the French occupation, between 1808 and 1813, but not abolished until 1820.) In 1834, the Spanish crown issued a law making limpieza unnecessary for government jobs and institutions, and shortly thereafter, ecclesiastical and private secular bodies also suppressed their purity requirements. Finally, in 1865, a royal decree abolished the limpieza information that had been demanded of prospective marriage partners and candidates for bureaucratic posts. After more than five hundred years of their initial appearance, Spain's requirements of purity of blood were dealt their final blow. Domínguez Ortiz, *Los Judeoconversos en España y América,* pp. 123–34.

64. Martz, "Implementation of Pure-Blood Statutes in Sixteenth-Century Toledo," pp. 245–71.

65. Pike, *Linajudos and Conversos in Seville,* pp. 154–55.

66. According to Nicolás López Martínez, the effort failed largely because a powerful group of conversos in that body prevented it, successfully invoking the bull of Nicholas V, which had condemned people who made distinctions between New and Old Christians. López Martínez, "El estatuto de limpieza de sangre en la catedral de Burgos," *Hispania* (Madrid) 19, no. 74 to 77 (1959): pp. 52–81. Efforts to establish a statute in the University of Salamanca (whose Colegio Mayor de San Bartolomé had some of oldest purity requirements) in the 1560s also failed, but the reasons for this are not clear. Carlos Carrete Parrondo, *El judaísmo español y la inquisición* (Madrid: Editorial Mapfre, 1992), p. 156.

67. Contreras, *Sotos contra Riquelmes.*

68. See, for example, Hernández Franco, *Cultura y limpieza de sangre,* pp. 13–14 and 62–63; and Poole, "The Politics of Limpieza de Sangre," p. 368.

CHAPTER 4

1. For a succinct discussion of Spanish society at the end of the fifteenth century, see Miguel Angel Ladero Quesada, "Spain, circa 1492: Social Values and Structures," in *Implicit Understandings: Observing, Reporting, and Reflecting on the Encounters between Europeans and Other Peoples in the Early Modern Era,* ed. Stuart B. Schwartz (Cambridge and New York: Cambridge University Press, 1994), pp. 96–133.

2. The term *Mexica* refers to the migratory people who in the fourteenth century settled on an island in the Valley of Mexico's central lake, founded the cities of Tenochtitlan and Tlatelolco, and became the dominant power of the Triple Alliance. Popularly known as the "Aztec empire," the Triple Alliance was established by the rulers of Tenochtitlan, Texcoco, and Tlacopan in 1428 and subsequently conquered most of central Mexico and other parts of Mesoamerica. Because the term *Aztec* was not used in the pre-Hispanic period, many historians of Mexico no longer use it, opting instead for *Mexica* or *Mexica Empire* to describe that tripartite political entity. They also use the more general *Nahuas,* which refers to all the Náhuatl-speaking people of central Mexico (the majority).

3. On the environmental effects of Spanish colonialism, see Elinor G. K. Melville, *A Plague of Sheep: Environmental Consequences of the Conquest of Mexico* (Cambridge and New York: Cambridge University Press, 1994); and Alfred W. Crosby Jr., *The Columbian Exchange: Biological and Cultural Consequences of 1492,* 30th anniversary ed. (Westport, CT: Praeger, 2003).

4. The ayuntamiento was a local governing body in charge of administering an urban center and the territory under its jurisdiction. It included a cabildo but was larger and thus consisted of town council members as well as a *corregidor* (or *alcalde mayor*) and two *alcaldes menores.*

5. See Enrique Semo, *Historia del capitalismo en México: Los orígenes, 1521–1763* (Mexico City: Ediciones Era, 1973), pp. 65–70.

6. Magnus Mörner discusses the evolution and failures of the two-republic social model in *La corona española y los foráneos en los pueblos de indios de América* (Stockholm: Almqvist & Wiksell, 1970).

7. See Edward Calnek, "Patterns of Empire Formation in the Valley of Mexico, Late Postclassic Period, 1200–1521," in *Inca and Aztec States, 1400–1800: Anthropology and History,* ed. George Collier et al. (New York and London: Academic Press, 1982), pp. 43–62; and Geoffrey W. Conrad and Arthur Andrew Demarest, *Religion and Empire: The Dynamics of Aztec and Inca Expansionism* (Cambridge: Cambridge University Press, 1984), pp. 17–20. Also refer to Nigel Davies, *The Toltec Heritage: From the Fall of Tula to the Rise of Tenochtitlán* (Norman: University of Oklahoma Press, 1980).

8. See Nigel Davies, *The Aztecs* (Norman and London: University of Oklahoma Press, 1973), pp. 41–42; and for a detailed discussion of Mexica rulers' dynastic unions with women of Toltec descent, see Susan D. Gillespie, *The Aztec Kings: The Construction of Rulership in Mexica History* (Tucson: University of Arizona Press, 1989), esp. pp. 21 and 25–56.

9. Works on Nahua forms of writing include James Lockhart, *The Nahuas After the Conquest: A Social and Cultural History of the Indians of Central Mexico, Sixteenth through Eighteenth Centuries* (Stanford, CA: Stanford University Press, 1992), pp. 326–64; Elizabeth H. Boone, *Stories in Red and Black: Pictorial Histories of the Aztecs and Mixtecs* (Austin: University of Texas Press, 2000); and Boone, "Aztec Pictorial Histories: Records without Words," in *Writing without Words: Alternative Literacies in Mesoamerica and the Andes,* ed. Elizabeth H. Boone and Walter D. Mignolo (Durham, NC: Duke University Press, 1994), pp. 50–76.

10. Enrique Florescano, *Memory, Myth, and Time in Mexico: From the Aztecs to Independence,* trans. Albert G. Bork (Austin: University of Texas Press, 1994), pp. 30–64. For more on Mexica religion, symbolism, and myth, see Miguel León-Portilla, *Los antiguos mexicanos a través de sus crónicas y cantares* (Mexico City: Fondo de Cultura Económica, 1987); Conrad and Demarest, *Religion and Empire,* pp. 37–44; David Carrasco, *Quetzalcoatl and the Irony of Empire: Myths and Prophecies in the Aztec Tradition* (Chicago and London: University of Chicago Press, 1992); Alfredo López Austin, *The Human Body and Ideology: Concepts of the Ancient Nahuas,* trans. Thelma Ortiz de Montellano and Bernard Ortiz de Montellano, 2 vols. (Salt Lake City: University of Utah Press, 1988); Inga Clendinnen, *Aztecs: An Interpretation* (Cambridge and New York: Cambridge University Press, 1991); Richard F. Townsend, *The Aztecs,* rev. ed. (London: Thames & Hudson, 2000 [1992]), pp. 116–62; and David Carrasco, ed., *Aztec Ceremonial Landscapes* (Niwot: University Press of Colorado, 1991).

11. On the political and territorial organization of the Triple Alliance, see Pedro Carrasco, *The Tenochca Empire of Ancient Mexico: The Triple Alliance of Tenochtitlan, Tetzcoco, and Tlacopan* (Norman: University of Oklahoma Press, 1999). Although some scholars have argued that the Triple Alliance never achieved a high level of political and territorial integration and therefore should not be considered an "empire," Carrasco defines the term loosely, as "a large-scale state organization in which one people dominates others" and in which "one king is supreme over other subordinate rulers" (p. 3).

12. Friedrich Katz, *The Ancient American Civilisations* (London: Weidenfeld and Nicolson, 1989 [1972]), pp. 138–47; and Conrad and Demarest, *Religion and Empire,* pp. 32–44.

13. See Ross Hassig, *Trade, Tribute, and Transportation: The Sixteenth-century Political Economy of the Valley of Mexico* (Norman and London: University of Oklahoma Press, 1985); and Frances Berdan, "The Economics of Aztec Trade and Tribute," in *The Aztec Templo Mayor,* ed. Elizabeth Hill Boone (Washington, DC: Dumbarton Oaks Research Library and Collection, 1987), pp. 161–83. On the Mexica's social structures, see Pedro Carrasco, "Social Organization of Ancient Mexico," in *Handbook of Middle American Indians,* vol. 10, ed. R. Wauchope, G. F. Ekholm, and I. Bernal (Austin: University of Texas Press, 1971), pp. 349–75.

14. See Anthony Pagden, *Spanish Imperialism and the Political Imagination* (New Haven, CT: Yale University Press, 1990), p. 6.

15. See David A. Brading, *The First America: The Spanish Monarchy, Creole Patriots, and the Liberal State, 1492–1867* (Cambridge [England]: Cambridge University Press, 1991), pp. 102–27; Jacques Lafaye, *Quetzalcóatl and Guadalupe: The Formation of Mexican National Consciousness, 1531–1813*, trans. Benjamin Keen (Chicago: University of Chicago Press, 1976), pp. 30–50; and Georges Baudot, "Amerindian Image and Utopian Project: Motolinía and Millenarian Discourse," in *Amerindian Images and the Legacy of Columbus*, vol. 9 of *Hispanic Issues*, ed. René Jara and Nicholas Spadaccini (Minneapolis: University of Minnesota Press, 1992), pp. 375–400.

16. John L. Phelan, *The Millennial Kingdom of the Franciscans in the New World: A Study of the Writings of Gerónimo de Mendieta, 1525–1604* (Berkeley: University of California Press, 1956), p. 58.

17. According to Jesús Larios Martín, the Spanish crown's decision to grant the native people the status of purity of blood was made relatively soon, indeed, even before it formally recognized indigenous nobility. Jesús Larios Martín, *Hidalguía e hidalgos de Indias* (Madrid: Asociación de hidalgos a fuero de España, 1958), pp. 4–5.

18. Spanish debates regarding Castile's right to rule in the Americas are discussed in Anthony Pagden, *The Fall of Natural Man: The American Indian and the Origins of Comparative Ethnology* (New York: Cambridge University Press, 1982); and in the first chapter of his *Spanish Imperialism and the Political Imagination* (New Haven, CT: Yale University Press, 1990).

19. "Parecer de los frailes Franciscanos sobre repartimientos de Indios," *Boletín del Archivo General de la Nación* 9 (1938): p. 176. In this remarkable document, which amounts to an attack on the colonial system of corvée labor (*repartimiento*), the Franciscans go as far as to suggest that Spanish rule over the native people is illegitimate; that it was unjust for one republic, composed of "natural lords of the land," to be subordinate to the other, which was new and foreign to the land ("*advenediza y extranjera*"). By no title, the document continues, were the Indians obligated to serve, or be slaves to, the Spaniards.

20. See Pagden, *Spanish Imperialism and the Political Imagination*, p. 22; Lewis Hanke, *All Mankind is One: A Study of the Disputation between Bartolomé de Las Casas and Juan Ginés de Sepúlveda in 1550 on the Intellectual and Religious Capacity of the American Indians* (DeKalb: Northern Illinois University Press, 1974); and Edmundo O'Gorman, *La invención de América* (Mexico City: Fondo de Cultura Económica, 1995 [first edition 1958]), pp. 27–28.

21. See Phelan, *The Millennial Kingdom*, p. 82; and Woodrow Borah, "The Spanish and Indian Law: New Spain," in *The Inca and Aztec States, 1400–1800: Anthropology and History*, ed. George Collier et al. (New York and London: Academic Press, 1982), pp. 265–88.

22. Pagden, *Spanish Imperialism*, p. 29.

23. On language policies in colonial and modern Mexico, see Shirley Brice Heath, *Telling Tongues: Language Policy in Mexico, Colony to Nation* (New York: Teachers College Press, 1972).

24. Richard M. Morse argues that Philip II strengthened the more Thomistic aspect of colonial rule, among other things by formally establishing the

Inquisition in American lands and promoting the spiritual mission of the colonial enterprise. Political and social hierarchies, he claims, were in theory
supposed to reflect the larger spiritual order. See Morse, "Toward a Theory
of Spanish American Government," *Journal of the History of Ideas* 15, no. 1
(January 1954): pp. 71–93. Also see Lomnitz-Adler, *Exits from the Labyrinth*,
pp. 262–65.

25. See Jonathan I. Israel, *Race, Class and Politics in Colonial Mexico, 1610–
1670* (London: Oxford University Press, 1975), esp. pp. 25–59.

26. Stern, "Paradigms of Conquest," p. 9.

27. On how the Castilian concept of vecindad operated in colonial Spanish
America, see Herzog, *Defining Nations*, pp. 43–63; and Francisco Domínguez
y Compañy, "La condición de vecino: Su significación e importancia en la vida
colonial hispanoamericana," in *Crónica del VI congreso histórico municipal
interamericano (Madrid-Barcelona, 1957)* (Madrid: Instituto de Estudios de
Administración Local, 1959), pp. 703–20.

28. See María Elena Martínez, "Space, Order, and Group Identities in a
Spanish Colonial Town: Puebla de los Angeles," in *The Collective and the Public
in Latin America: Cultural Identities and Political Order*, ed. Luis Roniger and
Tamar Herzog (Brighton, UK, and Portland, OR: Sussex Academic Press, 2000),
pp. 13–36; Norman Martin, *Los vagabundos en la Nueva España* (Mexico City:
Editorial Jus, 1957), p. 42; and Israel, *Race, Class and Politics*, pp. 6–10.

29. Silvio Zavala, "La utopía de Tomás Moro en la Nueva España," in *La
utopía mexicana del siglo XVI: Lo bello, lo verdadero y lo bueno* (Mexico City:
Grupo Azabache, 1992), pp. 76–93, and Fintan B. Warren, *Vasco de Quiroga
and his Pueblo-Hospitals of Santa Fe* (Washington, DC: Academy of American
Franciscan History, 1963).

30. See Woodrow Borah, *Justice by Insurance: The General Indian Court
of Colonial Mexico and the Legal Aides of the Half-Real* (Berkeley: University
of California Press, 1983); and Susan Kellogg, *Law and the Transformation
of Aztec Culture, 1500–1700* (Norman: University of Oklahoma Press, 1995).
Other works on the role of law and legal tribunals in Spanish colonial societies include Steve J. Stern, "The Social Significance of Judicial Institutions in
an Exploitative Society: Huamanga, Peru, 1570–1640," in *The Inca and Aztec
States*, pp. 289–320; Ward Stavig, "Ambiguous Visions: Nature, Law, and Culture in Indigenous-Spanish Land Relations in Colonial Peru," *Hispanic American Historical Review* 80, no. 1 (2000): pp. 77–111; Charles R. Cutter, *The
Legal Culture of Northern New Spain, 1700–1810* (Albuquerque: University
of New Mexico Press, 1995); and Lauren Benton, *Law and Colonial Cultures:
Legal Regimes in World History: 1400–1900* (Cambridge and New York:
Cambridge University Press, 2002), pp. 81–102.

31. Borah, "The Spanish and Indian Law," pp. 278–82. The Juzgado de Indios
was based in Mexico City and was not extended to other provincial jurisdictions. Therefore, if they wanted to use the court, communities outside of the central valley had to send representatives to the capital.

32. See Richard E. Greenleaf, *Zumárraga y la Inquisición mexicana* (Mexico
City: Fondo de Cultura Económica, 1988), pp. 86–93; and Mariano Cuevas,

Historia de la Iglesia en México, vol. 1, 3rd ed. (El Paso, TX: Editorial "Revista Católica," 1928), pp. 369–80. For published documents relating to various cases of native idolatry from the 1530s and 1540s, see *Procesos de indios idólatras y hechiceros* (Mexico City: Secretaría de Gobernación and Archivo General de la Nación, 2002).

33. Richard E. Greenleaf, "The Inquisition and the Indians of New Spain: A Study in Jurisdictional Confusion," *The Americas* 22, no. 2 (1965): p. 139. Church authorities and the inquisitor general ordered an investigation of Don Carlos's case to see if he should have been reconciled instead of relaxed. The results of the inquiry are not clear, but Zumárraga was privately admonished. In a 1574 letter, Mexican inquisitors noted that Don Carlos's punishment had been considered too severe by many people in New Spain and even by the Suprema. AHN, Inquisición, Libro 1050, fols. 212–20: letter by inquisitors Bonilla and Ávalos to the Suprema, October 20, 1574.

34. See Inga Clendinnen, *Ambivalent Conquests: Maya and Spaniard in Yucatan, 1517–1570* (New York: Cambridge University Press, 1991), esp. pp. 72–111; Clendinnen, "Reading the Inquisitorial Record in Yucatán: Fact or Fantasy," *The Americas* 38, no. 3 (1982): pp. 327–45; and Greenleaf, "The Inquisition and the Indians of New Spain," pp. 140–41.

35. For an alternative view on why the native people were removed from the Inquisition's jurisdiction, see Jorge Klor de Alva, "Colonizing Souls: The Failure of the Indian Inquisition and the Rise of Penitential Discipline," *Cultural Encounters: The Impact of the Inquisition in Spain and the New World,* ed. Mary Elizabeth Perry and Anne J. Cruz (Berkeley: University of California Press, 1991), pp. 3–21.

36. See Greenleaf, "The Inquisition and the Indians of New Spain," pp. 138–66; and Roberto Moreno de los Arcos, "New Spain's Inquisition for Indians from the Sixteenth to the Nineteenth Century," in *Cultural Encounters: The Impact of the Inquisition in Spain and the New World,* pp. 23–32. Greenleaf notes that there are indications that in the eighteenth century, the crown was moving toward placing the native people under the full jurisdiction of the Inquisition.

37. See Richard Greenleaf, "The Mexican Inquisition and the Indians: Sources for the Ethnohistorian," *The Americas* 34, no. 3 (1978): pp. 315–44; and "The Inquisition and the Indians of New Spain."

38. See Juan de Solórzano Pereira, *Política Indiana,* vol. 1 (Madrid: Compañía Ibero-Americana de Publicaciones, 1930 [1648]), pp. 417–29. Note that the native people's special juridico-religious status survived for a short while after independence. In the 1822 Constitution, Emperor Iturbide classified all of the inhabitants of the "empire" as "citizens" but singled out the Indians as people that were to receive "apostolic privileges" and be designated as *"ciudadanos agraciados por la silla Apostólica."*

39. See Laura A. Lewis, "The 'Weakness' of Women and the Feminization of the Indian in Colonial Mexico," *Colonial Latin American Review* 5, no. 1 (1996): 73–94.

40. See Greenleaf, "The Inquisition and the Indians of New Spain," pp. 150–55; and Martha Few, *Women Who Live Evil Lives: Gender, Religion, and the*

Politics of Power in Colonial Guatemala (Austin: University of Texas Press, 2002), p. 30.

41. As Lauran Benton has stressed, the existence of distinct and overlapping legal jurisdictions in colonial Spanish America and elsewhere contributed to the permeability of cultural boundaries by creating spaces for people to manipulate and contest categories. Benton, *Law and Colonial Cultures*, pp. 81–102.

42. See, for example, AGN, Inquisición, vol. 486 (2), fols. 451–58 (or 404–10); AGN, Inquisición, vol. 372, exp. 14, AGN, Inquisición, vol. 684, exp. 11, fols. 130–40; and AGN, Inquisición, vol. 1044, fols. 50–50v.

43. See, for example, AGN, Civil 1094: Francisco Alonso de Besada against Marcelo Rojas, 1798–1799.

44. Refer to AGN, Inquisición, vol. 684, exp. 11.

45. Lockhart refers to the altepetl as "ethnic states" in order to highlight their strong ethnic and corporate identities during the pre-Hispanic and colonial period. See chapter 2 in *The Nahuas After the Conquest*, pp. 14–58, esp. p. 27.

46. A number of scholars have studied the reconstitution of pre-Hispanic dynasties under Spanish rule. For central Mexico, see, for example, Charles Gibson, *The Aztecs under Spanish Rule: A History of the Indians of the Valley of Mexico, 1519–1810* (Stanford, CA: Stanford University Press, 1964); Delfina E. López Sarrelangue, *La nobleza indígena de Pátzcuaro en la época virreinal* (Mexico City: Universidad Nacional Autónoma de México, 1965), pp. 52–53; and Robert Haskett, *Indigenous Rulers: An Ethnohistory of Town Government in Colonial Cuernavaca* (Albuquerque: University of New Mexico Press, 1991).

47. See Charles Gibson, *Tlaxcala in the Sixteenth Century* (New Haven, CT: Yale University Press, 1952); Jaime Cuadriello, *Las glorias de la república de Tlaxcala: O la conciencia como imagen sublime* (Mexico City: Instituto de Investigaciones Estéticas, UNAM, and Museo Nacional de Arte, INBA, 2004); and R. Jovita Baber, "The Construction of Empire: Politics, Law and Community in Tlaxcala, New Spain, 1521–1640" (PhD diss., University of Chicago, 2005).

48. The main rulership of the province of Michoacán was transmitted through royal bloodlines until 1577, when no eligible successor remained. López Sarrelangue, *La nobleza indígena de Pátzcuaro*, pp. 52–53. Also see James Krippner-Martínez, *Rereading the Conquest: Power, Politics, and the History of Early Colonial Michoacán, Mexico, 1521–1565* (University Park: Pennsylvania State University Press, 2001).

49. William B. Taylor, "Cacicazgos coloniales en el Valle de Oaxaca," *Historia Mexicana* 20 (1970): pp. 1–41. Also see Kevin Terraciano, *The Mixtecs of Colonial Oaxaca: Ñudzahui History, Sixteenth through Eighteenth Centuries* (Stanford, CA: Stanford University Press, 2001).

50. On Cholula, see Francisco González Hermosillo, "La élite indígena de Cholula en el siglo XVIII: El caso de don Juan de León y Mendoza," in *Círculos de poder en la Nueva España,* ed. Carmen Castañeda (Mexico City: CIESAS and Grupo Editorial Miguel Angel Porrúa, 1998), pp. 61–62.

51. The establishment of the repartimiento, combined with the new forms of calculating tribute quotas, led to a more regularized and regimented form of

exploitation, one that suited the developing silver mining industry and the rising fiscal demands of a Spanish state consumed by its wars in Europe but that contributed to the demographic decline. See Peter Bakewell, "Conquest after the Conquest: The Rise of Spanish Domination in America," in *Spain, Europe and the Atlantic World,* ed. Richard Kagan and Geoffrey Parker (New York: Cambridge University Press, 1995), pp. 296–315. In part because of its negative effects on the native population, the repartimiento declined in the first third of the seventeenth century and was formally abolished in 1633.

52. Carrasco, "La transformación de la cultura indígena durante la colonia." *Historia Mexicana* 25, no. 2 (1975), p. 177. Others draw similar conclusions. See, for example, Lockhart *Nahuas After the Conquest,* p. 177; and Haskett, *Indigenous Rulers,* pp. 158–59.

53. After independence from Spain, Mexico suppressed noble titles and thus also cacicazgos. Some of the descendants of the colonial native nobility were initially able to maintain some of their landed estates, but in the course of the nineteenth century, properties that had been parts of indigenous rulerships tended to be divided among family members or bought by *hacendados* (owners of haciendas or landed estates), thus eroding long-standing patterns of hereditary landholding.

54. The order was first sent to the Audiencia of Perú but was then extended to all the Indies. See Richard Konetzke, *Colección de documentos para la historia de la formación social de Hispanoamérica 1493–1810,* vol. 1 (Madrid: Consejo Superior de Investigaciones Científicas, 1953), p. 360.

55. Sometimes a finer distinction was made between the members of the main royal lineages, labeled *caciques principales* or *caciques y principales,* and those that ruled in less important areas. With time, however, the terms *cacique* and *principal* both acquired more general meanings. The latter, for example, was applied to all those who occupied public office. Carrasco, "La transformación de la cultura," p. 182.

56. Francisco de Solano, *Cedulario de tierras: Compilación de legislación agraria colonial 1497-1820* (Mexico City: Universidad Nacional Autónoma de México, 1984), p. 89. On Spanish colonial laws regarding the purchase and alienation of land, see William B. Taylor, "Land and Water Rights in the Viceroyalty of New Spain," *New Mexico Historical Review* 50, no. 3 (1975): pp. 189–211.

57. For a list of some indigenous rulers who under Viceroy Mendoza were given permission to carry swords and be "treated like Spaniards," see *Los virreyes españoles en América durante el gobierno de la Casa de Austria,* ed. Lewis Hanke with the collaboration of Celso Rodríguez, vol. 1 (Madrid: Atlas, 1976), pp. 69–70.

58. Lockhart, *The Nahuas After the Conquest,* p. 132. Note that some cacicazgo titles included Spanish last names.

59. See Guido Munch, *El cacicazgo de San Juan Teotihuacan durante la colonia, 1521–1821* (Mexico City: Instituto Nacional de Antropología e Historia, 1976), p. 8.

60. López Sarrelangue, *La nobleza indígena,* p. 105.

61. Guillermo S. Fernández de Recas, *Cacicazgos y nobiliario indígena de la Nueva España* (Mexico City: Instituto Bibliográfico Mexicano de la Biblioteca

Nacional de México, 1961), p. xvii. Although it had earlier origins, the mayorazgo was codified in the 1505 Leyes de Toro and continued to be be modified throughout the sixteenth century. For a general work on the Castilian mayorazgo, see Bartolomé Clavero, *Mayorazgo: Propiedad feudal en Castilla 1369–1836* (Madrid: Siglo XXI de España Editores, 1989); and for the institution in late medieval Andalusía, see Miguel Ángel Ladero Quesada, *Los señores de Andalucía: Investigaciones sobre nobles y señoríos en los siglos XIII a XV* (Cádiz: Universidad de Cádiz, 1998), pp. 30–31.

62. In the Iberian Peninsula and in New Spain there were two main types of mayorazgos. The first and most common followed the crown's laws regarding succession, which were based upon the principles of primogeniture, inalienability, and indivisibility. In the irregular form, the rules of inheritance were determined by the founder. See Guillermo S. Fernández de Recas, *Mayorazgos de la Nueva España* (Mexico City: Instituto Bibliográfico Mexicano, Biblioteca Nacional de México, 1965), p. xii. Although primogeniture became increasingly important in Spain during the fifteenth and sixteenth centuries, Castilian legal traditions as old as the Siete Partidas (the thirteenth-century Castile law code that was still being used in the early modern period) still allowed for certain types of feminine succession, and practices varied by region.

63. See J. Rounds, "Dynastic Succession and the Centralization of Power in Tenochtitlan," in *The Inca and Aztec States 1400–1800: Anthropology and History,* ed. George A. Collier, Renato I. Rosaldo, and John D. Wirth (New York: Academic Press, 1982), pp. 63–89; and Kellogg, *Law and the Transformation of Aztec Culture,* pp. 92–94.

64. For cacicas in Oaxaca, see Ronald Spores, "Mixteca *Cacicas:* Status, Wealth, and the Political Accommodation of Native Elite Women in Early Colonial Mexico," in *Indian Women of Early Mexico,* ed. Schroeder, Susan, Stephanie Wood, and Robert Haskett (Norman and London: University of Oklahoma Press, 1997), pp. 185–97. And for the case of an eighteenth-century cacica from central Mexico, see Robert Haskett, "Activist or Adulteress? The Life and Struggle of Doña Josefa María of Tepoztlan," *Indian Women of Early Mexico,* pp. 145–64.

65. See López Sarrelangue, *La nobleza indígena de Pátzcuaro,* p. 95; and González Hermosillo, "La élite indígena de Cholula," pp. 62–63.

66. See Luis Lira Montt, "La prueba de la hidalguía en el derecho Indiano," *Revista Chilena de Historia del Derecho* (Santiago) 7 (1978): pp. 131–52.

67. Local authorities (the *alcaldes ordinarios* or first instance-judges who were also members of cabildos) were ordered not to interfere or attempt to deprive legitimate caciques of their rights to rulerships. See, for instance, Konetzke, *Colección,* vol. 1, pp. 243–44.

68. In both purity and nobility probanzas, the term *tiempo immemorial* could refer to different spans of time depending on who used it and when. In the eighteenth-century Andes, native communities and individuals normally used it to refer to one or two generations, specifically to the late Hapsburg period or before the Bourbons implemented their modernizing reforms. Scarlett O'Phelan Godoy, "Tiempo inmemorial, tiempo colonial: Un estudio de casos," *Revista*

Ecuatoriana de Historia 4 (1993): pp. 3–20. Doris M. Ladd states that in the late eighteenth century, the term in Mexico referred to forty years, but she does not indicate how she determined its meaning. Ladd, *The Mexican Nobility at Independence, 1780–1826* (Austin: Institute of Latin American Studies, University of Texas, 1976), p. 86.

69. See Amada López de Meneses, "Grandezas y títulos de nobleza a los descendientes de Moctezuma II," *Revista de Indias* 22 (1962): pp. 341–52.

70. Tacuba's cacicazgo is discussed in Fernández de Recas, *Cacicazgos y nobiliario indígena*, p. xvii.

71. See López Sarrelangue, *La nobleza indígena de Pátzcuaro*, pp. 210–11. López Sarrelangue discusses the Tarascan cacicazgo in pp. 169–228.

72. Kellogg, *Law and the Transformation of Aztec Culture*, pp. 160–212.

73. Ibid, p. 87; and Susan Kellogg, "The Woman's Room: Some Aspects of Gender Relations in Tenochtitlan in the Late Pre-Hispanic Period," *Ethnohistory* 42, no. 4 (1995): p. 572.

74. Born 1579, Chimalpahin was a descendant of the pre-Hispanic lesser nobility of Chalco, one of the polities that struggled to remain independent during the Postclassic period. He wrote two major historical works in Náhuatl. The first, the "Relaciones," was mainly a dynastic history of the kingdom of Chalco but also included substantial information about other kingdoms in central Mexico and various other topics. The second, the "Diario," recorded all sorts of events in New Spain from 1589 to 1612, in the pre-Hispanic tradition of annals. For an introduction to Chimalpahin's life and works, see Susan Schroeder, *Chimalpahin and the Kingdom of Chalco* (Tucson: University of Arizona Press, 1991), esp. pp. 7–30. Also see Domingo Francisco de San Antón Muñón Chimalpahin Quauhtlehuanitzin, *Codex Chimalpahin: Society and Politics in Mexico Tenochtitlan, Tlatelolco, Texcoco, Culhuacan, and Other Nahua Altepetl in Central Mexico*, 2 vols., trans. Arthur J. Anderson and Susan Schroeder (Norman and London: University of Oklahoma Press, 1997); and Chimalpahin Quauhtlehuanitzin, *Annals of His Time: Don Domingo de San Antón Muñón Chimalpahin Quauhtlehuanitzin*, ed. and trans. James Lockhart, Susan Schroeder, and Doris Namala (Stanford, CA: Stanford University Press, 2006).

75. The maps that native communities submitted with their relaciones have been studied and published by a number of scholars, including Barbara E. Mundy, *The Mapping of New Spain: Indigenous Cartography and the Maps of the Relaciones Geográficas* (Chicago: The University of Chicago Press, 1996).

76. Carrasco, "La transformación," p. 183. Tezozómoc, a descendant of the rulers of Texcoco, wrote an extensive account of his ancestors' kingdom. See Hernando de Alvarado Tezózomoc, *Crónica mexicana* (Mexico City: Secretaría de Educación Pública, 1944).

77. Schroeder, *Chimalpahin and the Kingdom of Chalco*, p. 24.

78. Bautista Pomar, one of the first mestizos to elaborate a regional history, produced the *Relación de Texcoco* as a response to the government's request for relaciones geográficas. Ixtlilxóchitl also wrote a historical account of Texcoco and its governors, *Historia de la nación chichimeca*. Muñoz Camargo was

responsible for various works, including *Descripción de la ciudad y provincia de Tlaxcala*, a copy of which was submitted to the viceregal government in the 1580s, possibly as a relación geográfica. The historical material from this work provided the author with the basis for his *Historia de Tlaxcala*. Some scholars believe that Muñoz Camargo used the geographic and descriptive components of the *Descripción de la ciudad y provincia de Tlaxcala* for another work whose conclusion or "epilogue" has recently been located and published. See Andrea Martínez Baracs and Carlos Sempat Assadourian, eds., *Suma y epíloga de toda la descripción de Tlaxcala* (Tlaxcala: Universidad de Tlaxcala and Centro de Investigaciones y Estudios Superiores en Antropología Social, 1994), pp. 5–18.

79. Enrique Florescano, "La reconstrucción histórica elaborada por la nobleza indígena y sus descendientes mestizos," in *La memoria y el olvido: Segundo simposio de las mentalidades* (Mexico City: Instituto Nacional de Antropología e Historia, 1985), pp. 11–20.

80. Baracs and Sempat Assadourian, eds., *Suma y epíloga de toda la descripción de Tlaxcala*, p. 230. The text also discusses the origins of the people of Tlaxcala and of other parts of central Mexico, as well as some of the pre-Hispanic founders of the noble lineages and "mayorazgos" of the town of Atligüetza (pp. 239–47).

81. Although other sources claim that Cortés took Texcoco by force, Ixtlilxóchitl the author describes king Ixtlilxóchitl's encounter with the Spaniards as friendly. Fernando de Alva Ixtlilxóchitl, *Historia de la nación chichimeca* (Madrid: Historia 16, 1985), pp. 272–73.

82. Roberto González Echevarría, *Myth and Archive: A Theory of Latin American Narrative* (Durham, NC, and London: Duke University Press, 1998), pp. 43–92, esp. 71–77.

83. Thanks in part to the efforts of Carlos Sigüenza y Góngora, a lawyer and one of the first important creole writers of the Americas, all of the properties of the rulership (titled Cacicazgo Alva y Cortés de San Juan de Teotihuacán) were eventually reconfirmed, and those that had been illegally expropriated were returned. See Munch, *El cacicazgo de San Juan Teotihuacán*, pp. 20–27 and 47–48.

84. See Magnus Mörner, "La infiltración mestiza en los cacicazgos y cabildos de indios (siglos XVI–XVIII)," in *XXXVI Congreso Internacional de Americanistas (España 1964): Actas y Memorias,* vol. 2 (Seville: Congreso Internacional de Americanistas, 1966), pp. 155–60. For examples of cacicazgos that were transferred to Spaniards or their descendants (a process that varied by region and depended in part on demographics), see Fernández de Recas, *Cacicazgos y nobiliario indígena*, pp. 69–81; and Charles Gibson, "The Aztec Aristocracy in Colonial Mexico," *Comparative Studies in Society and History* 2, no. 2 (January 1960): pp. 191–92. In the Valley of Oaxaca, Taylor found only two cases in which native nobles married non-Indians. In one case, a female principal married a Spaniard, and in the other, a mulatto. Taylor, "Cacicazgos coloniales," pp. 6–7.

85. Religious and secular officials initially promoted unions between Spanish males and indigenous noble women precisely because they allowed conquerors

and colonists to acquire native properties, titles, and cacicazgos. See Konetzke, *Colección*, vol. 1, pp. 63–67. For the 1576 law barring mestizos from inheriting cacicazgos, see *Leyes de Indias* (Madrid: Biblioteca Judicial, 1889), p. 72. The law was subsequently qualified so that mestizos descending from male caciques would be able to inherit the title.

86. On the different uses and manipulation of limpieza de sangre status in the greater Puebla area, see Norma Angélica Castillo Palma, "Los estatutos de 'pureza de sangre' como medio de acceso a las élites: el caso de la región de Puebla," in *Círculos de Poder en la Nueva España,* edited by Carmen Castañeda (Mexico City: CIESAS and Grupo Editorial Miguel Angel Porrúa, 1998), pp. 105–29.

87. Mörner, "La infiltración mestiza," pp. 158–59. According to Mörner, the 1576 law regarding the succession of cacicazgos was ignored throughout colonial Spanish America (p. 158).

88. See Juan de Palafox y Mendoza, *Manual de estados y profesiones de la naturaleza del indio* (Mexico City: Coordinación de Humanidades, Universidad Nacional Autónoma de México y Miguel Angel Porrúa, 1986), pp. 55–59 and 60–61.

89. Enrique Florescano provides a good synthesis of recent literature on the primordial titles in "El canon memorioso forjado por los títulos primordiales," *Colonial Latin American Review* 11, no. 2 (2002): pp. 183–230. Also see James Lockhart, *Nahuas and Spaniards: Postconquest Central Mexican History and Philology* (Los Angeles: UCLA Latin American Center Publications, University of California, Los Angeles, 1991), pp. 39–64; and Serge Gruzinski, *La colonización de lo imaginario: Sociedades indígenas y occidentalización en el México español, siglos XVI–XVIII,* trans. Jorge Ferreiro (Mexico City: Fondo de Cultura Económica, 1991), pp. 104–48.

90. See Florescano, "El canon memorioso," pp. 196–97. The Techialoyan codices, a subgroup of the títulos primordiales, were produced in a workshop in Mexico City by a group of indigenous painters who provided their services in surrounding areas, in parts of what today are the states of Hidalgo, Tlaxcala, and Morelos. The literature on the Techialoyan codices is substantial and growing. It includes Donald Robertson, *Mexican Manuscript Painting of the Early Colonial Period,* foreword by Elizabeth Hill Boone (Norman and London: University of Oklahoma Press, 1994), pp. 190–95; Donald Robertson and Martha Barton Robertson, "Techialoyan Manuscripts and Paintings, with a Catalog," in *Handbook of Middle American Indians,* vol. 14, part 3, Guide to Ethnohistorical Sources (Austin: University of Texas Press, 1975), pp. 265–80; María Teresa Jarquín Ortega, "El códice Techialoyan García Granados y las congregaciones en el altiplano central de México," in *De Tlacuilos y escribanos,* ed. Xavier Noguez and Stephanie Wood (Zamora: El Colegio de Michoacán and El Colegio Mexiquense, 1998), pp. 49–58; Stephanie Wood, "El problema de la historicidad de Títulos y los códices del grupo Techialoyan," in *De tlacuilos y escribanos: Estudios sobre documentos indígenas coloniales del centro de México,* ed. Xavier Noguez and Stephanie Gail Wood (Zamora: El Colegio de Michoacán, 1998), pp. 167–221.

91. For examples from the Cuernavaca region, see Haskett, *Indigenous Rulers*, pp. 156–58.

92. See Gruzinski, *La colonización de lo imaginario,* pp. 126–28; Lockhart, *Nahuas and Spaniards,* pp. 57–64; Florescano, *Memory, Myth, and Time,* pp. 115–20; and Robert Haskett, "El legendario don Toribio en los títulos primordiales de Cuernavaca," in *De Tlacuilos y escribanos,* ed. Xavier Noguez and Stephanie Gail Wood (Zamora, Michoacán: El Colegio de Michoacán, 1998), pp. 137–66. The extent to which Christianity and Spanish genealogical formulas influenced native ideas of community and lineage differed by region and social group. For example, according to Matthew Restall, late colonial títulos primordiales produced by Mayan elites downplayed the significance of the Spanish conquest and stressed continuities between the pre-Hispanic and colonial communal forms. See Matthew Restall, *Seven Myths of the Spanish Conquest* (Oxford and New York: Oxford University Press, 2003), p. 122.

93. The royal decree, which was sent to religious and secular officials in the viceroyalties of New Spain and Peru, is reproduced in Richard Konetzke, *Colección de documentos para la historia de la formación social de Hispanoamérica 1493–1810,* vol. 3, bk. 1 (Madrid: Consejo Superior de Investigaciones Científicas, 1962), pp. 66–69.

94. Archivo General de la Nación (hereafter AGN), Bienes Nacionales, vol. 553, exp. 8. The Spanish term *capellanía* combined elements of the English chaplaincy (in which priests received fixed salaries in return for seeing to the religious needs of the corporation or other group whom they served) and chantry (a pious work). In the latter, the priest or chaplain held a stipulated number of masses per year for the benefit of the patron or founder and in return received revenues from the pious work. See John Frederick Schwaller, *The Church and Clergy in Sixteenth-Century Mexico* (Albuquerque: University of New Mexico Press, 1997), p. 111.

95. Ibid, fol. 60v. For a cacicazgo case involving the issue of indigenous purity and accusations of black ancestry, see AGN, Tierras 224 (2).

96. AGN, General de Parte, vol. 37, doc. 71, fols. 92–92v: "El Virrey manda que se le guarden las exempciones y los privilegios con el de Armas a Ursula García Cortés y Moctezuma y sus hijos, que conforme a sus calidades de caciques principales y cristianos viejos le corresponden," 1751.

97. See, for example, Mörner; *La corona española y los foráneos en los pueblos de indios;* and Christopher H. Lutz, *Santiago de Guatemala, 1541–1773: City, Caste, and the Colonial Experience* (Norman: University of Oklahoma Press, 1994), pp. 45–78 and 79–112.

CHAPTER 5

1. See José Antonio Maravall, *Las comunidades de Castilla* (Madrid: Alianza Editorial, 1994).

2. In the late 1520s, various conquerors tried to convince the crown to allow them to make native people into their personal vassals, including the *comendador* Diego de Ordás. See Enrique Otte, "Nueve Cartas de Diego de Ordás,"

Historia Mexicana 14 (1964): pp. 102–29; and AGI, Indiferente 737, n. 3. Debates over the institution of the encomienda during the 1520s and 1530s are discussed in the classic work by Silvio A. Zavala, *La encomienda indiana*, 3rd ed. (Mexico City: Editorial Porrúa, 1992), pp. 40–73.

3. Robert Himmerich y Valencia, *The Encomenderos of New Spain, 1521–1555* (Austin: University of Texas Press, 1991), p. 12.

4. The term *wages of conquest* is borrowed from Hugo G. Nuttini, *The Wages of Conquest: The Mexican Aristocracy in the Context of Western Aristocracies* (Ann Arbor: University of Michigan Press, 1995).

5. Although many encomiendas survived well into the seventeenth century —and in places such as Yucatán until the end of the colonial period—during the second half of the sixteenth century, some began to be repossessed by royal authorities. Zavala, *La encomienda indiana*, pp. 101–8. Information on seventeenth-century encomiendas in the Puebla-Tlaxcala region can be found in AGI, México 1952; and AGI, México 1953.

6. See the 1543 royal decree sent to Viceroy Mendoza. Konetzke, *Colección*, vol. 1, pp. 220–21. And for examples of royal grants (namely, pensions and stipends derived from native tribute) given to the families and descendants of the conquerors and first colonists, see AGI, México 1.

7. Colonists used various types of documents to claim royal grants, including *informaciones de oficio y parte* and *informaciones de méritos y calidades*. These two genres were similar to the reports of merits and services but stressed different types of services rendered to the crown or community. Examples of informaciones (or relaciones) de méritos can be found in AGI, Indiferente 193; and of informaciones de oficio y parte, in AGI, México 599, 1064–67, and 1088–1100. Also see AGI, México 1952 and 1953, which contain royal decrees regarding encomiendas, grants, pensions, and so forth.

8. Various laws regarding the maintenance of archives for the children of conquerors were issued in the second half of the sixteenth century. See, for example, the 1591 royal decree sent to Mexico's viceroy, in AGI, México 1064, leg. 2.

9. Some of the reports submitted by Juan de Cervantes Casaús's descendants can be found in AGI, Patronato 62, r. 1; AGI Patronato 62, r. 4; and AGI, Indiferente 113, n. 155.

10. See Jesús Larios Martín, "Ciencias complementarias de la nobiliaria," in *Apuntes de nobiliaria y nociones de genealogía y heráldica*, ed. Francisco de Cadenas y Allende et al. (Madrid: Ediciones Hidalguía, 1960), p. 29; Lira Montt, "La prueba de la hidalguía," pp. 131–32, and Marqués de Siete Iglesias, "¿Qué es nobleza de sangre?" in *Apuntes de nobiliaria y nociones de genealogía y heráldica*, pp. 105–6.

11. See Jesús Larios Martín, *Hidalguía e hidalgos de Indias* (Madrid: Asociación de hidalgos a fuero de España, 1958), pp. 4–5; and Richard Konetzke, "La formación de la nobleza en Indias," *Estudios Americanos* (Seville) 3, no. 10 (1951): pp. 332–39. And for examples of coats of arms granted to New Spain's conquerors, see AGI, Patronato 169, n. 1, r. 3: Royal decree granting Gonzalo Rodríguez, a vecino in Puebla, a coat of arms because of his services in the conquests of Mexico and the province of Pánuco, 1538; and AGI, Patronato 169,

n. 1, r. 5: Royal decree granting Alonso Galeote, a vecino of Puebla, a coat of arms for his services in the taking of Mexico City and in the conquest of the province of Pánuco, 1538.

12. Nuttini, *The Wages of Conquest*, p. 164.

13. AGI, México 168: Letter by various conquerors and settlers of New Spain, February 17, 1564.

14. AGI, México 1, n. 275; AGI, Indiferente 1530, n. 7.

15. See, for example, AGI, México 168: Letter from García Aguilar to the crown, 1570. García de Aguilar's encomienda was inherited by his son-in-law Felipe de Arellano. His eighteenth-century descendants and their mayorazgo carried the name Ramírez de Arellano. See Mariano Fernández de Echeverría y Veytia, *Historia de la fundación de la ciudad de la Puebla de los Ángeles,* vol. 1 (Puebla: Imprenta Labor, 1931), p. 9; and AGI, México 208, r. 3.

16. Gonzalo Gómez de Cervantes, *La vida económica y social de Nueva España al finalizar el siglo XVI* (México: Antigua Librería Robredo, de José Porrúa e Hijos, 1944), esp. pp. 77–79.

17. Bernard Lavallé, *Las promesas ambiguas: Criollismo colonial en los Andes* (Lima: Instituto Riva-Agüero de la Pontífica Universidad Católica del Perú, 1993), p. 23.

18. For earlier decrees restricting emigration to the Americas to pure Old Christians, see AGI, Indiferente 419, leg. 7, fols. 763v–764; AGI, Indiferente 420, leg. 8, fols. 92v–93r. At least until the 1520s, the crown occasionally granted temporary travel permits to individuals that fell under the prohibited categories, many of them merchants. See AGI, Indiferente 421, leg. 11, fol. 139; and AGI, Indiferente 420, leg. 10, fols. 1v–2r.

19. See, for example, AGI, México 1064, leg. 2, fol. 155; and the 1539 order *(real provisión)* by Charles V banning Jews, Moors, and conversos and the children and grandchildren of people who had been burned or reconciled from going to and residing in Spanish America. Konetzke, *Colección,* vol. 1, pp. 192–93.

20. Luis Lira Montt, "El estatuto de *limpieza de sangre* en el derecho Indiano," in *XI Congreso del Instituto Internacional del Derecho Indiano* (Buenos Aires: Instituto de Investigación de Historia del Derecho, 1997), p. 39.

21. AHN, Inquisición de México, libro 1050, fol. 75: Letter from Inquisitor Peralta, 1604.

22. Some of the conversos who arrived in New Spain later went to the Philippines, which offered many commercial opportunities and, until the 1590s, a relatively lax religious environment. See Eva Alexandra Uchmany, "Criptojudíos y cristianos nuevos en las filipinas durante el siglo XVI," in *The Sepharadi and Oriental Jewish Heritage Studies,* ed. Issachar Ben-Ami (Jerusalem: Magnes Press, Hebrew University, 1982), pp. 85–103.

23. See John Tate Lanning, "Legitimacy and *Limpieza de Sangre* in the Practice of Medicine in the Spanish Empire," *Jahrbuch für Geschichte von Staat, Wirtschaft, und Gesellschaft Lateinamerikas* 4 (1967): p. 43. There is a substantial scholarship on Jews and conversos in colonial Spanish America. For Mexico, the literature includes Alfonso Toro, *Los judíos en la Nueva España,*

2nd ed. (Mexico City: Fondo de Cultura Económica, 1993); Alicia Gojman Goldberg, *Los conversos en la Nueva España* (Mexico City: Universidad Nacional Autónoma de México, n.d.); Seymour B. Liebman, *The Jews in New Spain: Faith, Flame, and the Inquisition* (Coral Gables, FL: University of Miami Press, 1970); Eva Alexandra Uchmany, *La vida entre el judaísmo y el cristianismo en la Nueva España, 1580–1606* (Mexico City: Archivo General de la Nación and Fondo de Cultura Económica, 1992); Stanley M. Hordes, "The Inquisition as Economic and Political Agent: The Campaign of the Mexican Holy Office against the Crypto-Jews in the Mid-Seventeenth Century," *The Americas* 39, no. 1 (1982): pp. 23–38; and Solange Alberro, "Crypto-Jews and the Mexican Holy Office in the Seventeenth Century," in *The Jews and the Expansion of Europe to the West 1450–1800*, ed. Paolo Bernardini and Norman Fiering (New York and Oxford: Berghahn Books, 2001), pp. 172–85.

24. AGN, Inquisición, vol. 189, exp. 17.

25. Fray Agustín Salucio, *Discurso sobre los estatutos,* fol. 2v.

26. For example, the crown granted the audiencias and cabildos of Guatemala and Quito the power to determine the limpieza status of candidates for public office. See J. Joaquin Pardo, ed., *Prontuario de Reales Cédulas 1529–1599* (Guatemala: Unión Tipográfica, 1941), p. 14; AGI, Indiferente 424, leg. 22, fols. 262v–263 and 406r–v.

27. AGI, México 280. Probanza of Francisco Gutiérrez de León, priest and vecino of Puebla, April 14, 1539.

28. AGI, México 280. The precentor was in charge of the music provided during cathedral services. Not a few probanzas de limpieza de sangre for Spaniards in Mexico were requested by their relatives in Spain. See, for example, AGI, México 2606; AGN, Inquisición, vol. 194, exp. 3; AGI, México 121, r. 1.

29. AGI, México 282.

30. AGI, México 281. For more examples of informaciones de limpieza de sangre made by alcaldes or corregidores in Spain for people going to New Spain or already there, see AGN, Inquisición, vol. 194, exp. 3; John Carter Brown Library, Rare Book Collection, Libro de Informaciones (hereafter JCBL/LI), vol. 1, fols. 17–64; JCBL/LI, vol. 1, fols. 243–74; JCBL/LI, vol. 1, fols. 331–50; and JCBL/LI, vol. 1, fols. 685–720.

31. AGI, México 280. The volume also contains a 1552 letter sent to the crown by Mexico City's cathedral chapter requesting that all who were named to it be Old Christians.

32. AGI, México 2606. A prebend was a stipend or income from a position, usually ecclesiastical. Prebends were provided by a cathedral or church to clergymen as a kind of payment for their services or simply as an honorary recognition.

33. AGI, México 121, r. 1.

34. AGI, México 121, r. 1. The volume also includes the información submittted by Miguel de Asurcia, another applicant for the title of royal scribe at the turn of the sixteenth century.

35. See Schwaller, *The Church and Clergy in Sixteenth-Century Mexico,* pp. 81–109.

36. For examples of informaciones de oficio y parte with limpieza de sangre information, see AGI, México 241, n. 4, fols. 1–22: Información de oficio y parte of the priest Bartolomé de Aguayo, 1642; and AGI, México 241, n. 11: Información de oficio y parte of the priest Francisco de Castillo Milán, 1644. Requesting a benefice in the cathedral chapter of Mexico or Puebla, Milán presented a report of his merits and information regarding his legitimacy, limpieza de sangre, and other qualifications.

37. AHN, Inquisición de México, libro 1050: Letter from the Mexican Inquisition to the Suprema, November 1604.

38. Limpieza records submitted by candidates to the Franciscan Order's novitiate in Puebla de los Ángeles can be consulted at the John Carter Brown Library, Rare Book Collection, Libros de Informaciones, 14 volumes. Mexico's Archivo General de la Nación has hundreds of limpieza documents submitted by candidates to the Jesuit Order in New Spain from the early seventeenth century until 1767, the year that the Jesuits were expelled from Spanish America. See AGN, Archivo Histórico de Hacienda, vols. 11–15, 317, and 636–38; and AGN, Jesuitas, vols. I-15, I-24, II-10, II-18, II-33, IV-2, IV-24, IV-25, IV-37, and IV-59.

39. According to Domínguez Ortiz, crypto-Judaism was perceived as a serious problem in Spanish America only when cristãos novos began to have a strong presence there. *Los judeoconversos en España y América* (1971), p. 134.

40. Seymour B. Liebman, ed., *The Enlightened: The Writings of Luis de Carvajal, el Mozo*, trans. Seymour B. Leibman (Coral Gables, FL: University of Miami Press 1967), pp. 22–23.

41. See AGN, Inquisición, vol. 77, exp. 34, fols. 191v–194v; and AGN, Judicial, vol. 5, exp. 5.

42. The Suprema sent colonial Inquisition tribunals frequent reminders of the purity requirement for wives of familiars. See, for example, AHN, Inquisición de México, libro 1049, fols. 591–591v; and AHN, Inquisición de México, libro 1051, fol. 58.

43. AHN, Inquisición de México, libro 1051, fol. 47.

44. For example, in 1658, Martín García Rendón was denied a habit by the Franciscan Order because of witness declarations that he was a descendant of Pablo de la Cruz, who had been reconciled in Spain. Hoping that a more thorough investigation would help restore his family's honor, he requested a probanza from the Inquisition. AHN, Inquisición de México, leg. 2276.

45. Herzog, *Defining Nations*, p. 65.

46. See Stafford Poole, "Criollos and Criollismo," in *Encyclopedia of Mexico: History, Society and Culture*, ed. Michael S. Werner (Chicago: Fitzroy Dearborn, 1997), p. 371.

47. Lavallé, *Las promesas ambiguas*, p. 20.

48. Himmerich y Valencia, *The Encomenderos of New Spain*, p. 63.

49. AGI, México 343.

50. See José F. de la Peña, *Oligarquía y propiedad en Nueva España (1550–1624)* (Mexico City: Fondo de Cultura Económica, 1983), pp. 149–51. Puebla's conquerors and first colonists also underwent a social and political decline, but it was neither as sudden nor as sharp as that of their counterparts in the capital.

Some members of Puebla's more traditional families, those that had settled there in the 1530s, continued to have an important presence in municipal government at the end of the sixteenth century and, indeed, throughout the colonial period. For the first half of the colonial period, see de la Peña, *Oligarquía y propiedad en la Nueva España*, pp. 162–80; and for the second, Gustavo Rafael Alfaro Ramírez, "El reclutamiento oligárquico en el cabildo de la Puebla de los Ángeles, 1665–1765" (master's thesis, Universidad Autónoma de Puebla, Facultad de Filosofía y Letras, 1994).

51. AGI, México 295: "Relación del estado en que se hayan las cosas eclesiásticas en la Nueva España," report sent by Pedro Ramírez, 1606.

52. AGI, México 293; and AGI, México 2606.

53. Archivo del Ayuntamiento de Puebla (Puebla), Actas de Cabildo [hereafter AAPAC], vol. 15, doc. 89, fols. 52–53v; AGI, México 138, r. 2. In the latter document, a fourth category was deployed: *gachupines* (also *cachupines*). Of uncertain origins, the word here referred to friars who were born in Spain and had taken the habit there but were trying to monopolize religious offices and benefices in Mexico. Eventually the word became a derogatory name for Spaniards. On lingering tensions between creole friars and those born in Spain over the alternativa, see AGI, México 348: Letter from the bishop of Puebla, 1658.

54. See AGI, México 1064, libro. 2: Royal decree of 1591.

55. Government officials were especially concerned that creoles would forge alliances with blacks, mulattos, and other "uprooted" individuals. For example, at one point Mexico City's audiencia even supported giving encomiendas to all the descendants of the conquerors and first colonists because it feared that otherwise they "might unite with mulattoes, blacks and other lost people and attempt some kind of movement." AGI, Indiferente 1530, n. 7: "Parecer del Virrey y la Audiencia de México sobre el estado de los repartimientos y de las encomiendas en dicha Audiencia," 1597.

56. On European theories of colonial degeneration due to climate, see Lavallé, *Las promesas ambiguas*, pp. 45–61.

57. Juan López de Velasco, *Geografía y descripción universal de las Indias*, vol. 248 of *Biblioteca de Autores Españoles*, ed. Don Marcos Jiménez de la Espada (Madrid: Ediciones Atlas, 1971), pp. 13–20.

58. Gregorio García, *Origen de los indios del Nuevo Mundo* (Mexico City: Fondo de Cultura Económica, 1981).

59. Lavallé, *Las promesas ambiguas*, pp. 50–59.

60. Lavallé, *Las promesas ambiguas*, pp. 48–50; and Stuart B. Schwartz, "Colonial Identities and the *Sociedad de Castas*," *Colonial Latin America Review* 4, no. 1 (1995): p. 194.

61. Stoler, *Race and the Education of Desire*, p. 32.

62. AGI, México 347.

63. AGI, México 1064, libro 2.

64. See Juan de Cárdenas, *Problemas y secretos maravillosos de las Indias* (Madrid: Alianza Editorial, 1988 [1591]), esp. pp. 208–9 and 217. Also refer to Jorge Cañizares-Esguerra, "New World, New Stars: Patriotic Astrology and the Invention of Indian and Creole Bodies in Colonial Spanish America 1600–1650," *American Historical Review* 104, no. 1 (1999): p. 60.

65. See Brackette Williams, "Classification Systems Revisited: Kinship, Caste, Race, and Nationality as the Flow of Blood and the Spread of Rights," in *Naturalizing Power: Essays in Feminist Cultural Analysis*, ed. Sylvia Yanagisako and Carol Delaney (New York and London: Routledge, 1995), pp. 201–36.

66. See AGI, México 2606; AGI, México, leg. 295; and AGI México 822.

67. Lavallé, *Las promesas ambiguas*, pp. 59–61.

68. Solórzano Pereira, *Política Indiana*, vol. 1, pp. 442–43.

CHAPTER 6

1. See, for example, Patricia Seed, *To Love, Honor, and Obey in Colonial Mexico: Conflicts Over Marriage Choice, 1574–1821* (Stanford: Stanford University Press, 1988), p. 251 n. 25; and Cope, *The Limits of Racial Domination*, p. 24. Note that in certain places, parish books for people of mixed ancestry were never kept, and in those that they were (mainly in larger cities), the timing varied.

2. AHN, Inquisición, libro 1266. The word *mozárabe* eventually came to designate Christians who had lived under Muslim rule (especially in Toledo) and adopted aspects of Islamic culture.

3. Francisco Domínguez y Compañy notes that in sixteenth-century Havana and other Spanish American towns, the children of Spanish males, even if classified as mestizo or mulatto, were considered vecinos, and some were able to access land and even political posts. Domínguez y Compañy, "La condición de vecino," pp. 713–14.

4. Of the remaining fifty-four, forty-four had Castilian wives and ten were single. See "Relación de los vecinos que había en le Ciudad de los Ángeles el año de 1534," *Epistolario de Nueva España*, vol. 3, pp. 137–40.

5. For example, in the 1534 report, Pedro Gallardo, Cristóbal Martín, and Cristóbal de Morales were all listed as married to women "from the land." When their (legitimate) children were registered in the Sagrario's baptismal records, however, no mention of their mothers being indigenous was made, and they were not classified as mestizos. Academia Mexicana de Genealogía y Heráldica, Libros de Bautismos de Españoles del Sagrario de Puebla (hereafter LBESP), vol. 1, fols. 1r, 4r–5v, and 20r. The same pattern of classification can be found in the Sagrario for the children of other conquerors and vecinos who were married to native women.

6. The first time the category of mestizo(a) was used in the Sagrario's baptismal records was on August 3, 1544. Significantly, the word appears crossed out in the following manner: ~~mestiça~~. The entry was recorded for the daughter of Benito Mendez and his wife, who is not named, but presumably was indigenous. The next time the term appeared was in the year 1550. LBESP, vol. 1 (1545–91), fols. 1v and 10.

7. AHN, Inquisición de México, libro 1049, fols. 54r–57v: Report from Pedro de Vega regarding the population of Mexico City, Puebla, and other cities, 1595. The report was based on a census taken in New Spain in 1592. For Mexico City, Vega estimated a population of 60,000, consisting of 40,000 lay Spaniards; 2,000 religious (friars and nuns); 400 clergymen; 1,100 students;

2,000 mestizos; 1,500 free blacks and mulattos; 10,000 slaves; and 3,000 "foreigners." The estimate for the Spanish population was based on a count of male heads of households times eight (assumed to be the average number of people in a Spanish household, including parents, children, and servants).

8. See AAPAC, vol. 5, doc. 167; AAPAC, vol. 6, docs. 117, 124, 264; and AAPAC, vol. 8, doc. 97. In 1556, the city council ordered "mestizos, mulatos, indios," and free blacks not to live in the city or occupy any of its lots without first obtaining special licenses. Biblioteca Nacional de Antropología e Historia (Mexico City), Microfilm Collection (hereafter BNAHMC), Serie Puebla, roll 81, fols. 47v–48.

9. The Sagrario's baptismal records are consistent with Peter Boyd-Bowman's study of African slaves in mid-sixteenth century Puebla, in which he concluded that few had surnames. Boyd-Bowman, "Negro Slaves in Early Colonial Mexico," *The Americas* 26, no. 2 (1969), p. 145.

10. LBESP, vol. 1, fol. 30r. While the terms *mulata* and *negra* appear relatively soon, that of *india* begins to be used only in the last decades of the sixteenth century and even then only sporadically. See, for example, LBESP, vol. 1, fol. 131v; and LBESP, vol. 3, fol. 27v.

11. Elizabeth Anne Kuznesof stresses the same point in her study of parish records from sixteenth-century Lima and Veracruz. "Ethnic and Gender Influences on 'Spanish' Creole Society in Colonial Spanish America," *Colonial Latin American Review* 4, no. 1 (1995): p. 164.

12. AGI, México 168: Letter from Gonzalo Díaz de Vargas to the Spanish king, May 2, 1556. My translation and interpolations.

13. See AGI, México 280: Letter from Fray Cruzate requesting royal funds to establish a home for the daughters of Spanish males and indigenous women, June 12, 1549; AGI, Indiferente 427, leg. 30, fols. 73r–73v: Decree ordering New Spain's viceroy and royal audiencia to assign tutors to orphaned mestizo boys and girls and to look out for their well-being, February 18, 1555; and AGI, México 1064, leg. 2, fols. 136–136v: Decree to the viceroy of New Spain, requesting a report on the status of the monastery for orphaned young mestizos, March 3, 1585. Also refer to Antonio F. García-Abásolo, *Martín Enríquez y la Reforma de 1568 en Nueva España* (Sevilla: Excelentísima Diputación Provincial de Sevilla, 1983), pp. 212–57; and *Leyes de Indias*, vol. 2 (Madrid: Biblioteca Judicial, 1889), p. 128.

14. Charles Gibson, "The Identity of Diego Muñoz Camargo," *Hispanic American Historical Review* 30, no. 2 (1950): pp. 199–205.

15. Ibid., p. 207.

16. For a listing of colonial parish records and the books kept by year, refer to David J. Robinson, ed., *Research Inventory of the Mexican Collection of Colonial Parish Registers* (Salt Lake City: University of Utah Press, 1980).

17. Eva Alexandra Uchmany, "El mestizaje en el siglo XVI novohispano," *Historia Mexicana* 37, no. 1 (1987): pp. 31–34.

18. BNAHMC, Serie Puebla, roll 81, fol. 13v. A 1590 report by Viceroy Velasco (the son) described the Spaniards arriving on every fleet as a miserable lot and as thieves with many immoral habits. Velasco indicated that he was establishing

a rural police force or Hermandad to deal with all the "lost" people of the vice-royalty, "white and black." AGI, México 22, n. 24.

19. Andrea Martínez Baracs and Carlos Sempat Assadourian, eds., *Suma y epíloga de toda la descripción de Tlaxcala,* p. 169.

20. Some guilds, such as those for silk producers, were closed to blacks, but others allowed them membership and some mobility. The latter included the guilds for gold beaters, hat makers, glove makers, needle makers, candle makers, and leather dressers (the last two accepted them as masters). Robert LaDon Brady, "The Emergence of a Negro Class in Mexico, 1524–1640," (PhD diss., University of Iowa, 1965), pp. 65 and 83. Also see Richard Konetzke, "Ordenanzas de gremios durante la época colonial," in *Estudios de Historia Social de España* (Madrid: Consejo Superior de Investigaciones Científicas, 1949), pp. 483–524.

21. BNAHMC, Serie Puebla, roll 81, fols. 52–52v and roll 98, fols. 89–89v.

22. Cope, *The Limits of Racial Domination,* pp. 18–24.

23. In 1536, the crown made the succession of encomiendas limited to individuals of legitimate birth, which affected many of the children of Spanish–Indian unions. Thirteen years later, it barred mestizos from acquiring native labor through the repartimiento and from serving in royal or public posts. Richard Konetzke, "Estado y Sociedad en las Indias," *Estudios Americanos* 3, no. 8 (1951): p. 57.

24. Mörner, *Race Mixture in the History of Latin America,* pp. 42–43; C. E. Marshall, "The Birth of the Mestizo in New Spain," *Hispanic American Historical Review* 19 (1939): pp. 160–84; and Richard Konetzke, "El mestizaje y su importancia en el desarrollo de la población hispano-americana durante la época colonial," *Revista de Indias* 7, no. 24 (April-June, 1946): p. 230.

25. AGI, México 1064, leg. 2.

26. See, for example, Aguirre Beltrán, *La población negra de México,* pp. 153–54; Ben Vinson III, *Bearing Arms for his Majesty: The Free-colored Militia in Colonial Mexico* (Stanford, CA: Stanford University Press, 2001), p. 3; and Robert Jackson, "Race/caste and the Creation and Meaning of Identity in Colonial Spanish America," *Revista de Indias* 55, no. 203 (1995): pp. 150–73.

27. Among the Spanish writers who linked the Indians to the Jews were Diego Durán, José de Acosta, and Gregorio García. The theory was popular in the Atlantic world as a whole. See Richard H. Popkin, "The Rise and Fall of the Jewish Indian Theory," in *Menasseh ben Israel and his World,* ed. Yosef Kaplan, Henry Méchoulan, and Richard H. Hopkin (Leiden, Netherlands: E. J. Brill, 1989), pp. 63–82.

28. Fray Antonio Vázquez de Espinosa, *Descripción de la Nueva España en el Siglo XVII* (Mexico City: Editorial Patria, 1944), pp. 49–50. The similarity between the *i* and the *j,* as well as between the *u* and the *n,* in early modern manuscripts has led many a reader to confuse the word *indio* for *judio,* and vice versa.

29. Ibid., pp. 41–45. Vázquez de Espinosa suggested that the Indians descended from Issachar, who in the Bible (Genesis, chap. 49) is likened to a domesticated beast of burden ("a strong ass"), satisfied with a pleasant piece of land and willing to become a slave to the Canaanites.

30. AHN, Inquisición de México, libro 1047, fols. 430–34: Correspondence from the Mexican Inquisition to the Suprema, November 5, 1576.

31. *Diccionario de Autoridades,* vol. II (Madrid: Editorial Gredos, 1990 [1732]), pp. 141 and 204.

32. AHN, Inquisición, libro 1051, fols. 223–224v: Letter to the Suprema from Dr. Francisco Bazan de Albornoz and Dr. Juan Gutiérrez Flores regarding heretic Indians ("indios herejes"), Mexico, 1619. The word *ladino* had first been used in the Iberian Peninsula to refer to Muslims and "foreigners" who were able to use the Castilian language so well that Spaniards were not able to tell their accents apart from their own. The word was also eventually applied to Jews and in particular to the language spoken by the Sephardim. In the colonial context, depending on the region, it referred to Hispanicized native people, mestizos, or blacks and others who were fluent in Spanish and had adopted other elements of Castilian culture but were not quite considered Spaniards. On the term's meanings in Spain, see Covarrubias, *Tesoro de la lengua Castellana,* p. 697; and Corominas, *Diccionario crítico etimológico,* vol. I, pp. 9–10.

33. AGI, México 347.

34. Francisco Morales, O.F.M., *Ethnic and Social Background of the Franciscan Friars in Seventeenth-Century Mexico* (Washington, DC: Academy of American Franciscan History, 1973), p. 16.

35. Jerónimo de Mendieta, *Historia eclesiástica indiana,* vol. II, *Biblioteca de Autores Españoles,* vol. 261 (Madrid: Ediciones Atlas, 1973), pp. 59–61.

36. See Gruzinski, *La colonización de lo imaginario,* pp. 146–83, esp. 150–57 and 170–72; and Inga Clendinnen, "Ways to the Sacred: Reconstructing 'Religion' in Sixteenth Century Mexico," *History and Anthropology* 5 (1990): pp. 105–41.

37. The term is borrowed from Gruzinski, *La colonización de lo imaginario,* p. 156.

38. See Herzog, *Defining Nations,* pp. 43–63, esp. 44–45.

39. García, *Origen de los indios del Nuevo Mundo,* pp. 79–128. The book was first published in Valencia, Spain, in 1607.

40. García, *Origen de los indios del Nuevo Mundo,* p. 102.

41. AHN, Inquisición 1050, fol. 341. The word *nación* was also sometimes used to refer to social groups (such as peasants or soldiers), women, and members of a kingdom (as in the "Castilian nation"). In the late 1700s, it started to be used in a more modern political territorial sense (as in nación española), but even then, several of the term's older connotations were still in use. Pedro Álvarez de Miranda, *Palabras e ideas: El léxico de la Ilustración temprana española (1680–1760)* (Madrid: Real Academia Española, 1992), pp. 211–26. Also see Monica Quijada, "¿Qué nación? Dinámicas y dicotomías de la nación en el imaginario hispanoamericana del siglo XIX," in *Imaginar la nación,* ed. François-Xavier Guerra and Monica Quijada (Münster and Hamburg: Lit, 1994), p. 22. Nicholas Hudson points out that in early modern Europe, the concepts of race and nation both derived from "lineage" or "stock." Hudson, "From 'Nation' to 'Race': The Origin of Racial Classification in Eighteenth-Century Thought," *Eighteenth-Century Studies* 29, no. 3 (1996): pp. 247–64.

42. García, *Origen de los indios del Nuevo Mundo,* p. 73.

43. As Stoler has observed, when sexual symbols are used to represent colonial domination, they are more than metaphors and not just about gender but about other social relations, including class and race. See Stoler, "Carnal Knowledge," pp. 54–55.

44. *Cartas de Indias* (Madrid: Ministerio de Fomento, 1877), p. 299.

45. Robin Blackburn, "The Old World Background to European Colonial Slavery," *William and Mary Quarterly* 54, no. 1 (1997): pp. 70 and 73–75.

46. According to James H. Sweet, antiblack imagery and the association of "blackness" and slavery in Spain surfaced as early as the eighth century, when Muslim rulers introduced increasing numbers of sub-Saharan African slaves into the peninsula. Sweet, "The Iberian Roots of American Racist Thought," pp. 145–50. Also see David B. Davis, *Challenging the Boundaries of Slavery* (Cambridge, MA, and London: Harvard University Press, 2003), pp. 7–8. And on blacks in southern Iberia, see Ruth Pike, "Sevillian Society in the Sixteenth Century: Slaves and Freedmen," *Hispanic American Historical Review* 7, no. 3 (1967): pp. 344–59.

47. "White slaves" (*esclavos blancos*) included Muslims, Berbers, and Jews who had had been captured in North Africa. Although they were initially allowed in Spanish America, Spanish kings issued various decrees, starting in 1501, which prohibited the practice. Aguirre Beltrán attributed the decision to fears that the presence of Muslims and other "infidels" in the colonies would undermine the Christianizing mission. Aguirre Beltrán, *La población negra*, pp. 104 and 156.

48. See Matthew Restall, "Black Conquistadors: Armed Africans in Early Spanish America," *The Americas* 57, no. 2 (2000): pp. 167–205; Restall, *Seven Myths of the Spanish Conquest*, pp. 44–63; and Domínguez y Compañy, "La condición de vecino," pp. 713–14. For vecino titles granted to blacks in Puebla during the 1530s and 1540s, see AAPAC, vols. 1 and 4.

49. See Pagden, *Fall of Natural Man*, p. 33; William D. Phillips Jr., "The Old World Background of Slavery in the Americas," in *Slavery and the Rise of the Atlantic System*, ed. Barbara L. Solow (Cambridge, MA: Cambridge University Press, 1991), pp. 43–61; John Thornton, *Africa and Africans in the Making of the Atlantic World, 1400–1800* (Cambridge: Cambridge University Press, 1998), pp. 13–125; and Peter Wade, "Negros, indígenas e identidad nacional en Colombia," in *Imaginar la nación*, ed. François-Xavier Guerra and Monica Quijada (Münster and Hamburg: Lit, 1994), pp. 259–61.

50. Juan de Solórzano y Pereira, *De Indiarum Iure. Liber III: De retentione Indiarum*, ed. C. Baciero et al. (Madrid: Consejo Superior de Investigaciones Científicas, 1994), pp. 412–63, esp. 429–31.

51. Henrique Urbano, ed., *Tradición y modernidad en los Andes* (Cusco, Peru: Centro de Estudios Regionales Andinos, "Bartolomé de las Casas," 1992), pp. xxxiv–xxxv.

52. See, for example, the 1580 report by the viceroy Martín Enríquez, who warned his successor of the need for labor in the mines. *Instrucciones que los virreyes de Nueva España dejaron a sus sucesores* (Mexico: Imprenta Imperial, 1867), p. 245.

53. Letter from the archbishop of Mexico to the king, June 30, 1560, in Paso y Troncoso, *Epistolario de Nueva España*, vol. 9 (Mexico City: Antigua Librería Robredo, de José Porrúa e Hijos, 1939–42), pp. 53–55.

54. See Albornoz, "Tratado sobre la esclavitud," in *Biblioteca de Autores Españoles*, vol. 65 (Madrid: M. Rivadeneyra, 1873), pp. 231–33; and *Biblioteca de Autores Españoles*, vol. 65, pp. lxxxvi–lxxxviii. For more on Spanish opponents of black slavery, see Colin A. Palmer, *Slaves of the White God: Blacks in Mexico, 1570–1650* (Cambridge, MA: Harvard University Press, 1976), pp. 167–72.

55. See Enriqueta Vila Vilar, *Hispano-América y el comercio de esclavos* (Seville: Escuela de Estudios Hispanoamericanos, 1977), esp. pp. 23–91.

56. James H. Sweet, *Recreating Africa: Culture, Kinship, and Religion in the African-Portuguese World, 1441–1770* (Chapel Hill and London: University of North Carolina Press, 2003), pp. 3, 15–19, and 87–96. As of the 1580s, slaves increasingly derived from Central Africa, particularly, Kongo and Angola.

57. García-Abásolo, *Martín Enríquez y la Reforma de 1568*, p. 261.

58. The Spanish began to use the curse of Ham to explain black slavery in the last third of the sixteenth century; the Portuguese began to do so a century earlier. See Palmer, *Slaves of the White God*, p. 39; and Russell-Wood, "Before Columbus," p. 154. And for a discussion of the uses of the biblical myth in broader Europe, see Benjamin Braude, "The Sons of Noah and the Construction of Ethnic and Geographical Identities in the Medieval and Early Modern Periods," *William and Mary Quarterly* 54, no. 1 (1997): pp. 103–42.

59. See, for example, AGI, Indiferente 425, leg. 24, fol. 13r.

60. Fray Prudencio de Sandoval, *Historia de la vida y hechos del Emperador Carlos V*. Vol 82 of *Biblioteca de Autores Españoles* (Madrid: Ediciones Atlas, 1955 [1606]), p. 319.

61. Sandoval, *Historia de la vida y hechos del Emperador Carlos V*, p. 319.

62. Patterson, *Slavery and Social Death: A Comparative Study* (Cambridge, MA: Harvard University Press, 1982), pp. 6 and 9.

63. As Claudio Lomnitz-Adler has pointed out, the Spanish system of slavery seemed to be premised on the idea that individual blacks, under the supervision of their masters and church officials, could be brought into the Christian fold, but that as "nations" they were inherently disloyal to the crown and Catholic faith and hence not viable as communities. Lomnitz-Adler, *Exits from the Labyrinth*, pp. 267–68.

64. For Puebla, see BNAHMC, Serie Puebla, roll 98, fols. 89v–94; and AAPAC, libro 9, fol. 22.

65. Refer to Nicole von Germeten, *Black Blood Brothers: Confraternities and Social Mobility for Afro-Mexicans* (Gainesville: University Press of Florida, 2006). Recent works on the population of African descent in colonial Mexico also include Adriana Naveda Chávez-Hita, *Pardos, mulatos y libertos: Sexto Encuentro de Afromexicanistas* (Xalapa, Mexico: Universidad Veracruzana, 2001); Ben Vinson, Bobby Vaughn, and Clara García Ayluardo, *Afroméxico: El pulso de la población negra en México, una historia recordada, olvidada y*

vuelta a recordar (México, City: Centro de Investigación y Docencia Económica, 2004); Luz M. Martínez Montiel, *Presencia africana en México* (Mexico City: Consejo Nacional para la Cultura y las Artes, 1995); Luz M. Martínez Montiel and Juan Carlos Reyes G., *Memoria del III Encuentro Nacional de Afromexicanistas* (Colima, Mexico: Gobierno del Estado, Instituto Colimense de Cultura, 1993); and the special issue of *Signos históricos* II, no. 4 (2000).

66. See, for example, the request for a papal dispensation for his "defect of birth" submitted by Nicolas Antonio de Anijo, a physician in the city Puebla who in 1707 tried to be ordained as a priest. AGI, México 709.

67. In the eyes of colonial officials, free blacks and mulattos demonstrated their political disloyalty through their rebellious tendencies and refusal to pay tribute to the crown, which they supposedly owed because they were living in the lands of Castilian monarchs and enjoying the benefits of the Spanish system of "peace and justice," and because they had achieved their liberty. The claim that blacks were disloyal was also tied to the perception (whether justified or not) of their mobility and lack of fixed residence, which automatically implied lack of integration and hence another violation of the duties of a vecino. See AGI, Indiferente 427, leg. 30, fols. 248r–249r: Royal decree ordering that blacks and mulattos be made into tributaries, 1574; AGI, Contaduría 677: Registers of black and mulatto tribute for Mexico, 1576–78; and AGI, México 22, no. 24: Memorial of Villamanrique's government (included in the letters of his successor, Viceroy Luis de Velasco, the younger), 1590.

68. See Vinson III, *Bearing Arms for His Majesty*. Also see the collection of articles on black militia participation in colonial Latin America in *Journal of Colonialism and Colonial History* 5, no. 2 (2004). Thanks primarily to their military contributions in regions vulnerable to foreign encroachment, free (and in some cases enslaved) blacks were able to obtain, if not the political rights of vecindad, economic ones, such as access to land. See Jane G. Landers, *Black Society in Spanish Florida* (Urbana: University of Illinois Press, 1999), pp. 21–23 and 202–28; Landers, "Acquisition and Loss on a Spanish Frontier: The Free Black Homesteaders of Florida, 1784–1821," in *Against the Odds: Free Blacks in the Slave Societies of the Americas,* ed. Jane G. Landers (London and Portland, OR: Frank Cass, 1996), pp. 85–101; and Kimberly S. Hanger, "Patronage, Property and Persistence: The Emergence of a Free Black Elite in Spanish New Orleans," in *Against the Odds,* pp. 44–64.

69. See Frederick Bowser, "Africans in Spanish American Colonial Society," in *The Cambridge History of Latin America,* vol. II, ed. Leslie Bethell (Cambridge and New York: Cambridge University Press), pp. 366–67.

70. A number of laws at the turn of the century tried to curb the trend. In 1601, for example, Viceroy Gaspar de Zúñiga y Azevedo limited the number of blacks and mulattos who could accompany any Spaniard to three. AGI, México 270: Decree regarding accompaniments of blacks and mulattos, 1601.

71. See note 32 in this chapter.

72. See María Elena Martínez, "The Black Blood of New Spain: *Limpieza de Sangre,* Racial Violence, and Gendered Power in Early Colonial Mexico," *William and Mary Quarterly,* 3rd ser., vol. LXI (July 2004): pp. 479–520.

73. Compare, for example, the fantasies that surfaced in 1612 with the fears that Spaniards in Mexico City had about the possibility that blacks and mulattos would try to rebel in the year 1666. Martínez, "The Black Blood of New Spain"; and AHN, Inquisición, libro 1060, fols. 175–205v.

74. Corominas, *Diccionario crítico etimológico de la lengua castellana*, pp. 722–24. Corominas disagreed with Covarrubias's claim that the word *casta* derived from the Latin *castus*, which alluded to chastity.

75. Domínguez Ortiz made the same observation in *La clase de los conversos en Castilla en la edad moderna*, p. 55.

76. "Castizos," stated Covarrubias, "we call those that derive from good lineage and caste." *Tesoro de la lengua castellana*, p. 282.

77. Because the word *casta* referred to people who were "mixed," it meant the opposite of what *caste* meant when the British (who borrowed it from the Portuguese) applied it to the Hindu system of social differentiation, which was based on endogamous social groups. In Spanish America, then, the sistema de castas was a function of the instability, not rigidity, of "caste." See Julian Pitt-Rivers, "On the Word 'Caste,' " in *The Translation of Culture: Essays to E. E. Evans-Pritchard*, ed. T. O. Beidelman (London: Tavistock, 1971), pp. 234–35. Iberians also used the word *casta* to designate the place of origin of slaves who had been born in Africa (as in *casta angola*) and thus applied it to "pure" blacks. According to Leslie Rout, all blacks were considered part of the castas, even if they had no native or Spanish ancestry, because it was African blood itself, not necessarily mixture, that was deemed to have a degenerating effect. Leslie B. Rout, *The African Experience in Spanish America* (Cambridge: Cambridge University Press, 1976), p. 127.

78. AGN, Inquisición, Caja 163, fols. 1–37v.

79. AGI, México 280. My translation and interpolations.

80. See Williams, "Classification Systems Revisited," pp. 201–36.

81. García, *Origen de los indios del Nuevo Mundo*, p. 65.

82. Lewis, *Hall of Mirrors*, pp. 22–25.

83. JCBL/LI, vol. 1, fols. 487–91. Also see JCBL/LI, vol. 2, fols. 207–14: información of Alonso Gómez, made in the Villa de Niebla (Spain), 1617.

84. AGI, México 121, r. 1.

85. Covarrubias Orozco, *Tesoro de la lengua castellana*, p. 751. For Corominas, the word *mestizo* was of uncertain origin, but he speculated that it might have come from the Latin *mixtus*. Corominas, *Diccionario crítico etimológico de la lengua castellana*, vol. 3, p. 359.

86. Forbes writes that, in Mexico, the term *mulato* continued to be used for the descendants of blacks and Indians into the 1650s and that within the Spanish empire, the term generally meant a person who was half African and half something else. As such, it could be applied to various combinations. Jack D. Forbes, *Black Africans and Native Americans: Color, Race and Caste in the Evolution of Red-Black Peoples* (New York: Basil Blackwell, 1988), pp. 162–65. Forbes also notes that the term *mulato* initially appeared in legislation relating to the Americas (p. 173), but it is not clear whether it was first used in the colonial or Iberian context.

87. Solórzano Pereira, *Política Indiana*, vol. 1, p. 445.

88. Covarrubias, *Tesoro de la lengua castellana*, p. 768.

89. See Doris Garraway, "Race, Reproduction and Family Romance in Moreau de Saint-Méry's Description . . . de la partie française de l'isle Saint-Domingue," *Eighteenth-Century Studies* 38, no. 2 (2005): 227–46.

90. The Mexican Holy Office, for instance, used the word *castizo* in the 1570s and stated that it was a term commonly applied in New Spain to the children of mestizos (and presumably Spaniards). AHN, Inquisición de México, libro 1047, fols. 430–34: Correspondence from the Mexican Inquisition to the Supreme Council of the Inquisition, November 5, 1576. Also see AHN, Inquisición, libro 1064: Summary report of the bigamy case against Bartolomé Hernández, "castizo," native of the city of los Ángeles (Puebla), 1578.

91. In 1539, for example, Viceroy Mendoza instructed Mexico City, Puebla, and other cities not to allow *negros* or *moriscos,* whether free or slave, as well as Indians, to carry arms without special permission. BNAHMC, Serie Puebla, roll 81, fol. 12v. Viceroy Mendoza also ordered that any "negro, negra o morisca" who made pulque be punished with two hundred lashes. Condumex (Mexico City), Fondo CMLXI-36, fol. 46. Also see AAPAC, vol. 1, doc. 234: Puebla's city council orders penalties for anyone helping "runaway moriscos or black slaves," March 2, 1537. Noting the association that Spaniards in Peru made between blacks and moriscos, Lockhart speculated that the latter, who were usually described as white, were either Muslim Spaniards or slaves from Morocco, but in Mexican sources there is not enough information to determine whether that was the case. James Lockhart, *Spanish Peru, 1532–1560* (Madison: University of Wisconsin Press, 1974), p. 196.

92. See AHN, Inquisición, libro 1064.

93. AGN, Inquisición, vol. 372, exp. 14; AHN, Inquisición, libro 1065; and AGN, Inquisición, vol. 684, exp. 4. Note the deployment of the word *raza* to describe moriscos. For more on Beatriz de Padilla's case, see Solange Alberro, "Beatriz de Padilla, Mulatta Mistress and Mother," in *Colonial Spanish America: A Documentary History,* eds. Kenneth Mills and William Taylor (Wilmington, DE: SR Books, 1998), pp. 178–84.

94. See, for example, Philip II's 1582 letter to Mexican secular and religious officials, which clarifies that any previous decrees limiting the access of mestizos to the priesthood should be understood to apply only to the children of Indian and Spanish unions, not to their subsequent descendants. See Konetzke, Colección de documentos para la historia, pp. 543–44.

95. AGN, Inquisición, vol. 82, exp. 4, fol. 118.

96. See AHN, Inquisición de México, libro 1057; and Morales, *Ethnic and Social Background of the Franciscan Friars in Seventeenth-Century Mexico,* pp. 16–17.

97. *Lobo* (wolf) and *coyote* are zoological terms, while *pardo* and *moreno* refer to skin color and were applied to people of partial African descent. In casta paintings, the classification *chino* was designated to the child of a black and native woman, but colonial officials often used it as a generic name for Asians, particularly from the Philippines. Thus, when the religious official in charge

of the Provisorato or Inquisition for indigenous people changed his title in the eighteenth century, he became "Provisor de Indios y Chinos del Arzobispado" because his jurisdiction extended to the Philippines. AHN, Inquisición, leg. 2286 (1).

98. See AGN, Bienes Nacionales, vol. 578, exp. 21; and AHN, Inquisición, libro 1067, fols. 316–18, and 500–500v. Casta nomenclature came mainly from a zoological vocabulary, particularly from the breeding of horses and cattle. See Nicolás León, *Las castas del México colonial* (Mexico City: Talleres Gráficos del Museo Nacional de Arqueología, Historia y Etnografía, 1924), p. 27; and Daisy Rípodas Ardanaz, *El matrimonio en Indias: Realidad social y regulación jurídica* (Buenos Aires: Fundación para la Educación, la Ciencia y la Cultura, 1977), p. 26.

99. Ramón A. Gutiérrez, *When Jesus Came, the Corn Mothers Went Away: Marriage, Sexuality and Power in New Mexico, 1500–1846* (Stanford, CA: Stanford University Press, 1991), pp. 196–200; Jackson, "Race/caste and the Creation and Meaning of Identity," p. 155; and Steven W. Hackel, *Children of Coyote, Missionaries of Saint Francis: Indian-Spanish Relations in Colonial California, 1769–1850* (Chapel Hill: Omohundro Institute of Early American History and Culture and University of North Carolina Press, 2005), pp. 59–60.

100. See, among others, Patricia Seed, "Social Dimensions of Race: Mexico City, 1753," *Hispanic American Historical Review* 62, no. 4 (1982): pp. 568–606; Cope, *The Limits of Racial Domination*, pp. 49–67; Schwartz, "Colonial Identities and the *Sociedad de Castas,*" pp. 185–201; and Richard Boyer, *Cast [sic] and Identity in Colonial Mexico: A Proposal and an Example* (Storrs, CT; Providence, RI; and Amherst, MA: Latin American Studies Consortium of New England, 1997).

101. Foucault used the phrase in his discussion of the importance of blood in the early modern period, which he suggested stemmed primarily from its function as a central sign for a person's place within the largely birth-determined system of estates and from its role as a symbol of the sovereign's power of life and death over his subjects. Foucault, *The History of Sexuality*, pp. 135–50.

CHAPTER 7

1. Stoler, *Race and the Education of Desire*, p. 30.
2. See the 1575 Inquisition letter describing problems with doing probanzas de limpieza de sangre in Spanish America. AHN, Inquisición, leg. 2269.
3. AHN, Inquisición de México, libro 1050, fols. 212–20: Correspondence from the Mexican Inquisition, 1574–75.
4. AHN, Inquisición de México, libro 1049, fols. 591–591v: Copy of the letter from Peruvian inquisitors regarding genealogical information for the wives of familiars, April 14, 1603.
5. AHN, Inquisición de México, libro 1047, fols. 380–381v: Letter to the Council of the Indies from the Mexican Inquisition, September 23, 1575; and AHN, Inquisición de México, leg. 2269. When port inspectors suspected the use of a false genealogy or travel permit, they were supposed to request

investigations by appropriate Spanish tribunals. See AGN, Inquisición, vol. 77, exp. 34, fols. 191v–194v: Correspondence of the Mexican Holy Office, 1582.

6. AHN, Inquisición de México, libro 1049, fols. 433–34.

7. AHN, Inquisición de México, libro 1058, fols. 152–53: Letter from Medina Rico to the Suprema, 1660. A *visita* was an administrative tour ordered by the crown in order to study particular colonial affairs.

8. AHN, Inquisición de México, libro 1050, fol. 12v.

9. AHN, Inquisición de México, libro 1054.

10. AHN, Inquisición de México, libro 1049, fols. 33v–34v. Birbiesca Roldán suspected that the commissioner in charge of investigating his lineage in his place of birth (Villa de Moguer, Spain) and other enemies that he had left behind there had declared against him, but other documents suggest that his confirmation was delayed because his wife's genealogical investigation was not yet complete. See AHN, Inquisición de México, libro 1048, fols. 335–335v; and AHN, Inquisición de México, libro 1049, fols. 231–32.

11. Covarrubias, *Tesoro de la lengua castellana*, p. 773.

12. Huntington Library (hereafter HL), MS 35149. Other witnesses mentioned an announcement made in Zacatecas about Francisco de Cobarruvias's limpieza de sangre, but they don't elaborate by whom or why. Perhaps it had been made when he received his title of familiar, which had been before his probanza was completed.

13. HL, MS 35150. For another sixteenth-century probanza in which witnesses argued that their knowledge of the lineage in question was reliable because they were from small Spanish towns, see AGN, Inquisición, vol. 202, exp. 10.

14. AGN, Inquisición, vol. 325, exp. 3.

15. In the sixteenth century, the Spanish Inquisition did conduct genealogical investigations in the parts of Italy in which it had jurisdiction. See, for example, the references to purity probanzas done in Sicily for the wives of familiares and officials. AHN, Inquisición, leg. 1254.

16. AHN, Inquisición de México, libro 1049, fols. 167–167v.

17. For examples in which "public opinion" is particularly underscored in witness testimonies, see HL, MSS 35145, 15149, and 35144; AGI, México 280; and AGN, Inquisición, vol. 65, exp. 4, fols. 64–87v.

18. Vera referred to a royal decree stating that all of the Holy Office's consultores should be chosen from audiencia magistrates and judges who had proven their limpieza and the purity of their wives. The decree hints at how the issue of limpieza cut across different institutions, even those that did not have formal purity requirements, and at how the tendency among colonial officials to want to work for the Inquisition meant that many of them underwent genealogical investigations. HL, MS 35145.

19. Because Santiago de Vera's paternal grandfather had married twice, the Seville commissioner also had to determine who his biological grandmother was and her purity status. AGN, Inquisición, vol. 77, exp. 34: Correspondence of the Mexican Inquisition, 1582.

20. AHN, Inquisición de México, libro 1048, fols. 139–140v: Letter from the Mexican Inquisition to the Suprema, October 22, 1583; and HL, MS 35145.

21. The Mexican inquisitors denied Vera's petition. In a 1584 letter, they thanked Seville's tribunal for exposing the truth about his wife's ancestry and blamed an uncle in Spain for having arranged to produce false genealogies and probanzas. AGN, Inquisición, vol. 177, exp. 34.

22. AGN, Judicial, vol. 5, exp. 5.

23. Ibid.

24. AGN, Inquisición, vol. 233 (1).

25. AGN, Inquisición, vol. 77, exp. 34.

26. AHN, Inquisición de México, libro 1051, fols. 184–85: Letter from the Mexican inquisitors to the Suprema, May 29, 1619.

27. AHN, Inquisición de México, libro 1056, fol. 374.

28. AHN, Inquisición de México, libro 1049, fols. 429–429v and 506–7. Also see the case of Juan Ruiz Martínez, a priest who in the mid-sixteenth century applied for a benefice in Oaxaca's cathedral chapter. His petition led to two inquiries in Spanish towns, one in his native town of Villa del Campanario, the other in Montañez. The Council of the Indies approved the two probanzas, but after receiving a report accusing Ruiz Martínez of being a confeso, it ordered a new investigation and close examination of the scribes, witnesses, and archives that had been involved in the first procedures. AGI, Indiferente General, 1210.

29. AHN, Inquisición de México, libro 1048, fols. 139–140v: Letter from the Mexican Inquisition to the Suprema, October 22, 1583.

30. See AGN, Inquisición, vol. 177, exp. 34; AGN, Inquisición, vol. 202, exp. 10; and HL, MS 35144.

31. AGN, Inquisición, vol. 372, exp. 23.

32. See AHN, Inquisición de México, libro 1050; and AHN, Inquisición de México, libro 1047, fols. 171v–172.

33. For the Puebla region, see Ida Altman, *Transatlantic Ties in the Spanish Empire: Brihuega, Spain, and Puebla, Mexico, 1560–1620* (Stanford, CA: Stanford University Press, 2000); and Guadalupe Albi Romero, "La sociedad de Puebla de los Ángeles en el siglo XVI," *Jahrbuch für Geschichte von Staat, Wirtschaft, und Gesellschaft Lateinamerikas* 7 (1970): pp. 76–145.

34. Nuttini, *The Wages of Conquest*, pp. 48–49 and 155–82.

35. Doña Mariana de Ircio y de Velasco's paternal grandfather was Viceroy Luis de Velasco (senior), who arrived in New Spain in 1550. Her mother was María de Mendoza, daughter of the illegitimate sister of Viceroy Antonio de Mendoza and a miner, Martín de Ircio, both of whom must have arrived in Mexico not too long after the conquest.

36. AHN, Inquisición de México, libro 1051. The probanzas done for Juan de Altamirano and doña Mariana Ircio y de Velasco in New Spain were later put to good use by their descendants. They were among the documents presented, for example, by the couple's son, don Fernando Altamirano y Velasco, when he received the title of count of Santiago Calimaya (1616), when he became corregidor, and when he was named capitan general of Guatemala and president of its audiencia. For more on the Velasco lineage, its endogamic practices, and its various titles of nobility, see de la Peña, *Oligarquía y propiedad en Nueva España*, pp. 200–209.

37. Solórzano Pereira, *Política Indiana*, pp. 442–43.

38. Anthony Pagden, "Identity Formation in Spanish America," in *Colonial Identity in the Atlantic World, 1500–1800,* ed. Nicholas Canny and Anthony Pagden (Princeton, NJ: Princeton University Press, 1987), p. 63.

39. On the ambiguity of the Castilian concept of nación with respect to territory (patria) and bloodlines and the conflicted loyalties of creoles, see Lomnitz-Adler, "Nationalism as a Practical System," pp. 333–34 and 342.

40. AHN, Inquisición, libro 1051, fol. 57: Unsigned letter from Mexico to the Suprema, received in Madrid on April 10, 1612. A note at the top of the document (presumably written by a member of Suprema) attributes the letter to the archbishop of Mexico. Although the archbishop is not named, he was probably Fray García Guerra, who died in February 1612.

41. Solange Alberro, *Inquisición y sociedad en méxico, 1571–1700* (Mexico City: Fondo de Cultura Económica, 1988), p. 54. For a study of the Mexican Inquisition's familiars in the sixteenth century, see Javier Eusebio Sanchiz Ruiz, "La *limpieza de sangre* en Nueva España: El funcionariado del tribunal del Santo Oficio de la Inquisición, siglo XVI" (master's thesis, Universidad Nacional Autónoma de México, Facultad de Filosofía y Letras, 1988). I thank Professor Sanchiz Ruiz for generously giving me a copy of his master's thesis.

42. AHN, Inquisición de México, libro 1053, fols. 214–15.

43. AHN, Inquisición de México, libro 1058, fols. 185–185v. Also see AHN, Inquisición de México, libro 1057, fol. 125v.

44. See AHN, Inquisición, libro 1051, fols. 22, 287–289v and 290–292v.

45. AHN, Inquisición de México, libro 1057, fols. 127–30. To lessen corruption, Medina Rico introduced a series of changes in payment procedures that were meant to make officials more accountable. See, for example, AHN, Inquisición de México, libro 1057, fols. 125–41; and AHN, Inquisición de México, libro 1058, fols. 151–153v.

46. AHN, Inquisición de México, libro 1056, fols. 373–382v: Report from the visitador Pedro Medina Rico on the proofs of limpieza for the Mexican Holy Office's ministers and familiars, 1657. The report includes a list of all the Inquisition officials and familiares whose probanzas the visitador considered unacceptable.

47. AHN, Inquisición de México, libro 1057, fols. 117–18: Letter from Dr. Juan de Aguirre, 1659.

48. AHN, Inquisición de México, libro 1057, fols. 127–30.

49. AHN, Inquisición de México, libro 1057, fols. 137–41: Letters from the archbishop of Mexico and from Medina Rico, 1658.

50. AHN, Inquisición de México, libro 1055, fols. 313–314v: Letters from inquisitors don Francisco Estrada y Escobedo, don Juan Saenz de Mañozca, and don Bernabe de la Higuera y Amarilla, Mexico, July 20, 1650, and August 8, 1651. The Suprema apparently did not rescind its order; *"que se guarde lo proveido"* (let what had been decided stand) was its response.

51. It had become so customary for the children of Inquisition ministers and familiars to inherit their honors that in 1658 the Holy Office informed Pedro de Soto López, who was attempting to become a familiar simply by establishing that his father had held the title, that the process was no longer going to operate

that way. AHN, Inquisición de México, libro 1057. Also see AHN, Inquisición de México, libro 1056, fols. 277–282: Petition and genealogy of Joseph Rey y Alarcón, 1656. The file includes a letter from the father of the petitioner indicating that he expected his son to inherit his title.

52. AHN, Inquisición, libro 1063, fols. 200–200v. At the end of the letter, the members of the Suprema jotted down that they would look into the matter further, but it is unclear that they did. In fact, the council did not change its policy of requiring that proof of purity be established in lugares de naturaleza, which mainly referred to communities in Spain. Thus, in the eighteenth century, Mexican inquisitors continued to complain that it was hard to comply with that requirement because of how long creole families had been in New Spain. See, for example, AHN, Inquisición, leg. 2279 (1): Letter to the Suprema, 1725.

53. Brading, *The First America,* pp. 2 and 293–313; Lavallé, *Las promesas ambiguas,* pp. 63–77, esp. 64–65; and Herzog, *Defining Nations,* p. 146.

54. Brading, *The First America,* p. 390; and HL, MS 35174.

55. La Faye, *Quetzalcóatl and Guadalupe,* pp. 59–61; and Brading, *The First America,* pp. 363–72.

56. Pagden, "Identity Formation in Spanish America," p. 67. For Pagden and other scholars, Mexican creoles could exalt and appropriate the native past to a greater degree than their Peruvian counterparts because, by the seventeenth century, the indigenous people of the central valley were presumed to be too devastated or too acculturated to find inspiration in their imperial past to oppose Spanish rule. See Pagden, p. 67; and Lafaye, *Quetzalcóatl and Guadalupe,* pp. 65–66.

57. John Leddy Phelan, "Neo-Aztecism in the Eighteenth Century and the Genesis of Mexican Nationalism," in *Culture in History: Essays in Honor of Paul Radin,* ed. Stanley Diamond (New York: Columbia University Press, 1960), p. 761.

58. See, for example, JCBL/LI, vol. IV, fols. 819–23; vol. V, fols. 165–171; and vol. VI, fols. 762–67.

59. Pagden, *Spanish Imperialism and the Political Imagination,* p. 10.

CHAPTER 8

1. Edmundo O'Gorman, *Fundamentos de la historia de América* (Mexico City: Imprenta Universitaria, 1942), pp. 87–99. Also see Stephen Greenblatt, *Marvelous Possessions: The Wonder of the New World* (Chicago: University of Chicago Press, 1991).

2. AHN, Inquisición, libro 1266. The document containing the Inquisition's deliberations is not dated. Given the reference to Solórzana Pereira's *Política Indiana* (published in the mid-seventeenth century) and the other papers amid which the report is found, however, it is probable that it was produced in the last third of the seventeenth century.

3. See *Política Indiana,* vol. I, bk. 2, chap. 30.

4. The category of zambahigo referred mainly to people of indigenous and African ancestry, but sometimes of Spanish as well. In the Suprema's discussion

of the purity statutes, for example, zambahigos are defined as the children of "white Indians" and "black Indians," terms referring, respectively, to people of Spanish–Indian and African–Indian descent. Note the emphasis on skin color.

5. AHN, Inquisición, libro 1266.

6. AHN, Inquisición, libro 1266.

7. Alfonso Pérez de Lara, *De anniversariis, et capellaniis, libri dvo. Qvibus vltra generalem anniuersariorum & capellaniarum materiam, specialiter disputatur de annuo relicto: pro virginibus maritādis: pro infantibus expositis nutriendis: pro redimendis captiuis: pro relaxādis carceratis: pro mōte pietatis: pro celebrādo festo Corporis Christi, cum præcedentijs processionis: de trāsferēdis cadaueribus, absqué tributo. De quarta funerali: de probatione generis & qualitatis sanguinis ad capellaniam requisitæ, et ad alia statuta. Opvs qvidem, vt pivm et practicabile, ita & vtile vtroque foro versantibus, iudicibus, aduocatis, clericis, & monachis, & quibuscunque alijs piorum executoribus* (Matriti[Madrid]: ex typographia Illephonsi Martini, 1608), esp. bk. 2, chap. 4, fols. 333–36. This work appears to have been widely circulated throughout Europe, for it was subsequently published several times in various European, especially Italian, cities.

8. See Méchoulan, *El honor de Dios,* pp. 58–59

9. Juan Escobar del Corro, *Tractatus bipartitus de puritate et nobilitate probanda* (Lyon: Sumptibus Rochi Deville and L. Chalmette, 1737). The work was first published in 1633.

10. Solórzano Pereira based his argument on two points. First, he pointed out that technically, a person stopped being a neophyte ten years after having been baptized. And second, he contended that interpretations of the statutes that advocated that at least two hundred years had to pass before conversos could be considered Old Christians could be applied only to the descendants of converted Jews and Muslims because they were special cases. *Política Indiana,* vol. 1, pp. 436–37.

11. Solórzano Pereira considered mestizos the best possible "mix" in the colonies, even though he also warned that their growth was considered dangerous because of their "vices" and "depraved customs." *Política Indiana,* vol. 1, pp. 446–48.

12. For a brief overview of general demographic, social, and economic patterns in seventeenth-century Spanish America, see John E. Kicza, "Native American, African, and Hispanic Communities During the Middle Period in the Colonial Americas," *Historical Archaeology* 31, no. 1 (1997): pp. 9–17.

13. The Requerimiento, or "Requirement," was a military and political ritual that defined the terms under which war could legally be launched on the native people. A manifesto that was supposed to be read before war was legally declared, it was designed by Spanish jurists and theologians in 1513 to establish Spain's political authority over the Americas. It is reproduced and translated in Lewis Hanke, ed., *History of Latin American Civilization: Sources and Interpretation,* vol. 1, *The Colonial Experience* (London: Methuen and Co., 1969), pp. 93–95. Also see Seed, *Ceremonies of Possession,* pp. 69–99.

14. See Luciano Pereña, "Defensor oficial de la Corona," in Juan de Solórzano y Pereira, *De Indiarum Iure: Liber III: "De retentione Indiarum,"* ed. C. Baciero, F. Cantelar, A. García, J. M. García Añoveros, F. Maseda, L. Pereña, and

J. M. Pérez-Prendes (Madrid: Consejo Superior de Investigaciones Científicas, 1994), pp. 20–61; and book 3 of *Indiarum Iure,* in which Solórzano explains why it is just that Spain remain in the Americas and retain its titles, ibid., pp. 208–485.

15. See Thomas Cohen, "Nation, Lineage, and Jesuit Unity in Antonio Possevino's Memorial to Everard Mercurian (1576)," in *A Companhia de Jesus na Península Ibérica nos séculos XVI e XVII: Espiritualidade e cultura* (Porto: Editora Universidade do Porto, 2004), pp. 543–61.

16. AHN, Inquisición, libro 1050, fols. 110–11.

17. The complete title of the book is *Luz y methodo de confesar idólatras y destierro de idolatrías debajo del tratado siguiente. Tratado de avisos y puntos importantes de la abominable seta de la idolatría, para examinar por ellos al penitente en el fuero interior de la consciencia, y exterior judicial. Sacados no de los libros, sino de la experiencia en las aberiguaciones con los rabbies de ella* (Puebla: Imprenta de Diego Fernández de León, 1692). John Carter Brown Library, Rare Book Collection. The book was dedicated to don Isidro de Sariñana y Cuenca. Note that Villavicencio's text had precedents, including the works by Hernando Ruiz de Alarcón (1629) and Jacinto de la Serna (1656). The latter two works, which described rituals associated with idolatry, were not printed in the seventeenth century but probably circulated nonetheless. See Gruzinski, *The Conquest of Mexico,* pp. 148–49. Also refer to the undated manuscript by P. R. López de Martínez, in BNAHMC, Serie Puebla, Roll 100.

18. Hernando Ruiz de Alarcón had already alluded to the problem of distinguishing idolatrous practices among the native people from simple "customs" in his colonial treaty (written in the 1620s but unpublished until modern times) on native idolatry. Indeed, colonial priests, many of whom were not well educated on certain doctrinal matters, had to be taught, precisely through manuals such as that of Villavicencio, what concepts such as "idolatry" and "superstition" meant and how to identify them. See Hernando Ruiz De Alarcón, *Treatise on the Heathen Superstitions: That Today Live Among the Indians Native to This New Spain, 1629,* ed. Ross Hassig and J. Richard Andrews (Norman: University of Oklahoma Press, 1999). And on the production of writings on idolatry by colonial scholars, see Magdalena G. Chocano Mena, "Colonial Scholars in the Cultural Establishment of Seventeenth Century New Spain" (PhD diss., State University of New York at Stony Brook, 1994), pp. 161–201.

19. See Villavicencio's *Luz y methodo de confesar idólatras,* part 1, p. 28; and chaps. 6, 10, and 11.

20. Ibid., part 1, p. 20.

21. Ibid., part 1, pp. 93–95. After the 1692 riot, many church officials advocated reinforcing the segregation of native people in order to keep them under stricter vigilance.

22. On drinking in colonial Mexico, see William B. Taylor, *Drinking, Homicide and Rebellion in Colonial Mexican Villages* (Stanford, CA: Stanford University Press, 1979).

23. AHN, Inquisición de México, libro 1050, fol. 75.

24. Judith Laikin Elkin, "Imagining Idolatry: Missionaries, Indians, and Jews," in *Religion and the Authority of the Past,* ed. Tobin Siebers (Ann Arbor:

University of Michigan Press, 1993), pp. 75–97. On idolatry in the Andes, see Kenneth R. Mills, *Idolatry and its Enemies: Colonial Andean Religion and Extirpation, 1640–1750* (Princeton, NJ: Princeton University Press, 1997); and Mills, "The Limits of Religious Coercion in Midcolonial Peru," in *The Church in Colonial Latin America,* ed. John F. Schwaller (Wilmington, DE: Scholarly Resources, 2000), pp. 147–80.

25. See note 38, p. 332.

26. Morales, *Ethnic and Social Background of the Franciscan Friars,* pp. 12–14.

27. Cited in Morales, *Ethnic and Social Background of the Franciscan Friars,* pp. 16–17. The translation is by Morales.

28. JCBL/LI, vol. 4, fols. 491–504.

29. JCBL/LI, vol. 5, fols. 165–171v.

30. JCBL/LI, vol. 6, fols. 761–67.

31. The five friars who reviewed Diego Valdés Moctezuma's case stated that the investigation was not complete because not enough information was gathered about his grandparents, but decided to accept the candidate because two of his brothers had already professed in the Province of the Holy Gospel without any kind of dispensation.

32. JCBL/LI, vol. 4, fols. 819–23. According to notes made by the friars, Manuel de Salazar had requested to be accepted into the order on a number of occasions, and they finally decided to accept his candidacy after being convinced of his religious devotion.

33. See Morales, *Ethnic and Social Background of the Franciscan Friars,* pp. 143–44.

34. See Brading, *The First America,* pp. 373–75.

35. Jaime Cuadriello, "Cortés as the American Moses: The Mural Writing of Patriotic History," (lecture, University of Southern California, Los Angeles, November 22, 2005); and Cuadriello, *Las glorias de la república de Tlaxcala: O la conciencia como imagen sublime* (Mexico City: Instituto de Investigaciones Estéticas, UNAM, and Museo Nacional de Arte, INBA, 2004), p. 78.

36. Colin A. Palmer, "Religion and Magic in Mexican Slave Society, 1570–1650," in *Race and Slavery in the Western Hemisphere: Quantitative Studies,* ed. Stanley L. Engerman and Eugene D. Genovese (Stanford, CA: Center for Advanced Studies in the Behavioral Sciences, 1975), p. 314.

37. Lomnitz-Adler, *Exits from the Labyrinth,* pp. 267–68.

38. By 1646, New Spain's creole black population amounted to 116,529; and that of enslaved Africans, to 35,089. In the capital, most of the population of African descent consisted of free creoles. See Herman Bennett, *Africans in Colonial Mexico: Absolutism, Christianity, and Afro-Creole Consciousness, 1570–1640* (Bloomington and Indianapolis: Indiana University Press, 2003), pp. 1 and 18–27.

39. JCBL/LI, vol. 1, pp. 3–13.

40. JCBL/LI, vol. 1, fols. 487–91. For a probanza that used similar language but was made in Spain, see JCBL/LI, vol. 2, fols. 207–14: Information regarding Alonso Gómez, made in the Villa de Niebla, 1617.

41. AGI, Indiferente 2072, no. 44. As of the 1530s, Spanish laws barred mulattos (along with other categories) from going to the Indies without first obtain-

ing a special license. For some unstated reason, the Council of the Indies did not give Catalina and her son, "the free mulattoes," permission to go to Mexico.

42. AHN, Inquisición, libro 1066, fols. 379–382v and 389.

43. AHN, Inquisición, libro 1066, fols. 387–390v.

44. JCBL/LI, vol. 12, fols. 612–29. Because Diego Joseph Rodríguez Vargas's información is out of place and incomplete, it was not possible to determine whether he was accepted into the novitiate or not.

45. By the eighteenth century, *pardo* and *moreno* were the most common terms used for free colored militiamen in Mexico. Though the former at some point referred to the children of blacks and native people, in central New Spain it eventually became a synonym for *mulato*.

46. On how the ways in which subordinate groups understand, accommodate, or resist domination are shaped by the process of domination itself (resistance and domination thus operating within a common discursive framework), see Roseberry, "Hegemony and the Language of Contention," pp. 355–66.

47. Thomas C. Holt, "Slavery and Freedom in the Atlantic World: Reflections on the Diasporan Framework," in *Crossing Boundaries: Comparative History of Black People in Diaspora,* ed. Darlene Clark Hine and Jacqueline McLeod (Bloomington and Indianapolis: Indiana University Press, 1999), p. 37.

48. AGN, Bienes Nacionales, vol. 578, exp. 21: Investigation of the nobility and purity of blood of don Juan Velasco and doña Jerónima Muñoz, parents of Fray Nicolás de Velasco and Fray Miguel de Velasco, Querétaro, 1702–5.

49. For example, see JCBL/LI, vol. 4, fol. 826.

CHAPTER 9

1. Recent studies of the paintings include Ilona Katzew, *Casta Painting: Images of Race in Eighteenth Century Mexico* (New Haven, CT, and London: Yale University Press, 2004); Magali M. Carrera, *Imagining Identity in New Spain: Race, Lineage, and the Colonial Body in Portraiture and Casta Paintings* (Austin: University of Texas Press, 2003); María Elena Martínez, "The Spanish Concept of Limpieza de Sangre and the Emergence of the 'Race/Caste' System in the Viceroyalty of New Spain" (PhD diss., University of Chicago, 2002), pp. 1–42; and María Concepción García Sáiz, *Las castas mexicanas: Un género pictórico americano* (Milan: Olivetti, 1989). Thus far, more than one hundred sets have been rediscovered, but many remain undated and anonymous. For Peru, one series, commissioned by Viceroy Amat, has been identified. See Juan Carlos Estenssoro, Pilar Romero de Tejada y Picatoste, Luis Eduardo Wuffarden, and Natalia Majluf, eds., *Los cuadros del mestizaje del virrey Amat: La representación etnográfica en el Perú colonial* (Lima: Museo del Arte de Lima, 1999).

2. Painters who contributed to the genre include Juan Rodríguez Juárez, Miguel Cabrera, José de Páez, José Alfaro, Ignacio María Barreda, Andrés de Islas, Mariano Guerrero, Luis Berrueco, Ignacio de Castro, José de Bustos, and José Joaquín Magón. A few of the artists, including Andrés de Islas, José de Ibarra, Miguel Cabrera, and Juan Patricio Morlete Ruiz, were of mixed descent.

3. For details on commissioned casta sets, see Efrain Castro Morales, "Los cuadros de castas de la Nueva España," *Jahrbuch für Geschichte von Staat, Wirtschaft, und Gesellschaft Lateinamerikas* no. 20 (1983): pp. 678–68; Ilona Katzew, "Casta Painting: Identity and Social Stratification in Colonial Mexico," in *New World Orders: Casta Painting and Colonial Latin America*, ed. Ilona Katzew (New York: Americas Society Art Gallery, 1996), pp. 13–14; and María Concepción García Sáiz, "The Contribution of Colonial Painting to the Spread of the Image of America," in *America: Bride of the Sun: 500 Years of Latin America and the Low Countries: 1.2–31.5.92: Royal Museum of Fine Arts, Antwerp*, ed. Bernadette J. Bucher (Brussels, Belgium: Flemish Community, Administration of External Relations, 1992), pp. 172–73.

4. Katzew, *Casta Painting*, pp. 7 and 17.

5. On natural history and the emergence after the mid-seventeenth century of new ways of linking "things both to the eye and discourse," see Foucault, *The Order of Things*, pp. 128–32.

6. Katzew, *Casta Painting*, pp. 2 and 7.

7. By the 1790s, the population had grown to about 4.5 to 5 million, and in 1810, to more than 6 million. Of those 6 million, about 22 percent were castas, 60 percent were indigenous people, and 18 percent were creoles. Peter Bakewell, *A History of Latin America: Empires and Sequels, 1450–1930* (Malden, MA: Blackwell, 1997), pp. 256 and 277–78; and Mark A. Burkholder and Lyman L. Johnson, *Colonial Latin America* (New York and Oxford: Oxford University Press, 1998) p. 278.

8. Silver production began to rise in 1670 and grew at a steady pace from 1700 to 1810. Bakewell, *A History of Latin America*, p. 258.

9. See Elisa Vargas Lugo's introduction to Francisco Perez Salazar's *Historia de la pintura en Puebla* (Mexico City: Universidad Nacional Autónoma de México, Instituto de Investigaciones Estéticas, 1963), esp. pp. 13–16; and Manuel Toussaint, *Pintura colonial en México* (Mexico City: Universidad Nacional Autónoma de México, Instituto de Investigaciones Estéticas, 1990).

10. María Concepción García Sáiz, "The Artistic Development of Casta Painting" in *New World Orders*, p. 31. See p. 31 and plate 1 for reproductions of the two paintings as well as Katzew, *Casta Painting*, pp. 10–11.

11. Robin Blackburn, *The Making of New World Slavery: From the Baroque to the Modern, 1492–1800* (New York and London: Verso, 1997), pp. 19 and 234.

12. García Sáiz, "The Artistic Development," pp. 31–32.

13. A few sets produced in the late eighteenth century included various family units within a single landscape.

14. The series, which is undated, is reproduced in García Sáiz, *Las castas mexicanas*, pp. 102–11.

15. See the sets in Katzew, *Casta Painting*, pp. 19–20, 30–31, 36, 86, 91, 98–99, 100, 116–19, 124–27, 132–34, 144–46, 153, and 156–59.

16. García Sáiz, *Las castas mexicanas*, p. 38. When black men are pictured with Spanish women, they are usually depicted as belonging to a relatively privileged socioeconomic status and often appear as coachmen. See plates 21 and 34 in García Sáiz, *New World Orders*.

17. See plates 20 and 49 in García Saíz, *New World Orders*, both of which feature black women attacking their mulatto children or Spanish males with household objects (e.g., a spoon). Also see plate 42 in the same book and García Saíz, *Las castas mexicanas*, pp. 146, 155, and 162.

18. This 1763 Cabrera series consists of sixteen numbered canvases, most of which are owned by the Museo de América in Madrid and are reproduced in Joseph J. Rishel and Suzanne Stratton-Pruitt, eds., *The Arts in Latin America, 1492–1820* (New Haven, CT, and London: Yale University Press, 2006), pp. 404–409.

19. García Saíz, *Las castas mexicanas*, p. 81.

20. Katzew, *Casta Painting*, pp. 4, 94–109, and 111–61. Katzew also notes that as of the 1760s, the paintings echo themes present in the writings of Bourbon reformers, such as the problems of drinking, idleness, and gambling and the need for more order, better education, and stronger work ethics.

21. Aguirre Beltrán, *La población negra de México*, pp. 247–48.

22. AGN, Inquisición, vol. 195, exp. 55, fols. 240–243v.

23. Seed, *To Love, Honor, and Obey in Colonial Mexico*, pp. 25, 96–98, and 146–47. Also see Dennis Nodín Valdés, "The Decline of the Sociedad de Castas in Mexico City" (PhD diss., University of Michigan, 1978), pp. 40–42. For examples of late seventeenth-century petitions by mulatto slaves and mestizos to marry Spanish and castiza women in Mexico City, see AGN, Inquisición, caja 163, folder 16, exps. 4–6; and AGN, Inquisición, caja 163, folders 18 and 20.

24. Some families took matters into their own hands and investigated the bloodlines of the would-be spouse. See the 1703 testimony of Juan de Valdez regarding the purity of don Ignacio Márquez de los Ríos Valdés, in AHN, Inquisición, leg. 2284.

25. AGI, México 827: Testimonies taken by priests from Puebla's cathedral on the city's economic and social conditions from 1690 to 1723, document produced in 1724. Also refer to Guy P. C. Thomson, *Puebla de los Ángeles: Industry and Society in a Mexican City, 1700–1850* (Boulder, CO: Westview, 1989).

26. BNM, MS 2929: Instructions from the Duke of Linares to his successor, March 22, 1723.

27. AHN, Inquisición, leg. 2280. Eighteenth-century New Spain had several other epidemics, the most severe occurring in 1785 and 1786.

28. Jonathan Brown, *Latin America: A Social History of the Colonial World* (Belmont, CA: Wadsworth/Thomson Learning, 2005), pp. 296–300.

29. Richard J. Salvucci, *Textiles and Capitalism in Mexico: An Economic History of the Obrajes, 1539–1840* (Princeton, NJ: Princeton University Press, 1987), pp. 84–86 and 97–134.

30. Katzew, *Casta Painting*, pp. 56–61. The manuscript was signed by Pedro Anselmo Chreslos Jache, but Katzew speculates that this name was fictitious.

31. In the 1760s, Spain allowed New Spain to trade with its other colonies, and in 1778, it abolished the Cádiz monopoly on commerce with Spanish America. Furthermore, in 1789, it made its policy of "free trade" uniform for all its American possessions. In addition to modifying trade policies, the Bourbon reforms included reducing the power of the church, strengthening military forces, reorganizing political administration, and promoting science, the last

in order to better exploit botanical and mineral resources in Spanish America. See David A. Brading, "Bourbon Spain and its American Empires," in *Colonial Spanish America,* ed. Leslie Bethell (Cambridge: Cambridge University Press, 1987), pp. 112–62; Kenneth R. Maxwell, "Hegemonies Old and New: The Ibero-Atlantic in the Long Eighteenth Century," in *Colonial Legacies: The Problem of Persistence in Latin American History,* ed. Jeremy Adelman (New York and London: Routledge, 1999), pp. 69–90; and Jean Sarrailh, *La España ilustrada de la segunda mitad del siglo XVIII,* 4th ed. (Mexico City: Fondo de Cultura Económica, 1992 [1st ed. 1954]).

32. For more on tobacco, see Susan Deans-Smith, *Bureaucrats, Planters, and Workers: The Making of the Tobacco Monopoly in Bourbon Mexico* (Austin: University of Texas Press, 1992).

33. Pedro Pérez Herrero, "El méxico borbónico: ¿'un éxito' fracasado?" in *Interpretaciones del siglo XVIII mexicano: El impacto de las reformas borbónicas,* ed. Josefina Zoraida Vázquez (Mexico City: Nueva Imagen, 1992), pp. 117 and 127; Bakewell, *A History of Latin America,* pp. 271–72; and Richard L. Garner and Spiro E. Stefanou, *Economic Growth and Change in Bourbon Mexico* (Gainesville: University Press of Florida, 1993), pp. 25–27 and 241–45.

34. Garner, *Economic Growth,* pp. 246–58.

35. The jump in purchases of European cloth hurt the region's traditional export-import merchants, obraje owners, and artisans in major cities. See Salvucci, *Textiles and Capitalism in Mexico,* pp. 3 and 135–69; and Richard J. Salvucci, Linda K. Salvucci, and Aslán Cohen, "The Politics of Protection: Interpreting Commercial Policy in Late Bourbon and Early National Mexico," in *The Political Economy of Spanish America in the Age of Revolution, 1750–1850,* ed. Kenneth J. Andrien and Lyman L. Johnson (Albuquerque: University of New Mexico Press, 1994), p. 97.

36. Carlos Marichal, "La bancarrota del virreinato: Finanzas, guerra, y política en la Nueva España, 1770–1808," in *Interpretaciones del siglo XVIII mexicano,* pp. 153–86. Also see John H. Coatsworth, "The Limits of Colonial Absolutism: Mexico in the Eighteenth Century," in *Essays in the Political, Economic and Social History of Colonial Latin America,* ed. Karen Spalding (Newark: University of Delaware, Latin American Studies Program, Occasional Papers and Monographs no. 3, 1982), pp. 25–51.

37. The Mexican government's debt surged from 3 million pesos in the 1770s to more than 31 million pesos in 1810. Thus, much of the wealth that was generated by New Spain did not remain there. See Brian R. Hamnett, "Absolutismo ilustrado y la crisis multidimensional en el periodo colonial tardío, 1760–1808," in *Interpretaciones del siglo XVIII mexicano,* p. 72; and Brown, *Latin America,* p. 419.

38. Refer to Garner, *Economic Growth,* p. 255; Richard Salvucci, "Economic Growth and Change in Bourbon Mexico: A Review Essay," *The Americas* 51, no. 4 (1994): pp. 219–31; and Paul Gootenberg, "On Salamanders, Pyramids, and Mexico's 'Growth–without–Change': Anachronistic Reflections on a Case of Bourbon New Spain," *Colonial Latin America Review* 4, no. 1 (1995): pp. 117–27.

39. Some Spaniards and creoles attempted to preserve their social preeminence by buying titles of nobility. Charles III alone granted at least twenty-three titles (excluding those of marquise and count) to Mexico, most of which were awarded to individuals who provided important military and economic services. Recipients therefore included wealthy miners. See Ladd, *The Mexican Nobility at Independence*, p. 17.

40. Castro Morales, "Los cuadros de castas," pp. 679–81.

41. AHN, Inquisición, leg. 2280. The inquisitors admitted to not always demanding that the investigations be done in Spain but simply conducting "extra-official" inquiries into the purity, calidad, and reputation of the wives of candidates.

42. AHN, Inquisición, leg. 2282.

43. From the start of the eighteenth century to independence, New Spain imported about 20,000 slaves. By the end of the colonial period, the African-descended population ("Afromestizos") amounted to about 10 percent of Mexico's total population, or about 624,461. See Gonzalo Aguirre Beltrán, "The Slave Trade in Mexico," *Hispanic American Historical Review* 24 (1944): p. 427; and Dennis Nodín Valdés, "The Decline of Slavery in Mexico," *The Americas* 44, no. 2 (1987): p. 177.

44. On the use of different strategies by African-descended people in Cholula to ascend the social ladder and erase the stigma of their slave past, including intermarrying with mestizos and the indigenous population, see Norma Angélica Castillo Palma, "Matrimonios mixtos y cruce de la barrera de color como vías para el mestizaje de la población negra y mulata (1674-1796)," *Signos históricos* II, no. 4 (2000): 107-37.

45. Castro Morales, "Los cuadros de castas," pp. 679–81.

46. Attesting to the growing application of limpieza policies are Inquisition records, which contain limpieza de sangre documents for aldermen, alcaldes (judges), and university professors that were not produced by the Holy Office itself but by town councils, royal officials, colleges, seminaries, and so forth. See, AHN, Inquisición, leg. 2284. For examples of town councils with purity requirements, see AGN, Ayuntamientos, vol. 197, fols. 1–22v, 49, and 65; and AGN, Ayuntamientos, vol. 186. For examples of educational stipends for which the applicant submitted proof of purity, see AGN, Archivo Histórico de Hacienda, vol. 2019, exp. 5; AGN, Archivo Histórico de Hacienda, vol. 2019, exp. 9; and AGN, Ayuntamientos, vol. 186. And for a purity certification granted by the Convento de las Religiosas Capuchinas de Puebla, see JCBL/LI, vol. 11, fols. 667–71. Also refer to the probanza that Francisco Grijalva presented in the 1730s to be ordained as priest in the archbishopric of Puebla, which stated that proofs of limpieza were necessary to ensure "that all those that become part of the ecclesiastical estate are individuals of good quality [*calidad*], pure Spaniards, without the mixture of the race or ancestry of Jews, heretics, conversos, mulattos, or people who have been penanced by the Holy Office or punished by the secular justice for another crime that causes infamy." Cited in Castillo Palma, "Los estatutos de 'pureza de sangre,' como medio de acceso a las élites," p. 120 (my translation). Note how by the eighteenth century

purity was equated with Spanish ancestry and how mulattos explicitly formed part of the impure categories.

47. Like elsewhere in the Spanish colonies, in Mexico the impulse to exclude people of African ancestry from the universities and certain professions intensified as of 1750. For example, the University of Mexico, which had been trying to exclude "blacks, mulatos, chinos, morenos," and former slaves since the seventeenth century, stepped up its attempts to enforce purity requirements at that time. Tate Lanning, "Legitimacy and *Limpieza de Sangre*," p. 47, n. 41.

48. On the Royal Pragmatic's implications in Mexico, see Seed, *To Love, Honor, and Obey,* pp. 200–204.

49. For various probanzas done for military men and their wives, see AGN, Indiferente de Guerra, vol. 130; and for purity certifications for tax collectors and other representatives of the royal treasury and their wives, see AGN, Matrimonios, vol. 45, exp. 2, fols. 9–20 (year 1800); AGN, Matrimonios, vol. 45, exp. 3 (year 1801); and AGN Matrimonios, vol. 39, exp. 3, fols. 22–58 (year 1802). Some of the petitions for purity certification submitted by military men (mainly to royal audiencias) explicitly refer to the Royal Pragmatic and other royal decrees compelling officers to obtain licenses to marry and to submit proof of blood purity for themselves and their wives.

50. See AGN, Indiferente de Guerra, vol. 130; Acervo Histórico del Palacio de Minería (hereafter AHPM), 1804/IV/127/d.2; and AHPM, 1805/V/133/d.7.

51. The concept of impurity was sometimes also used against Asians ("chinos") and their descendants. See JCBL/LI, vol. 9, fol. 297v.

52. AHN, Inquisición, leg. 2288.

53. The text reads, "como vulgarmente se piensa, la sangre denegrida jamás sale, porque la experiencia enseña, que a la tercera, cuarta, o quinta generación, pulula, produciendo dos blancos un negro, que llaman tornatrás, o saltatrás." AHN, Inquisición, leg. 2288.

54. AHN, Inquisición, leg. 2288.

55. For some examples, see AHN, Inquisición, leg. 2282; AHN, Inquisición, leg. 2286 (1); and AGN, Bienes Nacionales, vol. 578, exp. 21. Although the concept of calidad was already used in the sixteenth century, it became much more common in the eighteenth. By then, it referred to a number of factors, including economic status, occupation, purity of blood, and birthplace, in short, to "reputation as a whole." Robert McCaa, "*Calidad, Clase,* and Marriage in Colonial Mexico: The Case of Parral, 1788–90," *Hispanic American Historical Review* 64, no. 3 (1984): pp. 477–501.

56. See BNM, MS 18701.

57. Terms such as *negra atezada* (dark black woman), *negra lora* (lighter than *atezada*), and others that refer to degrees of "blackness" are not uncommon in sixteenth-century Spanish records. See, for example, AGI, Indiferente 425, leg. 24, fol. 104; AGI, Indiferente 425, leg. 23, fols. 510r–v; and AGI, Indiferente 2074, N. 50.

58. In the Iberian context, one of the central contributions to the topic of skin color was made by Benito Gerónimo Feijoo (1676–1764), a Benedictine friar and one of the main thinkers of the Spanish Enlightenment. See A. Owen Aldridge, "Feijoo and the Problem of Ethiopian Color," in *Racism in the*

Eighteenth Century, ed. Harold E. Pagliaro (Cleveland, OH, and London: The Press of Case Western Reserve University, 1973). According to Roxann Wheeler, skin color became a central aspect of British race theory in the last third of the eighteenth century, a phenomenon she partly attributes to natural history and its concern with physical characteristics. Wheeler, *The Complexion of Race: Categories of Difference in Eighteenth-Century British Culture* (Philadelphia: University of Pennsylvania Press, 2000).

59. See AGN, Tierras, vol. 2979, exp. 165; AGN, Inquisición, vol. 1148, exp. 11; AGN, Inquisición, vol. 1201, exp. 8; HM 35174; and AGN, Inquisición, vol. 1201, exp. 8, fols. 338–411. In the latter half of the eighteenth century, some witnesses started to use categories such as "Spanish European" (*europeo español*) and "European of the Kingdoms of Castile" (*europeo de los Reinos de Castilla*). See JCBL/LI, vol. 11, fols. 651–72; JCBL/LI, vol. 13, fol. 292; and AGN, Inquisición, vol. 1148, exp. 11.

60. AGN, Bienes Nacionales, vol. 578, exp. 21. On the concept of physiognomy in the eighteenth-century Hispanic world, see Rebecca Haidt, *Embodying the Enlightenment: Knowing the Body in Eighteenth-Century Spanish Literature and Culture* (New York: St. Martin's, 1998), pp. 63–150; and Carrera, *Imagining Identity in New Spain,* p. 9.

61. JCBL/LI, vol. 9, fols.1023–38. Also see JCBL/LI, vol. 10, fols. 294–306v; JCBL/LI, vol. 4, fols. 491–504; JCBL/LI, vol. 6, fols. 197–203v; JCBL/LI, vol. 6, fols. 818–823v; and AHN, Inquisición, leg. 2284.

62. See Asunción Lavrin, "Indian Brides of Christ: Creating New Spaces for Indigenous Women in New Spain," *Mexican Studies/Estudios Mexicanos* 15, no. 2 (1999): pp. 225–60; and Ann Miriam Gallagher, R. S. M., "Las monjas indígenas del monasterio de Corpus Christi de la ciudad de México, 1724–1821," in *Las mujeres latino-americanas: Perspectivas históricas,* ed. Asunción Lavrin, trans. Mercedes Pizarro de Parlange (Mexico City: Fondo de Cultura Económica, 1985), pp. 177–201.

63. Key works on the origins and development of the cult of the Virgin of Guadalupe include D. A. Brading, *Mexican Phoenix: Our Lady of Guadalupe; Image and Tradition Across Five Centuries* (Cambridge and New York: Cambridge University Press, 2001); Lafaye, *Quetzalcóatl and Guadalupe,* pp. 211–53 and 274–98; Edmundo O'Gorman, *Destierro de las sombra: Luz en el origin de la imagen y culto de Nuestra Señora de Guadalupe del Tepeyac* (Mexico City: Universidad Nacional Autónoma de México, 1991), pp. 27–61; and William Taylor, "The Virgin of Guadalupe in New Spain: An Inquiry into the Social History of Marian Devotion," *American Ethnologist* 14, no. 1 (1987): pp. 9–33.

64. Katzew, *Casta Painting,* p. 17. Also see Guillermo Tovar de Teresa, *Miguel Cabrera: Pintor de Cámara de la Reina Celestial* (Mexico City: InverMéxico Grupo Financiero, 1995); and Abelardo Carillo y Gariel, *Miguel Cabrera* (Mexico City: Instituto Nacional de Antropología e Historia, 1966).

65. La Faye, Quetzalcóatl and Guadalupe, p. 230.

66. JCBL, Rare Book Collection, *Oración á nuestra señora de Guadalupe, compuesta por el Illmo. Señor D. Francisco Antonio de Lorenzana, arzobispo de México.* Printed in Mexico by don Joseph Antonio de Hogal, 1770.

67. See the 1526 letter that a group of Franciscan friars wrote to Charles V, in Joaquín García Icazbalceta, ed., *Colección de documentos para la historia de México*, vol. II (Mexico City: Joaquín García Icazbalceta, 1866), pp. 155–57.

68. Clavijero wrote in part to refute arguments by the Comte de Buffon, the Abbé Raynal, the Scottish historian William Robertson, and the Prussian naturalist Cornelius de Pauw about how all nature, physical and human, degenerated in the Americas. See Phelan, "Neo-Aztecism in the Eighteenth Century," pp. 760–70; Brading, *The First America*, pp. 450–62 (esp. pp. 461–62); and Cañizares-Esguerra, *How to Write the History of the New World*, pp. 246–47.

69. Rout, *The African Experience*, pp. 143–44.

70. JCBL, Rare Book Collection, *Oración á nuestra señora de Guadalupe*.

71. Seed, *To Love, Honor, and Obey*, pp. 205–6. Also refer to Martínez-Alier (now Stolcke), *Marriage, Class and Colour in Nineteenth-Century Cuba*, pp. 11–15; and Susan Kellogg, "Depicting Mestizaje: Gendered Images of Ethnorace in Colonial Mexican Texts," *Journal of Women's History* 12, no. 3 (2000): p. 73.

72. Twinam, "Racial Passing," pp. 249–72. Twinam notes that the fifteen applications that were submitted between 1795 and 1816 were all from *pardos* and *mulatos*. Twinam, "Racial Passing," p. 250. None were from Mexico. Also refer to Rodulfo Cortés, *El régimen de las "gracias al sacar" en Venezuela durante el período hispánico*, vol. I (Caracas: Academia Nacional de la Historia, 1978).

73. AHPM, 1791/V/52/d.1; and AHPM, 1791/II/49/d.5. For informaciones de limpieza de sangre submitted by applicants to the mining seminar, see AHPM, 1784/IV/7/d.7; 1785/III/20/d.27; 1791/II/49/d.5; 1791/II/49/d.6; 1791/II/49/d.9; 1793/II/61/d.19; 1798/II/93/d.14; 1798/II/93/d.19; 1800/IV/107/d.11; and 1801/II/110/d.5. These probanzas were handled by the Real Tribunal General de Minería but included the participation of alcaldes, intendants, corregidores, and subdelegates from different mining regions (such as Taxco, Guanajuato, Pachuca, and Sinaloa). They were approved by the Real Audiencia.

74. Mainly intended to encourage indigenous rulers and nobles to produce proof of their purity in order to have their titles to offices and lands validated, the 1697 decree circulated in various parts of Mexico. Copies of the decree appear in a host of colonial legal documents, including indigenous petitions to entail estates, struggles over cabildo offices or lands, and claims regarding pure bloodlines. See, for example, Bancroft Library, MS M-M 13; and AGN, Bienes Nacionales, vol. 553, exp. 8.

75. Jaime Cuadriello, *Las glorias de la república de Tlaxcala*, pp. 26–27, 63–86 passim.

76. On Gálvez's maneuvering to diminish the role of creoles in audiencias, town councils, and cathedral chapters while he was minister of the Indies (1776–86). See Bakewell, *A History of Latin America*, p. 270–72; and Kenneth Mills and William B. Taylor, eds., "Royal *Cédula* that American and European Vassals are to be Equal" (Madrid, January 1778), in *Colonial Spanish America: A Documentary History* (Wilmington, DE: Scholarly Resources, 1998), pp. 270–72.

77. See the 1725 "representation" sent to Philip V by Juan Antonio de Ahumada, a lawyer in Mexico City's audiencia. It built on older arguments

about the rights of creoles as well as anticipated some of the more militant ones of the last third of the eighteenth century. BNM, MS 19124. Also refer to Brading, *The First America,* pp. 379–81.

78. BNM, MS 1110: "Representación de la ciudad de Mexico hecha a S.M. en 1771, sobre asuntos de interés común para toda la América Septentrional," 1771. The 1771 Representación was a response to Gálvez's attempts to establish the dominance of peninsulars in the ayuntamiento and audiencia and to break the power of the Consulado of Mexico. It was also a reaction to a secret report allegedly sent to the crown that denigrated creoles and argued that they were not suitable for upper-rank positions. In a 1792 letter to Charles IV, the ayuntamiento reiterated the same points it had made in 1771. See David A. Brading, *The Origins of Mexican Nationalism* (Cambridge: Centre of Latin American Studies, University of Cambridge, 1985), p. 15; and Brading, *The First America,* pp. 479–83.

79. Brading, *The First America,* p. 483.

80. Although the Mexican Inquisition's complaints about the difficulty of doing probanzas increased in the eighteenth century, it continued to send some cases to Spain, where genealogies for Spaniards in the colonies continued to be investigated. These investigations still entailed probing into the candidate's ancestry and overall Christian conduct and reputation. For references to problems associated with doing probanzas, see AHN, Inquisición, legs. 2280–83. For examples of cases sent to Spain, see HL MSS 35173 and 35174; AGN, Inquisición, vol. 1148, exp. 11; AGN, Inquisición, vol. 1287, exp. 2; AGN, Inquisición, vol. 1229, exp. 10; and AGN, Inquisición, vol. 1409, exp. 6.

81. The increasing production of genealogies and genealogical trees appears in a host of Inquisition cases, not just those that pertained to limpieza de sangre. See, for example, AHN, Inquisición, libro 1066, fols. 379–382v and 387–390v; and AHN, Inquisición, legs. 2278, 2279, 2281–82, 2284, 2287–88, and 2291. Most of these cases stress both limpieza and nobleza de sangre.

82. AHN, Inquisición, leg. 2284.

83. AHN, Inquisición, leg. 2282. Also see the probanzas of don Luis María Moreno de Monroy Guerrero Villaseca y Luyando, a lieutenant colonel and alderman, and of don Manuel Joachin Barrientos Lomelín y Cervantes, a canon in Mexico City's Cathedral, lawyer in the royal audiencia, and university rector. AHN, Inquisición, leg. 2282 and 2284.

84. Cuadriello, "Cortés as the American Moses."

CONCLUSION

1. See, for example, Castro, *España en su historia.*

2. As late as the eighteenth century, Franciscan friars examining an información in New Spain expressed the opinion that birth records establish legitimacy, while oral testimonies (reputation) determined limpieza de sangre status. See JCBL/LI, vol. 13, fols. 304–6.

3. Michel-Rolph Trouillot, *Silencing the Past: Power and the Production of History* (Boston: Beacon, 1995), pp. xix, 25, and passim.

4. Cuadriello, *Las glorias de la república de Tlaxcala,* pp. 26–27 and 63–86.

Bibliography

Adelman, Jeremy. "Introduction: The Problem of Persistence in Latin American History." In *Colonial Legacies: The Problem of Persistence in Latin American History,* edited by Jeremy Adelman, 1–13. New York and London: Routledge, 1999.

———. *Sovereignty and Revolution in the Iberian Atlantic.* Princeton: Princeton University Press, 2006.

Aguirre Beltrán, Gonzalo. "The Slave Trade in Mexico." *Hispanic American Historical Review* 24 (1944): 412–31.

———. *La población negra de México: Estudio etnohistórico.* 3rd ed. Mexico City: Fondo de Cultura Económica, 1989 [1946].

Alberro, Solange. "Beatriz de Padilla, Mulatta Mistress and Mother." In *Colonial Spanish America: A Documentary History,* edited by Ken Mills and William Taylor, 178–84. Wilmington, DE: SR Books, 1998.

———. "Crypto-Jews and the Mexican Holy Office in the Seventeenth Century." In *The Jews and the Expansion of Europe to the West 1450–1800,* edited by Paolo Bernardini and Norman Fiering, 172–85. New York and Oxford: Berghahn Books, 2001.

———. *Inquisición y sociedad en México, 1571–1700.* Mexico City: Fondo de Cultura Económica, 1988.

Albi Romero, Guadalupe. "La sociedad de Puebla de los Ángeles en el siglo XVI." *Jahrbuch für Geschichte von Staat, Wirtschaft, und Gesellschaft Lateinamerikas* 7 (1970): 76–145.

Albornoz, Bartolomé de. "Tratado sobre la Esclavitud," 231–33. *Biblioteca de Autores Españoles,* vol. 65. Madrid: M. Rivadeneyra, 1873.

Aldridge, A. Owen. "Feijoo and the Problem of Ethiopian Color." In *Racism in the Eighteenth Century,* edited by Harold E. Pagliaro, 263–77. Cleveland, OH, and London: The Press of Case Western Reserve University, 1973.

Alfaro Ramírez, Gustavo Rafael. "El reclutamiento oligárquico en el cabildo de la Puebla de los Ángeles, 1665–1765." Master's thesis, Universidad Autónoma de Puebla, Facultad de Filosofía y Letras, 1994.

Alpert, Michael. *Crypto-Judaism and the Spanish Inquisition.* New York: Palgrave, 2001.

Altman, Ida. *Emigrants and Society: Extremadura and America in the Sixteenth Century.* Berkeley: University of California Press, 1989.

———. *Transatlantic Ties in the Spanish Empire: Brihuega, Spain, and Puebla, Mexico, 1560–1620.* Stanford, CA: Stanford University Press, 2000.

Álvarez de Miranda, Pedro. *Palabras e ideas: El léxico de la ilustración temprana española (1680–1760).* Madrid: Real Academia Española, 1992.

Amelang, James. "The Purchase of Nobility in Castile, 1552–1700: A Comment." *Journal of European Economic History* 11, no. 1 (1982): 219–26.

Anderson, Benedict. *Imagined Communities.* London: Verso, 1991.

Appelbaum, Nancy P., Anne S. Macpherson, and Karin Alejandra Rosemblatt, eds. *Race and Nation in Modern Latin America.* Chapel Hill and London: University of North Carolina Press, 2003.

Arnorldsson, Sverker. *La conquista española de América según el juicio de la posteridad; vestigios de la leyenda negra.* Madrid: Insula, 1960.

Atienza Hernández, Ignacio. " 'Refeudalisation' in Castile during the Seventeenth Century: A Cliché?" In *The Castilian Crisis of the Seventeenth Century: New Perspectives on the Economic and Social History of Seventeenth-Century Spain,* edited by I. A. A. Thompson and Bartolomé Yun Casalilla, 249–76. Cambridge and New York: Cambridge University Press, 1994.

Aubert, Guillaume. " 'The Blood of France': Race and Purity of Blood in the French Atlantic World." *William and Mary Quarterly,* 3rd series, vol. LXI (July 2004): 439–78.

Baber, R. Jovita. "The Construction of Empire: Politics, Law and Community in Tlaxcala, New Spain, 1521–1640." PhD diss., University of Chicago, 2005.

Baer, Yitzhak. *A History of the Jews in Christian Spain.* Vol. 2. Translated from the Hebrew by Louis Schoffman. Philadelphia: Jewish Publication Society of America, 1978.

Bailyn, Bernard. *Atlantic History: Concept and Contours.* Cambridge, MA: Harvard University Press, 2005.

Bakewell, Peter. "Conquest after Conquest: The Rise of Spanish Domination in America." In *Spain, Europe and the Atlantic World,* edited by Richard Kagan and Geoffrey Parker, 296–315. New York: Cambridge University Press, 1995.

———. *A History of Latin America: Empires and Sequels, 1450–1930.* Malden, MA: Blackwell, 1997.

Balibar, Étienne. "Is there a 'Neo-Racism'?" In *Race, Nation, Class: Ambiguous Identities,* edited by Étienne Balibar and Immanuel Wallerstein, translation of Étienne Balibar by Chris Turner, 17–28. London and New York: Verso, 1991.

———. "Racism and Nationalism." Translated by Chris Turner. In *Race, Nation, Class: Ambiguous Identities,* edited by Étienne Balibar and Immanuel Wallerstein, 37–67. London and New York: Verso, 1991.

Banton, Michael. *Racial Theories.* Cambridge: Cambridge University Press, 1998.

Barkan, Elazar. "Race and the Social Sciences." *Cambridge History of Science* 7 (2003): 693–707.

Baudot, Georges. "Amerindian Image and Utopian Project: Motolinía and Millenarian Discourse." In *Amerindian Images and the Legacy of Colum-*

bus. Vol. 9 of *Hispanic Issues,* edited by René Jara and Nicholas Spadaccini, 375–400. Minneapolis: University of Minnesota Press, 1992.

Beinart, Haim. "The Conversos in Spain and Portugal in the 16th to 18th Centuries." In *The Sephardi Legacy,* vol. 2, edited by Haim Beinart, 43–67. Jerusalem: Magnes Press and Hebrew University, 1992.

———. *Conversos on Trial: The Inquisition in Ciudad Real.* Translated by Yael Guiladi. Jerusalem: Magnes Press, 1981.

———. "The Expulsion from Spain: Causes and Results." In *The Sephardi Legacy,* vol. 2, edited by Haim Beinart, 11–42. Jerusalem: Magnes Press and Hebrew University, 1992.

———. *The Expulsion of the Jews from Spain.* Translated by Jeffrey M. Green. Oxford and Portland, OR: Littman Library of Jewish Civilization, 2002.

Bennassar, Bartolomé. *L'Inquisition Espagnole XVe–XIXe.* Paris: Hachette, 1979.

Bennett, Herman. *Africans in Colonial Mexico: Absolutism, Christianity, and Afro-Creole Consciousness, 1570–1640.* Bloomington and Indianapolis: Indiana University Press, 2003.

Benton, Lauren. *Law and Colonial Cultures: Legal Regimes in World History: 1400–1900.* Cambridge and New York: Cambridge University Press, 2002.

Berdan, Frances. "The Economics of Aztec Trade and Tribute." In *The Aztec Templo Mayor,* edited by Elizabeth Hill Boone, 161–83. Washington, DC: Dumbarton Oaks Research Library and Collection, 1987.

Bethencourt, Francisco. "The Auto da fe: Ritual and Imagery." *Journal of the Warburg and Courtlaud Institutes* 55 (1992): 155–68.

Biblioteca de Autores Españoles, vol. 65. Madrid: M. Rivadeneyra, 1873.

Blackburn, Robin. *The Making of New World Slavery: From the Baroque to the Modern, 1492–1800.* New York and London: Verso, 1997.

———. "The Old World Background to European Colonial Slavery." *William and Mary Quarterly* 54, no. 1 (1997): 65–102.

Boase, Roger. "The Morisco Expulsion and Diaspora: An Example of Racial and Religious Intolerance." In *Cultures in Contact in Medieval Spain,* edited by David Hook and Barry Taylor, 9–28. London: King's College London Medieval Studies, 1990.

Boone, Elizabeth Hill. "Aztec Pictorial Histories: Records without Words." In *Writing without Words: Alternative Literacies in Mesoamerica and the Andes,* edited by Elizabeth H. Boone and Walter D. Mignolo, 50–76. Durham, NC: Duke University Press, 1994.

———. *Stories in Red and Black: Pictorial Histories of the Aztecs and Mixtecs.* Austin: University of Texas Press, 2000.

Borah, Woodrow. *Justice by Insurance: The General Indian Court of Colonial Mexico and the Legal Aides of the Half-Real.* Berkeley: University of California Press, 1983.

———. "The Spanish and Indian Law: New Spain." In *The Inca and Aztec States, 1400–1800: Anthropology and History,* edited by George A. Collier, Renato I. Rosaldo, and John D. Wirth, 265–88. New York and London: Academic Press, 1982.

Bourdieu, Pierre. *Outline of a Theory of Practice*. Translated by Richard Nice. Cambridge and New York: Cambridge University Press, 1977.

Bourdieu, Pierre, and Loïc Wacquant. "On the Cunning of Imperialist Reason." *Theory, Culture and Society* 16, no. 1 (1999): 41–58.

Bowser, Frederick. "Africans in Spanish American Colonial Society." In *The Cambridge History of Latin America*, vol. II, edited by Leslie Bethell, 357–79. Cambridge and New York: Cambridge University Press.

Boyd-Bowman, Peter. "Negro Slaves in Early Colonial Mexico." *The Americas* 26, no. 2 (1969): 134–151.

Boyer, Richard. *Cast [sic] and Identity in Colonial Mexico: A Proposal and an Example*. Storrs, CT, Providence, RI, and Amherst, MA: Latin American Studies Consortium of New England, 1997.

Brading, David A. "Bourbon Spain and its American Empires." In *Colonial Spanish America*, edited by Leslie Bethell, 112–62. Cambridge: Cambridge University Press, 1987.

————. *The First America: The Spanish Monarchy, Creole Patriots, and the Liberal State, 1492–1867*. Cambridge: Cambridge University Press, 1991.

————. *Mexican Phoenix: Our Lady of Guadalupe: Image and Tradition Across Five Centuries*. Cambridge and New York: Cambridge University Press, 2001.

————. *The Origins of Mexican Nationalism*. Cambridge: Centre of Latin American Studies, University of Cambridge, 1985.

Brady, Robert LaDon. "The Emergence of a Negro Class in Mexico, 1524–1640." PhD diss., University of Iowa, 1965.

Braude, Benjamin. "The Sons of Noah and the Construction of Ethnic and Geographical Identities in the Medieval and Early Modern Periods." *William and Mary Quarterly* 54, no. 1 (1997): 103–42.

Brice Heath, Shirley. *Telling Tongues: Language Policy in Mexico, Colony to Nation*. New York: Teachers College Press, 1972.

Brown, Jonathan. *Latin America: A Social History of the Colonial World*. Belmont, CA: Wadsworth/Thomson Learning, 2005.

Burdick, John. "The Myth of Racial Democracy." *Report on the Americas* (NACLA) 25, no. 4 (February, 1992): 40–44.

Burkholder, Mark A., and Lyman L. Johnson. *Colonial Latin America*. New York and Oxford: Oxford University Press, 1998.

Calnek, Edward. "Patterns of Empire Formation in the Valley of Mexico, Late Postclassic Period, 1200–1521." In *The Inca and Aztec States, 1400–1800: Anthropology and History*, edited by George Collier et al., 43–62. New York and London: Academic Press, 1982.

Cañizares-Esguerra, Jorge. "New World, New Stars: Patriotic Astrology and the Invention of Indian and Creole Bodies in Colonial Spanish America 1600–1650." *American Historical Review* 104, no. 1 (1999): 33-68

————. *Puritan Conquistadors: Iberianizing the Atlantic, 1550–1700*. Stanford, CA: Stanford University Press, 2006.

Cárdenas, Juan de. *Problemas y secretos maravillosos de las Indias*. Madrid: Alianza Editorial, 1988 [1591].

Carillo y Gariel, Abelardo. *Miguel Cabrera*. Mexico City: Instituto Nacional de Antropología e Historia, 1966.

Caro Baroja, Julio. "Antecedentes españoles de algunos problemas sociales relativos al mestizaje." *Revista Histórica* (Lima) 28 (1965): 197–210.

———. *Los judíos en la España moderna y contemporánea.* Vol. 2. Madrid: Ediciones Arión, 1961.

———. *Los moriscos del Reino de Granada.* Madrid: Diana, 1957.

———. *Razas, pueblos y linajes.* Madrid: Revista de Occidente, 1957.

Carrasco, David, ed. *Aztec Ceremonial Landscapes.* Niwot: University Press of Colorado, 1991.

———. *Quetzalcoatl and the Irony of Empire: Myths and Prophecies in the Aztec Tradition.* Chicago and London: University of Chicago Press, 1992.

Carrasco, Pedro. "Social Organization of Ancient Mexico." In *Handbook of Middle American Indians,* vol. 10, edited by R. Wauchope, G. F. Ekholm, and I. Bernal, 349–75. Austin: University of Texas Press, 1971.

———. *The Tenochca Empire of Ancient Mexico: The Triple Alliance of Tenochtitlan, Tetzcoco, and Tlacopan.* Norman: University of Oklahoma Press, 1999.

———. "La transformación de la cultura indígena durante la colonia." *Historia Mexicana* 25, no. 2 (1975): 175–203. Carrera, Magali M. *Imagining Identity in New Spain: Race, Lineage, and the Colonial Body in Portraiture and Casta Paintings.* Austin: University of Texas Press, 2003.

Carrete Parrondo, Carlos. *El judaísmo español y la inquisición.* Madrid: Editorial Mapfre, 1992.

Cartagena, Alonso de. *Defensorium unitatis christianae (tratado en favor de los judíos conversos).* Madrid: C. Bermejo, Impresor, 1943.

Cartas de Indias. Madrid: Ministerio de Fomento, 1877.

Castillo Palma, Norma Angélica. "Los estatutos de 'pureza de sangre' como medio de acceso a las élites: el caso de la región de Puebla." In *Círculos de Poder en la Nueva España,* edited by Carmen Castañeda, 105–129. Mexico City: CIESAS and Grupo Editorial Miguel Angel Porrúa, 1998.

———. "Matrimonios mixtos y cruce de la barrera de color como vías para el mestizaje de la población negra y mulata (1674–1796)." *Signos históricos* II, no. 4 (2000): 107–37

Castro, Américo. *España en su historia: Cristianos, moros y judíos.* Barcelona: Editorial Crítica, 1984 [1948].

Castro Morales, Efrain. "Los cuadros de castas de la Nueva España." *Jahrbuch für Geschichte von Staat, Wirtschaft, und Gesellschaft Lateinamerikas,* no. 20 (1983): 671–90.

Cervantes, Miguel de. *Entremeses.* Mexico City: Editorial Porrúa, 1968.

Chance, John K., and William B. Taylor. "Estate *and* Class: A Reply." *Comparative Studies of Society and History* 21, no. 3 (1979): 434–41.

———. "Estate and Class in a Colonial City: Oaxaca in 1792." *Comparative Studies in Society and History* 19 (1977): 454–87.

Chasteen, John Charles. "Introduction: Beyond Imagined Communities." In *Beyond Imagined Communities: Reading and Writing the Nation in the Nineteenth-Century Latin America,* edited by Sara Castro-Klarén and John Charles Chasteen, ix–xxv. Washington, DC, Baltimore, and London: Woodrow Wilson Press and Johns Hopkins University Press, 2003.

Chimalpahin Quauhtlehuanitzin, Domingo Francisco de San Antón Muñón. *Annals of His Time: Don Domingo de San Antón Muñón Chimalpahin Quauhtlehuanitzin.* Edited and translated by James Lockhart, Susan Schroeder, and Doris Namala. Stanford, CA: Stanford University Press, 2006.

———. *Codex Chimalpahin: Society and Politics in Mexico Tenochtitlan, Tlatelolco, Texcoco, Culhuacan, and Other Nahua Altepetl in Central Mexico.* 2 vols. Translated by Arthur J. Anderson and Susan Schroeder. Norman and London: University of Oklahoma Press, 1997.

Chocano Mena, Magdalena G. "Colonial Scholars in the Cultural Establishment of Seventeenth Century New Spain." PhD diss., State University of New York at Stony Brook, 1994.

Clavero, Bartolomé. *Mayorazgo: Propiedad feudal en Castilla, 1369–1836.* Madrid: Siglo XXI de España Editores, 1989.

Clendinnen, Inga. *Ambivalent Conquests: Maya and Spaniard in Yucatan, 1517–1570.* New York: Cambridge University Press, 1991.

———. *Aztecs: An Interpretation.* Cambridge and New York: Cambridge University Press, 1991.

———. "Reading the Inquisitorial Record in Yucatán: Fact or Fantasy." *The Americas* 38, no. 3 (1982): 327–45.

———. "Ways to the Sacred: Reconstructing 'Religion' in Sixteenth Century Mexico." *History and Anthropology* 5 (1990): 105–41.

Coatsworth, John H. "The Limits of Colonial Absolutism: Mexico in the Eighteenth Century." In *Essays in the Political, Economic and Social History of Colonial Latin America,* edited by Karen Spalding, 25–51. Newark: University of Delaware, Latin American Studies Program, Occasional Papers and Monographs No. 3, 1982.

Cohen, Thomas. "Nation, Lineage, and Jesuit Unity in Antonio Possevino's Memorial to Everard Mercurian (1576)." In *A Companhia de Jesus na Península Ibérica nos séculos XVI e XVII: Espiritualidade e cultura,* 543–61. Porto, Portugal: Editora Universidade do Porto, 2004.

Conrad, Geoffrey W., and Arthur Andrew Demarest. *Religion and Empire: The Dynamics of Aztec and Inca Expansionism.* Cambridge: Cambridge University Press, 1984.

Contreras, Jaime. *El Santo Oficio de la Inquisición en Galicia, 1560–1700: Poder, sociedad y cultura.* Madrid: Akal, 1982.

———. *Historia de la Inquisición Española (1478–1834).* Madrid: Arco/Libros, 1997.

———. "Limpieza de sangre, cambio social y manipulación de la memoria." In *Inquisición y conversos,* 81–101. Toledo: Caja de Castilla-La Mancha, 1994.

———. *Sotos contra Riquelmes: Regidores, inquisidores y criptojudíos.* Madrid: Anaya & M. Muchnik, 1992.

Contreras, Jaime, and Jean Pierre Dedieu. "Estructuras geográficas del Santo Oficio en España." In *Historia de la Inquisición en España y América: Las estructuras del Santo Oficio,* vol. 2, edited by Joaquín Pérez Villanueva and Bartolomé Escandell Bonet, 3–48. Madrid: Biblioteca de Autores Cristianos, Centro de Estudios Inquisitoriales, 1993.

Cooper, Frederick. *Colonialism in Question: Theory, Knowledge, History.* Berkeley: University of California Press, 2005.

Cooper, Frederick, and Ann L. Stoler. "Tensions of Empire: Colonial Control and Visions of Rule." *American Ethnologist* 16, no. 4 (1989): 609–21.

Cope, Douglas R. *The Limits of Racial Domination: Plebeian Society in Colonial Mexico City, 1660–1720.* Madison: University of Wisconsin Press, 1994.

Corominas, Joan. *Diccionario crítico etimológico de la lengua castellana.* 4 vols. Berne: Editorial Francke, 1954.

Cortés, Rodulfo. *El régimen de las "gracias al sacar" en Venezuela durante el período hispánico.* Vol. I. Caracas: Academia Nacional de la Historia, 1978.

Covarrubias Orozco, Sebastián de. *Tesoro de la lengua castellana o española.* Edited by Felipe C. R. Maldonado Madrid: Editorial Castalia, 1995 [1611].

Crosby, Alfred W., Jr. *The Columbian Exchange: Biological and Cultural Consequences of 1492.* 30th anniversary ed. Westport, CT: Praeger, 2003.

Cuadriello, Jaime. "Cortés as the American Moses: The Mural Writing of Patriotic History." Lecture given at the University of Southern California, Los Angeles, November 22, 2005.

———. *Las glorias de la república de Tlaxcala: O la conciencia como imagen sublime.* Mexico City: Instituto de Investigaciones Estéticas, Universidad Nacional Autónoma de México, and Museo Nacional de Arte, INBA, 2004.

Cuevas, Mariano. *Historia de la Iglesia en México.* 3rd ed., vol. 1. El Paso, TX: Editorial "Revista Católica," 1928.

Cutter, Charles R. *The Legal Culture of Northern New Spain, 1700–1810.* Albuquerque: University of New Mexico Press, 1995.

Davies, Nigel. *The Aztecs.* Norman and London: University of Oklahoma Press, 1973.

———. *The Toltec Heritage: From the Fall of Tula to the Rise of Tenochtitlán.* Norman: University of Oklahoma Press, 1980.

Davis, David B. *Challenging the Boundaries of Slavery.* Cambridge, MA, and London: Harvard University Press, 2003.

———. "Constructing Race: A Reflection." *William and Mary Quarterly* 54, no. 1 (1997): 7–18.

Deans-Smith, Susan. *Bureaucrats, Planters, and Workers: The Making of the Tobacco Monopoly in Bourbon Mexico.* Austin: University of Texas Press, 1992.

Dedieu, Jean Pierre. *L'administration de la foi: L'inquisition de Tolède XVIe–XVIIIe siècle.* Madrid: Casa de Velázquez, 1989.

———. "'Christianization' in New Castile: Catechism, Communion, Mass, and Confirmation in the Toledo Archbishopric, 1540–1650." In *Culture and Control in Counter-Reformation Spain,* edited by Anne J. Cruz and Mary Elizabeth Perry, 1–24. Minneapolis: University of Minnesota Press, 1992.

———. "*Limpieza,* Pouvoir et Richesse: Conditions d'entrée dans le corps des ministres de l'inquisition: Tribunal de Tolède, XIVe–XVIIe siècles." In *Les sociétés fermées dans le monde Ibérique (XVIe–XVIIIe siècle),* 168–87. Paris: Editions du Centre National de la Recherche Scientifique, 1986.

Diccionario de Autoridades. Madrid: Editorial Gredos, 1990 [1732].

Domínguez Ortiz, Antonio. *La clase social de los conversos en Castilla en la edad moderna*. Madrid: Instituto Balmes de Sociología, Departamento de Historia Social, Consejo Superior de Investigaciones Científicas, 1955.

———. *The Golden Age of Spain, 1516–1659*. Translated by James Casey. New York: Basic Books, 1971.

———. *Los judeoconversos en España y América*. Madrid: Ediciones Istmo, 1971.

———. *Los judeoconversos en la España moderna*. Madrid: Editorial MAPFRE, 1992.

Domínguez Ortiz, Antonio, and Bernard Vincent. *Historia de los moriscos: Vida y tragedia de una minoría*. Madrid: Alianza Editorial, 1997 [1985].

Domínguez y Compañy, Francisco. "La condición de vecino: Su significación e importancia en la vida colonial hispanoamericana." In *Crónica del VI congreso histórico municipal interamericano (Madrid-Barcelona, 1957)*, 703–20. Madrid: Instituto de Estudios de Administración Local, 1959.

Douglas, Mary. *Purity and Danger: An Analysis of the Concepts of Pollution and Taboo*. London: Routledge, 1995.

Edwards, John. "The Beginnings of a Scientific Theory of Race? Spain, 1450–1600." In *From Iberia to Diaspora: Studies in Sephardic History and Culture*, edited by Yedida K. Stillman and Norman A. Stillman. Leiden, Boston, and Cologne: Brill, 1999.

———. *Christian Córdoba: The City and its Region in the Late Middle Ages*. New York: Cambridge University Press, 1982.

Elliot, John H. *Imperial Spain, 1469–1716*. London: Edward Arnold Publishers, 1963.

Escobar del Corro, Juan. *Tractatus bipartitus de puritate et nobilitate probanda*. Lyon: Sumptibus Rochi Deville & L. Chalmette, 1737.

Estensoro, Juan Carlos, Pilar Romero de Tejada y Picatoste, Luis Eduardo Wuffarden, and Natalia Majluf, eds. *Los cuadros del mestizaje del virrey Amat: La representación etnográfica en el Perú colonial*. Lima: Museo del Arte de Lima, 1999.

Fausto-Sterling, Anne. *Sexing the Body: Gender Politics and the Construction of Sexuality*. New York: Basic Books, 2000.

Fernández de Echeverría y Veytia, Mariano. *Historia de la fundación de la ciudad de la Puebla de los Ángeles en la Nueva España*. 2 vols. Puebla: Imprenta Labor, 1931.

Fernández de Recas, Guillermo S. *Cacicazgos y nobiliario indígena de la Nueva España*. Mexico City: Instituto Bibliográfico Mexicano de la Biblioteca Nacional de México, 1961.

———. *Mayorazgos de la Nueva España*. Mexico City: Instituto Bibliográfico Mexicano, Biblioteca Nacional de México, 1965.

Few, Martha. *Women Who Live Evil Lives: Gender, Religion, and the Politics of Power in Colonial Guatemala*. Austin: University of Texas Press, 2002.

Florescano, Enrique. "El canon memorioso forjado por los títulos primordiales." *Colonial Latin American Review* 11, no. 2 (2002): 183–230.

———. *Memory, Myth, and Time in Mexico: From the Aztecs to Independence.* Translated by Albert G. Bork. Austin: University of Texas Press, 1994.

———. "La reconstrucción histórica elaborada por la nobleza indígena y sus descendientes mestizos." In *La memoria y el olvido: Segundo simposio de las mentalidades*, 11–20. Mexico City: Instituto Nacional de Antropología e Historia, 1985.

Forbes, Jack D. *Black Africans and Native Americans: Color, Race and Caste in the Evolution of Red-Black Peoples.* New York: Basil Blackwell, 1988.

Foster, George. *Culture and Conquest: America's Spanish Heritage.* New York: Wenner-Gren Foundation for Anthropological Research, 1960.

Foucault, Michel. *The Archaeology of Knowledge.* Translated from the French by A. M. Sheridan Smith. New York: Pantheon, 1972.

———. *The History of Sexuality.* Vol. 1. Translated by Robert Hurley. New York: Vintage, 1990.

———. *The Order of Things: An Archaeology of the Human Sciences.* New York: Vintage, 1973.

Fredrickson, George M. *Racism: A Short History.* Princeton, NJ, and Oxford: Princeton University Press, 2002.

Freedman, Paul. *Images of the Medieval Peasant.* Stanford, CA: Stanford University Press, 1999.

French, John D. "The Missteps of Anti-Imperialist Reason: Bourdieu, Wacquant and Hanchard's *Orpheus and Power.*" *Theory, Culture and Society* 17, no. 1 (2000): 107–28.

Gallagher, Ann Miriam, R. S. M. "Las monjas indígenas del monasterio de Corpus Christi de la ciudad de México, 1724–1821." In *Las mujeres latino-americanas: perspectivas históricas*, edited by Asunción Lavrin, translated by Mercedes Pizarro de Parlante, 177–201. Mexico City: Fondo de Cultura Económica, 1985.

Gampel, Benjamin R. "Does Medieval Navarrese Jewry Salvage Our Notion of *Convivencia*?" In *In Iberia and Beyond: Hispanic Jews Between Cultures*, edited by Bernard Dov Cooperman, 97–122. Newark: University of Delaware Press, 1998.

García, Gregorio. *Origen de los indios del Nuevo Mundo.* Mexico City: Fondo de Cultura Económica, 1981.

García-Abásolo, Antonio F. *Martín Enríquez y la Reforma de 1568 en Nueva España.* Seville: Excelentísima Diputación Provincial de Sevilla, 1983.

García-Baquero González, Antonio. *Andalucía y la Carrera de Indias, 1492–1824.* Seville: Biblioteca de la Cultura Andaluza, 1986.

García Cárcel, Ricardo. *La leyenda negra: Historia y opinión.* Madrid: Alianza Editorial, 1992.

———. *Orígenes de la inquisición española: El Tribunal de Valencia, 1478–1530.* Barcelona: Ediciones Península, 1976.

García Icazbalceta, Joaquín, ed. *Colección de documentos para la historia de México.* Vol. II. Mexico City: Joaquín García Icazbalceta, 1866.

García Ivars, Flora. *La represión en el tribunal inquisitorial de Granada, 1550–1819.* Madrid: Ediciones Akal, 1991.

García Sáiz, María Concepción. "The Artistic Development of Casta Painting." In *New World Orders: Casta Painting and Colonial Latin America,* edited by Ilona Katzew, 30–41. New York: Americas Society Art Gallery, 1996.

———. *Las castas mexicanas: Un género pictórico americano.* Milan: Olivetti, 1989.

———. "The Contribution of Colonial Painting to the Spread of the Image of America." In *America: Bride of the Sun: 500 Years of Latin America and the Low Countries: 1.2–31.5.92: Royal Museum of Fine Arts, Antwerp.* Edited by Bernadette J. Bucher 177–78. Brussels, Belgium: Flemish Community, Administration of External Relations, 1992.

Garner, Richard L., and Spiro E. Stefanou. *Economic Growth and Change in Bourbon Mexico.* Gainesville: University Press of Florida, 1993.

Garraway, Doris. "Race, Reproduction and Family Romance in Moreau de Saint-Méry's *Description . . . de la partie française de l'isle Saint-Domingue.*" *Eighteenth-Century Studies* 38, no. 2 (2005): 227–46.

Germeten, Nicole von. *Black Blood Brothers: Confraternities and Social Mobility for Afro-Mexicans.* Gainesville: University Press of Florida, 2006.

Gibson, Charles. "The Aztec Aristocracy in Colonial Mexico." *Comparative Studies in Society and History* 2, no. 2 (January 1960), pp. 169–96.

———. *The Aztecs under Spanish Rule: A History of the Indians of the Valley of Mexico, 1519–1810.* Stanford, CA: Stanford University Press, 1964.

———, ed. *The Black Legend: Anti-Spanish Attitudes in the Old World and the New.* New York: Knopf, 1971.

———. "The Identity of Diego Muñoz Camargo." *Hispanic American Historical Review* 30, no. 2 (1950): 199–205.

———. *Tlaxcala in the Sixteenth Century.* New Haven, CT: Yale University Press, 1952.

Gil, Juan. *Los conversos y la Inquisición sevillana.* Vol. 1. Seville: Universidad de Sevilla: Fundación El Monte, 2000.

Gillespie, Susan D. *The Aztec Kings: The Construction of Rulership in Mexica History.* Tucson: University of Arizona Press, 1989.

Gilroy, Paul. "One Nation under a Groove: The Cultural Politics of 'Race' and Racism in Britain." In *Anatomy of Racism,* edited by David Theo Goldberg, 263–82. Minneapolis and London: University of Minnesota Press, 1990.

———. *'There ain't no Black in the Union Jack': The Cultural Politics of Race and Nation.* Chicago: University of Chicago Press, 1991.

Gojman Goldberg, Alicia. *Los conversos en la Nueva España.* Mexico City: Universidad Nacional Autónoma de México, Escuela Nacional de Estudios Profesionales Acatlán, and B'nai B'rith, n.d.

Gómez de Cervantes, Gonzalo. *La vida económica y social de Nueva España al finalizar el siglo XVI.* Mexico City: Antigua Librería Robredo, de José Porrúa e Hijos, 1944.

González Echevarría, Roberto. *Myth and Archive: A Theory of Latin American Narrative.* Durham, NC, and London: Duke University Press, 1998.

González Hermosillo, Francisco. "La élite indígena de Cholula en el siglo XVIII: El caso de don Juan de León y Mendoza." In *Círculos de poder en la Nueva*

España, edited by Carmen Castañeda, 59–103. Mexico City: CIESAS and Grupo Editorial Miguel Angel Porrúa, 1998.

Gootenberg, Paul. "On Salamanders, Pyramids, and Mexico's 'Growth–without–Change': Anachronistic Reflections on a Case of Bourbon New Spain." *Colonial Latin America Review* 4, no. 1 (1995): 117–27.

Graizbord, David L. *Souls in Dispute: Converso Identities in Iberia and the Jewish Diaspora, 1580–1700.* Philadelphia: University of Pennsylvania Press, 2004.

Greenblatt, Stephen. *Marvelous Possessions: The Wonder of the New World.* Chicago: University of Chicago Press, 1991.

Greenleaf, Richard E. "The Inquisition and the Indians of New Spain: A Study in Jurisdictional Confusion." *The Americas* 22, no. 2 (1965): 138–66.

———. "The Mexican Inquisition and the Indians: Sources for the Ethnohistorian." *The Americas* 34, no. 3 (1978): 315–44.

———. *Zumárraga y la Inquisición mexicana.* Mexico City: Fondo de Cultura Económica, 1988.

Gruzinski, Serge. *La colonización de lo imaginario: Sociedades indígenas y occidentalización en el México español, siglos XVI–XVIII.* Translated by Jorge Ferreiro. Mexico City: Fondo de Cultura Económica, 1991.

Guerra, François-Xavier. "Identidades e independencia: La excepción americana." In *Imaginar la nación,* edited by François-Xavier Guerra and Monica Quijada, 93–134. Münster, Hamburg: Lit, 1994.

Guillaumin, Colette. "The Idea of Race and its Elevation to Autonomous Scientific and Legal Status." In *Sociological Theories: Race and Colonialism,* 37–67. Paris: UNESCO, 1980.

———. *Racism, Sexism, Power and Ideology.* London and New York: Routledge, 1995.

Gutiérrez, Ramón A. *When Jesus Came, the Corn Mothers Went Away: Marriage, Sexuality and Power in New Mexico, 1500–1846.* Stanford, CA: Stanford University Press, 1991.

Hackel, Steven W. *Children of Coyote, Missionaries of Saint Francis: Indian-Spanish Relations in Colonial California, 1769–1850.* Chapel Hill: Omohundro Institute of Early American History and Culture and University of North Carolina Press, 2005.

Haidt, Rebecca. *Embodying the Enlightenment: Knowing the Body in Eighteenth-Century Spanish Literature and Culture.* New York: St. Martin's Press, 1998.

Haliczer, Stephen. *Inquisition and Society in the Kingdom of Valencia, 1478–1834.* Berkeley: University of California Press, 1990.

———. "The Moriscos: Loyal Subjects of his Catholic Majesty Philip III." In *Christians, Muslims, and Jews in Medieval and Early Modern Spain: Interaction and Cultural Change,* edited by Mark D. Meyerson and Edward D. English, 265–89. Notre Dame, IN: University of Notre Dame Press, 1999.

———. "Sexuality and Repression in Counter-Reformation Spain." In *Sex and Love in Golden Age Spain,* edited by Alain Saint-Saëns, 81–94. New Orleans: University Press of the South, 1999.

Hall, Stuart. "Gramsci's Relevance for the Study of Race and Ethnicity." In *Stuart Hall: Critical Dialogues in Cultural Studies,* edited by David Morley and Kuan-Hsing Chen, 411–40. London and New York: Routledge, 1996.

———. "On Postmodernism and Articulation." In *Stuart Hall: Critical Dialogues in Cultural Studies,* edited by David Morley and Kuan-Hsing Chen, 131–50. London and New York: Routledge, 1996.

———. "Race, Articulation and Societies Structured in Dominance." In *Unesco Reader, Sociological Theories: Race and Colonialism,* 305–45. Paris: UNESCO, 1980.

Hamnett, Brian R. "Absolutismo ilustrado y la crisis multidimensional en el período colonial tardío, 1760–1808." In *Interpretaciones del siglo XVIII mexicano: El impacto de las reformas borbónicas,* edited by Josefina Zoraida Vázquez, 67–108. Mexico City: Nueva Imagen, 1992.

Hanger, Kimberly S. "Patronage, Property and Persistence: The Emergence of a Free Black Elite in Spanish New Orleans." In *Against the Odds: Free Blacks in the Slave Societies of the Americas,* edited by Jane G. Landers, 44–64. London and Portland, OR: Frank Cass, 1996.

Hanke, Lewis. *All Mankind is One: A Study of the Disputation between Bartolomé de Las Casas and Juan Ginés de Sepúlveda in 1550 on the Intellectual and Religious Capacity of the American Indians.* DeKalb: Northern Illinois University Press, 1974.

———. ed. *History of Latin American Civilization: Sources and Interpretations.* Vol. 1, *The Colonial Experience.* London: Methuen and Co., 1969.

———. "A Modest Proposal for a Moratorium on Grand Generalizations: Some Thoughts on the Black Legend." *Hispanic American Historical Review* 51, no. 1 (1971): 112–27.

Hannaford, Ivan. *The Idea of Race: The History of an Idea in the West.* Washington, DC: Woodrow Wilson Center Press and Johns Hopkins University Press, 1996.

Harrison, Faye V. "The Persistent Power of 'Race' in the Cultural and Political Economy of Racism." *Annual Review of Anthropology* 24 (1995): 47–74.

Haskett, Robert. "Activist or Adulteress? The Life and Struggle of Doña Josefa María of Tepoztlan." In *Indian Women of Early Mexico,* edited by Susan Schroeder, Stephanie Wood, and Robert Haskett, 145–64. Norman and London: University of Oklahoma Press, 1997.

———. *Indigenous Rulers: An Ethnohistory of Town Government in Colonial Cuernavaca.* Albuquerque: University of New Mexico Press, 1991.

———. "El legendario don Toribio en los títulos primordiales de Cuernavaca." In *De Tlacuilos y escribanos,* edited by Xavier Noguez and Stephanie Gail Wood, 137–66. Zamora, Michoacán: El Colegio de Michoacán, 1998.

Hassig, Ross. *Trade, Tribute, and Transportation: The Sixteenth-Century Political Economy of the Valley of Mexico.* Norman and London: University of Oklahoma Press, 1985.

Henningsen, Gustav. "The Archives and the Historiography of the Spanish Inquisition," translated by Lawrence Scott Rainey. In *The Inquisition in Early Modern Europe: Studies on Sources and Methods,* edited by Gustav

Henningsen, John Tedeschi, and Charles Amiel, 54–78. Dekalb: Northern Illinois University, 1986.

Héritier-Augé, Françoise. "Semen and Blood: Some Ancient Theories Concerning Their Genesis and Relationship." In *Fragments for a History of the Human Body*, vol. 3, edited by Michel Feher with Ramona Naddaff and Nadia Tazi, 159–75. New York: Urzone, 1989.

Hernández Franco, Juan. *Cultura y limpieza de sangre en la España moderna: Puritate sanguinis*. Murcia: Universidad de Murcia, 1996.

Herzog, Tamar. *Defining Nations: Immigrants and Citizens in Early Modern Spain and Spanish America*. New Haven, CT, and London: Yale University Press, 2003.

———. *Upholding Justice: Society, State, and the Penal System in Quito (1650–1750)*. Ann Arbor: University of Michigan Press, 2004.

Himmerich y Valencia, Robert. *The Encomenderos of New Spain, 1521–1555*. Austin: University of Texas Press, 1991.

Hodes, Martha. *White Women, Black Men*. New Haven, CT: Yale University Press, 1997.

Holt, Thomas C. "Marking: Race, Race-making and the Writing of History." *American Historical Review* 100, no. 1 (1995): 1–20.

———. *The Problem of Race in the 21st Century*. Cambridge, MA, and London: Harvard University Press, 2000.

———. "Slavery and Freedom in the Atlantic World: Reflections on the Diasporan Framework." In *Crossing Boundaries: Comparative History of Black People in Diaspora*, edited by Darlene Clark Hine and Jacqueline McLeod, 33–44. Bloomington and Indianapolis: Indiana University Press, 1999.

Hordes, Stanley M. "The Inquisition as Economic and Political Agent: The Campaign of the Mexican Holy Office against the Crypto-Jews in the Mid-Seventeenth Century." *The Americas* 39, no. 1 (1982): pp. 23–38.

Hudson, Nicholas. "From 'Nation' to 'Race': The Origin of Racial Classification in Eighteenth-Century Thought." *Eighteenth-Century Studies* 29, no. 3 (1996): 247–64.

Instrucciones que los virreyes de Nueva España dejaron a sus sucesores. Mexico: Imprenta Imperial, 1867.

Israel, Jonathan I. *Race, Class and Politics in Colonial Mexico, 1610–1670*. London: Oxford University Press, 1975.

Ixtlilxóchitl, Fernando de Alva. *Historia de la nación chichimeca*. Madrid: Historia 16, 1985.

Jackson, Robert H. "Race/caste and the Creation and Meaning of Identity in Colonial Spanish America." *Revista de Indias* 55, no. 203 (1995): 150–73.

Jarquín Ortega, María Teresa. "El códice Techialoyan García Granados y las congregaciones en el altiplano central de México." In *De Tlacuilos y escribanos*, edited by Xavier Noguez and Stephanie Wood, 49–58. Zamora, Michoacán: El Colegio de Michoacán, 1998.

Javier Pescador, Juan. *The New World Inside a Basque Village: The Oiartzun Valley and Its Atlantic Emigrants, 1550–1800*. Reno: University of Nevada Press, 2004.

Journal of Colonialism and Colonial History 5, no. 2 (2004).

Kamen, Henry. *Inquisition and Society in Spain in the Sixteenth and Seventeenth Centuries.* Bloomington: Indiana University Press, 1985.

———. "Limpieza and the Ghost of Américo Castro: Racism as a Tool of Literary Analysis." *Hispanic Review* 64, no. 1 (1996): 19–29.

———. *The Spanish Inquisition: A Historical Revision.* New Haven, CT, and London: Yale University Press, 1998.

Kamen, Henry, and Joseph Pérez. *La imagen de la España de Felipe II: "Leyenda negra" o conflicto de intereses.* Valladolid: Universidad de Valladolid, 1980.

Katz, Friedrich. *The Ancient American Civilisations.* London: Weidenfield and Nicolson, 1989 [1972].

Katzew, Ilona. "Casta Painting: Identity and Social Stratification in Colonial Mexico." In *New World Orders: Casta Painting and Colonial Latin America,* edited by Ilona Katzew, 8–29. New York: Americas Society Art Gallery, 1996.

———. *Casta Painting: Images of Race in Eighteenth-Century Mexico.* New Haven, CT, and London: Yale University Press, 2004.

Keen, Benjamin. "The Black Legend Revisited: Assumptions and Realities." *Hispanic American Historical Review* 49, no. 4 (1969): 703–19.

———. "The White Legend Revisited: A Reply to Professor Hanke's 'Modest Proposal.'" *Hispanic American Historical Review* 51, no. 2 (1971): 336–55.

Kellogg, Susan. "Depicting Mestizaje: Gendered Images of Ethnorace in Colonial Mexican Texts." *Journal of Women's History* 12, no. 3 (2000): 69–92.

———. *Law and the Transformation of Aztec Culture, 1500–1700.* Norman: University of Oklahoma Press, 1995.

———. "The Woman's Room: Some Aspects of Gender Relations in Tenochtitlan in the Late Pre-Hispanic Period." *Ethnohistory* 42, no. 4 (1995): 563–76.

Kenneth Mills, "The Limits of Religious Coercion in Midcolonial Peru." In *The Church in Colonial Latin America,* edited by John F. Schwaller, 147–80. Wilmington, DE: Scholarly Resources, 2000.

Kicza, John E. "Native American, African, and Hispanic Communities during the Middle Period in the Colonial Americas." *Historical Archaelogy* 31, no. 1 (1997): 9–17.

Klor de Alva, Jorge. "Colonizing Souls: The Failure of the Indian Inquisition and the Rise of Penitential Discipline." In *Cultural Encounters: The Impact of the Inquisition in Spain and the New World,* edited by Mary Elizabeth Perry and Anne J. Cruz, 3–21. Berkeley: University of California Press, 1991.

Konetzke, Richard. *Colección de documentos para la historia de la formación social de Hispanoamérica, 1493–1810.* Vol. 1. Madrid: Consejo Superior de Investigaciones Científicas, 1953.

———. *Colección de documentos para la historia de la formación social de Hispanoamérica 1493–1810.* Vol. 3, bk.1. Madrid: Consejo Superior de Investigaciones Científicas, 1962.

———. "Estado y Sociedad en las Indias." *Estudios Americanos* (Seville) 3, no. 8 (1951): 33–58.

———. "La formación de la nobleza en Indias." *Estudios Americanos* 3, no. 10 (1951): 329–57.

———. "El mestizaje y su importancia en el desarrollo de la población hispano-americana durante la época colonial." *Revista de Indias* 7, no. 24 (April–June, 1946): 215–37.

———. "Ordenanzas de gremios durante la época colonial." *Estudios de Historia Social de España*, 483–524. Madrid: Consejo Superior de Investigaciones Científicas, 1949.

Krippner-Martínez, James. *Rereading the Conquest: Power, Politics, and the History of Early Colonial Michoacán, Mexico, 1521–1565.* University Park: Pennsylvania State University Press, 2001.

Kruger, Steven F. "Conversion and Medieval Sexual, Religious, and Racial Categories." In *Constructing Medieval Sexuality*, edited by Karma Lochrie, Peggy McCracken, and James A. Schultz, 164–76. Minneapolis and London: University of Minnesota Press, 1997.

Kuznesof, Elizabeth Anne. "Ethnic and Gender Influences on 'Spanish' Creole Society in Colonial Spanish America." *Colonial Latin American Review* 4, no. 1 (1995): 153–76.

Lacqueur, Thomas. *Making Sex: Body and Gender from the Greeks to Freud.* Cambridge, MA, and London: Harvard University Press, 1990.

Ladd, Doris M. *The Mexican Nobility at Independence, 1780–1826.* Austin: Institute of Latin American Studies, University of Texas, 1976.

Ladero Quesada, Miguel Ángel. *Los señores de Andalucía: Investigaciones sobre nobles y señoríos en los siglos XIII a XV.* Cádiz: Universidad de Cádiz, 1998.

———. "Spain, circa 1492: Social Values and Structures." In *Implicit Understandings: Observing, Reporting, and Reflecting on the Encounters between Europeans and other Peoples in the Early Modern Period,* edited by Stuart B. Schwartz, 96–133. Cambridge and New York: Cambridge University Press, 1994.

Lafaye, Jacques. *Quetzalcóatl and Guadalupe: The Formation of Mexican National Consciousness, 1531–1813.* Translated by Benjamin Keen. Chicago: University of Chicago Press, 1976.

Laikin Elkin, Judith. "Imagining Idolatry: Missionaries, Indians, and Jews." In *Religion and the Authority of the Past,* edited by Tobin Siebers, 75–97. Ann Arbor: University of Michigan Press, 1993.

Landers, Jane G. "Acquisition and Loss on a Spanish Frontier: The Free Black Homesteaders of Florida, 1784–1821." In *Against the Odds: Free Blacks in the Slave Societies of the Americas,* edited by Jane G. Landers, 85–101. London and Portland, OR: Frank Cass, 1996.

———. *Black Society in Spanish Florida.* Urbana: University of Illinois Press, 1999.

Larios Martín, Jesús. "Ciencias complementarias de la nobiliaria." In *Apuntes de nobiliaria y nociones de genealogía y heráldica,* edited by Francisco de Cadenas y Allende, Vicente de Cadenas y Vicent, Julio Atienza, Jesus Lario Martín, Antonio de Vargas-Zúñiga, and Marqués de Siete Iglesias, 29–49. Madrid: Ediciones Hidalguía, 1960.

———. *Hidalguía e hidalgos de Indias.* Madrid: Asociación de hidalgos a fuero de España, 1958.

Lavallé, Bernard. *Las promesas ambiguas: Criollismo colonial en los Andes.* Lima: Instituto Riva-Agüero de la Pontífica Universidad Católica del Perú, 1993.

Lavrin, Asunción. "Indian Brides of Christ: Creating New Spaces for Indigenous Women in New Spain." In *Mexican Studies/Estudios Mexicanos* 15, no. 2 (1999): 225–60.

Lea, Henry Charles. *Historia de la Inquisición española.* Vol. 2. Translated by Angel Alcalá and Jesús Tobío, edited by Angel Alcalá, prologue by Angel Alcalá. Madrid: Fundación Universitaria Española, 1982–83.

———. *A History of the Inquisition in Spain.* Vol. 2. New York: Macmillan, 1906.

León, Nicolás. *Las castas del México colonial.* Mexico City: Talleres Gráficos del Museo Nacional de Arqueología, Historia, y Etnografía, 1924.

León-Portilla, Miguel. *Los antiguos mexicanos a través de sus crónicas y cantares.* Mexico City: Fondo de Cultura Económica, 1987.

Levine, Philippa, ed. *Gender and Empire.* Oxford and New York: Oxford University Press, 2004.

Levine Melammed, Renee. "Crypto-Jewish Women Facing the Spanish Inquisition: Transmitting Religious Practices, Beliefs, and Attitudes." In *Christians, Muslims, and Jews in Medieval and Early Modern Spain: Interaction and Cultural Change,* edited by Mark D. Meyerson and Edward D. English, 197–219. Notre Dame, IN: University of Notre Dame Press, 1999.

———. *Heretics or Daughters of Israel? The Crypto-Jewish Women of Castile.* New York: Oxford University Press, 1999.

Lewis, Laura A. *Hall of Mirrors: Power, Witchcraft, and Caste in Colonial Mexico.* Durham, NC, and London: Duke University Press, 2003.

———. "The 'Weakness' of Women and the Feminization of the Indian in Colonial Mexico." *Colonial Latin American Review* 5, no. 1 (1996): 73–94.

Leyes de Indias. Madrid: Biblioteca Judicial, 1889.

Liebman, Seymour B., ed. *The Enlightened: The Writings of Luis de Carvajal, el Mozo.* Translated by Seymour B. Leibman. Coral Gables, FL: University of Miami Press, 1967.

———. *The Jews in New Spain: Faith, Flame, and the Inquisition.* Coral Gables, FL: University of Miami Press, 1970.

Lira Montt, Luis. "El estatuto de *limpieza de sangre* en el derecho Indiano." In *XI Congreso del Instituto Internacional del Derecho Indiano,* 31–47. Buenos Aires: Instituto de Investigación de Historia del Derecho, 1997.

———. "La prueba de la hidalguía en el derecho Indiano." *Revista Chilena de Historia del Derecho* (Santiago) 7 (1978): 131–52.

Liss, Peggy. *Mexico Under Spain, 1521–1556: Society and the Origins of Nationality.* Chicago: University of Chicago Press, 1975.

Lockhart, James. *The Nahuas After the Conquest: A Social and Cultural History of the Indians of Central Mexico, Sixteenth Through Eighteenth Centuries.* Stanford, CA: Stanford University Press, 1992.

———. *Nahuas and Spaniards: Postconquest Central Mexican History and Philology.* Los Angeles: UCLA Latin American Center Publications, University of California, Los Angeles, 1991.

———. *Spanish Peru, 1532–1560*. Madison: University of Wisconsin Press, 1974.

Lockhart, James, and Stuart B. Schwartz. *Early Latin America*. New York: Cambridge University Press, 1983.

Lomnitz-Adler, Claudio. *Exits from the Labyrinth: Culture and Ideology in the Mexican National Space*. Berkeley: University of California Press, 1992.

———. "Nationalism as a Practical System: Benedict Anderson's Theory of Nationalism from the Vantage Point of Spanish America." In *The Other Mirror: Grand Theory through the Lens of Latin America*, edited by Miguel Angel Centeno and Fernando López-Alves, 329–59. Princeton, NJ: Princeton University Press, 2001.

López Austin, Alfredo. *The Human Body and Ideology: Concepts of the Ancient Nahuas*. 2 vols. Translated by Thelma Ortiz de Montellano and Bernard Ortiz de Montellano. Salt Lake City: University of Utah Press, 1988.

López de Meneses, Amada. "Grandezas y títulos de nobleza a los descendientes de Moctezuma II." *Revista de Indias* 22 (1962): 341–52.

López de Velasco, Juan. *Geografía y descripción universal de las Indias*. Vol. 248 of *Biblioteca de Autores Españoles*. Edited by don Marcos Jiménez de la Espada. Madrid: Ediciones Atlas, 1971.

López Martínez, Nicolás. "El estatuto de limpieza de sangre en la catedral de Burgos." *Hispania* (Madrid) 19, no. 74–77 (1959): 52–81.

López Sarrelangue, Delfina E. *La nobleza indígena de Pátzcuaro en la época virreinal*. Mexico City: Universidad Nacional Autónoma de México, 1965.

López Vela, Roberto. "Estructuras administrativas del Santo Oficio." In *Historia de la Inquisición en España y América: Las estructuras del Santo Oficio*, edited by Joaquín Pérez Villanueva and Bartolomé Escandell Bonet, 63–274. Vol. 2. Madrid: Biblioteca de Autores Cristianos, Centro de Estudios Inquisitoriales, 1993.

———. "Inquisición y monarquía: Estado de la cuestión (1940–1990)." *Hispania* 3, no. 176 (1990): 1133–40.

Lorence, Bruce A. "The Inquisition and the New Christians in the Iberian Peninsula: Main Historiographic Issues and Controversies." In *The Sepharadi and Oriental Jewish Heritage Studies*, International Congress on the Sepharadi and Oriental Jewry, and Issachar Ben-Ami, 13–72. Jerusalem: Magnes Press, Hebrew University, 1982.

Los virreyes españoles en América durante el gobierno de la Casa de Austria. Vol. 1. Edited by Lewis Hanke with the collaboration of Celso Rodríguez. Vol. 273 of *Biblioteca de Autores Españoles*. Madrid: Atlas, 1976.

Luis Sánchez Lora, José. *Mujeres, conventos, y formas de religiosidad Barroca*. Madrid: Fundación Universitaria Española, 1988.

Luis Vives, Juan. *The Education of a Christian Woman: A Sixteenth Century Manual*. Chicago: University of Chicago Press, 2000.

Lutz, Christopher H. *Santiago de Guatemala, 1541–1773: City, Caste, and the Colonial Experience*. Norman: University of Oklahoma Press, 1994.

Lynch, John. *Spain under the Habsburgs*. Vol. 1. New York: Oxford University Press, 1964.

Mahmood, Saba. *The Politics of Piety: The Islamic Revival and the Feminist Subject*. Princeton, NJ, and Oxford: Princeton University Press, 2005.

Maltby, William S. *The Black Legend in England: The Development of Anti Spanish Sentiment, 1558–1660.* Durham, NC: Duke University Press, 1971.

Maravall, José Antonio. *Las comunidades de Castilla.* Madrid: Alianza Editorial, 1994.

———. *Poder, honor, y élites en el siglo XVII.* Madrid: Siglo Veintiuno Editores, 1984.

Marichal, Carlos. "La bancarrota del virreinato: Finanzas, guerra, y política en la Nueva España, 1770–1808." In *Interpretaciones del siglo XVIII mexicano: El impacto de las reformas borbónicas,* edited by Josefina Zoraida Vázquez, 153–86. Mexico City: Nueva Imagen, 1992.

Márquez Villanueva, Francisco. "Conversos y cargos consejiles en el siglo XV." *Revista de Archivos, Bibliotecas y Museos* 63 (1957): 503–40.

———. "Noticias de la Inquisición sevillana." Plenary address, conference titled "Los conversos y la historia de España de 1248 a 1700," Saint Louis University (Madrid Campus), May 21–22, 2004.

Marshall, C. E. "The Birth of the Mestizo in New Spain." *Hispanic American Historical Review* 19 (1939): 160–84.

Martin, Norman. *Los vagabundos en la Nueva España.* Mexico City: Editorial Jus, 1957.

Martínez, María Elena. "The Black Blood of New Spain: *Limpieza de Sangre,* Racial Violence, and Gendered Power in Early Colonial Mexico." *William and Mary Quarterly,* 3rd series, vol. LXI (July 2004): 479–520.

———. "Space, Order, and Group Identities in a Spanish Colonial Town: Puebla de los Angeles." In *The Collective and the Public in Latin America: Cultural Identities and Political Order,* edited by Luis Roniger and Tamar Herzog, 13–36. Brighton, UK, and Portland, OR: Sussex Academic Press, 2000.

———. "The Spanish Concept of Limpieza de Sangre and the Emergence of the 'Race/Caste' System in the Viceroyalty of New Spain." PhD diss., University of Chicago, 2002.

Martínez-Alier (now Stolcke), Verena. *Marriage, Class and Colour in Nineteenth-Century Cuba: A Study of Racial Attitudes and Sexual Values in a Slave Society.* Ann Arbor: University of Michigan Press, 1989 [1974].

Martínez Baracs, Andrea, and Carlos Sempat Assadourian, eds. *Suma y epíloga de toda la descripción de Tlaxcala.* Tlaxcala: Universidad de Tlaxcala and Centro de Investigaciones y Estudios Superiores en Antropología Social, 1994.

Martínez Montiel, Luz M. *Presencia africana en México.* Mexico City: Consejo Nacional para la Cultura y las Artes, 1995.

Martínez Montiel, Luz M., and Juan Carlos Reyes G. *Memoria del III Encuentro Nacional de Afromexicanistas.* Colima, Mexico: Gobierno del Estado, Instituto Colimense de Cultura, 1993.

Martz, Linda. "Implementation of Pure-Blood Statutes in Sixteenth-Century Toledo." In *In Iberia and Beyond: Hispanic Jews Between Cultures,* edited by Bernard Dov Cooperman, 245–71. Newark: University of Delaware Press, 1998.

Maxwell, Kenneth R. "Hegemonies Old and New: The Ibero-Atlantic in the Long Eighteenth Century." In *Colonial Legacies: The Problem of Persistence in Latin American History,* edited by Jeremy Adelman, 69–90. New York and London: Routledge, 1999.

McAlister, Lyle N. "Social Structure and Social Change in New Spain." *Hispanic American Historical Review* 43, no. 3 (1963): 349–70.

McCaa, Robert. "*Calidad, Clase,* and Marriage in Colonial Mexico: The Case of Parral, 1788–90." *Hispanic American Historical Review* 64, no. 3 (1984): 477–501.

McCaa, Robert, and Stuart B. Schwartz. "Measuring Marriage Patterns: Percentages, Cohen's Kappa, and Log-Linear Models." *Comparative Studies of Society and History* 25, no. 4 (1983): 711–20.

McCaa, Robert, Stuart B. Schwartz, and Arturo Grubessich. "Race and Class in Colonial Latin America: A Critique." *Comparative Studies of Society and History* 21, no. 3 (1979): 421–33.

McClintock, Anne. *Imperial Leather: Race, Gender and Sexuality in the Colonial Contest.* New York: Routledge, 1995.

———. "'No Longer in a Future Heaven': Gender, Race and Nationalism." In *Dangerous Liaisons: Gender, Nation and Postcolonial Perspectives,* edited by Anne McClintock, Aamir Mufti, and Ella Shohat. Minneapolis and London: University of Minnesota Press, 1997.

Méchoulan, Henry. *El honor de Dios.* Translated from the French by Enrique Sordo. Barcelona: Editorial Argos Vergara, 1981.

Melville, Elinor G. K. *A Plague of Sheep: Environmental Consequences of the Conquest of Mexico.* Cambridge and New York: Cambridge University Press, 1994.

Mendieta, Jerónimo de. *Historia eclesiástica indiana.* Vol. 2. Vol. 261 of *Biblioteca de Autores Españoles.* Madrid: Ediciones Atlas, 1973.

Menocal, María Rosa. *The Ornament of the World: How Muslims, Jews, and Christians Created a Culture of Tolerance in Medieval Spain.* Boston: Little, Brown, 2002.

Meyerson, Mark D. *A Jewish Renaissance in Fifteenth-Century Spain.* Princeton, NJ: Princeton University Press, 2004.

———. *The Muslims of Valencia in the Age of Fernando and Isabel: Between Coexistence and Crusade.* Berkeley: University of California Press, 1991.

Mills, Kenneth R. *Idolatry and its Enemies: Colonial Andean Religion and Extirpation, 1640–1750.* Princeton, NJ: Princeton University Press, 1997.

———. "The Limits of Religious Coercion in Midcolonial Peru." In *The Church in Colonial Latin America,* edited by John F. Schwaller, 147–80. Wilmington, DE: Scholarly Resources, 2000.

Mitre Fernández, Emilio. *Los judíos de Castilla en tiempo de Enrique III: El pogrom de 1391.* Valladolid: Secretariado de Publicaciones, Universidad de Valladolid, 1994.

Molas Ribalta, Peré. "El exclusivismo de los gremios de la Corona de Aragón: Limpieza de sangre y limpieza de oficios." In *Les sociétés fermées dans le monde Ibérique, XVIe–XVIIIe siècles. Définitions et problématique: Actes de la table ronde des 8 et 9 février 1985.* 63–80. Paris: Editions du Centre National de la Recherche Scientifique, 1986.

Molina Martínez, Miguel. *La leyenda Negra.* Madrid: Nerea, 1991.

Monter, E. William. *Frontiers of Heresy: The Spanish Inquisition from the Basque Lands to Sicily.* Cambridge: Cambridge University Press, 1990.

Monter, E. William. "The Death of Coexistence: Jews and Moslems in Christian Spain, 1480–1502." In *The Expulsion of the Jews: 1492 and After,* edited by Raymond B. Waddington and Arthur H. Williamson, 5–14. New York and London: Garland, 1994.

Moore, R. I. *The Formation of a Persecuting Society: Power and Deviance in Western Europe, 950–1250.* Oxford: Basil Blackwell, 1990.

Morales, Francisco, O. F. M. *Ethnic and Social Background of the Franciscan Friars in Seventeenth Century Mexico.* Washington, DC: Academy of American Franciscan History, 1973.

Moreno de los Arcos, Roberto. "New Spain's Inquisition for Indians from the Sixteenth to the Nineteenth Century." In *Cultural Encounters: The Impact of the Inquisition in Spain and the New World,* edited by Mary Elizabeth Perry and Anne J. Cruz, 23–32. Berkeley: University of California Press, 1991.

Mörner, Magnus. *La corona española y los foráneos en los pueblos de indios de América.* Stockholm: Almqvist & Wiksell, 1970.

———. "La infiltración mestiza en los cacicazgos y cabildos de indios (siglos XVI–XVIII)." In *XXXVI Congreso Internacional de Americanistas (España 1964): Actas y Memorias.* Vol. 2. Seville: Congreso Internacional de Americanistas, 1966.

———. *Race Mixture in the History of Latin America.* Boston: Little, Brown, 1967.

Morse, Richard M. "Toward a Theory of Spanish American Government." *Journal of the History of Ideas* 15, no. 1 (January 1954): 71–93.

Munch, Guido. *El cacicazgo de San Juan Teotihuacan durante la colonia, 1521–1821.* Mexico City: Instituto Nacional de Antropología e Historia, 1976.

Mundy, Barbara E. *The Mapping of New Spain: Indigenous Cartography and the Maps of the Relaciones Geográficas.* Chicago: University of Chicago Press, 1996.

Nader, Helen. *Liberty in Absolutist Spain: The Habsburg Sale of Towns, 1516–1700.* Baltimore: Johns Hopkins University Press, 1990.

Naveda Chávez-Hita, Adriana. *Pardos, mulatos y libertos: Sexto Encuentro de Afromexicanistas.* Xalapa, Mexico: Universidad Veracruzana, 2001.

Netanyahu, Benzion. *The Origins of the Inquisition in Fifteenth Century Spain.* New York: Random House, 1995.

———. "The Racial Attack on the Conversos: Américo Castro's View of Its Origins." In *Toward the Inquisition: Essays on Jewish and Converso History in Late Medieval Spain,* 1–39. Ithaca, NY: Cornell University Press, 1997.

Nirenberg, David. *Communities of Violence: Persecution of Minorities in the Middle Ages.* Princeton, NJ: Princeton University Press, 1996.

———. "El concepto de la raza en la España medieval." *Edad Media: Revista de Historia* 3 (Spring 2000): 50–54.

———. "Conversion, Sex, and Segregation: Jews and Christians in Medieval Spain." *American Historical Review* 107, no. 4 (2002): 1478–92.

————. "Mass Conversions and Genealogical Mentalities: Jews and Christians in Fifteenth-Century Spain." *Past and Present* 174 (2002): 18–33.

Novinsky, Avita. "Some Theoretical Considerations about the New Christian Problem." In *The Sepharadi and Oriental Jewish Heritage Studies,* edited by Issachar Ben-Ami, 4–12. Jerusalem: Magnes Press, Hebrew University, 1982.

Nuttini, Hugo G. *The Wages of Conquest: The Mexican Aristocracy in the Context of Western Aristocracies.* Ann Arbor: University of Michigan Press, 1995.

O'Gorman, Edmundo. *Destierro de las sombra: Luz en el origen de la imagen y culto de Nuestra Señora de Guadalupe del Tepeyac.* Mexico City: Universidad Nacional Autónoma de México, 1991.

————. *Fundamentos de la historia de América.* Mexico City: Imprenta Universitaria, 1942.

————. *La invención de América.* Mexico City: Fondo de Cultura Económica, 1995.

O'Phelan Godoy, Scarlett. "Tiempo inmemorial, tiempo colonial: Un estudio de casos." *Revista Ecuatoriana de Historia* 4 (1993): pp. 3–20.

Oración á nuestra señora de Guadalupe, compuesta por el Illmo. Señor D. Francisco Antonio de Lorenzana, arzobispo de México. Mexico City: Don Joseph Antonio de Hogal, 1770.

Otte, Enrique. "Nueve Cartas de Diego de Ordás." *Historia Mexicana* 14 (1964): 102–29.

Outlaw, Lucius. "Toward a Critical Theory of 'Race.'" In *Anatomy of Racism,* edited by Theo Goldberg, 62–68. Minneapolis: University of Minnesota Press, 1990.

Pagden, Anthony. *The Fall of Natural Man: The American Indian and the Origins of Comparative Ethnology.* New York: Cambridge University Press, 1982.

————. "Identity Formation in Spanish America." In *Colonial Identity in the Atlantic World, 1500–1800,* edited by Nicholas Canny and Anthony Pagden, 51–93. Princeton, NJ: Princeton University Press, 1987.

————. *Spanish Imperialism and the Political Imagination.* New Haven, CT: Yale University Press, 1990.

Palafox y Mendoza, Juan de. *Manual de estados y profesiones de la naturaleza del indio.* Mexico City: Coordinación de Humanidades, Universidad Nacional Autónoma de México y Miguel Angel Porrúa, 1986.

Palmer, Colin A. "Religion and Magic in Mexican Slave Society, 1570–1650." In *Race and Slavery in the Western Hemisphere: Quantitative Studies,* edited by Stanley L. Engerman and Eugene D. Genovese, 311–28. Stanford, CA: Center for Advanced Study in the Behavioral Sciences, 1975.

————. *Slaves of the White God: Blacks in Mexico, 1570–1650.* Cambridge: Harvard University Press, 1976.

"Parecer de los frailes franciscanos sobre repartimiento de Indios." *Boletín del Archivo General de la Nación* (Mexico City) 9 (1938): 173–80.

Pardo, J. Joaquin, ed. *Prontuario de Reales Cédulas, 1529–1599.* Guatemala City: Unión Tipográfica, 1941.

Paso y Troncoso, Francisco del, ed. *Epistolario de Nueva España.* 16 vols. Mexico City: Antigua Librería Robredo, de José Porrúa e Hijos, 1939–42.

Pateman, Carole. *The Sexual Contract.* Stanford, CA: Stanford University Press, 1988.

Patterson, Orlando. *Slavery and Social Death: A Comparative Study.* Cambridge, MA: Harvard University Press, 1982.

Peña, José F. de la *Oligarquía y propiedad en Nueva España (1550–1624).* Mexico City: Fondo de Cultura Económica, 1983.

Pereña, Luciano. "Defensor oficial de la Corona." In Juan de Solórzano y Pereira, *De Indiarum Iure: Liber III: "De retentione Indiarum,"* edited by C. Baciero, F. Cantelar, A. García, J. M. García Añoveros, F. Maseda, L. Pereña, and J. M. Pérez-Prendes, 20–61. Madrid: Consejo Superior de Investigaciones Científicas, 1994.

Pérez de Lara, Alfonso. *De anniversariis, et capellaniis, libri dvo. Qvibus vltra generalem anniuersariorum & capellaniarum materiam, specialiter disputatur de annuo relicto: pro virginibus maritadis: pro infantibus expositis nutriendis: pro redimendis captiuis: pro relaxadis carceratis: pro mote pietatis: pro celebrado festo Corporis Christi, cum præcedentijs processionis: de trasferedis cadaueribus, absquè tributo. De quarta funerali: de probatione generis & qualitatis sanguinis ad capellaniam requisitæ, et ad alia statuta. Opvs qvidem, vt pivm et practicabile, ita & vtile vtroque foro versantibus, iudicibus, aduocatis, clericis, & monachis, & quibuscunque alijs piorum executoribus.* Matriti [Madrid]: ex typographia Illephonsi Martini, 1608.

Perez de Salazar, Francisco. *Historia de la pintura en Puebla.* Mexico City: Universidad Nacional Autónoma de México, Instituto de Investigaciones Estéticas, 1963.

Pérez Herrero, Pedro. "El méxico borbónico: ¿'un éxito' fracasado?" In *Interpretaciones del siglo XVIII mexicano: El impacto de las reformas borbónicas,* edited by Josefina Zoraida Vázquez, 109–51. Mexico City: Nueva Imagen, 1992

Perry, Mary Elizabeth. *Gender and Disorder in Early Modern Seville.* Princeton, NJ: Princeton University Press, 1990.

———. "Moriscas and the Limits of Assimilation." In *Christians, Muslims, and Jews in Medieval and Early Modern Spain: Interaction and Cultural Change,* edited by Mark D. Meyerson and Edward D. English, 274–89. Notre Dame, IN: University of Notre Dame Press, 1999.

Peters, Edward, *Inquisition.* Berkeley: University of California Press, 1989.

Phelan, John Leddy. "Neo-Aztecism in the Eighteenth Century and the Genesis of Mexican Nationalism." In *Culture in History: Essays in Honor of Paul Radin,* edited by Stanley Diamond, 760–70. New York: Columbia University Press, 1960.

———. *The Millennial Kingdom of the Franciscans in the New World: A Study of the Writings of Gerónimo de Mendieta, 1525–1604.* Berkeley: University of California Press, 1956.

Phillips, William D. "The Old World Background of Slavery in the Americas." In *Slavery and the Rise of the Atlantic System,* edited by Barbara L. Solow, 43–61. Cambridge, UK: Cambridge University Press, 1991.

Phillips, William D., Jr., *Enrique IV and the Crisis of Fifteenth-Century Castile, 1425–1480*. Cambridge, MA: Harvard University Press, 1978.

Phillips, William D., Jr., and Carla Rahn Phillips. "Spain in the Fifteenth Century." In *Transatlantic Encounters: Europeans and Andeans in the Sixteenth Century*, edited by Kenneth J. Andrien and Rolena Adorno, 11–39. Berkeley: University of California Press, 1991.

Pike, Ruth. *Linajudos and Conversos in Seville: Greed and Prejudice in Sixteenth- and Seventeenth-Century Spain*. New York and Washington, DC: Peter Lang, 2000.

———. "Sevillian Society in the Sixteenth Century: Slaves and Freedmen." *Hispanic American Historical Review* 7, no. 3 (1967): 344–59.

Pineda, Juan de. *Diálogos familiares de la agricultura cristiana*. Vol. 3. Edited by Juan Meseguer Fernández. Vol. 163 of *Biblioteca de Autores Españoles*. Madrid: Ediciones Atlas, 1963–64.

Pitt-Rivers, Julian. "On the Word 'Caste.'" In *The Translation of Culture: Essays to E. E. Evans-Pritchard*, edited by T. O. Beidelman, 231–54. London: Tavistock, 1971.

Poliakov, Léon. *The History of Anti-Semitism*. Vol. 1. Translated from the French by Richard Howard. New York: Schocken, 1974.

———. *The History of Anti-Semitism*. Vol. 2. Translated by Natalie Gerardi. Philadelphia: University of Pennsylvania Press, 1973.

Poole, Stafford. "Criollos and Criollismo." In *Encyclopedia of Mexico: History, Society and Culture*, edited by Michael S. Werner. Chicago: Fitzroy Dearborn, 1997.

———. "The Politics of Limpieza de Sangre: Juan de Ovando and his Circle in the Reign of Philip II." *The Americas* 55, no. 3 (January 1999): 359–89.

Popkin, Richard H. "The Rise and Fall of the Jewish Indian Theory." In *Menasseh ben Israel and his World*, edited by Yosef Kaplan, Henry Méchoulan, and Richard H. Hopkin, 63–82. Leiden, Netherlands: E. J. Brill, 1989.

Postigo Castellanos, Elena. *Honor y privilegio en la corona de Castilla: El Consejo de las Órdenes y los caballeros de hábito en el s. XVII*. Almazán, Soria: Junta de Castilla y León, 1988.

Procesos de indios idólatras y hechiceros. Mexico City: Secretaría de Gobernación and Archivo General de la Nación, 2002.

Quevedo, Francisco de. *Dreams and Discourses*. Translated by R. K. Britton. Warminster, UK: Aris & Phillips, 1989.

Quijada, Monica. "¿Qué nación? Dinámicas y dicotomías de la nación en el imaginario hispanoamericana del siglo XIX." In *Imaginar la nación*, edited by François-Xavier Guerra and Monica Quijada. Münster and Hamburg: Lit, 1994.

Quintanilla Raso, María Concepción. "La nobleza en la historia política castellana en la segunda mitad del siglo XV: Bases de poder y pautas de comportamiento." In *Congreso Internacional Bartolomeu Dias e a sua época: Actas*, vol. 1, 181–200. Oporto, Portugal: Universidade do Porto, 1989.

———. "Nobleza y señoríos en Castilla durante la baja edad media: Aportaciones de la historiografía reciente." *Anuario de Estudios Medievales* (Barcelona) 14 (1984): 613–39.

Restall, Matthew. "Black Conquistadors: Armed Africans in Early Spanish America." *The Americas* 57, no. 2 (2000):167–205.

———. *Seven Myths of the Spanish Conquest*. Oxford and New York: Oxford University Press, 2003.

Rípodas Ardanaz, Daisy. *El matrimonio en Indias: Realidad social y regulación jurídica*. Buenos Aires: Fundación para la Educación, la Ciencia y la Cultura, 1977.

Rishel Joseph J., and Suzanne Stratton-Pruitt, eds. *The Arts in Latin America, 1492–1820*. New Haven, CT, and London: Yale University Press, 2006.

Robertson, Donald. *Mexican Manuscript Painting of the Early Colonial Period*. Foreword by Elizabeth Hill Boone. Norman and London: University of Oklahoma Press, 1994.

Robertson, Donald, and Martha Barton Robertson. "Techialoyan Manuscripts and Paintings, with a Catalog." In *Handbook of Middle American Indians*, vol. 14, part 3, Guide to Ethnohistorical Sources, 265–80. Austin: University of Texas Press, 1975.

Robinson, David J., ed. *Research Inventory of the Mexican Collection of Colonial Parish Registers*. Salt Lake City: University of Utah Press, 1980.

Roseberry, William, "Hegemony and the Language of Contention." In *Everyday Forms of State Formation: Revolution and the Negotiation of Rule in Modern Mexico,* edited by Gilbert M. Joseph and Daniel Nugent, 355–66. Durham, NC: Duke University Press, 1994.

Roth, Cecil. *The Spanish Inquisition*. New York: W. W. Norton, 1964.

Roth, Norman. *Conversos, Inquisition and the Expulsion of the Jews from Spain*. Madison: University of Wisconsin Press, 2002.

Rounds, J. "Dynastic Succession and the Centralization of Power in Tenochtitlan." In *The Inca and Aztec States, 1400–1800: Anthropology and History,* edited by George A. Collier, Renato I. Rosaldo, and John D. Wirth, 63–89. New York: Academic Press, 1982.

Rout, Leslie B. *The African Experience in Spanish America*. Cambridge: Cambridge University Press, 1976.

Ruano, Eloy Benito. *Toledo en el siglo XV: Vida política*. Madrid: Consejo Superior de Investigaciones Científicas, Escuela de Estudios Medievales, 1961.

Ruiz, Teófilo F. "The Holy Office in Medieval France and in Late Medieval Castile: Origins and Contrasts." In *The Spanish Inquisition and the Inquisitorial Mind,* edited by Angel Alcalá, 33–51. Highland Lakes, NJ: Atlantic Research and Publications, 1987.

Ruiz De Alarcón, Hernando. *Treatise on the Heathen Superstitions: That Today Live Among the Indians Native to This New Spain, 1629*. Edited by Ross Hassig and J. Richard Andrews. Norman: University of Oklahoma Press, 1999.

Russell-Wood, A.J.R. "Before Columbus: Portugal's African Prelude to the Middle Passage and Contribution to Discourse on Race and Slavery." In *Race, Discourse, and the Origins of the Americas: A New World View,* edited by Vera Lawrence and Rex Nettleford, 134–65. Washington, DC, and London: Smithsonian Institution Press, 1995.

Salucio, Fray Agustín. *Discurso sobre los estatutos de limpieza de sangre.* Edited by Antonio Pérez y Gómez. Valencia: Artes Gráficas Soler, 1975 [1599].

Salvucci, Richard. "Economic Growth and Change in Bourbon Mexico: A Review Essay." *The Americas* 51, no. 4 (1994): 219–31.

Salvucci, Richard J. *Textiles and Capitalism in Mexico: An Economic History of the Obrajes, 1539–1840.* Princeton, NJ: Princeton University Press, 1987.

Salvucci, Richard J., Linda K. Salvucci, and Aslán Cohen. "The Politics of Protection: Interpreting Commercial Policy in Late Bourbon and Early National Mexico." In *The Political Economy of Spanish America in the Age of Revolution, 1750–1850,* edited by Kenneth J. Andrien and Lyman L. Johnson, 95–114. Albuquerque: University of New Mexico Press, 1994.

Sanchiz Ruiz, Javier Eusebio. "La *limpieza de sangre* en Nueva España: El funcionariado del tribunal del Santo Oficio de la Inquisición, siglo XVI." Master's thesis, Universidad Nacional Autónoma de México, Facultad de Filosofía y Letras, 1988.

Sanders, Ronald. *Lost Tribes and Promised Lands: The Origins of American Racism.* Boston: Little, Brown, 1978.

Sandoval, Fray Prudencio de. *Historia de la vida y hechos del Emperador Carlos V.* Vol. 82 of *Biblioteca de Autores Españoles.* Madrid: Ediciones Atlas, 1955 [1606]).

Sapir Abulafia, Anna. "The Intellectual and Spiritual Quest for Christ and Central Medieval Persecution of Jews." In *Religious Violence between Christians and Jews: Medieval Roots, Modern Perspectives,* edited by Anna Sapir Abulafia, 61–85. Houndmills, Basingstoke, Hampshire, UK, and New York: Palgrave, 2002.

Sarrailh, Jean. *La España ilustrada de la segunda mitad del siglo XVIII.* 4th ed. Mexico City: Fondo de Cultura Económica, 1992 [1st ed. 1954].

Schroeder, Susan. *Chimalpahin and the Kingdom of Chalco.* Tucson: University of Arizona Press, 1991.

Schwaller, John Frederick. *The Church and Clergy in Sixteenth-Century Mexico.* Albuquerque: University of New Mexico Press, 1997.

Schwartz, Stuart B. "Colonial Identities and the *Sociedad de Castas.*" *Colonial Latin American Review* 4, no. 1 (1995): 185–201.

Schwartz, Stuart B., and Frank Salomon. "New Peoples and New Kinds of People: Adaptation, Readjustment, and Ethnogenesis in South American Indigenous Societies (colonial era)." In *The Cambridge History of the Native Peoples of the Americas III (2): South America,* 443–501. Cambridge: Cambridge University Press, 1999.

Scott, Joan W. "Gender: A Useful Category of Historical Analysis." In *Gender and the Politics of History,* 28–50. New York: Columbia University Press, 1988.

Seed, Patricia. *Ceremonies of Possession in Europe's Conquest of the New World, 1492–1640.* Cambridge: Cambridge University Press, 1995.

———. "Social Dimensions of Race: Mexico City, 1753." *Hispanic American Historical Review* 62, no. 4 (1982): 568–606.

———. *To Love, Honor, and Obey in Colonial Mexico: Conflicts Over Marriage Choice, 1574–1821.* Stanford, CA: Stanford University Press, 1988.

Seed, Patricia, and Philip F. Rust. "Estate and Class in Colonial Oaxaca Revisited." *Comparative Studies of Society and History* 25, no. 4 (1983): 703–10.

Semo, Enrique. *Historia del capitalismo en México: Los orígenes, 1521–1763*. Mexico City: Ediciones Era, 1973.

Sicroff, Albert A. *Los estatutos de limpieza de sangre: Controversias entre los siglos XV y XVII*. Translated from the French by Mauro Armiño. Madrid: Tauros Ediciones, 1985.

Siete Iglesias, Marqués de. "¿Qué es nobleza de sangre?" In *Apuntes de nobiliaria y nociones de genealogía y heráldica,* edited by Francisco de Cadenas y Allende, Vicente de Cadenas y Vicent, Julio Atienza, Jesus Lario Martín, Antonio de Vargas-Zúñiga, and Marqués de Siete Iglesias, 105–118. Madrid: Ediciones Hidalguía, 1960.

Signos históricos II, no. 4 (2000).

Socolow, Susan. *The Women of Colonial Latin America*. Cambridge: Cambridge University Press, 2000.

Solano, Francisco de. *Cedulario de tierras: Compilación de legislación agraria colonial 1497–1820* (Mexico City: Universidad Nacional Autónoma de México, 1984,

Solórzano Pereira, Juan de. *De Indiarum Iure. Liber III: De retentione Indiarum,* edited by C. Baciero, F. Cantelar, A. García, J. M. García Añoveros, F. Maseda, L. Pereña, and J. M. Pérez-Prendes. Madrid: Consejo Superior de Investigaciones Científicas, 1994.

———. *Política Indiana*. Vol. 1. Madrid: Compañía Ibero-Americana de Publicaciones, 1930 [1648].

Spores, Ronald. "Mixteca *Cacicas:* Status, Wealth, and the Political Accommodation of Native Elite Women in Early Colonial Mexico." In *Indian Women of Early Mexico,* edited by Susan Schroeder, Stephanie Wood, and Robert Haskett, 185–197. Norman and London: University of Oklahoma Press, 1997.

Starr-LeBeau, Gretchen D. *In the Shadow of the Virgin: Inquisitors, Friars, and Conversos in Guadalupe, Spain*. Princeton, NJ: Princeton University Press, 2003.

Stavig, Ward. "Ambiguous Visions: Nature, Law, and Culture in Indigenous-Spanish Land Relations in Colonial Peru." *Hispanic American Historical Review* 80, no. 1 (2000): 77–111.

Stern, Steve. "Paradigms of Conquest: History, Historiography, and Politics." *Journal of Latin American Studies* 24 (1992): 1–34.

Stern, Steve J. *The Secret History of Gender: Women, Men, and Power in Late Colonial Mexico*. Chapel Hill and London: University of North Carolina Press, 1995.

———. "The Social Significance of Judicial Institutions in an Exploitative Society: Huamanga, Peru, 1570–1640." In *The Inca and Aztec States, 1400–1800: Anthropology and History,* edited by George A. Collier, Renato I. Rosaldo, and John D. Wirth, 289–320. New York and London: Academic Press, 1982.

Stolcke, Verena. "Conquered Women." *Report on the Americas (NACLA)* 24, no. 5 (1991): 23–38.

———. "Invaded Women: Gender, Race, and Class in the Formation of Colonial Society." In *Women, 'Race' and Writing in the Early Modern Period*, edited by Margo Hendricks and Patricia Parker, 272–86. London: Routledge, 1994.

———. "A New World Engendered: The Making of the Iberian Transatlantic Empires" In *A Companion to Gender History*, edited by Teresa A. Meade and Merry E. Weisner-Hanks, 371–92. Oxford: Blackwell, 2003.

Stoler, Ann Laura. "Carnal Knowledge and Imperial Power: Gender, Race and Morality in Colonial Asia." In *Gender at the Crossroads of Knowledge: Feminist Anthropology in the Postmodern Era*, 51–101. Berkeley: University of California Press, 1991.

———. *Race and the Education of Desire: Foucault's "History of Sexuality" and the Colonial Order of Things*. Durham, NC, and London: Duke University Press, 1995.

———. "Rethinking Colonial Categories: European Communities and the Boundaries of Rule." *Comparative Studies in Society and History* 31, no. 1 (January 1989): 134–61.

Sweet, James H. "The Iberian Roots of American Racist Thought." *William and Mary Quarterly* 54, no. 1 (1997): 143–66.

———. *Recreating Africa: Culture, Kinship, and Religion in the African-Portuguese World, 1441–1770*. Chapel Hill and London: University of North Carolina Press, 2003.

Tate Lanning, John. "Legitimacy and *Limpieza de Sangre* in the Practice of Medicine in the Spanish Empire." *Jahrbuch für Geschichte von Staat, Wirtschaft, und Gesellschaft Lateinamerikas* 4 (1967): 37–60.

Taylor, William. "The Virgin of Guadalupe in New Spain: An Inquiry into the Social History of Marian Devotion." *American Ethnologist* 14, no. 1 (1987): 9–33.

Taylor, William B. "Between Global Process and Local Knowledge: An Inquiry into Early Latin American Social History, 1500–1900." In *Reliving the Past: The Worlds of Social History*, edited by Oliver Zunz, 115–90. Chapel Hill and London: University of North Carolina Press, 1985.

———. "Cacicazgos coloniales en el Valle de Oaxaca." *Historia Mexicana* 20 (1970): 1–41.

———. *Drinking, Homicide and Rebellion in Colonial Mexican Villages*. Stanford, CA: Stanford University Press, 1979.

———. "Land and Water Rights in the Viceroyalty of New Spain." *New Mexico Historical Review* 50, no. 3 (1975): 189–211.

Terraciano, Kevin. *The Mixtecs of Colonial Oaxaca: Ñudzahui History, Sixteenth through Eighteenth Centuries*. Stanford: Stanford University Press, 2001.

Tezózomoc, Hernando de Alvarado. *Crónica mexicana*. Mexico City: Secretaría de Educación Pública, 1944.

Thomson, Guy P. C. *Puebla de los Ángeles: Industry and Society in a Mexican City, 1700–1850*. Boulder, CO: Westview, 1989.

Thompson, I.A.A. "*Hidalgo* and *pechero*: The language of 'estates' and 'classes' in early-modern Castile." In *Language, History and Class*, edited by Penelope J. Corfield, 53–78. Cambridge: Basil Blackwell, 1991.

———. "The Purchase of Nobility in Castile, 1552–1700." *Journal of European Economic History* 11 (1982): pp. 313–60.

Thornton, John. *Africa and Africans in the Making of the Atlantic World, 1400–1800.* Cambridge: Cambridge University Press, 1998.

Toro, Alfonso. *Los judíos en la Nueva España.* 2nd ed. Mexico City: Fondo de Cultura Económica, 1993.

Toussaint, Manuel. *Pintura Colonial en México.* Mexico City: Universidad Nacional Autónoma de México, Instituto de Investigaciones Estéticas, 1990.

Tovar de Teresa, Guillermo. *Miguel Cabrera: Pintor de Cámara de la Reina Celestial.* Mexico City: InverMéxico Grupo Financiero, 1995.

Townsend, Richard F. *The Aztecs.* London: Thames & Hudson, 2000 [1992].

Trachtenberg, Joshua. *The Devil and the Jews: The Medieval Conception of the Jew and its Relation to Modern Antisemitism.* New Haven, CT: Yale University Press; London: H. Milford Oxford University Press, 1943.

Trouillot, Michel-Rolph. *Silencing the Past: Power and the Production of History.* Boston: Beacon, 1995.

Tucci Carneiro, Maria Luiza. *Preconcepto Racial: Portugal e Brasil-Colônia.* São Paolo: Editora Brasiliense, 1988.

Twinam, Ann. "Pedro de Ayarzo: The Purchase of Whiteness." In *The Human Tradition in Colonial Latin America,* edited by Kenneth J. Andrien, 194–210. Wilmington, DE: Scholarly Resources, 2002.

———. *Public Lives, Private Secrets: Gender, Honor, Sexuality, and Illegitimacy in Colonial Spanish America.* Stanford, CA: Stanford University Press, 1999.

———. "Racial Passing: Informal and Official 'Whiteness' in Colonial Spanish America." In *New World Orders: Violence, Sanction, and Authority in the Colonial Americas,* edited by John Smolenski and Thomas J. Humphrey, 249–72. Philadelphia: University of Pennsylvania Press, 2005.

Uchmany, Eva Alexandra. "Criptojudíos y cristianos nuevos en las filipinas durante el siglo XVI." In *The Sepharadi and Oriental Jewish Heritage Studies,* edited by Issachar Ben-Ami, 85–103. Jerusalem: Magnes Press, Hebrew University, 1982.

———. "El mestizaje en el siglo XVI novohispano." *Historia Mexicana* 37, no. 1 (1987): 29–48.

———. *La vida entre el judaísmo y el cristianismo en la Nueva España, 1580–1606.* Mexico City: Archivo General de la Nación and Fondo de Cultura Económica, 1992.

Urbano, Henrique, ed. *Tradición y modernidad en los Andes.* Cusco, Peru: Centro de Estudios Regionales Andinos, "Bartolomé de las Casas," 1992.

Valdés, Dennis Nodín. "The Decline of Slavery in Mexico." *The Americas* 44, no. 2 (1987): 167–94.

———. "The Decline of the Sociedad de Castas in Mexico City." PhD diss., University of Michigan, 1978.

Vázquez de Espinosa, Fray Antonio. *Descripción de la Nueva España en el siglo XVII.* Mexico City: Editorial Patria, 1944.

Vila Vilar, Enriqueta. *Hispano-América y el comercio de esclavos.* Seville: Escuela de Estudios Hispanoamericanos, 1977.

Villavicencio, Diego Jaymes Ricardo de. *Luz y methodo de confesar idólatras y destierro de idolatrías debajo del tratado siguiente. Tratado de avisos y puntos importantes de la abominable seta de la idolatría, para examinar por ellos al penitente en el fuero interior de la consciencia, y exterior judicial. Sacados no de los libros, sino de la experiencia en las aberigüaciones con los rabbies de ella.* Puebla: Imprenta de Diego Fernández de León, 1692. Rare Book Collection. John Carter Brown Library.

Vincent, Bernard. *Minorías y marginados en la España del siglo XVI.* Granada: Diputación Provincial de Granada, 1987.

Vinson, Ben, III. Bearing *Arms for His Majesty: The Free-Colored Militia in Colonial Mexico.* Stanford, CA: Stanford University Press, 2001.

Vinson, Ben, III, Bobby Vaughn, and Clara García Ayluardo. *Afroméxico: El pulso de la población negra en México, una historia recordada, olvidada y vuelta a recordar.* Mexico City: Centro de Investigación y Docencia Económica, 2004.

Viotti da Costa, Emilia. *The Brazilian Empire: Myths and Histories.* Chicago: Dorsey, 1988.

Wachtel, Nathan. *Foi du Souvenir: Labyrinthes Marranes.* Paris: Éditions du Seuil, 2001.

———. "Marrano Religiosity in Hispanic America in the Seventeenth Century." In *The Jews and the Expansion of Europe to the West, 1450–1800,* edited by Paolo Bernardini and Norman Fiering, 149–71. New York and Oxford: Berghahn Books, 2001.

Wade, Peter. "*Negros, indígenas e identidad nacional en Colombia.*" In *Imaginar la nación,* edited by François-Xavier Guerra and Monica Quijada. Münster and Hamburg: Lit, 1994.

———. *Race, Nature and Culture: An Anthropological Perspective.* London and Sterling, VA: Pluto, 2002.

Walker Bynum, Caroline. "The Female Body and Religious Practice in the Later Middle Ages." In *Fragments for a History of the Human Body,* vol. I, edited by Michel Feher with Ramona Naddaff and Nadia Tazi, 162–219. New York: Urzone, 1989.

Warren, Fintan B. *Vasco de Quiroga and his Pueblo-Hospitals of Santa Fe.* Washington, DC: Academy of American Franciscan History, 1963.

Wertheimer, Elaine C. *Jewish Sources of Spanish Blood Purity Concerns.* Brooklyn, NY: Adelantre, the Judezmo Society, 1977.

West, Cornel. "Race and Social Theory: Toward a Genealogical Materialist Analysis." In *The Year Left 2: An American Socialist Yearbook,* edited by Mike Davis et al., 74–90. London: Verso, 1987.

Wheeler, Roxann. *The Complexion of Race: Categories of Difference in Eighteenth-Century British Culture.* Philadelphia: University of Pennsylvania Press, 2000.

Williams, Brackette. "Classification Systems Revisited: Kinship, Caste, Race, and Nationality as the Flow of Blood and the Spread of Rights." In *Naturalizing Power: Essays in Feminist Cultural Analysis,* edited by Sylvia Yanagisako and Carol Delaney, 201–36. New York and London: Routledge, 1995.

Wolff, Philippe. "The 1391 Pogrom in Spain: Social Crisis or Not?" *Past and Present* 50 (1971): 4–18.

Wood, Stephanie. "El problema de la historicidad de títulos y los códices del grupo Techialoyan." In *De tlacuilos y escribanos: estudios sobre documentos indígenas coloniales del centro de México,* edited by Xavier Noguez and Stephanie Wood, 167–221. Zamora, Mexico: El Colegio de Michoacán and El Colegio Mexiquense, 1998.

Wynter, Sylvia. "1492: A New World View." In *Race, Discourse, and the Origins of the Americas: A New World View,* edited by Vera Lawrence and Rex Nettleford, 5–57. Washington, DC, and London: Smithsonian Institution Press, 1995.

Yun Casalilla, Bartolomé. "The Castilian Aristocracy in the Seventeenth Century: Crisis, Refeudalisation, or Political Offensive?" In *The Castilian Crisis of the Seventeenth Century: New Perspectives on the Economic and Social History of Seventeenth-Century Spain,* edited by I.A.A. Thompson and Bartolomé Yun Casalilla, 277–300. Cambridge and New York: Cambridge University Press, 1994.

Zavala, Silvio A. *La encomienda indiana.* 3rd ed. Mexico City: Editorial Porrúa, 1992.

———. "La utopía de Tomás Moro en la Nueva España." In *La utopía mexicana del siglo XVI: Lo bello, lo verdadero y lo bueno,* 76–93. Mexico City: Grupo Azabache, 1992.

Index

Acosta, José de, 138, 336n27
Africans, 4, 8, 12, 105, 340n70, 341n73; as bozales, 135; category of negro in sistema de castas, 1, 144, 161, 162–63, 164, 166–67, 259, 335n10, 341n77, 342n91, 356n47; confraternities of, 159, 160, 161; conversos compared to, 158, 159; in craft guilds, 336n20; as creoles, 135, 160–61, 350n38; as free, 144, 147, 155, 159–60, 220–24, 238, 243, 269, 335n7, 340nn67,68, 350n38, 351n45, 356n47; as ladinos, 160–61; and limpieza de sangre, 163–64, 201, 201–6, 207, 213, 214, 220–25, 233, 235, 238, 243–44, 245–47, 249, 253, 254, 255, 256–59, 267, 267–68, 268, 271–73, 274, 275, 290n21, 356nn46,47; and principle of the free womb, 144, 157, 222, 335n11; religious status of, 21, 121, 156, 157–59, 167–68, 201, 205, 220–24, 225, 270, 272, 339n63; as slaves, 2, 3, 9, 10, 20, 60, 121, 135, 136, 143, 144–45, 152, 154–61, 164–65, 168, 169, 218, 221, 222, 225, 238, 240, 243, 244, 267, 271–72, 290n19, 335nn7,9, 338n46, 339nn56,58,63, 340n68, 341n77, 342n91, 350n38, 355n43. *See also* mulattos; sistema de castas
Aguirre, Juan de, 194–95
Aguirre Beltrán, Gonzalo, 273, 290n21, 338n47, 355n43
Ahumada, Juan Antonio de, 359n77
Albornoz, Bartolomé, 157
alcabala, 241–42

alcaldes: alcaldes mayores, 131, 176, 317n4; alcaldes menores, 317n4; alcaldes ordinarios, 130, 132, 175, 324n67, 355n46. *See also* corregidores
Alencastre Noroña y Silva, Fernando de, 229, 239
Alfaro, José, 352n2
Alfaro Ramírez, Rafael, 333n50
Almaguer, Antonio de, 130, 131
Alpert, Michael, 300n41
Altamirano, Juan de, 191, 345n36
Altamirano Pizarro, Juana, 191
Altamirano y Velasco, Fernando, 345n36
Álvarez de Hita, Bernabé, 195–96
Álvarez de Miranda, Pedro, 337n41
Alzate y Ramírez, José Antonio de, 257–58, 259
Anderson, Benedict, 12, 14, 292n34
Antequera, bishop of, 139, 150
Arce y Miranda, Andrés: "Noticias de los escritores de la Nueva España," 242–43
archival practices: and limpieza de sangre, 6, 17–18, 19, 20–21, 62, 65, 69, 76, 87, 123, 125, 142, 173, 175–76, 177–78, 199, 215–17, 218, 225–26, 264, 269, 274–75, 360n2; and sistema de castas, 142, 143–46, 166, 167, 173, 175–76, 216, 225–26, 264, 268, 334nn1,5; of Spanish Inquisition, 6, 18, 65, 69, 175–76
Arellano, Felipe de, 330n15
Arellanos, Manuel, 229–31
Aristotle, 48, 139, 237
Asperilla, Pedro Hernández de, 173–74
Aubert, Guillaume, 306n44

mestizos (*continued*)
238, 242–43, 244, 248–49, 250,
256–58, 259–60, 263, 267–68, 274,
275; vs. mulattoes, 152, 154, 157,
164–65, 168, 202, 233, 235, 249,
256, 258–59, 263, 274; policies of
Mexican Inquisition regarding,
148–50, 162, 165–66, 169–70, 217,
342n90; policies of Spanish crown
regarding, 116, 118, 119, 122, 139,
145, 147–48, 153, 205–6, 225, 259,
327nn85,87, 336n23, 342n94;
Solórzano Pereira on, 164, 304–5,
348n10, 348n11
Mexican Inquisition, 18, 129, 133, 222,
225, 261; calificadores (censors) of,
178–79, 215; commisioners of,
169–70, 189, 190, 195, 215, 246;
establishment of, 101–2, 143, 169, 190,
319n24; familiares of, 134, 173–74,
178, 187, 189, 190, 192–93, 194,
195–96, 243, 245–47, 266, 312n25,
332n42, 344n12, 346nn46,51;
genealogical investigations by, 104,
130, 134–35, 165–66, 167, 169–70,
173–74, 175–78, 180, 186–89,
191–92, 215, 216, 243, 245–47,
312n25, 332n44, 344nn10,12,
345nn21,28,36, 346n46, 347n52,
355nn41,46, 359nn80,81; policies
regarding African descent, 220–21,
245–47, 262, 268; policies regarding
castizos, 165–66, 169–70, 342n90;
policies regarding creoles, 190,
191–95, 243–44; policies regarding
idolatry and heresy, 149–50, 153,
165, 211–12, 217; policies regarding
mestizos, 148–50, 162, 165–66,
169–70, 217, 342n90; purity requirements for members of, 194–95,
346nn46,51; relations with Spanish
Inquisition, 65, 149, 165, 173–74,
175–76, 186–87, 189–90, 191–95,
198–99, 243, 246, 268, 310n9,
311n15, 312n25, 321n33, 332n42,
345n21, 346nn45,50
Mexican institutions: cathedral chapters, 134, 137, 138–39, 150, 331n31,
345n28, 359n76; colleges, 244, 245,
259; confraternities in, 159, 160,
161; Convent of Corpus Christi,
249, 251, 258; courts (audiencias)
in, 91, 99, 100, 105–6, 110, 119–20,

124, 125, 130, 131–32, 136, 139,
161, 178, 181, 193, 258, 261, 333n55,
358n73, 359nn76,78; craft guilds,
147, 239–40, 241, 242, 244–45,
336n336; municipalities (ayuntamientos), 91, 106, 260, 261, 275, 317n4,
335n8, 359n78; purity requirements
for members of, 20–21, 173–74, 175,
193, 194–95, 207, 213, 244–47, 249,
258, 262, 263, 268, 270, 272, 331n31,
332n38, 346n46, 355n46, 356n47;
religious orders, 96, 97, 98, 102, 133,
134, 137, 150–51, 163–64, 166, 174,
192, 194, 269, 272, 319n19, 332n38,
350n25; town councils (cabildos) in,
91, 98, 100, 106, 116, 127, 129–31,
134, 136, 137, 147, 174, 195, 244–45,
317n4, 324n67, 355n46, 359n76;
University of Mexico, 152, 197, 242,
356n47. *See also* Mexican Inquisition
Mexico, colonial: Atlixco, 210; the
Bajío, 240; Chalco, 113, 115, 325n74;
Cholula, 106, 355n44; Consulado
of Mexico, 359n78; government
debt in, 354n37; Maya region, 117;
Michoacán, 99, 106, 112, 131,
322n48; Mixtec region, 117; Oaxaca,
94, 106, 111, 118, 239, 249, 326n84,
345n28; Pánuco, 97, 126; vs. Peru,
111, 113, 121, 164, 196, 212, 347n56;
Querétaro, 223–24, 248; Salamanca,
245–46; San Juan de Ulúa, 176; Santa
Cruz Tlatlaccotepetl, 209; Santa Fe,
99; Sonora, 97; Spanish conquest,
91, 95, 96, 111, 114, 117–18, 119,
123, 126, 210, 217, 220, 261, 326n81;
taxes in, 241–42; Tepeji de la Seda,
111, 119, 120; Texcoco, 115, 325n78;
Third Provincial Council, 103;
Tlalmanalco, 115; Tlaxcala, 145–46,
217–19, 240, 248, 273, 326n78;
Tocuba, 106; Toluca, 217; Veracruz,
176, 189, 335n11; Yucatán, 102,
329n5; Zacatecas, 189, 344n12;
Zapotec region, 117. *See also* Mexican
Inquisition; Mexican institutions;
Mexico, colonial, native population
of; Mexico, colonial, Spanish population of; Mexico, independent;
Mexico, pre-Hispanic; Mexico City;
Puebla; sistema de castas
Mexico, colonial, native population
of, 3, 4, 14, 336n29, 352n7; category

degeneration, 137–39, 140–41, 193, 202, 358n68; White Legend of, 8, 10. *See also* Mexico, colonial; Peru; sistema de castas

Spanish crown: Alfonso VI, 261; Catholic Kings (Ferdinand and Isabella), 26, 33–34, 35, 40, 50, 78–79, 91, 129, 156, 298n25, 299nn31,32,34,35, 303n8, 305n25; Charles II, 118, 205, 229, 240; Charles III, 227, 355n39; Charles IV, 359n78; Charles V, 44, 79, 106, 156, 267, 303n8, 330n19; Enrique IV, 30, 31, 33, 44, 91, 297n20; Ferdinand VII, 14; Juan II, 29–30, 44; Ordenanza del Patronazgo, 132–33; Philip II, 44–45, 51, 63–64, 78–79, 82, 100, 106, 113, 117, 127, 129, 136, 145–46, 156, 188, 267, 303n8, 319n24, 342n94; Philip IV, 70, 311n14, 314n41; Philip V, 229, 359n77; policies regarding African slaves, 154, 155–56, 157; policies regarding creoles, 192, 193, 259–60, 359nn76,77,78; policies regarding free Africans, 220, 221; policies regarding immigration, 20, 46, 123, 128–29, 141, 173, 174, 176, 185, 198, 266–67, 330nn18,19, 343n5, 351n41; policies regarding inheritance, 324n62; policies regarding Jews, 9, 35, 96, 299nn31,34,35, 330n19; policies regarding limpieza de sangre, 25, 29–30, 42, 43–45, 50, 70, 73, 74, 77–78, 81–82, 84, 86–87, 123, 128–35, 140, 141, 199, 201, 202, 225, 245, 267, 270, 274, 296n17, 312n27, 314n41, 316n63; policies regarding marriage, 245, 256, 258, 262–63, 273–74, 356n49; policies regarding mestizos, 116, 118, 119, 122, 139, 145, 147–48, 153, 205–6, 225, 259, 327nn85,87, 336n23, 342n94; policies regarding Mexican Inquisition, 101–2; policies regarding native population of colonial Mexico, 5, 16, 20, 91, 92, 95–105, 106–7, 109–12, 114–15, 116, 118, 120–21, 122, 123, 124, 125, 128–29, 133–34, 137, 141, 153, 155, 156, 168, 201, 205–6, 220, 221, 225, 259, 270, 271, 273, 274, 319n17, 321n36, 328n2; policies regarding rehabilitaciones

for conversos, 45, 303n8; policies regarding relaciones geográficas, 113; policies regarding Spaniards in colonial Mexico, 91–92, 95, 99, 106, 124–25, 129–30, 132–34, 136, 139, 141, 155, 192, 259–60, 329nn6,7, 355n39, 359n76; policies regarding Spanish Inquisition, 33–35, 63–64, 298nn25,29, 299n32, 312n27, 321n36; policies regarding white slaves, 338n47; real cédula of 1697, 118, 119, 122, 205, 259, 358n74; Real Gabinete de Historia Natural, 227–28; Real Patronato, 132–33; Real Pragmática of 1623, 70, 74, 312n27, 314n41; reforms of Bourbons, 21, 84, 229, 240–41, 258–59, 324n68, 353n20, 354n31; relations with Catholic Church, 9, 33, 34–35, 40, 91, 97, 98, 128, 132–34, 141, 206, 298nn25,29; relations with nobles, 31, 49, 77–79, 85, 305n25, 314nn42,47, 355n39; royal lands (mercedes de tierra), 107; Royal Pragmatic on Marriages/Pragmatic Sanction, 245, 256, 258, 262–63, 356n49

Spanish Inquisition: abolished, 316n63; archival practices of, 6, 18, 65, 69, 175–76; autos de fe, 36–37, 86, 101, 300n38; commissioners (comisarios) of, 64, 65–69, 87, 179, 182, 185–86, 189–90, 193–94, 313n31, 344n19; consultores of, 64, 181–82, 190, 344n18; and crypto-Judaism among conversos, 1, 26, 33, 34, 35, 36, 37–40, 41, 46, 50, 54, 55, 57, 58, 86, 299n35, 300n40, 305n33, 307nn47,49; edicts of grace, 54–55, 307n47; establishment of, 9, 26, 31–35, 39, 41, 43, 151, 175–76, 297n22, 298nn26–29; estates of conversos confiscated by, 34, 299nn32,34; executions authorized by, 36, 37, 55; familiares of, 64, 72–73, 75, 87, 176, 198, 267, 313n31, 344n15; genealogical investigations by, 2, 19, 43, 62, 64–70, 76, 77, 86, 87, 142, 146, 169, 173–74, 175, 176–77, 178–82, 183, 184, 185–87, 189–90, 191–92, 193–94, 198, 216, 265–66, 267, 272, 305n33, 310n11, 311n14, 312nn23,27, 313n32,